HEALTH AND SAFETY: HAZARDOUS AGENTS

by
Dr Chris Hartley LLB (Hons) MIBiol MSc PhD PGCE FIOSH RSP
Visiting Fellow, Aston University
Independent Health and Safety Consultant

edited by
Professor Peter Waterhouse BA BSc PhD FIOSH RSP

Published by IOSH Services Limited

THE AUTHOR

Dr Chris Hartley is a Visiting Fellow at the Health and Safety Unit at Aston University and works as an independent health and safety consultant specialising in occupational health and hygiene.

Chris originally qualified in biochemistry and worked as a biochemist in several hospitals. He then developed an interest in health and safety matters and gained the Aston University MSc in Occupational Safety and Hygiene.

He has lectured widely on occupational health and hygiene subjects, principally at Aston and South Bank Universities. He also has extensive experience of consultancy work in a wide range of organisations and workplaces. He was course manager for the Postgraduate Diploma for HSE inspector trainees, and subsequently programme director for the BSc course in Health and Safety Management at Aston University.

Chris's research has focused on expertise in hazardous substance risk assessment and in 2000, jointly with Professor Richard Booth, he was awarded the IOSH Academic Journal Award for best paper.

From 1993 to 1999, he was Chief Examiner in occupational health and hygiene for the National Examination Board in Occupational Safety and Health, and since 1997 he has been External Examiner for the MSc in Occupational Health and Ergonomics at the National University of Ireland (Galway).

He is a Fellow of IOSH, a Registered Safety Practitioner, a Member of the British Occupational Hygiene Society, and was a Graduate Member of the former British Institute of Occupational Hygienists (now Faculty of Occupational Hygiene). In addition, Chris has recently obtained a law degree.

THE EDITOR

Dr Peter Waterhouse is Honorary Visiting Professor of Occupational Safety in the Robens Centre of the European Institute of Health and Medical Sciences at the University of Surrey.

He was employed as a safety adviser in the chemical industry for 23 years and has served as a Chief Examiner for the National Examination Board in Occupational Safety and Health in safety technology, occupational health and hygiene, and health and safety law. He has also assisted the Employment National Training Organisation in the development of vocational standards for health, safety and environmental protection advisers.

Peter is a Fellow of the Institution, a Registered Safety Practitioner and a former President. He has also served as Vice-Chairman of the Institute of Risk Management and President of the British Health and Safety Society.

PUBLISHER'S NOTE

IOSH and IOSH Services Limited assume no responsibility for the contents of this book, in whole or in part, nor for interpretations or concepts advanced by the author.

All rights reserved. No part of this publication may be reproduced in any material form (including photocopying or storing it in any medium by electronic or photographic means and whether or not transiently or incidentally to some other use of this publication) without written permission of the copyright owner. Applications for the copyright owner's permission to reproduce any part of this publication should be addressed to the publisher.

Warning: The doing of an unauthorised act in relation to a copyright work may result in both a civil claim for damages and criminal prosecution.

© Copyright Dr Chris Hartley 2003
Revised 2005

Printed in England by The Lavenham Press Limited

ISBN 0 9013 5734 0

ACKNOWLEDGEMENTS

Thanks are due to the various people who made this book possible.

First, I would like to thank Peter Waterhouse, who kept me on track and read the drafts, for his expert guidance and cheerful enthusiasm. Second, I am grateful to the production editor David Porteous who put the whole book together.

I am grateful for the support of my colleagues in the Health and Safety Unit at Aston University, in particular Richard Booth, Roger Clarke, Mark Cooper, Hani Raafat and Diane Markley. Thanks are also due to Brenda Wilkins for the front-page photograph in Chapter 5, Helen Toll for the stress diagram in Chapter 12, and to other past students who gave useful feedback.

I would also like to thank the following for their valued help and advice: Margo Campbell, Lesley Gannon, Gerry Lee and Mark Piney.

I am very grateful to various individuals and organisations for permission to use their images and I have tried to acknowledge fully all external sources.

Finally, special thanks to Marie and Rohan for their continuing patience and support.

Dr Chris Hartley
Malvern, September 2003

Images from BOHS Technical Guides 7 and 12 are reproduced with permission of the BOHS.

The extract from BS EN 1032: 2003 (page 215) is reproduced with the permission of the BSI under licence number 2004DH0007. British Standards can be obtained from BSI Customer Services, 389 Chiswick High Road, London, W4 4AL. Tel +44 (0)20 8996 9001, email cservices@bsi-global.com.

© Crown copyright material is reproduced with the permission of the Controller of HMSO and Queen's Printer for Scotland.

Contents

Foreword

Introduction

1: **Setting perspectives in occupational health** 1

2: **Human physiology** 31

3: **Chemical agents** 59

4: **Biological agents** 145

5: **Noise** 177

6: **Vibration** 213

7: **Thermal environment** 231

8: **Non-ionising radiation** 263

9: **Ionising radiation** 283

10: **Lighting** 305

11: **Agents of physical misfit** 323

12: **Agents of psychosocial misfit** 361

13: **Personal protection** 381

Appendices

  1: NEBOSH syllabus 413

  2: Vocational standards knowledge requirements 427

  3: Selected list of websites 431

Index

Foreword

People have a right to have their health and safety protected from work activities. There will always be risks – our world would not function without some. But in a civilised society we expect people at work to be protected from risks that are excessive, unnecessary and preventable.

The evolution of health and safety management has meant an initial bias towards managing risks with the most obvious, immediate and dramatic outcomes – those related to safety. We have achieved some enormous reductions in work-related fatalities and major injuries. Robust inspection has had its effect.

But the workplace has changed enormously since the Health and Safety at Work etc Act 1974 was passed. There are now fewer manufacturing plants where accidents traditionally occurred. Technological advances make better controls possible, even robots to carry out extremely dangerous tasks. But new risks are overtaking those in which we have established world-leading management expertise.

This volume takes us towards the new direction for managing health and safety in the workplace. The effects of the hazardous agents covered in this book tend to be longer term. It is often difficult to say when the problem actually began or where it was caused. Because of this we have work still to do.

It is now time to give greater priority to occupational health and focus more on agents that cause harm less quickly, less obviously than safety failure, but just as devastatingly. We need to address all the agents that affect our physical and mental wellbeing to the detriment of enjoying life as a whole. We have the advantage of a developed risk management framework that means we can tackle both old and emerging risks.

The HSC has embarked on a review of its strategy, building on the good work that has gone on before. The work of the Revitalising Health and Safety and Securing Health Together strategies galvanised partnerships and led to industry sectors and businesses, together with their trade unions and safety representatives across Great Britain, setting and meeting challenging health and safety targets. The new strategy will aim to do more to tackle new and emerging health issues. We want to make sure that everyone joins us in tackling these with the same energy and commitment that has made a difference to safety.

With 3.6 million businesses and a workforce of some 28 million in Great Britain, health and safety cannot be the concern of the HSC and HSE alone. More and more people are realising what benefits good health and safety management brings to the workplace. Our closer links with the Department of Work and Pensions provide greater opportunity for shared agendas, particularly getting people back into work who have been ill or injured as a result of their work.

This volume provides a wide-ranging overview of risk control for hazardous agents. I am sure that it will prove a valuable resource in your work raising the standards and conditions in which people work: ensuring that good health and safety conditions are accepted as a cornerstone of a civilised society.

Bill Callaghan
Chair, Health and Safety Commission
September 2003

Introduction

In general terms, occupational safety and health is concerned with the prevention or control, to a tolerable level, of the risks to life, limb and human wellbeing, as well as physical assets, that arise from work. Within this broad range there are a number of specific subdivisions, one of which is the risk to human wellbeing from hazardous agents. This is the subject of this book.

Unfortunately, the failure to control the risk from hazardous agents at a tolerable/acceptable level – in other words, the incidence of occupational diseases and ill health – does not always become apparent until after years of exposure to the conditions, and this leads many to ignore the risk until it is too late.

The eminent occupational health academic Professor Malcolm Harrington has described the role of occupational health services as providing a balance of functions: the early detection and control of workplace hazards; the recognition of occupational disease without missing non-occupational illness; the provision of effective health surveillance; the facilitation of treatment, rehabilitation and return to work; and ensuring that the business of the employer can be conducted safely without detriment to the health of the workforce.

Within an occupational health service, the occupational hygienist and other specialists are concerned with the risk management of hazardous agents. The aim of this book is to provide occupational safety and health practitioners with the necessary underpinning knowledge and understanding of a range of health hazards that will enable them to provide competent advice and assistance to management in the prevention and control of health risks. Equally important, this knowledge will be useful to occupational safety and health practitioners in their role of explaining health risks and the consequent need for precautions to employees and members of the community at large.

The range of hazardous occupational health agents includes chemical, physical, biological, psychosocial and ergonomic. The opening chapter sets general perspectives including occupational health challenges. This is followed by a basic review of human physiological systems and body defence mechanisms. Subsequent chapters consecutively review the risk assessment and control of chemical agents, biological agents, noise, vibration, the thermal environment, and non-ionising and ionising radiation. These are followed by chapters on agents of physical misfit, which deals with ergonomics, and on agents of psychosocial misfit, which deals with the impact of stress and violence at work – both highly topical and important issues in the modern workplace. The final chapter deals with personal protection – not only does it contain descriptions of the different types of equipment available but also it focuses centrally on the achievement of an effective strategy for the use of personal protective equipment.

The unifying theme of these chapters is providing the reader with the means of identifying the hazards, assessing the risk, and choosing appropriate prevention or control measures with respect to the full range of hazardous agents.

The book is intended to provide the knowledge and understanding requirements for the occupational health and hygiene aspects of university courses in occupational safety and health, NEBOSH Diploma courses and NVQ/SVQ Levels 3 and 4 standards for health, safety and environmental protection. It also provides basic knowledge and understanding for occupational hygiene qualifications.

Professor Peter Waterhouse
Editor

1: Setting perspectives in occupational health

(Hunter 1978. Reproduced by permission of Hodder Arnold.)

All substances are poisons, there is none that is not a poison, the right dose differentiates a poison and a remedy. (Paracelsus, 1493–1541)

…the doctor no longer knows everything about everything. (E. R. Merewether, Chief Medical Inspector of Factories, addressing the American Public Health Association in 1942)

INTRODUCTION

Exposure of people to harmful agents, that is, substances, energies and environments, occurs to some extent in all workplaces. At the national level, such exposure results in a large occupational ill health burden, although, until relatively recently, collected national statistics on occupational disease did not reflect this very clearly. The problem is that it is often difficult to link disease found in the community with occupational factors. There are many reasons for this, including statistical data collection systems, medical training and practice, and the multicausal and/or chronic nature of some diseases. Indeed, by their very nature, some apparently 'occupational' diseases will probably never be linked to their workplace causes. Some of today's ill health statistics do not reflect current working conditions. The symptoms of some chronic occupational diseases are the result of working conditions which existed many years ago, about which obviously nothing can now be done. Furthermore, even where occupational causes of disease are clearly recognised, this does not necessarily mean that suitable regulatory action will be taken, since other factors, political, economic and social, may intervene. Selected examples of some occupational health 'disasters', which support this point, are discussed later in this chapter. The historical photograph above shows the dust exposure involved in the maintenance of an asbestos carding machine.

Changes in work and patterns of occupational disease

Over the last 50 years, there has been an increasingly rapid change in the nature of the world of work in developed countries. Manufacturing and mining jobs have declined and there has been a continuing increase in office-based work. Reflecting this decline in manufacturing and mining, the number of manual jobs has decreased while non-manual occupations in other sectors have increased. This decline in manual work continues. In the UK, in 1991, 42 per cent of those in employment had manual jobs, while in 1997, this figure was down to 39 per cent (Jones *et al.* 1998). This survey also reported that 52 per cent of men and 71 per cent of women were in non-manual occupations. Furthermore, there are now many more women and part-time workers of both sexes represented in the national workforce compared to 50 years ago. The number of people working in small and medium-sized enterprises (SMEs) has also significantly increased over the last 50 years. At the same time, many large organisations have 'delayered' and 'downsized' in response to increasingly tough international economic competition. In 1993, 89 per cent of businesses employed less than four persons and this constituted 22 per cent of total employment; only 37 per cent of people worked in organisations with 500 or more people (McCaig 1998). It can be seen that not only have the types of job changed, but so have the structures within which people are employed. Both these factors have implications for occupational health provision.

This transformation in the world of work has been translated into profound changes in patterns of occupational disease. Although numbers of manual jobs have decreased, levels of musculoskeletal disorders, ill health due to stress and compensated disability from lower back pain (LBP) have significantly increased over the last 20 years. At the same time, there has been a continuing progressive decrease in the number of classical (usually acute) industrial chemical poisonings. This is partly due to a decline in manufacturing, but also because of the application of more effective management and control of exposure to substances. There is now comprehensive health and safety legislation actively promoted by the European Union and, in spite of problems of competency in some areas, the ethos of risk assessment has become firmly established.

Ideas on the nature of occupational disease are changing. It was satisfactory to picture the classical industrial poisonings as a simple biomedical model, that is, a toxic chemical entered the body, interfered with metabolic processes and the result was clinical disease. However, it is now argued that it is necessary to adopt a wider approach to understand many modern occupational diseases, and to apply a 'bio-psychosocial' model is more appropriate.

According to McCaig (1998), a 'bio-psychosocial' model describes:

> ...the interaction of physical or psychological exposures related to the work task and the effects of wider organisational influences on the individual.

This model has been particularly developed for musculoskeletal and mental health problems, which today present a challenge to occupational health practitioners. Furthermore, the effect of management systems and work organisation on ill health means that occupational health considerations need to be accounted for in management decision-making.

Although the true size of the national occupational ill health burden is not exactly defined, the UK's statistical base has been much improved with the 1990, 1995 and 1999 Household Surveys (Hodgson 1993; Jones 1998; Jones 2001) (discussed below). This gives considerably improved direction to preventive efforts. It is known that where exposure to harmful agents is reduced, by applied controls, to 'as low as reasonably practicable' (ALARP), then levels of consequent disease will also be reduced. To achieve this, competent, systematic and proactive health risk assessment and management of occupational health agents is required, and this is the unifying theme of this book.

The scope of occupational health and contributing specialists is covered in the next section. The two sections thereafter give a brief historical review highlighting the development of strategies for managing and controlling occupational health risks and their underpinning statutory regulation. Finally in this chapter, the current occupational health 'problem', future preventive strategy and the modern risk management framework are also discussed.

Scope of occupational health

The overall role of occupational health has been defined as:

> ...the promotion and maintenance of the highest degree of physical, mental and social wellbeing of workers in all occupations. (International Labour Office/World Health Organisation 1950)

FIGURE 1.1: Nature of occupational health[1]

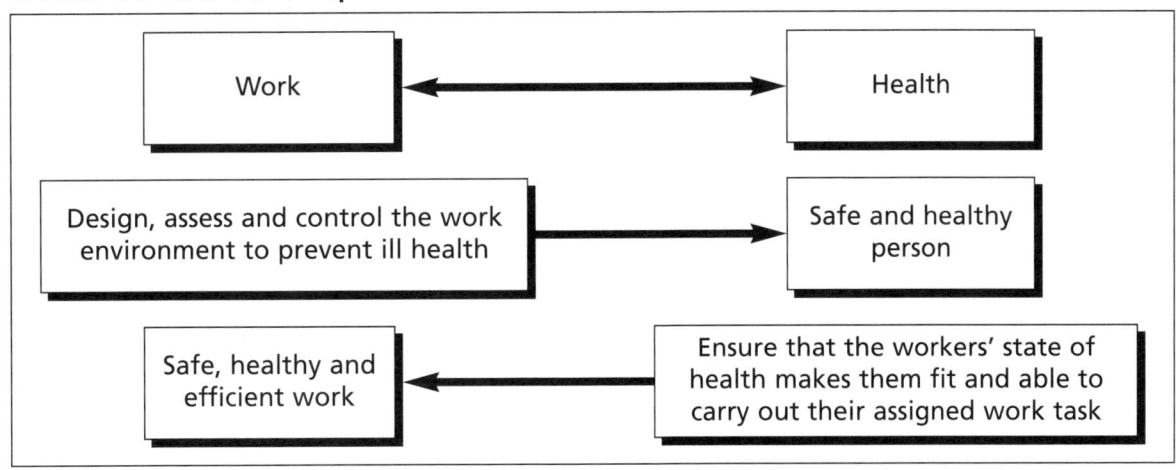

```
    Work  <----------------->  Health

Design, assess and control the work  ----->  Safe and healthy
environment to prevent ill health             person

Safe, healthy and  <-----  Ensure that the workers' state of
efficient work              health makes them fit and able to
                            carry out their assigned work task
```

Occupational health is a multidisciplinary area principally concerned with preventing people from becoming ill because of their work. It is difficult to define exactly since each of the various contributing professional specialisms has its own viewpoint. Harrington *et al.* (1998) represent occupational health as concerned with the two-way relationship between work and health, that is, both the effect of the work environment on the health of the worker as well as the worker's state of health in so far as this may affect his or her ability to do the job. Occupational health (and safety) practitioners are concerned overall with preventing ill health and discomfort by designing and controlling the work environment and making sure that people are fit for the jobs that they do.

Occupational health services

The role of occupational health services is succinctly summarised by Harrington *et al.* (1998) below:

> *The challenge for occupational health services is to provide a balance of functions: detect and control workplace hazards early; recognise occupational disease without missing non-occupational illness; provide effective health surveillance; facilitate treatment, rehabilitation and return to work; and ensure that the business of the employer can be conducted safely without detriment to the health of the workforce.*

A wide range of specialist disciplines are involved in the provision of occupational health services including:
- occupational health physicians;
- occupational health nurses;
- occupational hygienists;
- epidemiologists;
- toxicologists;
- ergonomists;
- occupational psychologists;
- radiation protection specialists;
- engineers (eg for ventilation and noise control applications); and
- health and safety practitioners.

In terms of numbers, occupational health physicians, occupational health nurses and health and safety practitioners are the largest groups of specialists involved in occupational health. However, the provision of occupational health services to workers across the UK is far from universal and Harrington *et al.* (1998) estimate that over 90 per cent of workplaces do not have occupational health cover. The employees of large organisations are most likely to have some occupational health service provision, while for those working in SMEs, this is unlikely to be available.

---
[1] Workplace health promotion to enhance people's wellbeing could be added to this definition.

Occupational health physicians and nurses

The British Medical Association (BMA) defines an occupational health physician as:

> *A doctor who in relation to any particular workplace takes full medical responsibility for advising those working therein including contractors working on the site on all matters connected directly or indirectly with the work. These may have a bearing on health as it affects work and the effect of work on health including that of the public at large, either in general or as an individual.* (Cited by Kloss, 1998)

The Royal College of Nursing defines the functions of the occupational health nurse in similar terms to the BMA, except for the significant addition of the provision of a routine treatment service (Kloss 1998).

Generally, the medical and nursing specialists are concerned with:

1. **Pre-employment medical screening** – This may involve a screening health questionnaire and clinical examination; policy on pre-employment screening needs to allow for the provisions of the Disability Discrimination Act 1998.
2. **Health surveillance** – This is a very broad term and includes periodic clinical examination[2], the assessment of visual function, the assessment of hearing by audiometry, the assessment of respiratory function by spirometry, and biological monitoring for absorption of toxic substances (eg lead in blood).
3. **Treatment** – This is usually confined to industrial workplaces and although the provision of first aid requirements in workplaces is a statutory requirement, it is usually administered by trained first-aiders[3].
4. **Health education** – This includes giving workers advice and information about healthy lifestyles and general fitness.
5. **Rehabilitation** – People returning to work after a significant period of absence are assisted in re-adjusting; occupational health personnel liaise with management about the nature and suitability of proposed work tasks for returning workers, taking into account their health status.
6. **Advice and counselling** – This can cover a wide range of subjects, both work and non-work; stress counselling is now widely applied in many larger organisations.
7. **Record-keeping** – The keeping of high quality health and exposure records is very important for many reasons; in preventing ill health, this data is crucial for future epidemiological surveys in identifying and quantifying chronic occupational health risks.

Today, there is also more involvement of medical specialists in the risk assessment and management aspects of exposure to harmful agents.

The Employment Medical Advisory Service (EMAS)

The Employment Medical Advisory Service (EMAS) was created by the Employment Medical Advisory Service Act 1972 and it was made directly accountable to the Secretary of State responsible for employment. Part II of the Health and Safety at Work etc Act 1974 amended the 1972 Act and provided a new code governing the function of EMAS.

According to Ballard (1999), it was originally intended that EMAS would co-ordinate the activities of the then medical inspectors of factories, the 'appointed' factory doctors and the medical advisors to rehabilitation centres. The posts of 'Employment Medical Advisor' and 'Employment Nursing Advisor'

---

[2] There are statutory requirements for some periodic medical examinations for workers exposed to specified harmful agents, eg vinyl chloride monomer in defined processes (COSHH, regulation 11). Otherwise, health surveillance, under COSHH, regulation 11, needs to be carried out where appropriate.

[3] The Health and Safety (First Aid) Regulations 1981.

were created by the 1972 Act. In 1998, these job titles for the two groups were changed to 'HM Medical Inspector' and 'HM Inspector of Health and Safety (Occupational Health)' respectively.

The main functions of EMAS are to:
- provide specialist support to the Health and Safety Executive (HSE) – at both policy level and on the ground to assist general health and safety inspectors;
- investigate complaints regarding ill health made by individual employees and others;
- investigate health issues raised by general practitioners and other medical personnel;
- carry out workplace inspection and investigation of occupational health risks and, where appropriate, take enforcement action;
- provide occupational health advice at the workplace to employers and employees; and
- carry out epidemiological research.

Occupational hygienists

Occupational hygiene is an area of specialist expertise located within the health and safety knowledge domain. Its subject content extends across traditional academic divisions and provides an integrated risk-based approach to managing occupational health risks. The general remit of occupational hygiene is as follows:

1. Identification of chemical, physical, biological, ergonomic and psychological hazards.
2. The evaluation of exposure to hazards – this may involve the measurement of exposure and the use of complex technical equipment.
3. Interpretation of results and determination of risks.
4. The design and application of control measures including engineering controls such as local exhaust ventilation.
5. Provision of education and training in occupational hygiene principles.
6. Research and development – largely concerned with the development of technical monitoring methods (particularly for air contaminants), tolerability standards for selected agents, and the modification and improvement of technical control measures.

The discipline had its origins in the USA (as 'industrial hygiene') and it became established in the UK (as 'occupational hygiene') in the 1950s. The terms 'industrial hygiene' and 'occupational hygiene' are broadly interchangeable. In fact, with the decline in numbers of blue-collar industrial jobs, the term 'occupational hygiene' is increasingly prevalent in the USA. The American Industrial Hygiene Association (AIHA) defines industrial hygiene as:

...that science and art devoted to recognition, evaluation and control of those environmental factors or stresses, arising in or from the workplace, which may cause sickness, impaired health and wellbeing, or significant discomfort and inefficiency among workers or among the citizens of the community.

However, the UK definition of occupational hygiene is somewhat narrower:

The applied science concerned with the identification, measurement, appraisal of risk and control to acceptable standards of physical, chemical and biological factors arising in or from the workplace which may affect the health or wellbeing of those at work or in the community. (British Occupational Hygiene Society (BOHS))

It is apparent that the forté of the occupational hygienist is to apply the risk assessment and management framework to health risks:

Occupational hygienists make professional judgments about the state of hygiene in workplaces. They make appraisals of employee exposure to chemical and physical agents, sentiently, supplemented where necessary by actual measurements. This is at the heart of occupational hygiene. (Roach 1992)

> *Occupational hygiene is concerned with conditions in the working environment that lead to ill health. It is involved in identifying and anticipating those conditions and in evaluating and controlling them. The training which occupational hygiene professionals have undergone makes them uniquely suited to much of the work of assessment.* (HSE 1988)

Occupational hygiene has been particularly involved in developing and improving workplace monitoring techniques for evaluating exposure to harmful agents (both chemical and physical), deriving tolerability standards, and developing technical control measures for reducing exposure to harmful agents.

In summary, the risk management framework has been applied to occupational health hazards, for many years, by occupational hygienists and those utilising occupational hygiene principles. Other professionals (listed below) have focused on, among other things, ergonomic aspects and harmful psychosocial agents.

Occupational epidemiologists

Harrington & Gardiner (1995) define epidemiology as:

> *The science of the occurrence of disease in human populations.*

Occupational epidemiologists collect information on ill health levels and exposure patterns for defined working populations. They attempt to find a biologically plausible statistical link between the level of disease and exposure to the workplace agent. A fuller discussion of basic concepts in epidemiology is given in Chapter 3.

Occupational toxicologists

Occupational toxicologists evaluate the toxicity of substances which are used at work. They provide hazard data for the packaging and labelling of substances and preparations, and vital information for workplace risk assessment. Toxicologists also investigate the mechanisms of action of harmful substances in animal, human and other biological systems. For further details on toxicology and the role of toxicologists, see Chapter 3.

Ergonomists

Ergonomics is concerned with design of work taking into account the human characteristics of the worker, that is, the aim is to achieve a high degree of fit between the human characteristics of the worker and the demands of work. The ultimate goal is to provide a suitable environment for a work task without excessive physical or mental strain. For a fuller description of the ergonomic approach, see Chapter 11.

Occupational psychologists

Occupational psychologists are concerned with the performance of people at work and with developing an understanding of how organisations function and how individuals and groups behave at work. Their aim is to increase the effectiveness and efficiency of people at work as well as job satisfaction. Occupational psychologists are increasingly concerned in the evaluation, prevention and control of occupational stress.

Radiation protection specialists

Radiological protection is the science and practice of limiting harm to human beings from radiation. Specialists are principally concerned with the management of risks from ionising radiation, that is, radiation capable of producing ionisation in matter, principally arising in the nuclear industry, hospitals and in specific industrial applications such as non-destructive testing.

Engineers

Many different specialist engineers may be involved in working in the area of occupational health, for example, in ventilation and noise control applications.

Health and safety practitioners
This large group of specialists is principally involved in the application and facilitation of practical risk assessment and management in the area of occupational health agents.

Occupational health hazards
As discussed above, the unifying theme is to apply competent, systematic risk assessment and management to hazards where human health risks arise. It is convenient to divide these hazards into the categories shown in Table 1.1.

TABLE 1.1: Categories of health hazards

Hazard	Examples
Chemical	Exposure to: • Organic solvents • Welding fumes • Heavy metals (eg lead, cadmium) • Isocyanates • Asbestos and silica • Around 110,000 chemicals registered with the European Inventory of Existing Commercial Substances (EINECS)[4]
Physical	Exposure to: • Noise • Vibration • Extreme thermal environments • Ionising radiation • Non-ionising radiation • Extremes of pressure
Biological	Exposure to: • Bacteria • Viruses • Fungal spores • Genetic material • Enzymes • Animal proteins
Pyschosocial/ergonomic	Exposure to: • Excessive work demands beyond a person's ability to cope • Work involving repetitive movements, excessive force and awkward postures • Poor work organisation

Historical background and perspectives
The aim of this section is to discuss the inadequacies, associated with weak legislation and lack of enforcement, of the traditional reactive approach to health risk control, together with the past focus on compensation for, rather than prevention of, occupational ill health.

Historical background
Exposure to harmful agents and consequent ill health has long been a problem for people at work. People were subjected to 'occupational' health hazards long before the Industrial Revolution. In the Stone Age, the knapping (breaking) of flints would have produced clouds of silica dust. However, it is

---
[4]Source: European Foundation for the Improvement of Living and Working Conditions (1996).

unlikely that many of our ancestors would have died of silicosis due to the high prevalence of more immediate causes of death.

For many years, mining has been recognised as a hazardous occupation. However, in the earliest times, miners tended to be serfs who were thought to be readily replaceable and thus there was no perceived need for mine owners to improve working conditions. Among the first recorded observations on miners and their diseases were those made by the physicians Agricola (1494–1555) and Paracelsus (1493–1541). In the Middle Ages, the status of the miner changed from serf to skilled worker. The demand for currency required an increasing supply of gold and silver and consequently mines tended to be dug deeper and working conditions in general worsened. Agricola described the prevailing diseases in mining communities and although levels of mortality from pulmonary diseases were not recorded nor causes known, these conditions would have included silicosis, tuberculosis and lung cancer (the latter due to exposure to radioactive ores). Mortality was high, as indicated by this comment of Agricola (cited by Schilling, 1981):

> *In the mines of the Carpathian Mountains, women are found who have married seven husbands, all of whom this terrible consumption has carried off to a premature death.*

Paracelsus, also cited by Schilling (1981), similarly recognised the diseases of the mining community:

> *We must have gold and silver, and also other metals, iron, tin, copper, lead and mercury. If we wish to have these, we must risk both life and body in struggle with many enemies that oppose us.*

Another physician, Bernardino Ramazzini (1633–1714), published the first systematic study of trade diseases and recommended that doctors should always enquire about a patient's occupation. He advised against dusty work in confined spaces and commented on lack of ventilation in workplaces. Furthermore, he advised patients to stop work immediately the symptoms of disease appeared. In his book *De Morbis Artificium*, he described many diseases arising from a range of occupations:

> *I hesitate and wonder whether I shall bring bile to the noses of doctors – they are so particular about being elegant and immaculate – if I invite them to leave the apothecary's shop which is usually redolent of cinnamon and where they linger as in their own domain, and to come to the latrines and observe the diseases of those who clean out the privies.*

The Industrial Revolution in Great Britain

In the late 18th century, the Industrial Revolution began in Great Britain with the development of the factory system. The dreadful working conditions aroused concern about the effects of work on the health and wellbeing of workers, particularly young children.

In 1775, Percival Pott drew attention to soot as a cause of scrotal cancer in children working as chimney sweeps. This is the first example of a documented 'occupational' cancer. The condition was caused by irritation of the skin of the scrotum by chimney soot. Hunter (1978) cites Pott's original evocative comments:

> *The fate of these people seems singularly hard: in their early infancy they are most frequently treated with great brutality, and almost starved with cold and hunger; they are thrust up narrow and sometimes hot chimneys, where they are bruised, burned and almost suffocated, and when they get to puberty become peculiarly liable to a most noisome, painful and fatal disease.*

Previously, in 1773, the philanthropist Jonas Hanway had drawn attention to the miserable condition of the 'climbing boys' and suggested that such apprentices should be licensed. In 1814, an Act was passed by Parliament forbidding the climbing of chimneys by children, but by the 1860s, the employment of boys for this purpose was increasing. It was not until the Climbing Boys Act 1875, promoted by Lord Shaftesbury, that this practice was finally stopped. In 1831, the physician Charles Thackrah published the first seminal British work on occupational disease – it was entitled:

The Effects of the Principal Arts, Trades and Professions, and of Civic States and Habits of Living, on Health and Longevity, with Suggestions for the Removal of many of the Agents which produce Disease and shorten the duration of Life.

This work attracted the attention of both the medically qualified and the layman when it appeared. Hunter (1978) credits it with stimulating factory and health legislation, which mitigated some of the worst effects of industrialisation. Michael Sadler quoted this book extensively in Parliament during the reading of the 1833 Factory Bill. Thackrah comments on many subjects including postural deformities in young children, lung disease in tailors, miners, metal grinders and other groups, and lead poisoning in pottery glaze-dippers. He made specific recommendations for eliminating lead poisoning in pottery workers:

Could not the process be effected without the immersion of the hands in the metallic solution? Or could it not be effected by a machine? Or could not some article less noxious be substituted for the lead? I am told that cheapness of the leaden glaze is the chief recommendation. The total disuse of lead in glaze is highly desirable. (Cited by Hunter, 1978)

Thackrah also describes 'modern' disorders concerned with the ill effects of bad posture and wear and tear problems arising from the chronic overuse of limbs.

Measurement of occupational mortality was first introduced into England and Wales in the middle of the 19th century. William Farr used population census figures to calculate mortality rates in certain occupations (Schilling 1981). This drew attention to the high risks of injury and disease faced by factory workers and miners at the time. The epidemiologist Edward Greenhow (1814–1888) compared the mortality figures of lead-mining towns with those towns without lead mines and concluded that there was excessive mortality due to inhalation and/or other exposure to lead dust (Schilling 1981). From this work, he also came to the general conclusion that much pulmonary disease in the industrial districts of England and Wales was due to inhalation of dust and fumes arising at work. The first factory inspectors were appointed in 1833, against much opposition, and with, initially, very limited powers. In 1862, the first Chief Medical Officer to the Local Government Board, Sir John Simon, who had been much influenced by Thackrah's work, commented:

The canker of industrial disease gnaws at the very root of our national strength. (Posner 1973)

Some pioneers for improved conditions occasionally inspired the hostility of both colleagues and manufacturers. The physician John Thomas Arlidge (1822–99) studied the diseases of potters and a colleague wrote of him:

He made an unfortunate beginning of his career by compiling statistics of the people working in the potteries which gravely reflected on the humanity of the manufacturers. He was instrumental in the appointment of factory surgeons for earthenware and china manufacture upon which this entailed much expense. His medical friends were up against him and up to his death this feeling never died out. (Posner 1973)

In the mid-19th century, there was general concern about lead poisoning, particularly in the pottery industry, where this overshadowed the much older problem of potter's rot (silicosis). Illustrating the problem of arousing concern about chronic ill health conditions, Arlidge commented:

In one sense, indeed, it is unfortunate that it does not for the most part awake attention by any immediate tangible consequences. Its disabling action is very slow but it is ever progressive, and until it has already worked its results it is let pass as a matter of indifference – an inconvenience of the trade. (Posner 1973)

During the 19th century, increasing evidence was collected on the rise in levels of industrial disease and this led, in 1898, to the appointment of Sir Thomas Legge as the first Medical Inspector of Factories within the Factory Department of the Home Office. Legge took a rigorous, modern, scientific approach to the investigation and management of occupational health problems. He is best remembered for his investigative work on lead poisoning and his axioms (rules), which are given below, are principally concerned with the achievement of effective control of exposure:

1. Unless and until the employer has done everything – and everything means a good deal – the workman can do next to nothing to protect himself, although he is naturally willing enough to do his share.
2. If you can bring an influence to bear external to the workman (ie one over which he can exercise no control), you will be successful; and if you cannot or do not, you will never be wholly successful.
3. Practically all industrial lead poisoning is due to the inhalation of dust and fumes; and if you stop their inhalation, you will stop the poisoning[5].
4. All workmen should be told something of the danger of the material with which they come into contact and not be left to find out for themselves – sometimes at the cost of their lives.

At the turn of the 20th century, new statutory regulations required those in specific occupations to be examined by 'Certifying Surgeons', namely workers involved in making lead paints, lucifer matches, and explosives (with dinitrobenzene), vulcanising rubber (with carbon disulphide) and enamelling iron plates. Notification requirements were introduced for disease caused by lead, phosphorus, arsenic and anthrax. At this time, there was a high general prevalence of acute lead poisoning and also 'phossy jaw' in matchmakers.

During the First World War, concern heightened about the effects of work on the health and efficiency of workers. The hazards of TNT (trinitrotoluene) and organic solvents used in aircraft manufacture were given particular attention. There was a rapid growth in the provision of first aid and industrial medical and nursing services. However, these were short-lived phenomena and numbers declined soon after the war.

Schilling (1963) asserts that the first 30 years of the 20th century were concerned with preventing industrial disease and accidents, but that in subsequent years, the emphasis shifted from not only protecting, but also improving, the health of the working population.

During the early years of the 20th century, the discipline of industrial hygiene developed in the USA, with occupational hygiene following in the UK in the early 1950s. The Robens Report was published in 1973 with the subsequent introduction of the Health and Safety at Work etc Act in 1974. Also in 1973, the UK joined the European Economic Community (EEC), now the European Union, and became subject to the requirements of European directives. Following the adoption of a series of directives on health and safety matters during the 1980s and early 1990s, a battery of risk assessment-driven regulations were enacted into UK law and these covered both health and safety risks. These regulations underpin the risk assessment and management framework which today unifies the efforts of occupational health (and safety) practitioners.

Occupational health disasters

In the 20th century, there have been various occupational health disasters and two examples will be discussed briefly in order to illustrate the inadequacy of the traditional reactive approach to health

---

[5]Due to the efforts of Legge and his colleagues, the annual numbers of notified cases of lead poisoning were reduced from 1,278 in 1898 to 104 in 1931. Lead production over this period is estimated to have increased from 200,000 to 210,000 tons per annum (Lane 1947, cited by Hunter, 1978).

hazard management. Furthermore, even where ill health problems were recognised and clearly linked to causes, this did not necessarily mean that suitable action was taken, since, as will be demonstrated, other political, economic and social factors may intervene.

The cases are, first, bladder cancer arising from exposure to aromatic amines (2-naphthylamine in particular), predominantly in the chemical and rubber industry, and second, the ill health experience following widespread exposure to asbestos dust. (For more details on these case studies, the reader should consult Atherley (1978) – now, sadly, out of print.)

Compensation rather than prevention – Bladder cancer and aromatic amines

By the mid-1930s, bladder cancer due to exposure to aromatic amines was widely recognised as a significant risk to workers in the UK chemical industry and there was pressure for it to be 'scheduled' under the 'Workman's Compensation' legislation[6]. According to Atherley (1978), the chemical industry at the time thought that this would have been a premature step and that confirmation of the link between aromatic amine exposure and bladder cancer was required in the form of an epidemiological survey. Furthermore, the industry offered a 'gentlemen's agreement' where men with the disease would 'not be worse off' than if the disease had been scheduled. This was accepted by the trade unions and, due to the intervention of the Second World War, an epidemiological survey was not carried out until 1948. The carcinogenic role of 2-naphthylamine and benzidine was then clearly established.

Following the survey, action included scheduling tumours of the bladder under National Insurance legislation, while ICI ceased to manufacture 2-naphthylamine in 1949 and its manufacture in Britain was totally discontinued in 1952. Five years later, a voluntary code of practice recommending control and medical procedures was introduced by the chemical industry. The Carcinogenic Substances Regulations 1967 (which were a direct result of this whole episode), together with other regulations, forbade the manufacture and importation into Great Britain of these and related substances.

It is worth noting that there was a 14-year interval between the scheduling of the disease under National Insurance compensation legislation and the introduction of legislation to prevent and control the disease. The Robens Committee (1972) commented unfavourably on this general tendency:

> *Prevention and compensation are two sides of one problem. Most people would say that prevention should be the first consideration. In practice the situation in this country is such that whenever there is a degree of conflict between better accident prevention provisions on the one hand, and compensation principles and procedures on the other, it is the latter which dictates what should be done.* (Robens 1972)

Case *et al.* (1954), in an epidemiological survey, also identified an excess of bladder tumours in the rubber industry and this was subsequently linked to the presence of both 1-naphthylamine and 2-naphthylamine as impurities in Nonox S, an antioxidant used to prevent the deterioration of rubber in tyres. According to Case (1966), the rubber-manufacturing employers decided against a similar survey to that done in the chemical industry, apparently because it did not want to 'alarm employees'. (Later in 1966, Case was to report the incidence of bladder tumours in men engaged in certain occupations. In workers involved in the distillation of 2-naphthylamine, 100 per cent of men were affected.)

In the case of this occupational health disaster, compensation clearly took precedence over prevention of the disease.

Complacency – Ill health from exposure to asbestos dust

Asbestos is the term used to describe several mineral fibrous silicates, principally crocidolite, amosite, chrysotile and anthophyllite. Asbestos is now known to cause asbestosis (progressive fibrosis), carcinoma of the lungs, mesothelioma of the pleura and peritoneum, and other pathological conditions.

---
[6]Various Workman's Compensation Acts 1897–1946.

The hazardous nature of this material was noted by the Chief Inspector of Factories, who in his annual report for 1898 commented:

> *The evil effects of asbestos dust have also attracted my attention, a microscopic examination of this mineral dust which was made by H. M. Medical Inspector clearly revealed the sharp, glass-like, jagged nature of the particles, and where they are allowed to rise and remain suspended in the air of a room, in any quantity, the effects have been found to be injurious, as might have been expected.*

Murray (1907) reported cases of asbestosis disease in people he examined in 1900 (Hunter 1978). Following case reports of asbestosis in the 1920s, Merewether & Price (1930) carried out an inquiry, which resulted ultimately in the Asbestos Industry Regulations 1931. In the inquiry report, Merewether commented that full development of asbestosis could be prevented in a workplace if the concentration of asbestos fibres was maintained below that found in the spinning processes of a factory processing raw materials (because the observed incidence of asbestosis disease was low with such processes). In the 30 years following this report, no progress was reported in developing a working hygiene standard for exposure to airborne asbestos dust.

Lynch & Smith (1935) in the USA reported a link between asbestos exposure and carcinoma of the lung. A near contemporary report by Merewether, cited by Atherley (1978), suggested that 17.7 per cent of a male population with asbestosis had died of lung malignancy. However, no full-scale epidemiological studies were made on asbestos factory workers until Doll (1955), who investigated employees with at least 20 years' exposure in an asbestos textile plant. He found that this group experienced ten times the lung cancer deaths of non-asbestos workers of the same age.

However, the very high degree of complacency in the asbestos-manufacturing companies is illustrated by this observation, in 1949, by Dr Kenneth Smith, the medical director of a Johns-Manville plant in Canada where seven men had been found to have asbestosis:

> *It must be remembered that although these men have the X-ray evidence of asbestosis, they are working today and definitely are not disabled from asbestosis. They have not been told of this diagnosis, for it is felt that as long as the man feels well, is happy at home and at work, and his physical condition remains good, nothing should be said. When he becomes disabled and sick, then the diagnosis should be made and the claim submitted by the Company. The fibrosis of this disease is irreversible and permanent so that eventually compensation will be paid to each of these men. But as long as the man is not disabled, it is felt that he should not be told of his condition so that he can live and work in peace and the Company can benefit by his many years of experience. Should the man be told of his condition today there is a very definite possibility that he would become mentally and physically ill, simply through the knowledge that he has asbestosis.* (Epstein 1979)

Consider the comment below (Lloyd-Davies 1957) in an industrial medicine textbook about dust in an asbestos factory (this was just two years *after* the publication of Doll's 1955 report linking asbestos exposure and lung cancer mentioned above):

> *A rough but useful means of judging the dustiness of a work room is to look at the back of a girl's hair to see how much asbestos is caught there.* (Lloyd-Davies 1957)

The Asbestos Industry Regulations 1931 required the use of exhaust ventilation systems "to ensure that no asbestos dust was allowed to escape into the air of any room in which people worked". However, these Regulations had a great weakness, since they applied controls only to the asbestos-manufacturing industry itself and not to the many industries in which asbestos was processed and used. Following growing concern, these Regulations were reviewed in the mid-1960s and subsequently replaced by the Asbestos Regulations 1969.

In 1968, the British Occupational Hygiene Society (BOHS) published an exposure standard for chrysotile asbestos dust and this was based on the proposition that the risk of "the earliest demonstrable effects on the lung due to asbestos" would be less than one per cent for an accumulated exposure of 100 fibre-years (ie exposure at two fibres/ml for 50 years or four fibres/ml for 25 years). The standard noted the significant risk of lung cancer associated with asbestosis and the risk of mesothelioma of the pleura and peritoneum, associated particularly with crocidolite exposure. The standard specifically noted the lack of quantitative information linking exposure to asbestos dust and incidence of both lung cancer and mesothelioma (BOHS 1968).

Since BOHS published its hygiene standard, attitudes towards asbestos have changed radically, from complacency to anxiety. Prosecutions were very rare under the Asbestos Industry Regulations 1931 during the 40 years they were in force, while between 1969 and 1978, 51 firms were prosecuted for 120 different contraventions of the 1969 Asbestos Regulations. (The Asbestos Regulations 1969 have now been replaced by the current, proactive, risk assessment-driven Control of Asbestos at Work Regulations 2002 (CAW).)

The Parliamentary Commissioner (1975) investigated asbestosis at the Acre Mill asbestos factory in Hebden Bridge, Yorkshire, and examined the Factory Inspectorate's conduct. He found that for many years both the employer and the Factory Inspectorate were unaware of the full extent of the dangers from exposure to the asbestos dust. The Commissioner also found that there was little contact over the years between the Factory Inspectorate and the workforce at the mill. How much asbestosis would have been prevented if the workforce had been adequately consulted is a matter for speculation.

In conclusion, the true magnitude of the overall asbestos disaster is evoked by the epidemiologist Richard Peto who commented in 1982:

There will be a total of about 50,000 asbestos-induced deaths in Britain in the next 30 years or so. Because it is so widespread, asbestos may well be the worst occupational carcinogen (cancer-causing substance) ever.

Sadly, this prediction is currently in the process of coming true and it is only recently that the EU countries have agreed to ban the marketing and use of chrysotile asbestos (the only type currently permitted) from January 2005.

Development of occupational health legislation

The emergence of health and safety legislation in a piecemeal fashion has been well documented and much analysed. Robens (1972) cites the preface to *A History of Factory Legislation* (Webb 1910) which commented:

This century of experiment in factory legislation affords a typical example of English practical empiricism. We began with no abstract theory of social justice or the rights of man. We seem always to have been incapable even of taking a general view of the subject we were legislating upon. Each successive statute aimed at remedying a single ascertained evil. It was in vain that objectors urged that other evils, no more defensible, existed in other trades or among other classes, or with persons of ages other than those to which the particular Bill applied. Neither logic nor consistency, neither the over-nice consideration of even-handed justice nor the quixotic appeal of a general humanitarianism, was permitted to stand in the way of a practical remedy for a proved wrong.

Detailed law needs to be constantly extended and elaborated to deal with new problems arising from the rapid pace of current industrial development. Robens (1972) identified this traditional approach as unsatisfactory because it was cumbersome and inflexible and could not respond rapidly enough to such change. Robens categorised existing health and safety legislation into three major groups: first, that covering large sectors of the working population (eg those in factories, offices, shops, railway premises, mines and quarries); second, legislation requiring special control over certain industrial activities and substances; and third, legislation covering emissions and effluents from workplaces. This unwieldy body of highly prescriptive law was broadly composed of nine main statutes and 500 statutory instruments.

Oldershaw (1989) focuses specifically on occupational health legislation, illustrating the reactive nature of its development:

> *For well over a hundred years in the UK, legislation has been passed with the aim of combating an established ill health condition clearly resulting from a particular work activity. Disease has been found and steps have been taken to stop the process, prevent exposure, ban the substance thought to be responsible, substitute the substance or, finally, to physically control exposure to the material perhaps by engineering or personal protective means.*

This may have been a slow or laborious process but one which had the merit of allowing the explicit demonstration of the effectiveness of applied controls in preventing a clearly recognised health effect. However, there are significant drawbacks where the ill health is serious, chronic or irreversible. Robens (1972) makes a similar point when citing the Chief Inspector of Factories Annual Report for 1970:

> *The proliferation of more subtle hazards, and particularly potential carcinogens, must also be the subject of continuous vigilance. Cancer-producing chemicals share with asbestos and other fibrogenic dusts a latent period before the disease is manifest. Any failure at the present time to bring these risks under control can only therefore be reaped as a bitter harvest, not by us but by the next generation.*

For a long period, the control of toxic substances relied on section 63 of the Factories Act 1961, which stated:

> *In every factory in which, in connection with any process carried on, there is given off any dust or fume or other impurity of such a character and to such extent as to be likely to be injurious or offensive to the persons employed, or any substantial quantity of dust of any kind, all practicable measures shall be taken to protect the persons employed against inhalation of the dust or fume or other impurity and to prevent its accumulating in any workroom, and in particular, where the nature of the process makes it practicable, exhaust appliances shall be provided and maintained, as near as possible to the point of origin of the dust or fume or other impurity, so as to prevent it entering the air of any work room.*

There were relatively few prosecutions under this legislation, since there was a lack of air monitoring techniques to quantify such 'dust or fume' as well as any methods to determine its 'injurious' nature. This was combined with a lack of expertise to decide what constituted 'practicable measures'. Up until the 1940s, there were very few defined tolerable limits or air quality standards. In addition, there was little guidance on ventilation design principles for factories and workplaces. In the USA, the American Conference of Governmental Industrial Hygienists (ACGIH) first published an industrial ventilation manual in 1951.

Special regulations made under the Factories Acts prohibited the use of some substances and controlled the circumstances in which specified materials (such as asbestos, chromic acid and lead) could be used in manufacturing processes. There were other relevant statutory provisions such as the Agriculture (Poisonous Substances) Act 1952 where 40 chemicals were scheduled and these had prescribed precautions for their use. However, Robens (1972) commented:

> *Many toxic substances in many industrial circumstances are not directly regulated by statutory provision.*

The subsequent Health and Safety at Work etc Act 1974, section 6, placed new general duties on the manufacturers and suppliers of chemical substances. However, this had limited effectiveness, even after passing of other complementary regulations dealing with the toxicity of new substances (Notification of New Substances Regulations 1982 (NONS)[7]), and the classification, packaging and labelling of substances (Classification, Packaging and Labelling Regulations 1984, now replaced by the Chemicals (Hazard Information and Packaging for Supply) Regulations 2002 (CHIP)). The HSE (1985) stated that more than 100,000 substances were registered with the European Inventory of Existing Commercial Substances (EINECS). These would not be treated as 'new substances' for the purposes of the NONS Regulations and, for such substances, premarket testing would not be required. This number of substances gives an indication of the logistical problems in managing the risks from chemical agents in the workplace.

The traditional approach to the use of substances was *de facto* to assume that they were safe until there was overwhelming evidence that this was not the case, at which point action would be taken. Unfortunately, such action often concentrated on compensation at the expense of preventive strategies, as discussed in the aromatic amines case study above. The HSE published a toxic substances philosophy in 1976 as a guidance note (HSE 1976). This suggested that *all* substances should be regarded as potentially harmful and that all exposure should be kept as low as reasonably practicable. There was an increasingly strong feeling that specific regulations concerned with controlling all toxic substances were required.

Concerns about exposure to chemical and physical agents, in the UK and the rest of Europe, provided the impetus for a series of European Community directives aimed at preventing or controlling exposure at work. In response, several sets of UK regulations were enacted and these are summarised in Figure 1.2, which illustrates the current position.

FIGURE 1.2: Summary of risk assessment-driven regulations

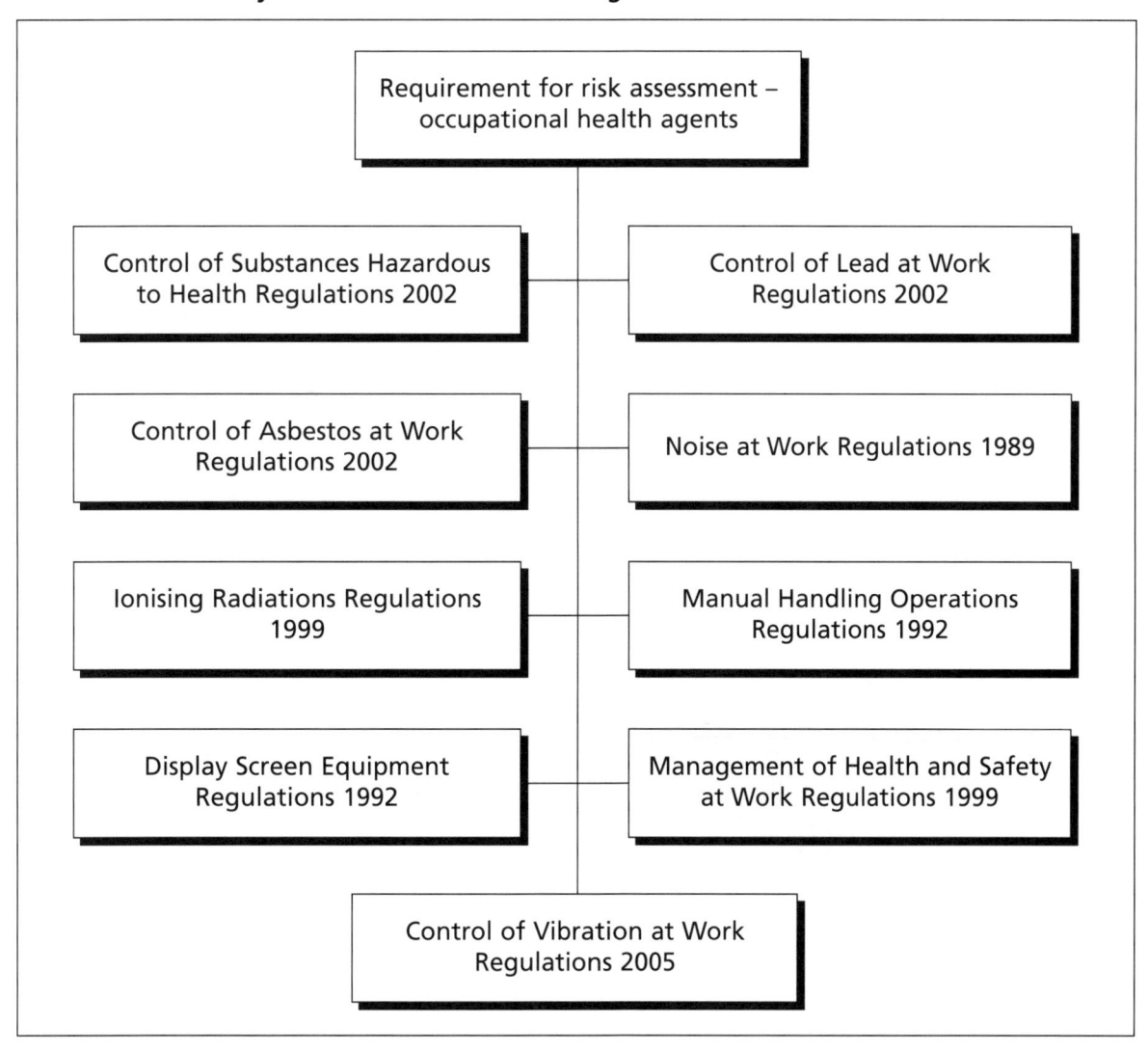

- Requirement for risk assessment – occupational health agents
  - Control of Substances Hazardous to Health Regulations 2002
  - Control of Lead at Work Regulations 2002
  - Control of Asbestos at Work Regulations 2002
  - Noise at Work Regulations 1989
  - Ionising Radiations Regulations 1999
  - Manual Handling Operations Regulations 1992
  - Display Screen Equipment Regulations 1992
  - Management of Health and Safety at Work Regulations 1999
  - Control of Vibration at Work Regulations 2005

---

[7]These Regulations were revised in 1993.

Following the enactment of regulations for work with lead, ionising radiations and asbestos, the original Control of Substances Hazardous to Health Regulations (COSHH), issued in 1988, broadened the requirement for competent risk management to all situations where people were exposed to "substances hazardous to health" arising as a result of work activity. The COSHH Regulations required, for the first time, the systematic identification of all such substances used by an employer, an assessment of the health risks arising, implementation of prevention or adequate control measures, and a regular review of this whole process. In 1992, further risk assessment-driven regulations followed, covering display screen equipment, manual handling operations and, crucially, the management of health and safety at work. The latter regulations contain the requirement to carry out risk assessments for all hazards at work.

The current occupational health problem

This section will explore some important aspects of current occupational health challenges and describe how we can deal with them. The following two comments and Figure 1.3 illustrate the extent of the occupational health problem in the UK:

> *In 1995 an estimated 2.5 million[8] individuals in Great Britain were suffering from an illness which they believe was caused or made worse by their work. One-fifth of these reported that they were suffering from more than one such condition.* (HSC 1996)

> *Work-related ill health costs the UK economy 13 million lost working days a year.* (HSC 1998)

Furthermore, the HSE has estimated that occupational ill health costs the economy four to five billion pounds annually (HSE 1994).

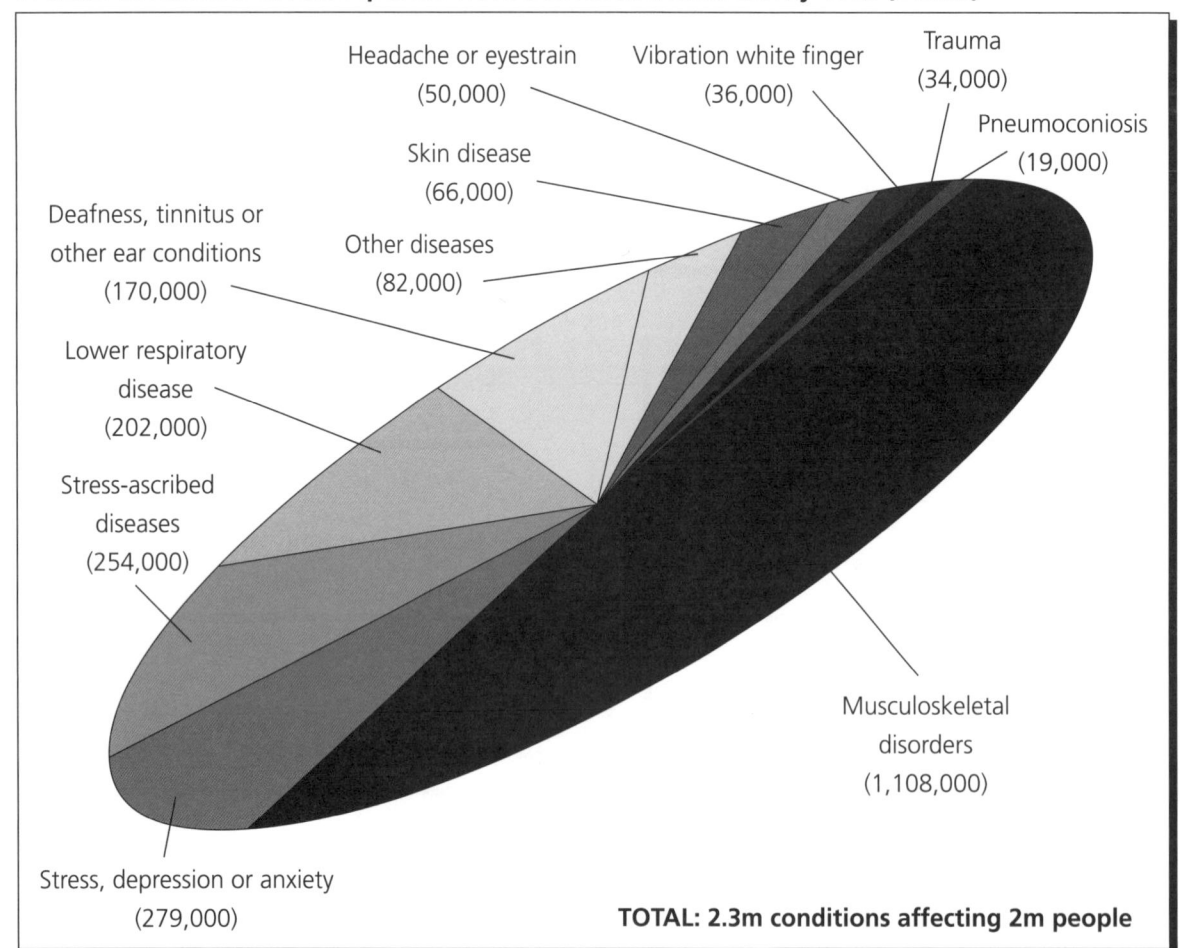

FIGURE 1.3: Results of self-reported work-related ill health survey 1995 (SWI95)

- Headache or eyestrain (50,000)
- Vibration white finger (36,000)
- Trauma (34,000)
- Pneumoconiosis (19,000)
- Skin disease (66,000)
- Deafness, tinnitus or other ear conditions (170,000)
- Other diseases (82,000)
- Lower respiratory disease (202,000)
- Stress-ascribed diseases (254,000)
- Musculoskeletal disorders (1,108,000)
- Stress, depression or anxiety (279,000)

TOTAL: 2.3m conditions affecting 2m people

(DETR, from Jones et al. 1998)

---

[8]This figure was subsequently revised down to two million in later publications.

Every year, many more people in the UK die prematurely from occupational diseases than are killed in workplace accidents. As a direct comparison with the above survey, for example, 272 workers died in accidents at work between April 1995 and March 1996 (HSC 1996). As regards occupationally-induced cancer alone, the HSE has commented:

> *The existing routine sources of information on occupational cancer greatly underestimate its scale; and the best available estimate is that four per cent of cancer deaths have occupational causes, with a range of acceptable figures from two to eight per cent, which would correspond to between 3,000 and 12,000 deaths per year in Britain today.* (HSC 1996)

As mentioned above, there is no effective national system to identify and collect data on occupational disease. The HSC has acknowledged the difficulty in collecting such data:

> *We can measure the extent of ill health caused by work only quite roughly. Our current best estimate suggests that it directly gives rise to at least 2,000 premature deaths each year, and contributes to a further 8,000. We estimate that at least 80,000 new cases of work-related disease occur each year and that more than 500,000 people suffer continuing damage to health from work.* (HSC 1991)

Problems with occupational ill health and causation

The question as to whether an accident happened at work is reasonably straightforward, while the judgment as to whether a particular illness was caused by work is often problematic. A major problem when considering ill health and disease in the wider community is separating that proportion caused by work and that caused by other factors such as smoking, diet, lifestyle and general environment. For example, lung carcinoma (cancer) is a relatively common multicausal disease. In the general population, lung carcinoma is strongly linked with smoking habits. However, occupational exposure to chromates, arsenic, asbestos and other chemical agents is also associated with an increased risk of this disease. The disease is clinically the same whether the cause is cigarette smoking or other chemical exposure. In an individual case, adequate records may not be available to indicate occupational exposure to toxic substances (assuming a doctor asks the right questions about work history) and, therefore, a connection with work may not be made.

Furthermore, other substances causing lung cancer and other common diseases have not yet been recognised and Nicholson (1984) comments:

> *Any plausible frequency distribution of the relative risks of site-specific human occupational cancers would certainly have a large number of points with relative risk less than 5 were they to be known. In terms of accepted human carcinogens, we have clearly identified only the tip of the iceberg.*

This is in effect saying that, currently, there is human exposure to a large number of low potency carcinogens, which are presently unrecognised.

In the past, the only cases of occupational ill health which were widely recognised were those that were acute in nature, that is, symptoms occurred within a relatively short period following exposure (often at a high level) to the agent. This usually allowed the connection to be made between cause and effect and, thus, appropriate control measures could be identified and applied. With chronically-induced disease, exposures are generally at lower levels and over a long-term period. The time interval between first exposure and development of observable health effects may be 20 to 40 years in the case of some substances which cause cancer. After such a long latency period, together with the multicausal nature of some diseases and frequent poor record-keeping practice in the past, it may be difficult to make the connection between occupational cause and ill health effect. Consequently, this makes it difficult to obtain accurate statistical estimates of the prevalence and incidence of current occupational disease.

SETTING PERSPECTIVES IN OCCUPATIONAL HEALTH

Sources of national occupational health statistics

The HSE publishes annual statistics (see www.hse.gov.uk/statistics) on occupational disease which fall into several major categories. The HSE's stated policy is to make the fullest use of a range of sources. Different sources give varying estimates of the extent and severity of work-related diseases. Major statistical data sources are listed below:

1. Industrial Injuries Scheme and 'prescribed' diseases under social security legislation.
2. Data collected from the Reporting of Injuries, Diseases and Dangerous Occurrences Regulations 1995 (RIDDOR).
3. Voluntary schemes for reporting work-related respiratory, skin and other diseases operated by professional medical bodies.
4. Household surveys giving estimates of the numbers of people who think they have ill health caused or made worse by their work (Labour Force Surveys on self-reported work-related ill health).
5. Death certificates which are mainly useful for monitoring the most serious forms of occupational lung disease.

Industrial Injuries Scheme – Prescribed diseases

These are diseases whose occupational cause is well established. Cases are individually confirmed by medical examination and checking of the person's work history. Typical numbers claiming industrial disablement benefit for selected diseases are given in Table 1.2. The scheme compensates people (or their dependants) who are killed or injured by an accident at work or who suffer from a 'prescribed' disease. Diseases are usually prescribed in conjunction with defined occupations or work activities. Disablement benefit is awarded to sufferers where "their body or mind is impaired for more than 15 weeks".

TABLE 1.2: Claims for industrial disablement benefit by year – Selected prescribed diseases

Industrial disease	84/5	85/6	86/7	87/8	88/9	89/0	90/1	91/2	92/3	93/4	94/5	95/6	96/7	97/8	98/9	99/0
Occupational deafness	1492	1179	1381	1515	1128	1506	1041	972	901	882	763	531	513	215	316	226
Dermatitis	619	785	464	368	285	301	432	411	419	392	368	328	336	271	220	208
Byssinosis and pneumoconiosis	806	836	776	652	732	741	784	786	853	1006	866	845	594	872	870	866
Tenosynovitis	390	619	376	322	294	423	556	649	911	800	787	548	513	415	344	348
VWF	3	641	1366	1673	1056	2601	5401	2369	1447	1425	1747	3016	3288	3033	3155	3212
Asthma	166	166	220	222	220	216	293	553	510	506	514	410	298	222	196	168
Lung cancer (asbestos)	8	34	55	59	54	58	55	54	72	77	55	51	26	42	38	42
Lung cancer (non-asbestos)					4	5	4	6	3	–	4	2	1	3	7	1

After 1986 figures represent new cases 'assessed' for disablement as opposed to those actually receiving the benefit in the data which were listed before this time. (HSC 1999, 2001)

This is irrespective of whether the claimant is working or suffering loss of earnings. Individual entitlement depends on a medical assessment of degree of disability suffered. The sufferer is compared to a healthy person of the same age and sex and their disability expressed as a percentage. Until 1986, a benefit was paid where disability was recognised and accepted. This was payable (on a sliding scale) irrespective of the actual level of impairment. At this point in time a new rule was introduced, where for most prescribed diseases, benefit would only be payable if disability exceeded 14 per cent. This change greatly reduced the number of people qualifying for benefit.

Using prescribed disease A8 tenosynovitis ('Inflammation of the tendons of the hand, forearm or associated tendon sheaths') as an example, qualifying cases fell from 390 (1984–85) to four (1986–87). The 376 cases shown in Table 1.2 were those *assessed* for benefit. In 1981, there were 2,275 'spells' of Industrial Injury Benefit (now abolished) awarded for cases of this disease (HSE 1985). In the case of vibration white finger (VWF), of the 5,401 assessed cases in 1990–91, only 31 had sufficient disability from VWF alone to receive benefit. Some may have reached the 14 per cent threshold by aggregation of other disability – most likely in this case from occupational deafness.

Changes in the eligibility rules for benefit affect the numbers putting in a claim, that is, once people realise that a successful claim is unlikely, they are less likely to apply for assessment. Therefore, one must be cautious in interpreting social security data in terms of the national occupational disease trends. The VWF figure for 1990–91 represents a peak; in 2000–01, 3,317 people were assessed for benefit for VWF (HSC 2001).

Occupational cancer statistics

The statistical data for cancer greatly underestimates the true situation. Concerning lung cancer caused by asbestos or other hazardous substances, the HSC has stated:

> *Exposure to asbestos is by far the most important known occupational cause of cancer, in terms of incident cases and mortality. Because of the difficulty of determining the cause of individual cases, the numbers awarded disablement benefit considerably understate the likely true number, which is at least equal to the number of mesotheliomas and may be even greater.* (HSC 1996)

Table 1.3 lists annual deaths from mesothelioma. This cancer is very rare in the general population and very closely linked with asbestos exposure. Other asbestos-induced deaths due to lung cancer are much more difficult to detect (since this cause of death is common in the general population) and are, therefore, much less likely to be included in the collected statistics.

TABLE 1.3: Deaths from mesothelioma

Year	Number of deaths
1968	153
1993	1143
1994	1241
1995	1318
1996	1301
1997	1330
1998	1535
1999	1695
2000	1631
2001	1848

(Source: UK death certificates)

Reporting of Injuries, Diseases and Dangerous Occurrences Regulations 1995 (RIDDOR)

These Regulations define a list of 'reportable' diseases, placing a duty on the employer to inform the HSE (or other relevant authority) where cases occur. The list of diseases is combined with a list of work activities and a particular disease is only reportable if the activity requirement is also satisfied (HSE

SETTING PERSPECTIVES IN OCCUPATIONAL HEALTH

1999). The list is very similar to the 'prescribed' disease list described above, though with notable omissions such as the common condition of occupational deafness. Dermatitis was added to the list with the 1995 revision of the Regulations. Table 1.4 highlights the extent of the inadequacy of data collected by the RIDDOR system. The figures refer to *total* national reported cases of occupational disease.

TABLE: 1.4: Total cases of occupational disease reported under RIDDOR

Year	Cases
1986/87	276
1987/88	332
1988/89	309
1989/90	323
1990/91	306
1991/92	395
1992/93	331
1993/94	363
1994/95	559
1995/96	404
1996/97	1644
1997/98	1887
1998/99	2196
1999/00	2534
2000/01	2378

(HSC 1999, 2001)

There are many fundamental problems with the RIDDOR system, resulting in grossly inadequate data collection. The system has been marginally improved with the 1995 revised Regulations and their wider reporting requirements. From the collection year 1996–97 onwards, significantly increased reported numbers can be seen. The newly-reportable occupational diseases principally responsible for this increase are cramp of the hand/forearm, tenosynovitis of the hand/forearm, carpal tunnel syndrome and occupational dermatitis.

National population surveys

Some insight into overall levels of occupational disease may be gained from other sources such as national population surveys. Two large surveys were carried out in 1990 (Hodgson *et al.* 1993) and 1995 (Jones *et al.* 1998) with a smaller survey in 1999 (Jones *et al.* 2001).

For methodological reasons, the best available prevalence data is believed to be that obtained from the 1995 survey. However, the 1999 survey did highlight an increase in the relative prevalence of stress conditions and a decrease in musculoskeletal disorders compared with the previous two surveys.

In the 1990 Labour Force Survey (LFS), carried out by the then Office for Population, Censuses and Surveys (OPCS), adult respondents in England and Wales were asked whether they had:

> ...in the past 12 months suffered from any illness, disability, or other physical problem that was caused or made worse by [their] work? Please include any work you have done in the past.

Follow-up questions established: the nature of the illness and the job that was thought to have caused it; whether work was thought to have caused the condition or to have simply made it worse; and the number of days on sick leave during the year due to the complaint. Based on the results of this survey, the following estimates of self-reported work-related illness were published (Hodgson *et al.* 1993):

- 700,000 people took 13 million days off in 1989–90 because of what they regarded as 'work-related illness';
- another 670,000 people in work were affected but took no time off; and

- 750,000 retired and unemployed people reported that they were affected by the long-term consequences of work.

From the 1995 survey of self-reported work-related ill health (SWI95), similar estimates were obtained. Overall, there was a national prevalence of around 2.3 million cases of work-related ill health and two million individuals were affected (some with more than one condition). The results were as follows:
- 712,000 affected people were no longer in work;
- 575,000 were affected but took no time off work; and
- 545,000 people lost 19.5 million working days because of illness.

The main categories of illness are shown by the SWI95 survey in Figure 1.3. In Figure 1.4, results are presented as disease 'caused' by work and disease 'caused and made worse' by work.

The results from these national self-reporting surveys indicate the prevalence of different classes of ill health and give some necessary direction to prevention strategies. However, it is worth noting that some ill health conditions are underrepresented in the 1990 and SWI95 national surveys, for example, the prevalence of work-related cancer.

FIGURE 1.4: Results of the SWI95 survey

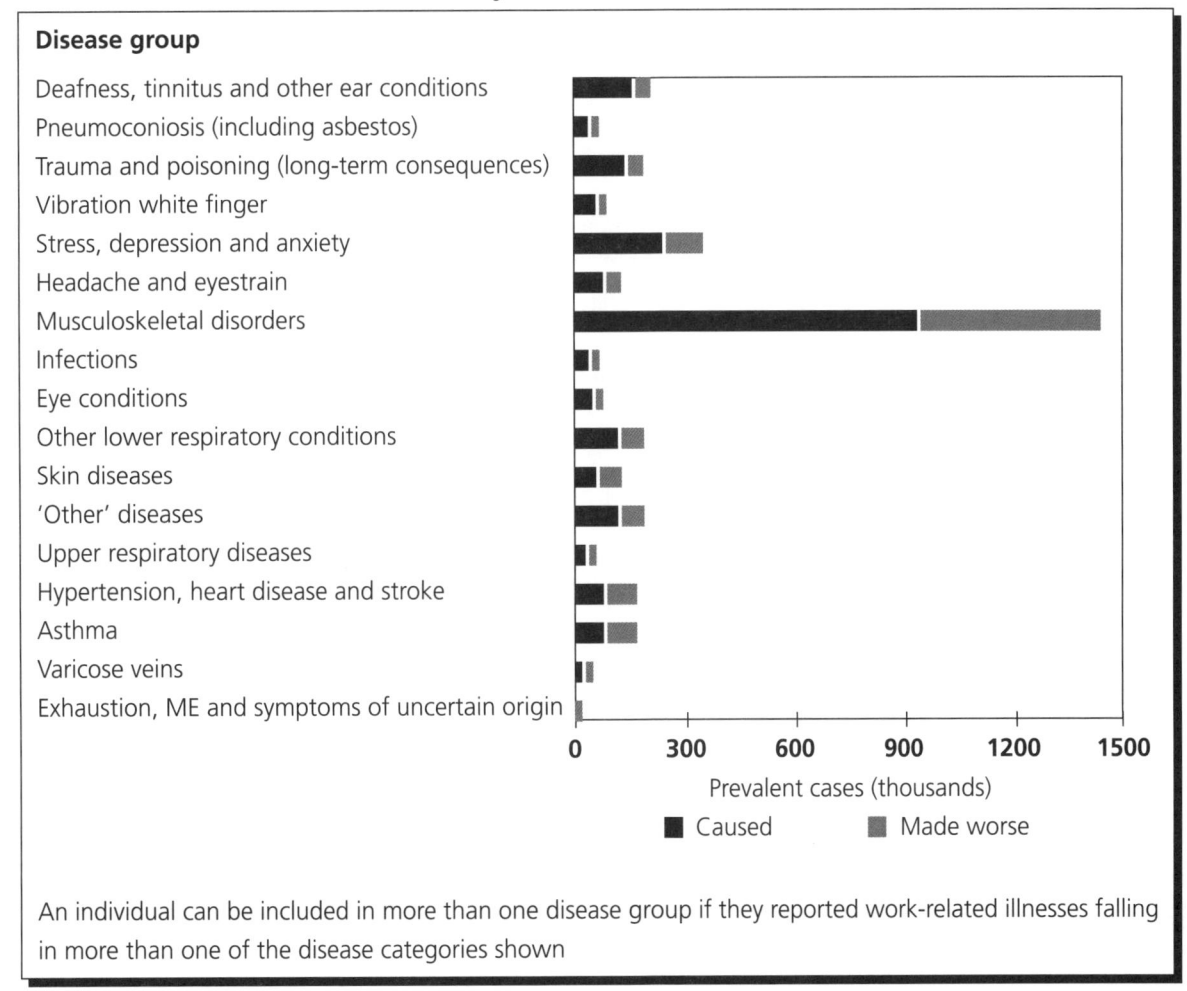

An individual can be included in more than one disease group if they reported work-related illnesses falling in more than one of the disease categories shown

(Jones et al. 1998)

The numbers indicated in the LFS contrast starkly with information gathered from the traditional sources discussed earlier. The 1990 LFS estimates that around seven per cent of all General Practitioner consultations involve work-related ill health and there has been some independent validation of this figure.

Following the implementation of the original RIDDOR code (1985), the HSC asked its Medical Advisory Committee to develop proposals for a more comprehensive data collection system for occupational ill health. The Medical Advisory Committee produced a report (HSE 1988a) and argued for various measures including:

> *The encouragement of case registers for specific types of illness and disease related to occupation – doctors would be alerted to report particular diseases to a central body collecting information on that disease.*

Only this latter recommendation was actually put into practice. In 1989, the Surveillance of Work-related Respiratory Disease (SWORD) scheme was implemented at the London Chest Hospital. SWORD is a reporting system for cases of occupationally-related respiratory disease which have been seen for the first time by occupational and chest physicians.

TABLE 1.5: Total cases of respiratory disease reported to SWORD and OPRA

Year	Cases
1994	3267
1995	2741
1996	3322
1997	3903
1998	3009
1999	4418
2000	3854

(HSC 1999, 2001)

In 1993, the University of Manchester (Centre for Occupational Health) set up a similar case register for work-related skin diseases (known as 'EPIDERM') to which dermatologists report cases. The figures in Table 1.6 relate to new cases of diagnosed contact dermatitis.

TABLE 1.6: Total cases of skin disease reported to EPIDERM and OPRA

Year	Cases
1995	3448
1996	3555
1997	3741
1998	4579
1999	4950
2000	4398

(HSC 1998a, 2001)

Figures from the SWORD and EPIDERM schemes demonstrate (regularly) that data from the Industrial Injuries Scheme (on prescribed respiratory and skin diseases) underreport true levels of occupational ill health.

There are now several other surveillance schemes for medical specialists covering a wider range of conditions including the reporting of work-related diseases by: communicable disease specialists (SIDAW – Surveillance of Infectious Disease at Work); rheumatologists (MOSS – Musculoskeletal Occupational Surveillance Scheme); psychiatrists (SOSMI – Surveillance of Occupational Stress and Mental Illness); and audiologists (OSSA – Occupational Surveillance Scheme for Audiologists). Since January 1996, occupational physicians have reported cases of various disorders to their own scheme – OPRA (Occupational Physicians Reporting Activity). The surveillance schemes are co-ordinated within an occupational disease intelligence network (ODIN) based at Manchester University. These schemes have much improved the method and quality of data collection on the above types of work-related ill health.

Data from both the RIDDOR and the statutory Industrial Injuries Scheme significantly underestimate

SETTING PERSPECTIVES IN OCCUPATIONAL HEALTH

true levels of work-related ill health. Furthermore, it is unlikely that these sources of statistical data on occupational ill health will improve dramatically in the near future. However, the national survey approach has improved our perspective of the occupational ill health problem and this type of survey is likely to be repeated in the future. It is important to bear in mind that poor quality occupational ill health data makes it difficult to decide as to what share of national resources should be allocated to prevention strategies.

One useful approach is to collect and examine data which serves as an indicator of national occupational health performance. For example, information on the number and quality of assessments generated by risk assessment-driven regulations (eg the COSHH Regulations 2002 or the Noise at Work Regulations 1989 (NAW)), together with the adequacy of implemented control measures. Other useful data could be from medical surveillance generated by the required risk assessments. Where these indicators showed that occupational health performance was improving, then this would suggest an impact on the underlying problem.

Future preventive approach

Risk management approach

Modern occupational health legislation requires a proactive risk management approach as opposed to the reactive approach applied to managing health hazards in the past. In 1991, the HSE first published an influential guide, *Successful Health and Safety Management* (the revised edition HSG65 was published in 1997), dealing with the issues and principles involved for organisations seeking to achieve successful health and safety management. This guide was intended to help organisations effect an improvement in their health and safety performance.

The important elements (shown in Figure 1.5) were linked with achievement of successful health and safety management.

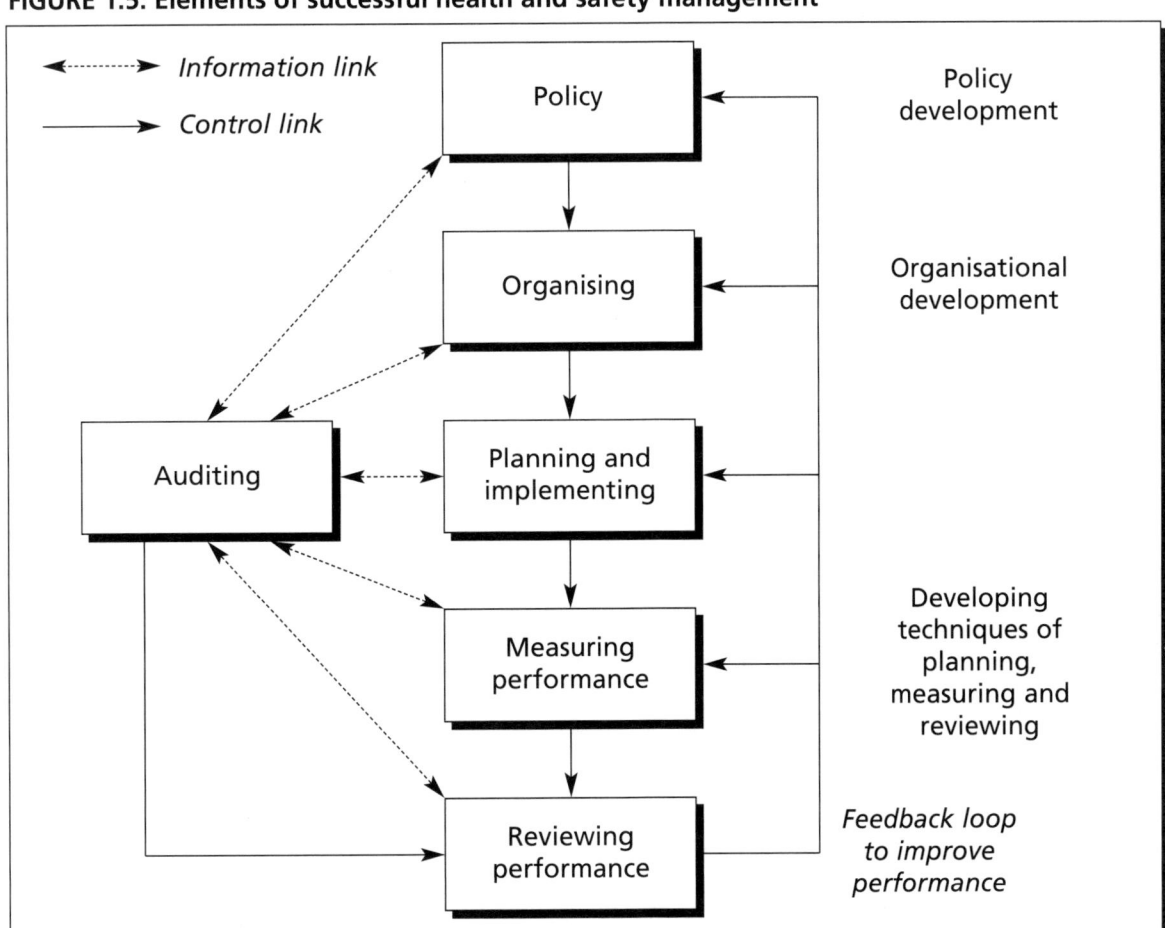

FIGURE 1.5: Elements of successful health and safety management

(HSE 1997)

Each of these elements is briefly outlined below:

Policy
Organisations which are successful at managing health and safety have effective and well-developed health and safety policies.

Organising
Successful organisations are structured in such a way that they can put health and safety policy into effective practice.

Planning and implementing
They have a planned and systematic approach to policy implementation and use risk assessment methods to decide priorities and set objectives for hazard elimination and risk reduction. Performance standards are established and performance is measured against them, a practice discussed further below.

Measuring performance
Performance is measured against predetermined standards. This reveals where and when action is needed to improve performance. There should be proactive self-monitoring to determine the success of action taken to control risks and intensive reactive monitoring where a failure has been identified, for example, the occurrence of a case of occupational disease.

Auditing and reviewing performance
This involves learning from all relevant experience and applying lessons learned in a feedback loop. Auditing involves an independent assessment of the validity and reliability of planning and control systems.

Building on this approach, the British Standard Guide BS 8800 (BSI 1996) has been published, which aims, with detailed practical advice, to assist organisations to develop effective health and safety management systems.

For some time, there has been demand for a specification for the assessment and certification of occupational health and safety management systems. In response to this, the BSI has developed the Occupational Health and Safety Assessment Series (OHSAS) Specification, OHSAS 18001 (BSI 1999). This explains what organisations have to do to develop a certifiable health and safety management system, based on the BS 8800 approach. The complementary publication, OHSAS 18002 (BSI 2000), gives guidance on how to achieve this.

Performance standards for the control of hazards and risks
The HSE highlights performance standards as vital for effective control of health and safety risks (HSE 1997). The setting of standards can be seen to involve four essential stages:
1. Hazard identification.
2. Risk evaluation.
3. Risk control.
4. Implementing and maintaining control measures.

These steps represent the key stages in health and safety risk management and they have been incorporated into risk assessment-driven legislation, such as the COSHH, NAW and Management of Health and Safety at Work Regulations (MHSW). According to the HSE (1997), a distinctive approach may be needed in the case of health risks, because of the inherent features of such risks and the difficulties in making the connection between occupational cause and the harmful ill health outcome. It is concluded that where there are complex health risks, specialist expertise may be needed for risk assessment, which may require measurement of exposure involving complex technical equipment and trained personnel. Assessing the effectiveness of control measures in this context may also involve technical measurements of the work environment.

Definition of terms

The terms 'hazard', 'risk' and 'risk assessment' are used in many different contexts and need to be defined for the purpose of this publication. The definitions reproduced here are taken from BS 8800 (BSI 1996).

Hazard

A source or situation with a potential for harm in terms of human injury or ill health, damage to property, damage to the environment, or a combination of these.

Risk

The combination of the likelihood and consequence of a specified hazardous event occurring.

Risk assessment

The overall process of estimating the magnitude of the risk and deciding whether or not the risk is tolerable or acceptable.

Risk assessment and control

Risk assessment is a process where judgments are made about the harm that might arise from work activities and processes, and the likelihood that harm will occur. The essential objective is to determine whether existing or planned preventive or control measures are adequate.

This general framework is illustrated in Figure 1.6 and is now the important focus for the efforts of occupational health and safety practitioners.

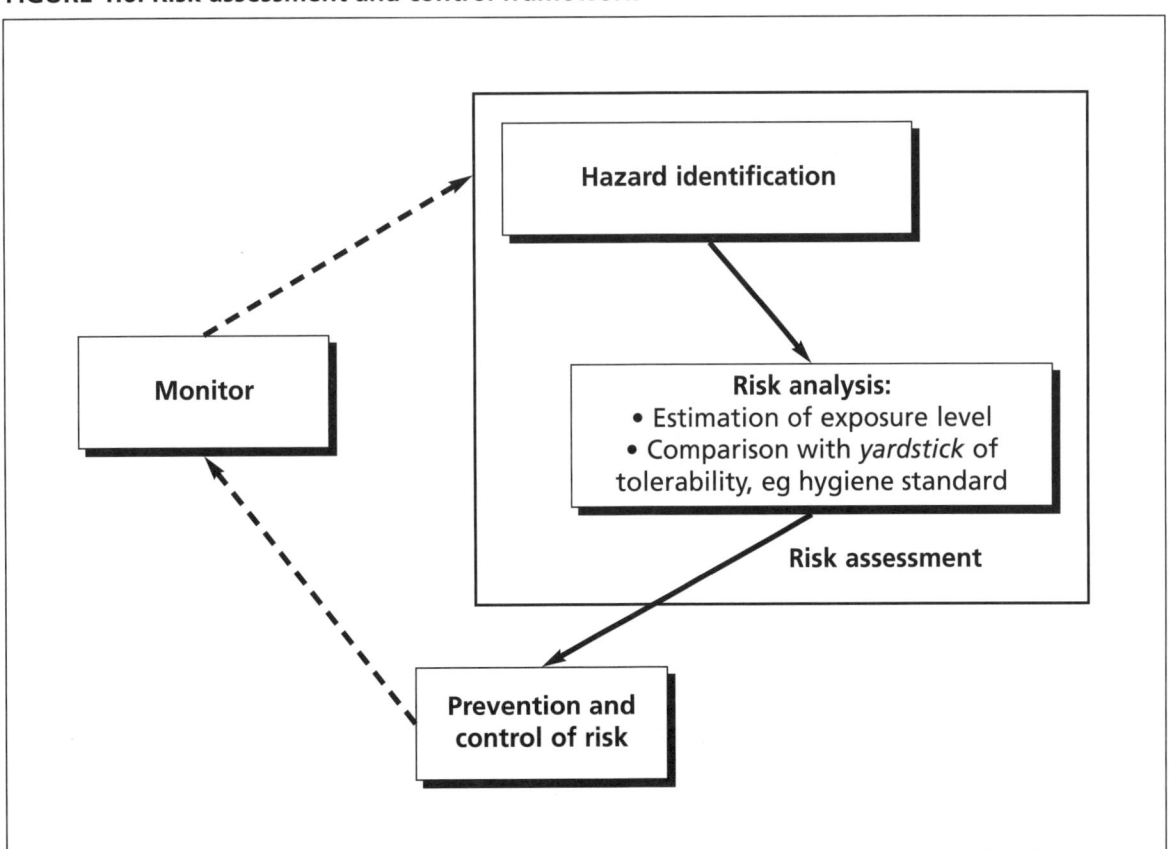

FIGURE 1.6: Risk assessment and control framework

Hazard identification

The first stage is to identify the hazard. This may result from an inspection of the process in question or may be suggested by the signs and symptoms of disease in exposed people. It is convenient to divide occupational health hazards into the following categories: chemical; physical; biological; psychosocial; and ergonomic.

Risk analysis

The second stage is to analyse the risk, that is, quantify exposure to the hazard and compare with a tolerability standard, for example, an HSE Occupational Exposure Limit (OEL).

Prevention and control

Having assessed the level of risk, the final stage is to decide on the best strategy for prevention or control. A wide range of options is available to achieve adequate control, which will depend in each case on particular circumstances. These range from a complete redesign of a process to eliminate the hazard, to the installation of a local exhaust ventilation system and a worker having to wear personal protective equipment. Principal control options are listed below.

TABLE 1.7: Principal control options

Control measure	Observations
Elimination	This is the removal of a hazard completely so that no risk can arise from it
Specification	This requires the work process to be designed so that hazards are 'designed out' or fully considered as regards prevention
Substitution	This is where one type of hazard is substituted for another (eg a noisy operation such as riveting might be substituted by welding), however, there may be new hazards with such a change in the process
Segregation	It is possible to segregate in space, ie carry out the operation in an isolated part of the work site, or segregate in time, ie where a process may be carried out in the middle of the night when there are fewer people around to be exposed
Engineering control measures	**Local exhaust ventilation** – control at source by extracting contaminated air close to its emission source and removing it from the workplace environment **Dilution ventilation** – this is used with low toxicity contaminants, which are diluted by the normal workplace air **Noise control** – this is reducing the noise emitted by a process, eg by containing the process in an acoustically-designed booth to protect the plant operator
Personal hygiene	This means having a high standard – preventing the ingestion of, or skin contact with, substances and biological agents; adequate welfare facilities including arrangements for eating/drinking (see Figure 1.7) and the provision of washrooms
Information, instruction and training	It is vital that both workers and managers have adequate information on hazards and risks and methods of control
Good housekeeping	Keeping the workplace clear, clean and tidy to prevent workplace contamination
Personal protective equipment	This is asking people to wear special clothing and protective devices during the time they are exposed to a hazard
Reduced time exposure	This is the control of a person's exposure simply by removing them from the work area

The list of control measures in Table 1.7 is often called the 'general hierarchy of control', with the least desirable measures coming at the bottom of the list. However, in a specific risk situation, it is advisable to use an optimal blend of the available options. Regulatory provisions, such as the

Control of Substances Hazardous to Health Regulations 2002 and the NAW Regulations 1989, preferentially require control at source or by engineering methods – where this is thought to be reasonably practicable – before other methods are considered. The welfare arrangements for taking a tea break on the roof of Paddington Station in the 1930s, shown in Figure 1.7, would not be acceptable today!

In conclusion, the current occupational health 'problem' poses many challenges to occupational safety and health professionals and the application of a broad risk management approach, encompassing the various types of harmful agents highlighted in this chapter, is now the key focus for their efforts.

FIGURE 1.7: Welfare arrangements – Tea break on the roof of Paddington Station

(Hulton Getty Picture Collection)

REFERENCES

American Industrial Hygiene Association, 1959, *Am Ind Hyg Assoc J*, **20,** 428.

Atherley G R C, 1978, *Occupational Health and Safety Concepts*, Applied Science. (Out of print.)

Ballard J, 1999, The Fall and Rise of EMAS, *Occupational Health Review*, July/August 1999, Industrial Relations Services.

British Occupational Hygiene Society (Committee on Hygiene Standards), 1968, Hygiene Standards for Chrysotile Asbestos Dust, *Ann Occ Hyg*, **11**, 47–69.

British Standards Institution, 1996, *Guide to Health and Safety Management Systems*, BS 8800, BSI, London.

British Standards Institution, 1999, *Occupational Health and Safety Management Systems*, Specification, OHSAS 18001: 1999, BSI, London.

British Standards Institution, 2000, *Occupational Health and Safety Management Systems*, Guidelines for the Implementation of OHSAS 18001 and OHSAS 18002: 2000, BSI, London.

Case R A M, Hosker M E, McDonald D B and Pearson J T, 1954, Tumours of the Urinary Bladder in Workmen Engaged in the Manufacture and Use of Certain Dyestuff Intermediates in the Chemical Industry, *BJIM*, **11**, 75–104.

Case R A M, 1966, Hunterian Lecture Tumours of the Urinary Tract as an Occupational Disease in Several Industries, *Ann Roy Coll Surg*, **39**, 213–235.

Chief Inspector of Factories, Annual Report for 1898.

Department of the Environment, Transport and the Regions, 1999, *Revitalising Health and Safety* (consultation document), DETR, London.

Doll R, 1955, Mortality from Lung Cancer in Asbestos Workers, *BJIM*, **12**, 81–86.

Epstein S, 1979, *The Politics of Cancer*, Doubleday.

European Foundation for the Improvement of Living and Working Conditions, 1996, *European Review on Research in Health and Safety at Work*.

Harrington J M and Gardiner K, 1995, *Occupational Hygiene* (2nd edition), Blackwell Science, Oxford.

Harrington J M, Gill F S, Aw T C and Gardiner K, 1998, *Occupational Health* (4th edition), Blackwell Science, Oxford.

Health and Safety Commission, 1991, *Annual Report 1989–1990*, HSE Books, Sudbury.

Health and Safety Commission, 1996, *Health and Safety Statistics 1995–1996*, HSE Books, Sudbury.

Health and Safety Commission, 1998, *Annual Report 1996–1997*, HSE Books, Sudbury.

Health and Safety Commission, 1998a, *Health and Safety Statistics 1997–1998*, HSE Books, Sudbury.

Health and Safety Commission, 1999, *Health and Safety Statistics 1998–1999*, HSE Books, Sudbury.

Health and Safety Commission, 2001, *Health and Safety Statistics 2000–2001*, HSE Books, Sudbury.

Health and Safety Executive, 1976, *Toxic Substances – A Precautionary Policy*, Guidance Note EH18, HMSO, London.

Health and Safety Executive, 1985, *Press Release 9*, September 1985.

Health and Safety Executive, 1988, *COSHH Assessment – A Step-By-Step Guide to Assessment and the Skills Needed for It*, HMSO, London.

Health and Safety Executive, 1988a, *Collecting Information on Disease Caused by Work* (discussion document), HMSO, London.

Health and Safety Executive, 1994, *The Costs to the British Economy of Work Accidents and Work-Related Ill Health*, HSE Books, Sudbury.

Health and Safety Executive, 1997, *A Guide to Health and Safety Management* (2nd edition), HSG65, HSE Books, Sudbury.

Health and Safety Executive, 1998, *The Changing Nature of Occupational Health*, HSE Books, Sudbury.

Health and Safety Executive, 1999, *A Guide to the Reporting of Injuries, Diseases and Dangerous Occurrences Regulations 1995* (2nd edition), L73, HSE Books, Sudbury.

Hodgson J T, Jones J R, Elliot R C and Osman J, 1993, *Self-Reported Work-Related Illness*, Research Paper 33, HSE Books, Sudbury.

Hunter D, 1978, *The Diseases of Occupations*, The English Universities Press Ltd, London.

International Labour Office/World Health Organisation, 1950, *Proceedings of the First Meeting of the Joint Committee*.

Jones J R, Hodgson J T, Clegg T A and Elliot R C, 1998, *Self-Reported Work-Related Illness in 1995: Results from a Household Survey*, HSE Books, Sudbury.

Jones J R, Huxtable C S and Hodgson J T, 2001, *Self-Reported Work-Related Illness in 1998–99*, Results from a EUROSTAT Ill Health Module in the 1999 Labour Force Survey Summer Quarter 2001, www.hse.gov.uk/hthdir/noframes//euro9899.htm.

Kloss D, 1998, *Occupational Health Law* (3rd edition), Blackwell Science, Oxford.

Lloyd-Davies T A, 1957, *The Practice of Industrial Medicine*, Churchill.

Lynch K M and Smith W A, 1935, Pulmonary Asbestos III Carcinoma of Lung in Asbesto-Silicosis, *Am J Cancer*, **24**, 56–64.

McCaig R, 1998, in *The Changing Nature of Occupational Health*, HSE Books, Sudbury.

Merewether E R A and Price C W, 1930, *Report on Effects of Asbestos Dust on the Lungs and Dust Suppression in the Asbestos Industry*, HMSO, London.

Murray M, 1907, *Departmental Committee on Compensation for Industrial Diseases – Minutes of Evidence*, Cmnd 3496, 127–128, HMSO, London.

Nicholson W J, 1984, Quantitative Estimates of Cancer in the Workplace, *Am J Med*, **5**, 341–342.

Office for Population, Censuses and Surveys, *Labour Force Survey for 1997*.

Oldershaw P J, 1989, Traps for the Unwary, in *Perspectives on Occupational Health 2*, Clarke R C (Ed.), Proceedings of a seminar held by the British Health and Safety Society, May 1989, London.

Parliamentary Commissioner, 1975, *Danger to Health From Asbestos*, Report Supplement (Department of Employment), Case 253/V, HMSO, London.

Peto R, 1982, *New Statesman*, 10 October 1982.

Posner, 1973, John Thomas Arlidge (1822–99) and the Potteries, *BJIM*, **30**, 266–270.

Roach S A, 1992, *Health Risks from Hazardous Substances at Work (Assessment, Evaluation and Control)*, Pergamon Press.

Robens, 1972, *Report of the Committee on Health and Safety at Work 1970–1972*, Cmnd 5034, HMSO.

Schilling R S F, 1963, *Occupational Health Practice* (1st edition), Butterworths, London.

Schilling R S F, 1981, *Occupational Health Practice* (2nd edition), Butterworths, London.

Tweedale G, 2000, *Magic Mineral to Killer Dust*, Oxford University Press.

Waldron H A, 1989, *Occupational Health Practice* (3rd edition), Butterworths, London.

LEGISLATION

Health and Safety at Work etc Act 1974

Management of Health and Safety at Work Regulations 1999 (SI 1999/3242)

Reporting of Injuries, Diseases and Dangerous Occurrences Regulations 1995 (SI 1995/3163)

Workplace (Health, Safety and Welfare) Regulations 1992 (SI 1992/3004)

2: Human physiology

(Wellcome Library, London)

INTRODUCTION

This chapter introduces some fundamental anatomy and physiology to assist in a basic understanding of the body's structure and function. Some body defence mechanisms are also covered. The aim is to help the reader develop an understanding of the underlying mechanisms in occupational disease.

Because of the particular needs of the subject, some organs and organ systems are considered in more detail than others, for example, the respiratory system and the skin. The special sense organs, the ear and eye, are dealt with in Chapters 5 and 10 respectively.

Basic concepts and systems

Anatomy is the study of the structure of the human body and physiology is the study of its function. The body consists of a collection of cells, tissues, organs and (organ) systems which operate as an overall functional unit. Living things can be distinguished from non-living matter by the activities which they carry out, namely, respiration, excretion, nutrition, growth, reproduction, stimulus response and movement.

Cells are the basic unit of life and these exist in a dynamic equilibrium with their immediate environment. Cells need a continuous supply of nutrients and energy to maintain their form and activities. Cellular chemical reactions are collectively known as metabolism.

The French physiologist, Claude Bernard, described the body as involved in maintaining a "stable internal environment" for its cells and called this process 'homeostasis'. Many physiological parameters must be maintained between narrow limits, for example, internal body temperature must be close to 37°C as this represents the optimal temperature for metabolic reactions.

Homeostatic regulation is triggered by alterations in physiological parameters with the aim of producing a compensating change in the opposite direction. A basic homeostatic mechanism (see Figure 2.1) consists of a sensor, a co-ordinating centre and an effector mechanism.

HUMAN PHYSIOLOGY

FIGURE 2.1: Basic homeostatic mechanism

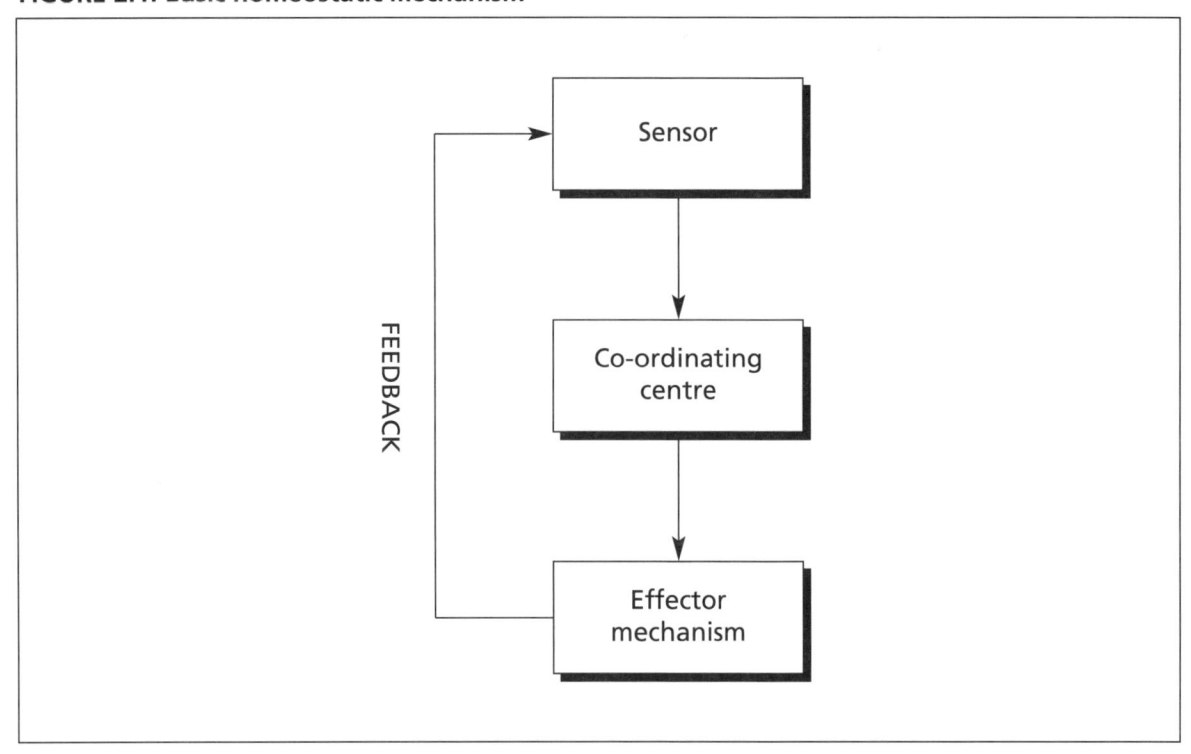

[Diagram: Sensor → Co-ordinating centre → Effector mechanism, with FEEDBACK loop from Effector mechanism back to Sensor]

1. **Sensor** – detection of physiological change by the body, eg lowering of body core temperature; messages sent via the nervous system to a co-ordination centre in the brain.
2. **Co-ordinating centre** – takes account of information from different sensors and sends messages to effectors.
3. **Effector mechanisms** – these act to compensate for changed conditions, eg skeletal muscles start involuntary contraction (shivering) to raise internal body temperature.
4. **Feedback** – information on the rising body temperature is now received by the sensor, which will respond accordingly.

Homeostasis is a fundamental physiological concept and the human body exhibits many examples of homestatic mechanisms, for example, the control of internal core body temperature, and the close control of the volume, composition and pH of body fluids. Each of these parameters is controlled within narrow preset limits.

From atoms to organisms (cells, tissues and organs)

What the body can do ultimately depends on the operations of its individual cells and their biochemical reactions. Cells are very small entities about 10^{-5}m in diameter. They can be viewed under an optical microscope (resolution of 0.2μm) and more of their fine structure can be seen under an electron microscope (resolution of 1 nanometre).

The general hierarchy of structural organisation in humans is illustrated in Table 2.1 together with Figure 2.2. The organ systems of the body and their basic functions are summarised in Table 2.2.

TABLE 2.1: Hierarchy of organisation

Level	Characteristics
Atoms	Includes: carbon, hydrogen, oxygen, nitrogen, magnesium, calcium, phosphorus
Molecules	Includes: fats, proteins, carbohydrates, nucleic acids, minerals
Cells	The cell is the unit of structure and function in living organisms; individual cells vary in size, structure and function

Table continued opposite

Tissues	Groups of similar cells that have a similar function. There are four basic types – epithelial, connective, nervous and muscle – and each has a characteristic role in the body: • epithelial tissue covers the surfaces of the body and lines its cavities • muscle tissue facilitates movement • connective tissue supports the body and protects its organs • nervous tissue provides a means of rapid internal communication by electrical impulses
Organs	An organ is a structure with at least two and often four tissue types; it carries out complex physiological processes. For example, the stomach is an organ. This has: • an epithelial lining (protective and produces digestive juices) • a muscular wall (churns and mixes food) • connective tissue (reinforces the soft muscular wall) • nervous tissue (co-ordinates the production of digestive juices and muscular contraction)
System	A system is a group of organs which operate together to perform a vital bodily function, eg the digestive system or the nervous system
Organism	Co-ordinated whole being

FIGURE 2.2: Levels of organisation

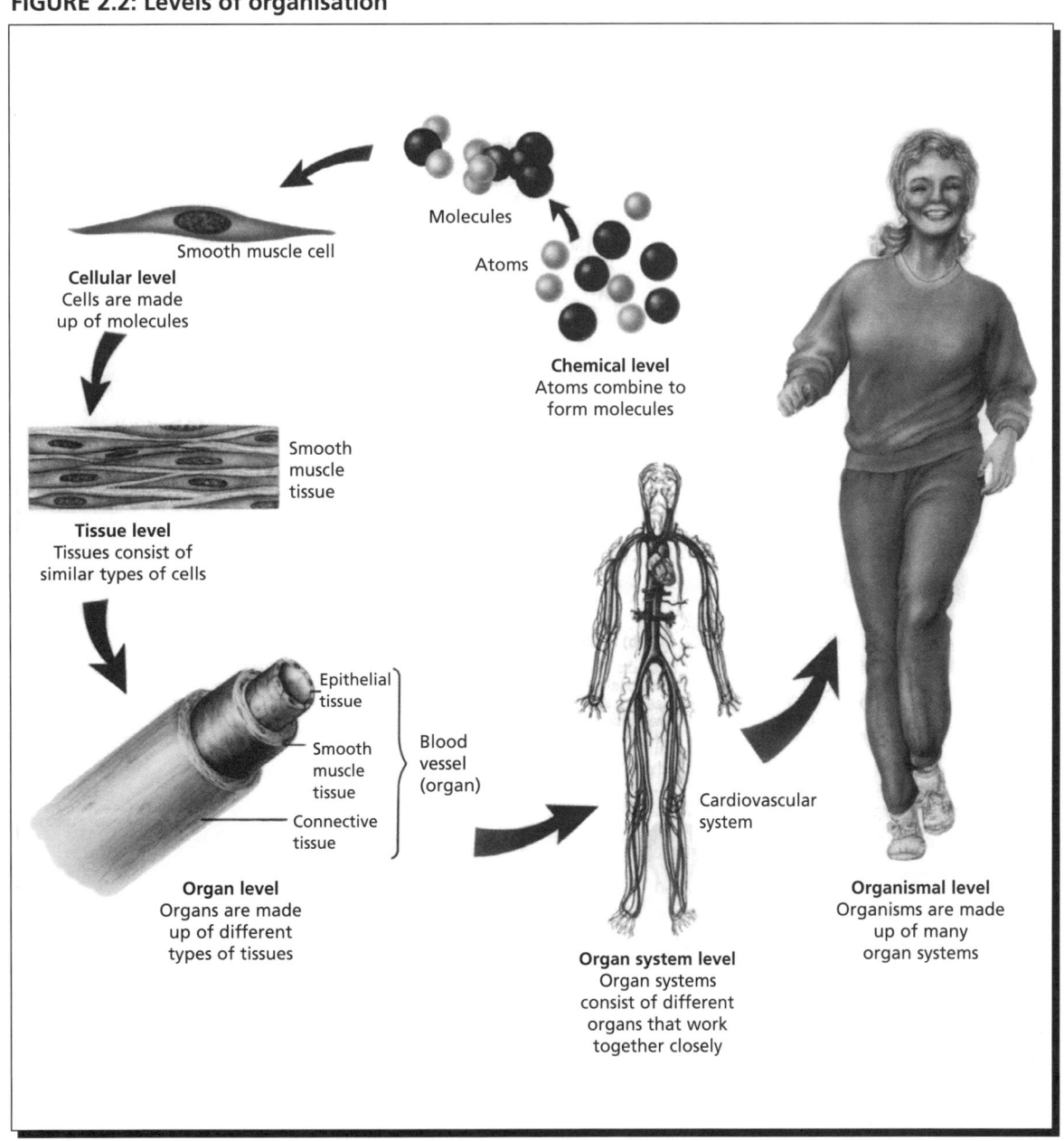

(Marieb 1989)

TABLE 2.2: Physiological systems of the body

System	Functions
Respiratory	Supplies the blood with adequate amounts of oxygen and removes carbon dioxide; gas exchange occurs across the alveolar (lung) membrane
Integumentary (skin)	Forms an external body covering and protects the internal organs and tissues from injury; synthesis of Vitamin D; involved in thermoregulation; contains sweat glands and pressure and pain receptors
Digestive	Breaks down foodstuffs into such a form that they can be absorbed from the gut into the blood and distributed to body cells for metabolic processes; food which is not digested is removed from the body as faeces
Nervous	Rapidly acting information and control system; information passed by chemicoelectrical impulses linking sensors, co-ordinators and activators (muscles and glands)
Skeletal	Protects and supports body organs; provides a framework for muscles to achieve movement; blood cells are formed within the bone marrow
Muscular	Allows manipulation of the environment; movement and facial expression; maintains posture and generates heat by work
Endocrine	Slower body control system when compared with the nervous system; glands secrete hormones, which regulate processes such as growth, reproduction and nutrition (metabolism) by body cells
Circulatory (cardiovascular and lymphatic)	Blood carries carbon dioxide, oxygen, nutrients and wastes to their appropriate destinations; powered by the heart; (works with the lymphatics). Lymphatic system collects fluid leaked from the blood circulation and returns it to the blood; disposal of cell and other debris in the lymphatic system; contains the white blood cells which support immune reactions to destroy invading bacterial cells and viruses
Urinary	Eliminates nitrogenous wastes from the body; regulates extracellular fluid concentration and volume as well as acid-base balance of the blood
Reproductive	Ensures production and delivery of male sperm and sex hormones, and female eggs and sex hormones; site provided for fertilisation and production of breast milk

Modes of entry

Listed below are the main routes of entry for harmful substances, organisms, energies and other agents into the body. The discussion here principally focuses on the uptake of harmful chemical and biological agents, but since this text is concerned with exposure to harmful agents in the widest sense, it is relevant to mention all their potential routes of entry into the body:

1. Inhalation via the respiratory system.
2. Ingestion via the gastrointestinal system.
3. Absorption through intact skin.
4. Injection through the skin.
5. Skin surface penetration (imbruement) – damage in the epidermis.
6. Irradiation – exposure to non-ionising and ionising radiation with/without deep body penetration.
7. Information – uptake via the nervous system and special sense organs; this applies to sensory, visual, auditory and psychosocial information.

Systemic circulation

The systemic circulation consists of the blood system, the extracellular fluid and the vessels of the lymphatic network. Once a chemical agent has penetrated a membrane barrier (respiratory, digestive system or skin), it may then enter the systemic circulation (see Figure 2.3) and reach the various organs of the body, such as the liver, kidney, pancreas and brain. Once a substance has gained access to the systemic circulation, it is concentrated and the harm it causes will depend on its selective toxicity. Each toxicant has its own selective toxicity, for example, cadmium is concentrated in the tissues of the kidney while fat-soluble solvents concentrate in nervous system tissue.

FIGURE 2.3: The systemic circulation

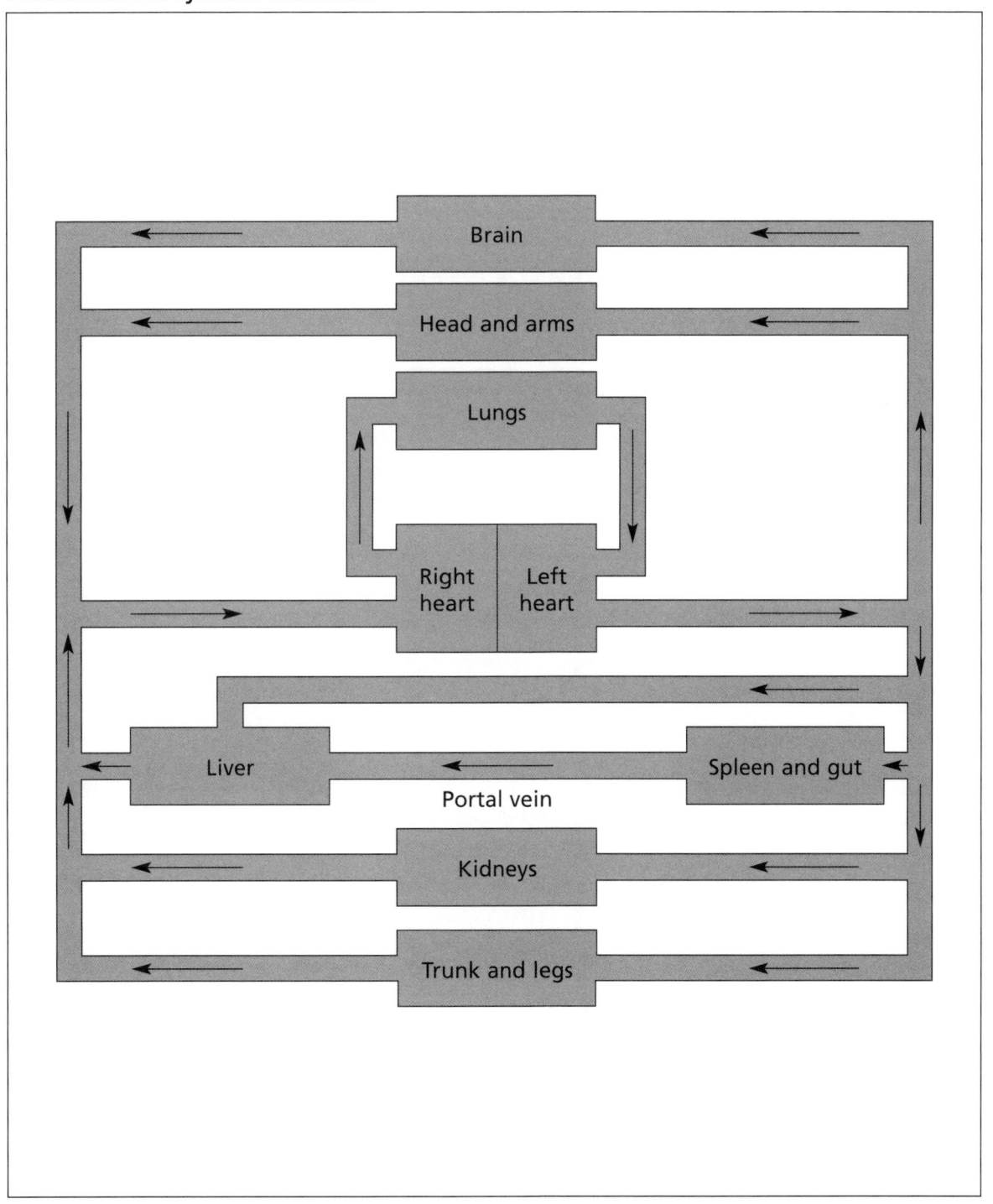

Physiological systems

In the current context, the physiological systems of the body are not of equal relevance and in the discussion below, certain systems, for example, the respiratory system and the skin, will be given a more detailed treatment than others.

HUMAN PHYSIOLOGY

Respiratory system

The function of the respiratory system is to transport air to the lung membrane and facilitate gas exchange between incoming oxygen and outgoing carbon dioxide, which is expelled from the body during expiration. (Oxygen is needed for tissue cells to carry out their metabolic functions and carbon dioxide is a waste product, which must be removed.)

The respiratory system is made up of the nose, mouth, throat, larynx, trachea, bronchi and lungs. It is lined by a wet, shiny membrane containing mucus-secreting cells which lubricate the inner surface. During inspiration, air enters the lungs through a series of branching tubes. Atherley (1978) divides the structure of the respiratory system as follows:

- the upper airways;
- the conducting airways; and
- the respiratory units. (See Figures 2.4, 2.5 and 2.6.)

An average human breathes approximately 10,000 litres of air per day. The exact figure will depend on the degree of exertion of an individual, for example, whether they have a sedentary job or an occupation which involves heavy manual labour. During inspiration, this air is heated to body temperature and humidified, that is, saturated with water vapour.

FIGURE 2.4: The upper airways

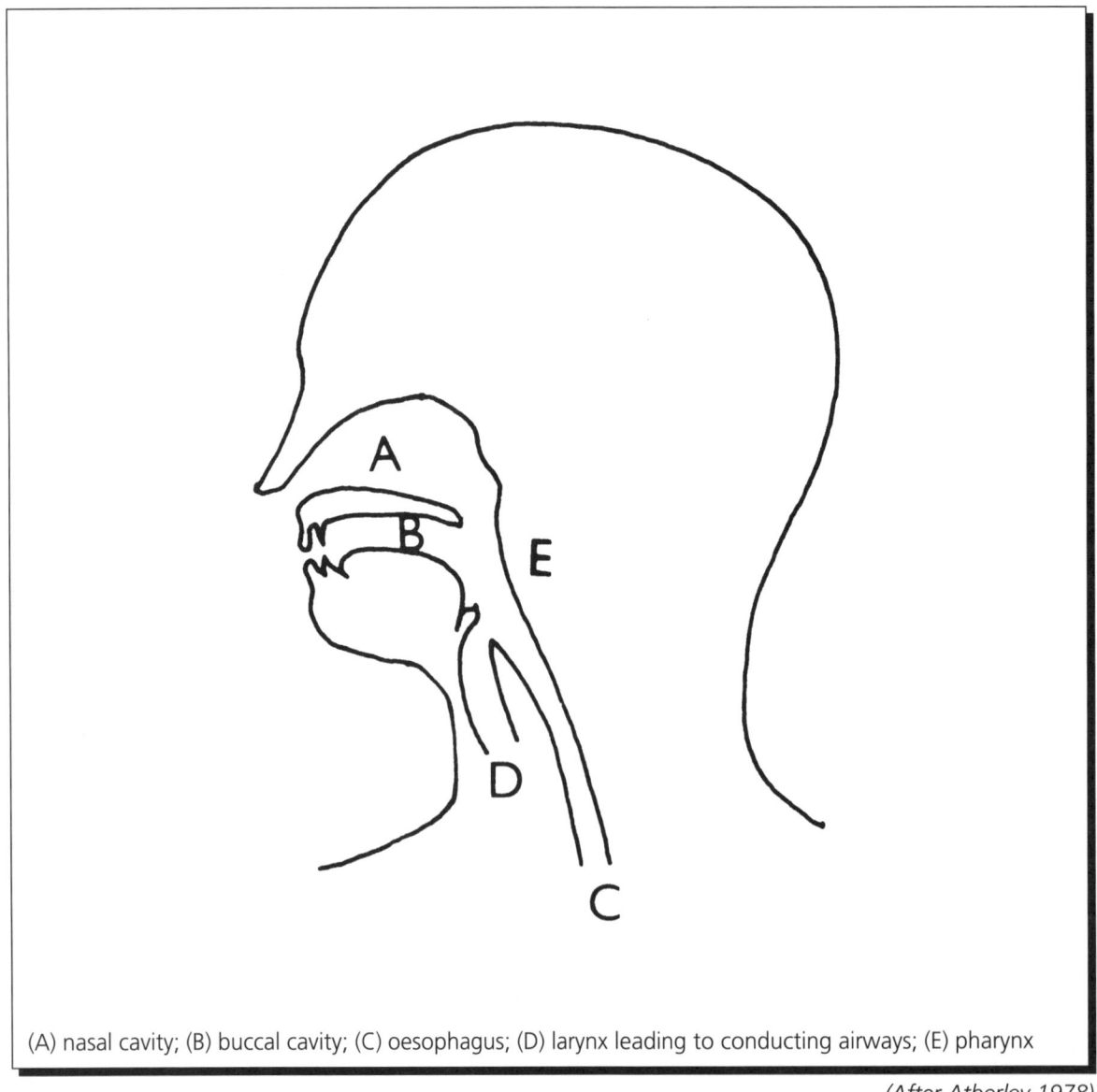

(A) nasal cavity; (B) buccal cavity; (C) oesophagus; (D) larynx leading to conducting airways; (E) pharynx

(After Atherley 1978)

Next, the air reaches the branching conducting airways. Branching increases the cross-sectional area of the airways and reduces the airflow rate.

FIGURE 2.5: The conducting airways

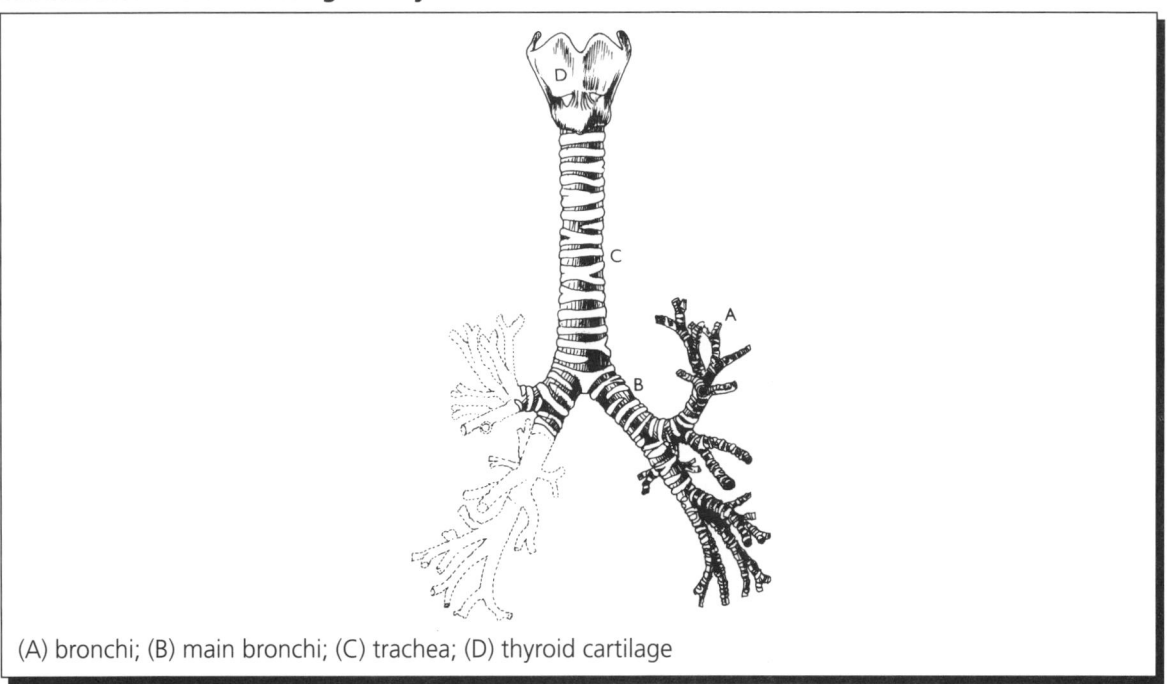

(A) bronchi; (B) main bronchi; (C) trachea; (D) thyroid cartilage

(After Atherley 1978)

Finally, the air encounters the lung membrane in the respiratory unit. The alveolar membrane is the point where gas exchange actually occurs and it has three important features which enhance gas transfer:

- very thin;
- very large surface area (100 to 200m^2); and
- high blood supply.

Blood and extracellular fluid transport oxygen and carbon dioxide around the body. The oxygen is carried by the haemoglobin (a complex protein) of the red blood cells and the carbon dioxide is dissolved in the blood fluid.

FIGURE 2.6: The respiratory unit

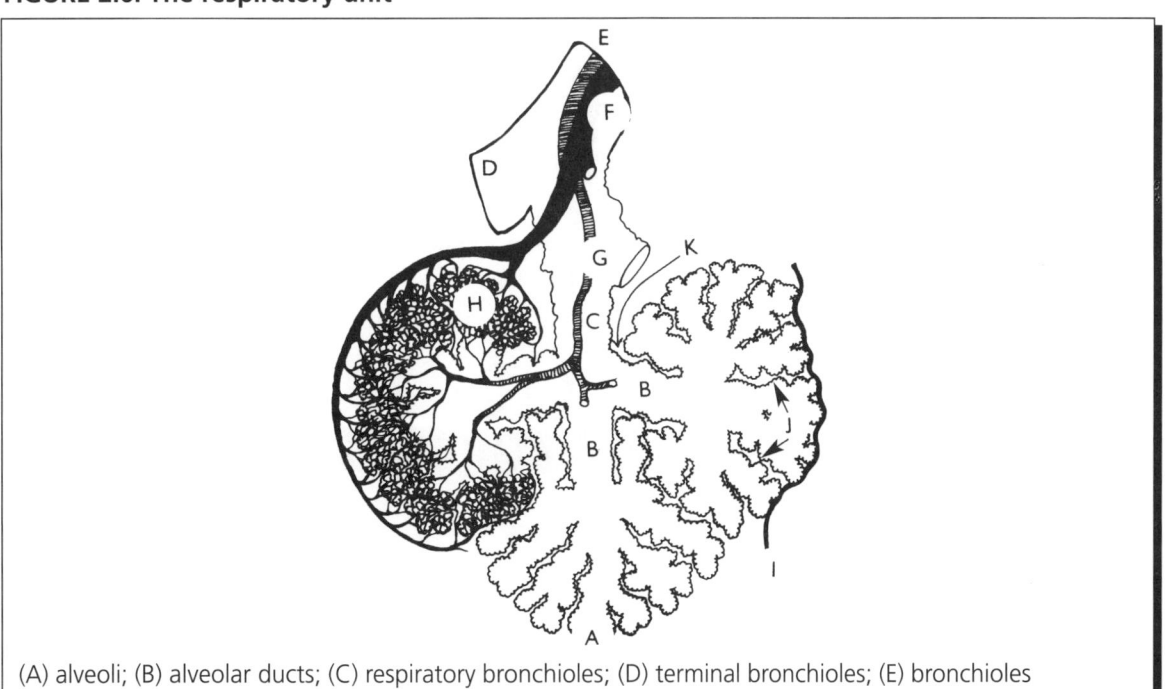

(A) alveoli; (B) alveolar ducts; (C) respiratory bronchioles; (D) terminal bronchioles; (E) bronchioles (bronchioles are not part of the respiratory unit); (F) pulmonary vein; (G) pulmonary artery; (H) blood capillary network; (I) pleural lining; (J) interstitial spaces enclosed by pleural lining; (K) interstitial space

(After Atherley 1978)

HUMAN PHYSIOLOGY

The factors that allow efficient gas exchange also make the lung membrane vulnerable to harmful airborne contaminants. Particle deposition in conjunction with a mucociliary escalator in the conducting airways (described later in this chapter) and the scrubbing out of water-soluble gases help to prevent harmful substances reaching the lung (alveolar) membrane. However, the large volume of air handled means that even low concentrations of contaminants may present a significant toxic burden in the body.

The skin

Function

The skin (Figures 2.7 and 2.8) can be regarded as a metabolically active organ involved in homeostasis and in the protection of the body (Foulds 1995). It has a wide range of functions, which are summarised below:

1. Protects the body from noxious agents; the horny layer represents a chemical barrier; it is relatively thick on the back of the hands; it can buffer mild acids but not alkalis; it cannot tolerate strong acids, alkalis and solvents.
2. Keeps internal body systems intact.
3. Barrier to physical agents.
4. Barrier to mechanical agents – skin can resist shearing due to the presence of elastin and collagen fibres.
5. Prevents loss of body fluids.
6. Reduces penetration of ultraviolet radiation (melanocyte cells).
7. Assists with regulation of body temperature.
8. Sensory organ – temperature; touch; pain; pressure.
9. Provides a surface for grip.
10. Vitamin D production.
11. Immune surveillance.
12. Cosmetic function.

The skin provides an essential barrier to the passage of chemical agents into the body. However, some substances are able to cross the barrier and enter the systemic circulation of the body.

FIGURE 2.7: The skin (integumentary system)

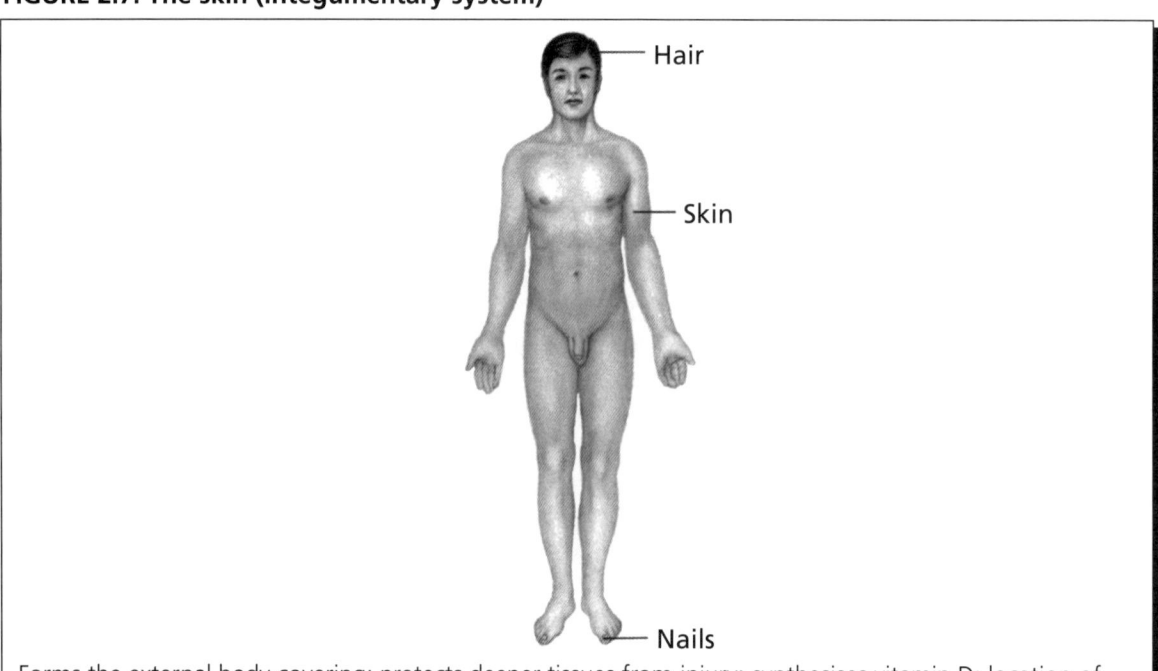

Forms the external body covering; protects deeper tissues from injury; synthesises vitamin D; location of cutaneous (pain, pressure, and temperature) receptors

(Marieb 1989)

Structure

The skin is one of the largest organs in the body with an average total surface area of 1.8m² and making up 16 per cent of body weight. It consists of three layers: the epidermis; the dermis; and the subcutis.

FIGURE 2.8: Structure of the skin

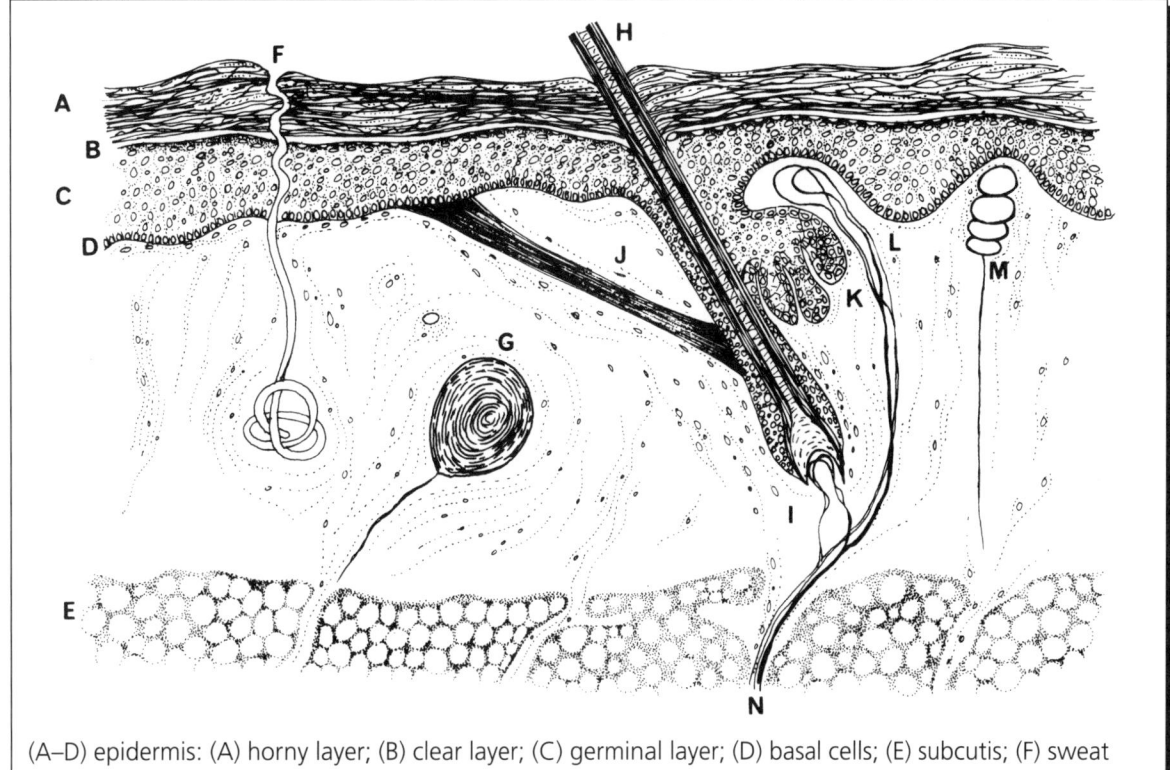

(A–D) epidermis: (A) horny layer; (B) clear layer; (C) germinal layer; (D) basal cells; (E) subcutis; (F) sweat gland duct; (G) nerve ending; (H) hair; (I) blood capillaries; (J) erector muscle of hair; (K) sebaceous gland; (L) blood capillaries; (M) nerve ending; (N) arteries and veins connected to systemic circulation

(After Atherley 1978)

Epidermis (A to D, Figure 2.8)

The epidermis is a layer of cells; epidermal cells are about 0.1mm thick. It is a protective layer and the main type of cell is the keratinocyte producing keratin, an important structural protein. The epidermis itself has four layers (basal, prickle, granular cell and horny) representing the progressive maturation of the initial keratinocytes formed in the basal layer. This involves the maturation of keratinocytes and the production of keratin. Each basal cell replicates every 200 to 400 hours. A maturing basal cell will take 14 days to reach the horny layer and be shed from the body. Upward movement of epidermal cells protects against wear and tear and discourages bacterial growth on the skin surface.

Dermis (between D and E, Figure 2.8)

This layer is a tough, supportive, connective tissue matrix. Its thickness varies with different parts of the body, for example, in the eyelids, it is around 0.6mm, and at the soles of the feet or the palms of the hand, it is greater than 3mm. Collagen, a structural protein, makes up 70 per cent of the dermis and contributes toughness and strength. Elastin fibres, a structural protein, are also present giving elasticity and they are more numerous near hair follicles and sweat glands. The ground substance glycosaminoglycans (GAGs) allow dermal structures some movement. The dermis contains fibroblast cells (which synthesise collagen), elastin, GAGs and other structures. The dermis also includes dendrocytes (immune function), mast cells, macrophages and lymphocytes. Immune system cells are dealt with in detail later in this chapter.

Subcutis (E, Figure 2.8)

This region contains loose connective tissue and fat. It may be greater than 3cm thick on the abdomen.

TABLE 2.3: Components of the skin

Skin structure	Function
Hair	This is found over the entire surface of the skin except for the glabrous skin, eg soles and palms. The density of hair follicles is greatest on the face. The scalp hair plays a role in protecting the skin from ultraviolet radiation exposure
Nail	This is a hard, dense keratin structure, which protects the tips of the fingers and toes
Sebaceous glands	These are associated with hair follicles and secrete oily sebum
Sweat and sweat glands	The sweat glands are located in the dermis and produce a watery secretion which evaporates from the skin surface. Sweat has a pH value of 4–6.8 and is an aqueous solution of sodium chloride, potassium chloride, ammonia, amino acids and small quantities of waste products and toxins. In controlling body temperature, skin blood flow may change over a range of 1 to 100ml min^{-1} per 100g of skin in the fingers and forearms. The sweat and sebaceous glands help the hydration and suppleness of the horny layer of the skin. Sweat also helps to maintain grip on the palms and the soles. There are two types of sweat gland: apocrine and eccrine. Eccrine glands are found in the dermis and the gland duct opens up on to the skin surface. An adult has approximately 2.5 million eccrine sweat glands universally distributed over the body surface. There are a high density in the palms, soles, armpits and head. The glands are under psychological and thermal control. The apocrine duct opens into the hair follicle and is larger than the eccrine duct. Its secretions are usually odourless, but any odour that might occur is often due to the action of skin bacteria. Men tend to sweat more than women
Nerves	Nerves are concentrated in the hands, face and genitalia. They are responsible for sensing pain, irritation, temperature sensitivity, pressure, vibration and touch. The autonomic nervous system controls the diameter of blood vessels and thus helps regulate blood flow. It also controls the action of the sweat glands and arrestor pilli muscles
Blood supply	The skin has a rich, adaptive blood supply, which is crucial for thermoregulation. The blood system is drained by the lymphatic system
Melanocyte	These cells are found in the basal layer of the epidermis. The horny layer melanocytes are uniformly distributed and form a UV-absorbing blanket. UV radiation is absorbed and UV-B (wavelength 280nm to 315nm) absorption darkens the skin immediately and causes photoxidation of preformed melanin pigment. Melanocyte cells are also stimulated to produce more melanin. UV exposure also induces keratinocyte division, increasing skin thickening. (This is discussed in Chapter 8.)

Digestive system

The digestive system is outlined in Figure 2.9. Food can be considered as a mixture of complex chemicals. When it is ingested, this mixture is broken down by the body into small 'building block' molecules, such as simple sugars, basic fats and amino acids. Food is broken down physically by the teeth and peristalsis, which increases its surface area to allow enzymes to break it down chemically. This occurs in the gastrointestinal tract, which is basically a long tube stretching from the mouth ultimately to the anus via the oesophagus, stomach, and small and large intestines. As food passes along this tube, it is gradually broken down, both physically, by mechanical muscular action, and chemically, by enzymes. Any food not absorbed by the processes of digestion eventually leaves the gastrointestinal tract as faeces via the anus.

FIGURE 2.9: Digestive system

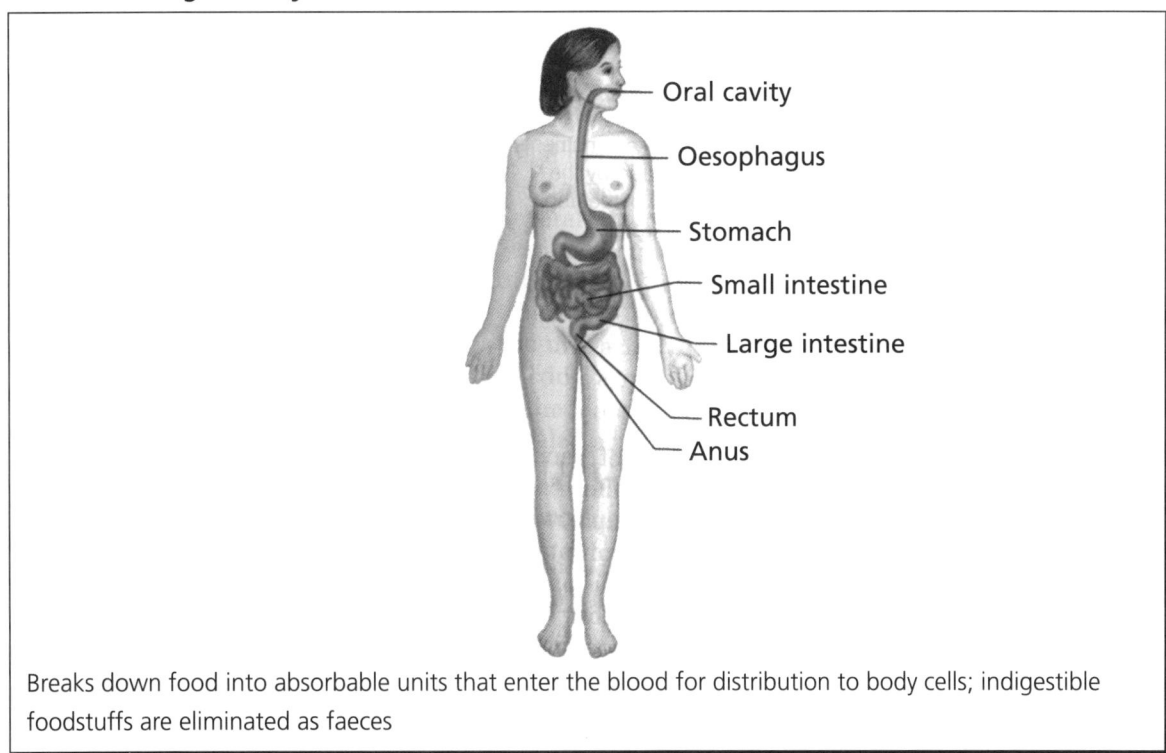

- Oral cavity
- Oesophagus
- Stomach
- Small intestine
- Large intestine
- Rectum
- Anus

Breaks down food into absorbable units that enter the blood for distribution to body cells; indigestible foodstuffs are eliminated as faeces

(Marieb 1989)

The gut membrane is thin, has a good blood supply and has a large surface area. Digested food passes through the gut membrane (mainly in the small intestine) and enters a blood vessel, the hepatic portal vein, through which it will pass to the liver. The liver is a large organ which has many functions closely associated with digestion and it has considerable detoxification capacity. The pancreas and the gall bladder function as part of the digestive system.

The digestive system provides a further potential mode of entry for toxic materials, which may contaminate food or water, to gain access to the systemic circulation and body organs. In an occupational health context, this is not a common route of entry in practice. However, if hygiene practices are poor in a particular workplace, the gut represents a route by which a relatively large amount of a harmful substance may gain entry to the body, and this is sometimes seen with, for example, lead workers.

Nervous system

The nervous system is a network of cells for rapid transfer and integration of information by transmission of chemico-electrical impulses. The system has a sensory aspect, a co-ordination and integration aspect, and a motor aspect. The system monitors stimuli, integrates the signals generated and determines the necessary motor output, in conjunction with the endocrine system. Special sense organs are concerned with the senses of taste, smell, vision, hearing and equilibrium.

The nervous system is composed of the central nervous system (CNS), which consists of the brain and the spinal cord, and the peripheral nervous system (PNS), which is mainly the sensory and motor nerve connections to the brain and spinal cord. An outline of the nervous system is given in Figure 2.10.

Functionally, the PNS can be subdivided into motor and sensory aspects:

- **Sensory aspects** – selected special sense organs and other body structures. (The ear is covered in Chapter 5 and the eye in Chapter 10.)
- **Motor aspects** – subdivided into somatic nervous system (voluntary muscle control) and autonomic (involuntary) nervous system. The autonomic system subdivides further into the sympathetic and parasympathetic nervous systems. The autonomic system is part of the motor aspect of the PNS which controls body activities automatically, eg the control of heart muscle and smooth muscle in internal organs. The parasympathetic and sympathetic systems afford fine control to body activities.

FIGURE 2.10: Nervous system

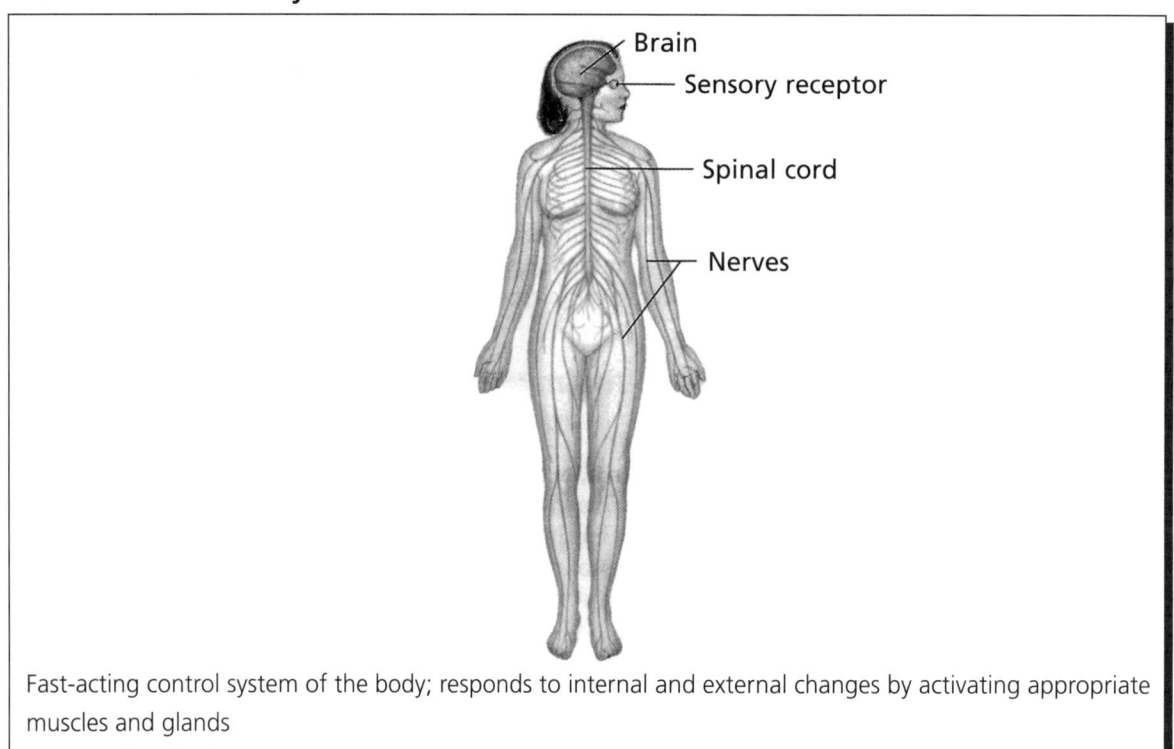

Fast-acting control system of the body; responds to internal and external changes by activating appropriate muscles and glands

(Marieb 1989)

The basic unit of the nervous system is the neurone, which is made up of dendrites, the cell body and the axon. The junction between neurones is known as the synapse and here chemicals (neuro-transmitters) are generated in the propagation of nerve impulses.

Nerve cells which carry impulses away from sense organs (skin receptors, eyes, ears, etc) and towards the brain and spinal cord are called sensory neurones. Those nerves which carry impulses away from the brain and spinal cord towards the muscles and glands are known as motor neurones. An insulating myelin sheath wraps itself around the nerve fibre. Both types of neurone are shown in Figure 2.11.

FIGURE 2.11: Sensory and motor neurones

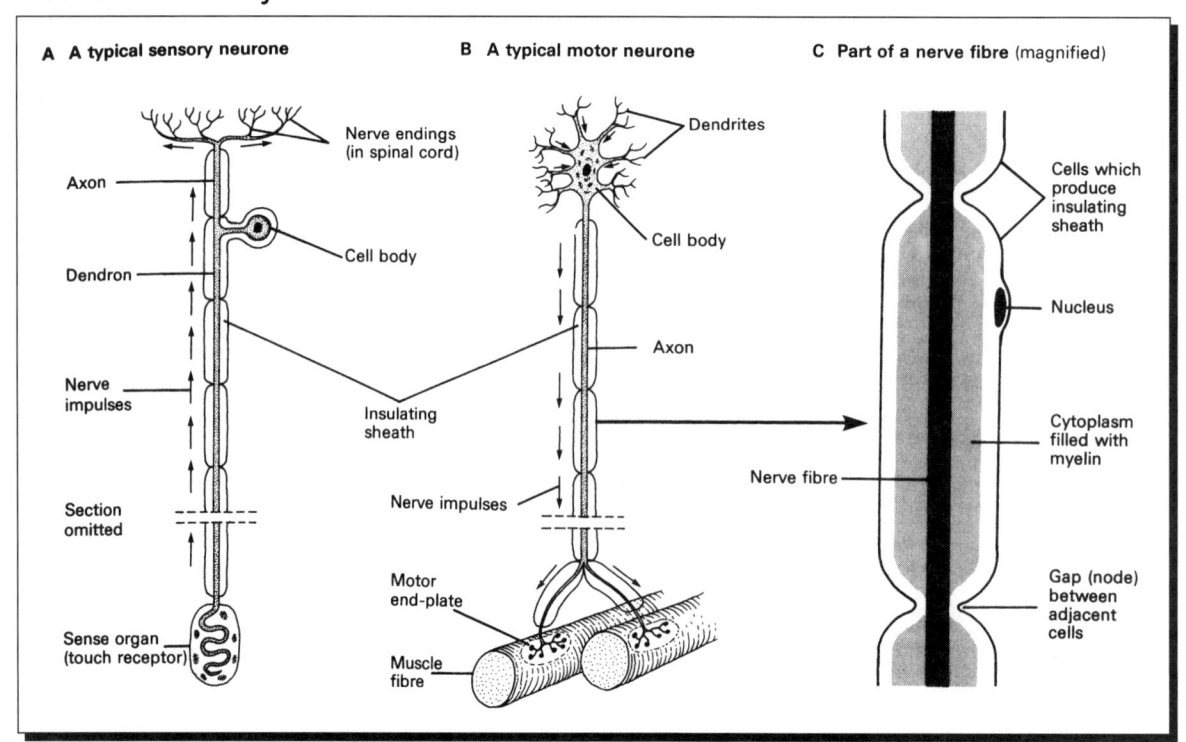

(Brian Beckett (© SSER Ltd) 1992)

Skeletal system

The skeletal system provides an internal support framework for the body. It protects and supports body organs and stores minerals, especially calcium and phosphorus. The bone marrow produces blood cells and tendons anchor skeletal muscles so that their contraction can cause movement. The skeletal system is outlined in Figure 2.12 and includes:

- bones (bone cells surrounded by a very hard matrix);
- joints;
- cartilage (rubbery smooth tissue on the end of bones in joints); and
- ligaments (fibrous cords which bind the bones together at joints).

More detail is given on the structure of joints in Chapter 11.

FIGURE 2.12: Skeletal system

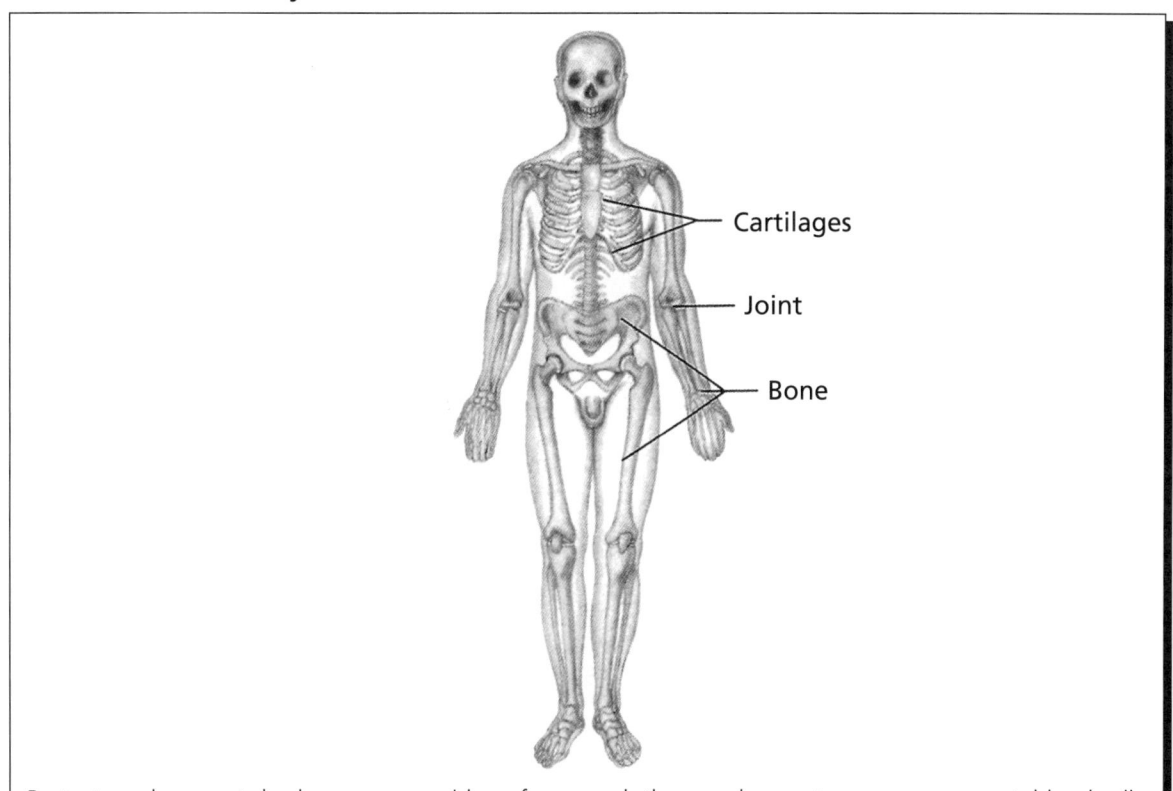

Protects and supports body organs; provides a framework the muscles use to cause movement; blood cells are formed within bones

(Marieb 1989)

Muscular system

This system functions to provide movement to the body and its parts and to generate heat. The structure of the muscular system is outlined in Figure 2.13. Muscles contract and shorten, and when skeletal muscles are attached to bones, this results in movement of the bone. Other internal muscles are mainly concerned with forcing fluid through narrow channels. There are three kinds of muscle classified according to their structure and function:

1. **Skeletal** – involved in voluntary control; characteristic striations.
2. **Smooth** – involuntary control.
3. **Cardiac** – striated, spontaneously active heart muscle.

Skeletal muscle makes up about 40 per cent of body weight and helps to form the contours of the body. It is involved in movement, the maintenance of posture, stabilising joints and generating heat. Smooth muscle mainly forms the walls of hollow internal organs and cardiac muscle is found in the heart. Smooth and cardiac muscles contract slowly and tirelessly, in contrast to skeletal muscle which contracts rapidly and tires easily.

HUMAN PHYSIOLOGY

FIGURE 2.13: Muscular system

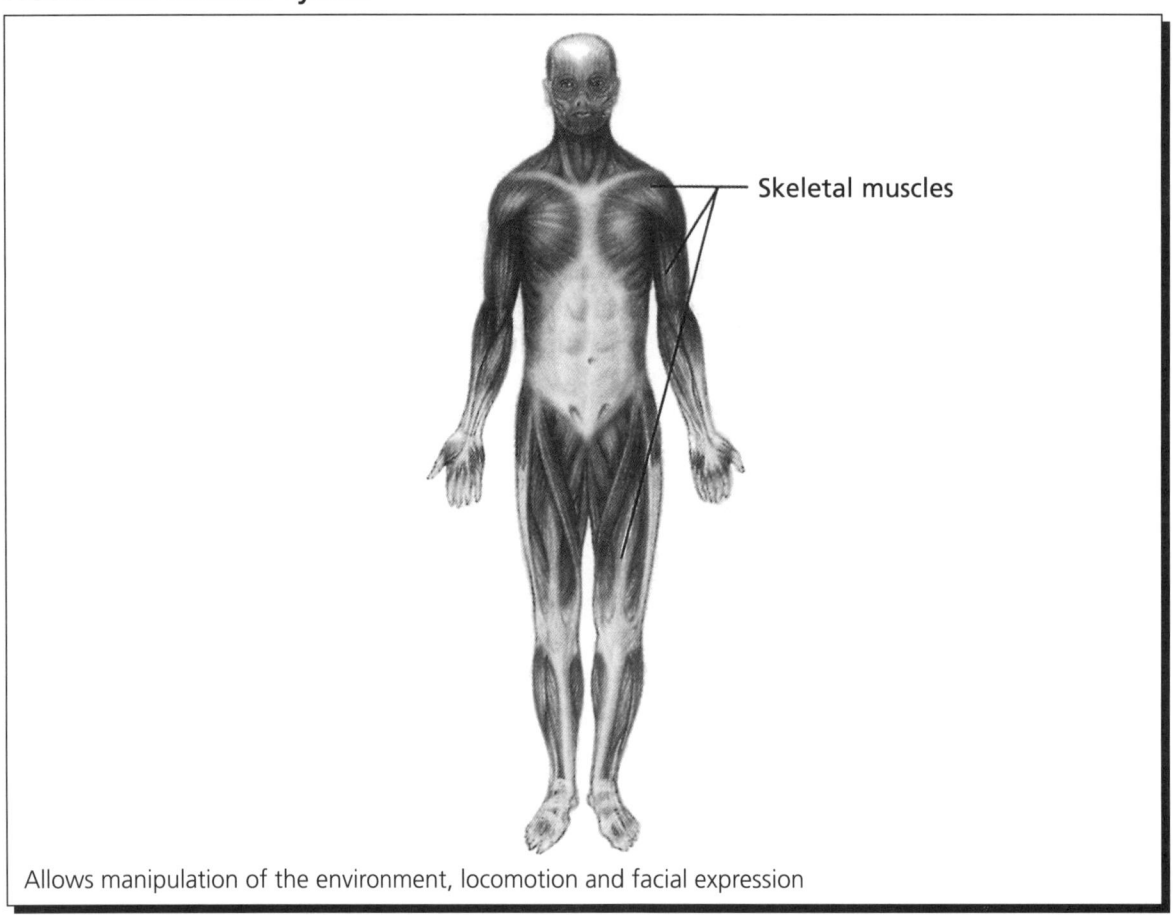

Skeletal muscles

Allows manipulation of the environment, locomotion and facial expression

(Marieb 1989)

FIGURE 2.14: Endocrine system

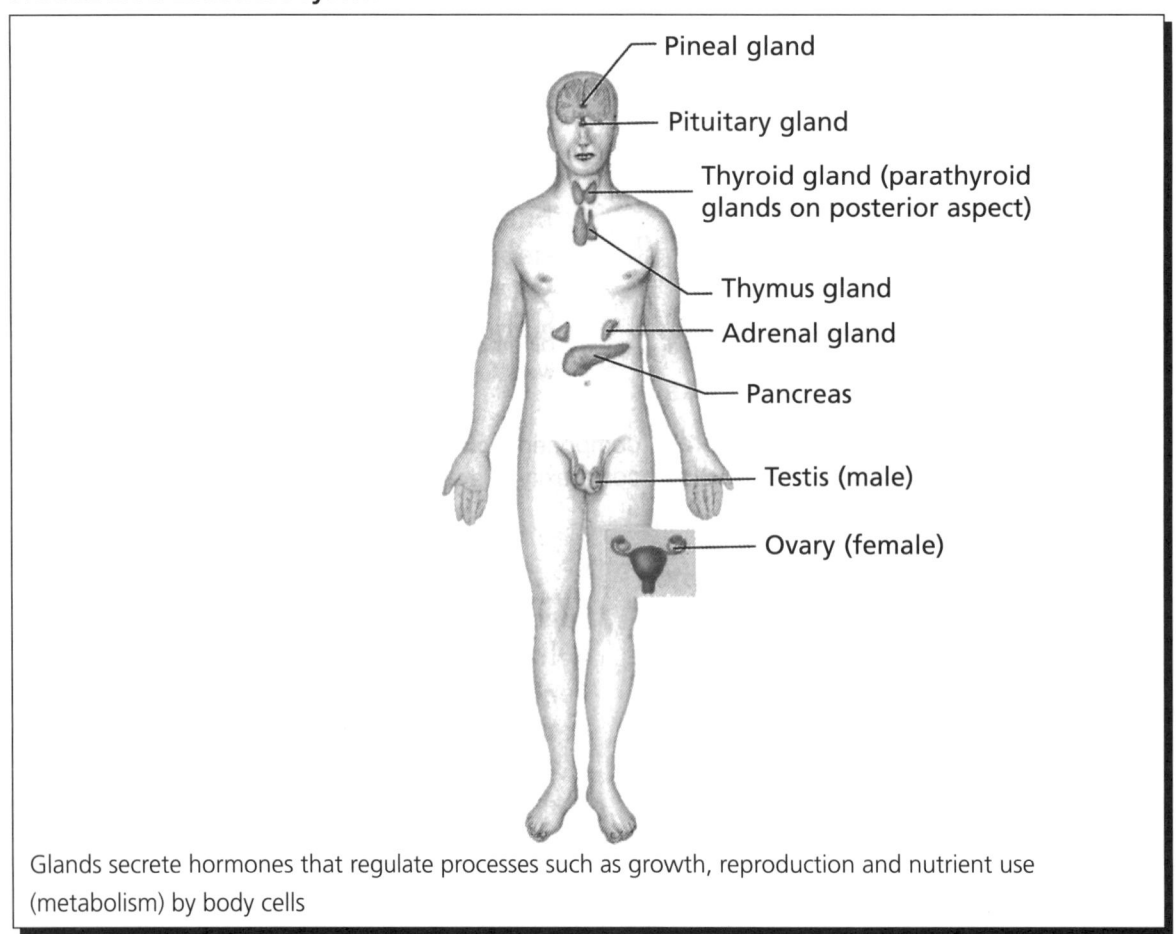

- Pineal gland
- Pituitary gland
- Thyroid gland (parathyroid glands on posterior aspect)
- Thymus gland
- Adrenal gland
- Pancreas
- Testis (male)
- Ovary (female)

Glands secrete hormones that regulate processes such as growth, reproduction and nutrient use (metabolism) by body cells

(Marieb 1989)

Endocrine system

The is a system of glands which secrete chemical mediators (hormones) into the blood. An outline of the endocrine system is given in Figure 2.14. This secretion of hormones produces a slower, more gradual action than the nervous system and is responsible for the control of prolonged or continuous processes, such as growth, development, reproduction and metabolism. The system is under overall control of the nervous system via the pituitary and hypothalamic glands, although many glands are involved in the production and secretion of hormones. Hormones are principally amino acid or steroid-based and each has a particular target site for its action. In an occupational health context, the adrenal hormones (adrenalin, nor-adrenalin and cortisol) are centrally involved in the body's response to stressful work conditions.

Circulatory system

This is a transport and delivery system and consists of two distinct organ systems: the cardiovascular system and the lymphatic system. These systems play a complementary role. The cardiovascular and lymphatic systems are outlined in Figures 2.15 and 2.17.

The cardiovascular system consists of the heart and blood vessels (arteries and veins), and the transport medium is blood. Blood carries oxygen, nutrients, hormones and other substances to the cells where exchanges are made for wastes which are carried away for removal from the body. Blood is a fluid tissue with living cells suspended in a non-living matrix (plasma). There are two types of blood cells: red cells (known as erythrocytes) and white blood cells (known as leucocytes and platelets). The principal function of the red blood cells is to transport oxygen while that of the white blood cells is to protect the body against disease. Platelets are involved in blood clotting. Blood is also involved in the distribution of body heat.

FIGURE 2.15: Cardiovascular system

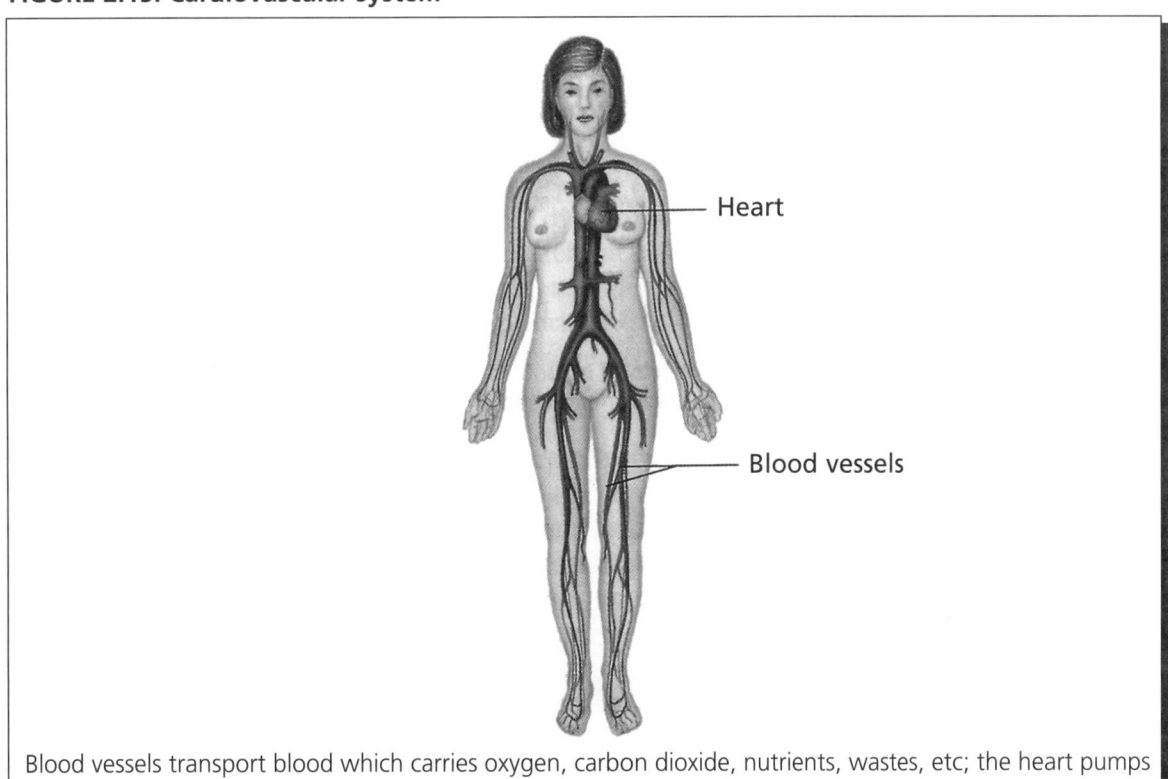

Blood vessels transport blood which carries oxygen, carbon dioxide, nutrients, wastes, etc; the heart pumps blood

(Marieb 1989)

The heart is the organ which drives the blood around the body, facilitating the various exchanges between tissue cells and the circulating fluid. With the exception of the pulmonary artery and pulmonary vein where this is reversed, the arteries always carry oxygenated blood away from the heart to the tissues and the veins carry de-oxygenated blood from the tissues back towards the heart. This is

HUMAN PHYSIOLOGY

shown diagrammatically in Figure 2.16. The closed cardiovascular system is a high-pressure system. Fluid plasma is forced out of the blood into tissues at the arterial end and re-enters at the venous end. However, not all of this fluid is returned at the venous end and some will remain in the tissue. This fluid eventually returns to the blood via the lymphatic system.

FIGURE 2.16: Systemic circulation

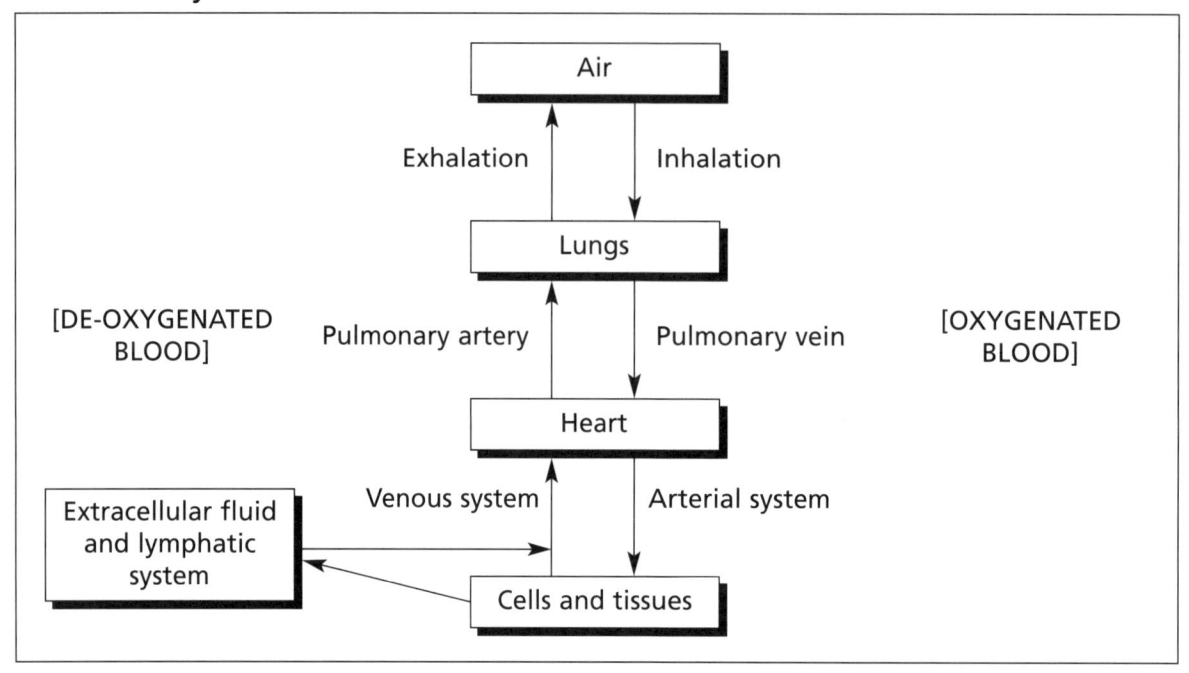

The lymphatic system consists of lymphatic vessels, lymph nodes and lymphoid organs such as the spleen and the thymus. The lymphatic system returns fluid, leaked from the blood into the extracellular fluid compartment, to the venous blood vessels so that the blood can be kept circulating continuously. This fluid is also cleansed by the lymphoid system which contains the cells involved in the immune response, a highly specific body defence mechanism against invading biological agents and tumour cells.

FIGURE 2.17: Lymphatic system

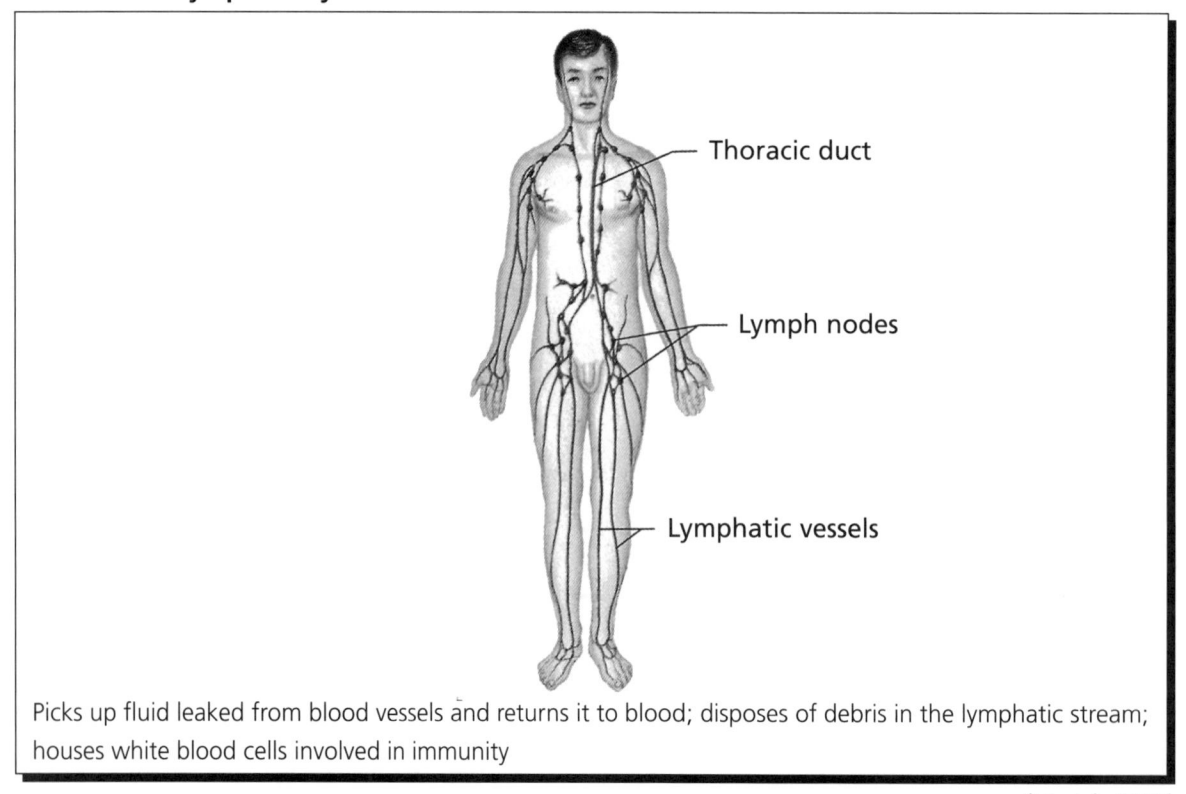

Picks up fluid leaked from blood vessels and returns it to blood; disposes of debris in the lymphatic stream; houses white blood cells involved in immunity

(Marieb 1989)

Urinary system

The urinary system, outlined in Figure 2.18, is concerned with getting rid of nitrogenous waste while regulating the water, electrolyte and acid-base balance of the blood and extracellular fluid. The kidney is the organ which maintains body fluid homeostasis. The fluid is filtered here, with required substances being re-absorbed in appropriate quantities and waste is allowed to leave the body.

FIGURE 2.18: Urinary system

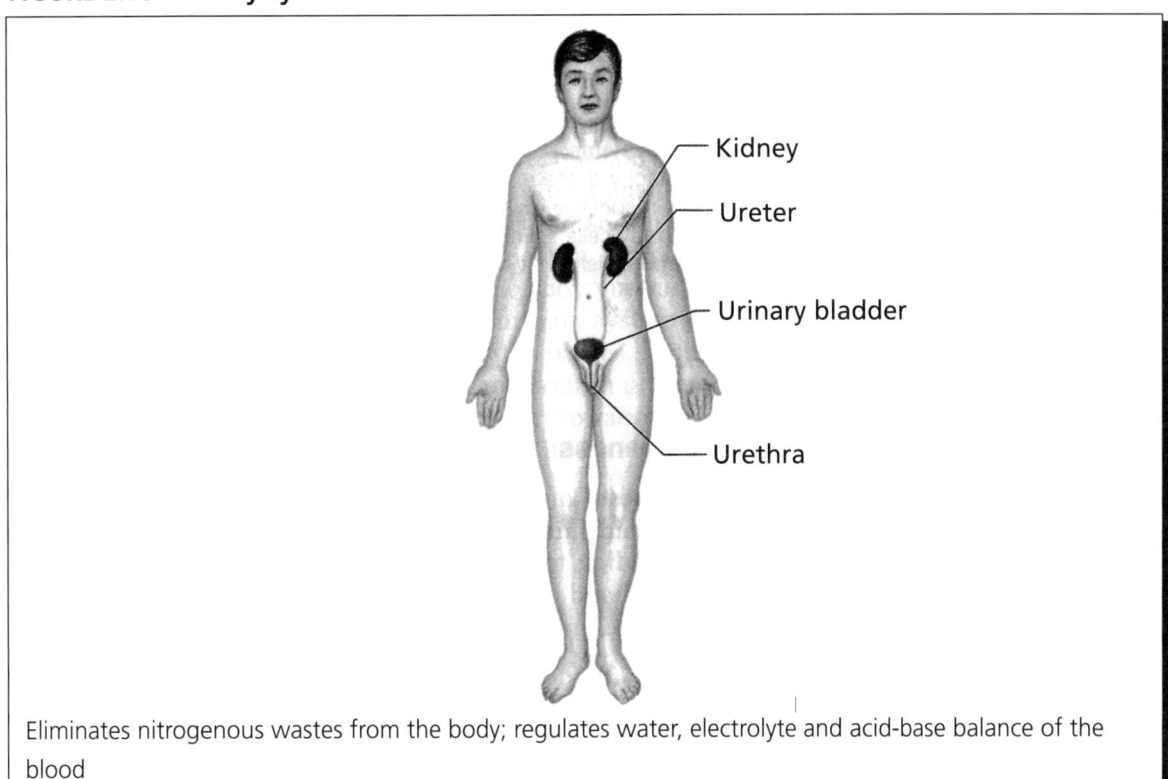

Eliminates nitrogenous wastes from the body; regulates water, electrolyte and acid-base balance of the blood

(Marieb 1989)

FIGURE 2.19: Reproductive system

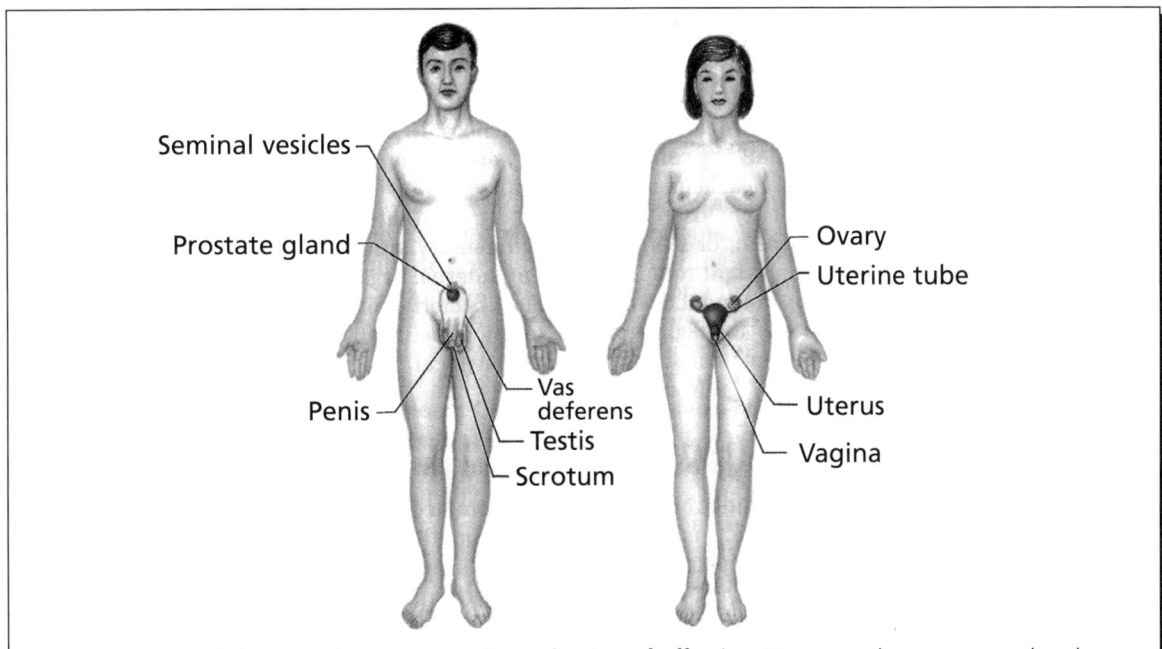

Overall function of the reproductive system is production of offspring. Testes produce sperm and male sex hormone; ducts and glands aid in delivery of viable sperm to the female reproductive tract. Ovaries produce eggs and female sex hormones; remaining structures serve as sites for fertilisation and development of the foetus

(Marieb 1989)

HUMAN PHYSIOLOGY

The kidney regulates the volume as well as the chemical composition of the body fluids (water-salt and acid-base balance). It has a very high blood supply and 25 per cent of the total blood volume passes through the kidney every minute. Urine is produced as a clear, yellow, slightly acid solution and it is excreted from the body via the bladder.

Reproductive system

The function of this system is the continuation of the species by producing offspring (see Figure 2.19). The male reproductive organs manufacture sperm and deliver this to the female reproductive tract. The female reproductive organs, that is, the ovaries, produce eggs which fuse with the sperm during fertilisation. This fertilised ovum represents the first cell of a new individual. The female uterus represents a safe environment for the embryo, later called the foetus, to develop. During this period, the foetus receives oxygen and nutrients from the mother via the placenta.

During the early stages of development, especially during the first 12 weeks when major body organs are developing, the foetus is most vulnerable to damage from toxins and infection. Other vulnerable points to toxic harm in the process are production of the functional sperm and egg as well as the actual pregnancy itself and development of the foetus.

Physiological defence mechanisms

The human body demonstrates a wide range of defensive capabilities which serve to maintain overall homeostasis. Selected defensive mechanisms, which are relevant in an occupational health context, are discussed below. These include: respiratory filtration; defensive cells; the inflammatory response; the immune response; metabolic transformation; and the skin barrier.

Respiratory filtration

This is the name for a group of defensive processes which collectively prevent aerosols[9] reaching the sensitive alveolar membrane. Particles are filtered by virtue of their aerodynamic behaviour causing them to deposit on the sides of the airways from where they are cleared by the ciliary escalator and other mechanisms. This process is discussed in detail below.

FIGURE 2.20: Ciliary escalator

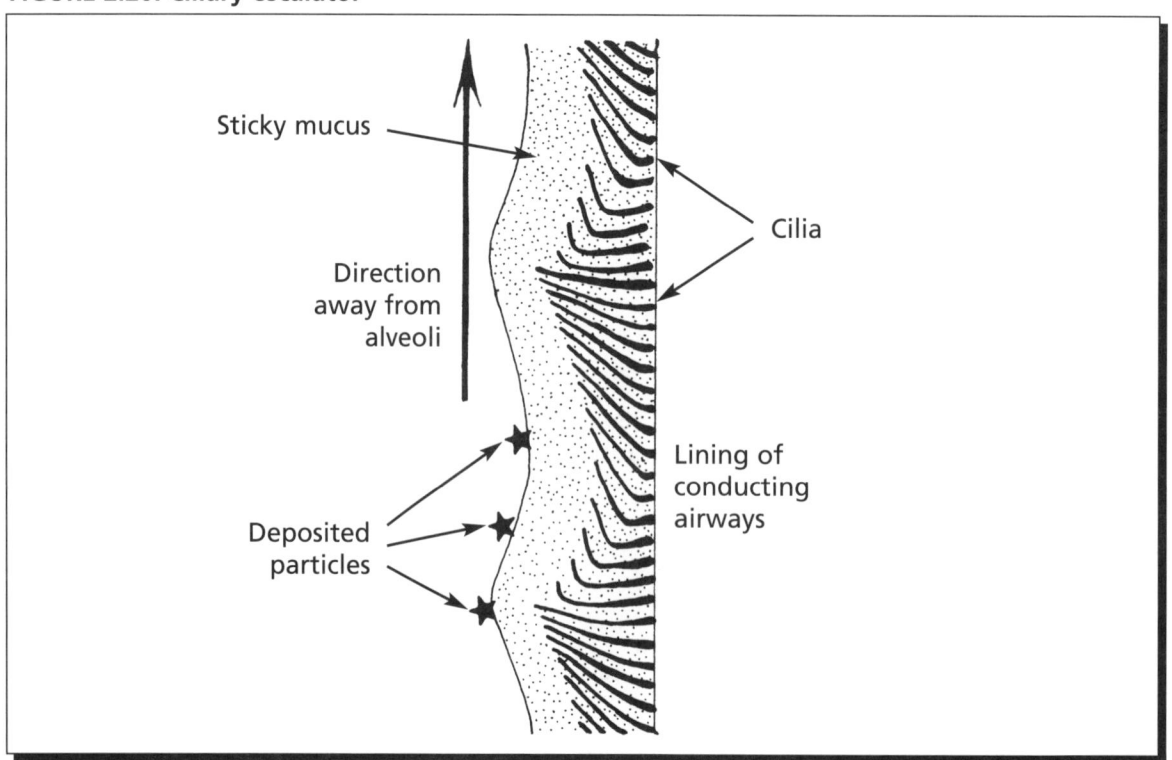

(After Atherley 1978)

---

[9] For definition of aerosol, see page 49.

The ciliary escalator is represented in Figure 2.20. This shows the deposited particles which adhere to the sticky mucous film lining the inner surface of the conducting airways. The 'beat' and direction of movement of the cilia transports the aerosol particles outwards, that is, back up the conducting airways to the pharynx where the particles are swallowed or expectorated.

Other glands in the surface of the respiratory tract lining produce defensive substances including antibodies against chemical and biological agents and lysozyme, an antibacterial substance.

Associated defensive processes

Coughing and sneezing can result in the forceful ejection of harmful substances and microbes from the respiratory system. The upper airways act as a humidifier which is sometimes defensive in function, for example, this mechanism may increase the diameter of some particles, thus altering their aerodynamic behaviour and aiding respiratory deposition. Goblet cells lining the tract secrete extra mucus in response to irritation caused by some toxic substances. (This is defensive up to a point, but excessive secretion can cause the blockage of small airways.)

Deposition dynamics

Aerosol is a scientific term which applies to any disperse system of liquid or solid particles suspended in a gas – usually air. (Vincent & Brosseau 1995)

Aerosols are discussed in more detail in Chapter 3. Four physical modes of deposition of aerosols in the respiratory system have been identified:
1. Sedimentation.
2. Interception.
3. Impaction.
4. Diffusion.

The behaviour of aerosol fractions, standardised by aerodynamic behaviour, is given in Table 2.4.

Sedimentation
This is the settlement of particles under gravity. The terminal velocity of the sedimenting aerosol is related to the density and the size (square of the diameter) of the aerosol. This generally holds for aerosols (assumed to be spherical) in the range of 1 to 20 microns.

However, many occupational aerosols are not spheres and the terminal velocity cannot be calculated from this simple relationship. In this case, a standardised aerodynamic diameter needs to be determined.

The equation below (Stokes equation) describes the terminal sedimentation velocity (V), which a particle will attain when falling through still air, and illustrates the factors that will affect this:

$$V = \frac{\rho g d^2}{18\eta}$$

(Where: ρ is the particle density; g is the acceleration due to gravity; d is the diameter of the particle; and η is the viscosity of the air.)

Aerodynamic diameter
This is the diameter of a uniform sphere which has the same terminal velocity as the aggregate or irregular particle. Where the uniform sphere has unit density (ie equals one), the aerodynamic diameter is expressed in terms of an equivalent unit density sphere (EUDS). Where not specified, aerodynamic diameter is normally taken as EUDS and this allows prediction of the deposition behaviour, of irregular particles, in the respiratory system. In Table 2.4, deposition site is related to particle diameter (μm EUDS).

Interception
This describes the process by which irregular particles such as fibres become caught on the walls of the small airways. The length and size of the fibre in relation to the size of the small airway are important factors influencing deposition by this mode.

Impaction
This is important where the airway curves and airstream particles carry on by their own momentum until colliding with the airway wall. The likelihood of deposition is related to the velocity of the aerosol's movement and the angular change in direction of the airstream.

Diffusion
This describes the process by which small aerosols move freely throughout space. Diffusion is brought about by random bombardment of the aerosol by molecules of the substance in which it is suspended (air, in this case). Small aerosol particles would obviously tend to be more susceptible to diffusive forces than larger particles.

Respiratory system deposition
The major purpose of respiratory filtration is to prevent aerosols reaching the sensitive alveolar membrane. Particles will deposit by the above modes on both inhalation and exhalation, although not necessarily at the same sites.

As before, the respiratory system is divided into the upper airways (Figure 2.4), the conducting airways (Figure 2.5), and the alveoli (Figure 2.6).

Upper airways
In this part of the respiratory system, the important factors are the presence of nasal hairs and a large change in airstream direction which creates highly turbulent flow. This results in significant impaction of particles with the airway surfaces on inhalation.

Conducting airways
At this part of the respiratory system, there are more streamlined airflow patterns. There is some deposition by impaction, particularly where the airways divide, that is, at bifurcations. Goblet cells in the mucus membrane produce a layer of sticky mucus lining the airways. This mucus, together with any deposited particles, is transported back up the airways by the ciliary escalator (see Figure 2.20). Aerosols, which are deposited on the escalator, are brought up to the pharynx and swallowed or expectorated. For insoluble or inactive particles, this may be effective. However, with water-soluble particles, this may not be a rapid enough response to prevent harm at the site of contact in the conducting airways. Cigarette smoke causes an increase in clearance time and appears to interfere with ciliary function.

Alveoli
Here the airflow rate is low and so diffusion is an important mode of deposition. The relationship between aerosol particle size and deposition site or fate is shown in Table 2.4.

TABLE 2.4: Aerosol particle size and deposition site

Diameter μm EUDS[10]	Deposition or fate
Greater than 70	Not drawn into the respiratory system
10 to 70	Upper airways
7 to 10	Conducting airways and ciliary escalator
0.5 to 7	Respiratory bronchioles and alveoli
Less than 0.5	Remain airborne or diffuse coming into contact with airway or lung membrane

[10] 1 micron (μm) = 10^{-6} m.

The information in Table 2.4 has been utilised in the design of air sampling equipment for characterising the hazard of occupational aerosols and this is discussed in further detail in Chapter 3. For air contaminant sampling and measurement, international definitions for health-related aerosol fractions have now been developed (BSI 1993). Three fractions have been distinguished:

1. **The inhalable fraction** – fraction of total airborne particles which is inhaled through the nose or mouth (nominally up to 100µm aerodynamic diameter).
2. **The thoracic fraction** – fraction of inhaled particles penetrating the respiratory system beyond the larynx (nominally 3µm to 20µm aerodynamic diameter; median 11.64µm).
3. **The respirable fraction** – fraction of inhaled particles penetrating to the non-ciliated parts of the lung (the alveolar region) (nominally 0.5µm to 7µm aerodynamic diameter; median 4.25µm). The above figures relate best to approximately spherical or globular particles and although 'aerodynamic diameter' can be evaluated for fibrous particles (fibres), in the context of asbestos monitoring the observed physical dimensions are used. In this context, a 'countable' fibre is defined as one which is greater than 5µm in length, less than 3µm in width and having a length to width ratio of at least 3:1 (HSE 1995).

When a particle impacts with the alveolar membrane, the effect will be determined by the physical and chemical nature of the particle. For example, fibrogenic dusts will initiate fibrotic tissue reactions in lung tissue which ultimately will result in loss of lung function.

Uptake of gases and vapours

The removal of harmful gases or 'scrubbing' represents an important respiratory system defence mechanism. This process removes water-soluble gases from the inhaled airstream, thus preventing them reaching and damaging the sensitive alveolar membrane. When a soluble gas is inhaled, it dissolves into the lining of the respiratory tract in the upper airways. Highly water-soluble gases, for example, ammonia, chlorine and sulphur dioxide, have an immediate affect on the eyes and upper respiratory tract causing pain, swelling and ulceration of mucus membranes. Exposed people, if they can, rapidly move out of the contaminated area. However, the essential objective, that is, protection of the alveolar membrane, has been achieved. Exposure to sufficiently high concentrations of soluble gas will saturate upper airway binding sites and gas will eventually reach the alveoli and cause harm. This may result in pulmonary oedema, where the alveolar membrane and blood capillaries are damaged with fluid and blood leaking out. This fluid seriously impairs normal gas exchange across the membrane.

With water-insoluble gases, for example, phosgene, there is little effect on the upper airways and these will pass down into the alveolar region. In this case, the gas will affect the lungs after a delay of up to 72 hours, causing pulmonary oedema.

With inhalation of organic vapours, the upper and conducting airway membranes are not absorbing and these will reach the alveolar region. The level by which they are absorbed into the systemic blood circulation will depend on their relative solubility in blood. For example, methanol vapour is very soluble in blood and a significant amount of that inhaled will be absorbed, while benzene is highly insoluble in blood and only a small fraction of that inhaled will be absorbed.

Defensive cells

Defensive cells and processes are found widely distributed around the body. Not all cells have a clear defensive function but most will respond to a threat by an alteration in structure or function, although brain cells and other highly specialised structures simply react by dying off. On the other hand, some cell groups are primarily defensive in function, for example, the white blood cells known as lymphocytes.

Defensive processes in which cells are involved

1. Phagocytosis.
2. Inflammatory response.
3. Immune response.
4. Tissue repair.

5. Secreting defensive substances.
6. Preventing excessive blood loss from circulatory system.

Phagocytosis, the inflammatory and immune responses and tissue repair are discussed below, although the secretion of defensive substances and the prevention of excessive blood loss are not dealt with further.

Phagocytosis

This is a vital component of the body's defence against biological and chemical agents (see Figure 2.21). Various types of large and small defensive cells are involved in this process. These are known as macrophages and microphages.

The basic sequence of events is as follows:
1. Phagocytic cells are attracted by small quantities of the invading particle. This is known as chemotaxis.
2. Adhesion of particle to phagocytic cell. This adhesion is a type of immune response involving binding between the particle and cell.
3. Ingestion of the particle by the phagocyte.
4. The lysosomal enzymes digest the particle to form a phagosome.

FIGURE 2.21: Phagocytosis

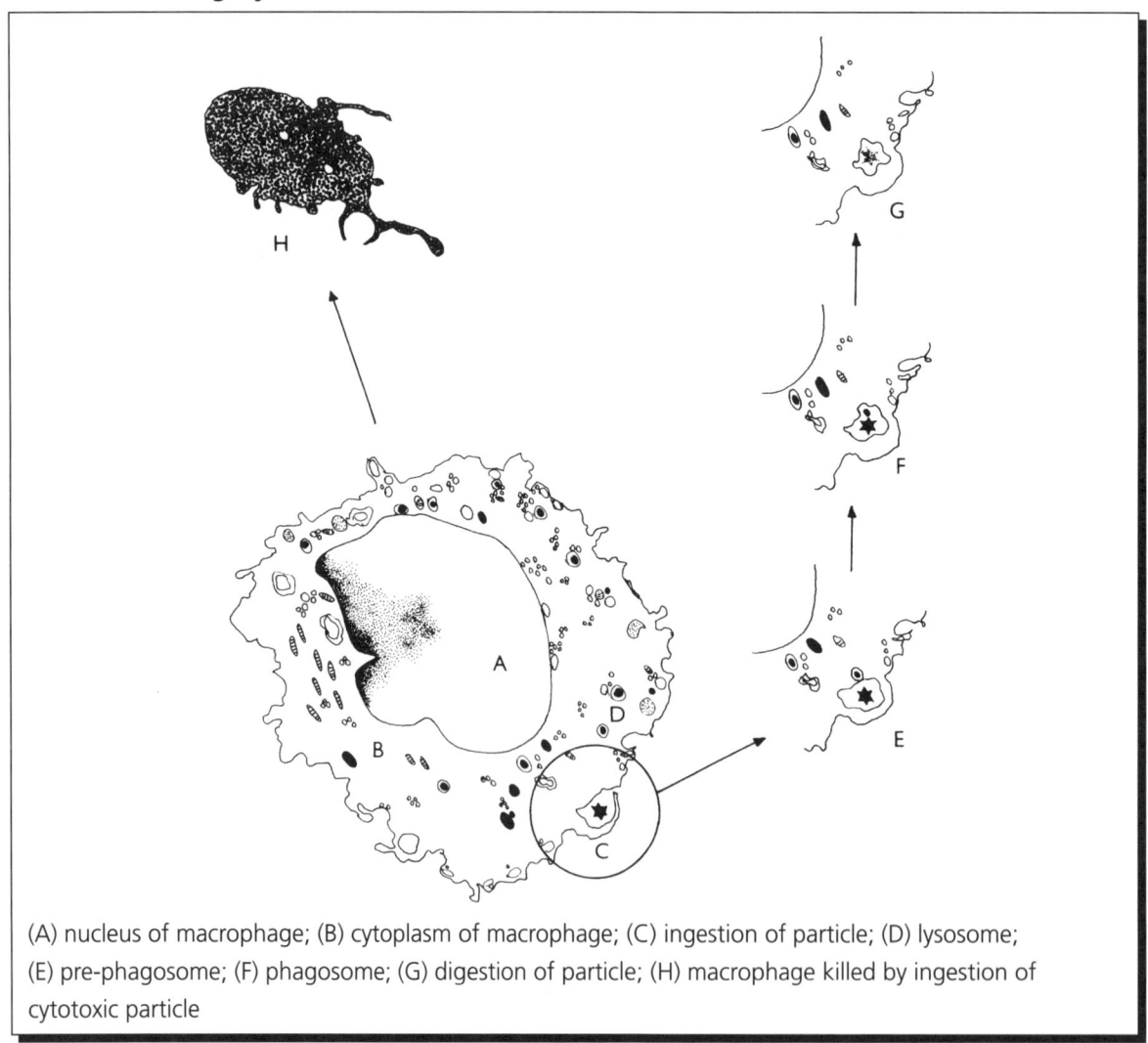

(A) nucleus of macrophage; (B) cytoplasm of macrophage; (C) ingestion of particle; (D) lysosome; (E) pre-phagosome; (F) phagosome; (G) digestion of particle; (H) macrophage killed by ingestion of cytotoxic particle

(After Atherley 1978)

The particle or biological agent may be rendered harmless or sometimes the phagocyte is killed; this is believed to happen with, for example, crystalline silica and asbestos fibres. This leads to further damage involving fibrosis, which is dealt with in Chapter 3.

Inflammatory response

This is the normal reaction of a tissue to harm which is insufficient to kill the tissue. It is a non-specific response to many different kinds of harm following their impact on the body (see Figure 2.22).

Acute inflammation

This is a response of short duration while chronic inflammation may last for weeks, months, or even years. Acute inflammation may subside completely or it may produce pus followed by making good with scar tissue. It may spread to involve a large area of tissue or may interfere with blood supply to cause tissue death and subsequent gangrene. It is a very important defensive process, but if called on to act for too long, it may itself become the source of disease. The primary characteristics are heat, swelling and pain. The basics of the process are given below:

1. Small blood vessels in the area of tissue affected by the harmful input constrict briefly.
2. The same blood vessels then dilate.
3. At the same time, the vessel walls increase in permeability.
4. Protein-rich fluid exudes from the blood vessels into the surrounding tissues causing them to swell.
5. White blood cells phagocytose the harmful input. These leucocytes migrate through the blood vessel wall and phagocytose the invading particles and any damaged tissue.
6. Tissue-dwelling macrophages join in and the area may be localised by fibrin because of blood clotting.

FIGURE 2.22: Inflammatory response

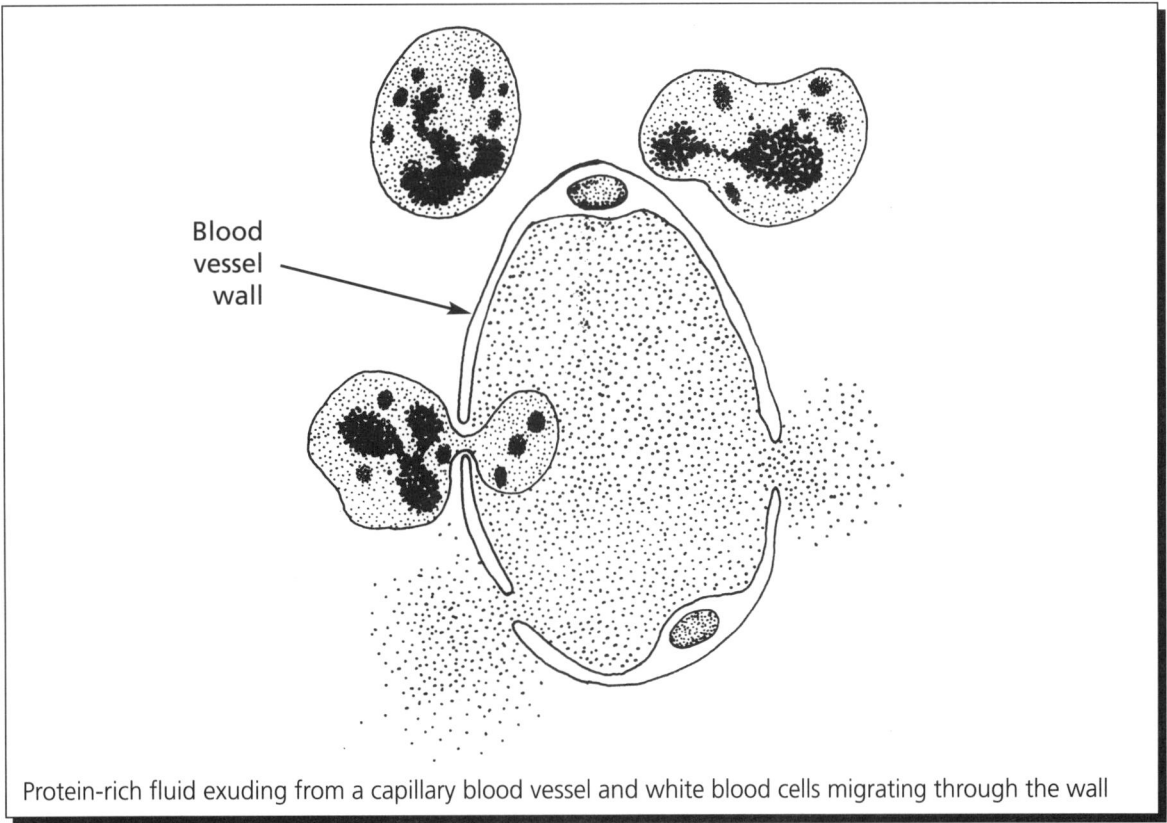

Protein-rich fluid exuding from a capillary blood vessel and white blood cells migrating through the wall

(After Atherley 1978)

Chronic inflammation

In contrast to acute inflammation, chronic inflammation may last for months or even years. Typical chronic inflammation involves the accumulation of macrophages and lymphocytes, together with the stimulation of fibroblast cells to produce excessive amounts of collagen. Collagen is an inflexible structural protein which is used in normal tissue repair or 'scarring', whereby gaps resulting from damage are made good. This repair process may become disordered (known as 'fibrosis') in certain patterns of chronic inflammation. With excessive production of collagen, the overgrowth of scar tissue shrinks and contracts, tearing and disrupting adjacent tissues. In the lung, this fibrosis results in emphysema, that is, the breakdown of air spaces and this results in a loss of lung capacity.

Chronic inflammation may develop as a sequel to acute inflammation or it may develop without a preliminary phase. Chronic inflammation occurs without an acute phase following exposure to fibrogenic dusts containing asbestos and crystalline forms of silica. Significant damage occurs when macrophage cells attempt to phagocytose these particles. Asbestos fibres are believed to puncture the macrophage cells releasing hydrolytic enzymes which cause local tissue damage, and this attracts more macrophages, some of which may suffer the same fate. In response, an excessive amount of collagenous scar tissue is formed. Silica particles appear to be particularly cytotoxic to macrophages which try to destroy them, and again, local tissue damage followed by fibrosis occurs.

Immune response

This describes a group of processes concerned with defence and preservation of normal body integrity. The immune response has three principal defensive functions, namely:

1. Surveillance.
2. Disposal of antigens.
3. Self-disposal.

The principal structures involved in the immune response are the lymph nodes, the spleen and the thymus (Figure 2.23).

Functions of the immune system

Surveillance
These mechanisms are thought to provide surveillance for genetic mutations, for example, cancer cells, which may result in the mutants being recognised and destroyed before they can cause harm. This is a very important function of the immune response.

Disposal of antigens
Biological and many chemical agents will provoke an immune response no matter by what route they enter the body. One form of this response is the production of antibodies (immunoglobulin proteins) which combine with the foreign substance, known as the antigen. This antigen-antibody complex may then be phagocytosed or otherwise destroyed.

Self-disposal
This involves the destruction of old or redundant body cells. Immunological mechanisms exist by which only the redundant or old cells are recognised and removed.

Types of immune response
There are two basic types of immune response:

1. The humoral or antibody-mediated immune response.
2. The cell-mediated immune response.

An immune response may be advantageous or disadvantageous. Examples of a disadvantageous immune response are conditions such as allergic asthma and allergic contact dermatitis. The normal or advantageous immune response is a very important and complex group of cellular and biochemical processes. It is important to link this process with inflammation and both can be regarded as part of the same continuous defensive process, that is, the immune response involved in recognising and preparing the antigen for the inflammatory response and its ultimate removal.

Features of the immune response
Three features characterise the immune response generally:

Specificity

The response of the immune system to an antigen is highly specific.

Memory

The response to a particular antigen will be remembered after a long period of time, even for as long as several years. This feature allows the body to mount a more effective and rapid response in terms of appropriate antibody production should the antigen be encountered for a second time.

Self-recognition

This is the ability of the immune response to distinguish between 'self' and 'non-self' and ensure that the body's own cells do not provoke an immune response. Antigens stimulate the production of antibodies which are immunoglobulin proteins. Human serum immunoglobulins are synthesised in plasma cells and there are five common types, subdivided based on their structure: Immunoglobulin G (IgG), M (IgM), A (IgA), E (IgE) and D (IgD). IgG and IgM form the bulk of circulating antibodies. IgA is found in secretions from the gut and respiratory pathway, while IgE is found in association with cell membranes, for example, it is involved in the release of histamine from cells following an immune response. IgE is also believed to be associated with phagocytosis by macrophages. The role of IgD is not known with certainty.

The immune system

The basic structures of the immune system are shown in Figure 2.23. The cells of the immune system, that is, the small, medium and large lymphocytes, all originate from the stem cells in the bone marrow. These stem cells differentiate into B-lymphocytes and T-lymphocytes, both which have particular roles in the immune response. B-cells are short-lived and are involved in the production of specific antibodies following antigenic stimulation. T-cells are involved in the regulation of the immune response and B-cell antibody production. Furthermore, T-cells live for a much longer time, from five to 10 years or more, and are the basis of the immune system's memory.

FIGURE 2.23: Immune system

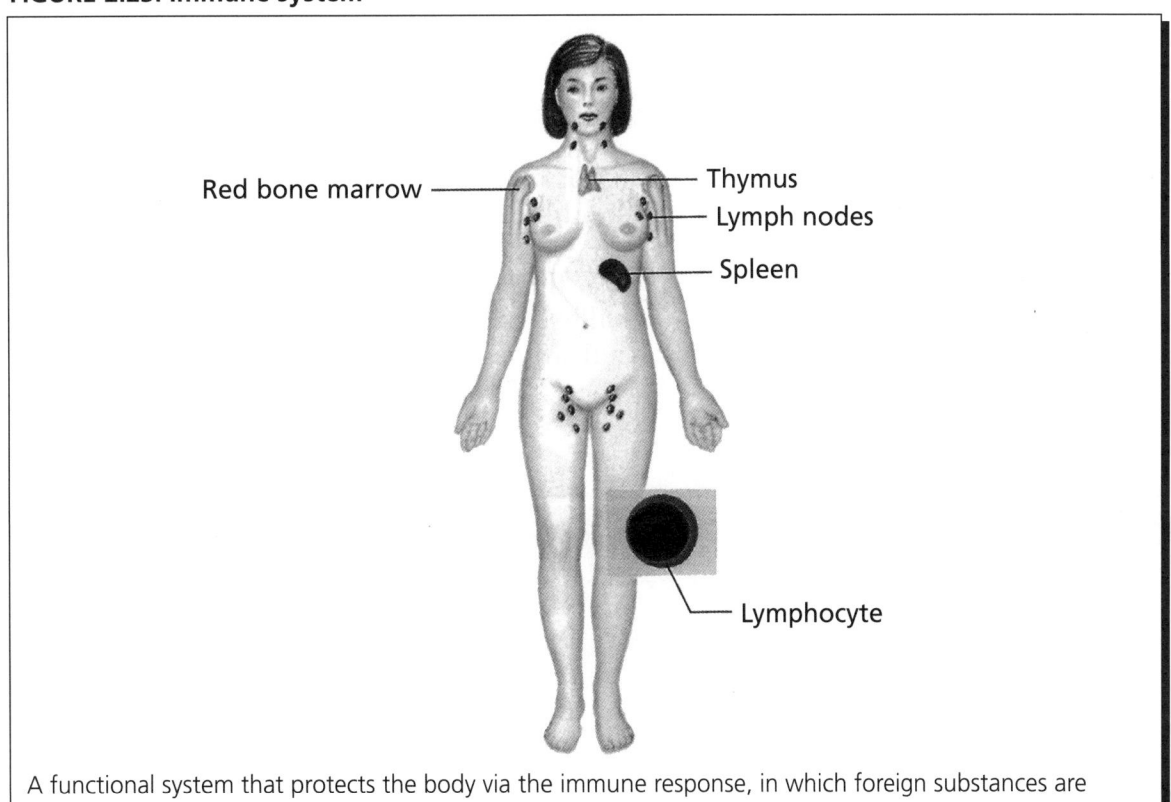

A functional system that protects the body via the immune response, in which foreign substances are attacked by lymphocytes and/or antibodies

(Marieb 1989)

Basic sequence of events in an immune response
1. Exposure to the antigen.
2. Antigen appears in the lymph nodes.
3. Appearance of the antigen stimulates lymphocyte division.
4. After about five days, antibodies are detectable in the lymph nodes; at the same time, large numbers of lymphocytes start to enter the bloodstream.
5. From the bloodstream, they gather in the spleen and bone marrow, and continue producing the antibody which, like the lymphocytes, starts to circulate freely in the bloodstream.
6. The combination of the antigen and the antibody forms a complex.
7. This complex enables the antigen to be either efficiently phagocytosed or otherwise rendered inactive.

Disadvantageous immune response
This is when the immune system functions inappropriately in response to an antigen. The collective name for these responses is hypersensitivity or allergy. Hypersensitivity (HS) reactions are complex and they are normally classified into five types, that is, I to V, based on the mechanism involved. The mechanism of allergic asthma is a Type I HS reaction, extrinsic allergic alveolitis is a mixed Type I and Type III HS reaction, and allergic contact dermatitis is a Type IV HS reaction. (Type V is not relevant here.)

Tissue repair
Damage to tissues and organs may result in gaps in their structure. This may result in damage to both supporting tissues and specialised cells. Repair involves the removal of dead cells and foreign particles by phagocytosis, followed by regeneration of support tissues and specialised cells. However, specialised cells vary in their ability to regenerate, for example, brain and muscle cells never regenerate while liver cells normally do so and bone cells always do so. If there is not too much tissue damage, then repair can take place without the formation of permanent scar tissue. Where tissue gaps are extensive or repair is delayed, then permanent scar tissue will form involving the fibrous, inflexible protein collagen. Occasionally, scar tissue formation can be overstimulated and an excessive amount of scar tissue is formed. The presence of inflexible scar tissue on the surface of the body causes few problems whereas its presence may result in serious problems in internal organs, for example, in the lungs where fibrosis results from exposure to both crystalline silica and asbestos fibres.

Metabolic transformation
Biotransformation and conjugation processes work together as an overall defensive process. The metabolic transformation of chemical agents which enter the body generally aims to increase the polarity and, thus, water solubility of such agents. This enables the transformed products to be excreted by the kidney, or these may become intermediates for other biochemical reactions. This process can be broadly divided into biotransformation and conjugation. The liver and kidney are the principal body organs involved in this activity.

Biotransformation
Biotransformation relies on basic chemical reactions such as oxidation, reduction and hydrolysis. Normally such reactions lead to a product, which is polar and water-soluble, since in this form it may be more efficiently removed from the body by the kidneys. For example, trichloroethylene is converted into trichloroacetic acid and trichloroethanol which are excreted in urine.

Usually the product is less harmful than its precursor, however, occasionally a more harmful substance is produced. This is known as bioactivation, as opposed to the more usual detoxification. The metabolic transformation of 2-naphthylamine by the body produces 2-aminonapthol, a potent bladder carcinogen, and is an example of a classic case of bioactivation. Furthermore, the conversion of n-hexane, a common industrial solvent, into 2,5-hexanedione, which causes peripheral neuropathy, is another example of bioactivation.

Conjugation

This describes a group of reactions by which endogenous substances (produced within the body) combine with the chemical agent in such a way that the active group of the latter is masked. The resulting conjugate is usually more water-soluble and, thus, will be excreted or possibly be the substrate for further reactions.

The barrier role of the skin

The structure of the skin is outlined in Figure 2.8 (see page 39). Penetration of the skin is a passive process which occurs without the assistance of cells in the skin. With different chemical agents, the penetration rate of the skin varies widely. Damage and disease may increase the penetration of the skin by harmful agents.

Skin absorption

The absorption pathway for substances is as follows:

1. Molecule absorbed at the surface of the stratum corneum. Hydrophilic substances will only pass through the skin slowly. At cell membranes and intercellular spaces, lipids and lipophilic compounds can also penetrate the skin.
2. Substance diffuses through the epidermis and dermis to reach blood capillaries and circulation.

Substances entering the systemic (blood) circulation via the skin route may have enhanced toxicity, since they bypass the liver, which is an important detoxification centre and acts as a first-stage filter after absorption following ingestion.

REFERENCES

Atherley G R C, 1978, *Occupational Health and Safety Concepts*, Applied Science Publishers Ltd, Barking (out of print).
Beckett B S, 1992, *Illustrated Human and Social Biology*, Oxford University Press, Oxford.
British Standards Institution, 1993, *Workplace Atmospheres – Size Fraction Definitions for Measurement of Airborne Particles*, BS EN 481, BSI, London.
Foulds I S, 1995, Organ Structure and Function: The Skin, Chapter 2 in *Occupational Hygiene* (2nd edition), Harrington J M and Gardiner K (Eds), Blackwell Science, Oxford.
Health and Safety Executive, 1995, *Asbestos Fibres in Air – Sampling and Evaluation by Phase Contrast Microscopy*, MDHS 39/4, HSE Books, Sudbury.
Marieb E N, 1989, *Human Anatomy and Physiology*, The Benjamin/Cummings Publishing Company, Redwood City, CA, USA.
Swedish Work Environment Association, 1987, *Your Body at Work*, Arbetsmiljo, Stockholm.
Vincent J H and Brosseau L M, 1995, The Nature and Properties of Workplace Airborne Contaminants, Chapter 6 in *Occupational Hygiene* (2nd edition), Harrington J M and Gardiner K (Eds), Blackwell Science, Oxford.

3: Chemical agents

(HSE 2001d)

INTRODUCTION

Large quantities of a very wide number of hazardous chemical substances are found and used in many industries and in virtually all workplaces people are to some extent exposed to such agents. In 1981, over 100,000 substances were listed in the European Inventory of Existing Commercial Substances (EINECS) with over 60,000 used in manufacturing quantities. The total list has increased by 10,000 since the inventory was initiated in 1981. Overall, excessive exposure to toxic substances results in a large occupational ill health problem. In some workplaces, such substances are an integral part of the process, for example, in paint or chemical manufacture where they may be raw materials, or intermediate or waste products. Harmful substances may also be part of the structural environment, for example asbestos, from which there may be an exposure risk to workers. Exposures may vary from very brief intermittent contact on the one hand, to continuous intense exposure on the other. There are not only risks from existing substances to be considered, but also potential problems with newly discovered chemical agents and the nature of the risk assessment to be undertaken.

Chemical agent risk management requires the identification of hazards, the evaluation of risks arising, and the application of prevention and control measures to achieve tolerable levels of risk. This very large range of chemical agents is regulated by the Control of Substances Hazardous to Health Regulations 2002 (COSHH) (as amended by the COSHH (Amendment) Regulations 2004 (SI 2004/3386)), the Chemicals (Hazard Information and Packaging for Supply) Regulations 2002 (CHIP) and the Notification of New Substances Regulations 1993 (NONS). Lead and asbestos are regulated respectively by the Control of Lead at Work Regulations 2002 (CLAW) (HSC 2002a) and the Control of Asbestos at Work Regulations 2002 (CAW) (HSC 2002b). Risk assessment and the application of appropriate prevention/control measures must be carried out for all agents which come within the definition of a "substance hazardous to health" under COSHH (regulation 2). (Biological agents come within this definition and the special considerations relating to these are considered in Chapter 4.)

Table 3.1 presents some typical hazardous chemical agents commonly found in the different industry sectors.

TABLE 3.1: Common hazardous substances and work processes

Occupational	Examples of hazardous chemical agents
Agriculture	Pesticides, herbicides, grain and organic dusts
Construction and demolition	Asbestos, solvents, welding fumes, cement dust, paints, diesel fumes, wood dust
Healthcare	Anaesthetic gases, solvents, sterilants, halogenated hydrocarbons, organic and mineral dusts
Mining and quarrying	Siliceous dusts, carbon monoxide, nitrogen oxides
Food	Flour dust, sugar dust and other organic dusts, solvents
Engineering	Halogenated hydrocarbons, soldering and welding fumes, mineral acids, alkalis, paints, metal fumes
Metals	Metal dusts and fumes, carbon monoxide, sulphur dioxide, silica dust
Paints	Pigments, solvents
Pharmaceuticals	Pharmacologically active dusts, solvents
Plastics	Plasticisers, vinyl chloride monomer, solvents, plastic fumes, isocyanates, epoxy resins, mineral fibres
Pottery	Silica dust, glazes
Printing	Printing inks, solvents
Rubber	Rubber fumes, solvents
Textiles	Textile fibres, solvents, halogenated hydrocarbons, dyes
All sectors	Cleaning and disinfectant chemicals, printing chemicals including carbon black

Hazard information on chemical agents can be collected via several routes – toxicology, epidemiology and observations on occupational disease and discomfort by physicians and other occupational health professionals, all of which constitute useful sources of information. Figure 3.1 attempts to illustrate where a relevant occupational health specialism has its principal input into the chemical agent risk assessment and control process.

Structure of chapter

In this chapter, the section on 'Chemical agent hazard information collection' covers:
1. The role and methods of occupational toxicology in the collection of hazard data on chemical agents.
2. The approach of human epidemiology in the analysis of disease frequency in defined populations in the determination of human health risk data.
3. Occupational diseases resulting from exposure to hazardous chemical agents. (This is a complicated subject and will be discussed principally using the physiological target organ systems described in Chapter 2.)

The section on 'Workplace chemical agent risk management' covers:
1. Hazard identification in workplace risk assessment.
2. Workplace assessment surveys and airborne contaminant monitoring.
3. Determination of tolerable risk criteria for exposure to chemical agents.
4. Prevention and control strategies with detailed measures for controlling exposure to hazardous chemical agents.

CHEMICAL AGENTS

FIGURE 3.1 Chemical agent – Risk assessment and control

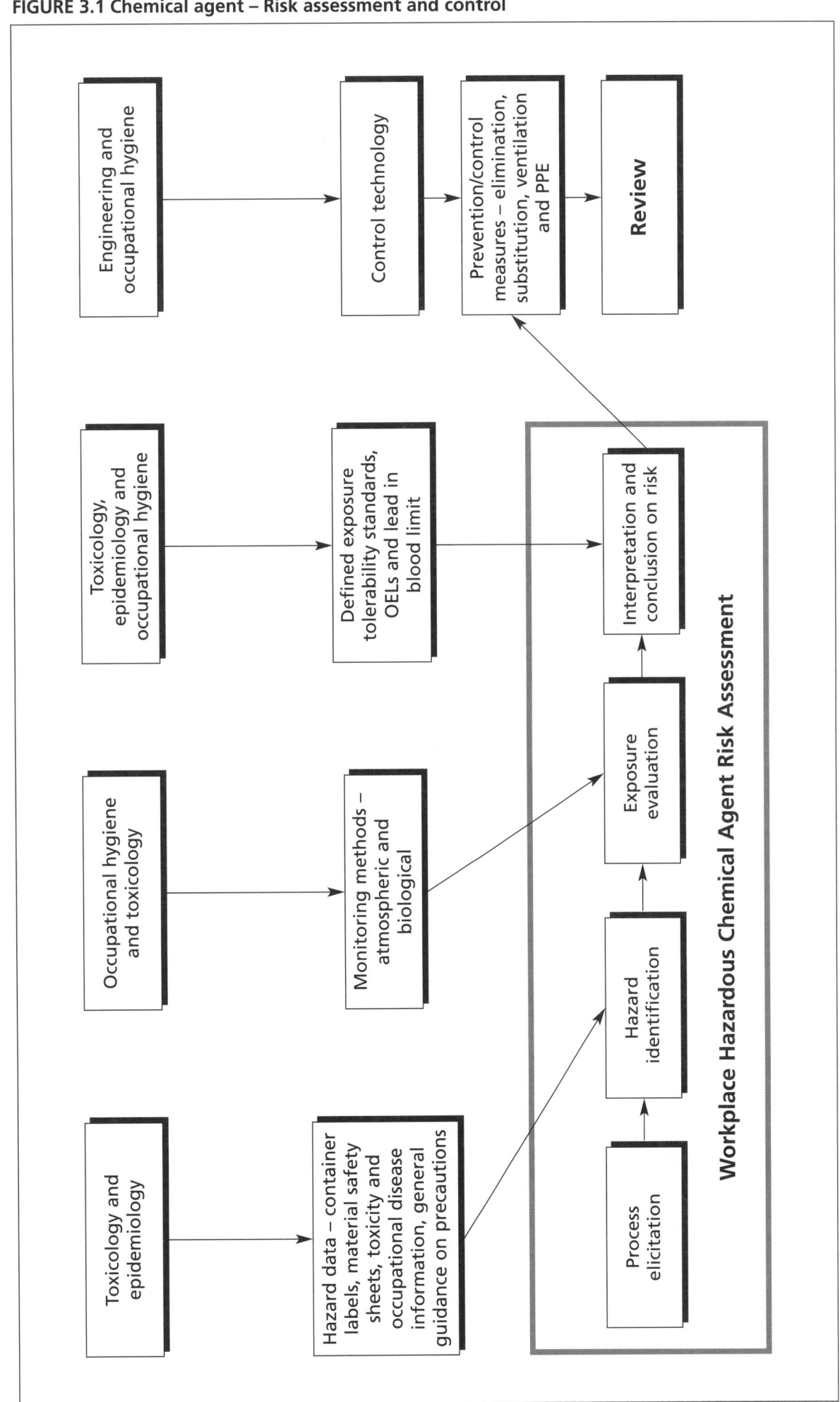

CHEMICAL AGENTS

Chemical agent hazard information collection
Hazardous substance data can be obtained from various sources:
1. Occupational toxicologists carrying out animal exposure studies, short-term testing (ie laboratory studies using *in vitro* cell test systems) and chemical analogy studies, which predict the likely toxic effects of substances based on their chemical structure when compared with related chemicals.
2. Occupational epidemiologists and physicians collecting data on human occupational exposure to chemical agents. Information ranges from individual case reports on exposure to statistical studies on large occupational population groups.

The following sections review the nature of this hazard information and how it is obtained and used.

Occupational toxicology
Toxicology can be considered the science of poisons; it studies the potential of substances to produce adverse effects, particularly in human and animal systems. The toxicity of potentially harmful substances is studied in different contexts, for example, food additives in the food industry, pesticides and herbicides in agriculture, and biologically active substances in the pharmaceutical industry.

The two important roles of occupational toxicology are:
1. **The identification of harmful effects of substances** – toxicity thresholds and mechanisms of toxicity, predicting toxicity of new substances.
2. **The provision of information for risk assessment** – setting tolerable limits for occupational exposure, development of biological monitoring methods, classification and labelling of substances, preparation of safety data sheets.

Key concepts and definitions
In the following sections some key concepts and definitions in occupational toxicology will be outlined.

Firstly, the physical nature of substances is very important and the different physical forms are discussed briefly below.

Physical state
Chemical agents can exist in three basic physical states, namely, solids, liquids and gases. Each of these is briefly discussed below:
1. **Solids** – Here atoms are located in fixed positions and molecules are held in a very regular pattern where they cannot move around, but they can vibrate. With cooling they vibrate less while with heating they vibrate more. Solids have different degrees of order, from highly-ordered crystalline solids to lowly-ordered amorphous solids.
2. **Liquid** – When enough energy (heat) is applied, a solid will melt and enter the liquid phase. Here, chemical bonds can be broken and re-made with individual molecules free to wander around and change places with one another.
3. **Gas** – With heat added, the molecules of a liquid will move faster. Two aspects prevent them from escaping: atmospheric pressure pressing down and the forces between the molecules. If sufficient heat is added, then these forces can be overcome and the liquid will boil and particles will escape from the surface of the liquid forming a gas. In this form, particles are found in the free atomic or molecular phase and they can quickly move far away from each other, diffusing to fill all the available space.

A key objective in occupational health and hygiene is to prevent harmful substances being transported through the workplace as airborne contaminants and gaining entry to the body via inhalation into the respiratory system. Airborne contaminants can be broadly divided into aerosols and gases, which can be classified as shown in Figure 3.2.

CHEMICAL AGENTS

FIGURE 3.2: Classification of airborne contaminants

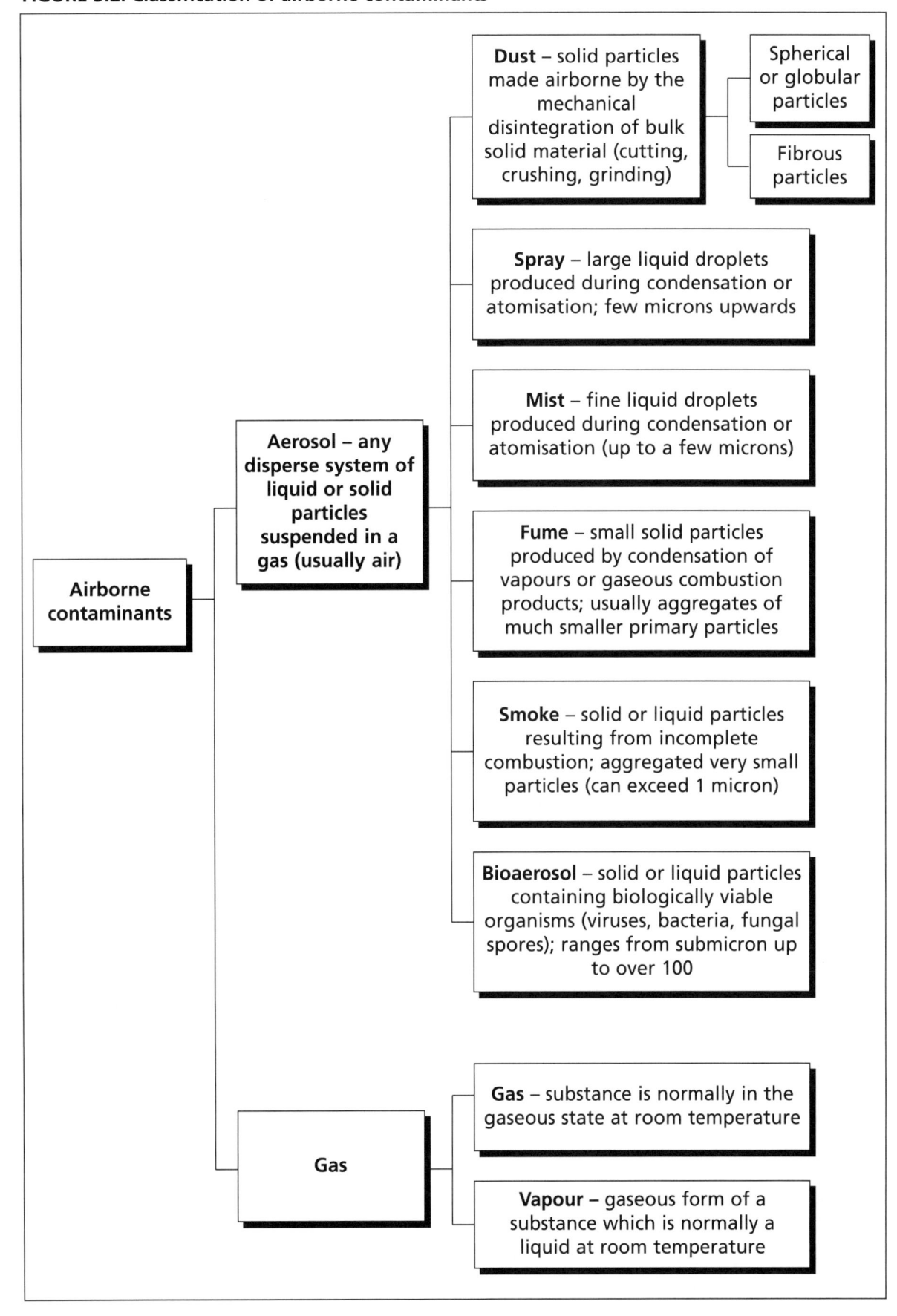

- **Airborne contaminants**
  - **Aerosol** – any disperse system of liquid or solid particles suspended in a gas (usually air)
    - **Dust** – solid particles made airborne by the mechanical disintegration of bulk solid material (cutting, crushing, grinding)
      - Spherical or globular particles
      - Fibrous particles
    - **Spray** – large liquid droplets produced during condensation or atomisation; few microns upwards
    - **Mist** – fine liquid droplets produced during condensation or atomisation (up to a few microns)
    - **Fume** – small solid particles produced by condensation of vapours or gaseous combustion products; usually aggregates of much smaller primary particles
    - **Smoke** – solid or liquid particles resulting from incomplete combustion; aggregated very small particles (can exceed 1 micron)
    - **Bioaerosol** – solid or liquid particles containing biologically viable organisms (viruses, bacteria, fungal spores); ranges from submicron up to over 100
  - **Gas**
    - **Gas** – substance is normally in the gaseous state at room temperature
    - **Vapour** – gaseous form of a substance which is normally a liquid at room temperature

Chemical exposure can result in a wide range of toxic effects, which vary in the extent and type of damage caused to body cells, tissues, organs and organ systems. Toxic chemicals may cause mild, reversible changes in the body while, at the other extreme, exposure may result in the death of the organism.

1. **Toxic effect** – This happens when a chemical agent (or its products) reaches an

appropriate site in the body at a sufficient concentration for a sufficient period of time which allows damage to occur. This is when a 'critical dose' reaches a 'target' organ or site.

2. **Dose** – Dose is the quantity of uptake of a substance into the body by inhalation, ingestion and skin absorption routes over a specified period of time. Inhalation dose can be estimated from personal monitoring of airborne contaminants while biological monitoring techniques give an indication of body dose from all routes. In animal exposure studies, dose is taken as the amount of substance administered by inhalation, oral or dermal routes over time. This is normally expressed in units of milligrams of substance per kilogram body weight of the animal (mg/kg).

3. **Dose response** – A dose response relationship links the level (dose) of exposure to an agent to the level of harm (response), for a defined effect, observed in a population. Dose response is a fundamental concept in toxicology and normally produces a characteristic s-shaped curve, as shown in Figure 3.3 below. The exact nature of the curve will vary with individual substances.

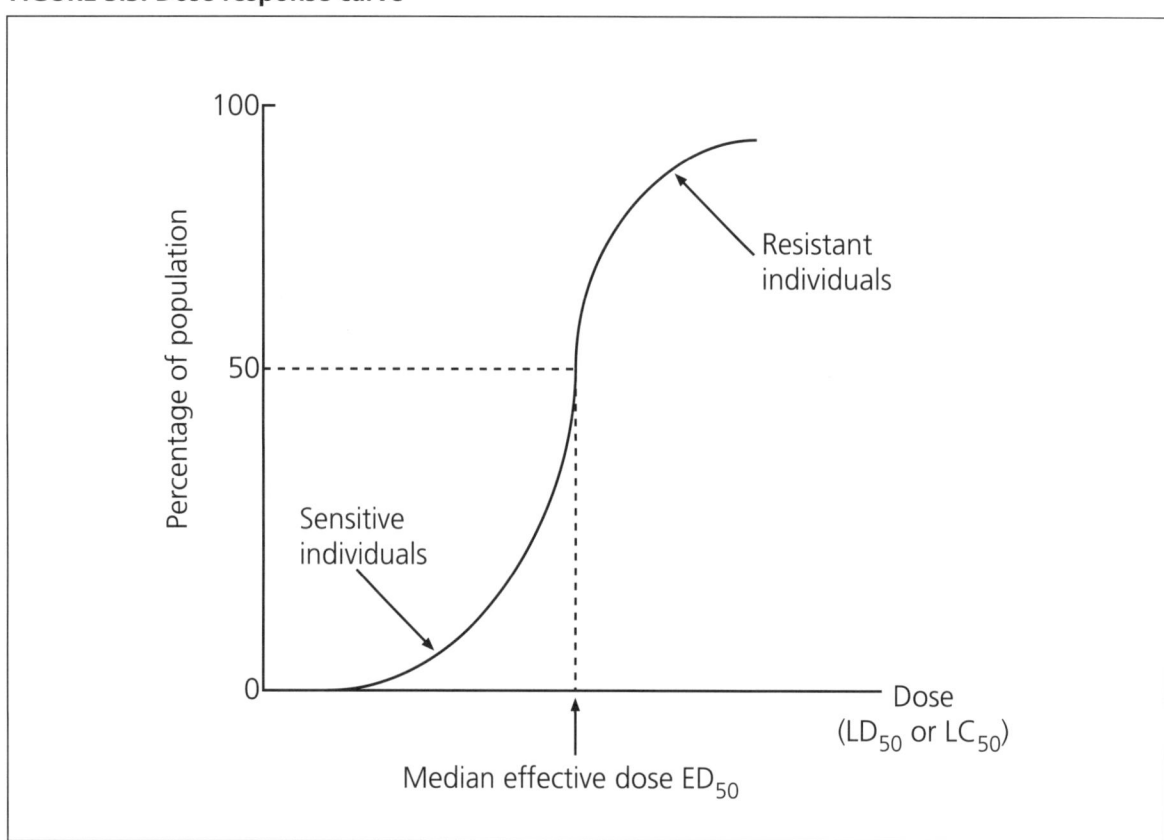

FIGURE 3.3: Dose response curve

Dose response data is used to derive indices of toxicity which are used in the legislative classification of chemical substances and preparations and in the setting of exposure limits embodying tolerable risk. Two indices are given below:

1. **Lethal dose 50% value (LD_{50} or LC_{50})** – The median effective dose of a substance which will kill 50% of a defined group of test animals is known as the LD_{50} value. If exposure is via inhalation, then this is known as the LC_{50} value. This parameter provides some indication of the relative toxicity of the chemical agent and its target organ(s), but doubts have been raised as to the usefulness of such mortality values. Determination of the LD_{50} or LC_{50} value is required under certain circumstances by the NONS Regulations 1993 and the CHIP Regulations 2002.

2. **No Observed Adverse Effect Level (NOAEL)** – This is the exposure dose, below which no observable effect occurs. Ideally, this should be used when setting tolerable exposure

limits. For some chemicals, eg carcinogens and allergens, there may be no discernible NOAEL.

Target organ or site

The target organ is the site in the body where a toxic agent exerts its major harm. Where a substance causes harm at more than one site, these can be ranked as major or minor target sites. This highlights the important concept of 'selective toxicity' where harmful substances often concentrate and exert their effects in one or two critical target sites, for example, absorption of cadmium by the body principally causes harmful effects in the kidney. Important targets for toxic chemicals include the respiratory system, skin, nervous system, kidney and liver.

Absorption and metabolic handling of toxic substances

The concentration of a toxic substance in the target tissue over a period of time (and, thus, the likelihood and degree of a harmful effect) depends on the exposure dose and other factors, including how the body handles the absorption, distribution, storage and excretion of the substance. In humans, the major sites of absorption are the respiratory system, the gastrointestinal tract and the skin. In experimental animals, other exposure routes for dose administration may be used, for example, subcutaneous (under the skin), intraperitoneal (injected into the body cavity), and intravenous (within a vein).

Absorption of a substance involves its passage across cell membranes, which are selectively permeable. The ability of a substance to cross a cell membrane depends on its physicochemical properties. Properties which facilitate uptake include:
- molecular size (not too large);
- high fat solubility;
- lack of polarity[11]; and
- structural similarity to body (endogenous) chemicals.

Non-polar (fat-soluble) substances, benzene for example, can diffuse across cell membranes. On the other hand, polar (non fat-soluble) substances, for example, sugars, amino acids and ions, cross membranes by special facilitated transport systems.

Once an agent has entered the systemic circulation (see page 35, Chapter 2) via inhalation, ingestion or skin absorption, it can, theoretically, accumulate and produce harmful effects at virtually any site in the body. As discussed above, the primary target(s) of a particular toxic agent depends on its chemical and toxicological properties, for example, carbon tetrachloride targets the liver and the blood-forming tissues are the primary target for inorganic lead, while organic lead exerts its effects predominantly on the central nervous system.

The respiratory system is usually the most important mode of entry in the workplace. As discussed in Chapter 2, the characteristics of the lung membrane make it vulnerable to air contaminant damage. The principal aim of respiratory defence is to prevent such damage.

The gastrointestinal system is not often a significant mode of entry to the body for toxic substances in the workplace. However, it is possible for large quantities of a toxic agent to gain entry via this route, particularly with work in conditions of poor hygiene. This can be the case where eating, drinking and smoking are permitted where there is processing of inorganic lead.

Respiratory filtration and the mucociliary escalator (see page 48, Chapter 2) may result in airborne chemical agents ultimately being swallowed. In some cases, this has been associated with disease, for example, exposure to asbestos fibres and stomach cancer. It is thought that the water-insoluble asbestos fibres cause harm on contact with the epithelial cell membrane.

The gastrointestinal membrane is similar to the lung membrane in that it is thin, well supplied with

---

[11]Polarity is a property of some covalent bonds; covalent bonds involve the sharing of electrons between two adjacent atoms. Where the electrons are not equally shared, then one end of the bond is more negative with respect to the other and there is thus a negative and positive end; the substance is said to possess polarity. Many, but not all, organic solvents are non-polar. Polar substances dissolve in polar solvents such as water.

blood vessels and has a very large surface area. These properties will maximise the absorption of toxic substances with the appropriate physicochemical properties.

The skin consists of three basic elements (see page 39, Chapter 2): an outer epidermis which acts as a protective layer and is non-wettable, the dermis which provides strength mainly through its collagen content, and the subcutis. The waterproofing characteristics of the epidermis (which presents a greasy surface) may aid in the absorption of fat-soluble organic materials and, thus, facilitate a route of entry for many substances.

Storage and distribution

After entering the bloodstream the chemical is available for distribution around the body. The nature and rate of this distribution will depend on the rate of blood flow through an organ or tissue, the ease of passage between the blood capillary wall and the cell membrane of the organ, and the affinity of the components of the tissue for the chemical. Toxic materials often concentrate in particular tissues, for example, cadmium will accumulate in the kidney, its site of toxic action, and lead in bone tissue, where it does not exert a toxic effect. Some storage sites will therefore act as a protective mechanism, which may prevent accumulation of high concentrations of the chemical in the most vulnerable target tissues.

Excretion

Following absorption and distribution of a chemical, it may be excreted either unchanged or as a metabolite. Generally, metabolites represent a more polar form of the original substance; they are more water-soluble and easier for the body to excrete. Metabolism may result in a less toxic metabolite, that is, detoxification, or sometimes in a more toxic metabolite. This is known as bioactivation or intoxication. The major routes of excretion are urinary (via the kidney), exhaled breath, and biliary (via the bile duct into the gastrointestinal tract). Other minor routes include the skin (via sweat), tears, saliva, hair and breast milk.

Duration and frequency of exposure

Toxicologists normally divide the exposure of animals to chemical agents into four categories:
1. **Acute** – exposure is less than 24 hours and is usually a single exposure.
2. **Subacute** – repeated exposure for one month.
3. **Subchronic** – repeated exposure for one to three months.
4. **Chronic** – repeated exposure for more than three months.

Characteristics of harmful effects

Immediate and delayed

It is possible to broadly divide the harmful effects of toxic substances into immediate (acute) and delayed (chronic):
1. **Immediate** – These effects occur within a relatively short time (up to 24 hours), usually following a single exposure, commonly to chemical agents that are rapidly absorbed. For example, the effects of chlorine gas poisoning will be apparent in a few minutes, while those of exposure to vapours of ethanol or chlorinated hydrocarbons will only become apparent after a few hours (unless of a very high concentration).
2. **Delayed** – These effects may occur after a much longer period following initial exposure and in some cases this may be many years later. For example, cancer may be caused by some chemicals up to 40 years following initial exposure.

Immediate effects are often quite different to delayed effects, even though both may be caused by exposure to the same substance. For example, exposure to benzene vapour can cause central nervous system depression (narcosis) as an immediate effect, while with repeated exposure, this agent may cause leukaemia as a delayed effect.

TABLE 3.2: Immediate and delayed effects

Immediate effects (acute)	Delayed effects (chronic)
Usually caused by a high exposure lasting anything from seconds to hours; accidental or single exposure	Usually related to lower, repeated exposures over months or years
Condition develops quickly within minutes or days, with signs or symptoms	Condition develops slowly over months or years; usually incremental damage with early changes going undetected
Usually damage is completely reversible unless fatal, eg narcosis	Damage is usually irreversible; damage may be arrested or it may become progressive, eg asbestosis

Reversible and irreversible effects

Some agents cause changes in the body which appear to be completely reversible, for example, the depressive effect of organic solvents on the central nervous system or exposure to some benign dusts. On the other hand, some agents exert irreversible changes in the body, for example, the fibrotic lung reactions resulting from exposure to asbestos or irreversible changes (mutations) in genetic material resulting from exposure to carcinogens.

Local and systemic

A local toxic effect occurs at the site of first contact between the organism and the chemical, while a systemic effect occurs only after the substance has been absorbed and concentrated in the body via the systemic circulation. This generally involves one or more organs and tissues.

Corrosive substances such as concentrated solutions of sulphuric acid or sodium hydroxide cause local toxic effects when coming into contact with the skin or eyes. Similarly, irritant gases are locally acting when they cause inflammation on making contact with the respiratory tract membrane following inhalation. Systemic effects are caused by absorption of, for example, carbon tetrachloride, which damages the liver, and organic lead compounds, which damage the central nervous system.

Allergy or hypersensitivity

This harmful effect causes inappropriate intervention of the immune system, usually involving excessive antibody formation. Once the body has become sensitised to a particular substance, harmful symptoms may occur on subsequent exposures to the substance in question, even at very low levels. Sensitisation reactions are irreversible and may cause very severe symptoms. Examples are allergic asthma and allergic contact dermatitis.

Mutagenicity

Mutagenicity is a toxic effect which causes a permanent change in the genetic material (ie the DNA) of the cell. The DNA is damaged or changed in such a way that the change is transferred to the next generation of cells. The type of cell where the mutation occurs will determine the type of potential health effect as shown in Figure 3.4.

In body cells, mutations are thought to be involved in the development of cancer in the individual concerned. If a substance causes mutations in reproductive cells, that is, sperm or ova, which are concerned with the transfer of genetic material to the next generation, then it may cause heritable health effects. This means that the genetic damage may be transmitted to offspring. Under the CHIP Regulations 2002, such a substance would be labelled with the risk phrase 'may cause heritable genetic damage' (R46). Toxicological methods to identify potential mutagenic substances are discussed later in this chapter.

FIGURE 3.4: Mutagenesis and cell type

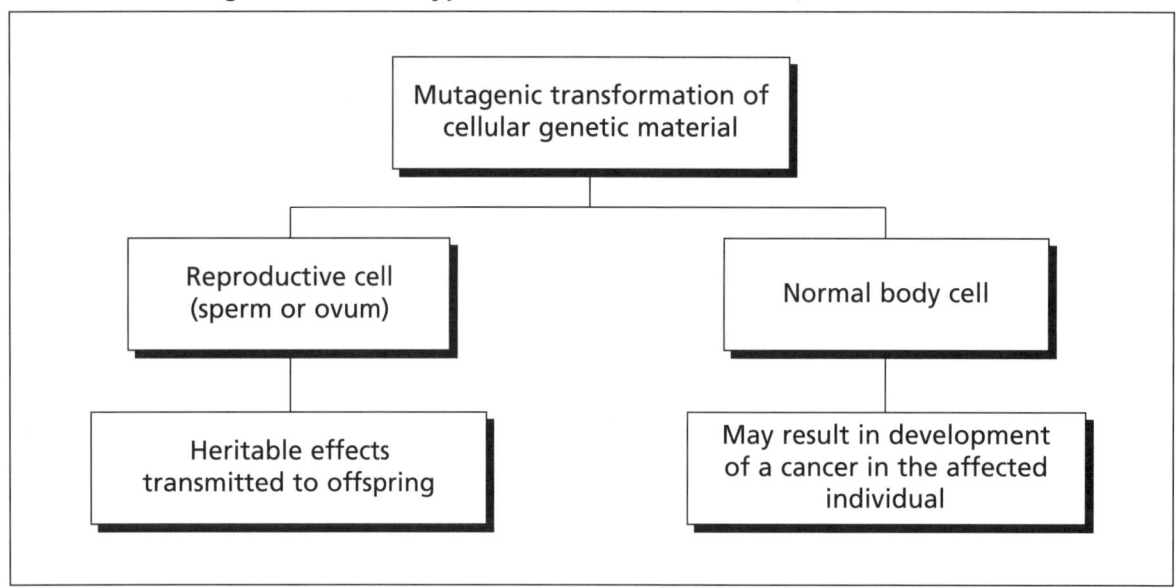

```
                    Mutagenic transformation of
                      cellular genetic material
                      /                    \
        Reproductive cell              Normal body cell
        (sperm or ovum)
              |                               |
         Heritable effects          May result in development
       transmitted to offspring      of a cancer in the affected
                                           individual
```

Carcinogenicity
This results from a toxic event (often a change in cellular DNA) which causes a loss of normal cellular growth control resulting in the development of a cancer.

Chemical carcinogen
This is a substance capable of causing cancer when it comes into contact with body cells.

Cancer
This is a general term for a large group of diseases. They begin when a group of body cells fails to respond to normal controls and continue to excessively divide and grow inappropriately. Such new growths are called tumours, or neoplasia, which may be benign or malignant. Malignant tumours grow faster than benign growths and may rapidly spread to other body tissues causing damage and disruption and forming secondary tumour growths, that is, metastases. Malignant cancer is invariably a very serious disease, often with a fatal outcome.

Cancer is caused by exposure to chemical agents, ionising radiation and some viruses. In general, cancer is caused by 'environmental' exposure to chemical agents in the widest sense including diet and the general environment as well as occupational sources. Induction of the disease is believed to be a multistage process: first, initiation, which is an interaction between the carcinogenic substance and the cellular DNA (in the case of genotoxic carcinogens); and second, promotion, where a promotor agent induces cell proliferation and tumour formation. Only at this stage is the ill health actually recognised.

Unfortunately, due to the nature of this disease it is often very difficult to identify many of the specific causative agents and definitively prove a link between a particular workplace chemical and cancer in workers. This is partly due to the time, often many years, between initial exposure to the substance and actual onset of the disease. This time between the initiation and promotion stages of cancer is known as the latency period.

During this period, when nothing apparently happens, a worker may have had several jobs, lived in different places and had a variety of exposures to different substances. Furthermore, many cancers which are common in the community are multicausal, that is, the same disease is associated with a range of exposures. For example, an increased risk of cancer of the lung is associated with exposure to diesel fumes, asbestos and various chromates as well as cigarette smoking and other chemical agents.

Because of these fundamental difficulties in recognising carcinogenic agents, the crucial role of competent, systematic risk assessment is emphasised, both with respect to the general body of workplace substances, where there are unidentified carcinogenic agents, and with formally defined carcinogens. The goal should always be elimination of the hazard or, if this is not possible, the reduction of exposures to as low as reasonably practicable. To emphasise this point, Doll (1992) has suggested that two to six per cent of all cancer deaths each year[12] may be attributed to occupational agents and a substantial number could be reduced if there was better control of workplace risks.

Genotoxic and epigenetic carcinogens

Carcinogenic substances can be broadly divided into two groups: genotoxic and epigenetic. Genotoxic carcinogens pose a clear qualitative cancer risk and they cause cancer by reacting directly with the DNA. They are theoretically effective at the lowest concentrations and they do not appear to have a safe level. These can be subdivided into 'primary carcinogens', which act directly and do not have to be bioactivated, and 'secondary carcinogens', which do have to be converted by the body into their active form.

Epigenetic carcinogens do not appear to have a direct effect on genetic material and require high or prolonged exposure to have an effect. In the case of these substances, it may be theoretically possible to define a 'safe level'.

Carcinogens and the COSHH Regulations

Because occupational cancer is a very serious disorder, carcinogens are specifically regulated by the COSHH Regulations 2002. 'Carcinogens' are defined in COSHH and there is a specific Approved Code of Practice to assist with compliance with carcinogen controls (HSC 2002).

Exposure to mixtures

Chemical exposure in the workplace commonly involves more than one material and, in some cases, a wide range of substances. Simultaneous exposure to two substances may alter the toxicity of one or both in several possible ways. These interactive effects may be additive, synergistic, potentiating or antagonistic.

Additive effect

The combined effect of two substances is equal to the sum of the individual effects of each when each substance is given alone (ie 2 + 3 = 5) – for example, exposure to xylene and methyl ethyl ketone, which are found together in some paints and both of which cause narcosis.

Synergistic effect

Here, the combined exposure effect is much greater than the sum of the effects of each individual substance alone (ie 9 + 10 = 90) – for example, carbon tetrachloride combined with ethanol exposure, in causing enhanced hepatotoxic effects. Also, an often cited example is that of cigarette smoking and exposure to asbestos leading to a much elevated lung cancer risk.

Potentiation

In this case, the first substance alone has no toxic effect, but when simultaneous exposure occurs with a second substance, the toxicity of the second substance is enhanced (ie 0 + 10 = 20) – for example, exposure to isopropanol and carbon tetrachloride. Here, isopropanol is not hepatotoxic, but it increases (significantly) the liver damage of carbon tetrachloride.

Antagonism

The combined effect of two chemicals is less than the effects observed when each chemical is administered alone (ie 4 + 6 = 8). This is a very important area of study in general toxicology and is the basis for the action of antidotes. In this case, the antidote competes for the same binding site in the cell as the toxic substance and therefore can lessen the impact of the latter substance.

Common hazardous chemical agents

The toxic properties of a range of common hazardous chemical agents are outlined in Table 3.3.

---

[12]There was a total of 159,714 UK cancer deaths in 1990.

CHEMICAL AGENTS

TABLE 3.3: Common hazardous chemical agents

Type	Substance	Harmful effects
Toxic	Lead (inorganic)	**Mode of entry** – respiratory system; gastrointestinal system **Acute effects** – significant central nervous system (CNS) damage and peripheral nervous system (PNS) damage; lassitude; abdominal cramps; constipation; blue line on gums **Chronic effects** – anaemia; peripheral motor neuropathy (wrist drop – rare); disturbance of haem synthesis and slowing of motor nerve conduction velocity **Subclinical** – mood changes; depression; anger; tension, confusion; neurobehavioural changes including short-term memory loss, impaired learning ability; psychomotor changes – hand/eye co-ordination reduced, speed and dexterity reduced **Target sites** – haematopoetic system; nervous system
	Lead (organic)	**Mode of entry** – skin; respiratory system **Acute effects** – effects on the CNS with psychiatric symptoms including insomnia; hyperexcitability and psychosis **Target sites** – nervous system
	Silaceous dusts	**Mode of entry** – respiratory system **Acute effects** – acute silicosis **Chronic effects** – silicosis; collagenous fibrosis of the lung caused by exposure to respirable crystalline silica; lung cancer **Target sites** – respiratory system
	Asbestos	**Mode of entry** – respiratory system **Chronic effects** – long-term exposure to asbestos fibres causes asbestosis, lung cancer and mesothelioma; asbestosis – collagenous fibrosis of the lung; symptoms are increasing shortness of breath and a dry cough; around 50 per cent of people with asbestosis go on to develop lung cancer (this is synergistically enhanced where there is smoking); mesothelioma of the pleura; stomach cancer **Target sites** – the respiratory system – exposure to fibres greater than 5µm in length and less than 3µm in diameter are thought to present the greatest hazard from asbestos; the gastrointestinal system – also target via fibres transported by ciliary escalator
	Trichloroethylene	**Mode of entry** – respiratory system; skin; occasionally gastrointestinal system **Acute effects** – narcosis; respiratory irritation; skin irritant dermatitis **Chronic effects** – addictive; peripheral neuropathy; suspect human carcinogen (liver carcinogen in animal studies) **Target sites** – nervous system; respiratory system; skin; liver

Table continued opposite

	Carbon monoxide	**Mode of entry** – respiratory system **Acute effects** – chest tightness; giddiness; nausea; unconsciousness (3,500ppm) **Chronic effects** – headache with brain damage with continued tissue anoxia **Target sites** – cardiovascular system; binds with haemoglobin in blood causing reduced oxygen-carrying capacity with consequent tissue oxygen starvation (anoxia)
	Isocyanates	**Mode of entry** – respiratory system; (toluene diisocyanate – volatile liquid) **Acute effects** – sensitisation and occupational asthma; irritation **Chronic effects** – chronic pulmonary disability **Target sites** – respiratory system
Corrosive substances	Mineral acids and bases	**Mode of entry** – skin; respiratory system **Acute effects** – direct chemical action on normal living tissue which results in disintegration and irreversible alteration of the site of contact, ulceration, necrosis and scar tissue formation **Target sites** – skin; eyes; nose and upper airways
Dermatitic substances	Primary contact agents – organic solvents; soaps and detergents	**Mode of entry** – direct toxic action on the skin **Chronic effects** – degreasing and inflammatory changes in the skin with repeated exposure; cumulative damage to the skin makes it more susceptible to harm; all exposed liable to develop these health effects (majority industrial dermatitis) **Target sites** – skin
	Secondary allergic agents	**Mode of entry** – skin **Chronic effects** – clinically similar to irritant contact dermatitis, but underlying mechanism due to an individual developing a hypersensitivity to a substance; repeated exposure usually over months or years
	Examples – platinum salts; latex; ammonia	Type 1 hypersensitivity reaction – urticaria, a widespread itchy rash on the skin; response occurs within minutes and individuals may react to many different chemicals coming into contact with the skin
	Examples – epoxy resins; chromates; formaldehyde; mercury and salts	Type IV hypersensitivity reaction – initial sensitising reaction may require high concentrations and/or prolonged contact; skin reaction after contact may be delayed for a week or more; allergic contact dermatitis only affects a small proportion of the workforce

Toxicological testing and hazard data

The collection of hazard data for chemical agents is discussed below. For convenience, information sources are divided into four types:

1. Chemical analogy.
2. Animal studies.
3. Short-term testing.
4. Human epidemiology.

Chemical analogy

By this method, the structural features of the substance under consideration are compared with other similar substances of known toxicity in order to predict its potential biological activity. Therefore, this can be seen as a method which may be applied to detect potentially harmful new substances.

Many studies have been carried out in the past modelling fragments of molecules with specific attributes and linking them to carcinogenicity. The chemical analogy approach needs to account for potential bioactivation of the substance, which may occur in biological systems.

This approach has been applied in studies on polycyclic aromatic hydrocarbons (PAHs) and carcinogenicity. Many of these substances are derived from the anthracene molecule (Figure 3.5). Anthracene itself is not carcinogenic, but many of the carcinogenic PAHs are derived from the weakly carcinogenic benz(a)anthracene. The addition of another benzene ring in selected positions results in powerful carcinogens, for example, benzo(a)pyrene and dibenz(a,h)anthracene. Knowledge of the impact of structural changes on biological function allows chemical analogy to predict the toxicity of new and unknown substances.

FIGURE 3.5: Polycyclic aromatic hydrocarbons

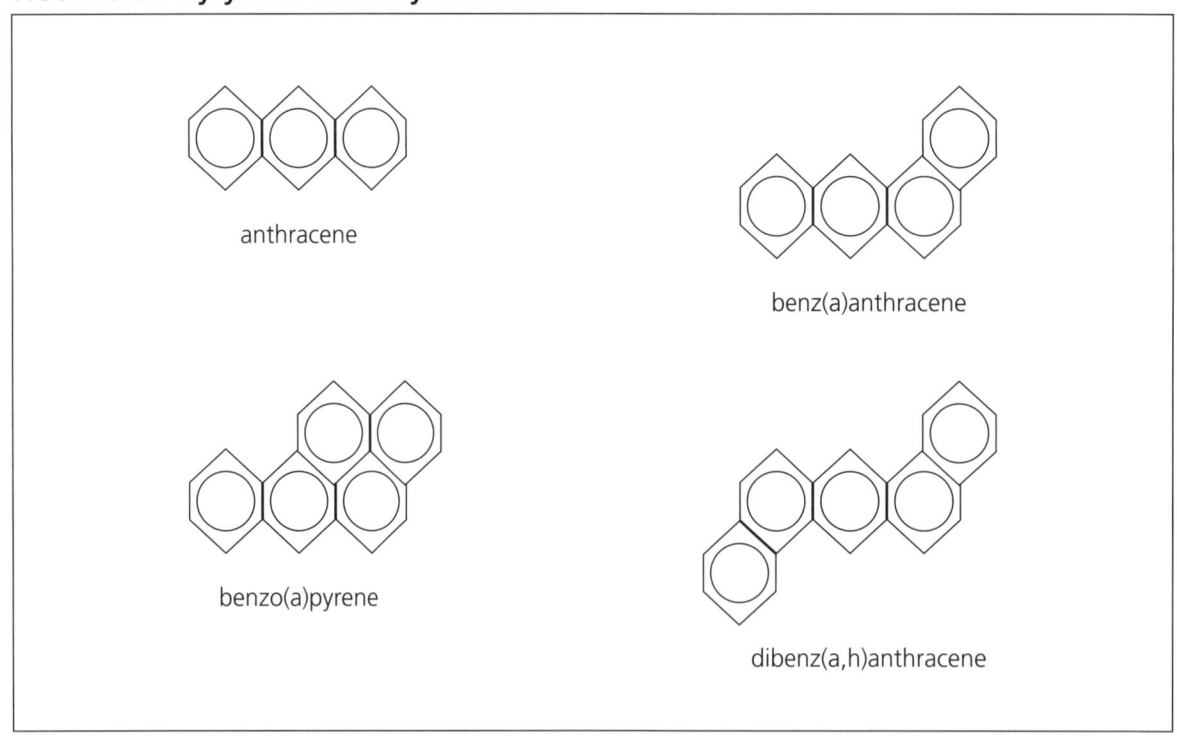

Animal studies

Acute toxicity testing

The aim is to provide an indication of toxicity using a nominal single dose. The exposure route is inhalation, ingestion or via the skin. The acute oral LD_{50} test has been used for many years. Test animals, normally rats, are each given a single dose of a test compound. The level of mortality and toxic effects are then determined over a two-week period. A range of dose levels is determined, empirically, with one dose where no deaths occur and one dose where all the animals die. The median lethal dose

is then determined, which is the point where 50 per cent of the animal group would be expected to die. This test has been widely criticised in that:
- lethality is an extreme criterion and unhelpful as a measure of toxicity in the workplace;
- this test is not relevant to occupational exposures;
- the use and suffering of large numbers of experimental animals is unacceptable ethically;
- cause of death may not be relevant to toxicological effects directly.

As Cross & Faux (1999) point out, a modified version of the test, called the 'fixed dose procedure', has been developed which attempts to avoid using death as the end point and focuses on 'evident toxicity'.

The results of acute toxicity testing are widely used in the classification of substances as either 'harmful', 'toxic' or 'very toxic', as shown in Table 3.6 (on page 77).

Skin irritation

Chemicals are tested for their potential to cause skin irritation. The test involves the application of a single dose of a substance to the shaved skin of the animal, usually a rabbit, and the effects are observed over 72 hours. Responses are graded from extreme damage, corrosion effects with tissue destruction, to no visible effect. Where a harmful effect can be anticipated, no testing is required. From the results of this test, a substance may be classified as an 'irritant' or, in the case of severe and irreversible effects, 'corrosive'.

Eye irritation

The eye irritation test is carried out in a similar manner. From the results of this test, a substance may be classified as an 'irritant'.

Skin sensitisation

Skin sensitisation is a common occupational problem. In this test, small amounts of the test agent are applied repetitively to the animal's skin. The skin response and the proportion of animals responding are evaluated. There is considerable interspecies variation in response.

Subacute and subchronic toxicity testing

Here, the test animal is exposed to repeated doses of the chemical agent at non-lethal levels for either 28 days (subacute testing) or 90 days (subchronic testing). Exposure may be by oral, dermal or inhalation routes (normally oral). During the test, the animal is assessed for clinical effects; at the end of the test period, the animal's tissues and organs are examined for signs of toxic damage. These tests allow some evaluation of the effects of prolonged exposure and determination as to whether these are reversible.

Chronic animal testing

This method involves animals being kept in a test environment for long periods, usually for several years. Exposure by inhalation is the most common human exposure in the workplace; however, creating and maintaining test atmospheres over very long periods is difficult and other modes of exposure have been validated as mimicking inhalation exposure. Relatively high doses are used in this work and results are extrapolated to lower dose estimates for interpretation purposes.

Test animals, usually rats or mice, are exposed to the test substance and allowed to live for most of their natural life span. At the termination of the experiment, the tissues and organs of the animals are examined in order to identify tumours or other harmful changes. Again, the approach is to compare test groups of animals with control groups. Different groups are used for the different sexes, dose levels and controls. In view of the numbers of animals required to achieve useful results, this method can be seen to be very expensive as well as time-consuming, irrespective of the ethical objections discussed in the next section. Furthermore, species specificity may be a problem since a substance may be found to be carcinogenic in one species but not in another. For example, 2-naphthylamine is carcinogenic in mice and humans, but not in the rat, a very common test animal.

CHEMICAL AGENTS

Ethics of animal testing

There is increasing concern about the ethical issues raised by using animals in the types of tests outlined. Nevertheless, test animals are the closest model to human systems and although cell culture systems are being developed and used, it is difficult to envisage the total abolition of animal testing in the near future.

Apart from the above concerns, for chronic animal toxicity studies, it takes a long time for results to be produced and thus there has been significant demand for accurate and specific 'short-term' tests, which are cheaper and deliver results over a much shorter time. These are discussed below.

Short-term tests

A range of tests has been developed where the objective is to provide valid toxicological information as rapidly and economically as possible. This category includes a wide range including *in vitro* tests using bacterial or mammalian cells and some *in vivo* tests using whole animals. These methods have been much applied in mutagenicity testing in bacterial cells and chromosomal aberration detection in mammalian cells in attempting to predict potential animal and human carcinogenicity.

The Ames method is probably the best-known mutagenicity test and this is outlined below. Mutagenic substances can be classified as Category 1, Category 2 or Category 3 under the CHIP Regulations 2002, as amended (see Table 3.6 on page 77).

The Ames test

In outline, the test is as follows. A bacterium, *Salmonella typhimurium*, is grown on a nutrient test plate. The strain used is histidine negative (his-). This means the nutrient medium must contain the amino acid histidine, since this bacterial strain lacks a gene for producing its own histidine and, therefore, it cannot grow. Initially, a little histidine is added to allow the bacterium to establish itself on the test plate, but this is rapidly used up. One culture plate is treated with the test chemical while another is treated with a known non-mutagen as a control. The principle of the test is that if the test chemical is a mutagen, then some of the his- bacteria will be mutated to his+ and now these will be able to grow without histidine supplied to the medium. The numbers of growing bacterial colonies are then compared on the test and control plates. A significant difference in the number of colonies indicates mutagenicity.

The test is good at distinguishing primary carcinogens, that is, those directly acting. However, it is not so good for secondary carcinogens, that is, those that have to be bioactivated in the body to their directly acting form. In one variant of the Ames test, liver extract is added to the culture to mimic conditions for bioactivation and detect secondary carcinogens. In addition, some variants of the test use the bacterium *E.coli* as the test organism. In a given case, a range of short-term tests is normally employed, using different techniques in the form of a test battery. This approach has been shown to be more accurate that just using one test alone. Another example is the 'sister chromatid exchange' test, which detects genetic damage. The principle is that substances which cause such damage are more likely to be carcinogenic.

Overall, for known animal carcinogens, there is good agreement with the results from short-term tests, particularly when these are used in test batteries. This supports the predictive usefulness of these tests.

New and existing substances

Many new substances are developed by the chemical industry every year and a significant number will ultimately be produced in manufacturing quantities, that is, in excess of one tonne per annum. Hazard evaluation as part of proactive risk assessment is necessary for these substances and a decision must be taken regarding the toxicological testing required.

In 1981, all existing commercial substances and preparations had to be registered with EINECS. From this time onwards, any non-registered substances were regarded as 'new' for the purposes of the testing regulations.

Under the NONS Regulations 1993, new substances are required to be tested in the toxicity regime outlined below. The requirements of the NONS Regulations (HSE 1994) can be seen to have two stages:

1. The first stage is to prepare a notification dossier. This includes basic information such as chemical name, structure, and physical and chemical properties, together with the results of basic specified toxicity testing (Table 3.4).
2. The dossier is submitted to the enforcing authority (HSE), which considers the information on a case-by-case basis to decide if further, more extensive toxicity testing (Table 3.5) is merited.

The testing requirements of the NONS Regulations are summarised below.

TABLE 3.4: NONS Regulations 1993 – Preliminary basic testing

Preliminary basic testing
Acute toxicity testing • Acute oral toxicity LD_{50} or acute dermal toxicity LD_{50} or acute inhalation toxicity LD_{50} • Skin irritation • Eye irritation • Skin sensitisation • Subacute toxicity testing – 28-day oral study or 28-day dermal study or 28-day inhalation study
Mutagenicity • *in vitro* non-mammalian cell assay (Ames test) • *in vitro* mammalian cell assay • Cytogenetic test – chromosomal aberrations in CHO* cells or human lymphocytes • *in vivo* mammalian cell assay: cytogenetic test – chromosomal aberrations in bone marrow cells • Micronucleus test – chromosomal damage in developing erythrocytes

*Chinese hamster ovary – a commonly used test cell line

TABLE 3.5: NONS Regulations 1993 – Additional testing

Additional testing
• These tests are required after consideration of the above tests where there is an indication of a specific toxicity and/or production of a new chemical reaches a specified level • Subchronic toxicity testing (90 days) – exposure by inhalation, oral or dermal route • Long-term (chronic) animal carcinogenicity testing • Reproductive toxicity testing

Classification of chemical agents

Chemical agents need to be adequately tested so that they can be appropriately categorised, packaged and labelled. These requirements are reviewed in the following sections. From a legal point of view, substances and preparations must be classified on the basis of 'category of danger', which is a requirement of the CHIP Regulations 2002.

In theory, there are many different ways in which chemical agents can be classified depending on the particular interest of the classifier:

- target organ (liver, kidney);
- use (pesticide, solvent);
- type of effect (cancer, mutation, liver injury);
- physical state (gas, dust, liquid);
- chemistry (aromatic amines, halogenated hydrocarbons);
- toxicity potential (very toxic, toxic, harmful, irritant).

CHEMICAL AGENTS

Chemicals (Hazard Information and Packaging for Supply) Regulations 2002 (CHIP)

Substances and preparations must be assigned to various 'categories of danger' based on the evaluation of specified toxicity testing.

The CHIP Regulations 2002 require:

- that substances and preparations be classified into respective defined categories of danger using appropriate toxicity testing;
- labelling with appropriate risk and safety phrases and symbols;
- appropriate packaging; and
- the supply of a concise safety data sheet.

Various publications have been produced to assist with compliance with the CHIP Regulations (HSC 2002c, 2002d, 2002e).

Risk and safety phrases

The CHIP Regulations 2002 require that 'risk' and 'safety' phrases are appropriately applied, in addition to designated hazard symbols, on containers and packages. They deal with the properties of the substance or preparation including the health, safety and environmental dangers. Selected examples are listed for illustrative purposes in Table 3.6. Examples of packaging and labelling are given below.

FIGURE 3.6: Packaging and labelling

(HSE)

Safety data sheet

The standard and content of these as received from manufacturers and suppliers varies widely. There have been some attempts to standardise their scope and content.

The approved guidance on regulation 6 of CHIP gives the following obligatory headings for a safety data sheet prepared under the Regulations (HSC 2002e).

1. Identification of the substance/preparation and company.
2. Composition/information on ingredients.
3. Hazard identification.
4. First aid measures.
5. Firefighting measures.
6. Accidental release measures.
7. Handling and storage.
8. Exposure controls/personal protection.
9. Physical and chemical properties.

TABLE 3.6: Categories of danger (CHIP Regulations 2002)

Category of danger	Test result	Toxicological basis	Risk phrases (examples)	Safety phrases (examples)
Very toxic	LD_{50} oral ≤ 25 mgkg^{-1} LD_{50} dermal ≤ 50 mgkg^{-1} LC_{50} ≤ 0.25 mgl^{-1} per 4hr	Acute toxicity testing	R28. Very toxic if swallowed R27. Very toxic in contact with the skin R26. Very toxic by inhalation	S36. Wear suitable protective clothing S37. Wear suitable gloves
Toxic	LD_{50} oral >25, ≤ 200 mgkg^{-1} LD_{50} dermal >50, ≤ 400 mgkg^{-1} LD_{50} oral >0.25, ≤ 1 mgl^{-1} per 4hr	Acute toxicity testing Subacute toxicity testing	R25. Toxic if swallowed R24. Toxic in contact with the skin R23. Toxic by inhalation	S36. Wear suitable protective clothing
Harmful	LD_{50} oral >200, $\leq 2,000$ mgkg^{-1} LD_{50} dermal >400, $\leq 2,000$ mgkg^{-1} LD_{50} oral >1, ≤ 5 mgkg^{-1} per 4hr	Acute toxicity testing Subacute toxicity testing	R22. Harmful if swallowed R21. Harmful in contact with the skin R20. Harmful by inhalation	S36. Wear suitable protective clothing S37. Wear suitable gloves
Corrosive		Skin irritation testing	R35. Causes severe burns (or burns, R34)	
Irritant		Skin irritation testing Eye irritation testing	R38. Irritating to skin R36. Irritating to eyes	S37. Wear suitable gloves
Sensitising		Skin sensitisation testing Inhalation sensitisation testing	R43. May cause skin sensitisation by skin contact R42. May cause sensitisation by inhalation	S22. Do not breathe dust
Carcinogenic	Categories 1 and 2 Category 3	Dossier of evidence	R45. May cause cancer R49. May cause cancer by inhalation R40. Possible risk of irreversible effects	
Mutagenic	Categories 1 and 2 Category 3	Dossier of evidence	R46. May cause heritable genetic damage R40. Possible risk of irreversible effects	
Toxic to reproduction	Categories 1 and 2 Category 2 Category 3	Dossier of evidence	R60. May impair fertility R61. May cause harm to the unborn child R62. Possible risk of impaired fertility R63. Possible risk to the unborn child	
Dangerous for environment	Aquatic and non-aquatic	Dossier of evidence	R50. Toxic to aquatic organisms	

CHEMICAL AGENTS

10. Stability and reactivity.
11. Toxicological information.
12. Ecological information.
13. Disposal considerations.
14. Transport information.
15. Regulatory information.
16. Other information.

Summary of toxicology

The role of toxicology in chemical agent risk assessment and control is summarised in Figure 3.1. In the above discussion, the use of toxicological methods has been seen to contribute to hazard data, which has been used in the classification, labelling and packaging of hazardous substances. Toxicology also has a role in the development of biological monitoring methods and in the derivation of tolerable exposure standards (see page 107).

Occupational epidemiology

Epidemiology is the science of determining the occurrence of disease in human populations. Occupational epidemiology seeks to determine the occurrence of disease in working populations. It is concerned with the evaluation of the association between workplace exposures, which may last a number of years, and diseases, which may have an insidious (secret or subtle) onset. For some diseases, as discussed above, the time between initial exposure and the first manifestation of ill health may be many years, and this makes connecting cause and effect difficult. Using different approaches, epidemiologists study both exposed persons (cohort studies) and persons with disease (case control studies). The object of an epidemiological study is to answer a question, which is usually posed in the negative, for example:

*Is there **no** association between lung cancer and exposure to material x?*

The ultimate aim is to determine whether there is a persuasive cause and effect relationship between the health effect and exposure to the suspect agent. There are several common types of study and the choice of the most suitable in a given case will depend on the situation, the question posed and the facilities available.

A study may be carried out as a snapshot at one point in time (cross-sectional) or at different points over a period of time (longitudinal). Epidemiological studies are carried out to determine both mortality and morbidity rates.

Mortality is the study of death rates whereas morbidity rates are the incidence of non-fatal ill health. Overall, epidemiology is concerned with the following:
- the identification of new hazards;
- controlling known risks;
- the establishment of hygiene standards;
- eliminating hazards;
- evaluating controls;
- setting priorities; and
- evaluation of health services.

Epidemiologists have a great interest in past records (sometimes going back up to 50 years), since with these they can define past populations (cohorts) of workers and, ideally, their exposures. They are also concerned with keeping adequate health and exposure records for the present which may be used in future epidemiology. That is the reason why there is a requirement in the COSHH Regulations 2002 for medical records and air monitoring results to be kept, in some cases, for 40 years. There are many potential sources of useful data for epidemiological studies and some are listed in Table 3.7.

TABLE 3.7: Epidemiological data sources

Health outcome data	Exposure data
Death certificates	Air monitoring surveys
Birth certificates	Noise monitoring surveys
Sickness absence records	Ionising radiation exposure data
Industrial accident or injury claims	Data on exposure to other agents
Medical practitioner records	Biological monitoring data
Hospital in-patient records	Job category data
Pension scheme records	Personnel data, eg length of service, type of work, location
Ad hoc morbidity data	
Health surveillance records	

(Harrington 1995)

Epidemiological data sources are summarised in Figure 3.7. The aim is to link the exposure data with the health outcome data in order to identify association and causation.

FIGURE 3.7: Linking exposure and health outcome data

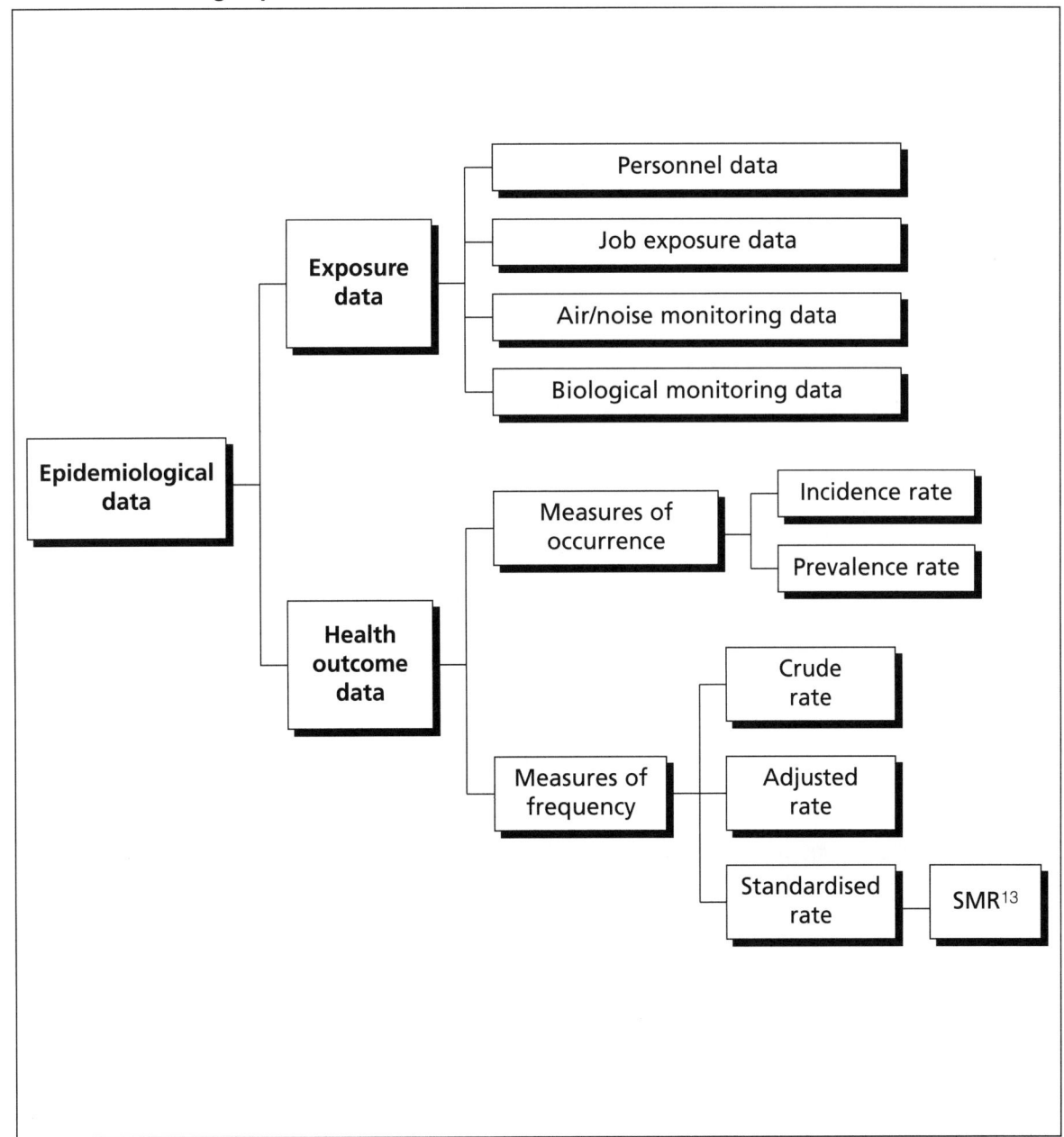

Epidemiological data
- Exposure data
  - Personnel data
  - Job exposure data
  - Air/noise monitoring data
  - Biological monitoring data
- Health outcome data
  - Measures of occurrence
    - Incidence rate
    - Prevalence rate
  - Measures of frequency
    - Crude rate
    - Adjusted rate
    - Standardised rate — SMR[13]

---

[13] Standardised Mortality Ratio.

CHEMICAL AGENTS

Exposure data

Unfortunately, as far as the working environment is concerned, recorded information on past exposures is often poor. Ideally, an epidemiologist would like to have the following type of data:

- exposure monitoring results with comprehensive task identification and process data;
- information on variation of exposure with work cycle, day of the week and specific operations; and
- the use of validated monitoring methods with high analytical accuracy.

Exposure data may be grouped as follows:
1. Ever/never employed in the industry.
2. Length of service in the industry.
3. Job categories/duties.
4. Job categories – ranked by exposure intensity.
5. Quantified exposure intensity categories.
6. Quantified exposure dose categories.

Health outcome data

Measures of occurrence

The commonest measures of occurrence are incidence and prevalence rates:
1. **Incidence** – relates to new cases and incidence rate relates to new cases over a given period of time.
2. **Prevalence** – relates to the existing number of cases of a disease at a point in time or over a defined period of time.

(Incidence rates are less useful with chronic disease which may have a vague or prolonged onset.)

Measures of frequency

These are rates which can be used to compare disease levels in different populations. There are three basic measures of frequency which may be used for a given event:
1. Crude.
2. Adjusted.
3. Standardised.

Comparison of crude rates may lead to the wrong conclusion being reached and it is important to be aware of the limitations of the different rates. For example, the crude death rate of town A (an industrial centre) is 12 per 10^6 per year and for town B (a seaside resort) it is 15 per 10^6 per year. The implication is that town B is a less healthy place than town A. However, this may be misleading, because no account has been taken of the age breakdown of the population of the two towns[14]. The solution is to apply an adjustment factor, which takes account of the age distribution of the two populations.

Standardised Mortality Ratio (SMR)

In epidemiology, it is often necessary to compare the mortality rate of an occupational group, the index population, with that of some other population, the standard population. This produces a summary statistic, the Standardised Mortality Ratio (SMR):

$$\text{SMR} = \frac{\text{Observed number of deaths in occupational group}}{\text{Expected number of deaths in standard population}} \times 100$$

The SMR represents the observed number of deaths in an occupational group divided by the number

---

[14]Elderly people often retire to the seaside.

expected had the mortality rates of the standard population at large been experienced. Usually, this figure is then multiplied by 100. Taking the normal population as 100, an SMR of greater than 100, indicates a larger than expected mortality experience in the selected group while less than 100 indicates less mortality than expected.

'Healthy worker effect'

In some epidemiological studies, cohorts of workers have had their disease outcomes compared with that of the general population and have been seen to have less illness than in the 'normal' population. This effect has been termed the 'healthy worker effect'.

This is because the normal population contains many elderly, sick, disabled and dying people who cannot work, while the working population is a more select group who are currently active and may be under periodic health screening and surveillance. The Office for National Statistics[15] intends to provide national population data on employed persons, which may be used for reference purposes in epidemiological studies.

Age-specific differences

The SMR overlooks age-specific differences within the index population (ie that of interest). For example, exposure may be more severe in younger workers while cumulative effects are more likely to be apparent in older workers.

Differences between the index and the normal population

The SMR does not take into account that socioeconomic class is closely linked to disease and the proportion of each social class in the index and normal population may not be the same.

Assembling data for epidemiological study

The collection of data for an epidemiological investigation is likened by Harrington (1995) to a criminal investigation in the questions that need to be asked. These are concerned with people, place and time:

1. To whom?
2. Where?
3. When?
4. By what? (why?)
5. How?
6. Is the result of any importance?

Measures of risk

These can be divided into relative risk (risk ratio) and attributable risk (rate difference):

1. **Relative risk** – this is the ratio of the disease rate in exposed persons divided by the disease rate in non-exposed persons. For example, if the rate of a disease in the exposed population was 150 per 100,000 and in the unexposed population 5 per 100,000, then the relative risk is 30. The magnitude of the relative risk is a measure of the strength of association of the risk factor and the disease.
2. **Attributable risk** – this is the difference between disease rates in exposed persons and disease rates in non-exposed persons. Using the same example as above, the risk attributable to the exposure factor is 145 per 100,000.

Causation or association

The statistical association of a risk factor (exposure) with a disease does not necessarily prove causation. The epidemiological hypothesis can never prove that A causes B, but it can give support (or not) to causation.

The types of information listed in Table 3.8 can provide such support.

---

[15]The Office for National Statistics was formerly known as the Office for Population, Censuses and Surveys.

TABLE 3.8: Properties supporting causation

Properties supporting causation	
Strength of association	Is the disease more common in a given group of workers? If so, how much more common?
Consistency	Has the association been described by other epidemiologists in a relevant population?
Specificity	Is the disease specific to certain groups of workers and/or specific industrial activities?
Time	Does exposure to the suspect agent always come before the onset of disease?
Biological gradient	Is there a good dose-response relationship?
Experimental evidence	Is there supporting animal data?
Biological plausibility	Is causality biologically reasonable?
Analogy	Has a similar suspect cause been shown for related causes or effects?

(Harrington 1995)

Validity

The validity of the results of an epidemiological investigation is obviously very important. Care in the design of a study has to be taken to ensure that findings are not influenced by:

1. Selection bias, which is concerned with the method of choosing the study group. For example, are they a survivor population?
2. Information bias, which is concerned with the quality and accuracy of the data gathered, eg errors by the interviewee.
3. Confounding factors which influence both the exposure and the outcome, eg age. The older the worker, the more likely he or she is to have been significantly exposed to the occupational hazard, and older workers are more likely to have the disease since most diseases are age-dependent. Confounding should be controlled at the planning stage with the careful matching of cases or the exposure group with controls.

Types of study

Various types of study design are used in epidemiology and the choice depends on the particular situation of interest. These are summarised in the diagram below.

FIGURE 3.8: Types of study

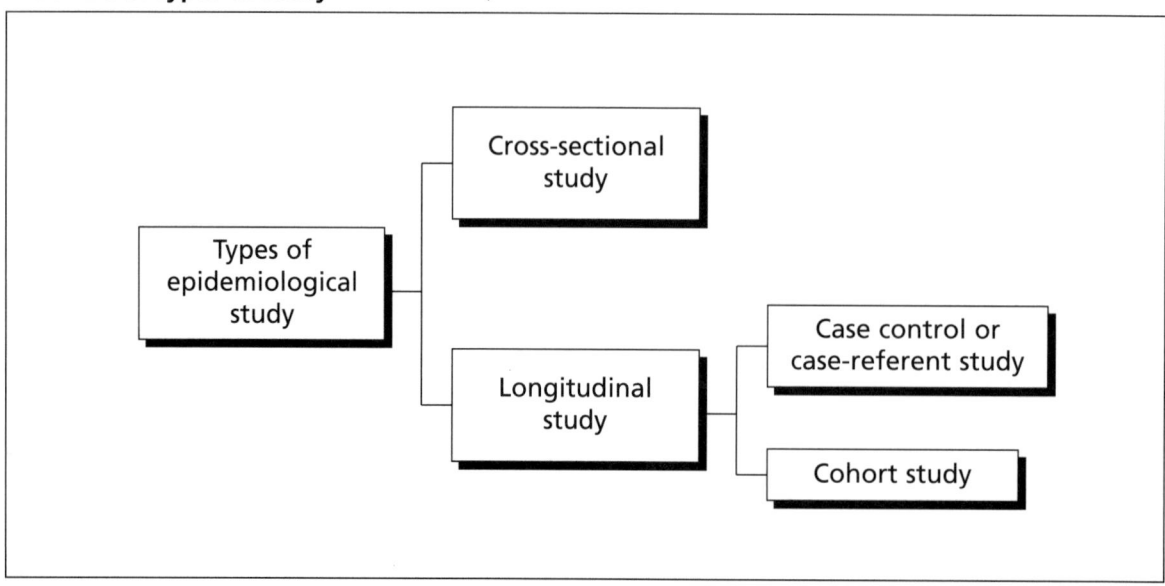

Types of epidemiological study
- Cross-sectional study
- Longitudinal study
  - Case control or case-referent study
  - Cohort study

Cross-sectional studies

These provide a quick, relatively cheap opportunity to study the problem in question. The population at risk is assessed within a narrow time frame. Investigators cannot look at exposure and outcome as a time-dependent relationship. All that may be feasible is an estimation of exposure prevalence or its outcome.

Longitudinal studies

These take longer to carry out and are more expensive, but the longer study time provides the opportunity to look at an exposure and its outcome as a time-related chain of events. There are two common types of longitudinal study:

1. Case control or case-referent study.
2. Follow-up study including cohort studies.

Case control study

The case control approach studies a group of people with a disease and compares them with matched controls, that is, a similar group in most respects but who do not have the disease. The respective past exposures of the two groups are analysed to try and identify possible causes. There have been problems with accuracy, particularly of exposure data, which may have been collected over 40 years previously.

Cohort study

A cohort study follows a group of people, an 'index' or 'test' cohort, exposed to the agent of interest to see who gets the disease and who does not. The disease rate of the index cohort is compared with a reference cohort, which sometimes may be the 'normal' population. Preferably, as discussed above, this should be a defined working population, differing only in an observed absence of exposure to the agent of interest. A cohort study may be carried out from past records (retrospective) or, more usually, forward in time (prospective). Follow-up studies should span a period of time in excess of the latency period for the disease in question.

Occupational disease and chemical agents

In Chapter 1, perspectives were developed with regard to patterns of occupational disease and current occupational health problems. This section will deal with occupational disease in detail for ill health caused by chemical agents.

Work exposure to health hazards may result in recognised occupational disease via the generalised mechanism below:

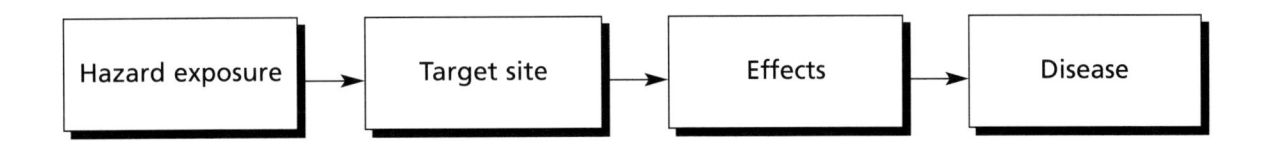

Hazard exposure → Target site → Effects → Disease

There is no universally accepted system for defining and classifying occupational disease. Approaches are generally based on a mixture of the harmful agent or target organ with special case categories. For example, this can be illustrated by the reference text, *Hunter's Diseases of Occupation* (Raffle et al. 1987), which has the following chapter structure:

1. Diseases associated with chemical agents.
2. Diseases associated with physical agents.
3. Diseases associated with microbiological agents.
4. Occupational cancer.
5. Occupational asthma.
6. Occupational diseases of the skin.

CHEMICAL AGENTS

FIGURE 3.9: Chemical agents – Main diseases and target sites

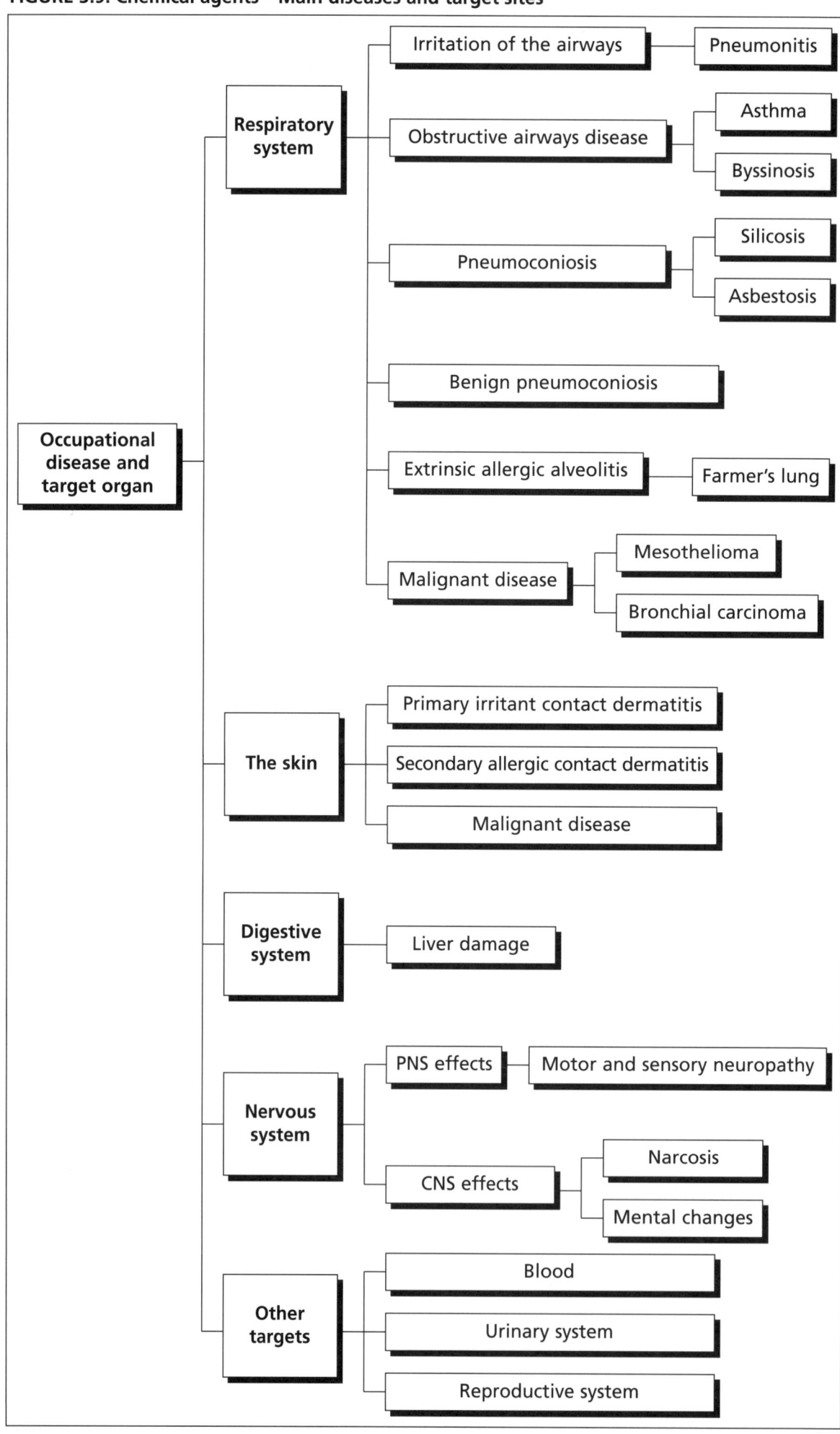

- **Occupational disease and target organ**
  - **Respiratory system**
    - Irritation of the airways
      - Pneumonitis
    - Obstructive airways disease
      - Asthma
      - Byssinosis
    - Pneumoconiosis
      - Silicosis
      - Asbestosis
    - Benign pneumoconiosis
    - Extrinsic allergic alveolitis
      - Farmer's lung
    - Malignant disease
      - Mesothelioma
      - Bronchial carcinoma
  - **The skin**
    - Primary irritant contact dermatitis
    - Secondary allergic contact dermatitis
    - Malignant disease
  - **Digestive system**
    - Liver damage
  - **Nervous system**
    - PNS effects
      - Motor and sensory neuropathy
    - CNS effects
      - Narcosis
      - Mental changes
  - **Other targets**
    - Blood
    - Urinary system
    - Reproductive system

The first three categories are then subdivided into more specific hazard types. Although occupational asthma, occupational cancer and skin diseases are associated with chemical agents, they are given a separate treatment to highlight their features and importance. An alternative approach, which will be used here, is to classify occupational disease caused by chemical agents by their principal target organ. This is summarised in Figure 3.9.

Respiratory system as a target

Respiratory system disorders may be grouped into the categories below:
1. Irritation of the airways.
2. Obstructive airways disease.
3. Pneumoconiosis.
4. Extrinsic allergic alveolitis.
5. Malignant disease.

(Disorders caused by infective biological agents are covered in Chapter 4.)

Irritation of the airways

Principally, this is caused by irritant gases and vapours. Symptoms vary depending on which part of the respiratory system is affected and this, in turn, depends on the water solubility and concentration of the contaminant. The terminology of acute inflammatory reactions follows the anatomy of the respiratory system, that is, rhinitis (nasal passage), tracheitis (trachea), bronchitis (bronchus) and pneumonitis (lung). There may be exudation of fluid and swelling, which may be particularly important in a small airway, or where the airway is narrowed or even totally obstructed.

Highly water-soluble gases, for example, ammonia, chlorine and sulphur dioxide, have an immediate affect on the eyes and upper respiratory tract causing pain, swelling and ulceration of mucus membranes. Exposed people, if they can, rapidly move out of the contaminated area.

With water-insoluble gases, for example, phosgene, there is little effect on the upper airways, but this will affect the lungs after a delay of up to 72 hours, causing pulmonary oedema. Some irritants will also cause irreversible lung damage, for example, nitrogen oxides and others predispose the lungs to chronic bronchitis and pneumonia.

Obstructive airways disease

Here the diameter (or 'calibre') of the airways is reduced. This may be reversible, as in asthma, or irreversible.

Occupational asthma

Asthma is a common disease in the general population and is characterised by attacks of breathlessness, wheezing and coughing, with and without sputum. It is an important occupational health problem and for the affected person continued exposure to the agent leads to deteriorating asthma and the risk of rare fatal attacks. Occupational asthma is caused by specific substances encountered at work. The causative mechanism involves a hypersensitive response to antigens. The antigen-antibody reaction ultimately causes the release of histamine, which results in the constriction of smooth muscle and narrowing of the conducting airways. (Hypersensitivity mechanisms were dealt with in Chapter 2.) The chemical agents which cause occupational asthma can be divided broadly into two groups:

1. **High molecular weight protein antigens** – For example, flour and grain. These agents are more likely to affect 'atopic' individuals, ie those who have a past history of eczema or asthma. However, overall, atopy is thought to be a predisposing factor only in the case of a few allergenic dusts which cause occupational asthma. Therefore, selecting out atopic people is not thought to be a particularly useful strategy in this context.
2. **Low molecular weight substances (haptens)** – These combine with body proteins to provoke an allergenic response, eg toluene diisocyanate, colophony, platinum salts and acid anhydrides. Atopy is not a risk factor with this group.

CHEMICAL AGENTS

Asthmatic symptoms may follow exposure immediately, but more commonly after several hours. Symptoms may develop during the evening or night and this delay can result in the connection with occupational exposure not being made.

While some chemical agents linked with asthma stimulate the immune system, for many substances immune changes have not yet been demonstrated. Asthmatics are often described as having become 'sensitised' to agents which cause their attacks, irrespective of underlying mechanisms, and causative agents are commonly known as 'respiratory sensitisers'.

The HSE (1998) has used the term 'asthmagen' to describe an agent which causes an asthmatic disorder and this may be considered to be synonymous with the term 'respiratory sensitiser'. However, the term 'sensitisation' itself is reserved for situations where immune changes show specific antibodies or related cellular changes in response to exposure to the chemical agent. According to the HSE (1994a), 'sensitisation' is:

- substance-specific;
- unpredictable – not all at risk will become sensitised;
- latent – it may occur after months or years of exposure; and
- irreversible, but symptoms will not occur on cessation of exposure.

The numbers of respiratory sensitisers (asthmagens) are increasing and these are listed in a compendium of asthmagens (HSE 1997). Furthermore, some respiratory sensitisers have been assigned a Workplace Exposure Limit (WEL) and they have an identifying sensitising 'Sen' notation (HSE 2005) (discussed later in this chapter). In addition, respiratory irritants in the workplace may provoke asthmatic attacks in those with occupational asthma or pre-existing non-occupational asthma. This is encompassed by the broader term 'work-related asthma'.

Byssinosis

This is an obstructive airways disease, which may progress to irreversible damage to the lungs and impaired airway function. It is caused by the inhalation of cotton dust and is accompanied by some immunological changes. The onset of symptoms usually occurs after several years of exposure. Commonly, symptoms first occur on a Monday morning when the worker returns to work after the weekend. During the early stages, symptoms disappear on the second day. However, with continued exposure the symptoms last longer and ultimately become continuous.

Pneumoconiosis

Collagenous pneumoconiosis

This is the permanent alteration of lung structure following inhalation of a mineral dust and the tissue reaction to its presence. It is caused by silica (quartz), coal and asbestos dust.

Silicosis

This is caused by exposure to dusts containing crystalline silicon dioxide, for example, quartz, which stimulates the production of fibrotic tissue. Fibrotic changes are detected on chest X-rays as small, round opacities throughout the lung. Radiological evidence of damage is apparent before the onset of clinical symptoms, primarily, breathlessness. Early diagnosis is essential since symptoms may progress, even after withdrawal from exposure, if a sufficiently large quantity of dust has been inhaled. The disease progresses with increasing breathing difficulty and death may result from heart and/or lung failure.

Coal miner's pneumoconiosis

This is a less severe condition than silicosis. It can be divided into two conditions: simple pneumoconiosis and progressive massive fibrosis.

Simple pneumoconiosis

Here, small, round opacities are seen in the lung which are thought to be coal dust. Radiological changes relate to the total amount of dust inhaled and there is a mild cough and black sputum.

However, the affected person is virtually without symptoms. This condition is important since it acts as a precursor to progressive massive fibrosis (PMF). It is not known why simple pneumoconiosis progresses to PMF in a relatively small proportion of miners.

Progressive massive fibrosis (PMF)

With PMF, large, irregular opacities can be seen in the upper lung area on chest X-rays. When the condition is moderate to severe, the sufferer is significantly disabled.

Asbestosis

Pulmonary fibrosis is caused mainly by chrysotile (white asbestos), although amosite (brown asbestos) and crocidolite (blue asbestos) are also fibrogenic. With asbestosis, there is increasing shortness of breath, a dry cough and weight loss. Radiological changes are observed in the lower lung. Asbestosis itself may be fatal but in addition around 50 per cent of sufferers may go on to develop lung cancer.

Benign pneumoconiosis

Non-collagenous pneumoconiosis

This group of conditions is based entirely on radiological evidence, which shows the deposition of particles in lung tissue, since patients are symptom-free. Barium, tin, antimony and lead will each cause benign or non-collagenous pneumoconiosis.

Extrinsic allergic alveolitis (EAA)

Organic substances often either induce asthma or may affect the alveoli and gas transfer region of the respiratory system. In EAA conditions, an allergic response to a wide range of antigens, particularly complex organic dusts, may occur in the alveoli. For example, farmer's lung, caused by exposure to spores in mouldy hay, is an important example of this condition in the UK. Symptoms develop four to eight hours after exposure when the person has fever, tiredness, chills, general aches and pains, shortness of breath and a cough. In contrast to asthma, there is an absence of wheeziness.

When the person is removed from exposure, symptoms disappear within 12 hours. Repeated exposures may lead to pulmonary fibrosis, that is, excessive production of collagenous scar tissue and impaired respiratory function. A range of organic dusts cause extrinsic allergic alveolitis and some examples are given in Table 3.9.

TABLE 3.9: Extrinsic allergic alveolitis

Exposure agent	Disease
Mouldy hay spores – *Thermoactinomycetes vulgaris*	Farmer's lung
Bird droppings – avian serum proteins	Bird fancier's lung
Mouldy sugar cane – *Thermoactinomycetes vulgaris*	Bagassosis
Mushroom compost – *Fusarium rectivirgula*	Mushroom worker's lung

Malignant disease

Mesothelioma

This is a cancer of the pleural membrane of the chest cavity. It is a rare condition in the general population and it is strongly associated with exposure to crocidolite. It is disputed as to how much mesothelioma is caused by other types of asbestos fibre, for example, chrysotile, amosite and tremolite. This disease can have a latency period of 50 years from first exposure to the onset of the clinical condition.

Bronchial carcinoma

Bronchial carcinoma has been caused by many agents used at work, as is shown in Table 3.10. This is a common cancer in the general population and it is often difficult to detect occupational causes.

Adenocarcinoma of the nose

This is caused by exposure to hardwood and leather dusts.

TABLE 3.10: Malignant disease and the respiratory system

Disease	Exposure agent
Bronchial carcinoma	• Ionising radiation; radon daughters; polonium-218, 214 and 210 • Arsenic • Nickel • Hexavalent chromium • Asbestos (synergy with smoking) • Crystalline silica • Polycyclic aromatic hydrocarbons (coke oven workers and other groups)
Adenocarcinoma of the nose	• Hardwoods and leather dust
Mesothelioma	• Asbestos

Skin as a target organ

Occupational skin disease is a common problem and there are many causes, principally minor cuts and abrasions with secondary infections (see Chapter 4) and chemical agents. (For the structure and function of the skin, see Chapter 2.) Skin disease associated with chemical agents is reviewed below based on the following groupings:

1. Contact dermatitis:
   - irritant;
   - allergic.
2. Pigmentation changes.
3. Malignant disease.
4. Oil folliculitis and acne.

Contact dermatitis

The commonest reaction of the skin to penetration through the barrier layer is an inflammation eczema. The signs are redness, swelling and blistering with the main symptom being itching. The chemical agents causing contact dermatitis can be divided into two groups: irritants and sensitisers (allergens).

Primary irritant contact dermatitis

This is sometimes known as non-immunological contact dermatitis (NICD) and the majority of occupational dermatoses are of this type. The irritants produce a direct effect on the skin with which they come into contact and they can be divided into those with strong and weak irritant properties.

In acute cases, the skin is red, swollen and itchy and there may also be blistering. The condition can resolve spontaneously. Continual contact with the irritating agent may cause the condition to become permanent.

Sulphuric acid will provoke a skin reaction in anyone it comes into contact with, whereas weak irritants require multiple exposure to cause irritant contact dermatitis. This condition is often caused by several weak irritants acting together. Concentration of the chemical agent, duration of exposure and frequency are important determinants in exposure situations.

Secondary allergic contact dermatitis

In this case, the causative agent is a skin sensitiser which exerts its effect via the immune system. Allergic contact dermatitis represents about 20 to 30 per cent of all eczemas and is a delayed hypersensitivity reaction (see Chapter 2). As with irritants, concentration, duration and frequency of exposure are crucial factors. Generally, there has to be more than one exposure to a sensitiser before sensitisation takes place and symptoms appear. Individuals differ in how easily they develop an allergy.

However, with some very potent sensitisers, a short exposure time is all that is required. The response is usually specific to one agent but may be delayed a week or more after contact. Once sensitisation has occurred, subsequent reactions can be provoked by the most minor exposures.

Allergic contact dermatitis may follow irritant contact dermatitis, for example, in cement workers (where chromate is a minor constituent of cement). Initially, a person may only develop an irritant dermatitis, but with repeated exposure they may become sensitised to chromate and develop allergic contact dermatitis.

Skin sensitisers are very common in the workplace as several thousand contact sensitisers are well known (HSE 1998a). It is important to note that many causative agents may be both irritants and sensitisers.

Important occupational contact irritants and sensitisers include:
- cement;
- chromates;
- epoxy resins;
- rubber-processing chemicals;
- latex;
- formaldehyde;
- glutaraldehyde;
- nickel and its salts; and
- cobalt and its salts.

Malignant disease

Repeated exposure over years to coal-tar products, pitch, tar and polycyclic aromatic hydrocarbons in refined mineral oil can cause skin cancer. Other skin cancers have been attributed to chemical agents including various hydrocarbons and arsenic compounds. Various agents have been found to cause scrotal cancer, for example, shale oil, mineral oil, pitch and tar.

Pigmentation changes

Hyperpigmentation may result from exposure to substances such as pitch and tar, and to poisoning by some mercury and arsenic compounds. Depigmentation (vitiligo) may also be caused by exposure to some industrial chemicals, for example, substituted phenols.

Oil folliculitis and chloracne

Exposure to cutting oils may block the sebaceous glands and cause the development of folliculitis around the areas of contact, commonly the forearms, thighs and abdomen. Another condition, chloracne, is caused by exposure to certain chlorinated hydrocarbons including dioxin. The face and neck are the most commonly affected and the condition may itch in contrast with oil folliculitis.

Digestive system as a target

Liver

Relatively few toxic materials will damage the liver and liver regeneration capacity is very high. Carbon tetrachloride is a potent hepatotoxin. Jaundice, a liver condition, is caused by trinitrotoluene (TNT), dinitrophenol (DNP) and phenol. Other occupational hepatotoxins include:
- trichloroethylene;
- beryllium; and
- chloroform.

Angiosarcoma is a rare cancer of the blood vessels of the liver first discovered in American PVC workers and associated with exposure to vinyl chloride monomer (VCM).

Nervous system as a target
The nervous system is an important target for toxic substances. The nervous system consists of the peripheral nervous system (PNS) and the central nervous system (CNS), and has both conscious and unconscious control (see Chapter 2). The unconscious control, that is, reflex activity, is exerted by the autonomic system. Both the PNS and the CNS can be damaged by occupational neurotoxins.

PNS effects
Toxic damage to the peripheral nervous system results in impairment of motor or sensory function or both. Most neurotoxins produce 'mixed function' nerve damage, with the exception of lead which appears to exclusively damage the motor function.

The general mechanism is structural damage to the nerve fibre which interferes with the conduction of nerve impulses. Organophosphates interfere with intrasynapse transmission by depleting acetyl cholinesterase activity. This prolongs the effects of acetyl choline and delays transmission of the impulse.

Some effects are described as 'subclinical', where changes are found of which the exposed person is unaware, for example, decreased motor nerve conduction velocity. Whether such changes always progress to explicit clinical damage is not clear.

CNS effects
Occupational ill health where the CNS is a target is reviewed below.

Narcosis
Exposure to organic solvents causes reversible depression of the CNS.

Mental changes
Psychotic symptoms may arise in workers exposed to excessive levels of some solvents (eg carbon disulphide) and manganese. High exposure to mercury compounds results in a condition known as 'erethism'. This is characterised by a general timidness, with aggressive verbal and physical outbursts, especially following mild criticism. Psychiatric problems arise in workers who are overexposed to tetraethyl lead compounds.

Some researchers have found that chronic low dose exposure to solvents can lead to 'organic psychosis'. The findings of this study have not been repeated in other work although a decrement in performance has been observed. Overall, the situation still needs clarification.

Parkinsonism
This condition is caused by depletion of the neurotransmitter dopamine in the nerve cell ganglion. Occupational exposure to methyl mercury and manganese can lead to this condition. This and the non-occupational form will respond to drugs and, therefore, the mechanisms are thought to be similar.

Blood as a target
Lead inhibits the activity of several enzymes in the haem synthesis pathway and, if exposure is prolonged and significant, this can result in anaemia. Benzene causes toxic damage to the cells of the bone marrow, which again may result in the onset of anaemia. Bone marrow damage can also lead to the malignant disease, leukaemia. Exposure to arsine results in the destruction, by haemolysis, of circulating red blood cells. The consequences are damage to kidney tubules and tissue hypoxia, that is, lack of oxygen due to decreased red cell numbers.

Urinary system as a target
The kidney is vulnerable to toxic damage because it has a very high blood supply and agents are concentrated in this organ, prior to excretion. Renal damage is often detected by the appearance of substances, for example, specific proteins in the urine indicating kidney dysfunction. Carbon tetrachloride, ethylene glycol and cadmium are potent nephrotoxic agents.

Reproductive system as a target

A reproductive hazard is any chemical, physical or biological agent which causes reproductive impairment in adults and/or developmental impairment in the embryo, foetus or child. Toxic damage may be caused by harmful chemical agents in both the male and female reproductive systems. Examples of chemical agents which impair the reproductive process include metals (lead, mercury), pesticides (aldrin), sterilising agents (ethylene oxide), organic solvents (styrene) and anaesthetic gases (halothane).

Workplace hazardous substance risk management

The following sections follow the key stages of practical hazardous substance risk management, that is, risk assessment, the application of prevention and control measures, and review and audit of the process.

The risk assessment and control process

Figure 3.10 attempts to represent the basic steps in the risk assessment and control process.

FIGURE 3.10: Stages in risk assessment and control

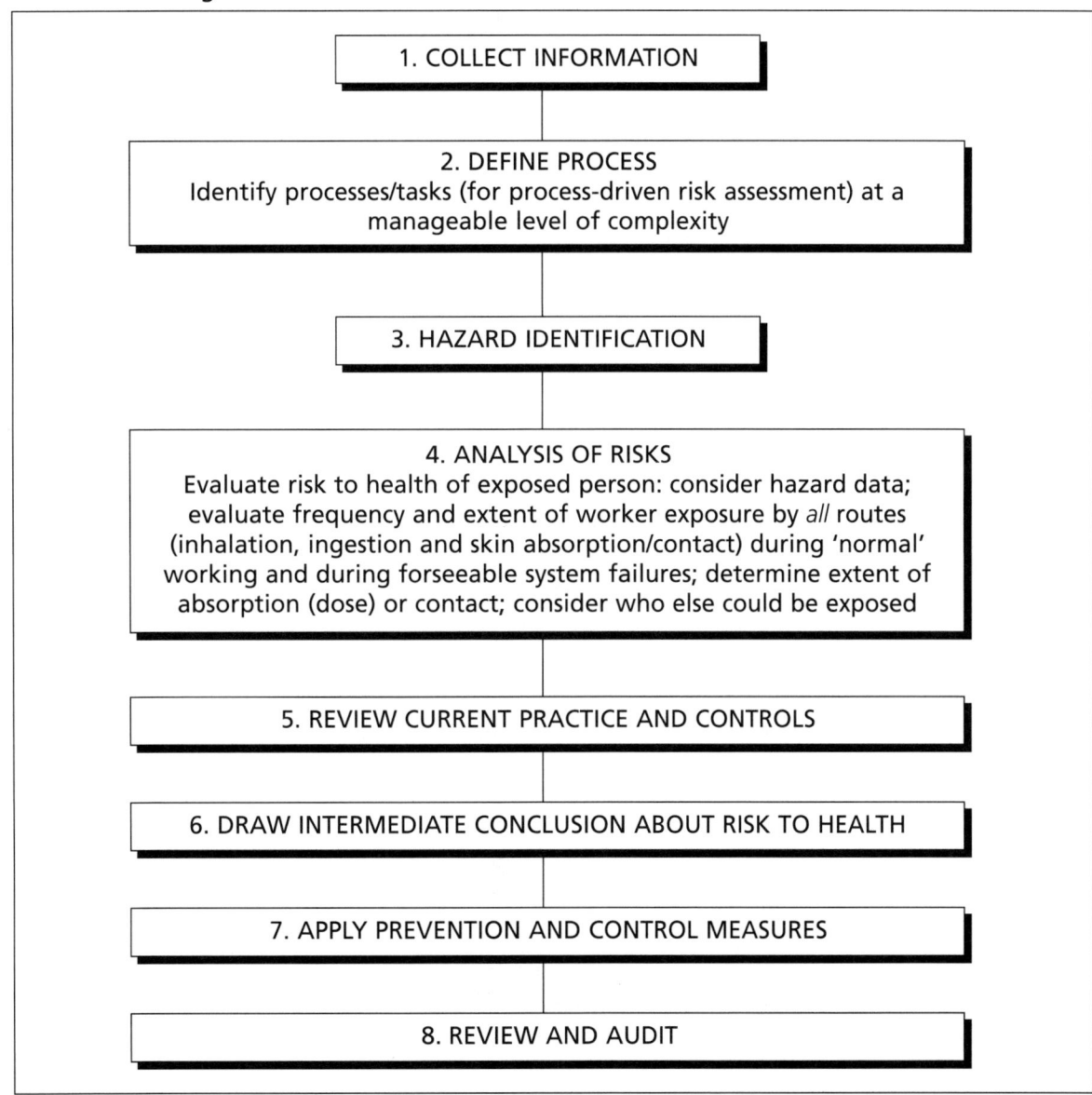

1. COLLECT INFORMATION

2. DEFINE PROCESS
Identify processes/tasks (for process-driven risk assessment) at a manageable level of complexity

3. HAZARD IDENTIFICATION

4. ANALYSIS OF RISKS
Evaluate risk to health of exposed person: consider hazard data; evaluate frequency and extent of worker exposure by *all* routes (inhalation, ingestion and skin absorption/contact) during 'normal' working and during forseeable system failures; determine extent of absorption (dose) or contact; consider who else could be exposed

5. REVIEW CURRENT PRACTICE AND CONTROLS

6. DRAW INTERMEDIATE CONCLUSION ABOUT RISK TO HEALTH

7. APPLY PREVENTION AND CONTROL MEASURES

8. REVIEW AND AUDIT

It can be seen that eight general stages are identified:
1. Collect information.
2. Define process.
3. Hazard identification.
4. Analysis of risks.
5. Review current practice and controls.

6. Draw intermediate conclusion about risk to health.
7. Apply prevention and control measures.
8. Review and audit.

An alternative version relating to the assessment of air contaminants as part of the design process for ventilation control is given in Figure 3.48 (see page 133).

Collection of information (Stage 1)

This entails the identification and collection of data on hazardous substances. It involves the compilation of a substance inventory and the collection of manufacturers' safety data sheets and other sources of hazard information. Assessment situations need to be identified, that is, situations with the following ingredients:

- 'substances hazardous to health' (as defined in COSHH, regulation 2);
- exposure arising from work; and
- person(s).

Define process (Stage 2)

The risk assessment is normally task or process-driven and a key part is defining this task at a manageable level of complexity, that is, not too simple and not too complex.

Hazard identification (Stage 3)

This is the identification of hazardous exposure within the task defined in Stage 2.

Analysis of risks (Stage 4)/Review current practice and controls (Stage 5)

The next step is to evaluate the exposure of operators to health risks. This is to allow an intermediate conclusion on health risk to be reached (Stage 6 in Figure 3.10). Normal working situations, as well as specific contingencies or foreseeable system failures, should be considered in the risk analysis. Similarly, an intermediate conclusion on health risk should be drawn with respect to each foreseeable failure. Some identified foreseeable failures may subsequently require a separate detailed risk assessment. There should be a review of current practice and controls.

Draw intermediate conclusion about risk to health (Stage 6)

When the necessary information has been collected and examined, a conclusion should be made regarding the overall tolerability of the health risk for the risk assessment in question. The following options have been found to be useful possibilities in practice (see Table 3.11). These reflect the level of overall risk tolerability based on the residual risk, together with the impact of any applied controls.

TABLE 3.11: Risk assessment conclusions

Conclusion
1. Risk to health unlikely
2. Risks significant – all adequate precautions in force
3. Risks significant – further precautions need to be applied
4. Uncertain about risk to health – further information required
5. Uncertain about precautions necessary – further information required

(Modified from HSE 1993)

Apply prevention and control measures (Stage 7)

A hierarchy of control is imposed by various statutory requirements in that control at source is the preferred option, followed by engineering control, and only if these can be shown not to be reasonably practicable is personal protective equipment to be considered. In a given situation, it is necessary to select and apply an appropriate 'blend' of control measures in order to reduce risks to tolerable levels.

Review and audit (Stage 8)
This involves evaluation of the whole risk assessment and control cycle on a regular basis and also in response to work process or other changes which may affect people's exposure.

The risk assessment survey
This is the application of the risk assessment process in practice. A risk assessment survey may be prompted by various factors, including statutory requirements. Harmful exposure may be suggested by the signs and symptoms of disease or complaints of irritation and discomfort in exposed workers. Indirect measures such as high sickness absence rates and an unexplained high staff turnover may also serve as useful indicators of unacceptable exposure.

The COSHH Regulations and assessment
The COSHH Regulations 2002 (as amended) (regulation 6(1)) require that:

> *An employer shall not carry out work which is liable to expose any employees to any substance hazardous to health unless he has: (a) made a suitable and sufficient assessment of the risk created by that work to the health of those employees and of the steps that need to be taken to meet the requirements of these Regulations; and (b) implemented the steps referred to in subparagraph (a).*

The basic ingredients of such an assessment are shown in Figure 3.11 below.

FIGURE 3.11: Assessment of health risks and COSHH, regulation 6

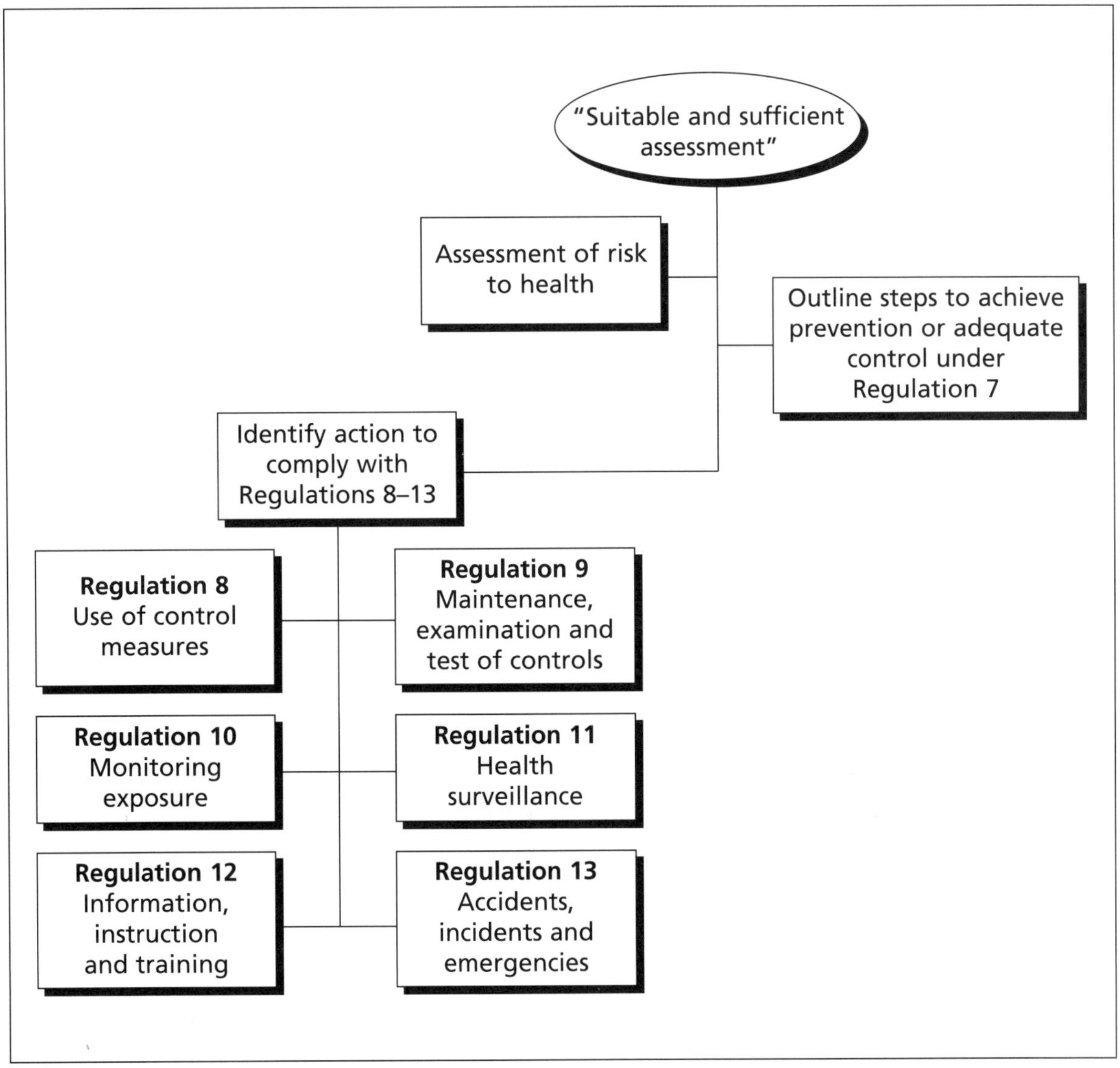

- "Suitable and sufficient assessment"
  - Assessment of risk to health
  - Outline steps to achieve prevention or adequate control under Regulation 7
  - Identify action to comply with Regulations 8–13
    - Regulation 8: Use of control measures
    - Regulation 9: Maintenance, examination and test of controls
    - Regulation 10: Monitoring exposure
    - Regulation 11: Health surveillance
    - Regulation 12: Information, instruction and training
    - Regulation 13: Accidents, incidents and emergencies

Similarly, the CLAW Regulations 2002 (regulation 5) require an assessment of risks to health from work with lead, and the CAW Regulations 2002 (regulation 5) require an assessment of work which exposes people to asbestos[16].

Many organisations have developed their own methods for identifying and carrying out required assessments under statutory regulations. This has often involved the development of standard formats, for example COSHH assessment forms.

Measurement of chemical exposure and analysis

Hazard identification results from an inspection of a work process and identifying situations where people have harmful exposures to chemical agents, relating to inhalation, ingestion and skin absorption and/or contact. As discussed above, practical hazard identification is supported by safety data sheets, which are obtained from manufacturers and suppliers.

Having identified chemical substances in the workplace as exposure hazards, the assessor examines the working process to decide which are likely to pose significant health risks. It is necessary to estimate or quantify the extent of exposure to the agent. This information is used to evaluate the level of risk to the worker's health using tolerability standards. In some workplace situations, this may only require subjective or semi-quantitative exposure evaluation, while on other occasions, detailed measurements using technical equipment will be required for a quantitative assessment. Principally, the measurement of chemical exposure means the monitoring of airborne contaminants. Airborne contaminant concentrations are usually measured in the person's breathing zone over time. These estimates are compared with air quality standards in order to determine whether further prevention and control measures are required.

It is also possible to estimate whole-body absorption, that is, entry into the body of chemical agents by all possible routes including skin absorption and ingestion as well as inhalation. This involves an approach known as 'biological monitoring'. Here, chemical agents, their metabolites or other suitable indicators of uptake are measured in body fluids such as blood or urine. The most commonly used biological monitoring measure is the lead in blood concentration. Overall, there are relatively few biological monitoring methods in comparison to the number of validated air contaminant monitoring methods available. Air contaminant and biological monitoring provide complementary information on chemical agent exposure and risk. Each approach has its advantages and disadvantages, which are discussed below.

Definitions

Air monitoring

This is the measurement of the concentration of airborne contaminants in the workplace and encompasses:

1. **Personal monitoring** – Air contaminant measurements made in the 'breathing zone' of exposed workers, usually by a device attached to the lapel.
2. **Static or area monitoring** – Air contaminant measurements are made at selected points in the general area of the workplace.
3. **Environmental monitoring** – Air contaminant measurements are made at the perimeter or outside the workplace.

Workplace air monitoring may be carried out for various reasons including:
- measuring long-term or short-term worker exposure;
- identifying operations giving rise to exposures;
- testing for leaks;
- testing the efficiency of engineering controls;
- assisting with ventilation design;
- assessing safety of entry into confined spaces;
- selection of personal protective equipment;

---

[16]A key requirement is a "duty to manage" asbestos in buildings.

- ensuring compliance with statutory regulations, eg the COSHH, Lead or Asbestos Regulations.

Biological monitoring

Biological monitoring allows the body's uptake of substances by all routes to be determined. It may be defined as follows:

A regular measuring activity where selected, validated indicators of the uptake of toxic substances are determined to prevent health impairment. (Tola & Hernberg 1981)

Workplace survey

The principal aim of a survey is to evaluate personal exposure to the chemical agents being processed or used. The assessor determines the exposure of people to chemical agents by all potential routes of absorption. The approach described below reflects the general guidance and terminology used by the HSE (1997a). The approach to carrying out a risk assessment survey for chemical agents can be divided into three stages:

1. Initial assessment.
2. Preliminary survey.
3. Detailed survey.

In the measurement of contaminant exposure, by far the most applied techniques involve the monitoring of various airborne contaminants. Much of the subsequent discussion, in the sections below, relates to the use of technical equipment and strategies for this purpose.

Initial assessment

An important early objective is to identify work processes and tasks, in detail, to try to understand the exposure of workers. The following questions could be asked at this stage:

1. What chemical agents are present (raw materials, intermediates, products)?
2. Are there any manufacturers' safety data sheets for the chemical agents?
3. How hazardous are the chemical agents?
4. What is the airborne form of the chemical agents (dust, fume, vapour, gas, mist)?
5. If a dust is present – is it fibrous and/or respirable?
6. Are workers exposed to mixtures of chemical agents?
7. Is there a likelihood of inhalation, skin absorption or ingestion?
8. At which processes or operations is exposure likely to occur?
9. Which groups of workers or individuals are likely to be exposed?
10. What is the likely pattern and duration of exposure?
11. What are the current exposure control measures?

Preliminary survey

Following the initial assessment, the next stage is to carry out a preliminary monitoring survey of the workplace. This will provide basic information on the efficiency of process and engineering control measures and an estimation of the personal exposure of operators. The survey should consider routine and non-routine exposures. The latter include maintenance, process shutdown and possible system failure. Detailed knowledge is required of the processes involved, the substances used and the individual assigned tasks of workers. Air contaminant monitoring equipment is used to measure exposure while other technical equipment, for example, anemometers, is used to check control measure effectiveness (discussed later in this chapter).

Variability of exposure

The atmospheric concentration of contaminants is not constant in a given workplace; it varies both from location to location and with time over the working cycle. There are random variations due to

CHEMICAL AGENTS

such factors as climatic conditions and regular variations due to the work cycle. This is illustrated in Figure 3.12. Both elements contribute to the overall exposure picture. For most chemical agents, it is normally the day-to-day or weekly averages, as an indication of inhalation exposure dose, which are of interest. Within reasonable limits, momentary peak contaminant exposures can be regarded as tolerable.

Exposure via ingestion and skin contact and/or absorption routes

The survey is also concerned with total absorption, which includes ingestion and absorption through the skin. Safety data sheets should indicate if there is a significant skin absorption hazard; for substances listed in EH40 (HSE 2005), these are assigned an 'Sk' notation. Exposure is assessed by evaluation of the potential for skin contact with the contaminant, for example, with dust particles deposited on surfaces[17] or in the handling of organic solvents, together with whether protective gloves and overalls are worn. Also, eye contact hazards need to be considered in this context.

FIGURE 3.12: Factors affecting the variability of exposure

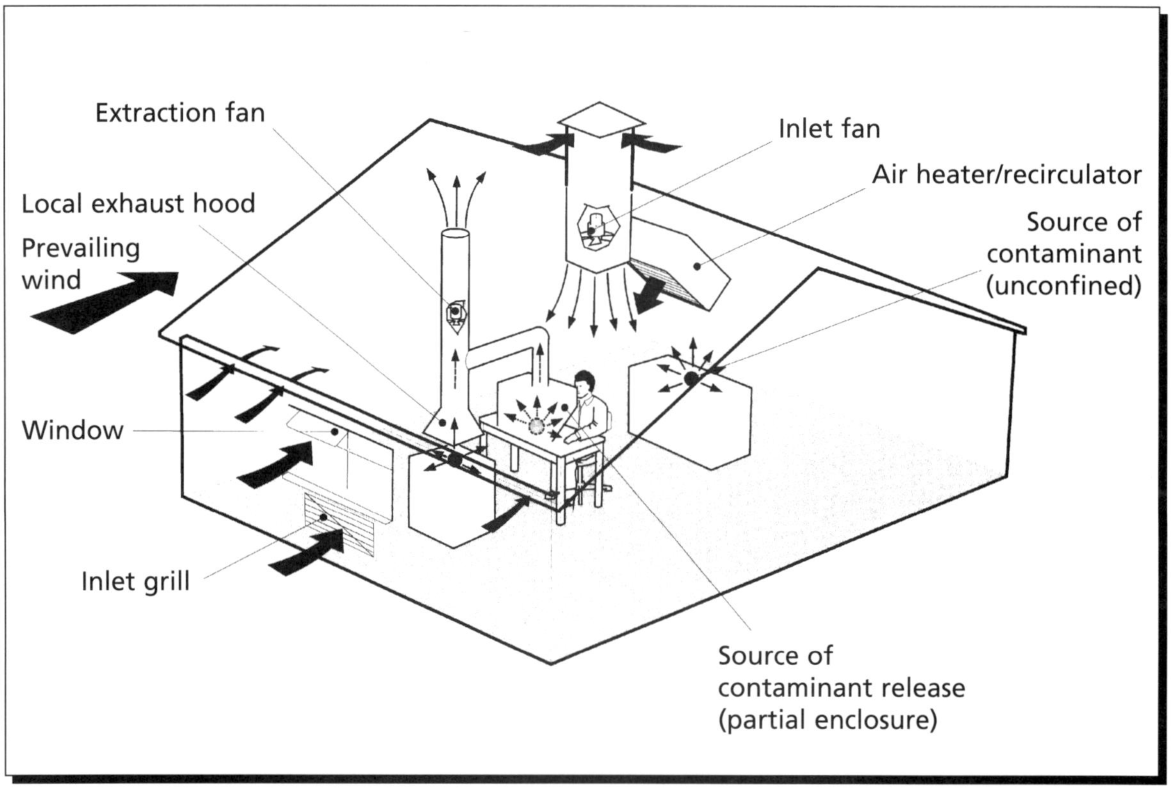

(HSE 1997a)

Detailed survey

Depending on the results of the preliminary survey, a subsequent more detailed air monitoring survey may be carried out. This may be the case where the preliminary survey shows that:
- personal exposure of people is very variable;
- large numbers of people may be at risk of unacceptable exposure; or
- a significant number of personal sampling results are close to exposure limits.

Sampling strategies

The HSE (1997a), in HSG173, identifies three levels of sampling strategy in approaching an exposure problem.

First level

As a first stage this is to obtain relatively crude information to determine if an exposure problem exists at all.

---

[17]Wipe sampling may be carried out to evaluate contaminant deposition.

CHEMICAL AGENTS

FIGURE 3.13: Approaches to air monitoring

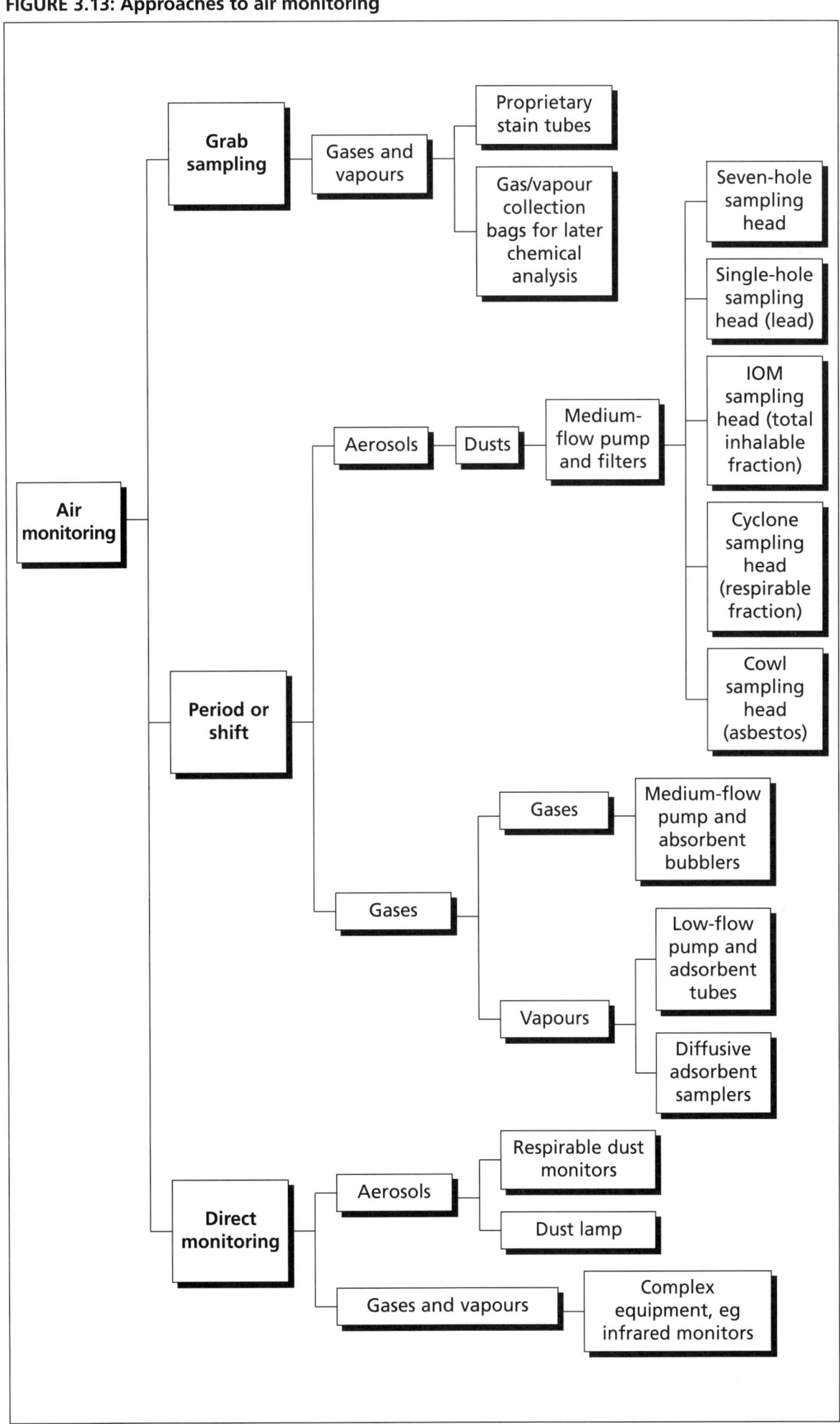

```
Air monitoring
├── Grab sampling
│   └── Gases and vapours
│       ├── Proprietary stain tubes
│       └── Gas/vapour collection bags for later chemical analysis
├── Period or shift
│   ├── Aerosols ── Dusts ── Medium-flow pump and filters
│   │   ├── Seven-hole sampling head
│   │   ├── Single-hole sampling head (lead)
│   │   ├── IOM sampling head (total inhalable fraction)
│   │   ├── Cyclone sampling head (respirable fraction)
│   │   └── Cowl sampling head (asbestos)
│   └── Gases
│       ├── Gases ── Medium-flow pump and absorbent bubblers
│       └── Vapours
│           ├── Low-flow pump and adsorbent tubes
│           └── Diffusive adsorbent samplers
└── Direct monitoring
    ├── Aerosols
    │   ├── Respirable dust monitors
    │   └── Dust lamp
    └── Gases and vapours
        └── Complex equipment, eg infrared monitors
```

97

CHEMICAL AGENTS

Second level

This is appropriate for most routine air monitoring and involves the accurate measurement of personal exposures in terms of time-weighted averages for interpretation against Occupational Exposure Limit (HSE 2002).

Third level

This is much less common and involves the application of more sophisticated technical sampling methods.

Air monitoring techniques

As might be expected from the vast range and nature of potential workplace exposures to airborne chemical agents, many different types of air monitoring equipment are available. Selected approaches to air monitoring are discussed below and these may be conveniently divided into:

1. Grab sampling.
2. Period or shift sampling.
3. Direct monitoring.

The exact choice of equipment and method to be employed will be determined by the particular circumstances and objectives of the monitoring exercise. The approaches and the equipment used are summarised in Figure 3.13.

Grab sampling

Grab sampling involves taking a sample of air over a relatively short period of time, usually a few minutes, in order to measure the airborne concentration of contaminant. This is illustrated in Figure 3.14 where the discrete measured values are highlighted with crosses. The actual exposure concentration is shown by the trace line which represents the underlying peak profile. This is unseen with this measurement method.

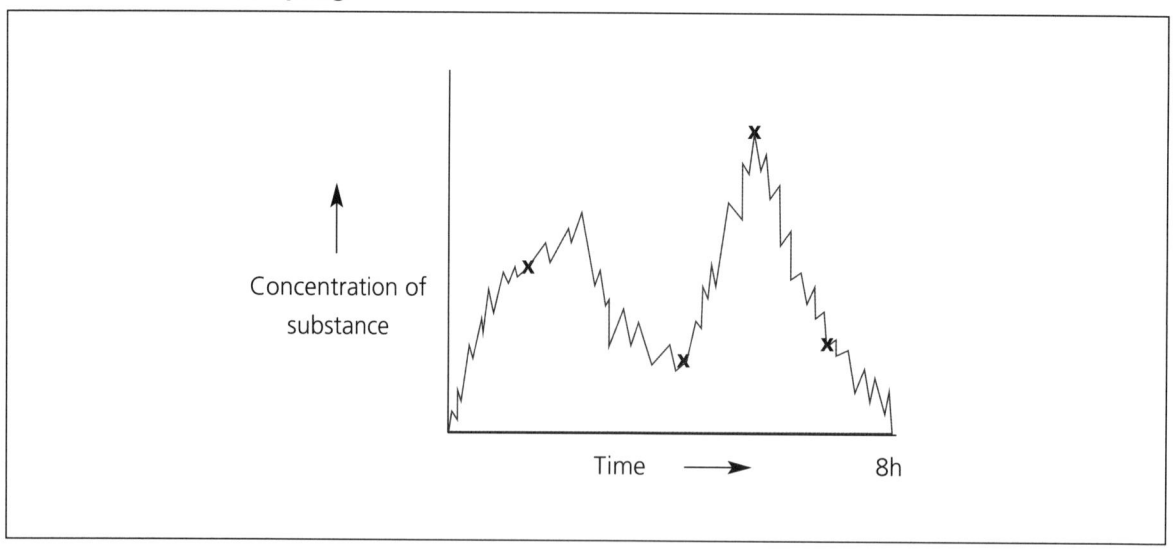

FIGURE 3.14: Grab sampling

Stain detector tubes

Stain detector tubes are used in the measurement of airborne concentrations of gases and vapours. Proprietary tubes are available which operate on a common principle. A sealed glass tube is packed with a particular chemical which reacts with the air contaminant. The tube seal is broken, a hand pump attached, and a standard volume of contaminated air is drawn through the tube. The packed chemical undergoes a colour change, which passes along the tube in the direction of the airflow. The tube is calibrated so that the extent of colour change indicates the concentration of contaminant sampled. This is the same principle on which the breathalyser works.

FIGURE 3.15: Stain tube and hand pump

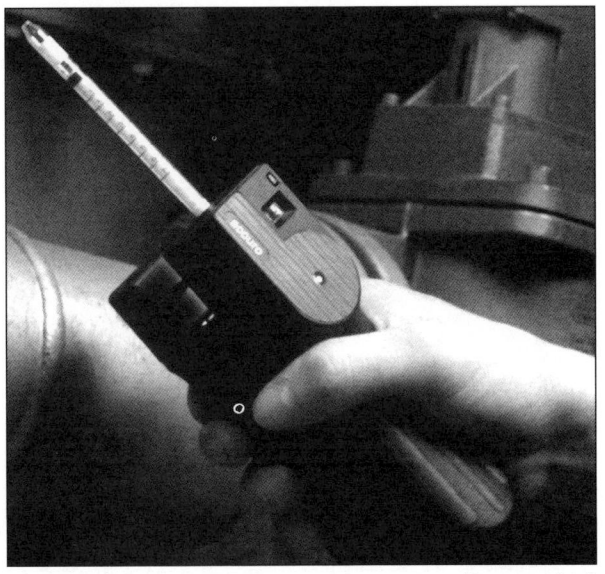

(Draeger Ltd)

The hand pump must be kept in good repair and recalibrated at intervals to ensure that it is drawing the standard volume of air. Care must be taken to ensure that a good seal is obtained between the pump and the tube. A leak on the pump will cause an underestimation of the measured level of contaminant. This method of grab sampling measurement has several advantages:

1. It is a quick, simple and versatile technique.
2. Stain tubes are available for a wide range of chemical contaminants (several hundred).
3. Measurement results are provided immediately.
4. It can be an economical approach.

However, it is important to be aware of the limitations of stain tubes:

1. The measurement result obtained relates to the concentration of airborne contaminant at the inlet at the precise moment the air is drawn in. Short-term stain tubes do not measure individual worker exposure.
2. Variations in contaminant levels throughout the work period or work cycle are difficult to monitor by this technique.
3. Other chemicals may sometimes interfere with a stain tube reaction, for example, xylene will interfere with tubes calibrated for toluene. Manufacturers give information on known cross-sensitivities of tubes. (This emphasises the need to consider the range of chemicals used in a process rather than just the major ones or the one of interest.)
4. Tubes are not re-usable.
5. Random errors associated with this technique can vary by ±25% depending on tube type.

A planned sampling strategy rather than occasional tube sampling will give a better picture of airborne contaminant levels. However, since tubes are not re-usable this method could be more costly than some long-term sampling techniques.

Other grab sampling techniques

These may involve collecting a sample of the workplace atmosphere in a suitable container, for example, using an air pump and a special gas bag to collect samples of gases and vapours. The container is transported to a laboratory for detailed chemical analysis.

Period or shift sampling

This may involve sampling air for several hours or even over the whole work shift. Air sampling may be carried out using personal or static sampling. Results give the average level of airborne contaminant across the sample period. From this value, the time-weighted average (TWA) over an eight-hour period

CHEMICAL AGENTS

can be calculated. This is illustrated in Figure 3.16 where the average concentration measured over the eight-hour period is xppm. The underlying actual exposure level is again represented by the trace line. The technical equipment used in this approach is shown in Figures 3.17, 3.18, 3.19 and 3.20.

FIGURE 3.16: Period or shift sampling

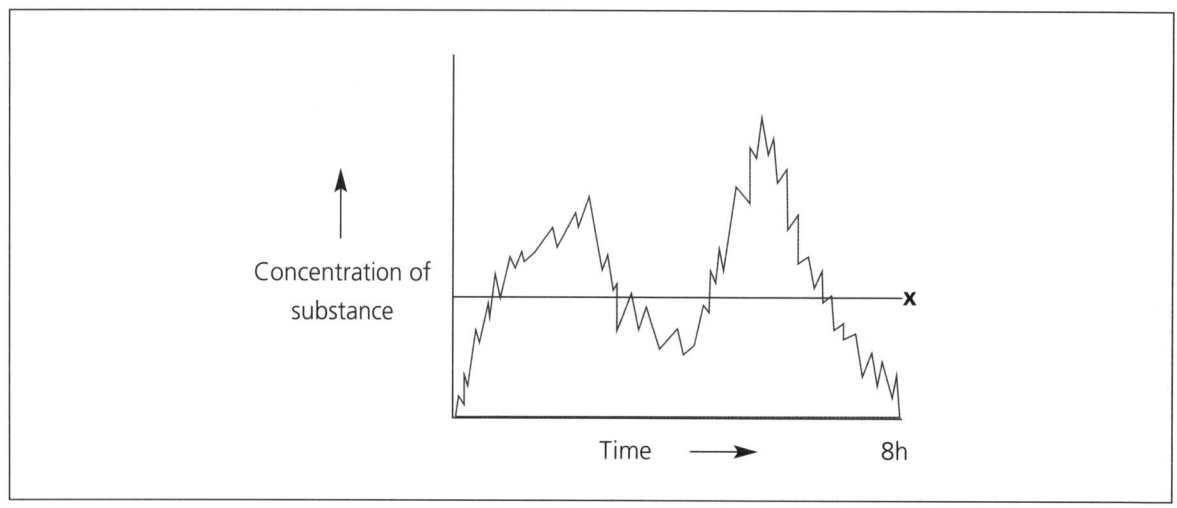

Long-term sampling methods are generally reliable, versatile and accurate. They are commonly used to check compliance with air quality exposure limits. Some measurement devices may be suitable for shift monitoring and also give a real-time direct display of contaminant levels.

Long-term stain tubes are available for this purpose and these are connected to a low-flow pump, which draws air through the tube at a set constant rate. After the sampling period, the tube is examined to give the amount of contaminant that has passed through the tube, from which the average level of contamination can be calculated.

Gas and vapour monitoring

Where accurate methods are required for the sampling of solvent vapours, an adsorption technique is used. Air is drawn by an attached portable low-flow pump through a tube usually containing adsorbent charcoal granules. The solvent vapour is trapped in the tube by adsorption on the charcoal granules. After sampling, the tube is sealed and taken to the laboratory where the contaminant is removed (desorbed), either chemically or by heat. This is followed by quantitative analysis, often using gas chromatographic techniques to determine the mass of contaminant adsorbed. The mass adsorbed divided by the total air volume sampled (pump flow rate multiplied by sampling time) gives the average airborne concentration of solvent vapour throughout the sampling period.

FIGURE 3.17: Period or shift sampling – Personal monitoring

(Munro Environmental)

CHEMICAL AGENTS

Diffusive monitors

For some gases and vapours, direct indicating diffusion tubes are available and these devices may be used for up to eight hours. These are easy to use as they do not require a sampling pump. Sampling by this method can be carried out by suitably trained non-specialists.

FIGURE 3.18: Direct reading diffusion stain tube

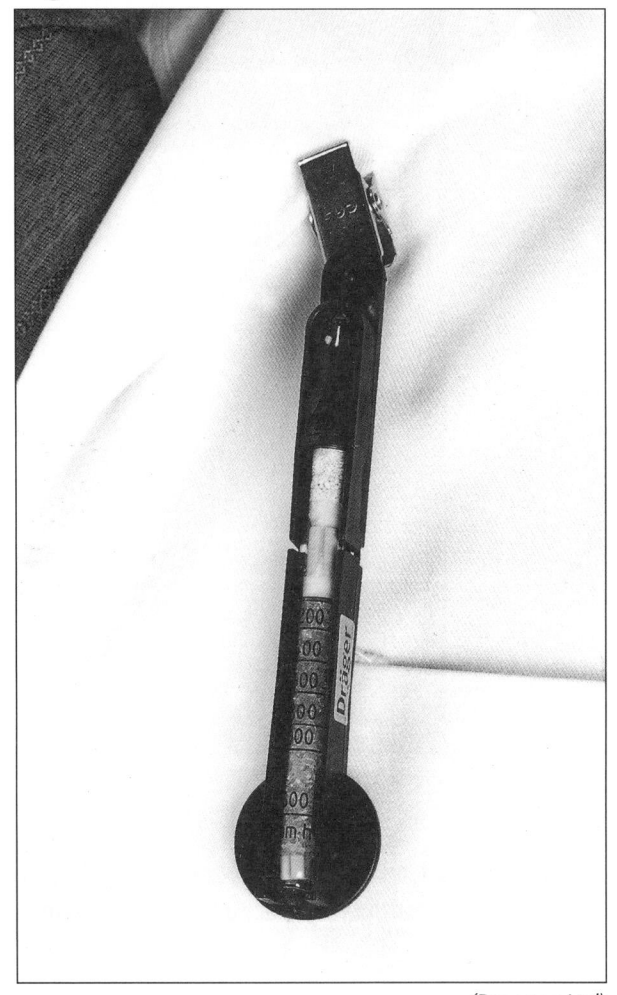

(Draeger Ltd)

Diffusive monitors or lapel badges (Figures 3.19 and 3.20) containing various adsorbents are also becoming much more widely used.

FIGURE 3.19: Passive badge monitor

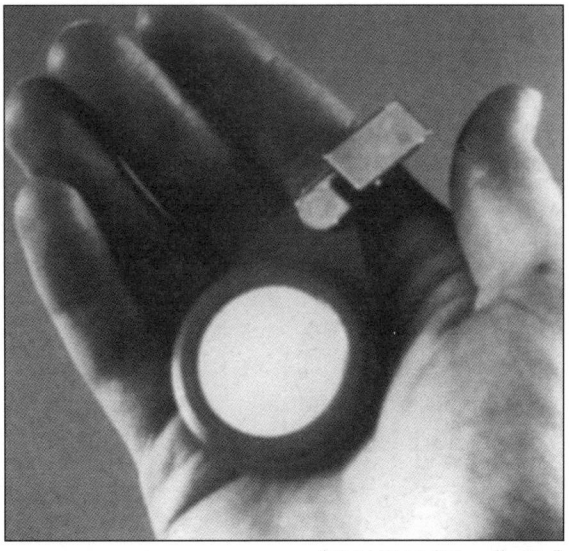

(3M UK Ltd/Casella Ltd)

Where charcoal is used, the chemical contaminant is trapped in the badge or diffusive monitor by the adsorbent granules. After sampling, the analytical procedure is the same as above for the pumped method of air collection. With the diffusive monitor, the total air volume sampled is calculated from a theoretical flow rate for the passive monitor and collection time.

FIGURE 3.20: Diffusive monitor

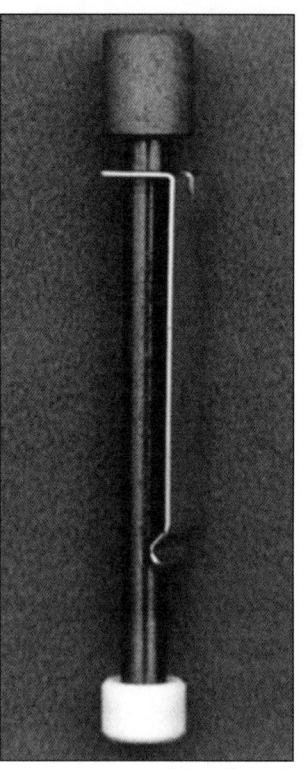

(Casella Ltd)

Gas chromatography
This is a common and versatile analytical technique, allowing both the identification and quantification of individual components in a mixture of substances. Separation of components of mixtures occurs after injecting a vaporised sample into a gas stream, which passes though a separating column. Components of the mixture pass through the column at different rates and emerge, sequentially, into a detector, which allows the identification and quantification of each component. This information, when taken with total air sample volume, allows calculation of average contaminant concentration.

Dust monitoring
In the measurement of airborne dusts, the collection device is a filter which is positioned in a holder attached to a medium-flow pump. After sampling, measurement of the contaminant on the filter may be made by determining the weight change of the filter (gravimetric) or by using other analytical techniques. The specific analytical technique used is determined by the dust of interest. For example, if the dust contains lead, then atomic absorption spectrophotometry may be used, or if it contains asbestos, then light microscopy is the standard method of analysis (HSE 1995). Also, the type of sampling device (which holds the filter) and the type of filter used depends on the nature of the dust and whether the aim is to collect the 'total inhalable', 'thoracic' or 'respirable' fraction (see Chapter 2).

Atomic absorption spectrophotometry
Atomic absorption spectrophotometry is a commonly used technique for the quantitative determination of metals. Absorption of electromagnetic radiation in the visible and ultraviolet region of the spectrum by atoms results in changes in their electronic structure. This is observed by passing radiation characteristic of a particular element through an atomic vapour of the sample. The sample is vaporised by aspiration into a flame or by contact with an electrically heated surface. The absorbed radiation excites electrons and the degree of absorption is a quantitative measure of the concentration of

'ground-state' atoms in the vapour. With a calibrated instrument, it is possible to determine the weight of a metal captured on a filter. This, taken with total sample air volume, allows calculation of the average concentration of the metal airborne contaminant over the sampling period.

Fibrous dust monitoring

In the measurement of airborne asbestos fibres, the collection device is a membrane filter with an imprinted grid (HSE 1995). The filter is positioned in an open-faced filter holder, fitted with an electrically conducting cowl and attached to a medium-flow pump. After sample collection, the filter is 'cleared', that is, made transparent and mounted on a microscope slide for visual evaluation. The airborne concentration of 'countable' fibres is evaluated using phase contrast microscopy. 'Countable' fibres are defined as particles with a length of >5µm, a width of <3µm and a length:width ratio of >3:1. Fibres having a width of <0.2µm may not be visible by the phase contrast method and this technique represents only a proportion of the total number of fibres present. However, the specified control limits for asbestos fibres take this into account (HSC 2002f).

A known proportion of the total exposed filter area is scanned using a phase contrast microscope and a tally made of all countable fibres in the examined area of the filter. Fibres are counted using a graticule, which is a calibrated eyepiece mounted in the objective lens of the microscope. The graticule allows a known area, or 'field', of the filter to be examined. Knowledge of the air sample volume, together with the calculated total number of fibres on the whole filter, allows calculation of the average fibre concentration over the sample period.

Direct monitoring

A wide range of instruments is used in the direct detection of aerosols, gases and vapours. These devices make a quantitative analysis giving a real-time display of contaminant level on a meter, chart recorder, data logger or other display equipment. There is a wide variety of commercially available direct monitoring instruments which are based on different physical principles of detection. Many of the physical principles involved and the range of instruments available are considered by Ashton & Gill (2000). A trace from a direct monitoring instrument is illustrated in Figure 3.21. From such information, it is also possible to work out the time weighted average concentrations during the sampling period with a suitable integrating device.

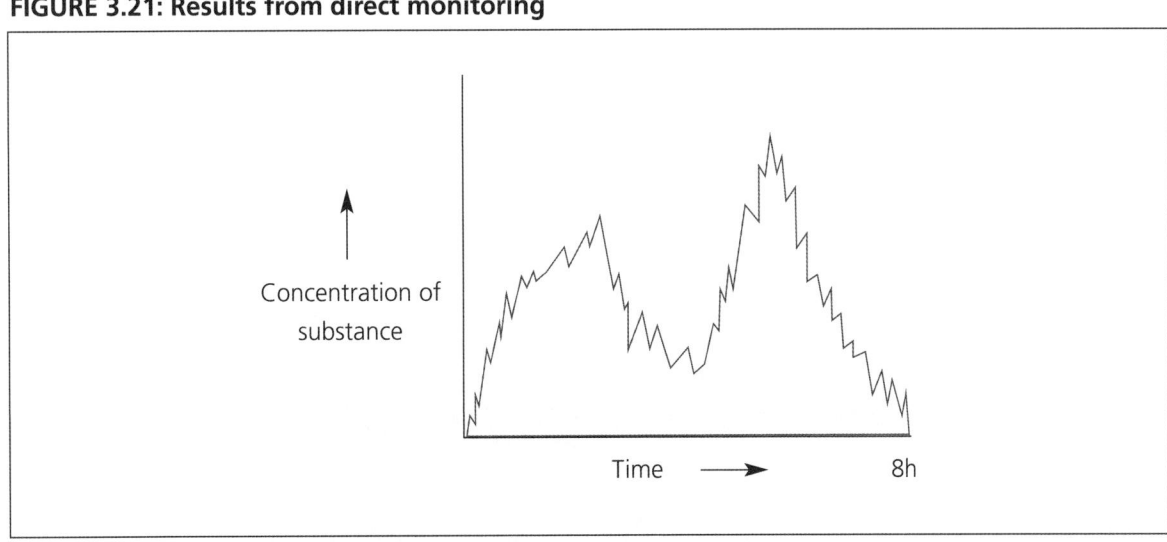

FIGURE 3.21: Results from direct monitoring

Direct monitoring is particularly useful where there is a need to have immediate readings of contaminant levels, for example, in the case of fast-acting chemicals. Also periods of peak concentration during the work cycle or work shift can be detected and this may be useful in determining a control strategy. This approach may help determine at which point in a particular process to install a local ventilation system and this will be discussed in relation to the monitoring of gases and vapours and dusts and fibres.

CHEMICAL AGENTS

Gases and vapours

Many direct reading instruments are available which are specific for particular gases, for example, carbon dioxide, carbon monoxide, nitrogen oxides, hydrogen sulphide and mercury vapour. These can be linked to a chart recorder, data logger or warning device.

A portable infrared gas analyser which allows direct monitoring of gases and vapours in the workplace is shown in Figure 3.22. In infrared spectrometry, the basic principle utilised is that many gases and vapours will absorb infrared radiation and, under standard conditions, the extent of absorption is directly proportional to the concentration of the chemical agent. This instrument takes a sample of air, detects the extent of absorption of an infrared beam, and displays the result as the concentration of the airborne contaminant in question. Before use, the instrument must be set up and calibrated for the particular chemical to be measured. Because so many chemical agents absorb infrared radiation, this is an extremely versatile instrument.

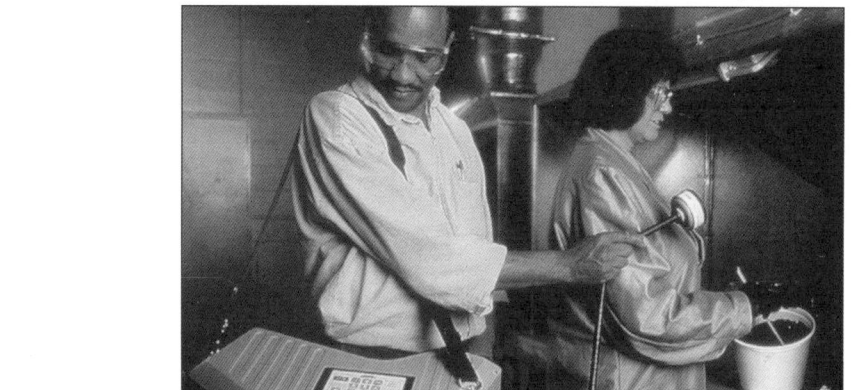

FIGURE 3.22: Portable infrared gas and vapour monitor (MIRAN SapphIRe)

(Thermo Electron Corporation, Franklin, MA, USA)

The organic vapour monitor featured in Figure 3.23 is a portable, direct reading instrument. It is based on a photoionisation detector and it will monitor most organic vapours, total hydrocarbon concentrations and some inorganic gases.

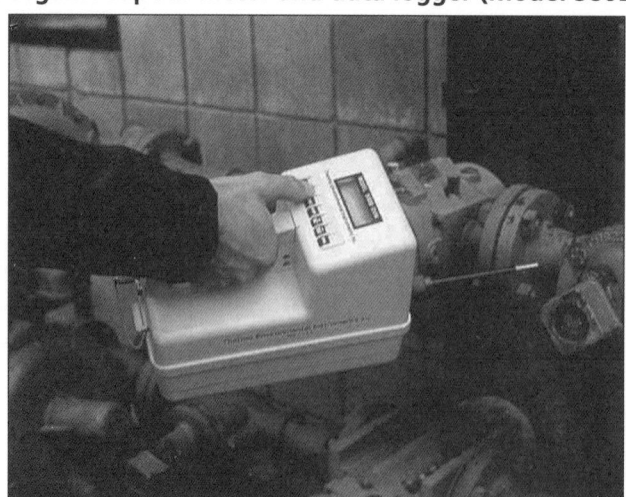

FIGURE 3.23: Portable organic vapour meter and data logger (Model 580B)

(Thermo Electron Corporation, Franklin, MA, USA)

Oxygen analysers

Deficiency of oxygen in the atmosphere of confined spaces is often experienced in industry, for example, inside large fuel storage tanks when 'empty of liquid'. Before such places may be entered to carry

CHEMICAL AGENTS

out inspections or maintenance work, the oxygen content of the atmosphere inside the vessel must be measured. Normal air contains approximately 21 per cent oxygen and it is generally accepted that when this is reduced to 16 per cent or below, people experience dizziness, increased heartbeat and headaches. Such environments should only be entered wearing air-supplied breathing apparatus.

Portable analysers are available which measure the concentration of oxygen in the air by the depolarisation produced at a sensitive electrode mounted in the instrument. Several different devices are available which vary in sensitivity, reliability and ease of maintenance. It is important that instruments are checked and calibrated before use. Long extension probes can be used which allow remote inspection of confined spaces.

Dusts and fibres

A dust lamp is a very useful and versatile direct reading instrument. Many particles of dust are too small to see with the naked eye under normal lighting conditions, but when a beam of strong light is passed through a cloud of dust, they reflect the light to the observer. This is known as forward light scattering, and as a result of this, the particles become readily visible. A natural occurrence of this phenomenon is observed when a shaft of sunlight shines into a dark building highlighting the airborne particles. Thus, if a portable lamp having a strong parallel beam is set up to shine through a dusty environment, the movement of the particles can be observed. Although this is not a quantitative method, the behaviour of dust emitted by work processes can be observed and corrective measures taken. It may be useful to photograph or make a videotape record of events. The use of a dust lamp is illustrated in Figures 3.24 and 3.25.

FIGURE 3.24: Dust lamp – Principle of operation

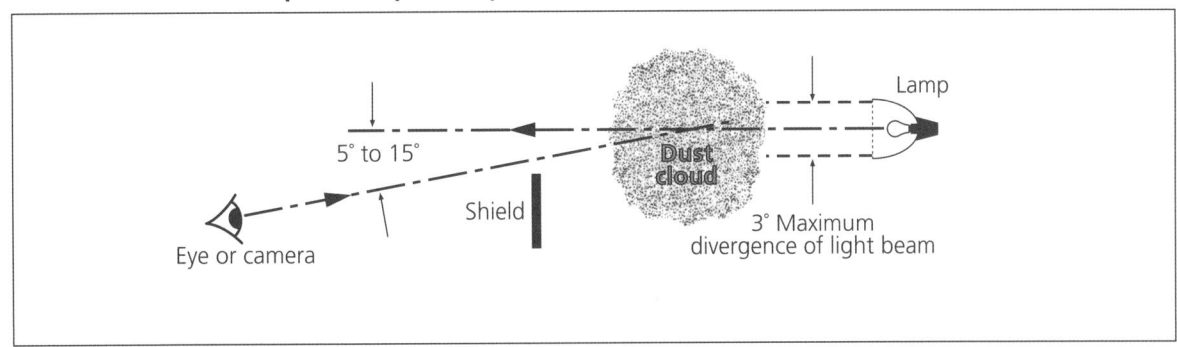

FIGURE 3.25: Disc-cutting stone – jets of fast moving dusty air (Tyndall illumination)

(HSE 2001d)

CHEMICAL AGENTS

Direct reading monitors for dusts are available, based on the principle of dust detection by the scattering of laser light. This type of instrument is shown in Figure 3.26. This will monitor inhalable thoracic and respirable fraction concentrations in ambient air as well as PM_{10}, $PM_{2.5}$ and $PM_{1.0}$ fractions[18].

FIGURE 3.26: Real-time dust monitor

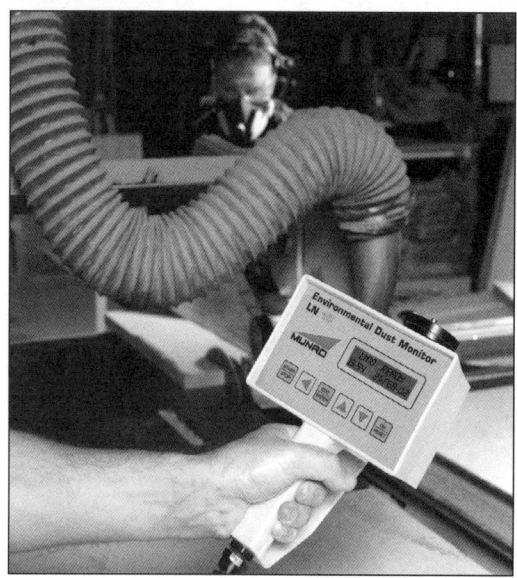

(Munro Environmental)

Validated methods

In order to be sure that the methods used in air contaminant monitoring are accurate and standardised, the HSE has developed and approved techniques for a range of contaminants in its *Methods for the Detection of Hazardous Substances* series, available online at www.hse.gov.uk/pubns/index.htm. A similar approach has been taken by the US National Institute for Occupational Safety and Health (NIOSH), which has published a *Manual of Analytical Methods*. Furthermore, in the UK there are several quality control schemes, some of which are administered by the HSE, which aim to ensure that laboratories offering occupational hygiene analytical services are producing satisfactory results.

Biological monitoring

Biological monitoring is a useful approach to evaluating exposure to chemical agents, and which often complements the information obtained by air monitoring methods. Biological monitoring allows the body's uptake of substances by all absorption routes to be determined, including skin absorption and gastrointestinal tract uptake following ingestion. It is also used in the evaluation of exposure where respiratory protection equipment and other PPE is worn. Tola & Hernberg (1981) define biological monitoring as:

> *A regular measuring activity where selected, validated indicators of the uptake of toxic substances are determined to **prevent** health impairment.* (Author's emphasis)

Biological monitoring involves the measurement and assessment of workplace chemical agents or their metabolites in body tissues, secretions, excreta or expired air (or combinations of these) in exposed workers. For example, measurement of the chemical agent itself may be carried out for lead and cadmium in blood, cobalt and nickel in urine, and tetrachloroethylene in exhaled breath. Evaluation of metabolites is also carried out, for example, bromide in blood is used to assess methyl bromide exposure and mandelic acid in urine to indicate exposure to styrene.

For interpreting selective biological monitoring measurements, Biological Monitoring Guidance Values (BMGVs) have been derived by the HSE. There are far fewer biological limits in comparison to air quality standards and BMGV limits for only 15 substances/categories are listed in EH40 (HSE 2005). A BMGV is

---

[18] A PM_{10} sampling head allows the mass concentration of particles generally less than 10μm in diameter to be measured, while a $PM_{2.5}$ sampler will allow measurement of particles less than 2.5μm in diameter and the $PM_{1.0}$ sampler will measure particles less than 1μm in diameter.

set where it is likely to be of practical value, where a suitable monitoring method exists and where there are enough data to validate the proposed biological limit. BMGVs are based on:

- the relationship between biological concentration and health effects;
- the relationship between biological concentration and exposure at the WEL; or
- representative biological samples fromn workplaces already applying good occupational hygiene practice.

In comparison to air quality standards (WELs), BMGVs are non-statutory (although blood lead concentration is used as a statutory guide to lead intoxication in the Control of Lead at Work Regulations 2002), but they are intended to be used as an aid to achieving adequate control under COSHH (regulation 7). Guidance on the practical implementation of biological monitoring schemes is given in a further publication (HSE 1997c).

Determination of risk tolerability

New control framework for substances hazardous to health

The COSHH Regulations 2002 (as amended) (regulation 7) require prevention of exposure to hazardous substances, or where this is not reasonably practicable, then exposure must be 'adequately' controlled. Protective measures should be applied appropriate to the activity and consistent with the risk assessment. There is a refocusing of 'adequate' control by specifically emphasising and requiring employers to apply principles of good control practice, as well as ensuring that any WEL is not exceeded. In addition, exposure to defined carcinogens/mutagens and asthmagens must be reduced to as low as is reasonably practicable. (Carcinogens/mutagens are substances with a risk phrase R45, R46 or R49, or substances or processes in COSHH Schedule 1 (which lists carcinogens); asthmagens are those substances with risk phrases R42 or R42/43 or which are listed in Section C of *Asthmagen? Critical assessments of the evidence for agents implicated in occupational asthma*, HSE Books 1997 (as updated).)

The new regulatory framework has the following key features:

- the principles of good practice are outlined in Schedule 2A (COSHH Regulations 2002, as amended) (see Table 3.11a below);
- replacement of the previous two-tier standards system (Maximum Exposure Limit (MEL) and Occupational Exposure Standard (OES)) with a single Workplace Exposure Limit (WEL) system where only 'scientifically robust' former exposure standards are retained (HSC 2003); legal compliance requires that WELs should not be exceeded;
- the WEL values will be linked to improved good practice advice, for example the *COSHH Essentials* guidance (HSE 2003).

TABLE 3.11a: Schedule 2A, COSHH Regulations 2002 (as amended)

Principles of good practice for the control of exposure to substances hazardous to health	
(a)	Design and operate processes and activities to minimise emission, release and spread of substances hazardous to health
(b)	Take into account all relevant routes of exposure – inhalation, skin absorption and ingestion – when developing control measures
(c)	Control exposure by measures that are porportionate to the health risk
(d)	Choose the most effective and reliable control options which minimise the escape and spread of substances hazardous to health
(e)	Where adequate control of exposure cannot be achieved by other means, provide, in combination with other control measures, suitable personal protective equipment
(f)	Check and review regularly all elements of control measures for their continuing effectiveness
(g)	Inform and train all employees on the hazards and risks from the substances with which they work and the use of control measures developed to minimise the risks
(h)	Ensure that the introduction of control measures does not increase the overall risk to health and safety

Setting exposure standards

When measurements of airborne contamination levels or other parameters have been made, it is necessary to interpret them against a standard. With exposure to chemical agents in the workplace, there are two broad philosophical options:
1. Achieve zero exposure.
2. Permit defined tolerable levels of exposure.

Given that zero exposure to chemical agents is not possible in most cases, and taking into account industrial realities, the usual option is to define and permit 'tolerable' exposure. The key question is how to derive tolerable limits for exposure to chemical agents?

Generally, exposure standard-setting can be regarded as a two-stage process:
1. The first stage is collection and evaluation of the health and scientific data. This includes information from human epidemiology, animal studies, short-term testing and other experience from the use of the substance.
2. The second stage involves setting of the actual exposure limit value, usually by a committee, which takes into account the previously mentioned health and scientific data and, crucially, relevant socioeconomic and political factors.

Thus, the final derived value is usually a compromise between health requirements and the costs and practicability of implementation.

In both the British WEL and American TLV systems, discussed below, concentrations are given in parts per million (ppm), that is, parts of vapour or gas by volume per million parts of contaminated air, and also in milligrams of substance per cubic metre of air (mg m^{-3}).

Threshold Limit Values (TLVs)

Threshold Limit Values (TLVs) were first published in the 1940s, in the USA, by the American Conference of Governmental Industrial Hygienists (ACGIH). At this time, toxicologists believed that they were setting virtually 'safe' limits, hence the term 'threshold'. However, it is now known that, for many health effects, this is not the case and the preface to the current list (ACGIH 2002) states:

Threshold Limit Values refer to airborne concentrations of substances and represent conditions under which it is believed that nearly all workers may be repeatedly exposed day after day without adverse health effects.

This system of limits is still used in many countries around the world.

UK exposure limits

For about 40 years the UK Factory Inspectorate republished the TLV list as authoritative guidance, but in 1984 this was discontinued and a British system of exposure standards was introduced. One reason for this change was that it was intended to adopt a tripartite approach to standard-setting and the need for a 'British' system within the context of the then European Community. Since 1984, there have been several types of UK occupational air quality standard including the two-tier 'Control Limit' and 'Recommended Limit' system and, until recently, the two-tier MEL and OES system. These two-tier systems defined exposure standards with different requirements for legal compliance and this has been abolished with the single-tier WEL system. As noted above, the WEL system now forms part of the requirements of 'adequate' control of exposure by inhalation. Limits should not be used as an index of toxicity distinguishing between safe and dangerous levels. Also, the absence of a substance from the list does not indicate that it is safe. The WEL values are set on the recommendation of the HSC Advisory Committee on Toxic Substances. This follows a scientific assessment by another committee, the Working Group on the Assessment of Toxic Chemicals. These committees consider whether to assign a limit and the precise substance concentration to be adopted. With only a few exceptions, levels embodied in the standards must be evaluated by personal monitoring techniques, ie a sampling device must be located in the person's breathing zone.

FIGURE 3.26a: Standard-setting process for WEL value

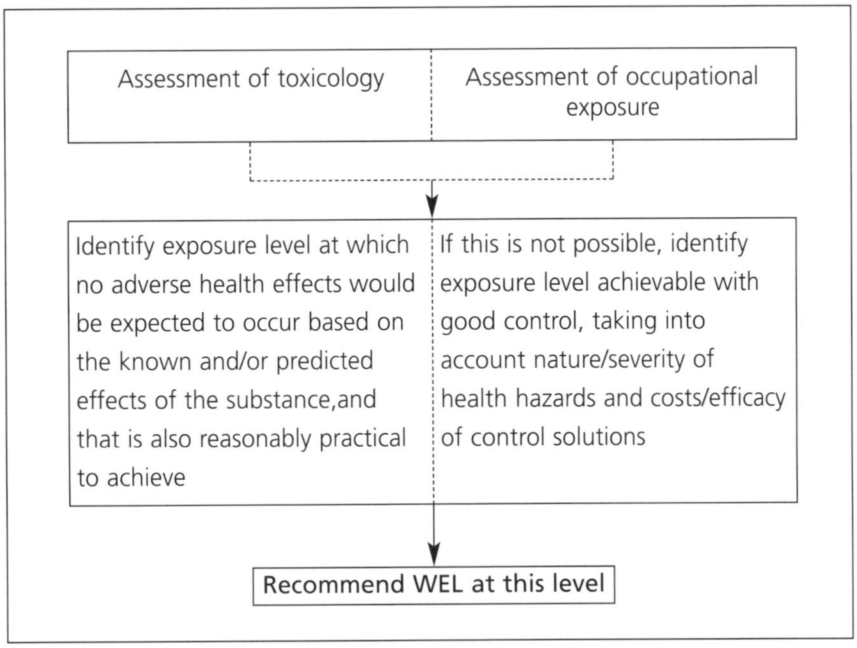

```
┌─────────────────────────────────┬─────────────────────────────────┐
│  Assessment of toxicology       │  Assessment of occupational     │
│                                 │  exposure                       │
└─────────────────────────────────┴─────────────────────────────────┘
                              │
                              ▼
┌─────────────────────────────────┬─────────────────────────────────┐
│ Identify exposure level at which│ If this is not possible, identify│
│ no adverse health effects would │ exposure level achievable with  │
│ be expected to occur based on   │ good control, taking into       │
│ the known and/or predicted      │ account nature/severity of      │
│ effects of the substance, and   │ health hazards and costs/efficacy│
│ that is also reasonably practical│ of control solutions            │
│ to achieve                      │                                 │
└─────────────────────────────────┴─────────────────────────────────┘
                              │
                              ▼
                  ┌───────────────────────────┐
                  │ Recommend WEL at this level│
                  └───────────────────────────┘
```

(HSE 2005)

Indicative Occupational Exposure Limit Values (IOELVs)

These are concentrations of a hazardous substance in air proposed by the European Commission under the framework of the Chemical Agents Directive (EC 1998). Member States are obliged to introduce an occupational exposure limit for these substances in accordance with national legislation and practice that takes the IOELV into account. IOELVs are based on recommendations by the European Commission's Scientific Committee on Occupational Exposure Limits (SCOEL). These European limits are incorporated into the list of WEL standards (HSC 2005).

Workplace Exposure Limits (WELs)

WELs refer to concentrations of substances hazardous to health in the air, expressed as a time-weighted average (TWA), ie averaged over a specified period of time (8 hours or 15 minutes). WELs are listed in Guidance Note EH40 (HSE 2005). When a substance is assigned a WEL, personal inhalation exposure must in all cases be reduced to below the limit. Some substances which have been assigned a WEL are also recognised as implicated in occupational asthma or categorised as carcinogens or mutagens, and in these cases all exposure (including inhalation) must be reduced to as low a level as is reasonably practicable.

Long-term and short-term exposure limits

For each WEL, time-weighted average values are listed for both eight hours and 15 minutes. The aim is to protect against both short-term effects (15-minute TWA), such as irritation of the skin, eyes or lungs or narcosis, and long-term health effects (8-hour TWA).

Time-weighted average (TWA) concentration

The limits refer to the maximum exposure concentration when *averaged* over a 15-minute period or an eight-hour day. The time-weighted average value, C_m, can be obtained from the following formula:

$$C_m = \frac{(C_1 \times t_1) + (C_2 \times t_2) + (C_n \times t_n)}{t_1 + t_2 + t_n}$$

(Where: C_1, C_2, C_n is concentrations measured during respective sampling periods; and t_1, t_2, t_n is duration of sampling periods.)

CHEMICAL AGENTS

A simple example is where the person working an eight-hour day was exposed for four hours at 160ppm vapour and then for four hours at 40ppm. The 8-hour TWA is calculated as follows:

$$C_m = \frac{(160 \times 4) + (40 \times 4)}{4 + 4} = 100\text{ppm}$$

Mixtures

Most of the listed exposure limits refer to single substances or closely related groups, for example, cadmium and its compounds and isocyanates. A few limits refer to complex mixtures or compounds, for example, white spirit or rubber fume. However, exposure in workplaces is often to mixtures of substances and such combinations may interact to increase, sometimes synergistically, the risks. Mixed exposure assessment should take into account the primary target organs of the major contaminants and possible interactions. General guidance on mixed exposures is given in EH40, together with a 'rule of thumb' formula which may be used where there is reason to believe that the effects of the constituents of a mixture are additive and the WELs are based on the same health effects:

$$\frac{C_1}{L_1} + \frac{C_2}{L_2} + \frac{C_3}{L_3} < 1$$

(Where: C_1, C_2 are time-weighted average concentrations of constituents; and L_1, L_2 are corresponding exposure limits.)

The use of this formula is only applicable where the additive substances have been assigned a WEL value. If the ratio is greater than 1, then the exposure limit for the mixture has been exceeded.

For example, if air contains 30ppm toluene (WEL = 50ppm) and 40ppm xylene (WEL = 50ppm), the formula gives:

$$\text{Additive ratio} = \frac{30}{50} + \frac{40}{50} = 1.4$$

The notional additive limit of 1 is therefore exceeded. If one of the substances has been assigned an MEL value, then the additive effect should be taken into account when deciding to what extent it is reasonably practicable to reduce exposure further.

Physical factors

Physical factors such as heat, ultraviolet light, high humidity and abnormal pressure place additional environmental stress on the body and are likely to increase the toxic effect of a substance. Most standards have been set at a level to encompass moderate deviations from the normal environment. However, for gross variations in conditions, for example, with heavy manual work where respiration rate is greatly increased, continuous activity at elevated temperatures or excessive overtime, a lower value for the exposure standard will need to be applied. This is held to be a matter of competent professional judgment.

Skin absorption

Some substances listed in EH40 have the designation 'Sk', which refers to the potential contribution to overall exposure of absorption through the skin. In this case, airborne contamination alone may not indicate total exposure to the chemical and the 'Sk' designation is intended to draw attention to the need to prevent skin absorption. In the application of the assigned exposure limit, it is assumed that additional exposure by the skin route is prevented.

The 'Sk' designation is assigned to substances where dermal exposure may:
- make a substantial contribution to body burden when compared with inhalation exposure at the WEL; and
- cause systemic effects in addition to any health effects based on evaluation of inhalation exposure only.

Sensitisation

Furthermore in EH40, the designation 'Sen' is assigned to selected substances to indicate their capacity to cause occupational asthma. The identified substances are those which:

- are assigned the risk phrase R42: 'May cause sensitisation by inhalation'; or R42/43: 'May cause sensitisation by inhalation and skin contact' in the CHIP *Approved supply list* (HSC 2002c); or
- are listed in the publication *Asthmagen?* (HSE 1997 as updated).

The COSHH Regulations 2002 (as amended) (regulation 7(5) and Appendix 1) focus specifically on prevention and control of exposure to carcinogens and mutagens.

Setting occupational exposure limits

Occupational exposure limits should, ideally, be derived from the quantitative relationship between the level of exposure to the harmful agent (dose) and its impact on an exposed working population (response). For example, in the case of chemical agents, an exposure of xppm over a specified time causes Y amount of harm in an exposed working population. In this context, 'harm' is the proportion of the exposed population, normally expressed as a percentage, who show a defined health effect. However, such dose response relations are very difficult to establish in humans, particularly in the case of chronic exposures and their health effects. Figure 3.27 illustrates a normal distribution of response curve that is thought to occur for many biological responses including toxic ones. Sensitive and resistant individuals are shown including a 'threshold' below which no-one would be affected, that is, a 'safe level'. Early toxicological work provided some support for thresholds. In the 1940s, the ACGIH was convinced by the idea of thresholds and the preface to its list of standards stated that they prevented "all workers" from harm. Today, this preface refers to "nearly all workers", reflecting the change of views on this subject (ACGIH 2002). There are particular difficulties with defining thresholds for carcinogens ('single hit' theory of causation) and allergens.

Sources of information, discussed previously, include chemical analogy, animal testing, short-term testing and human epidemiology. The ACGIH summarises toxicological information on substances for which TLVs have been adopted and shows that for some substances the hazards are clear, whereas for others there is much less information on human risks. This inherent uncertainty is not reflected in the listing of the adopted values.

The HSE (2001) published summaries of the information used in setting its MEL and OES values, and this will continue with the WELs. Such information can be useful in assessing the applicability of a standard to a particular workplace situation, although, obviously, statutory compliance is still required.

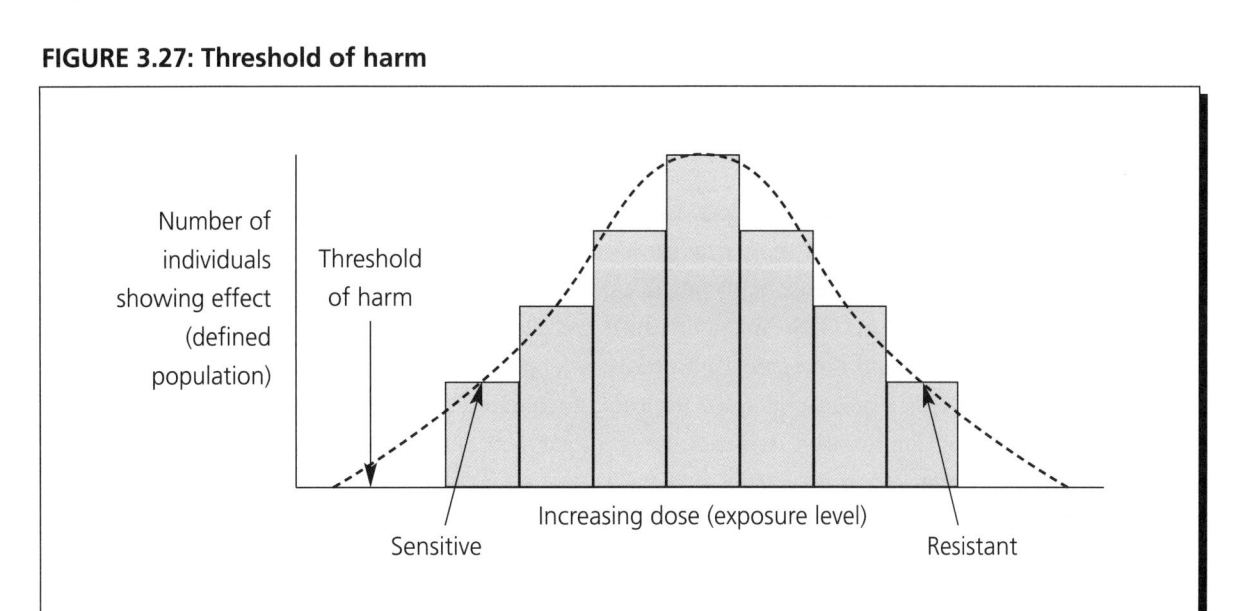

FIGURE 3.27: Threshold of harm

(Levy 1990)

Variation in international standards

There is considerable variation in international standards depending on the interpretation of the scientific data and the philosophy of regulations. International hygiene standards for trichloroethylene illustrate this variation as shown in Table 3.12.

TABLE 3.12: International occupational exposure standards for trichloroethylene

Country	mg m^{-3}	ppm
Australia*	267	50
UK*	550	100
USA (ACGIH)*	267	50
Sweden*	50	10
Hungary**	53	10
Former Soviet Union**	10	2

*Time-weighted average (TWA); **Maximum allowable concentration (MAC)

When compared with the United States, the former Soviet Union put greater emphasis on neurophysiological changes in experimental animals as well as behavioural effects in human beings. Although low levels were embodied in national regulations, this did not mean they were achieved in practice, as was acknowledged by former Soviet representatives.

In the European Union, there have been moves to harmonise exposure limits. However, there is also obviously a simultaneous need to harmonise compliance strategies.

Changes in hygiene limits

With new scientific evidence, hygiene limits are constantly being revised. The acute effects of vinyl chloride monomer (VCM) were identified in the 1930s as being primarily narcosis. To prevent narcosis during industrial use, a TLV of 500ppm was set in 1962. In further research, VCM was identified as affecting the liver, bones and kidneys and the adopted value TLV was lowered to 200ppm in 1971. In 1974, some chemical workers died of angiosarcoma, a rare liver cancer, which was traced to exposure to VCM, with the result that in 1978 the adopted value (ACGIH) was lowered to 5ppm[19]. As can be seen, the adopted TLV for VCM was reduced a hundred-fold in under 20 years.

The HSE in Guidance Note EH40 specifies the standards which are under particular consideration for possible change.

Enforcement of WELs

The COSHH Regulations 2002 (as amended) (regulation 7(1)) require that:

Every employer shall ensure that the exposure of his employees to substances hazardous to health is either prevented or, where this is not reasonably practicable, adequately controlled.

WELs form part of the compliance measures necessary to achieve 'adequate' control where exposure must be reduced below the level of the particular limit and in the case of carcinogens or mutagens and asthmagens to as low a level as is reasonably practicable.

The abolition of the previous OESs, many of which had dubious basis, the selection of more scientifically based limits as WELs, and the current emphasis on applying effective control principles take us in the right direction towards a policy contained in previous guidance on controlling exposure to toxic substances, where the HSE emphasised that exposure to toxic substances should always be reduced to as low a level as is reasonably practicable (HSE 1976).

COSHH Essentials and modification of the OEL framework

COSHH Essentials (HSE 2003) is a guide produced by the HSE to assist small and medium-sized

---

[19] VCM has a WEL of 3ppm (8-hour TWA) in the latest edition of EH40 (HSE 2005).

enterprises (SMEs) to comply with the COSHH Regulations. The user of the guide is helped to carry out a simple generic risk assessment, which it is claimed uses readily available information and allows the identification of appropriate control approaches. In 2002, *Electronic COSHH Essentials* was launched as a free Internet tool (www.COSHH-essentials.org.uk). According to the HSE, *COSHH Essentials* 'works' because it does not rely on measurement, which can be expensive for small firms, and that research has shown that business did not understand the previous two-limit OEL system (HSE 2002a).

Preventing and controlling exposure to chemical agents

Following risk assessment, the application of appropriate prevention or control measures is required. These control options need to be complemented and underpinned by adequate administrative arrangements, including provision for regular review.

The principal control options for chemical agents are listed below:
1. Elimination.
2. Specification.
3. Substitution.
4. Segregation.
5. Engineering control – ventilation.
6. Personal hygiene.
7. Good housekeeping.
8. Personal protection.
9. Reduced exposure time.
10. Change of work pattern.

A 'hierarchy of control' is imposed by various statutory requirements. Here, control at source is the preferred option, followed by engineering control measures, and only if it is not reasonably practicable to apply these measures to reduce risks to tolerable levels, is personal protective equipment allowed. A summary of the principal legal requirements relating to chemical agent risk assessment and control is presented in Table 3.13 on page 117. In a given situation, following risk assessment, it is necessary to select and apply an appropriate 'blend' of control measures.

Elimination

This is the removal of a hazard completely so that the risk disappears and it generally means process change. It is not an easy control option to achieve. However, there are many examples of chemical agents being successfully eliminated from work processes, such as powder-coating systems which have replaced solvent-based paints in some applications, and the development of lead-free paints and cadmium-free solders. In some cases, natural biological predators have replaced chemical pesticides.

As well as eliminating the chemical agent itself, it may be possible to eliminate the task which the operator performs and which leads to exposure, for example, employing remote handling by industrial robots. It is worth noting that exposure may still occur during maintenance and repair tasks. Sometimes, a process change may replace one type of hazard with another. For example, in a metal joining operation, riveting may replace welding, resulting in the elimination of welding fumes and the introduction of a noise hazard. This illustrates the point that, following the introduction of alternative control measures, there should be a further risk assessment to reflect the changed situation. Furthermore, it is important that there is always consideration of the overall risk situation which takes into account all types of hazard.

Specification

The design of a new workplace or process is an important strategic point at which to incorporate risk prevention and control features. Changing the design of a projected process is much easier and cheaper than trying to alter equipment and processes after installation. For example, at the design stage:

1. Process chemicals should be carefully selected.
2. Automation and remote handling to minimise exposure should be considered.
3. Quantities of toxic materials directly handled should be limited.
4. Lowest process temperatures possible to reduce fumes should be used.
5. Maintenance requirements should be minimised.
6. Emergency procedures should be considered with respect to exposures.
7. Use of alternative physical forms of chemical agents to reduce emissions should be considered. For example, reduced exposure to dusts and powders may be achieved by pressing them into pellets or making a liquid slurry; small amounts of oil have been added to mineral wool resulting in a significant reduction in the emission of respirable fibres (BOHS 1996). In electroplating, chromic acid mists have been reduced by covering tanks with foam.
8. Neighbouring activities in the work area should be considered. Is there a possibility of intermediates and cross-reactions? A classic example is that metal degreasing plants using halogenated hydrocarbons should not be positioned next to welding operations because of the toxic by-products produced. In purely process logic, this juxtaposition makes sense since metal cleaning is carried out before welding.

To re-emphasise the essential point, it is vital to have health and safety practitioners involved at the process design stage, since future health and safety problems may be averted by their intervention.

Existing processes

Of course, the above process considerations can be addressed concerning existing processes when seeking to control emissions. It may be possible to reduce exposure significantly by introducing modifications, sometimes minor, to the process. It is important that the production process is not considered immutable, that is, it cannot be changed just because this is the way things have always been done. All activities should be examined to see if improvements can be introduced which may reduce exposure.

Substitution

This involves the substitution of a chemical agent by a less harmful alternative. For example, carbon tetrachloride in dry cleaning has been replaced by the less toxic perchloroethylene. In the 1980s, because it was believed to be less toxic, 111-trichloroethane (111-TCE) was substituted for trichloroethylene (TCE) in metal degreasing applications. However, in the 1990s, 111-TCE, itself, was phased out because of its ozone-depleting characteristics. Solvent-based degreasing applications have now been widely replaced by water-based detergent systems. Similarly, water-based paints have replaced many solvent-based paints. Other examples include sandstone grinding wheels, which are high in quartz, being largely replaced by alumina synthetic abrasive wheels, and asbestos being replaced by asbestos-free materials such as glass wool, mineral wool and carbon fibre.

It is important to ensure that a 'safer' substitute is not considered so simply because there is less information available about its hazards. Where one chemical agent is substituted for another, then a re-assessment of risks is always needed. The HSE (1994b) gives guidance on a basic approach for introducing substitution.

Segregation

Where a hazardous chemical agent cannot be eliminated or substituted, another possibility is to enclose the process completely in order to prevent the spread of contamination. The individual worker is removed from close proximity to the emission source. This may be by means of a physical barrier, for example, handling toxic substances in a totally enclosed glove box or a partially enclosed fume hood. In addition, relocation of a process task to an isolated area of the plant to reduce, overall, the number of people potentially exposed is another possibility. A process may be segregated in time, that is, only operated at night when there are fewer people at work. However, another factor which should be taken into account in process evaluation is the additional stress imposed on night shift workers, who generally function less efficiently.

Engineering control – Ventilation

Ventilation provides fresh air, which is required in a workplace for several reasons including:

1. Respiration – to provide oxygen and dilute carbon dioxide.
2. The dilution and removal of airborne impurities created by occupants, eg body odours and tobacco smoke.
3. The removal of excess heat and maintenance of thermal comfort (see Chapter 7).
4. The dilution of other airborne contaminants generated by work processes, machinery and heating appliances. (This is the major concern of this chapter.)

A minimum standard of ventilation is required to provide fresh air for people and to dilute impurities. The exact requirements for ventilation will differ depending on the type and size of the building, the number of occupants and the particular work carried out. As shown in Figure 3.28, ventilation can be divided into local exhaust ventilation (LEV) and dilution ventilation (DV).

FIGURE 3.28: Approaches to ventilation

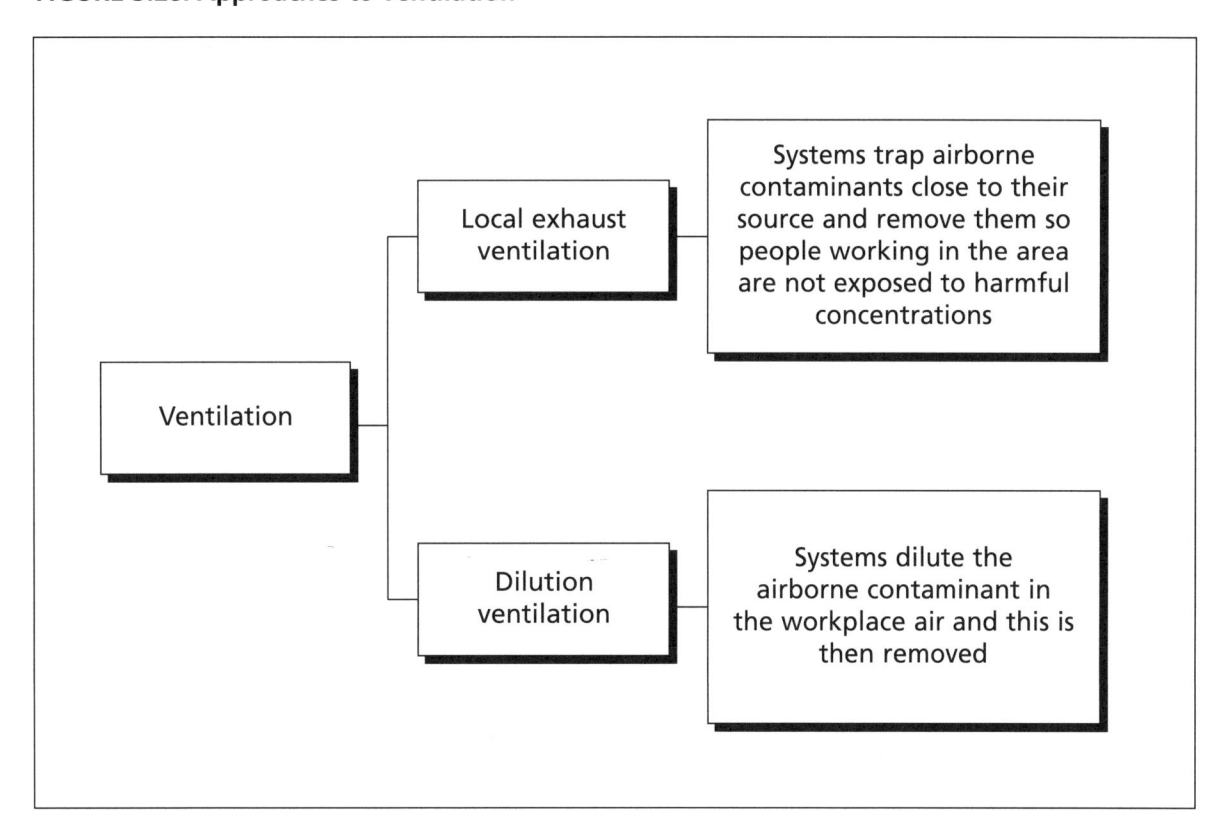

```
                          ┌─ Local exhaust ──── Systems trap airborne contaminants close to their
                          │   ventilation        source and remove them so people working in the
                          │                      area are not exposed to harmful concentrations
         Ventilation ─────┤
                          │
                          └─ Dilution ────────── Systems dilute the airborne contaminant in
                              ventilation        the workplace air and this is then removed
```

Local exhaust ventilation collects contaminated air close to its source and immediately removes it from the workplace air into the system ducting. It is eventually expelled in an appropriate state, normally having passed through an air-cleaning device. **Dilution ventilation** includes natural ventilation and/or mechanical ventilation components. The introduction of fresh air dilutes airborne contaminants to a tolerable level. This is followed by the removal of contaminated air at an appropriate rate, keeping contaminant concentrations well below tolerable air quality standards. Dilution ventilation may make use of natural ventilation resulting from doors, windows or roof vents, and/or use mechanical systems with inlet and/or outlet fans and ducting.

There are financial costs when providing artificial or mechanical ventilation, rather than relying on natural air movement, since there may be a requirement to move and heat a large volume of air. This, together with the installation and maintenance costs associated with a suitable mechanical system, may constitute a significant expense.

Ventilation systems are a very important control measure and their design, application and maintenance are considered in detail below.

Other modes of entry

It is important to keep in mind that ventilation only deals with inhalation exposure and in situations where the emission source is not fully enclosed, controlling potential exposure by ingestion and skin contact/absorption must always be kept in mind.

Personal hygiene

Adequate washing and eating facilities should be provided with instruction for workers on the hygiene measures they should take to prevent the spread of contamination. The use of lead at work is an example of where this is particularly important. This is a specific requirement of legislation on controlling chemical agents (see Table 3.13).

Good housekeeping

This has an important role in the protection of the health of people at work. Written procedures are necessary for preventing the spread of contamination, for example, the immediate clean-up of spillages, safe disposal of wastes, and the regular cleaning of workstations and areas. Dust exposure levels can be minimised by damping down with water, or other suitable liquid, close to the source of the dust. Also, where sweeping is unavoidable, then wetting of surfaces before commencing will minimise dust levels. In such situations, it is always preferable to use an industrial vacuum cleaner.

Personal protective equipment

Achieving a safe workplace should always be the first objective, but if it is not possible to reduce risks sufficiently by other methods, the worker may need to be protected from the environment by the use of personal protective equipment. This may be broadly divided as follows:

1. Hearing protection.
2. Respiratory protection.
3. Eye and face protection.
4. Protective clothing.
5. Skin protection.

Personal protection devices have a serious limitation in that they do nothing to attenuate the hazard at source, so that if they fail and this is not noticed, the wearer's protection is reduced and the risk increases correspondingly. Further, and importantly, PPE does nothing to protect the wearer unless it is *worn*.

Although personal protective equipment is often regarded as a last line of defence, in some situations it may be the only line of defence, for example, for some short-term maintenance tasks. This emphasises the need for an effective PPE strategy once the decision to apply this control option has been taken. The subject of PPE and its application is dealt with in detail in Chapter 13.

Reduced exposure time

Reducing the time of exposure to a health hazard, by rotation of workers, is a control measure which has been used in the past. But this does not take into account the possibly harmful effect of dose rate, for example, high levels over a short time even though followed by a long period of relatively low-level exposure.

Administrative controls

A control strategy has to be supported by administrative measures to ensure controls provided are used, adequately inspected and maintained (or reviewed if a procedure) and appropriate records are kept. Risk assessments and applied controls need to be periodically reviewed and audited. Monitoring of housekeeping, personal hygiene and the implementation of planned PPE schemes need to be carried out on a continuing basis.

TABLE 3.13: Summary of principal legal requirements

Legislation	Requirements
Control of Substances Hazardous to Health Regulations 2002 (as amended)	• Identification of 'substances hazardous to health' (defined in regulation 2); evaluation of risks; application of prevention and control measures and regular review (reg. 6) • Adequate control of exposure (reg. 7) • Control measures: use of (reg. 8); maintenance of (reg. 9) • Air monitoring – where appropriate (reg. 10) • Health surveillance – where appropriate (reg. 11) • Information, instruction and training (reg. 12) • Arrangements to deal with accidents, incidents and emergencies (reg. 13)
Control of Lead at Work Regulations 2002	• Assessment of health risks created by work involving lead (reg. 5) • Prevention and control of exposure to lead (reg. 6) • Restriction of eating, drinking and smoking (reg. 7) • Control measures: maintenance, examination and testing (reg. 8) • Air monitoring where exposure to lead is significant (reg. 9) • Medical surveillance where exposure to lead is significant (reg. 10) • Information, instruction and training (reg. 11) • Arrangements to deal with accidents, incidents and emergencies (reg. 12)
Control of Asbestos at Work Regulations 2002	• Duty to manage asbestos in non-domestic premises (reg. 4) • Identification of the type of asbestos (reg. 5) • Assessment of work which exposes employees to asbestos (reg. 6) • Plans of work (reg. 7) • Notification of work with asbestos (reg. 8) • Information, instruction and training (reg. 9) • Prevention/reduction of exposure (reg. 10) • Use of control measures (reg. 11) • Maintenance of controls (reg. 12) • Provision and cleaning of protective clothing (reg. 13) • Arrangements to deal with accidents, incidents and emergencies (reg. 14) • Duty to prevent the spread of asbestos (reg. 15) • Cleanliness of premises/plant (reg. 16) • Designated areas (reg. 17) • Air monitoring (reg. 18) • Standards for air testing (reg. 19) • Standards for analysis (reg. 20) • Health records and medical surveillance (reg. 21) • Washing and changing facilities (reg. 22) • Storage, distribution and labelling of raw asbestos and asbestos waste (reg. 23) • Supply of products containing asbestos for use at work (reg. 24)

Asbestos – Management and regulation

Up until around 1980, asbestos was widely used in the UK for industrial products and as a building material. Although a considerable amount has now been removed from buildings, much asbestos remains in situ within the fabric of occupied premises. The HSE estimates that currently there are half a million non-domestic premises with asbestos installations (HSE 2002b).

There is now comprehensive control of the use, supply and importation of asbestos and asbestos products. Similarly, there is strict regulation of asbestos work with many activities requiring a special licence from the HSE (HSC 2002b). However, these controls only protect workers from exposure to asbestos when the presence of the asbestos is known. The concern now is for people, for example, maintenance or building workers, who may be inadvertently exposed to asbestos fibres during their normal work activities. A significant proportion of those dying from asbestos-induced diseases have been found to have been engaged in construction/maintenance work in the past (Peto & Hodgson 1995). It is essential that any workers involved in building maintenance and associated tasks should know if premises contain or may contain asbestos and be aware of potential risks to their health unless precautions are taken.

FIGURE 3.29: Damaged asbestos lagging

(Hartley)

The CAW Regulations 2002 introduced an explicit duty to manage asbestos in non-domestic premises (regulation 4). This requirement applies to all non-domestic premises and became enforceable in May 2004. Duty-holders include those who have responsibility for controlling the maintenance and/or repair of non-domestic premises. This new 'duty to manage' aims to protect workers engaged in such tasks and the duty-holder will be required to:

- take reasonable steps to find asbestos in premises and to make a record of its location and condition;
- assess the risk arising from any asbestos installation and to prepare a risk management plan; and
- provide information on the location and condition of the material to anyone who is liable to disturb it.

Extensive guidance has been provided on the management of asbestos in non-domestic premises (HSC 2002b, HSE 2002b), together with other information targeting building maintenance and associated trades (HSE 2001a). In addition, there is detailed advice on surveying premises for asbestos-containing materials (HSE 2001b) and the application of asbestos exposure limits (HSE 2001c).

Ventilation

Since ventilation is a very important control measure for airborne contaminants in the occupational environment, the provision of ventilation systems will be discussed in detail. The principal types of ventilation systems and their design, application and maintenance are considered below. For convenience, this subject is divided into local exhaust ventilation and dilution ventilation. (For dilution ventilation, see page 140.)

Local exhaust ventilation

These systems remove the airborne contaminant close to its source of generation. A basic LEV system, as shown in Figure 3.30, usually has the following components:

1. An air collection device such as an enclosure or a hood. This is a collection point for gathering the contaminated air into the system.
2. Ducting to transport the extracted air through the system to the air-purifying device and ultimately to the outside atmosphere.
3. An air cleaner, which will be determined by the nature of the contaminant.
4. A fan, which provides the means for moving air through the system.
5. A discharge point to release air into the atmosphere.

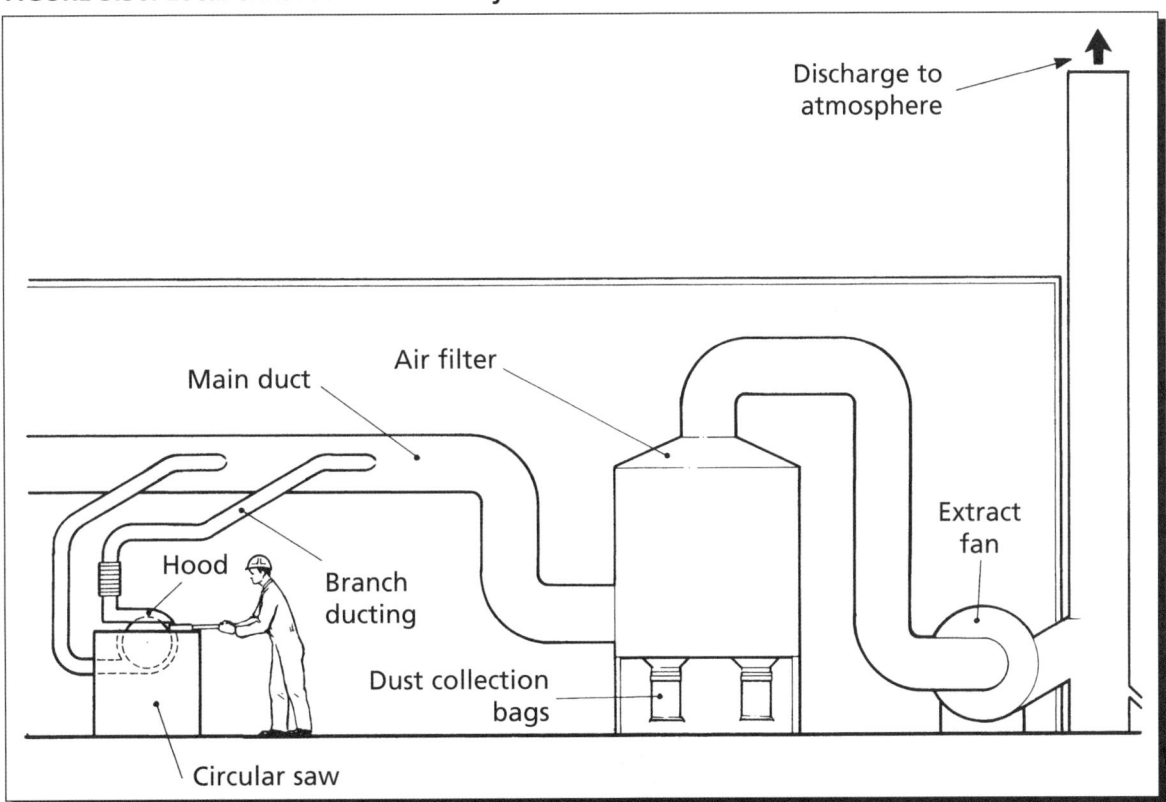

FIGURE 3.30: Local exhaust ventilation system

(HSE 1987 – rev. 2002)

Based on air collector design, local exhaust systems can be broadly divided into two groups: receptor and captor systems. This is summarised in Figure 3.31.

Receptor systems

Receptor systems are illustrated in Figure 3.32, where the left-hand diagram represents an enclosure (fume cupboard) and the right-hand diagram represents a receptor hood. Contaminant enters the receptor air collector of its own volition and the airflow generated by the system is to prevent the escape of contaminants into the work area. In quiet, ambient conditions, an inward airflow velocity of $0.5 ms^{-1}$ may be sufficient. However, where there is more potential for turbulence in the ambient environment, then an inward airflow of at least $1 ms^{-1}$ is required. In some difficult conditions, values in excess of $2 ms^{-1}$ may be required (BOHS 1991).

CHEMICAL AGENTS

FIGURE 3.31: Types of LEV system by collection device

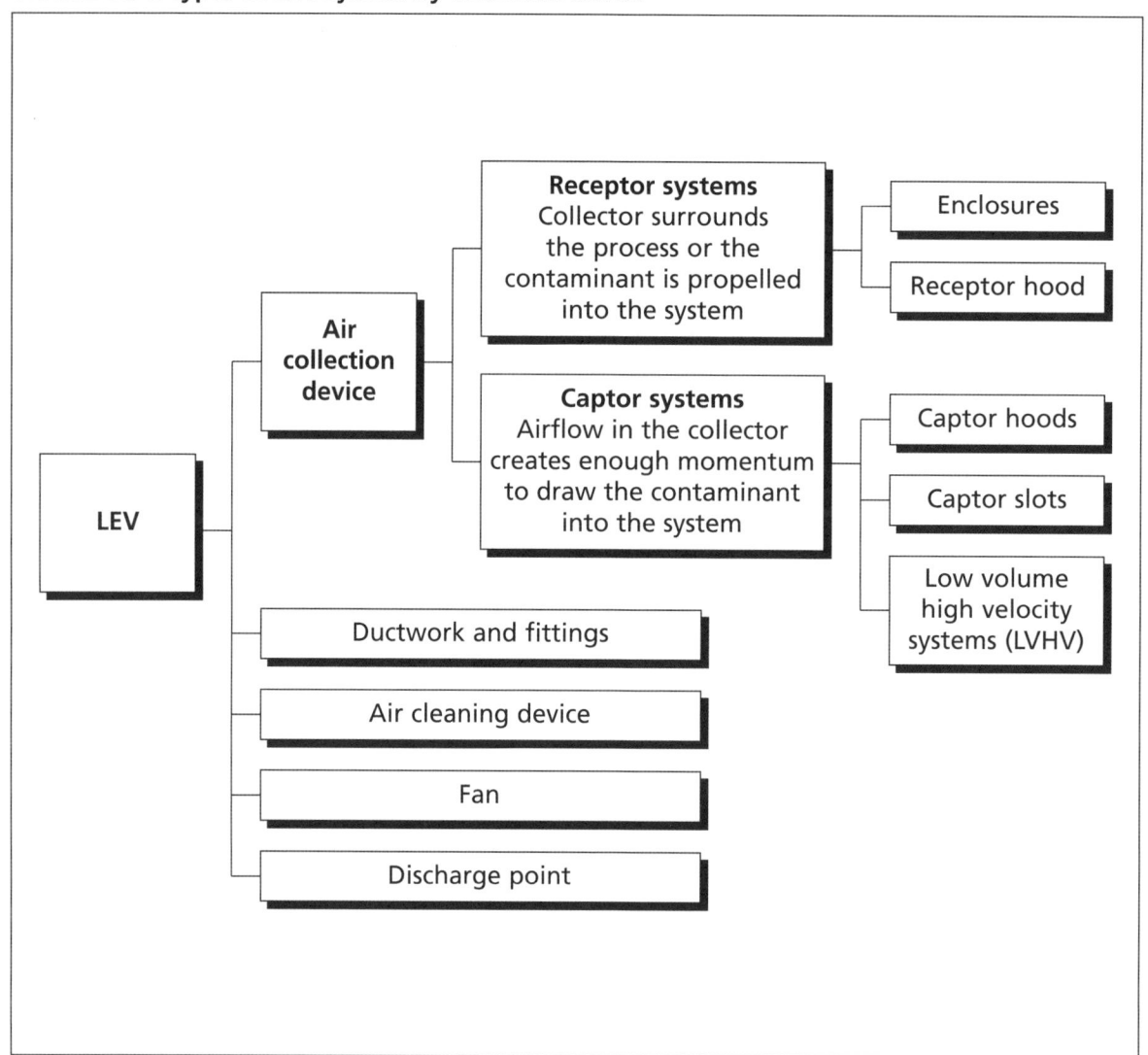

```
LEV ─┬─ Air collection device ─┬─ Receptor systems: Collector surrounds the process or the contaminant is propelled into the system ─┬─ Enclosures
     │                         │                                                                                                      └─ Receptor hood
     │                         └─ Captor systems: Airflow in the collector creates enough momentum to draw the contaminant into the system ─┬─ Captor hoods
     │                                                                                                                                       ├─ Captor slots
     │                                                                                                                                       └─ Low volume high velocity systems (LVHV)
     ├─ Ductwork and fittings
     ├─ Air cleaning device
     ├─ Fan
     └─ Discharge point
```

FIGURE 3.32: Receptor systems – Enclosure and receptor hood

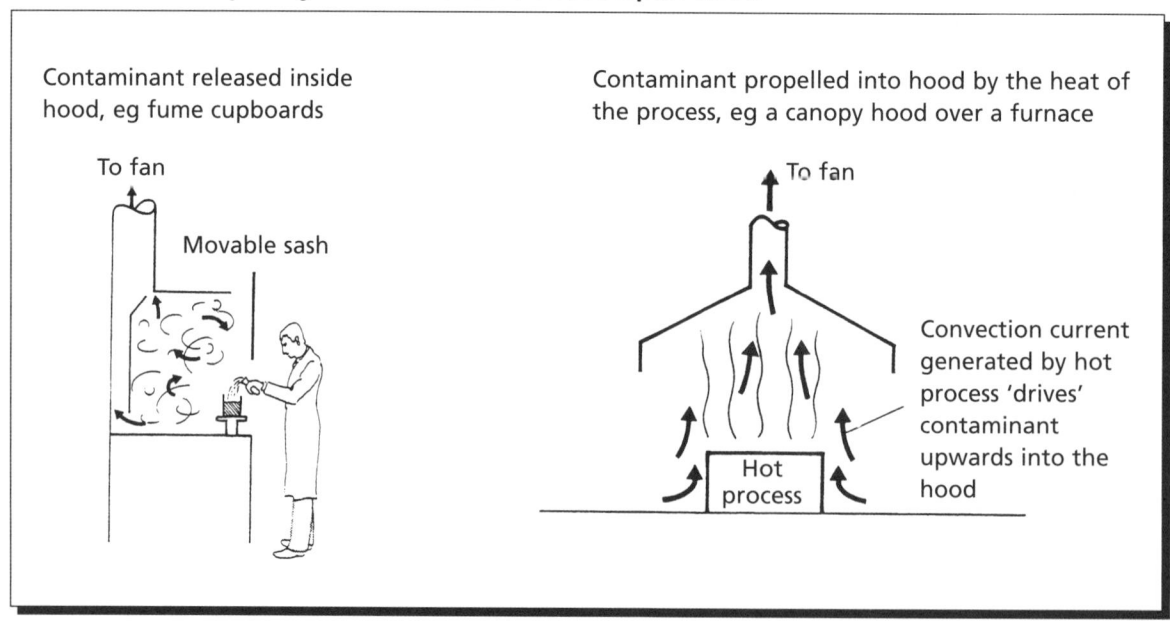

Contaminant released inside hood, eg fume cupboards

Contaminant propelled into hood by the heat of the process, eg a canopy hood over a furnace

Convection current generated by hot process 'drives' contaminant upwards into the hood

(BOHS 1991)

Captor systems

In this case, air flows into the system having 'captured' the contaminant at some point outside the system. To be effective, the rate of airflow into the hood must be capable of capturing the contaminant at its furthest point of generation (see Figure 3.33).

CHEMICAL AGENTS

FIGURE 3.33: Side draught captor hood

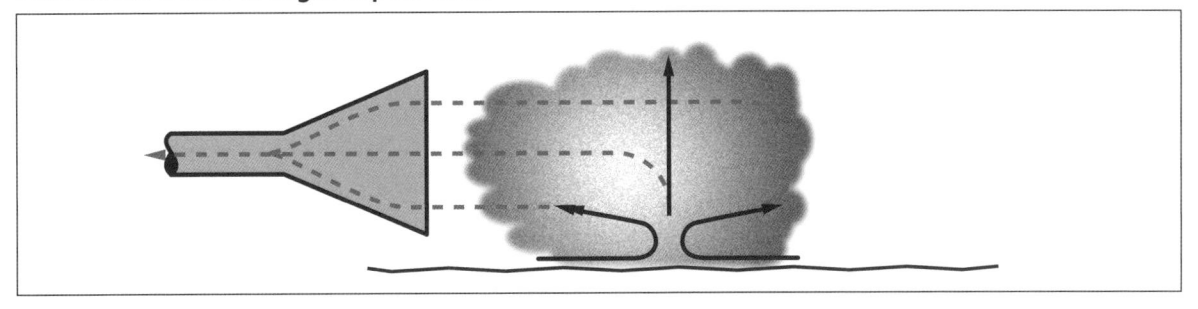

Captor hoods (Figure 3.34) or captor slots[20] (Figure 3.35) are placed either over the process or at the side, depending on the degree of access required.

FIGURE 3.34: Captor hoods

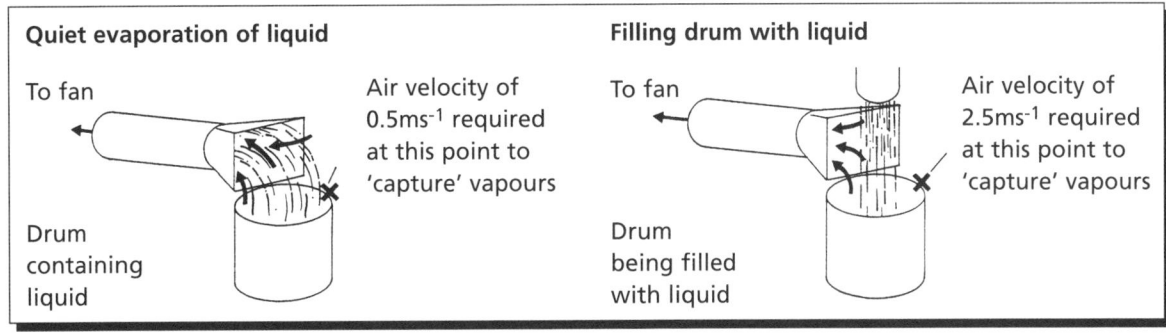

Quiet evaporation of liquid
- To fan
- Air velocity of 0.5ms^{-1} required at this point to 'capture' vapours
- Drum containing liquid

Filling drum with liquid
- To fan
- Air velocity of 2.5ms^{-1} required at this point to 'capture' vapours
- Drum being filled with liquid

(BOHS 1991)

Captor slots may be used for contaminant collection where it is not possible for practical reasons to use hoods. These are commonly used on vapour degreasing tanks where a high degree of access is required, together with extraction over a large surface area.

FIGURE 3.35: Captor slots and hood

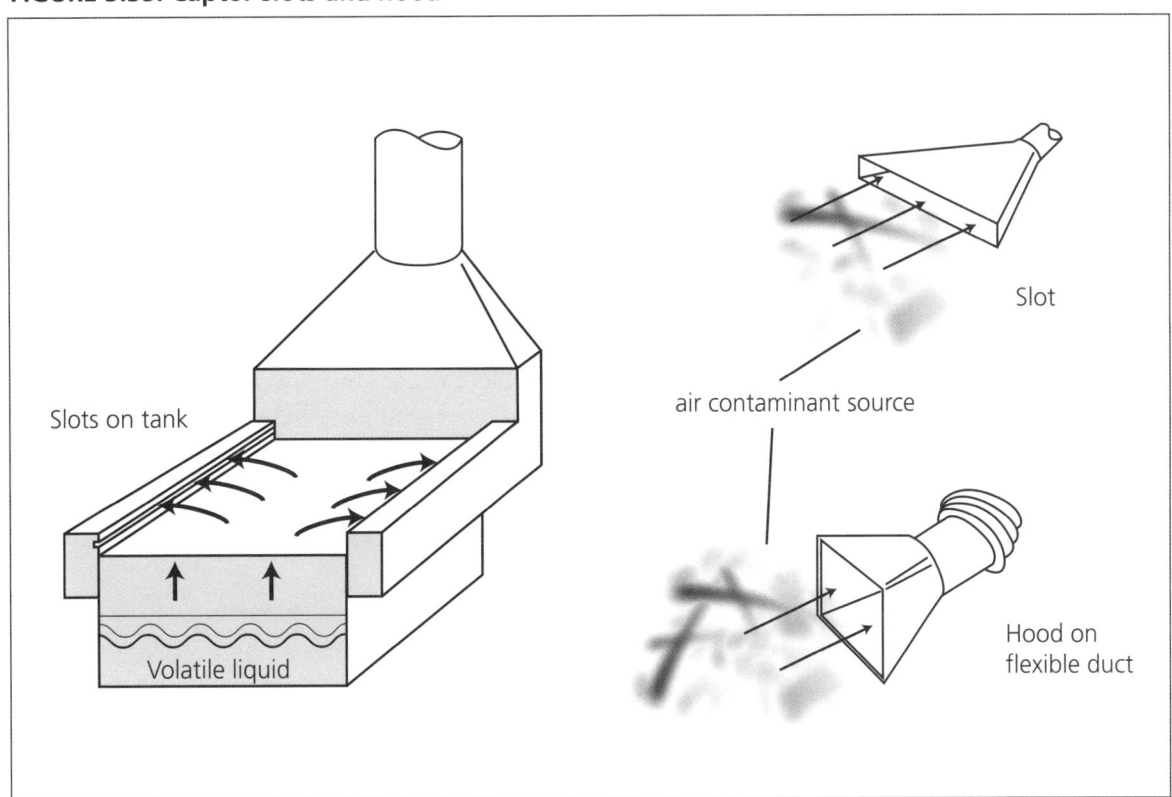

---

[20]Where the aspect ratio (width:length) of the captor hood is less than 0.2, these are called captor 'slots'.

'Capture velocity' is defined as the air velocity required at the source of contaminant emission which is sufficient to move pollutant to the mouth of the extract in order to be successfully captured by the system. Thus, this is the air velocity which the LEV system must generate at this emission point in order to be effective. In a given situation, the required capture velocity depends on the nature of the airborne contaminant and the process by which it is generated. Typical capture velocities for generation of a range of contaminants under specified conditions are listed in Table 3.14. Figure 3.34 illustrates the application of captor hoods and the requirement for different capture velocities under differing contaminant generation conditions. Correct siting of captor hoods is vital, since air velocity decreases very rapidly with distance from the hood. At a distance of one hood diameter from the hood, the air velocity reduces to one-tenth of face velocity. Furthermore, it is also very important to prevent the operator getting into the induced pathway of contaminated air, that is, the area between the emission source and the captor hood.

TABLE 3.14: Capture velocity

Source conditions	Examples	Capture velocity (ms^{-1})
Released into still air with no velocity	Degreasing tanks, still air drying	0.25–0.5
Released with low velocity into a slow airstream	Container filling, sieving, debagging, welding	0.5–1.0
Released at moderate velocity into highly turbulent air	Paint spraying, crushing	1.0–2.5
Released at high velocity into highly turbulent air	Grinding, fettling, abrasive blasting	2.5–10

(Adapted from Gill 1995)

The art of designing captor systems is to achieve the capture velocity required in a given situation, while minimising the total volume of air entering the system. This is because of the costly requirement for heated replacement air. The quantity of air passing through a system is the product of the area of the opening and the velocity of the air entering it. For example, where air at a velocity of $1ms^{-1}$ is extracted through a hood opening with an area of $1m^2$, there is a replacement air requirement for $1m^3 s^{-1}$.

Application of flanges

Normally, the work process is sited in front of the hood and a large volume of air will be drawn (inefficiently, in process control terms) from behind the hood. The addition of flanges, that is, a projecting flat rim or collar, to the hood or slot significantly decreases the quantity of air drawn from behind and in addition creates smoother airflow conditions. When added, flanges increase air velocity very significantly in front of the hood and Figure 3.36 illustrates the savings in total volume flow of air required for a system. Where possible, therefore, captor hoods should be converted into receptor hoods through the addition of sides and flanges.

Low volume high velocity (LVHV) captor systems

Dust particles given off by high speed grinding machines or pneumatic chipping tools require very high capture velocities. One way of achieving these high capture velocities at the point of emission is to extract via small apertures very close to the source of contaminant. By this method, high velocities can be achieved with relatively low air volume flow rates. This approach has been used with portable hand tools, for example grinders, and with welding guns as illustrated in Figure 3.37. Volume flow rates required with such a system are $0.0166–0.028 m^3 s^{-1}$ with duct transport velocities of $25–34 ms^{-1}$. With on-gun welding extraction, a high-vacuum suction hose is attached to the gun and extracts fumes and inert gas through an inlet with a small cross-section. These systems are not common, although

FIGURE 3.36: Effect of flanges on volume flow requirements

	Airflow required to give effective control		Saving compared to (a)
	$m^3 s^{-1}$	cfm	
(a) Plain extract opening above bench 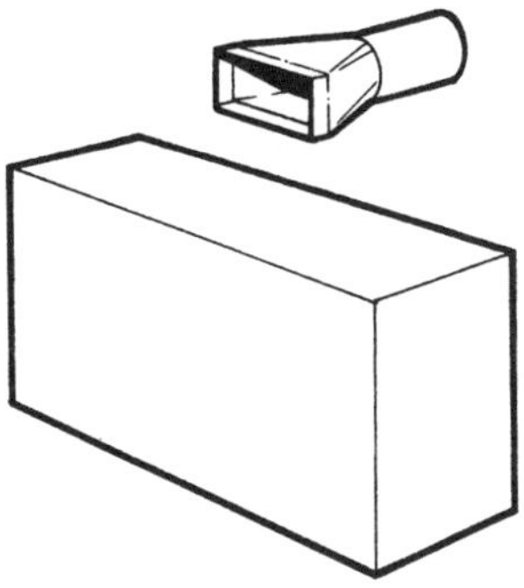	0.8	1,700	–
(b) Flange added at rear of bench 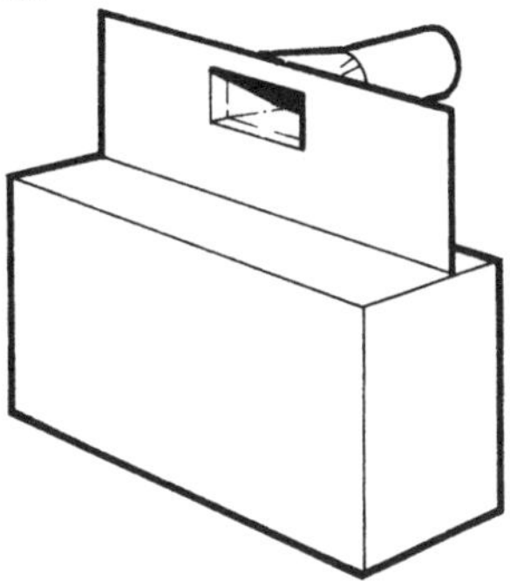	0.62	1,300	22%
(c) Enclosure extended at sides and above bench 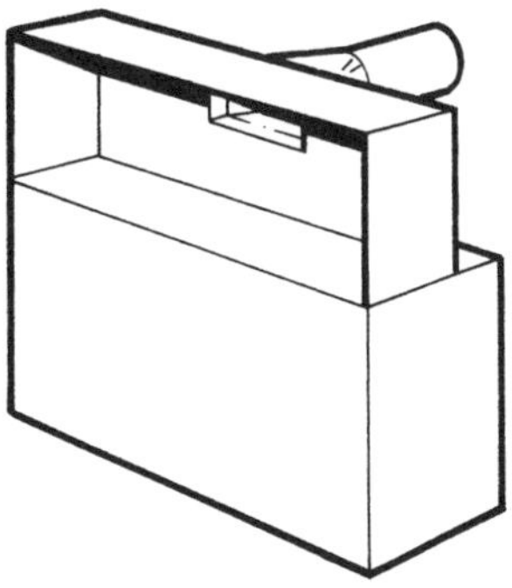	0.59	1,250	26%
(d) Transparent screen added at front of enclosure 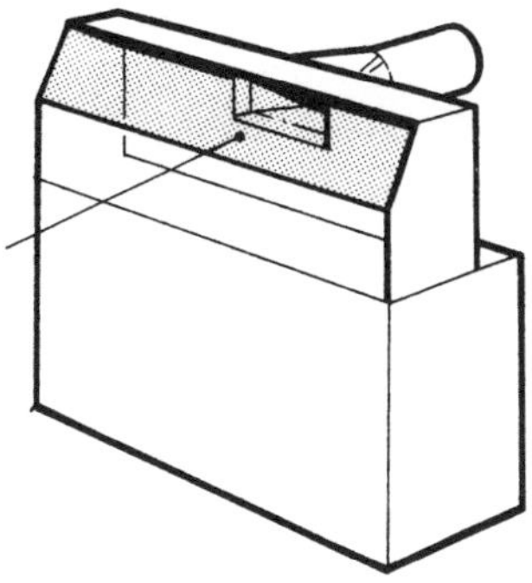 Transparent screen	0.32	680	61%

(HSE 1987 – rev. 2002)

CHEMICAL AGENTS

they are potentially very useful, for example, for work where access is restricted and conventional hoods are too bulky. However, they must be correctly adjusted and require a high standard of maintenance to remain effective.

FIGURE 3.37: Welding gun LVHV

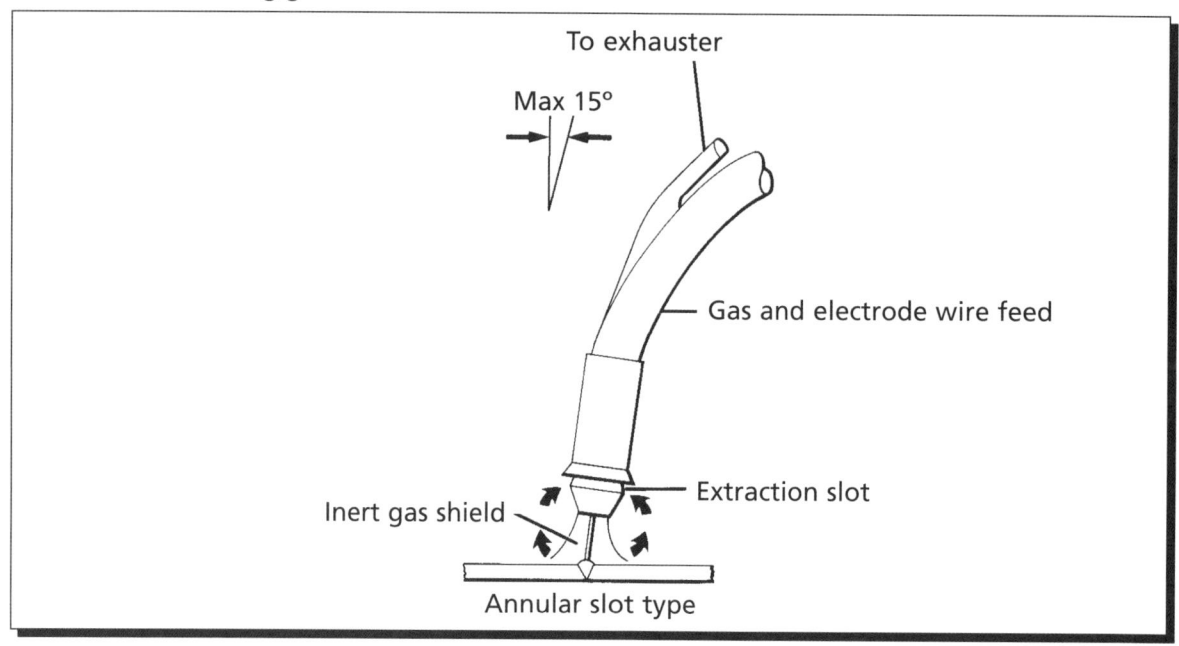

(HSE 1990)

Ducts and fittings

In a ventilation system, air is transported through ducting and normally there are bends and changes of direction to suit the needs of a particular installation and building. The transport velocity is the minimum air velocity required in all parts of the system, including ductwork and extraction devices, to ensure that contamination remains airborne and is, therefore, not deposited on the internal surfaces of the system. Transport velocities for selected air contaminants are given in Table 3.15.

TABLE 3.15: Transport velocity

Pollutant	Transport velocity (ms^{-1})
Fumes – zinc or aluminium	7 to 10
Fine dust – cotton fly, flour, fine powders	10 to 12.5
Industrial dust – asbestos, silica, grinding dust, cement	17.5 to 20
Heavy moist dust – lead, paint spray	Greater than 22.5

(Adapted from Gill 1995)

In each section of a ventilation system, the extracted air loses energy to overcome friction resulting from its passage through the ducting, air cleaners and other obstructions. The fan, which is the driving force for the whole system, has to compensate for this loss of energy. At the design stage, the energy loss for each section of a proposed system, expressed as a pressure drop, is calculated in order to determine the size and duty (capability) of the required fan. To minimise energy losses, sharp bends and sudden changes in duct diameter should be avoided in system design. Ducting is normally made from galvanised steel, but stainless steel, brick, fibreglass and plastics are also sometimes used.

Air cleaning devices

Contaminated air extracted from workplaces usually requires cleaning before it is discharged into the atmosphere and many types of device have been developed for this purpose. The air cleaning device is normally sited in front of the fan in the system, thus providing some degree of protection for it from, for example, corrosive or abrasive dusts. The different types of air cleaning devices are summarised in Figure 3.38.

CHEMICAL AGENTS

FIGURE 3.38: Summary of air cleaning devices

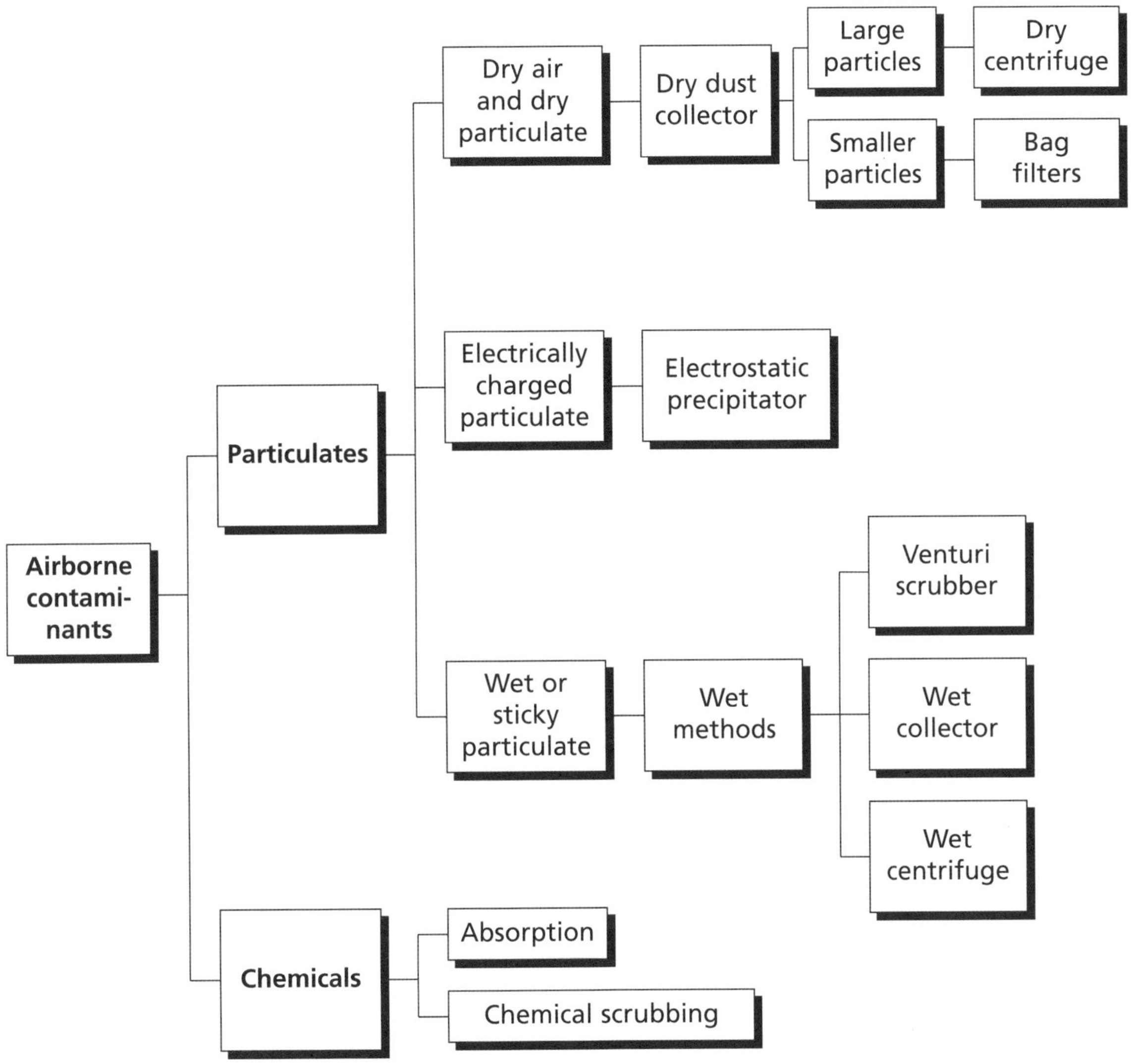

```
Airborne contaminants
├── Particulates
│   ├── Dry air and dry particulate ── Dry dust collector
│   │   ├── Large particles ── Dry centrifuge
│   │   └── Smaller particles ── Bag filters
│   ├── Electrically charged particulate ── Electrostatic precipitator
│   └── Wet or sticky particulate ── Wet methods
│       ├── Venturi scrubber
│       ├── Wet collector
│       └── Wet centrifuge
└── Chemicals
    ├── Absorption
    └── Chemical scrubbing
```

Dry dust collectors

It is common to use filters to clean air in ventilation and air-conditioning systems (Figures 3.39 and 3.40). These filters are designed to process high volumes of air with low-flow resistance. Special high resistance, high efficiency (HEPA) filters are used where there are hazardous dusts, for example, asbestos and in very highly controlled environments such as clean rooms.

CHEMICAL AGENTS

FIGURE 3.39: In-line air filter

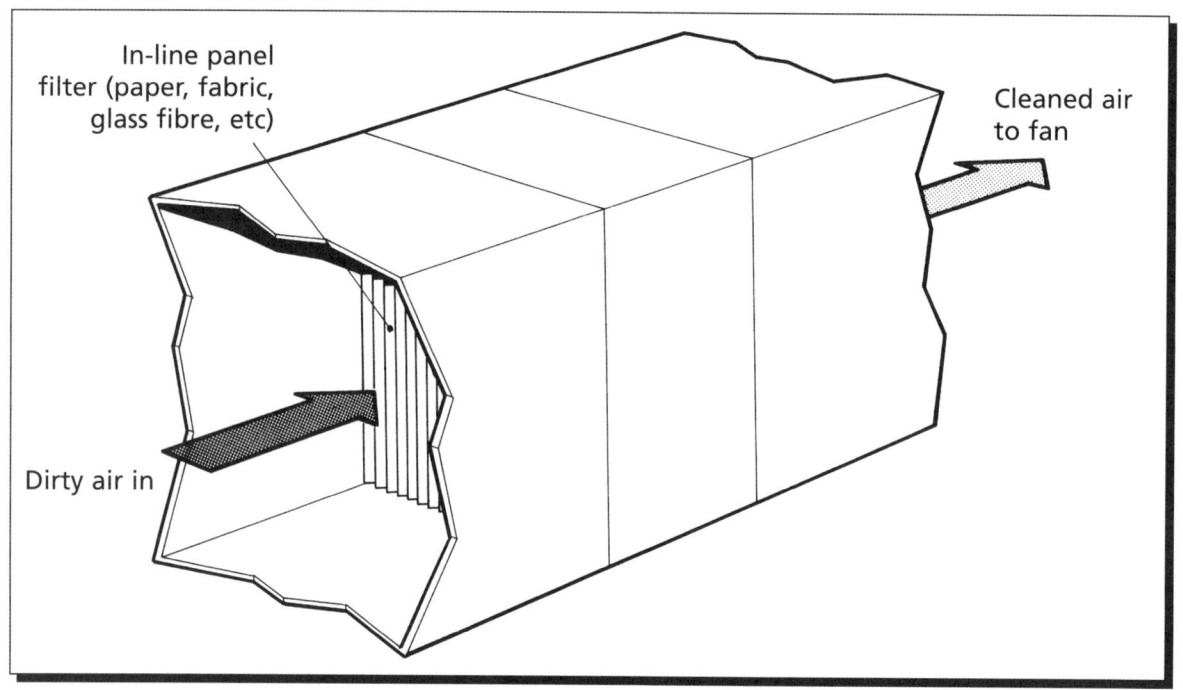

- In-line panel filter (paper, fabric, glass fibre, etc)
- Cleaned air to fan
- Dirty air in

(HSE 1987 – rev. 2002)

FIGURE 3.40: Bag filter

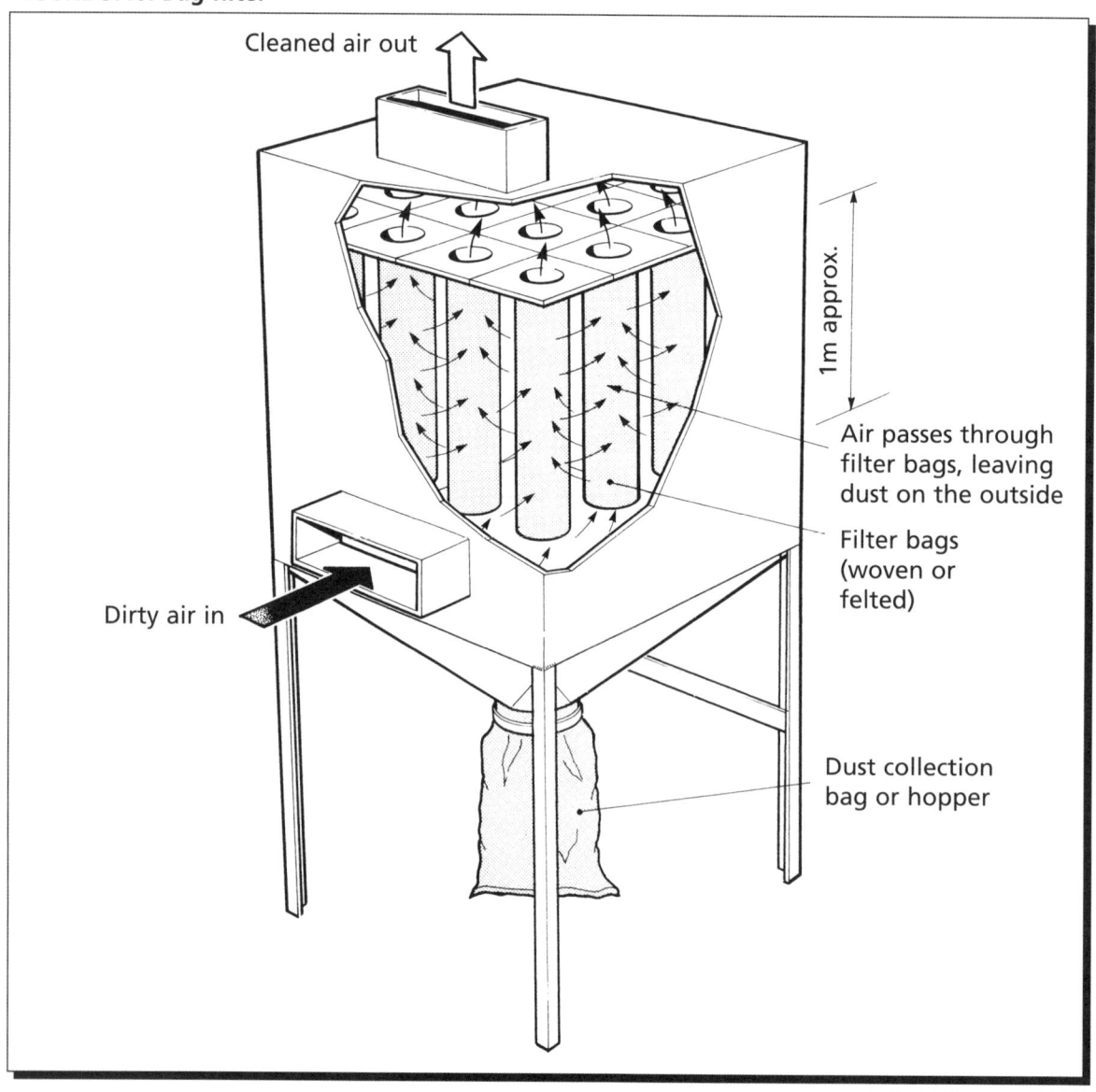

- Cleaned air out
- 1m approx.
- Air passes through filter bags, leaving dust on the outside
- Filter bags (woven or felted)
- Dirty air in
- Dust collection bag or hopper

(HSE 1987 – rev. 2002)

The cyclone is a dry centrifugal filtering device. Air enters the device tangentially as shown in Figure 3.41, and the centrifugal force generated throws the dust particles outwards. The dust particles fall into a hopper at the bottom of the cyclone and the cleaned air leaves via an exit at the top of the chamber. Typical dust collection efficiencies are 40 to 70 per cent for particles around 5µm in diameter (HSE 1993a).

FIGURE 3.41: Cyclone air cleaner

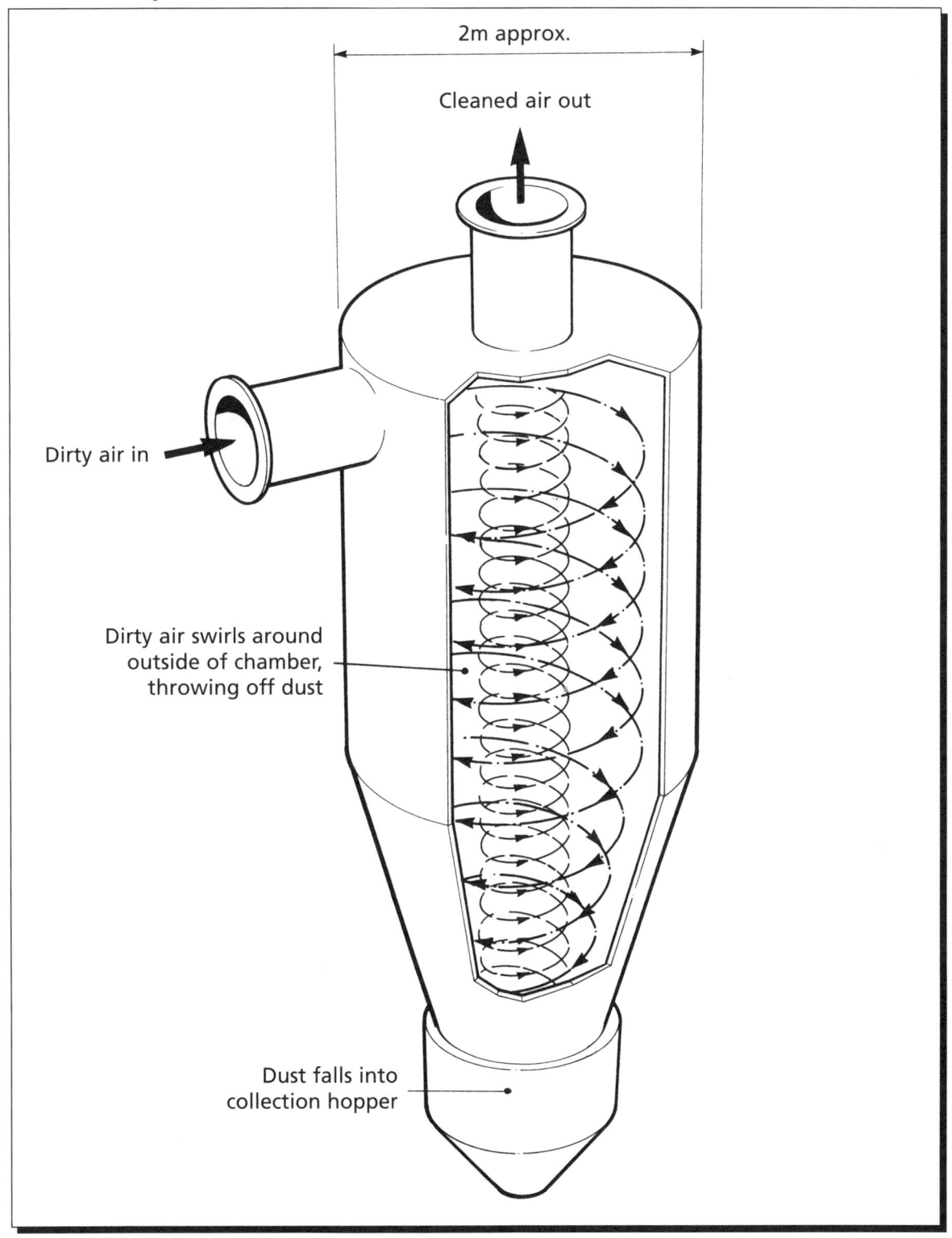

(HSE 1987 – rev. 2002)

Electrostatic precipitator
The electrostatic precipitator (Figure 3.42) induces an electrical charge on dust and fume particles. These particles are then collected on surfaces within the device with an opposing charge. Reported collection efficiencies are 92 to 98 per cent for particles around 5µm in diameter. This type of air cleaner has a high efficiency for fine dusts, mists and fumes from either hot or cold gases (Roach 1992).

CHEMICAL AGENTS

FIGURE 3.42: Electrostatic precipitator

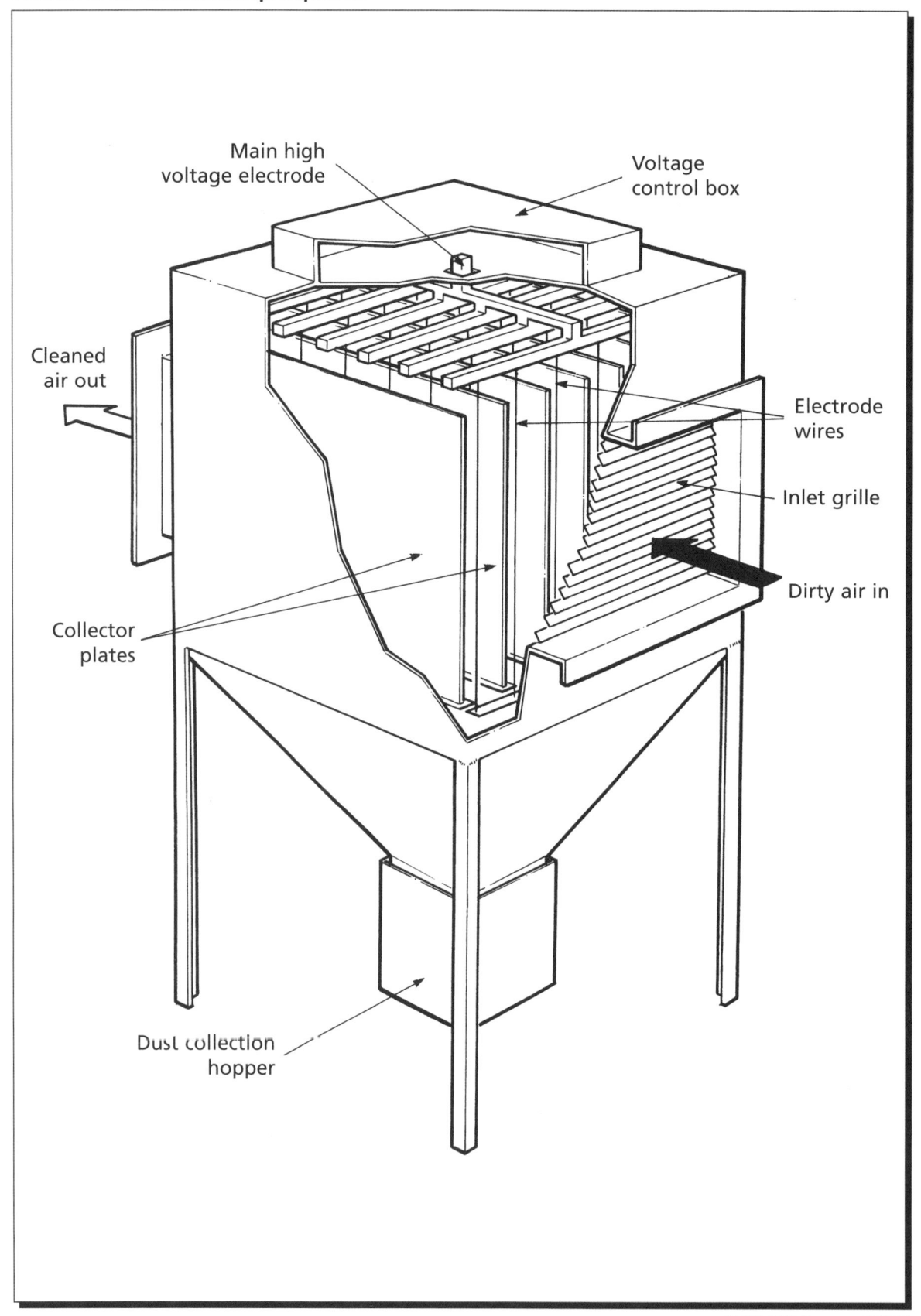

(HSE 1987 – rev. 2002)

Wet methods

With the venturi scrubber (Figure 3.43), dust passes through the inlet and water is injected. Highly turbulent conditions in the inlet break the water down into droplets, which associate with the dust particles. The dust-laden water droplets then separate out in a chamber, as in the cyclone. Water and sludge, from the dust, collect at the bottom of the separator, while clean air passes out at the exit as shown. Typical collection efficiencies are around 96 per cent for particles around 5μm in diameter.

FIGURE 3.43: Venturi scrubber

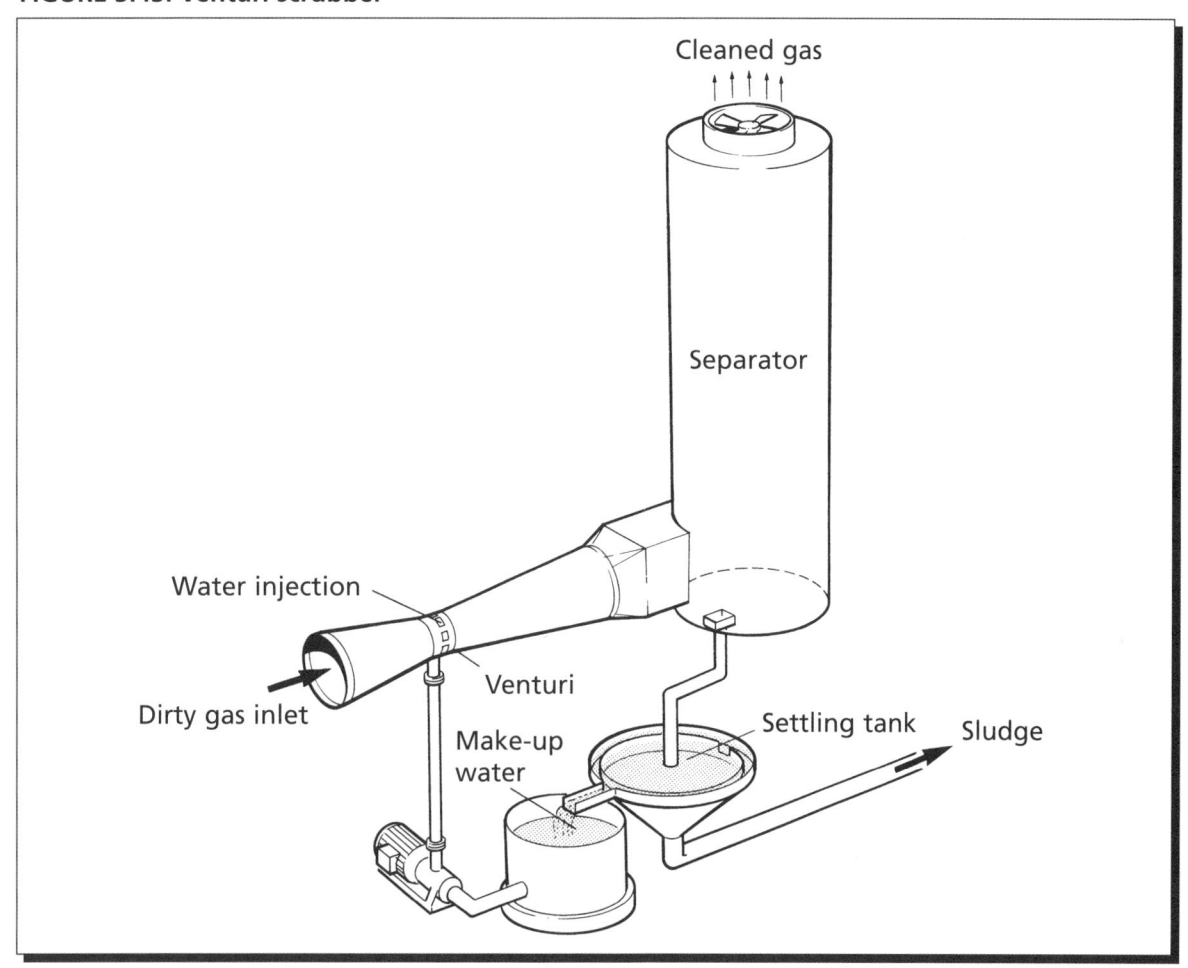

(HSE 1987 – rev. 2002)

Chemical methods (absorption and adsorption)

In absorption, the gas or vapour dissolves into a liquid medium in the trapping vessel as the air is bubbled through it. It may or may not react with the trapping medium. Intimate contact between the air and absorbent medium is required and the contaminated air must be broken down into very small bubbles. Many organic vapours can be collected on solid adsorbents such as activated charcoal and silica gel. This type of collector is sometimes used in local exhaust ventilation systems where air is recirculated, for example, in some laboratory fume cupboards.

Fans

The fan provides the means of moving air through the LEV system and there are many different types and sizes of fan. With fans of a similar design, relative performance depends on their diameter and the speed of rotation. A fan consists of two fundamental components:

1. The impeller (driver) which rotates on a shaft.
2. The casing which guides air to and from the impeller.

There are three basic types of fan:

1. Propeller.
2. Axial.
3. Centrifugal.

Propeller

These are usually used in general ventilation applications and they are not suitable for use with ductwork or for air filtration. Propeller fans may be used in air cooling and may be wall-mounted. According to Gill (1995), they have relatively low power and low efficiency (55 per cent), although aerofoil blades fitted to larger devices may increase efficiency to around 70 per cent.

CHEMICAL AGENTS

Axial

Axial fans (Figure 3.44) have a cylindrical casing, are compact and fit readily into ducting. However, they generate high noise levels particularly at high running speeds and silencers are often necessary. Downstream guide vanes streamline airflow and increase efficiency. The efficiency of axial fans can be up to 78 per cent (Gill 1995). Since the fan motor is positioned within the airstream, these devices should not be used where the air is at a high temperature or contains dusts or corrosive chemicals.

FIGURE 3.44: Axial fan

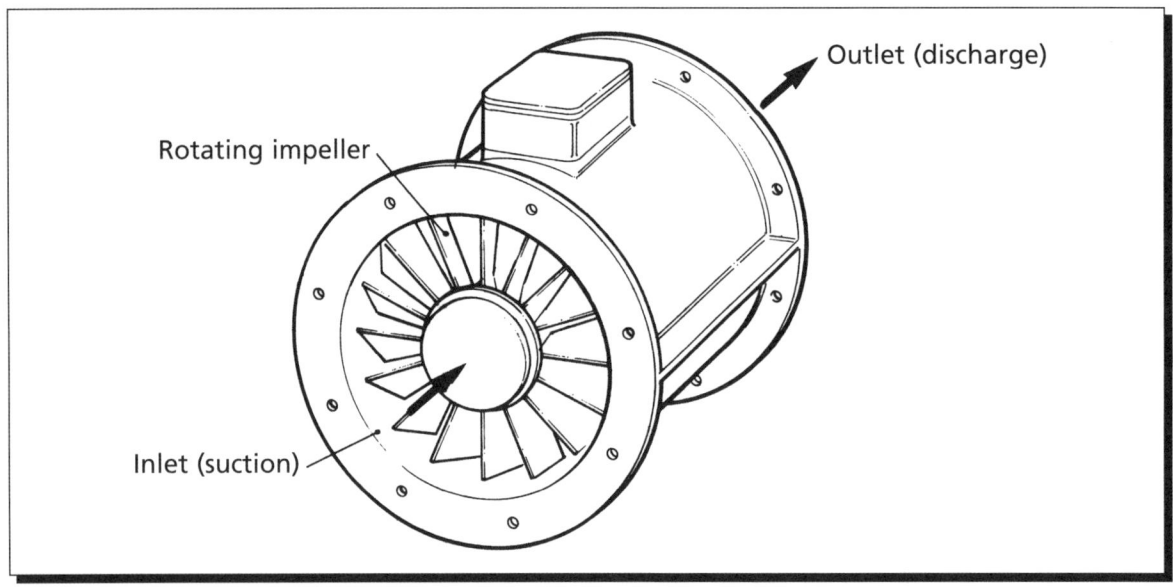

(HSE 1987 – rev. 2002)

Centrifugal

There are forward-bladed, backward-bladed and radial-bladed centrifugal fans. The radial-bladed type is most common. Air is drawn into the centre of the impeller and is collected by the rotating blades and thrown off at high velocity into the fan casing (see Figure 3.45). The casing collects the air and guides it towards the discharge outlet. Centrifugal fans can deliver the required airflow against high resistance and are the most common type of fan found in LEV systems. Efficiencies of up to 85 per cent have been reported where aerofoil blades are used on larger fans. Radial-bladed centrifugal fans may be used with abrasive dusts and corrosive chemicals and although the blades wear out quickly, they can be easily replaced.

FIGURE 3.45: Centrifugal fan

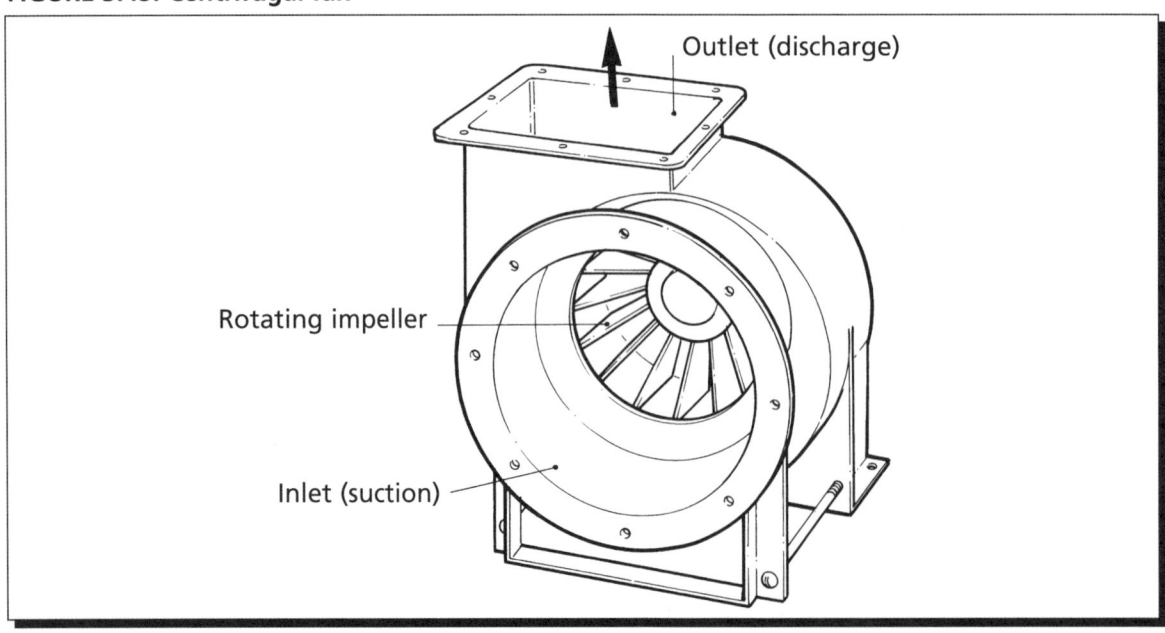

(HSE 1987 – rev. 2002)

CHEMICAL AGENTS

Discharge

The behaviour of the airstream close to the entry and the exit of the LEV system is very different. As illustrated in Figure 3.46, the discharge end of the system has a much greater influence, that is, causes much more disturbance of air in the surrounding environment than the air inlet side. This means it is important that careful consideration should be given to the positioning of discharge points. It is not uncommon to find them sited close to inlet points resulting in recycling of contaminants back into the workplace. Furthermore, discharge points should be positioned high enough above the building line, so that efficient mixing with the atmosphere is achieved. This can mean extending discharge stacks up to a height of three metres or more above the height of the building. In addition, where ductwork is sited outside a building, it should be of a robust construction and well supported in order to withstand wind and weather conditions. Because of its position and exposure, the discharge stack will need to be regularly inspected and maintained to ensure it is kept in good repair. Where discharge points are unavoidably positioned at a relatively low level, care must be taken to ensure that the discharge point does not blow air at passers-by.

FIGURE 3.46: Airflow disturbance at discharge

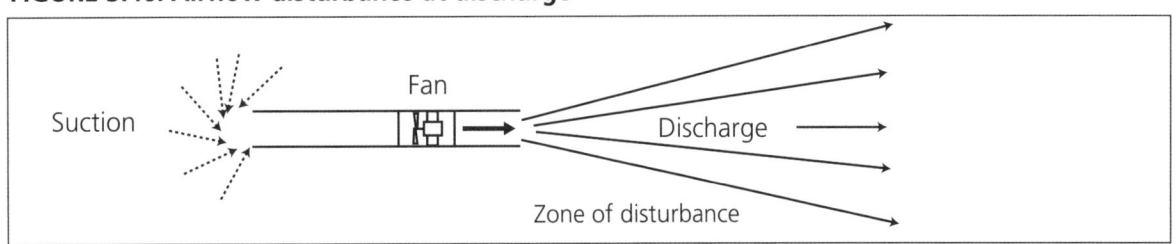

Devices such as weather caps are not recommended since they impede the upward momentum of discharged air and may deflect this air downwards for possible re-entry into the building (top diagram, Figure 3.47). Care should also be taken to take account of local wind effects resulting in the blowback of contaminants through the ductwork.

FIGURE 3.47: Discharge design

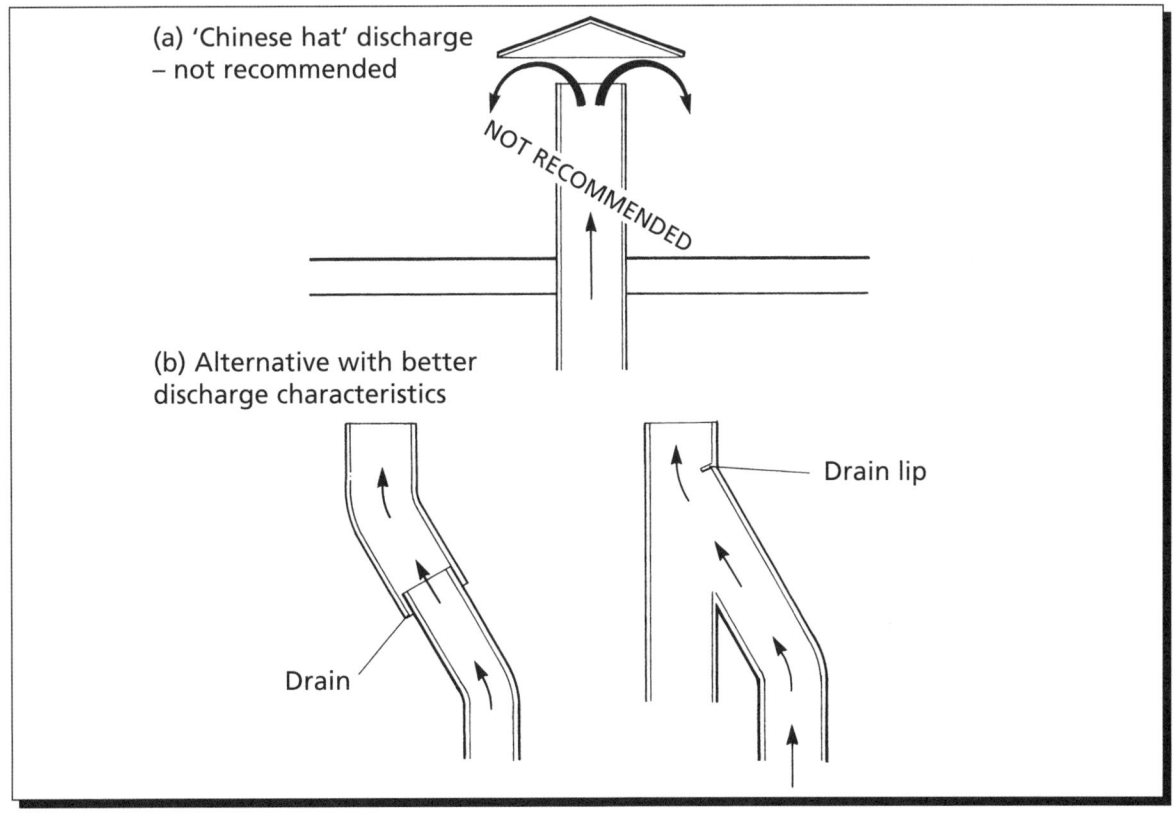

(HSE 1987 – rev. 2002)

Design of LEV systems

The basic components and types of local exhaust ventilation systems have been outlined above. However, designing LEV systems which will collect contaminant efficiently and reliably on a continuing basis is a complex and difficult task. To apply effective controls, it is first necessary to study how exposure arises. In a given situation, all emission sources need to be identified and prioritised, based on their relative contribution to worker exposure. Where exposures are significant, this will involve air contaminant monitoring and studying work processes and tasks. Piney (1985) suggests a simplified design approach, which has been adapted in Figure 3.48. From this diagram, it can be seen that there are several stages to be considered before the LEV option is decided on for controlling airborne pollutants. Commonly observed errors in LEV design are listed below.

In actual practice, Piney (1985) considers the following to be common errors in LEV design:

1. The design and position of the hood is based on misconceptions of how aerosols and gas/air mixtures travel in air.
2. Important exposure sources are left uncontrolled and continue to contribute significantly to exposure.
3. Restricted influence of captor hoods not appreciated – hood is positioned too far from the source of contaminant or the hood is too small.
4. Hood does not surround the process sufficiently.
5. Airflow rate is inadequate for various reasons.
6. Process-induced or extraneous draughts reduce hood efficiency.
7. LEV system does not withstand imposed duty.
8. System is not designed for ease of maintenance.
9. Exposure reduction is not assessed.
10. System is not regularly tested and maintained and its performance deteriorates unnoticed.

Evaluating the performance of ventilation systems

In addition to a well-designed LEV system, there is a requirement for a high and continuing level of performance. Regulation 9 of COSHH requires that engineering controls, in this case, LEV systems, be maintained in efficient working order and good repair. Furthermore, thorough examination and tests are required at least once every 14 months. The intended operating performance must be specified, together with an indication as to whether the plant still achieves this level of operation.

In order to evaluate ventilation system performance, the following tasks need to be carried out:

- measurement of air velocity;
- measurement of air volume flow rates;
- measurement of pressures at various points in the system; and
- observation of air movement characteristics.

There is a need to answer the following questions:

1. Are airborne contaminants successfully captured near to their point of release?
2. To what extent do current measured values differ from design specification intended values? What are air velocities at different points in the system? What pressure or suction is the fan developing? How much pressure (energy) is lost in different parts of the system? (This may be particularly important at filters or dust collectors.)

Ventilation system pressures

Monitoring ventilation system pressure and its change is an important measure of system performance. A pressure difference is required for air to flow in a ventilation system. Air will flow from areas of high pressure to low pressure. Such pressure differences can be induced either naturally or artificially, for example, a chimney and a fan respectively. Pressure appears in two forms: static pressure and velocity pressure. These are described below:

1. **Static pressure (P_s)** – Static pressure is the pressure exerted in all directions by a stationary fluid (gas or liquid). In a moving fluid, static pressure is measured at right

CHEMICAL AGENTS

FIGURE 3.48: Designing air contaminant control measures

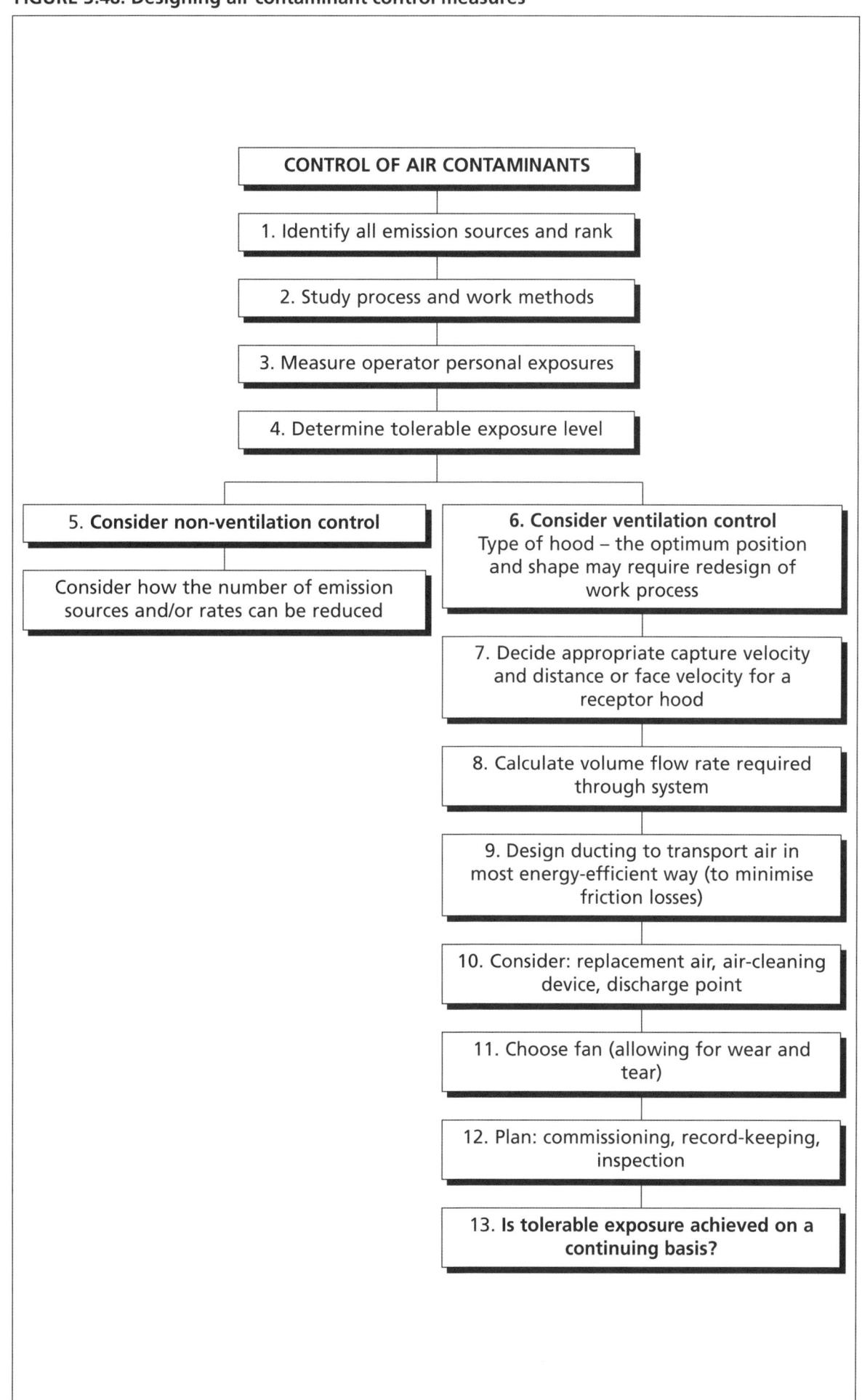

```
CONTROL OF AIR CONTAMINANTS
         │
1. Identify all emission sources and rank
         │
2. Study process and work methods
         │
3. Measure operator personal exposures
         │
4. Determine tolerable exposure level
         │
    ┌────┴─────────────────────┐
5. Consider non-ventilation    6. Consider ventilation control
   control                        Type of hood – the optimum position
                                  and shape may require redesign of
Consider how the number of        work process
emission sources and/or rates              │
can be reduced                  7. Decide appropriate capture velocity
                                   and distance or face velocity for a
                                   receptor hood
                                           │
                                8. Calculate volume flow rate required
                                   through system
                                           │
                                9. Design ducting to transport air in
                                   most energy-efficient way (to minimise
                                   friction losses)
                                           │
                                10. Consider: replacement air, air-cleaning
                                    device, discharge point
                                           │
                                11. Choose fan (allowing for wear and
                                    tear)
                                           │
                                12. Plan: commissioning, record-keeping,
                                    inspection
                                           │
                                13. Is tolerable exposure achieved on a
                                    continuing basis?
```

(Adapted from Piney 1985)

CHEMICAL AGENTS

angles to the direction of flow to eliminate the effects of velocity. Static pressure can be positive or negative with respect to normal atmospheric pressure.

2. **Velocity pressure (P_v)** – Velocity pressure is the kinetic energy of a fluid in motion. It provides the force for the drive of wind.
3. **Total pressure** – This is the sum of the velocity pressure and the static pressure.

In Figure 3.49, the duct pressures generated on both sides of a fan are illustrated. A U-tube is used to measure static, velocity and total pressures.

FIGURE 3.49: Duct pressures

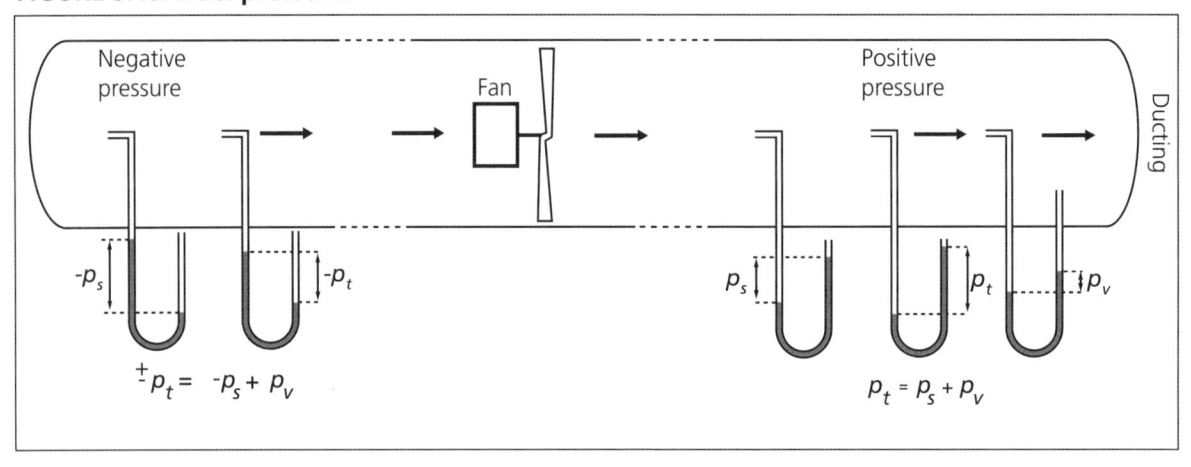

At the suction side of a ventilation system, that is, in front of the fan, the static pressure is negative and after the fan (the discharge side), it is positive. Velocity pressure (P_v) gives the 'push' to move air through the system and this parameter is always positive:

$$P_v = \rho v^2/2$$

(Where: ρ is the density of the air (1.2kgm^{-3} at 760mm pressure); and v is the air velocity.)

This simplifies to: $P_v = 0.6v^2$

(If v is in metres per second, P_v is in Newtons per square metre, ie pascals.)

Volume flow

When a quantity of air is moving within a system or duct, the volume flow rate is calculated using the following formula:

$$Q = vA$$

(Where: v is the average air velocity across the cross-section of the duct; A is the cross-sectional area of the duct; and Q is in cubic metres per second.)

Monitoring equipment

The equipment used for evaluating the performance of a ventilation system includes the following:

1. Pitot-static tube (Figure 3.50) – measures system pressures and air velocity.
2. Rotating vane anemometer (Figure 3.51) – measures air velocity.
3. Hot-wire anemometer (Figure 3.52) – measures air velocity.
4. Dust lamp (Figure 3.53) – traces and visualises airflow patterns.
5. Smoke tube tracers (Figure 3.54) – trace and visualise airflow patterns.

CHEMICAL AGENTS

Pitot-static tube

This measures velocity pressure inside a ventilation system irrespective of the static pressure at the point of measurement. With this instrument, velocity pressure is measured as the height of a column of liquid, which, using a simple equation, can be converted into pressure in pascals. (This equation involves the height of the liquid column in millimetres, the density of the liquid in the tube and a factor for acceleration due to gravity.) The velocity pressure is converted into air velocity using the equation below:

$$P_v = 0.6v^2$$

Measurements should be carried out in a straight section of ducting, with streamlined airflow and minimal turbulence. The measurement position should be at least 10 duct diameters from turbulent structures.

This instrument is sensitive to duct air velocities above $3ms^{-1}$; below this level an alternative method should be used since at low pressures it is difficult to measure the difference in height of the two columns of liquid.

FIGURE 3.50: Measuring velocity pressure with a pitot-static tube

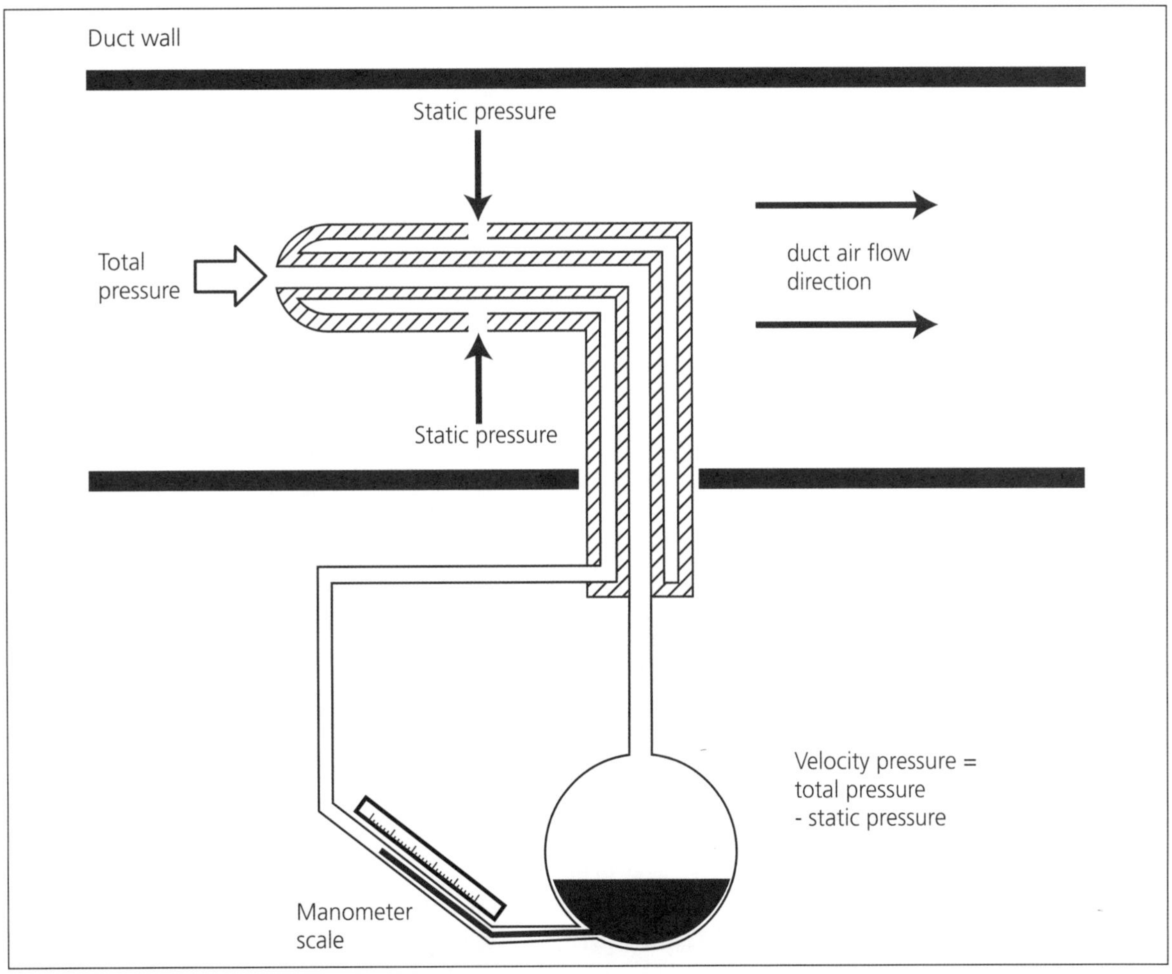

Rotating vane anemometer

This instrument has a rotating vane, which is connected electrically or mechanically to a display dial. In order to avoid errors when using the instrument, the axis of the rotating vane must be parallel to the airstream contours. The intrinsically safe version can be used in flammable atmospheres. This instrument can be used in large ducts, but not in narrow conduits, since vane size ranges from 25mm to 100mm in diameter. Furthermore, it is not advisable to use this instrument in dusty or corrosive atmospheres.

FIGURE 3.51: Rotating vane anemometer

(Airflow Developments Ltd)

Hot-wire anemometer

This uses a hot wire which is either a heated thermocouple or thermistor. The cooling power of the air is converted into an electrical reading and an allowance is made for ambient temperature. The device is non-directional (unless a cowl is fitted) and it can be inserted through a small hole in a ventilation duct to take measurements. It measures over a working range of air velocities from $0.1–30 \text{ms}^{-1}$. This instrument can also be used for measuring atmospheric wind velocity. As with the rotating vane instrument, to avoid errors it is important that the axis of the sensing head cowl is parallel to the airstream contours.

FIGURE 3.52: Hot-wire anemometer

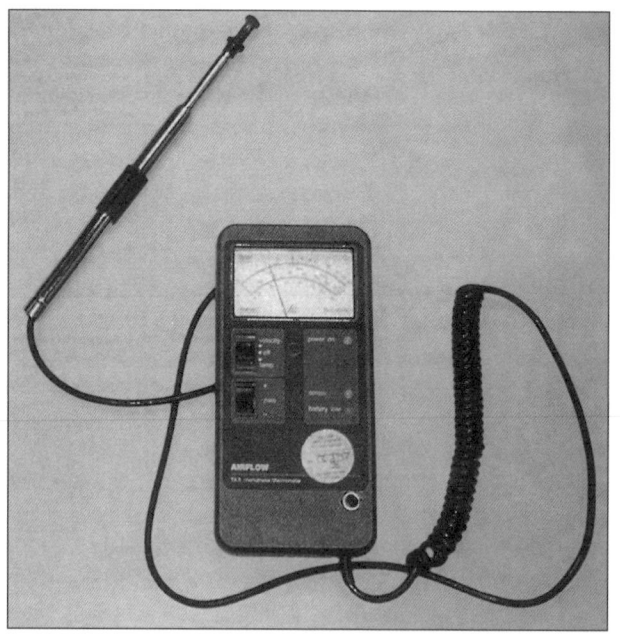

(Airflow Developments Ltd)

With the exception of the pitot-static tube, these wind speed measuring devices, that is, the rotating vane and hot-wire anemometers, will need to be regularly recalibrated against known air velocities in order to avoid errors.

Dust lamp

This instrument is used to visualise the distribution and movement of dust aerosols and was described earlier in this chapter (page 105).

FIGURE 3.53: Polishing stone – very poor dust control with a captor hood (Tyndall illumination)

(HSE 2001d)

This is a very useful and versatile instrument. Many particles of dust are too small to be seen by the naked eye, but when a parallel beam of strong light is shone through a cloud of dust, the particles reflect the light to the observer (forward light scattering).

Although this is not a quantitative method, it does allow the operation of a ventilation system to be directly observed and corrective measures to be taken if necessary. Other direct reading dust monitors (discussed earlier in this chapter) are available and can be similarly used to assess performance.

Smoke tube tracers

These devices produce a plume of smoke when air is forced through them, making it possible to visualise airflow patterns generated by the ventilation system.

FIGURE 3.54: Smoke tube

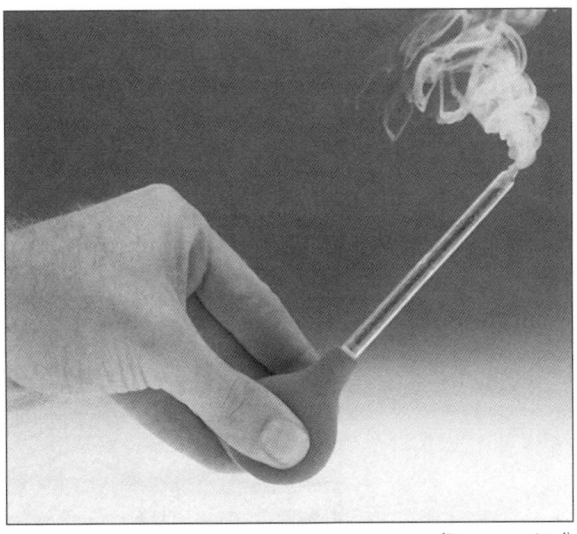

(Draeger Ltd)

Tracer gases, for example, Krypton 85, are used to measure ventilation air change rates in workrooms. (This is described on page 141.)

Predicting ventilation system performance

Rectangular captor hoods (Fletcher method[21])

The aim of captor hood design is to achieve a sufficiently high capture velocity to entrap and control the contaminant, while at the same time extracting a minimal volume of air from the workplace. The

---
[21] For circular hoods, the method of Garrison (1983) can be used.

CHEMICAL AGENTS

nomogram (Figure 3.56), generated by Fletcher (1977), can be used where a rectangular captor hood is required for a particular application.

Following observation of the work process, the following can be determined:
- the size of the contaminant source;
- the desired hood size and shape; and
- the closest distance the hood can be positioned to the source.

Taking into account the momentum of the contaminant at its point of release, a nominal capture velocity can be chosen from Table 3.14 (on page 122). With this information, it is possible to predict the face velocity (at the hood) which will generate the required capture velocity. The total air volume flow rate (Q in m^3s^{-1}) can then be calculated for the system ($Q = V_oA$). (This is step 8 in the LEV design process outlined in Figure 3.48.)

Using Figure 3.55 below as an example, W and L are the width and length of the hood, A is the area of the hood face (ie W x L) and X is the capture distance. V is the capture velocity at Z (distance X from the hood) and V_o is the hood face velocity. The method is as follows:

1. Find W/L and X/$\sqrt{A}$.
2. Using the Fletcher nomogram (Figure 3.56), join these two points with a straight line extended to cross the V/V_o line.
3. Knowing V, then find V_o.
4. Calculate the total volume flow rate required for the system.

Worked example – Calculation of volume flow rate

The objective is to design a hood to serve a welding station (see Figure 3.55). In this process, a lead-coated component is welded to tin in the fabrication of petrol tanks. The welding of lead will produce a fume that needs to be extracted.

The size of the proposed hood is 0.2m x 0.2m; this is to be positioned 0.36m from the source and a capture velocity of $1ms^{-1}$ is required.

1. W/L = 1; A = $0.04m^2$.
2. X/$\sqrt{A}$ = 0.36/0.2 = 1.8.
3. Using the Fletcher nomogram (Figure 3.56), join these two points with a straight extended line; V/V_o = 0.035.
4. Knowing V, then find V_o; here, V_o = 1/0.035 = $28.6ms^{-1}$.
5. Calculate the total volume flow rate required for the system: $Q = V_oA = 28.6 \times 0.04 = 1.14m^3s^{-1}$.

(The volume flow required can be drastically reduced by attaching a flange (Figure 3.36 on page 123).)

FIGURE 3.55: Rectangular captor hood

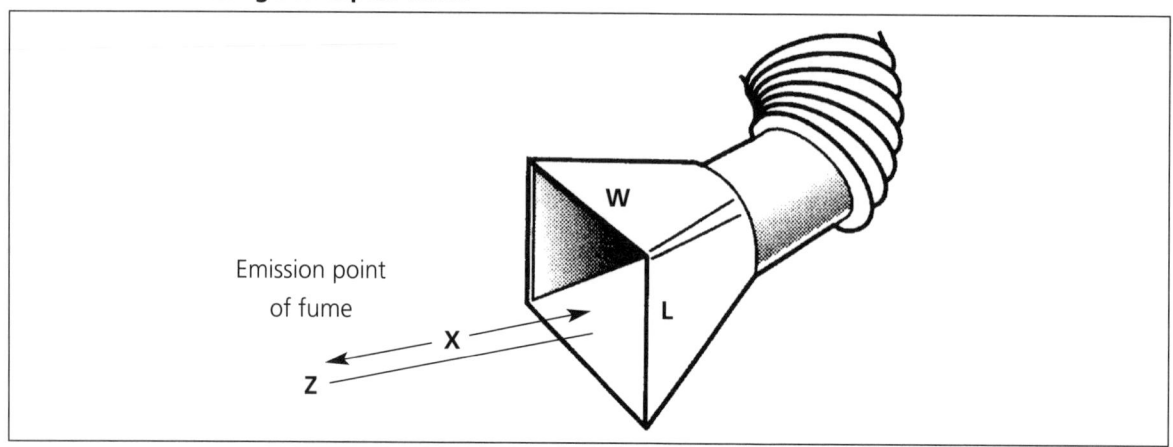

Once the total volume flow rate through the system has been determined, then the LEV designer designs the ducting to minimise friction losses, selects the air cleaner, considers the discharge point and, importantly, selects an appropriate fan to drive the system (see Figure 3.48 on page 133).

FIGURE 3.56: Fletcher nomogram

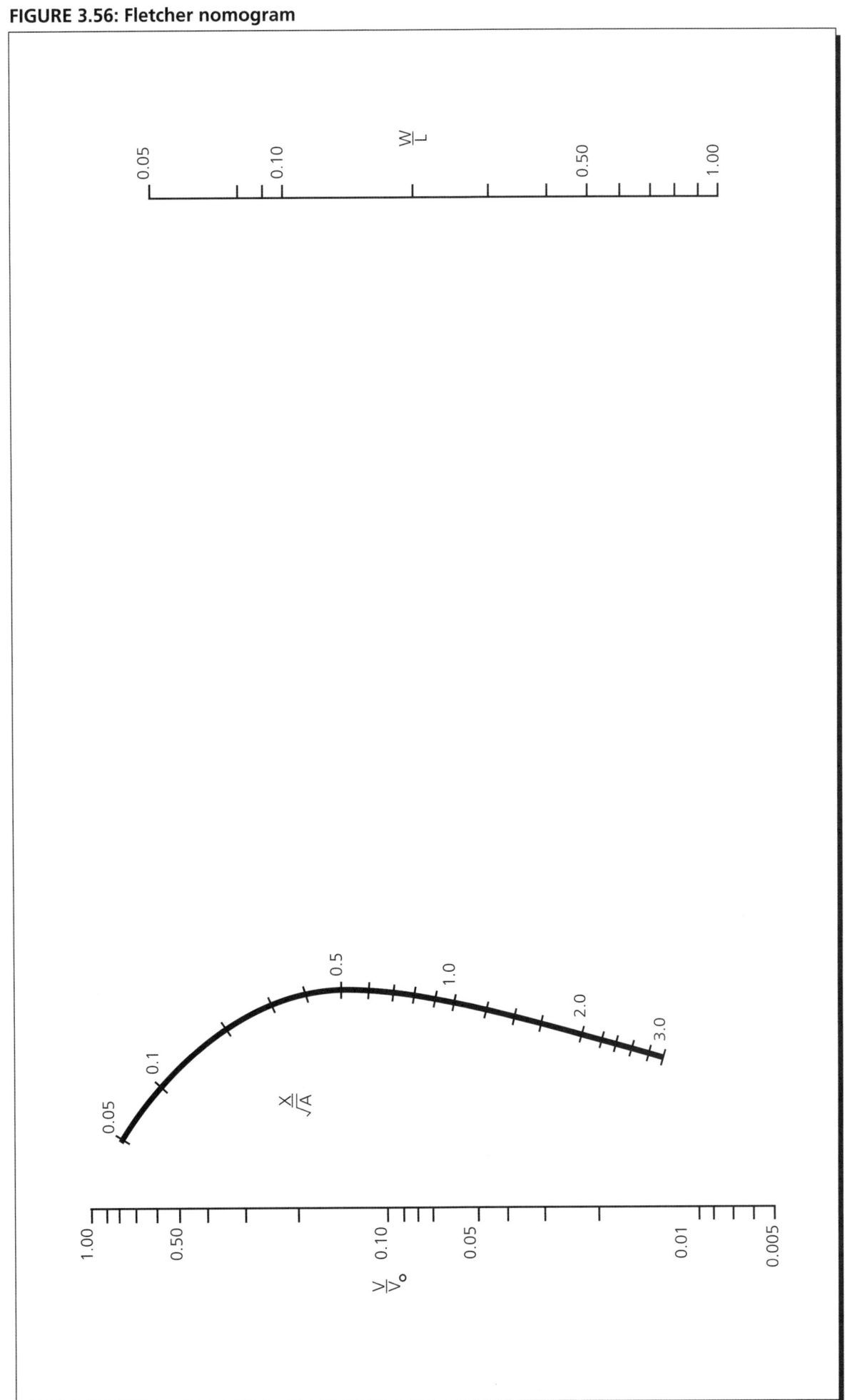

$\frac{W}{L}$ scale: 0.05, 0.10, 0.50, 1.00

$\frac{X}{\sqrt{A}}$ scale (curve): 0.05, 0.1, 0.5, 1.0, 2.0, 3.0

$\frac{V}{V_o}$ scale: 1.00, 0.50, 0.10, 0.05, 0.01, 0.005

(Fletcher 1977)

CHEMICAL AGENTS

Static measurements and fault-finding

Static pressure measurement points and diagnostic criteria are indicated in Figure 3.57. Simultaneous measurement of static pressures allows the different parts of the LEV system to be monitored and facilitates the diagnosis of problems. The deviation of static pressure from normal at the measurement points shown is indicative of certain faults, which are indicated below.

FIGURE 3.57: Use of static measurements in fault finding

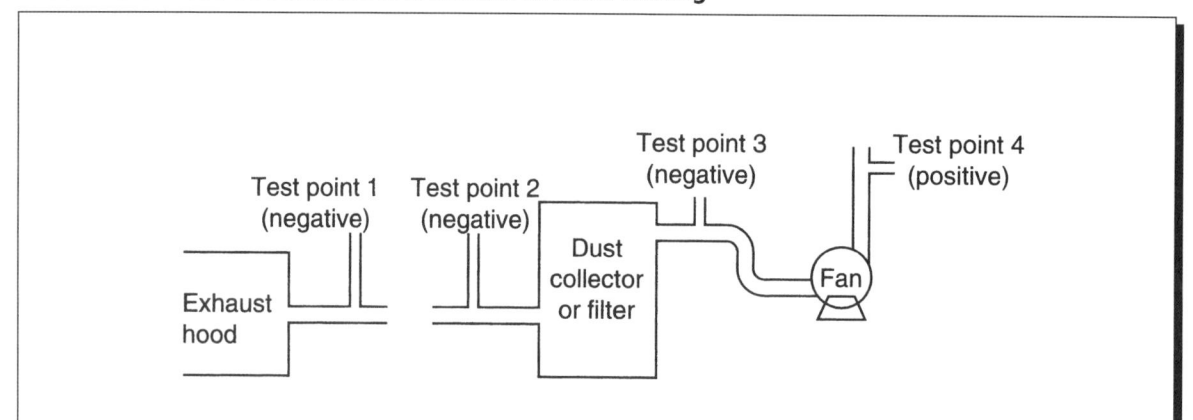

Static pressure at test point compared with normal				Typical fault
1	2	3	4	
Normal	Normal	Normal	Normal	System operating normally
Low	High	High	Low	Blockage in duct or closed damper between points 1 and 2
Low	Low	High	Low	Blocked filter dust collector
High	High	Low	High	Missing or damaged filter Low water level in wet dust collector
Low	Low	Low	Low	Faulty fan: incorrect fan speed, slipping drive belts, deposits on or damaged blades, incorrect electrical wiring
High	High	High	Low	Build-up of dust and debris in, or blockage of, hood, etc
Low	Low	Low	High	Blockage in exhaust stack

(HSE 1998b)

Dilution ventilation

Dilution ventilation is concerned with the general ventilation of a workroom so that any contamination is diluted by the introduction of fresh air. By this means, contaminant concentration levels are kept well below the appropriate air quality limits. Dilution ventilation should only be provided where:

- the pollutant is of low toxicity;
- only small quantities are released;
- contaminant can be sufficiently diluted before significant worker exposure.

A minimum standard of ventilation is required to provide fresh air for breathing and to dilute impurities. No local extraction system is 100 per cent efficient and some contaminant may escape and pollute the workroom air. In this situation, LEV may be applied to major emission sources with additional dilution ventilation ensuring compliance with exposure limits. Natural ventilation techniques, that is, doors, windows and roof vents, may be used in small buildings, while mechanical systems are employed in large office blocks and for larger industrial premises. In an industrial environment, dilution ventilation is usually employed when contamination is released over a wide area, for example, the use of volatile liquids in open surface tanks during dipping operations.

Ventilation standards

Adopting standards for dilution ventilation and fresh air requirements is a complex process. In 1986, the American Society of Heating, Refrigeration and Air-conditioning Engineers (ASHRAE) adopted a standard for dilution ventilation of $10ls^{-1}$ of outside air to be introduced per occupant. The HSE (2000) has published guidance (HSG202) on standards of general ventilation and fresh air requirements for the workplace. The fresh air supply rate should not fall below five to eight litres per second per occupant[22]. For factories and open-plan offices, HSG202 recommends a rate of at least eight litres per second per occupant. Higher fresh air supply rates of up to 36 litres per second per occupant are recommended for heavily contaminated buildings, for instance where 70 per cent of people smoke (CIBSE 1999).

Measuring air change rates

There are several methods of measuring air change rates in workplaces. The HSE (1992) outlines a tracer gas method for factories and offices. The overall amount of air entering and leaving a building is vital information in an assessment of the working environment. It is most often expressed in air changes per hour. The movement of large volumes of air can be measured by the use of a tracer gas, for example, Krypton 85, a low beta-emitter or sulphur hexafluoride. These are used to measure the ventilation air change rates in a building. This is done by releasing a pulse of the tracer gas and then tracking the build-up and rate of decay of the gas concentration as air is removed from the work area by ventilation. The rate of total air change may be calculated from this information.

Designing dilution ventilation

Careful planning is required to determine where inlet and outlet points are positioned in a dilution system. In designing dilution ventilation, it is necessary to have knowledge of:

- the rate of emission or evaporation rate of the chemical contaminant;
- the size of the workroom;
- how seasonal changes affect background natural ventilation; and
- general ventilation rates.

Where contaminant is emitted at various points in the workplace, then it is often possible to arrange the layout of the process to take the contaminated air away from workers. (This is known as displacement ventilation.) Efficient mixing can be encouraged if careful planning is undertaken as to how air enters and leaves the building. Provision for the following aspects should be included in the planned system:

- poor mixing in the ventilated area; and
- workers located close to or downstream from sources of contamination (see Figure 3.58).

The chemical contaminant is liberated at low velocity and the concentration nearby rises sharply. Ventilation currents disperse and dilute the contaminated air. The concentration falls as distance increases from the source. Employee exposure may be controlled by their location at a significant distance from the source. This approach is often found for solvent vapours in control rooms, photographic laboratories and small print rooms, where release rates are low and toxicity is low.

Advantages of dilution systems are that they are relatively simple, require only low fan power and have low capital costs. A disadvantage is that they require a high volume flow of air, which requires a large volume of heated replacement air.

---

[22]Guidance to regulation 6 of the Workplace (Health, Safety and Welfare) Regulations 1992.

CHEMICAL AGENTS

FIGURE 3.58: Dilution ventilation

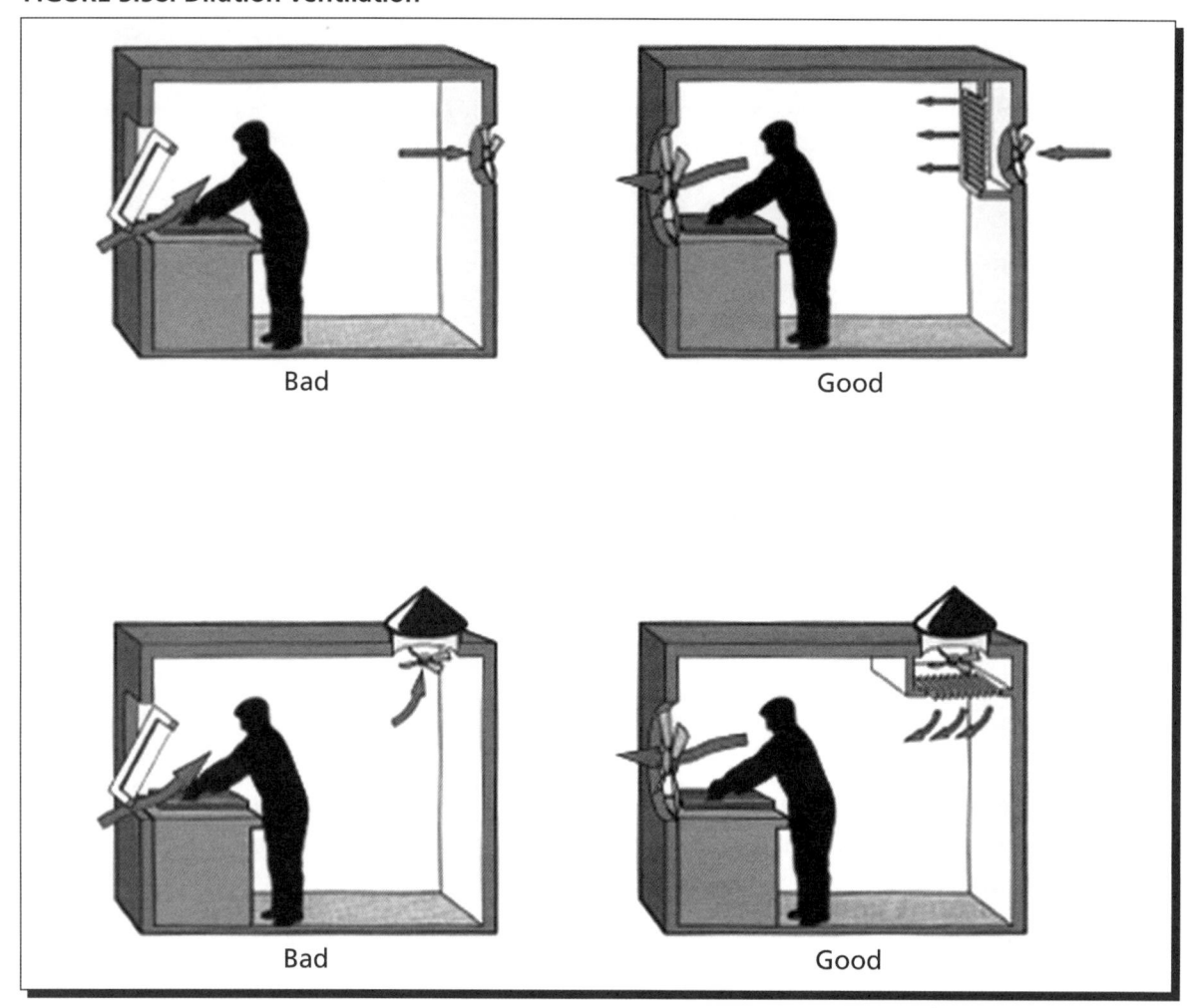

Bad	Good
Bad	Good

(HSE 1998c – rev. 2002)

REFERENCES

American Conference of Governmental Industrial Hygienists, *Documentation for Threshold Limit Values* (updated regularly), ACGIH, Cincinnati, OH, USA.

American Conference of Governmental Industrial Hygienists, 2002, *Threshold Limit Values for Chemical and Physical Agents and Biological Exposure Indices*, ACGIH, Cincinnati, OH, USA.

Ashton I and Gill F S, 2000, *Monitoring for Health Hazards at Work* (3rd edition), Blackwell Science, Oxford.

British Occupational Hygiene Society, 1991, *Controlling Airborne Contaminants in the Workplace*, Technical Guide No 7, H and H Scientific Consultants Ltd, Leeds.

British Occupational Hygiene Society, 1996, *The Manager's Guide to the Control of Hazardous Substances*, General Guide No 1, H and H Scientific Consultants Ltd, Leeds.

British Standards Institution, 1993, *Workplace Atmospheres – Size Fraction Definitions for Measurement of Airborne Particles*, BS EN 481, BSI, London.

Chartered Institution of Building Services Engineers, 1999, *Environmental Design*, Guide Volume A, CIBSE.

Claasen C and Doull J, 1991, *Cassarett and Doull's Toxicology: The Basic Science of Poisons* (4th edition), Macmillan.

Cross H J and Faux S P, 1999, Toxicological Basis of Hazard Identification, Chapter 3 in *Occupational Health – Risk Assessment and Management*, Sadhra S S and Rampal K G (Eds), Blackwell Science, Oxford.

Doll R, 1992, Carcinogenic Risk: Getting it in Proportion, in *Cancer in the Workplace*, Conference proceedings 15 October 1992, Health and Safety Executive and the Society of the Chemical Industry.

European Community, 1998, *Council Directive on the Protection of the Health and Safety of Workers From the Risks Related to Chemical Agents at Work*, 98/24/EC.

Fletcher B, 1977, Centreline Velocity Characteristics of Rectangular Unflanged Hoods and Slots, *Ann Occ Hyg*, **20**, 141–146.

Fletcher B, 1978, Effect of Flanges in Front of Exhaust Ventilation Hoods, *Ann Occ Hyg*, **21**, 265–269.

Garrison R P, 1983, Velocity Calculation for Local Exhaust Inlets, *Am Ind Hyg Assoc J*, **44**, 937–947.

Gill F S, 1995, Ventilation, Chapter 22 in *Occupational Hygiene* (2nd edition), Harrington J M and Gardiner K (Eds), Blackwell Science, Oxford.

Harrington J M, 1995, The Effects of Inhaled Materials on Target Organs, Chapter 4 in *Occupational Hygiene* (2nd edition), Harrington J M and Gardiner K (Eds), Blackwell Science, Oxford.

Hartley C B, 1999, Occupational Hygiene, Chapter 17 in *Safety at Work* (5th edition), Ridley J R and Channing J (Eds), Butterworth-Heinemann, Oxford.

Health and Safety Commission, 2002a, *Control of Lead at Work* (3rd edition), The Control of Lead at Work Regulations 2002, Approved Code of Practice and Guidance, L132, HSE Books, Sudbury.

Health and Safety Commission, 2002b, *Control of Asbestos at Work*, The Control of Asbestos at Work Regulations 2002, Approved Codes of Practice and Guidance, L27, L28, HSE Books, Sudbury.

Health and Safety Commission, 2002c, *The Approved Supply List: Information Approved for the Classification and Labelling of Substances and Preparations Dangerous for Supply* (7th edition), L129, HSE Books, Sudbury.

Health and Safety Commission, 2002d, *The Approved Classification and Labelling Guide*, L131, HSE Books, Sudbury.

Health and Safety Commission, 2002e, *The Compilation of Safety Data Sheets* (3rd edition), Approved Code of Practice, L130, HSE Books, Sudbury.

Health and Safety Commission, 2002f, *The Control of Asbestos at Work Regulations 2002*, Approved Codes of Practice and Guidance, L27, L28, HSE Books, Sudbury.

Health and Safety Commission, 2003, *Proposals to Introduce a New Occupational Exposure Limits Framework*, Consultative Document CD189, HSE Books, Sudbury.

Health and Safety Commission, 2005, *Control of Substances Hazardous to Health* (5th edition), The Control of Substances Hazardous to Health Regulations 2002 (as amended), Approved Code of Practice and Guidance, L5, HSE Books, Sudbury.

Health and Safety Executive, 1976, *Toxic Substances: A Precautionary Policy*, EH18, HMSO, London.

Health and Safety Executive, 1987, *An Introduction to Local Exhaust Ventilation* (1st edition), HS(G)37, HMSO, London.

Health and Safety Executive, 1990, *The Control of Exposure to Fume from Welding, Brazing and Similar Processes*, Guidance Note EH55, HMSO, London.

Health and Safety Executive, 1992, *Measurement of Air Change Rates in Factories and Offices*, MDHS Series 73, HSE Books, Sudbury.

Health and Safety Executive, 1993, *COSHH Assessment – A Step-By-Step Guide to Assessment and the Skills Needed for It* (2nd edition), HSE Books, Sudbury.

Health and Safety Executive, 1993a, *An Introduction to Local Exhaust Ventilation*, HSG37, HSE Books, Sudbury.

Health and Safety Executive, 1994, *Making Sense of NONS*, HS(G)117, HSE Books, Sudbury.

Health and Safety Executive, 1994a, *Preventing Occupational Asthma at Work*, L55, HSE Books, Sudbury.

Health and Safety Executive, 1994b, *7 Steps to Successful Substitution of Hazardous Substances*, HSG110, HSE Books, Sudbury.

Health and Safety Executive, 1995, *Asbestos Fibres in Air – Sampling and Evaluation by Phase Contrast Microscopy*, MDHS 39/4, HSE Books, Sudbury.

Health and Safety Executive, 1997, *Asthmagen? Critical Assessments of the Evidence for Agents Implicated in Occupational Asthma*, HSE Books, Sudbury.

Health and Safety Executive, 1997a, *Monitoring Strategies for Toxic Substances*, HSG173, HSE Books, Sudbury.

Health and Safety Executive, 1997b, *The Dust Lamp – A Simple Tool for Observing the Presence of Airborne Particles*, MDHS 82, HSE Books, Sudbury.

Health and Safety Executive, 1997c, *Biological Monitoring in the Workplace*, HSG167, HSE Books, Sudbury.

Health and Safety Executive, 1998, *Medical Aspects of Occupational Asthma*, Guidance Note MS25, HSE Books, Sudbury.

Health and Safety Executive, 1998a, *Medical Aspects of Occupational Skin Disease*, MS24, HSE Books, Sudbury.

Health and Safety Executive, 1998b, *Maintenance, Examination and Testing of Local Exhaust Ventilation*, HSG54, HSE Books, Sudbury.

Health and Safety Executive, 1998c, *The Printer's Guide to Health and Safety*, HSE Books, Sudbury.

Health and Safety Executive, 2000, *General Ventilation in the Workplace*, HSG202, HSE Books, Sudbury.

Health and Safety Executive, 2001, *Summary Criteria for Occupational Exposure Limits*, Guidance Note EH64 and Supplement, HSE Books, Sudbury.

Health and Safety Executive, 2001a, *Introduction to Asbestos Essentials*, HSG213, HSE Books, Sudbury.

Health and Safety Executive, 2001b, *Surveying, Sampling and Assessment of Asbestos-Containing Materials*, MDHS100, HSE Books, Sudbury.

Health and Safety Executive, 2001c, *Asbestos: Exposure Limits and Measurement of Airborne Dust Concentrations*, EH10, HSE Books, Sudbury.

Health and Safety Executive, 2001d, *Controlling Exposure to Stonemasonry Dust: Guidance for Employers*, HSG201, HSE Books, Sudbury.

Health and Safety Executive, 2002a, Press Release E080:02, 30 April 2002.

Health and Safety Executive, 2002b, *A Comprehensive Guide to Managing Asbestos in Premises*, HSG227, HSE Books, Sudbury.

Health and Safety Executive, 2003, *COSHH Essentials – Easy Steps to Control Chemicals*, HSG193, 2nd edition, HSE Books, Sudbury.

Health and Safety Executive, 2005, *Workplace Exposure Limits*, Guidance Note EH40, HSE Books, Sudbury.

Lee W R, 1987, Reproduction and Work, Chapter 27 in *Hunter's Diseases of Occupations*, Raffle P A B, Lee W R, McCallum R I and Murray R (Eds), Hodder and Stoughton, London.

Levy L S, 1990, *The Setting of Occupational Exposure Limits in the UK*, IChemE Symposium Series 117, Institute of Chemical Engineers.

Peto J and Hodgson J, 1995, Continuing Increase in Mesothelioma Mortality in Britain, *The Lancet*, **345**, 535–539.

Piney M D, 1985, 1986, Ventilation: Designing for the Future, *Health & Safety at Work*, July 1985, October 1985, January 1986.

Raffle P A B, Lee W R, McCallum R I and Murray R, 1987, *Hunter's Diseases of Occupations*, Hodder and Stoughton, London.

Roach S A, 1992, *Health Risks from Hazardous Substances (Assessment, Evaluation and Control)*, Pergamon Press.

Tola S and Hernberg S, 1981, Biological Monitoring Techniques, Chapter 17 in *Recent Advances in Occupational Health*, McDonald J C (Ed.), Livingstone.

LEGISLATION

Asbestos Licensing Regulations 1983 (SI 1983/1649) (as amended)

Chemicals (Hazard Information and Packaging for Supply) Regulations 2002 (SI 2002/1689)

Control of Asbestos at Work Regulations 2002 (SI 2002/2675)

Control of Lead at Work Regulations 2002 (SI 2002/2676)

Control of Substances Hazardous to Health Regulations 2002 (SI 2002/2677) (as amended by SI 2004/3386)

Notification of New Substances Regulations 1993 (SI 1993/3242) (as amended by the Notification of New Substances Regulations 2002 (SI 2002/2176))

Reporting of Injuries, Diseases and Dangerous Occurrences Regulations 1995 (SI 1995/3163)

4: Biological agents

(Hunter 1978. Reproduced by permission of Hodder Arnold.)

INTRODUCTION

Many people are in occupations where they are exposed, routinely or potentially, to biological agents. They may be exposed to such agents arising from the work process itself or from their work environment. For example, pathology laboratory workers are involved in handling and analysing infected biological samples, biotechnology research workers may be experimenting with different forms of bacteria, and farmers may be exposed to harmful biological agents arising from normal agricultural activities. The historical picture above illustrates two workers sorting woollen fleeces, an occupation associated with wool-sorter's disease, commonly known as anthrax. A wide spectrum of ill health is caused by occupational exposure to biological agents ranging from mild, self-limiting conditions (which get better on their own) to life-threatening illnesses such as hepatitis B infections in healthcare workers.

There are different definitions of the term 'biological agent'. For example, according to Beech & Ratti (1999), they are:

> ...principally micro-organisms and their products.

The term 'biological agent' is defined in regulation 2 of the Control of Substances Hazardous to Health Regulations 2002 (as amended) (COSHH) as:

> *Micro-organism, cell culture, or human endoparasite, whether or not genetically modified, which may cause infection, allergy, toxicity or otherwise create a hazard to human health.*

In the same Regulations, 'micro-organism' is defined as:

BIOLOGICAL AGENTS

A microbiological entity, cellular or non-cellular, which is capable of replication or of transferring genetic material.

This COSHH Approved Code of Practice (ACoP) (HSC 2005) elaborates that the term 'biological agent' refers to a general class of micro-organisms, cell cultures and human endoparasites, provided that they have one or more of the harmful properties specified in the above definition. Biological agents include bacteria, viruses, fungi, microscopic parasites (protozoa) and the microscopic infectious forms of larger parasites, for example, helminths (worms), which are pathogenic to humans.

Biological agents occur widely in a range of environments and some may have both useful and detrimental properties. For example, the common bacterium, *E. coli*, normally operates beneficially assisting with digestion in the gastrointestinal tract, but if it should gain access to the blood circulation, then it can cause harmful (pathogenic) reactions and disease, which may be severe in vulnerable people. This type of organism is described as an 'opportunistic pathogen'. Occupational groups routinely exposed to biological agents are listed below:

- hospital and laboratory workers;
- veterinary surgeons;
- medical and nursing staff;
- waste disposal workers;
- sewer workers;
- care workers and social workers;
- workers at risk of work-related violence;
- farm workers and poultry workers;
- zoo workers; and
- biotechnology workers.

Data on occupational infections (Tables 4.1 and 4.2) collected by several medical surveillance schemes is published by the Health and Safety Commission (HSC 1998), which comments that the figures are believed to represent an underestimation of the true incidence of such disease.

TABLE 4.1: Occupational infections reported to various medical surveillance schemes (October 1996 – September 1997, UK)

Diagnostic category	Estimated total
Diarrhoeal diseases	922
Hepatitis	17
Legionellosis	90
Leptospirosis	28
Ornithosis (Chlamydiosis)	12
Pulmonary tuberculosis	58
Q fever	4
Tinea	57
Scabies	84
Other	22
TOTAL	**1294**

(HSC 1998)

Some infective diseases caused by biological agents are reportable under the Reporting of Injuries Diseases and Dangerous Occurrences Regulations 1995 (RIDDOR) and these are listed in Table 4.11 (on page 165) (HSE 1996). The problems with disease data obtained from the RIDDOR scheme have been discussed in Chapter 1 and the RIDDOR figures on occupational infectious disease (not cited here) represent a greater underestimation of true incidence than those given above.

TABLE 4.2: Occupational infections by workplace (Reports from consultants in communicable disease control October 1996 – September 1997, UK)

Workplace	Number of cases
Social work activities	508
Production, processing, preserving meat products	47
Livestock farming	42
Veterinary activities	3
Sporting activities	26
Human health activities	185
Not specified	226
All cases	**1037**

(HSC 1998)

It is necessary to consider briefly some fundamental concepts in microbiology.

Basic microbiology

A micro-organism is a living creature too small to be seen with the naked eye. Microbiology is concerned with the study of these organisms, which include bacteria, viruses, algae and protozoa.

Most micro-organisms (87 per cent) are beneficial or harmless, with a few opportunist pathogens (10 per cent) which can cause disease in particularly susceptible individuals, for instance, those with a lower resistance. Around 3 per cent are thought to be pathogenic, that is, they will cause disease in normally healthy people.

Furthermore, protective micro-organisms inhabit the skin, mouth and intestine and these normally assist in inhibiting the growth of pathogens. Structurally, micro-organisms can be broadly divided into those with cells having a true nucleus (eukaryotic), those with cells without a nucleus (prokaryotic), and those which are non-cellular (see Figure 4.1).

Infection

Infection occurs when a biological agent enters the body and multiplies. The results of this may vary from life-threatening illness through minor health effects to no obvious symptoms at all. The biological agent gains entry to the body via several possible routes including ingestion, inhalation, through cuts or damaged skin (including puncture wounds with a sharp object), through the mucus membrane of the eye and during sexual intercourse.

The body has several mechanisms of defence (discussed in Chapter 2) including the non-specific inflammatory response and highly specific immune response. The immune response leads to the production of antibodies in response to the specific invading biological agent, which assist in the destruction of the invader. If the same biological agent invades again, the body is able to respond by much more rapidly producing appropriate antibodies and efficiently controlling any infection. The person is then said to have immunity to the particular biological agent.

A summary of potential sources of occupational exposure is given in Table 4.3.

TABLE 4.3: Sources of occupational exposure to infection

Category	Example
Industrial	Contact with contaminated materials, oils, coolants, dusts, aerosols
Humans	(a) Direct eg respiratory cross-infection due to crowding, ventilation, humidity
	(b) Indirect eg laboratory infection
Animals	(a) Direct eg contact with living animals
	(b) Indirect eg infection due to contact with materials and products derived from animals

(From Lee 1987)

BIOLOGICAL AGENTS

FIGURE 4.1: Family tree of micro-organisms

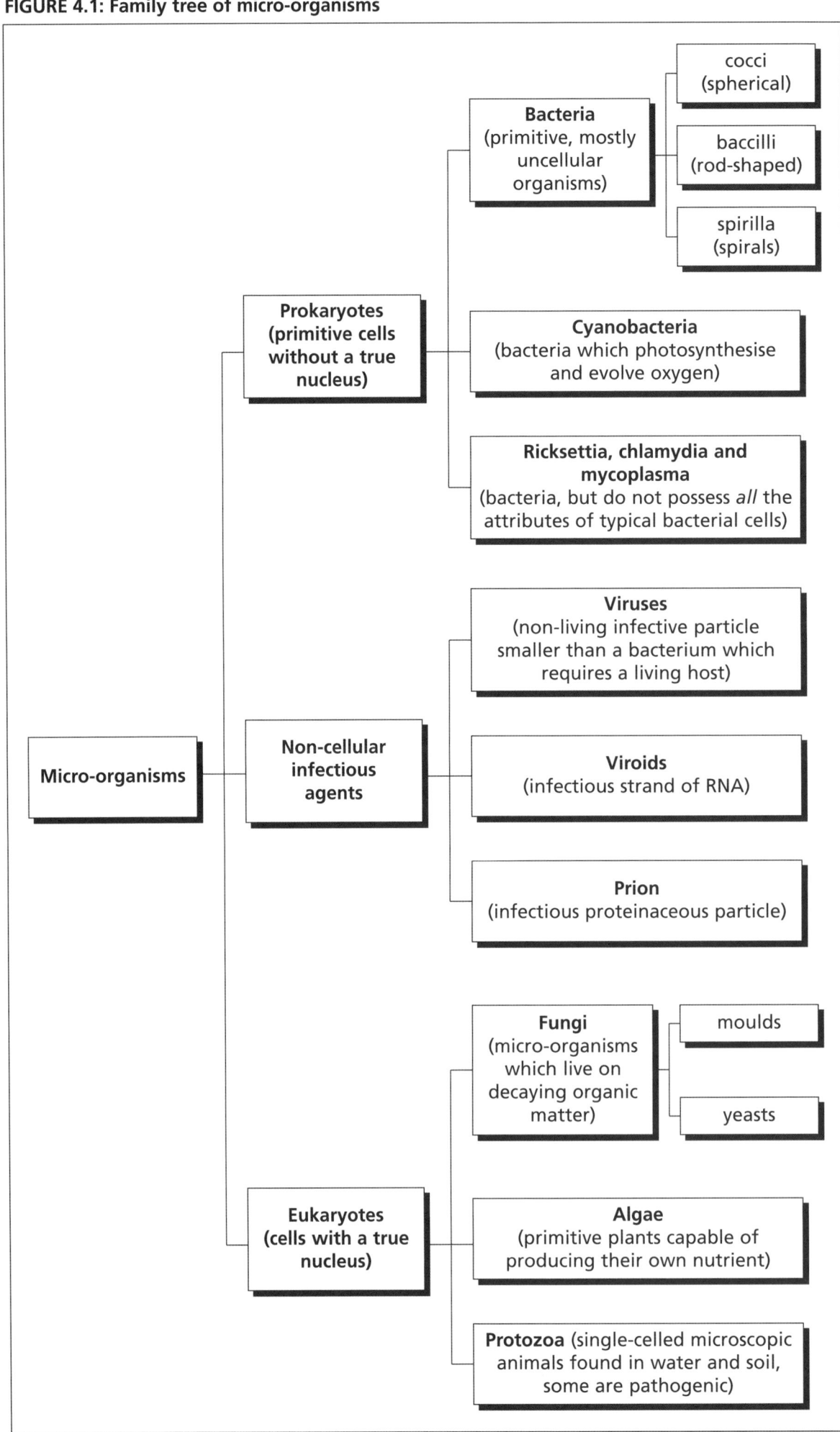

- **Micro-organisms**
  - **Prokaryotes** (primitive cells without a true nucleus)
    - **Bacteria** (primitive, mostly uncellular organisms)
      - cocci (spherical)
      - baccilli (rod-shaped)
      - spirilla (spirals)
    - **Cyanobacteria** (bacteria which photosynthesise and evolve oxygen)
    - **Ricksettia, chlamydia and mycoplasma** (bacteria, but do not possess *all* the attributes of typical bacterial cells)
  - **Non-cellular infectious agents**
    - **Viruses** (non-living infective particle smaller than a bacterium which requires a living host)
    - **Viroids** (infectious strand of RNA)
    - **Prion** (infectious proteinaceous particle)
  - **Eukaryotes** (cells with a true nucleus)
    - **Fungi** (micro-organisms which live on decaying organic matter)
      - moulds
      - yeasts
    - **Algae** (primitive plants capable of producing their own nutrient)
    - **Protozoa** (single-celled microscopic animals found in water and soil, some are pathogenic)

Occupational diseases transmitted from animals to humans are known as 'zoonoses', and examples include leptospirosis, anthrax and orf, all of which are discussed below.

Prokaryotes

Bacteria

Bacteria vary in shape (spherical, rod-shaped, spiral) and size from 1µm to 10µm. In contrast, viruses are very much smaller at around 0.02µm to 0.3µm. (The human eye has a resolution of around 100µm, a light microscope 0.1µm and an electron microscope 0.001µm.) When bacteria grow on a suitable substrate (agar), they can be observed as colonies which, depending on the organism, vary in colour, shape and general appearance (see Figure 4.2). In a clear liquid medium (broth), bacterial growth produces cloudiness (turbidity).

FIGURE 4.2: Bacteria – Shapes and arrangements

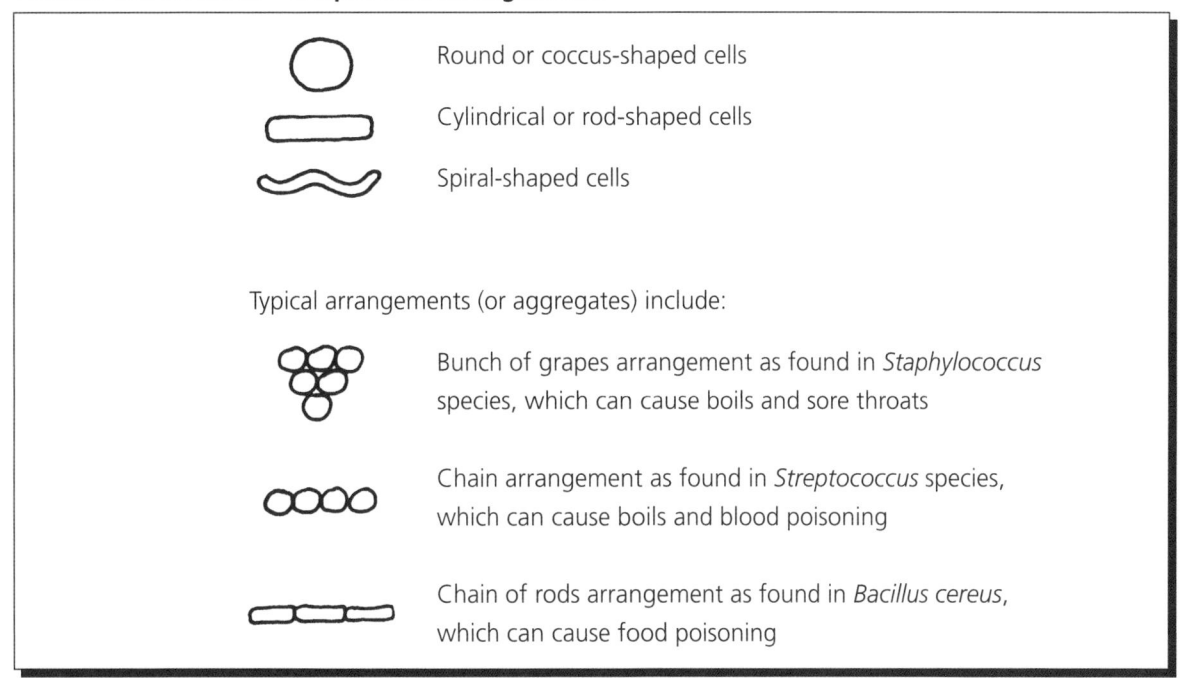

- ○ Round or coccus-shaped cells
- ▭ Cylindrical or rod-shaped cells
- ∼ Spiral-shaped cells

Typical arrangements (or aggregates) include:

- Bunch of grapes arrangement as found in *Staphylococcus* species, which can cause boils and sore throats
- Chain arrangement as found in *Streptococcus* species, which can cause boils and blood poisoning
- Chain of rods arrangement as found in *Bacillus cereus*, which can cause food poisoning

(After Price, Le Serve & Parker 1981)

Pathogenic bacteria can thrive in human and/or animal hosts and organic media, and they can often pass from one host to another. They may produce harmful metabolic poisons, that is, exotoxins and endotoxins, which can damage sensitive human tissues and organs. Exotoxins are toxic proteinaceous substances which are secreted by the pathogens. They can be classified by their principal target organ, for example, neurotoxin (nervous system), enterotoxin (gastrointestinal tract), cardiotoxin (heart) and nephrotoxin (kidney). Endotoxins are components of the cell wall in some bacteria and when these bacterial cells are destroyed in the gastrointestinal tract, the endotoxins released can exert harmful effects on the body. They may destroy defensive phagocytes and upset water and salt balance in the body.

By forming highly-resistant structures (spores), some bacteria can survive for considerable periods outside the body awaiting a suitable human or animal host. For example, the organism *Clostridium tetani* produces spores that may live in soil for many months. Following human infection, an exotoxin is produced by the bacterium, which causes muscular paralysis.

As discussed in Chapter 2, the human body has well-adapted defensive mechanisms to defend itself against micro-organisms. However, the effects of different organisms and strains vary; an additional factor is the susceptibility of the host and this depends on a person's general health and level of immunity.

Bacteria are the causative agents in many occupational diseases including leptospirosis, anthrax, brucellosis and tuberculosis.

BIOLOGICAL AGENTS

Cyanobacteria

These are pigmented micro-organisms which carry out photosynthesis and evolve oxygen. They occur in unicellular and filamentous forms and were formerly known as 'blue-green algae'. They have no particular relevance in an occupational context.

Rickettsiae

These are very small organisms which resemble the smallest bacteria and at one point they were thought to be viruses. They are round particles of about 0.2μm in diameter and can cause febrile diseases (fevers) in humans and animals as illustrated in Table 4.4 (on page 154). Q fever is a disease found in workers involved in housing, handling and transporting cows, goats and sheep. This condition is caused by the rickettsia *Coxiella burnetii* through the inhalation of contaminated dust or aerosol or in the drinking of infected milk. Chlamydiosis is a febrile disease found in poultry, farm and zoo workers, and is caused by the rickettsia bacterium *Chlamydia psittaci*. Chlamydiosis has both an avian form, caused by exposure to infected birds, and an ovine form, caused by exposure to infected sheep.

Non-cellular infectious agents

Viruses

Compared with bacteria, viruses generally are not usually an important cause of occupational infection. Viruses are small, very simple non-living infectious agents (0.02μm to 0.3μm in diameter), which may cause disease and genetic changes in animals, plants, algae, fungi, protozoa and bacteria. Viruses have a variety of shapes but consist principally of a protein coat (capsid) surrounding a strand of nucleic acid, which carries the genetic information of the virus particle (see Figure 4.3). They infect living cells and the genetic material of the virus takes over the metabolic machinery of the cell. The cell is directed to produce new viruses and finally the cell bursts, liberating new virus particles which are able to spread and similarly infect cells elsewhere. Among other diseases, viruses are the cause of viral hepatitis, rabies and acquired immune deficiency syndrome (AIDS).

FIGURE 4.3: Shapes of virus particles

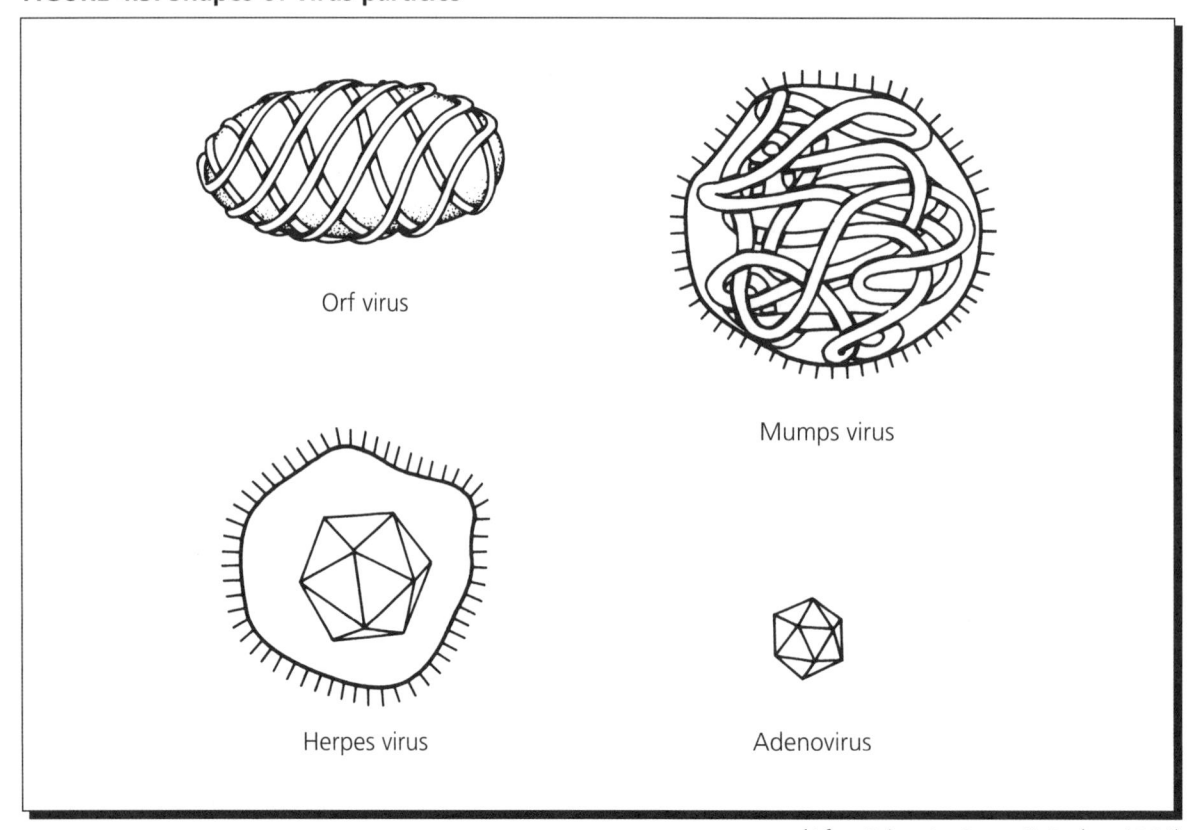

(After Price, Le Serve & Parker 1981)

FIGURE 4.4: Electron micrograph showing HIV particles being released from infected human lymphocyte

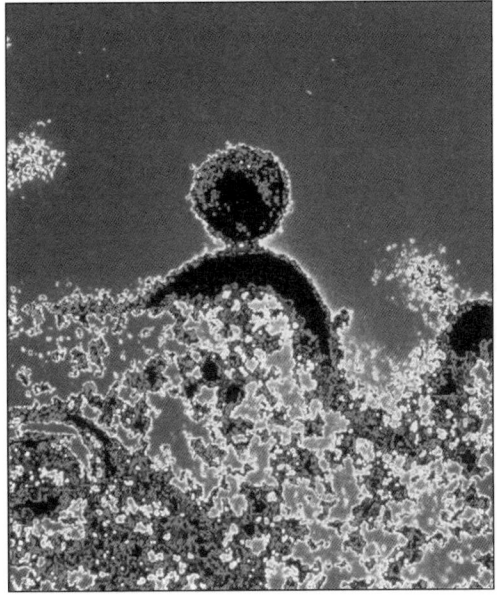

(Wellcome Photo Library)

Viroids
These are infectious strands of ribonucleic acid (RNA).

Prions
These are infective proteinaceous particles which are highly resistant to normal destructive control techniques. They are thought to be the causative agent in nervous system diseases such as scrapie in sheep and bovine spongiform encephalopathy (BSE) in cattle, which has been linked with new variant Creutzfeldt-Jakob disease (CJD) in humans. This group of nervous system diseases is known as the transmissible spongiform encephalopathies (TSEs).

Eukaryotes

Fungi
Fungi include mushrooms, moulds and yeasts, and being saprophytic organisms whose main source of food is decaying organic matter, they derive their energy from preformed macromolecules. Fungi can be colonies of single cells, but are more commonly complex multicellular structures. As with bacteria, they can be both harmful and beneficial. Fungi may be cultured on artificial media including agar, broth and compost, and in appearance, they range from the single-celled form of yeasts to those organisms with a mat (mycelium) of interlacing filaments (hyphae) found in moulds and mushrooms. Reproduction is by budding, hyphal extension or by the formation of extremely-resistant spores. Fungi are classified into different groups by virtue of their structural features and their mode of reproduction. Considering the very large number of fungal species, relatively few are pathogenic to humans. Some fungi produce toxic substances called mycotoxins.

Moulds are filamentous fungi often seen growing on water, soil and food. They reproduce by spore formation, which on release may act as airborne allergens (see Figure 4.5). Some fungi produce harmful toxins and cause ill health following the consumption of contaminated food. Poisoning may also be caused during the consumption of toxins in some mushrooms. Some fungal species may also invade superficial human tissues, particularly the skin and mucous membranes. The most common condition is ringworm (tinea). Deeper tissue penetration by fungi is found in people living in tropical regions. Candidiasis is a group of superficial infections of the skin or mucous membranes caused by species of the genus *Candida*. These vary from oral thrush to chronic infection of the mucous membranes. Yeasts are single-celled organisms which lack mycelia. They usually reproduce by budding (mitotic cell division) and occasionally by spore formation. They are found on soil and water and on the surfaces of fruit and vegetables. Mushrooms grow in the soil or on rotting organic material and reproduce by the release of spores. They consist of a network of filaments or strands.

FIGURE 4.5: Typical moulds (fungi) showing the release of spores

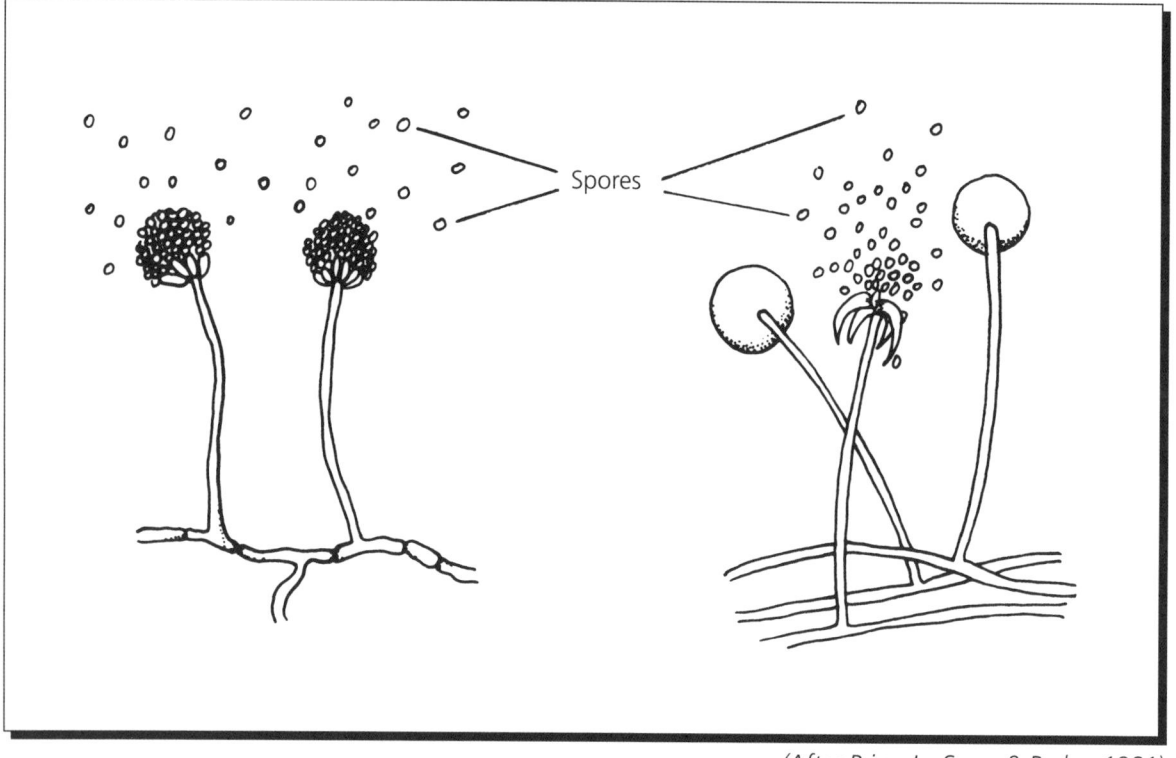

(After Price, Le Serve & Parker 1981)

Algae

These are photosynthetic organisms, which may be single or multicellular, and they are a vital part of the animal food chain. They are arranged in colonies or strands and are found in water, soil, plants and rocks. Only a few species of algae are pathogenic to humans.

Protozoa

These are single-celled animals (ranging in length from 2µm to 3,000µm) which are found in water and soil. Protozoa have the ability to move and they are classified by their mode of locomotion. They differ from bacteria in that they are eukaryotic, larger and do not have a cell wall.

Some species of protozoa are pathogenic to humans, for example, causing amoebic dysentery (amoebae), malaria (plasmodium), sleeping sickness (trypanosome) and toxoplasmosis (*Toxoplasma gondii*). The protozoan *Naegleria fowleri* is believed to be involved in 'humidifier fever', which is a form of extrinsic allergic alveolitis.

Larger parasites

Parasitic worms are also pathogens varying widely in the complexity of their structures and life cycles. Parasitic infections are common in developing countries, especially in the tropics, where conditions allow the parasite's life cycle to be completed. They are not a significant problem in the UK in an occupational context. The connection between the mite (a small insect) and itching has been long known. Scabies is an arachnid mite and a hazard to nurses and care attendants of infected patients.

Hazards from such parasites vary in different climates and they must be considered in workers returning from a period in the tropics.

Genetic engineering

Biotechnology is the use of biological organisms or processes in research, development, manufacturing and service industries. It integrates biology, chemistry and process engineering. Potential applications include chemicals production, waste treatment, energy generation, mineral extraction and electronics. The healthcare, food, drink and agricultural industries have been most active in applying biotechnology.

Traditionally, biotechnology has involved the enhancement of desirable (or the diminution of undesirable) characteristics of naturally occurring organisms via selection or mutation. Modern biotechnology is increasingly using recombinant DNA technology to confer entirely new capabilities and characteristics on the resulting genetically modified organisms (GMOs). The biological systems used include most commonly bacteria and fungi (yeasts), together with viruses, and animal, insect and plant cells. Commonly, viruses are used in vaccine production and as the agent of genetic transfer in genetic modification techniques.

A range of techniques have been developed to transfer eukaryotic genes, particularly human, into easily cultured cells in order to facilitate large-scale production of important proteins, for example, human growth hormone, insulin and the antiviral agent interferon. Much of the current interest in biotechnology comes from the use of techniques to develop micro-organisms expressing gene products from a variety of sources.

A typical biotechnology process involves several stages including inoculum preparation, growth of the organism in a bioreactor, separation of the organism from its growth medium, and product recovery and purification. A bioreactor is a vessel used for the growth of organisms or the operation of the biological process. The risk is that the incorporation of genetic material in this way may result in the inadvertent production of a dangerous bacterial or other pathogen. GMOs or their metabolites may pose a number of potential risks to human health including infection and toxic or allergenic effects and, therefore, strict regulation is necessary for this work. This includes the carrying out of a microbiological risk assessment and the application of suitable controls.

Exposure and health effects

Modes of entry
In the case of biological agents, knowledge of the mode of entry into the body is essential for the design of effective control measures. The key routes of entry are inhalation, passage through skin barrier and ingestion.

Inhalation
Many biological agents may gain access to the body via this route. They are present as airborne contaminants in mists (liquid droplet aerosols) and dusts. Some will form part of the respirable fraction of the total inhalable fraction and will, therefore, be capable of reaching the alveoli, establishing disease and gaining access to the systemic circulation. Examples of organisms infecting via the inhalation route include *Legionella pneumonphila* (legionellosis), *Bacillus anthracis* (anthrax), *Mycobacterium tuberculosis* (tuberculosis), and *Brucella abortus* (brucellosis). Respiratory system defences are very effective and well co-ordinated with ciliary hairs, mucus, (ciliary escalator) macrophages, circulating antibodies and antiviral agents, and the system is cleared by coughing and sneezing (see Chapter 2).

People in certain working environments are more susceptible to infections, for example, where lung damage (silicosis) has been caused by exposure to dust, workers are more susceptible to tuberculosis and bronchitis. Macrophages appear less able to kill the tubercle bacillus when quartz particles are present. Silicosis also damages lymphatic drainage of the lung, which is also important in the control of tuberculosis infections.

Skin
Where the protective surface of the skin is damaged by a break, cut or burn, then an infective organism may gain direct access to underlying tissues and the systemic circulation. For example, the bacterium *Bacillus anthracis* will initiate cutaneous anthrax in exposed areas of skin. Even with intact skin, the organism *Leptospira ichterohaemorrhagiae*, which causes leptospirosis (Weil's disease), can pass through and it also penetrates the mucous membranes of the nose and mouth.

Ingestion

This is where an infective organism gains access to the body via the digestive tract. Normally, the acidic nature of the stomach gastric juices is protective and destroys harmful agents. However, some biological agents will set up an infection via this route, for example, *Brucella abortus* will cause brucellosis in people drinking milk from infected animals. Ingestion of contaminated food may also induce gastrointestinal disorders, for example, camphylobacter and salmonella organisms are responsible for most occupationally-acquired diarrhoea principally found in healthcare workers.

Infectious occupational diseases

Many occupational diseases result from exposure to biological agents and infectious conditions. These are summarised in Table 4.4 with further selective discussion later in this chapter.

TABLE 4.4: Biological agents and infectious occupational disease

Organism	Disease	Source	Occupations at risk
Bacteria	Leptospirosis	Rodents, cattle, dogs	Farm workers, sewer workers
	Anthrax	Livestock	Wool and hide handling
	Brucellosis	Livestock	Vets, farm workers
	Tuberculosis	Humans	Healthcare workers
	Lyme disease	Ticks, wild animals	Workers in certain wooded areas
	Legionellosis	Various water systems	Various groups
	Tetanus	Various	Skin-breaking injury
Rickettsiae	Q fever	Infected dusts/aerosols	Animal transportation/handling, farm workers, abattoir workers, veterinarians
	Avian chlamydiosis	Birds	Poultry workers and zoo workers
	Ovine chlamydiosis	Sheep	Farm workers
Viral	Hepatitis A/B/C	Human body fluids	Healthcare workers
	AIDS	Human body fluids	Healthcare workers
	Rabies	Cats, dogs, wild animals	Vets, farm workers
	Orf	Sheep, goats	Shepherds, shearers, vets
	Newcastle disease	Birds	Poultry handlers, vets
Prion (BSE/TSE)	BSE and new variant Creutzfeldt-Jakob disease	Cattle	Vets, slaughterhouse workers, meat handlers
Fungal	Candidiasis	Humans	Dishwashers, cooks, bakers
	Histoplasmosis	Soil (enriched with bird droppings)	Farm workers, pigeon handlers
Mixed exposure	Humidifier fever	Air-conditioning systems	Office workers, print workers
	Sick building syndrome	Sealed buildings	Office workers

(Adapted from Perkins 1997, cited by Sadhra 1999)

Biological agents and the COSHH Regulations 2002 (as amended)

Risk assessment and control are applied to biological agents in a similar way as for chemical agents. However, there some important differences between the detailed methodology applied taking account of fundamental differences in the nature of the risks arising from chemical and biological agents. The COSHH Regulations 2002 (as amended) regard a biological agent as a "substance hazardous to health" and the employer must demonstrate that these have been identified, risks arising from work activities have been assessed, and adequate control or preventive measures put in place. A "suitable and sufficient" assessment must be carried out and regularly reviewed under regulation 6 of COSHH and the requirements for this are given in Figure 4.6.

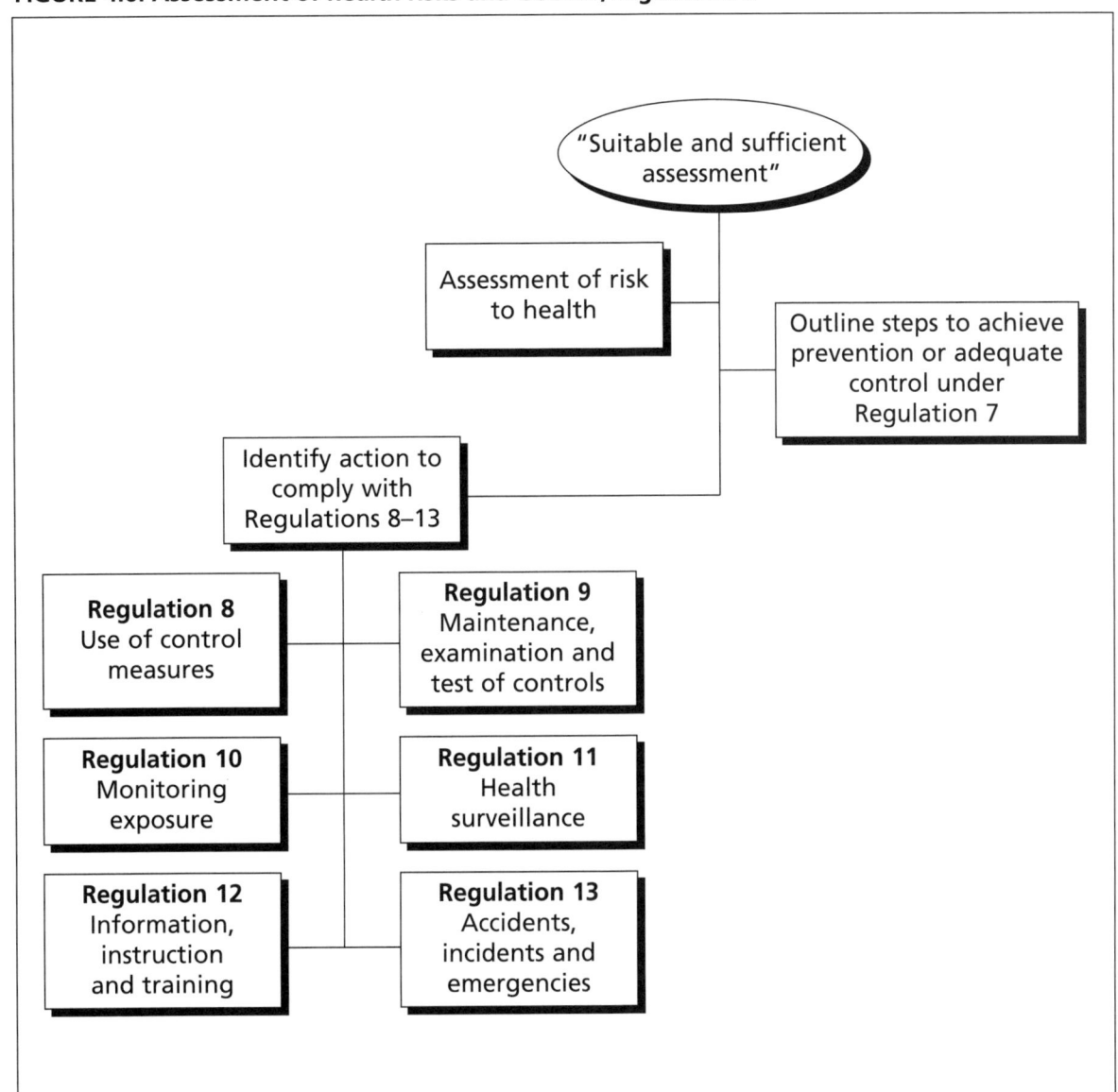

FIGURE 4.6: Assessment of health risks and COSHH, regulation 6

```
                          "Suitable and sufficient
                               assessment"
                                    │
                ┌───────────────────┴────────────────┐
          Assessment of risk                   Outline steps to achieve
             to health                         prevention or adequate
                                               control under
                                               Regulation 7
                │
        Identify action to
        comply with
        Regulations 8–13
                │
   ┌────────────┼──────────────┐
Regulation 8          Regulation 9
Use of control        Maintenance,
measures              examination and
                      test of controls

Regulation 10         Regulation 11
Monitoring            Health
exposure              surveillance

Regulation 12         Regulation 13
Information,          Accidents,
instruction           incidents and
and training          emergencies
```

Detailed compliance requirements for biological agents are found in Schedule 3 of the COSHH Regulations 2002 (as amended). These statutory requirements are elaborated on in Appendix 2 of the COSHH ACoP (HSC 2005). Initially, biological agents must be classified into one of four hazard groups based on their ability to cause infection, the severity of the disease which may result, the risk that the infection will spread to the community, and the availability of effective treatment.

Under the COSHH Regulations, biological agents must be treated in the same way as any other substance hazardous to health. However, there are some fundamental differences with this type of risk assessment, as indicated by the comment below:

> *The assessment of microbiological risk, while sharing many principles common to the assessment of any risk, brings different challenges due to the intrinsic nature of micro-organisms; the ability of micro-organisms to replicate, spread from person to person and mutate are not shared by, for example, chemical or physical agents. Similarly, intervention strategies such as vaccination and antibiotic treatment, which are applicable to limiting some microbiological risks, are not a feature of other assessments. Uncertainty is, however, a common crucial factor, as is the frequent lack of sufficient data to derive a complete MRA[23]. Although there is always the incentive to assign a quantitative value to an MRA, in some circumstances a semi-quantitative or qualitative value will suffice or simply has to be accepted.* (Advisory Committee on Dangerous Pathogens, HSC (1996))

---

[23] Microbiological risk assessment.

Key aspects are the potential of the biological agent to cause harm and the nature and degree of worker exposure to it. Appendix 2 of the COSHH ACoP gives practical guidance on risk assessment relating to the special features of biological agents. The assessment should reflect the ability such agents have to infect and replicate, and the possibility that there may be a significant risk to health at low exposures.

Hazard identification

Three general hazard situations can occur with biological agents in the workplace:
1. Exposure which does not arise out of work, eg getting a cold from someone else at work.
2. Exposure which arises out of work but which is incidental, ie the activity does not involve direct work on or use of the biological agent itself. For example, exposure to biological agents arising in food production, agriculture, sewage disposal or in animal husbandry.
3. Exposure to work where there is a deliberate intention to use or evaluate a biological agent, eg work in a microbiological research or diagnostic pathology laboratory.

The COSHH Regulations do not normally apply to the first category of hazard above. However, risk assessment must be carried out and control measures applied in the case of the other two types of situation.

Classification of biological agents

Schedule 3 of the COSHH Regulations 2002 (as amended) requires that biological agents are classified into hazard groups using the following criteria:
1. Their ability to cause infection.
2. The severity of the disease that may result.
3. The risk that such infection will spread to the community.
4. The availability of vaccines and effective treatment.

These infection criteria are the *only* ones to be used for classification purposes even though an infectious biological agent may have other harmful properties, for example, toxicity or allergenicity. Some biological agents are not infectious at all and such a non-infectious biological agent would fall into Group 1. However, substantial control measures may still be needed for it, since it may have other harmful properties.

The HSC has published an approved classification (HSC 1998a) which lists many biological agents along with their assigned hazard group classification. However, where a strain of a particular organism is attenuated or has lost virulence, as a result of genetic modification, it may be re-classified by the employer, for containment purposes, using the classification criteria listed above. The approved classification is not exhaustive and if a biological agent is not listed, this does not automatically mean that it falls into Group 1, that is, representing the lowest hazard group; the employer must again apply the criteria given above.

TABLE 4.5: Hazard group classification of biological agents (COSHH 2002) (as amended)

Hazard Group	Criteria
Group 1	Unlikely to cause human disease
Group 2	Can cause human disease; may be a hazard to employees; unlikely to spread to the community; there is usually effective treatment available
Group 3	Can cause severe human disease; may be a serious hazard to employees; may spread to the community; usually effective treatment available
Group 4	Causes severe human disease; serious hazard to employees; likely to spread to the community; no effective treatment available

Risk assessment

As with any risk assessment, the initial objective is to gain information by asking questions about the key ingredients of the risk situation, namely:
 1. What is/are the substance(s) hazardous to health (in this case, the biological agent(s))?
 2. What is/are the work task(s)?
 3. Who is/are the exposed person(s)?

The detailed requirements of an assessment are similar to those outlined previously in Chapter 3. As noted above, the potential of a biological agent to cause harm and the nature and degree of worker exposure to it are very important factors. In medical and veterinary care facilities and farming, the assessment needs to take into account the uncertainties about the presence of biological agents in patients and animals. The assessment needs to consider potentially harmful tissue samples during their handling, storage, transport and, where appropriate, waste disposal.

In the light of the special features of such biological hazards, the assessment should specifically consider each of the following questions:

What tasks are under consideration?

Observation of the operator's work task and the overall work system is very important to gaining an understanding of how an infectious biological agent could result in exposure and consequent disease in workers.

Questions regarding the use of sharp objects and aerosol generation would be relevant in this case. For example, does the work involve significant use of sharp objects, such as the use of powered saws and knives in meat processing or needles and ampoules in clinical laboratories? Does any activity involve significant aerosol generation or generation of dust clouds?

What biological agents may be present?

It is important to determine initially what biological agent hazards may be present, where they are and how they are transmitted. In addition:
 1. In which hazard group(s) does/do the biological agent(s) belong?
 2. What is the physical form of any biological agent(s)? For example, what is the possibility of them forming hardy forms, such as spores or cysts, which are resistant to disinfection?
 3. Could contaminant viruses be present in non-hazardous cell cultures? Are there tumour cells which may colonise an infected person or produce high levels of hazardous proteins?
 4. What types of disease may the biological agents cause?

Who could be exposed to the biological agent?

This may include not only the task operator but also other people such as cleaners, maintenance workers, supervisors and other colleagues:
 1. Could any workers be particularly susceptible to infection? (The position of pregnant women and exposure to biological agents is discussed below.)
 2. Have potentially exposed workers had a previous infection or immunisation?

Current controls

For the task in question, it is important to determine: What control measures are currently in use and what controls need to be applied? Is any local extract ventilation equipment such as a microbiological safety cabinet employed for the work? If so, is it effective at removing contaminated air? In addition, is the control measure actually used by personnel and is there an adequate maintenance schedule?

Examples of other questions related to controls are given below:
 1. In appropriate situations, is substitution with other less harmful organisms possible?
 2. Can the numbers of people potentially exposed be reduced?
 3. Is any personal protective equipment specified for the task being used?
 4. Is there a current air monitoring programme or is one required?

BIOLOGICAL AGENTS

5. Is there a current health surveillance programme or is one needed?
6. Is the current information, instruction and training provision for workers adequate? Do people understand the hazards of biological agents and the necessary precautions to be taken?

Pregnant women

Some infections (bacterial, viral and parasitic) contracted during pregnancy may affect the health of the mother and/or baby. These effects range from little impact to severe harm, which may result in disability and death. Usually, infection during pregnancy is no more likely than at other times. However, in some cases the infection may be more severe, for example, the chicken pox virus.

If the woman carrying out an activity is of child-bearing capacity, pregnant or a new mother, this must be taken account of in the risk assessment and it may be necessary to adopt further control measures, for example, hygienic breast-feeding facilities. Table 4.6 lists some agents known to present a risk to the foetus or new-born baby.

TABLE 4.6: Infectious biological agents and pregnancy

Infection	Occupational groups
Chlamydia psittaci	Agricultural workers, farmers, pet shop workers, veterinary surgeons
Cytomegalovirus	Nursery workers, healthcare workers
Hepatitis A	Nursery workers, primary school workers, sewage workers
Hepatitis B	Healthcare workers, dentists, laboratory workers, emergency service workers, social workers
HIV	Healthcare workers, dentists, laboratory workers, emergency service workers, social workers
Listeria	Laboratory workers, food workers, farmers, abattoir workers
Parvovirus	Healthcare workers, childcare workers, teachers
Rubella	Nursery workers, healthcare workers, laboratory workers
Toxoplasma	Veterinary surgeons, agricultural workers, ground staff, park keepers
Chicken pox	Healthcare workers, nursery workers, teachers

(Adapted from ACDP 1997)

Risk tolerability

When the necessary information has been collected and examined, a conclusion should be made regarding the overall tolerability of the health risk for the task in question. There are no specific occupational exposure limits for biological agents. The risk assessment should conclude that the overall risk from a given activity is either tolerable or intolerable (see Table 4.7). This reflects the level of overall risk tolerability based on the residual risk, taking into account the inherent level of risk together with the impact of any applied controls.

TABLE 4.7: Risk assessment conclusions

Conclusion
1. Risk to health unlikely
2. Risks significant – all adequate precautions in force
3. Risks significant – further precautions need to be applied
4. Uncertain about risk to health – further information required
5. Uncertain about precautions necessary – further information required

(Modified from HSE 1993)

Prevention and control of exposure

General aspects

COSHH (regulation 7) requires an employer to ensure that exposure to any biological agent is either prevented or, where this is not reasonably practicable, 'adequate' control is applied to limit exposure. Following risk assessment, the application of appropriate prevention or control measures is required. These control options need to be complemented and underpinned by adequate administrative arrangements, including provision for regular review. A hierarchy of control is imposed by COSHH 2002, regulation 7. Here, control at source is the preferred option, followed by engineering control measures. Only if it is not reasonably practicable to apply these measures to reduce risks to tolerable levels is personal protective equipment allowed.

So far as biological agents are concerned, regulation 7(10) directs attention to Schedule 3, which deals with the special provisions relating to biological agents. The selection of control measures should take into account the fact that biological agents do not have any air quality exposure limits, and their ability to infect and replicate at very small doses.

As regards control, the question may be asked as to whether the work activity can be carried out without using a biological agent or with a less harmful agent. Obviously, in some situations this question is inappropriate, for example, in a diagnostic pathology laboratory, the whole purpose is to identify and evaluate harmful biological agents. The position is similar in a research laboratory that is specifically investigating biological agents. Where prevention is not possible, then exposure must be adequately controlled.

Not all of the general measures listed below will be required in every situation and each should be used when it is considered: (a) to be applicable; and (b) that it will lead to a reduction in risk.

General control measures for biological agents include the following:

1. **Restricting employee exposure** – Keeping as low as practicable the number of employees exposed or likely to be exposed to the biological agent.
2. **Design of work processes** – Designing work processes and engineering controls so as to prevent or minimise the release of biological agents.
3. **Display of warning signs** – Displaying the biological agent sign and other appropriate warning signs.
4. **Emergency plans** – Preparation of emergency plans to deal with accidents involving biological agents.
5. **Decontamination/disinfection** – Specification of appropriate decontamination and disinfection procedures.
6. **Waste disposal** – After suitable treatment where appropriate, instituting procedures for the safe collection, storage and disposal of contaminated waste, including the use of secure and identifiable containers.
7. **Safe handling/transport** – Making arrangements for the safe handling and transport of biological agents, or materials which may contain such agents, within the workplace.
8. **Taking/handling and processing of samples** – Specifying procedures for taking, handling and processing samples which may contain biological agents.
9. **Personal protection measures** – Providing collective protective measures and, where exposure cannot be adequately controlled by other means, individual protective measures, in particular appropriate protective clothing and equipment.
10. **Vaccination** – Where appropriate, making available effective vaccines to employees who are not otherwise immune to the biological agents to which they are exposed or are liable to be exposed.
11. **Hygiene measures** – Taking appropriate hygiene measures compatible with the aim of preventing or reducing the accidental transfer or release of a biological agent, such as adequate provision of washing and toilet facilities and the prohibition of eating, drinking and application of cosmetics in the work area.

Monitoring techniques

With biological agents, exposure assessment is normally semi-quantitative. The routine use of atmospheric and personal sampling methods to obtain a quantitative estimate of exposure is not normally appropriate. The integrity of industrial process systems, for example, filters, seals and joints, may be assessed using atmospheric monitoring, where appropriate methods exist.

Monitoring biological agents includes taking and analysing a representative sample, from air, water, soil or other media, and the detailed arrangements will depend on the objective of the survey. It may be of interest to monitor both the kinds of micro-organisms present and their numbers. For monitoring bacteria and fungi, air samples are collected by the sampled air being drawn across a nutrient agar medium. Colony growth on the nutrient agar plates is examined at a later stage. Surface wipe samples and personal monitoring may be undertaken to give an estimate of overall contamination. A range of monitoring techniques are discussed by Ashton & Gill (2000).

Health surveillance

One objective of health surveillance is to determine the immune status of the potentially exposed workers, usually before and after vaccination. Routine antibody or other related testing is not normally appropriate until there are indications that an infection has occurred (HSC 2005). Where a person is believed to be suffering from an infection caused by work, then others who have been similarly exposed should be put under a health surveillance programme. Where workers are believed to be exposed to respiratory sensitisers of biological origin, then they should be put under an appropriate health surveillance regime.

Personal protective equipment

Where exposure to biological agents cannot be prevented or adequately controlled by other means, then appropriate personal protective equipment will be required. This may include gloves, coats, aprons, and boots together with eye and respiratory protection. In a specific situation, the risk assessment will determine the type of personal protective equipment required.

Detailed arrangements for the examination, maintenance and cleaning of personal protective equipment should be specified to prevent the equipment itself becoming the site of infection. Specific protective clothing and its usage are prescribed by the defined containment levels in Schedule 3 of COSHH 2002 (as amended). Personal protection strategy is dealt with in detail in Chapter 13.

Information, instruction and training for employees

It is vital that both workers and managers have adequate information on risks and methods of control. Information, instruction and training is required as would be appropriate with any hazardous substance. However, it is important to emphasise the key differences between the hazards posed by infective biological agents and chemical agents, including infection and replication of biological agents at very low exposure doses and possible person-to-person spread. Information should cover the following:

- legal requirements to control the risk of disease in humans;
- good occupational hygiene practices to control the spread of infection;
- personal protective equipment; and
- symptoms and controls for common diseases.

In addition, detailed written procedures are required and, where appropriate, notices must be displayed which include procedures to be followed:

- in the case of an incident which may have released a biological agent capable of causing severe human disease; and
- when handling a Group 4 biological agent or material which may contain such an agent.

Employees should also be informed about any incident resulting in the release of a biological agent which may cause severe human disease, the causes of the release and the rectifying measures applied.

Special control measures

Clinical waste

The HSC (1999) cites authoritative estimates that the UK healthcare sector, including NHS health trusts, nursing homes, GP and dental surgeries, generates about 400,000 tonnes of clinical waste per year. In this context, 'clinical waste' includes blood or other body fluids, excretions, drugs or other pharmaceutical products, swabs or dressings, and syringes, needles or other sharp instruments.

This is a very large potential source of exposure to biological agents (and other hazards) and it must be properly managed from its point of origin to its point of ultimate disposal. This involves risk assessment and management of the whole process, encompassing segregation, handling, transport and disposal of wastes in order to protect workers, the public and the environment. The HSC (1999) gives comprehensive guidance on the risk assessment and management of this waste.

Special control measures are prescribed by COSHH for health and veterinary care facilities, laboratories, animal rooms and industrial processes.

Health and veterinary care facilities

In health and veterinary care facilities, where there are human patients or animals which may be infected with a Group 3 or 4 biological agent (or are suspected of being), the employer must select the most suitable containment measures from those listed in Part II of the Schedule. This is summarised in Table 4.8.

Laboratories and animal rooms

Where work activities involve Group 2, 3 or 4 biological agents, then it is necessary to decide on the level of containment to control exposure of employees. This may occur in various types of laboratory and other work areas, for example:

- **Diagnostic clinical laboratories** – where the principal purpose is to carry out investigations on biological specimens which may contain biological agents, eg testing for the presence of, or identifying, a biological agent.
- **Research laboratories** – where the purpose is to investigate the biological specimens or animals, or to develop genetic manipulation techniques.
- **Animal rooms/houses** – much of the above work may also involve the housing and handling of animals, where animals have been deliberately infected or suspected of being naturally infected with biological agents.

The containment levels discussed below are directly focusing on infection control with different hazard groups of biological agents. In each case, not only infective hazards must be addressed in deciding control strategies but also toxic and allergenic hazards arising from exposure to biological agents in these types of work, for example, the risk of an extrinsic allergic alveolitis arising from exposure to proteins in laboratory animal faeces. Taking account of the risk assessment, in all cases protective measures must utilise the most suitable combination of controls prescribed in Schedule 3 and summarised in Table 4.8. This details requirements for Containment Levels 2, 3 and 4.

Under COSHH, minimum containment levels for biological agents assigned to specified hazard groups are:

- Level 2 for a Group 2 biological agent;
- Level 3 for a Group 3 biological agent; and
- Level 4 for a Group 4 biological agent.

Some flexibility is made in the prescribed level of containment for laboratories which do not intentionally work with biological agents and where there is known to be some uncertainty about the presence of Group 2, 3 or 4 agents. Here, Containment Level 2 is required for work. Containment Level 3 is required where a risk assessment is inconclusive and the activity is thought possibly to involve a serious health risk.

BIOLOGICAL AGENTS

TABLE 4.8: Summary of containment measures for health and veterinary care facilities, laboratories and animal rooms (Schedule 3, Part II, COSHH 2002 (as amended))

	CONTAINMENT MEASURES	CONTAINMENT LEVELS		
		2	3	4
1.	The workplace to be separated from other activities in the same building	No	Yes	Yes
2.	Input air and extract air to the workplace to be filtered to HEPA or equivalent	No	Yes, on extract air	Yes, on input and double on extract air
3.	Access – authorised persons only	Yes	Yes	Yes, air-lock key procedure
4.	Workplace sealable – to permit disinfection	No	Yes	Yes, for bench, floor, walls and ceiling
5.	Specified disinfection procedures	Yes	Yes	Yes
6.	Workplace negative air pressure required	No, unless mechanically ventilated	Yes	Yes
7.	Efficient vector control (eg for rodents and insects)	Yes, for animal containment	Yes, for animal containment	Yes
8.	Surfaces impervious to water and easy to clean	Yes, for bench	Yes, for bench and floor (and walls for animal containment)	Yes, for bench and floor (and walls for animal containment)
9.	Surfaces resistant to acids, alkalis, solvents and disinfectants	Yes, for bench	Yes, for bench and floor (and walls for animal containment)	Yes, for bench and floor (and walls for animal containment)
10.	Safe storage of biological agents	Yes	Yes	Yes, secure storage
11.	Observation window or alternative required, so occupant can be seen	No	Yes	Yes
12.	Laboratory to contain its own equipment	No	Yes, so far as is reasonably practicable	Yes
13.	Infected material, including any animal, to be handled in safety cabinet or isolator or equivalent	Yes, where aerosol produced	Yes, where aerosol produced	Yes, (Class III cabinet)
14.	Incinerator for disposal of animal carcasses	Accessible	Accessible	Yes, on site

TABLE 4.9: Summary of containment measures for industrial processes (Schedule 3, Part III, COSHH 2002 (as amended))

CONTAINMENT MEASURES	CONTAINMENT LEVELS		
	2	3	4
1. Viable micro-organisms contained in a system which physically separates the process from the environment (closed system)	Yes	Yes	Yes
2. Exhaust gases from closed system should be treated so as to:	Minimise release	Prevent release	Prevent release
3. Sample collection, addition of material to a closed system and transfer of viable micro-organisms to another closed system should be performed so as to:	Minimise release	Prevent release	Prevent release
4. Bulk culture fluids should not be removed from the closed system unless the viable micro-organisms have been:	Inactivated by validated means	Inactivated by validated chemical or physical means	Inactivated by validated chemical or physical means
5. Seals to be designed so as to:	Minimise release	Prevent release	Prevent release
6. Closed systems within a controlled area	Optional	Optional	Yes, and purpose-built
(a) biohazard signs should be posted	Optional	Yes	Yes
(b) access should be restricted to nominated personnel only	Optional	Yes	Yes, via air-lock
(c) personnel should wear personal protective equipment	Yes, work clothing	Yes	Yes, a complete change
(d) decontamination and washing facilities provided	Yes	Yes	Yes
(e) personnel should shower before leaving controlled area	No	Optional	Yes
(f) effluent from sinks and showers should be collected and inactivated before release	No	Optional	Yes
(g) controlled area adequately ventilated	Optional	Optional	Yes
(h) controlled area under negative pressure	No	Optional	Yes
(i) input and extract air HEPA filtered	No	Optional	Yes
(j) controlled area designed to contained spillage of entire contents	Optional	Yes	Yes
(k) controlled area sealable to permit fumigation	No	Optional	Yes
7. Effluent treatment before final discharge	Inactivated by validated means	Inactivated by validated chemical or physical means	Inactivated by validated chemical or physical means

Industrial processes

A wide diversity of industries use biotechnology applications which may involve the large-scale contained use of biological agents. In this case, protective measures for industrial processes are summarised in Table 4.9. These prescribe the detailed requirements for Containment Levels 2, 3 and 4.

The minimum containment levels specified are:
- Level 2 for a Group 2 biological agent;
- Level 3 for a Group 3 biological agent; and
- Level 4 for a Group 4 biological agent.

Where genetically modified organisms (GMOs) are handled under containment, then the Genetically Modified Organisms (Contained Use) Regulations 2000 would apply. These are designed to ensure the safe use and handling of GMOs. Among other things, these Regulations require that genetically modified micro-organisms be classified into low and high hazard categories (Groups 1 and 2 respectively), and also that work activities be classified into small-scale research and development (Type A) and general, large volume industrial operations (Type B). Risk assessment and containment measures for the various hazard and/or work activity combinations are specified in the Regulations.

Specific legislative requirements

An outline of relevant legislative requirements regarding biological agents is given in Table 4.10.

TABLE 4.10: Legislation and biological agents

Legislation	Requirements
Control of Substances Hazardous to Health Regulations 2002 (as amended)	Risk assessment and control of exposure to biological agents; Schedule 3 specifies Approved List and containment measures
Reporting of Injuries, Diseases and Dangerous Occurrences Regulations 1995	Reporting of specific diseases contracted as a result of exposure to biological agents at work
Genetically Modified Organisms (Contained Use) Regulations 2000	Require risk assessment (and, in some cases, notification to the HSE) of all activities involving the contained use of genetically modified organisms
Genetically Modified Organisms (Deliberate Release) Regulations 2002	Controls all deliberate releases of genetically modified organisms to the environment; with GM plants, consent must be obtained for field trials prior to commercialisation

List of employees exposed to certain biological agents

The employer must keep a list of employees exposed to a Group 3 or 4 biological agent. This list should include the type of work and biological agent(s) concerned, exposure record, and accidents and incidents. It should be kept for 10 years after the last known exposure. In the case of those biological agents exhibiting latent infections or other chronic features, then records must be kept for 40 years.

Notification of biological agents

An employer must inform the HSE if he or she intends to store or use (for the first time) Group 2, 3 or 4 biological agents. All Group 4 agents and other very dangerous viruses, such as Simian herpes B virus and Monkeypox virus, are subject to very strict notification requirements.

Some infectious diseases caused by biological agents are reportable under RIDDOR 1995 and these are listed in Table 4.11.

TABLE 4.11: Diseases due to biological agents reportable under RIDDOR 1995

Disease[24]	Work activity
Bacterial	
Leptospirosis (20)	(a) work in places which are, or are liable to be, infested by rats, field mice, voles or other small mammals; (b) work at dog kennels or involving the care or handling of dogs; or (c) work involving contact with bovine animals or their meat products or pigs or their meat products
Anthrax (15)	(a) work involving handling infected animals, their products or packaging containing infected material; or (b) work on infected sites
Tuberculosis (26)	Work with humans or animals, or human or animal remains or any other material which might be a source of infection
Legionellosis (19)	Work on or near cooling systems which are located in the workplace and use water; or work on hot water service systems located in the workplace which are likely to be a source of contamination
Brucellosis (16)	Work involving contact with: (a) animals or their carcasses (including any parts thereof) infected by *Brucella* or the untreated products of same; or (b) laboratory specimens or vaccines of, or containing, *Brucella*
Tetanus (25)	Work involving contact with soil likely to be contaminated by animals
Streptococcus suis (24)	Work involving contact with pigs infected with *Streptococcus suis*, or with the carcasses, products or residues of pigs so affected
Q fever (22)	Work involving contact with animals, their remains or their untreated products
(A) Avian chlamydiosis (17)	Work involving contact with birds infected with *Chlamydia psittaci*, or the remains or untreated products of such birds
(B) Ovine chlamydiosis (17)	Work involving contact with sheep infected with *Chlamydia psittaci* or the remains or untreated products of such sheep
Lyme disease (21)	Work involving exposure to ticks (including in particular work by forestry workers, rangers, dairy farmers, gamekeepers and other persons engaged in countryside management)
Extrinsic alveolitis (including farmer's lung) (46)	Work involving exposure to moulds, fungal spores or heterologous proteins during work in: (a) agriculture, horticulture, forestry, cultivation of edible fungi or malt working; (b) loading, unloading or handling mouldy vegetable matter or edible fungi while same is being stored; (c) caring for or handling birds; or (d) handling bagasse
Viral	
Hepatitis (18)	Work involving contact with: (a) human blood or human blood products; or (b) any source of viral hepatitis
Rabies (23)	Work involving handling or contact with infected animals
Mixed	
Any infection reliably attributable to the performance of the work specified opposite (27)	Work with micro-organisms; work with live or dead human beings in the course of providing any treatment or service or in conducting any investigation involving exposure to blood or body fluids; work with animals or any potentially infected material derived from any of the above
Occupational asthma (47)	Animals including insects and other arthropods (whether in their larval forms or not) used for the purposes of pest control or fruit cultivation or the larval forms of animals used for the purposes of research or education or in laboratories; crustaceans or fish or products arising from these in the food processing industry

[24] Diseases with RIDDOR 1995 numbering.

Biological agents and disease

Selected examples of important occupational diseases caused by biological agents are discussed below. These are subdivided into bacterial diseases, viral diseases and diseases resulting from mixed exposures.

Bacterial diseases

Leptospirosis (Weil's disease and cattle leptospirosis)

This is a disease of rodents which can also occur in dogs, pigs, cattle and man. The principal organism is *Leptospira icterohaemorrhagiae*, a Group 2 biological agent. (*L. harjo* is the strain transmitted from cattle to humans.) The disease is prevalent worldwide, particularly in areas where the population (including workers) is in contact with rats, or water or soil contaminated by rat urine, cattle urine or cattle faecal material. The organism enters through skin cuts and abrasions, intact skin and through the mucous membrane lining of the nose, mouth and conjunctiva. Leptospires may also be ingested via food or water contaminated by rat urine. The organism can survive for considerable periods in spore form outside the host (HSE 1993a).

Symptoms of the disease develop within one to two weeks of initial infection and are similar to hepatitis with varying severity. Normally, symptoms include an initial fever, high temperature, headache, vomiting and muscle pain. Jaundice may occur at a later stage. Other possible symptoms include haemorrhaging and liver or kidney failure; meningitis is also common with this condition. The disease is much more amenable to treatment if diagnosed early. The level of mortality depends on the age of the patient and the relative virulence of the organism.

Groups at risk include sewer and abattoir workers, veterinary surgeons, farmers (especially dairy farmers), construction workers, water and/or leisure industry workers, laboratory workers and miners. Prevention and control measures are necessary when contact is likely. The primary control measure is rodent eradication and control, and correct veterinary management of infected cattle. Other measures include:

1. Protective clothing (gloves and waterproof suits).
2. Drug therapy.
3. Information, instruction and training. Workers should be issued with a Weil's disease warning card to help ensure early reporting and treatment, which is vitally important.
4. Exposed personnel should have access to good hygiene and washing facilities.
5. Drainage of wet ground where possible to eliminate the infection reservoir.

Leptospirosis is a reportable illness under the requirements of RIDDOR 1995.

Anthrax (wool-sorter's disease)

This is primarily a disease of animals including cattle, sheep, pigs and goats – it is very rare in humans (but has developed a high profile since 11 September 2001). The principal organism is the bacterium *Bacillus anthracis*, a Group 3 biological agent. Infection usually occurs during the handling of contaminated skins, carcasses or other products. The organism is found in cattle, goats, horses, sheep, pigs and their products including hair, wool, skins and bone meal. The organism produces spores which enable the bacterium to survive harmful conditions for many years. The disease is very rare in the UK, although British tourists abroad have contracted it. There is a continuing risk from infected animals, their products and contaminated land. The spores are important in the transmission of the disease from animal to animal, and from animal to man by inanimate dusts and personal contact.

Cutaneous anthrax

This makes up about 95 per cent of all cases of anthrax and occurs as a result of an external infection, where spores enter the skin through a cut or abrasion to form a malignant pustule. A pimple or skin ulcer occurs two to five days after the initial infection by the spores or bacterium. These mostly occur around the head, neck and face area with far fewer on the limbs and trunk. Symptoms are malaise, fever, oedema, blisters, vomiting and collapse. The disease is sometimes fatal but more often than not there is full recovery with antibiotics, usually penicillin.

Pulmonary and gastrointestinal anthrax

Inhalation of spore-containing material and person-to-person infection is also possible, leading to much more serious conditions of pulmonary anthrax and pneumonia. There is also a rare ingestion or intestinal form of anthrax, which is not seen in humans in temperate zones.

Pulmonary anthrax results from the handling of infected animals and their products and occupations at risk include agricultural workers, veterinary surgeons, tannery workers and butchers.

Prevention and control measures include the following options:

1. Anthrax warning card for workers.
2. Vaccination of animals.
3. Sterilisation of hides by steam, disinfectant (formalin) or irradiation.
4. Good hygiene practice.
5. Effective ventilation.
6. Personal protective equipment including overalls, gloves and respirator.

Anthrax is a reportable illness under the requirements of RIDDOR 1995.

Tuberculosis

This disease affects humans, warm-blooded animals, birds and reptiles. The principal organism in humans is *Mycobacterium tuberculosis*, a Group 3 biological agent; in cattle, it is *Mycobacterium bovis*, also a Group 3 biological agent. These bacteria have a worldwide distribution and are particularly prevalent where living standards are low and there is poor nutrition.

These organisms are transmitted by contact with the tissues and carcasses of infected animals, either by inhalation or skin contact. Sputum is a highly infective agent. Sometimes the disease is asymptomatic and the condition is first discovered by chest X-ray. Tuberculosis can affect all body organs but, in 90 per cent of cases, the principal target is the lungs. The mycobacterium together with the body's white cells form a 'tubercle', which provokes fibrosis, the production of scar tissue and the exudation of fluid. In this process, the host tissue is destroyed and highly infective sputum is coughed up. This pulmonary form of the disease may lead to death.

Occupational groups at risk include farmers, veterinary surgeons, nurses, doctors, paramedical and laboratory workers, abattoir personnel and mortuary staff. The disease is spread rapidly by infected people and animals.

Prevention and control measures include:

1. Eradication of the organism in animal populations.
2. Vaccination (BCG in humans).
3. Personal protective equipment.
4. Information, instruction and training.

The incidence of tuberculosis in some communities has increased due to enhanced resistance to drugs and the lowered resistance of AIDS patients.

Tuberculosis is a reportable illness under the requirements of RIDDOR 1995.

Legionellosis (including legionnaire's disease)

This condition was first identified in 1976 following a large outbreak of pneumonia in people attending a conference in Philadelphia, USA. Legionellosis is a flu-like condition and it is most commonly caused by the bacterium *Legionella pneumophila*, a Group 2 biological agent. More than 40 individual species of *Legionella* have now been identified and 90 per cent of cases are associated with this organism. There are between 150 and 200 cases reported in the UK each year. *Legionella* bacteria are found in soil, rivers and streams, and in stagnant water in air-conditioning and water systems in hotels, hospitals and industrial premises. Water in these systems is often stored under such conditions as to encourage the growth of this organism. Growth of the bacterium is encouraged over the temperature range 20–45ºC. Below 20ºC, there is no proliferation of the organism, and above 60ºC, it does not survive. The organism may lie dormant and only grow when the water reaches a suitable temperature.

The sediment, sludge, scale and organic material in water systems act as a source of nutrient for the bacterium. Also, certain types of water fittings and pipework (and the materials used) may provide nutrient and make eradication difficult. Common organisms found in water systems, including algae, amoebae and other bacteria, may be an additional nutrient source. This enclosure in a 'biofilm' may protect the bacterium against biocides, which would normally be lethal to free organisms in water.

Risk assessment should take into account:

- the potential for water droplet formation;
- the temperature of the water;
- those groups at risk; and
- means of preventing or controlling the risk.

The bacterium is transmitted by aqueous mists which are inhaled deep into the lung by the exposed person. There is apparently no person-to-person transmission. Symptoms include fever, chills, headache and muscle pain. A dry cough and difficulty in breathing develops later and, in some patients, diarrhoea, vomiting, delirium and confusion. In some cases, symptoms of infection are restricted to a mild flu-like condition. However, legionellosis has a 12 per cent chance of mortality, which is higher in vulnerable groups such as diabetics, alcoholics and those with chronic respiratory or kidney conditions.

Prevention of exposure is principally achieved by the regular cleaning and disinfection of water systems, paying particular attention to shower or spray heads. An ACoP dealing with the prevention and control of legionellosis has recently been updated (HSC 2000).

Prevention and control measures include:

1. Temperature control to maintain temperatures above 60°C. However, care is needed when there are vulnerable groups, eg in old people's homes where temperatures greater than 43°C may cause scalding. Values between 20°C and 45°C should be avoided.
2. Avoiding water stagnation, eg in pipe 'deadlegs'.
3. Avoiding structural materials that harbour organisms or provide nutrients, eg leather, some rubbers and plastics.
4. Keeping systems clean and avoiding sediments.
5. Applying an effective water treatment programme with biocides to control scaling, corrosion and fouling.
6. Operating systems safely, particularly wet cooling towers and evaporative condensers, with effective maintenance and water quality monitoring.

Legionellosis is a reportable illness under the requirements of RIDDOR 1995.

Brucellosis

This condition is associated with work involving cattle and it is sometimes known as 'undulant fever'. There has been a dramatic reduction in UK incidence from 600 cases in the early 1970s, down to only seven cases in 1984 and one case in 1996. The principal organisms involved are in cattle, *Brucella abortus*, in pigs, *Brucella suis*, and in goats and sheep, *Brucella melitensis*. All three organisms are Group 3 biological agents. *Brucella abortus* is found worldwide and is transmitted via skin cuts and grazes following contact with infected animals and their discharges. At one time, milk and milk products were affected, but now this is controlled by pasteurisation. Other modes of input are ingestion, inhalation and passage through the conjunctiva of the eye.

Symptoms in humans are an intermittent fever with malaise, weakness and fatigue, while in cattle there is spontaneous abortion. Occupational groups at risk are those in contact with bovine animals and their untreated products, that is, veterinary surgeons, farm workers, laboratory workers, butchers and abattoir workers. Transmission is via contact with infected animals and their tissues, via skin cuts and grazes, ingestion (via the hands), and inhalation of aerosols.

Principal prevention measures have aimed to eradicate the organism from cattle. Although brucellosis is still a reportable disease under RIDDOR 1995, virtually no cases have been reported in the UK in recent years. Specific control measures include:

1. Regular testing of cattle for infection.
2. Pasteurisation of milk and milk products.
3. Preventing the importation of infected animals.
4. Personal protective equipment.
5. Information, instruction and training for those at risk.
6. Disinfection of contaminated areas.

Tetanus

This disease occurs in animals and humans and is commonly known as 'lockjaw'. It is caused by the rod-shaped bacterium *Clostridium tetani*, a Group 2 biological agent. This is found in the gastrointestinal tract of warm-blooded animals and in spore form in the soil. This endospore can germinate when it gains access to a cut or wound following contact with contaminated soil or clothing. The bacterium itself is localised in the wound and it is the exotoxin which enters the systemic circulation. This acts as a neurotoxin and results in involuntary muscle contraction, which is particularly noticeable in the jaw. Occupational groups at risk are agricultural and horticultural workers and others who may come into contact with contaminated soil or clothing.

Prevention and control measures include:
1. Cleaning of cuts and wounds.
2. Vaccination.
3. Antibiotics.
4. Good general hygiene practices.
5. Information, instruction and training for those at risk.

Tetanus is a reportable illness under the requirements of RIDDOR 1995.

Streptococcosis

Clinical symptoms of this condition are fever and often meningitis. There is a fatality rate of around eight per cent and definitive deafness and ataxia (lack of muscle co-ordination) has been reported in up to 50 per cent of survivors. Occupational groups at risk are those having close contact with pigs infected with *Streptococcus suis*, a Group 2 agent, or with the carcasses, products or residues of such animals. Normally, this condition is treated successfully with penicillin.

Disease induced by *Streptococcus suis* is reportable under the requirements of RIDDOR 1995.

Q fever

In Q or 'Query' fever the causative organism is *Coxiella burnettii*, a Group 3 agent, which is a rickettsia. Infection occurs in those occupational groups which have contact with animals, principally sheep and cattle, their remains or their untreated products. The organism can remain viable in dusts for many months. The onset of the disease is insidious with fever as the main symptom, sometimes accompanied by painful limbs, headache and photophobia. Q fever can be prevented in humans by immunisation but standard measures to avoid exposure sources should also be taken. Prevention and control measures include:
1. Personal protective equipment including gloves and coveralls.
2. Careful disposal of infected material and animal wastes.
3. Good personal hygiene.
4. Information, instruction and training for workers.

Q fever is a reportable illness under the requirements of RIDDOR 1995.

Chlamydiosis

Ovine chlamydiosis

This infection is caused by exposure to the organism *Chlamydia psittaci*, mainly from handling and contact with sheep (and possibly goats) and their products of conception (offspring/afterbirth). In humans, this infection may cause abortion and a flu-like illness. The non-avian strain is a Group 2 agent.

Prevention and control measures include:
1. Avoiding contact between pregnant women and pregnant ewes.
2. Strict segregation of protective clothing for cleaning.
3. Treatment with antibiotics.
4. Vaccination of breeding sheep.
5. Information, instruction and training for workers (visitors to farms must also be made aware of the risk).

Avian chlamydiosis

This disease is contracted in those having contact with birds (parrots, ducks and poultry) infected with *Chlamydia psittaci*, a Group 3 agent, or their remains or untreated avian products. In humans, a flu-like illness may develop leading to pneumonia and other serious health problems. Infection is transmitted by inhaling dust or aerosol containing bird faeces. Early diagnosis is important to successful treatment with antibiotics.

Prevention and control measures include:
1. Identify and reduce sources of production of dust.
2. Screen flocks for the infective organism.
3. High standard of flock husbandry.
4. Local exhaust ventilation in evisceration areas.
5. Personal protection including respiratory protection.
6. Good personal hygiene.
7. Information, instruction and training for workers (visitors to farms must also be made aware of the risk).

Both avian and ovine chlamydiosis are reportable conditions under the requirements of RIDDOR 1995.

Lyme disease

This disease occurs in occupational groups carrying out activities involving exposure to ticks. This includes forestry workers, rangers, dairy farmers, gamekeepers and other people engaged in countryside management. The condition occurs when a person is bitten by an insect (tick) infected with the bacterium *Borrelia burgdorferi*, a Group 2 agent. Deer and other wild animals are carriers of this parasitic insect. The first sign of the disease may be a faint, ring-shaped rash a few weeks after a bite with the subsequent development of an intermittent flu-like illness. At an early stage, the infection responds well to antibiotics, but if left untreated it may result in serious illness.

Prevention and control measures include:
1. Keeping skin covered – especially the legs.
2. Checking skin and clothing frequently, with removal of any ticks and covering any bites.
3. Information, instruction and training for those at risk. Those at risk should know the symptoms and realise the importance of immediately seeking medical help.

Lyme disease is a reportable illness under the requirements of RIDDOR 1995.

Extrinsic allergic alveolitis

Organic substances often either induce asthma or may affect the alveoli and gas transfer region of the respiratory system. In these conditions, an allergic response to a wide range of antigens, particularly complex organic dusts, may occur in the alveoli. 'Extrinsic allergic alveotitis' includes farmer's lung and describes similar diseases occurring in other occupational groups as shown in Table 4.12.

TABLE 4.12: Extrinsic allergic alveolitis

Exposure agent	Disease
Mouldy hay spores – *Thermoactinomycetes vulgaris* and *Micropolyspora faeni*	Farmer's lung
Bird droppings – avian serum proteins	Bird fancier's lung
Mouldy sugar cane – *Thermoactinomycetes vulgaris*	Bagassosis
Mushroom compost – *Fusarium rectivirgula*	Mushroom worker's lung
Mixed – fungi; amoebae; bacterial	Humidifier fever

Farmer's lung

If hay has been harvested when damp, it can become warm during storage and this promotes the growth of spore-forming actinomycetes. Farmer's lung is caused by inhalation of spore-containing dust from such mouldy hay. The principal organisms are *Thermoactinomycetes vulgaris* and *Micropolyspora faeni* which provoke an allergic response in the lung. The principal occupational groups at risk are farmers and agricultural workers.

Symptoms include a dry cough, general malaise, weakness, fever, a shortness of breath during exertion and joint pains. In contrast to asthma, there is an absence of wheeziness. When the person is removed from exposure, symptoms disappear within 12 hours. Damage to lung tissues may occur during the acute stage of the disease and this may progress to a chronic phase with repeated exposure to spore-forming dusts. This results in collagenous scar tissue (pulmonary fibrosis) which causes impaired respiratory function (symptoms of breathlessness and weakness) and also puts a strain on the heart. Sufferers may succumb to *cor pulmonale*, that is, heart failure caused by respiratory insufficiency.

Prevention and control measures include:

1. Suppression and/or removal of spore-forming dust.
2. Application of correct methods for harvesting and storage of the hay.
3. Machines which will thresh and harvest grasses and cereals as they are cut.
4. Personal protective equipment – effective respiratory protection equipment, suitable protective clothing.
5. Health surveillance – regular monitoring with lung function tests.
6. Information, instruction and training.

Humidifier fever

Humidifier fever is a flu-like illness caused by inhalation of fine droplets of water from humidifiers, which have become contaminated by micro-organisms. Exposure results from spray emitted from the contaminated system. The disease is considered to be an extrinsic allergic alveolitis – organic dust toxic syndrome. Humidifiers are used in the print industry to stabilise the size and condition of paper and they are also present in air-conditioning systems.

The symptoms of humidifier fever vary from mild fever with headache, malaise and muscle weakness, to acute illness with high fever, cough, chest tightness and breathlessness on exertion. The onset of symptoms is delayed, beginning four to eight hours after the start of the working day or shift. Symptoms usually occur on the first day back at work after a weekend or other break and tend to disappear after 12 to 16 hours. The disease has been associated with fungi, amoebae and endotoxin-producing bacteria and, in some cases, antibodies have been detected for contaminating organisms. Previous exposure appears to be the major risk factor for illness.

Contamination of humidifier systems is most likely to occur in internal reservoirs within the humidifiers and in holding tanks, especially if the water is re-circulated. Paper dust or other substances may act as a nutrient for the growth of micro-organisms if they are allowed to accumulate.

Prevention and control measures include:

1. Selection of humidifier design least likely to become contaminated, eg steam humidifiers, compressed air atomisers that take water directly from the mains and evaporative type humidifiers that do not create water spray.

2. Suitable cleaning regime – weekly may be necessary in process environments; every two to three months may be sufficient for offices.

Extrinsic allergic alveolitis is a reportable illness under the requirements of RIDDOR 1995.

Viral diseases

Bloodborne viral infections

These are infections where blood containing infectious agents, for example, from people who may be carriers of hepatitis virus, is transferred into the body of another person giving rise to infection. The main concern is with those agents that persist in the blood, possibly unknown to the carrier who may be without any symptoms. The principal agents are human immunodeficiency virus (HIV) that causes acquired immune deficiency syndrome (AIDS) and three of the viruses that cause hepatitis, that is, hepatitis B virus, hepatitis C virus and hepatitis D virus.

Bloodborne viruses may be transmitted to workers or to patients and/or clients in the course of many medical and paramedical procedures. Any activity in which there is a risk of blood transfer, for example, surgery, dentistry, venepuncture, acupuncture, body piercing or tattooing, requires adequate precautions to avoid exposure of the operator and decontamination of any equipment. Accidents with 'sharps', for example, blood-contaminated needles in healthcare work, are probably the commonest mode of occupational transmission of bloodborne viruses. The number of healthcare workers known to have become infected with HIV as a result of occupational exposure is small considering the frequency of exposure to blood and body fluids in clinical and laboratory work (HSC 1996a).

Hepatitis

This condition results from inflammation of the liver which is usually caused by an infective virus or a toxic chemical agent. In viral hepatitis, there are several variant forms, depending on the specific infective virus. For convenience, these are grouped into two categories:

1. Hepatitis A.
2. Hepatitis B, hepatitis C and hepatitis D.

Hepatitis A

Hepatitis A virus is not primarily bloodborne and infection with this agent arises principally from contact with faeces or with faecally-contaminated food and water. It is classified as a Group 2 biological agent. The virus multiplies in the liver and passes into faeces via the bile duct. Transmission is via the faecal-oral route, with the ingestion of material contaminated by faeces. Symptoms include fever, headaches, jaundice, loss of appetite, nausea, vomiting and abdominal pain from a tender inflamed liver. Recovery is normally complete within one to two weeks and recurrence is rare. The severity of the disease is closely related to age. Although the very severe form is rare, symptoms are generally more severe in adults than in children or adolescents who are often asymptomatic.

Prevention and control measures include:

1. Achieving high standards of personal hygiene.
2. Vaccination.

Hepatitis B, C and D

Hepatitis B virus is classified as a Group 3 biological agent. Infection may occur by contact with infected human blood or body fluids, often via injection by 'sharps' injuries which may be caused by a contaminated syringe or broken glass. The condition may occur from two to six months following initial contact. This is a prolonged, damaging illness and the acute inflammation of the liver may be life-threatening. A person with no symptoms may still carry the infection.

Symptoms include fever, nausea, malaise, jaundice and severe damage to liver tissue. The condition may develop into chronic hepatitis, cirrhosis and primary liver cancer. Occupational groups at highest risk are healthcare workers, laboratory personnel, emergency service workers and social workers who may have contact with other high risk groups, such as drug abusers.

Prevention and control measures include:
1. Taking measures to avoid sharps injuries.
2. No re-use of needles.
3. Avoiding direct contact with body fluids.
4. Using approved washing and disinfection techniques.
5. Applying adequate clinical waste disposal procedures.
6. Personal protective equipment – gloves, protective clothing and respiratory protection.
7. Vaccination.
8. Blood tests to check the effectiveness of control measures.
9. Information, instruction and training on the nature of the hazard and the precautions to be taken.

Hepatitis B has declined in recent years due to greater awareness of the hazards, implementation of safe working practices and vaccination programmes (ACDP 1997).

Both hepatitis C and D viruses are classified as Group 3 biological agents. They are acquired in a similar way to hepatitis B. There is a vaccine, which will protect against hepatitis D, but not against hepatitis C, which is very infective. The above precautions are also applicable to hepatitis C and D viruses.

Hepatitis is a reportable illness under the requirements of RIDDOR 1995.

Acquired immune deficiency syndrome (AIDS)

This disease is characterised by a weakening of the body's immune defence mechanism with the affected individual becoming vulnerable to a variety of diseases and infections. It is caused by the human immunodeficiency virus (HIV), which is classified as a Group 3 agent. AIDS results in a variety of health problems due to a large reduction in the capacity of the immune system to defend the body against infectious and other disorders.

HIV is transmitted from an infected individual by body fluids including blood and semen and other blood-containing secretions. Any person who is, occupationally or otherwise, exposed to these fluids, has a risk of contracting AIDS. The virus can be transmitted from one person to another by skin cuts or scratches. In an occupational context, contact with contaminated needles and other sharps or with infected blood or blood products may result in the disease. Casual contact with infected persons does not pose a risk. In a social context, important transmission routes of HIV have been well documented, that is, unprotected sexual intercourse with an infected person or the practice of sharing needles among drug addicts.

Occupational groups at risk include medical and healthcare staff, social workers and emergency service workers. As the number of HIV infections rises, then the risk to these occupational groups will similarly rise. Between July 1997 and January 2000, there were 258 recorded incidents of healthcare workers in England and Wales being exposed to HIV (Wafer 2000).

The symptoms of AIDS develop in stages – some individuals develop AIDS after a period with little or no symptoms at all and many have no symptoms for several years. Symptoms are fever, sweating, aches, unexplained weight loss and diarrhoea. Full AIDS includes specific lung diseases (eg pneumonia), skin diseases (including skin cancer), and bacterial and viral infections. Furthermore, some patients develop dementia and disorientation.

Prevention and control measures include:
1. Taking measures to avoid sharps injuries.
2. The use of disposable needles and equipment where possible.
3. Avoiding direct contact with body fluids.
4. The use of special devices for mouth-to-mouth resuscitation.
5. Wearing personal protective equipment and clothing (eg gowns, gloves, masks, goggles).
6. Disinfection of work surfaces.
7. Bagging, labelling and incineration of clinical waste.

8. Providing suitable information, instruction and training for those occupationally at risk.
9. Achieving high standards of personal hygiene, particularly handwashing.
10. Providing counselling for those who become infected.

Orf

Orf is a viral skin infection, which is acquired following contact with infected sheep (in particular lambs) and goats. It is caused by the orf virus, which is classified as a Group 2 agent. This virus is transmitted by contact with lesions on animals or with infected wool, fencing or hedges, with skin cuts and abrasions as the mode of entry. Orf infection causes painful skin lesions on the face, hands and arms, which usually heal within six to eight weeks. It occurs in slaughterhouse workers and shepherds.

Principal preventive measures include:

1. Vaccination of animals.
2. Good personal hygiene.
3. Covering cuts and scratches on hands and arms.

Orf is a reportable disease under the requirements of RIDDOR 1995.

Rabies

Rabies is a highly pathogenic virus, for which there is no treatment once the symptoms of disease have begun. The rabies virus is classified as a Group 3 agent. Most human infection occurs following bites from domestic animals, principally dogs. Infection is usually transmitted through the skin or less commonly the mucous membranes. Symptoms include fever, change in behaviour, anxiety, insomnia, headaches and restlessness. Without medical intervention, the duration of the illness is usually two to six days and death is often due to respiratory paralysis.

This involves occupational groups in activities where there is handling or contact with infected animals as well as diagnostic and other laboratory workers. In relation to laboratory work with rabies virus, the prime concern is to ensure that there can never be any accidental escape of the virus, which may infect the native animal population. (This is vital since the UK has been effectively rabies-free since 1922 with only two cases of the disease in animals outside quarantine.)

For most laboratory work, Containment Level 3 is considered appropriate for controlling risk. However, where work is intended that would propagate the rabies virus, then additional precautions must be applied. Under Schedule 3 of COSHH 2002 (as amended), strict notification requirements have been imposed regarding the intention to work on or transport, among other selected agents, the rabies virus.

Vaccination is effective and reliable, simple and harmless. It is therefore essential that any person intending to work with rabies is vaccinated and that an appropriate level of immunity is maintained. This is also appropriate for those working in animal quarantine.

Rabies is a reportable illness under the requirements of RIDDOR 1995.

Bovine spongiform encephalopathy (BSE)[25]

BSE is a fatal neurological disease of cattle which was first identified in Great Britain in 1986. This is the bovine form of a group of similar diseases, namely the transmissible spongiform encephalopathies (TSEs). BSE is thought to have been caused by the feeding of cattle with meat and bone meal infected with scrapie, a disease of sheep. The active agent involved in BSE (and all the TSEs) is very resistant to destruction by high temperature sterilisation or disinfection by chemical agents. It is thought that this agent is some form of transmissible protein, a prion. BSE in cattle resembles the human neurological disorder, Creutzfeldt-Jakob disease (CJD), first identified in 1926.

Those occupations at risk include farmers, veterinary surgeons, laboratory workers, abattoir workers and butchers. There are uncertainties regarding exposure to BSE and the ACDP (1996) commented that there are no known cases of BSE or CJD being transmitted occupationally. Furthermore, if BSE was to found to be transmissible to humans in an occupational context, the most likely routes would

---

[25]In the ACDP categorisation of biological agents (2nd edition, 2000), the biological agents for BSE and CJD are listed under the 'Unclassified viruses' section and both are assigned a Group 3 classification.

be through infected foodstuffs contaminating open wounds of skin damage, splashing mucous membranes or by ingestion. It is believed on present evidence that inhalation is unlikely to be a risk (ACDP 1996). However, because of the uncertainties, the following measures are recommended to eradicate the disease in cattle:

1. Animals suspected of having BSE should be destroyed and the carcasses incinerated.
2. Animals should not be fed animal products suspected of being sources of infection, eg bone meal.
3. All cattle carcasses must have 'specified bovine material' removed and destroyed as this is thought to contain the infective agent.

And in an occupational context:

4. High standards of personal hygiene to avoid contamination of cuts and mucus membranes.
5. Specific control measures – engineering, administrative and personal – are recommended for the various stages of meat and meat product processing work.

Mixed exposure

Occupational asthma

Asthma has been caused by exposure to a range of biological agents and their products including animals, insects, crustaceans, fish and their products. Asthma and hypersensitivity mechanisms have been dealt with in Chapter 2. Asthmatic symptoms (attacks of breathlessness, wheezing and coughing, with and without sputum) may follow exposure immediately, but more commonly after several hours.

Occupational asthma is a reportable disease under RIDDOR 1995 and it also a prescribed industrial disease under the Social Security Regulations.

REFERENCES

Advisory Committee on Dangerous Pathogens, 1995, *Categorisation of Biological Agents According to Hazard and Categories of Containment* (4th edition), HSE Books, Sudbury.

Advisory Committee on Dangerous Pathogens, 1996, *BSE (Bovine Spongiform Encephalopathy)*, HSE Books, Sudbury.

Advisory Committee on Dangerous Pathogens, 1997, *Infection Risks to New and Expectant Mothers in the Workplace*, HSE Books, Sudbury.

Advisory Committee on Dangerous Pathogens, 2000, *Second Supplement to Categorisation of Biological Agents According to Hazard and Categories of Containment*, HSE Books, Sudbury.

Ashton I and Gill F S, 2000, *Monitoring for Health Hazards at Work* (3rd edition), Blackwell Science, Oxford.

Beech J R and Ratti N, 1999, Biological Agents, Chapter 24 in *Occupational Health – Risk Assessment and Management*, Sadhra S S and Ramphal K G (Eds), Blackwell Science, Oxford.

Burton G R W, 1992, *Microbiology for the Health Sciences* (4th edition), Lippincott.

Health and Safety Commission, 1996, Advisory Committee on Dangerous Pathogens, *Microbiological Risk Assessment: An Interim Report*, HSE Books, Sudbury.

Health and Safety Commission, 1996a, Advisory Committee on Dangerous Pathogens, *Protection Against Bloodborne Infections in the Workplace: HIV and Hepatitis*, HMSO, London.

Health and Safety Commission, 1998, *Health and Safety Statistics 1997–1998*, HSE Books, Sudbury.

Health and Safety Commission, 1998a, Advisory Committee on Dangerous Pathogens, *Supplement to Categorisation of Biological Agents According to Hazard and Categories of Containment* (4th edition), HSE Books, Sudbury.

Health and Safety Commission, 1999, *Safe Disposal of Clinical Waste*, Health Services Advisory Committee (HSAC), HSE Books, Sudbury.

Health and Safety Commission, 2000, *Legionnaires' Disease: The Control of Legionella Bacteria in Water Systems* (3rd edition), Approved Code of Practice and Guidance, L8, HSE Books, Sudbury.

Health and Safety Commission, 2005, *Control of Substances Hazardous to Health* (5th edition), The Control of Substances Hazardous to Health Regulations 2002 (as amended), Approved Code of Practice and Guidance, L5, HSE Books, Sudbury.

Health and Safety Executive, 1993, *COSHH Assessment – A Step-By-Step Guide to Assessment and the Skills Needed for It* (2nd edition), HSE Books, Sudbury.

Health and Safety Executive, 1993a, *The Occupational Zoonoses*, HSE Books, Sudbury.

Health and Safety Executive, 1996, *A Guide to the Reporting of Injuries, Diseases and Dangerous Occurrences Regulations 1995*, L73, HSE Books, Sudbury.

Health and Safety Executive, 1997, *Anthrax – Safe Working and the Prevention of Infection*, HSG174, HSE Books, Sudbury.

Health and Safety Executive, 2000, *A Guide to the Genetically Modified Organisms (Contained Use) Regulations 2000*, L29, HSE Books, Sudbury.

Hunter D, 1978, *The Diseases of Occupations*, The English Universities Press Ltd, London.

Lee W R, 1987, Diseases Associated with Microbiological Agents, Section V in *Hunter's Diseases of Occupations*, Raffle P A B, Lee W R, McCallum R I and Murray R (Eds), Hodder and Stoughton.

Price A T, Le Serve A W and Parker D, 1981, *Biological Hazards – The Hidden Threat*, Thomas Nelson and Sons Ltd, Walton-on-Thames, Surrey.

Sadhra S S, 1999, Chapter 5 in *Occupational Health – Risk Assessment and Management*, Sadhra S S and Ramphal K G (Eds), Blackwell Science, Oxford.

Snashall D, 1997, Occupational Infections, Chapter 7 in *ABC of Work-Related Disorders*, Snashall D (Ed.), BMJ Publishing Group, London.

Wafer A, 2000, Doctors and HIV – Growing Risk, *BMA News Review*, 11 March 2000.

LEGISLATION

Control of Substances Hazardous to Health Regulations 2002 (SI 2002/2677) (as amended by SI 2004/3386)

Genetically Modified Organisms (Contained Use) Regulations 2000 (SI 2000/2831)

Genetically Modified Organisms (Deliberate Release) Regulations 2002 (SI 2002/2443)

Reporting of Injuries, Diseases and Dangerous Occurrences Regulations 1995 (SI 1995/3163)

5: Noise

(B. Wilkins)

INTRODUCTION

Noise is often referred to as 'unwanted sound'. According to Wright (1997), two million people in Britain are exposed to excessive noise for a significant period during their employment. High noise exposure, over time, may seriously damage an individual's hearing and have other harmful health effects. Deterioration in communication and speech results in a significantly reduced quality of life for those affected. The picture above illustrates the 'swaging' of metal tubes, a process which creates very high noise levels.

According to Kjellberg (1997), hearing loss is one of the most common of all physical impairments and noise is a major cause. In the 1995 UK survey of work-related ill health (SWI95), deafness was a commonly reported condition and its national prevalence (work-related) was estimated at 140,000 (Jones *et al*. 1998).

In 1980, Framework Directive 80/1107/EEC was adopted by the European Community (EC) which aimed to eliminate or limit exposure to chemical and physical agents in the workplace and protect exposed workers. Furthermore, in 1986, the EC adopted Directive 86/188/EEC which was specifically aimed at the protection of workers from the risk of exposure to noise. With respect to noise, these directives were incorporated into UK legislation with the Noise at Work Regulations 1989 (NAW) which provide a legal framework for the systematic identification of noise hazards, assessment of risks, and the application of appropriate prevention and risk control measures. There is a general duty to reduce noise levels as low as is reasonably practicable and to comply with specific requirements when exceeding defined noise 'Action Levels'. There is currently consultation under way on new UK noise regulations as a result of the recent EU Physical Agents (Noise) Directive 2002/10/EC.

There are many potential sources of noise exposure in the workplace, for example, noise generated by impacting metal surfaces with power tools and power presses, noise generated by air turbulence (such as leaking pneumatic control systems), local exhaust ventilation systems involving cyclone separators and jet aeroplane engines. A study, commissioned by the HSE to evaluate implementation of the NAW Regulations, reported that only 50 per cent of employers with 'noisy areas' had conducted a noise assessment and that considerable progress is still needed to implement the Regulations fully (Hillage 1998).

NOISE

Basic acoustics

Sound is a form of energy detected by the hearing mechanism. Sound is generated when a surface vibrates, setting adjacent molecules (usually air) into sympathetic vibration and creating minute pressure fluctuations above and below atmospheric pressure. Oscillating molecules collide with neighbours and rebound and, in turn, the neighbour now strikes the next molecule and so the disturbance is propagated through the medium as a wave. This sound wave may be transmitted through media of different physical states, that is, solid, liquid or gas, but it cannot pass through a vacuum. The sound may encounter materials where it may be reflected or absorbed, or transmitted. Where sound is reflected, this may be perceived as an echo.

Sound energy is propagated in all directions from the noise source. However, it is the pressure fluctuations that are detected by the human hearing mechanism and which can be measured by scientific instruments. The smallest acoustic pressure wave that can be detected by the ear is 20µPa (Nm^{-2}).

FIGURE 5.1: (a) Change of acoustic pressure with time at a fixed point; (b) Change of acoustic pressure with distance at one instant

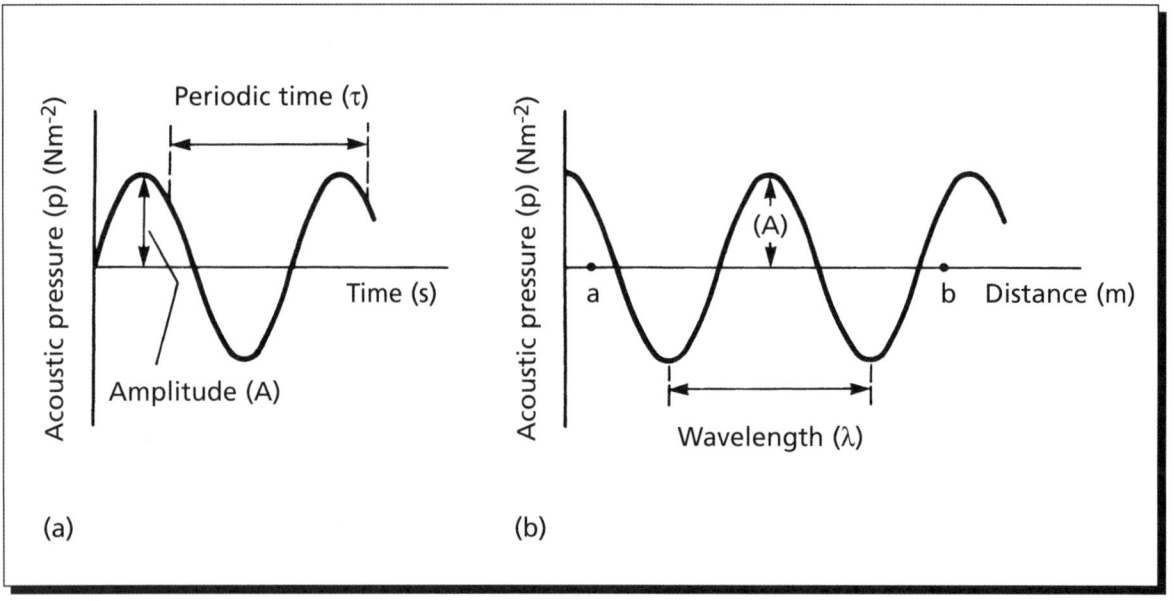

(Malerbi 1989. Reprinted by permission of Elsevier Limited.)

Oscillating air molecules exhibit simple harmonic motion and the resulting pressure fluctuations are basically sinusoidal. The graph of the sine wave (shown above) can trace the change in amplitude of acoustic pressure with time at a fixed point (Figure 5.1(a)) or with distance at a particular instant (Figure 5.1(b)). From this information, the frequency and velocity of the sound wave can be derived.

Only energy is transmitted as the pressure wave, since the air molecules themselves physically oscillate only over a very small distance from their equilibrium positions. The time taken for the motion to be transferred between successive particles and, therefore, the velocity of propagation of the disturbance depends on the medium's elasticity. For air under normal conditions at 20°C, this velocity is $340 ms^{-1}$.

Frequency

Frequency determines the 'pitch' of a sound, the subjective property of a tone which enables the ear to identify its frequency. Frequency is the rate at which pressure fluctuations take place, measured as the number of complete vibration cycles per unit time (expressed in Hertz (Hz) or cycles per second). Estimates vary but generally the human audible range extends from around 15Hz to 18,000Hz. The most sensitive frequencies extend from 500Hz to 5,000Hz. Acoustic pressures do exist at lower or higher frequencies beyond the audible range, that is, infrasonic and ultrasonic noise. Infrasonic noise is not heard but 'felt'. Unpleasant physiological and psychological effects (but not noise-induced hearing loss) have been associated with exposure to infrasound and ultrasound.

The distance between corresponding points in successive waves of compression and rarefaction is known as the wavelength, commonly given as the Greek letter 'lambda' (λ). The velocity of a sound wave can be expressed by the equation:

$$v = \lambda f$$

(Where: v is velocity in metres per second; λ is wavelength in metres; and f is frequency in Hz.)

Sound level

Sound intensity level

As sound energy is emitted from a point source, it will try to spread out in a spherical field. The quantity of sound energy reaching the ear results from its spread over an ever-increasing area and will depend on the distance from the source (see Figure 5.2). The sound energy per unit area is inversely proportional to the square of the distance from the source. This relationship is commonly known as the inverse square law. If the distance from the source is doubled, then the energy density is reduced to a quarter.

FIGURE 5.2: Inverse square law

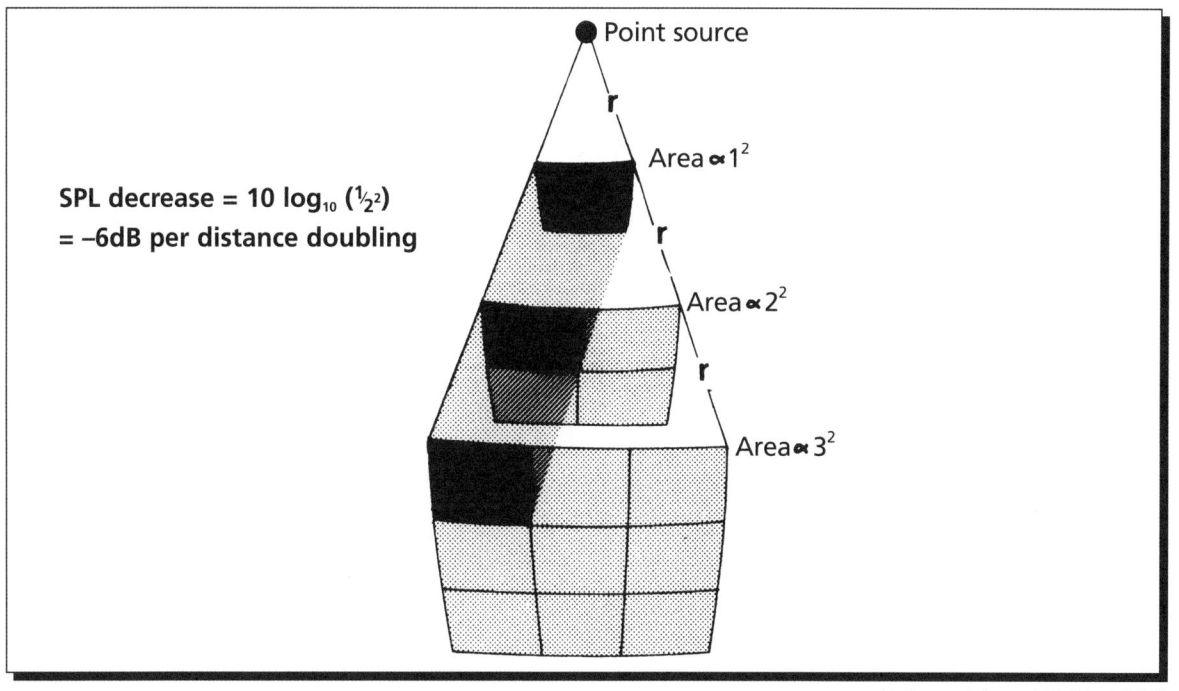

(Adapted from Webb 1976)

The intensity of a sound describes the rate of flow of sound energy and is measured in watts per square metre (Wm^{-2}). High intensity sound has more energy than low intensity sound. The highest sound intensity that is likely to be encountered in industry is about $1 Wm^{-2}$. Human perception of sound covers a wide range of intensities. The lowest intensity that the ear can detect, in a healthy young person at a frequency of 1,000Hz, is one million-millionth of a watt, that is, $10^{-12} Wm^{-2}$. This intensity is known as the threshold value or reference intensity. This sound intensity range from $10^{-12} Wm^{-2}$ to $1 Wm^{-2}$ is very large and unwieldy and a decibel scale is used to compress this range into a more comprehensible and manageable scale.

When expressing the magnitude of a sound, the ratio of the intensity level of the sound in question is compared with a reference intensity, based on the threshold of hearing.

Here, the ratio is taken of the intensity of the sound of interest and reference intensity value given above. The range of this ratio is compressed using a logarithmic scale (a bel scale) and the sound intensity can be expressed in decibels (dB) (see Figure 5.3):

$$\text{Sound intensity level (in decibels)} = 10 \log_{10} \frac{\text{Intensity of sound of interest (Wm}^{-2}\text{)}}{10^{-12} Wm^{-2} \text{ (reference value)}}$$

NOISE

Because the scale is logarithmic, an increase of three decibels represents a doubling of the sound energy that is flowing (Figure 5.3). A decibel scale is a scale of comparison and it is also used with other parameters, for example, sound pressure, sound power and in vibration measurement.

FIGURE 5.3: Decibel scale

Sound intensity units	Wm^{-2}
Loud noise	1 Wm^{-2}
Reference intensity (just perceptible sound)	10^{-12} Wm^{-2}
$\dfrac{1 \, (Wm^{-2})}{10^{-12} \, (Wm^{-2})}$	= 10^{12}
Scale compression by taking logarithms:	
Bels $\quad\quad \log_{10} \dfrac{1}{10^{-12}}$	= 12 (bels)
Decibels $\quad\quad 10\log_{10} \dfrac{1}{10^{-12}}$	= 120 (decibels)
(If the sound intensity is doubled, the decibel level increases by +3 ($10\log_{10} 2 = 3$))	

Sound pressure level

It is the sound intensity, that is, the energy content, which determines the perceived loudness of a sound. It is difficult to measure intensity directly, but the passage of sound energy through air is accompanied by fluctuations in atmospheric pressure. These fluctuations can be measured by a sound-level meter and related to the amount of sound energy that is flowing (ie the intensity).

The square of the sound pressure of a wave is proportional to its intensity. The relationship between pressure and intensity depends on the characteristic impedance of the medium through which the sound is passing.

This impedance is the product of $c\rho$ where ρ is the density of the medium and c is the velocity of sound in that medium. Hence, in air:

$$c\rho = 1.2 \times 340 = 400 \text{ (rayls)}$$

Intensity has the following relationship to pressure:

$$I = (p^2/c\rho) = (p^2/400) \, Wm^{-2}$$

(Where: I is intensity in Wm^{-2}; and p is pressure in Pa.)

For example, if the sound pressure in a very noisy machine room is 20Pa, then the sound intensity is 1Wm^{-2}. The relationship between the various measures of sound can be seen in Table 5.1.

The sound pressure level (SPL) expressed in decibels is defined as follows:

$$SPL \, (dB) = 10\log_{10}(p^2/p_{ref}^2) = 10\log_{10}(p/p_{ref})^2 = 20\log_{10}(p/p_{ref})$$

(Where: p is pressure of interest; and p_{ref} is the reference pressure, ie the sound pressure at the threshold of hearing, which is 20µPa or 2 x 10^{-5} Pa.)

When measured in air, the decibel values for pressure are numerically the same as those for intensity. Noise monitoring instruments are designed to measure pressure changes in the air and these are directly converted into decibels. Relationships between the various measures of sound are shown in Table 5.1.

Sound power level

This is a measure of the total acoustic power produced by a noise source, that is, the total sound energy radiated in unit time, and is measured in watts (W). This is a fixed property of a noise source irrespective of its environment. Sound power level is also commonly expressed in decibels, where the sound power of interest is related to a reference power (ie 10^{-12}W). This allows the sound power levels of different noise sources to be more easily compared.

TABLE 5.1 Relationship between various measures of sound

STIMULUS		RESPONSE		
Intensity (Wm^{-2})	Pressure (Pa)	Sound-level meter (SLM) (Bel)	(dB)	Physiological
10^3	600	15	150	Instantaneous damage
10^2	2×10^2	14	140	
10	6×10	13	130	Threshold pain
1	2×10	12	120	
10^{-1}	6	11	110	
10^{-2}	2	10	100	
10^{-3}	6×10^{-1}	9	90	Permanent hearing loss
10^{-4}	2×10^{-1}	8	80	Discomfort
10^{-5}		7	70	Annoyance
10^{-6}	2×10^{-2}	6	60	
10^{-7}		5	50	Comfortable audibility
10^{-8}	2×10^{-3}	4	40	
10^{-9}		3	30	
10^{-10}	2×10^{-4}	2	20	
10^{-11}		1	10	
10^{-12}	2×10^{-5}	0	0	Threshold of hearing

(Malerbi 1989)

A-weighted decibels

The response of the ear to different frequencies is not linear and it is most sensitive to sound over the range of 500Hz to 5,000Hz. Therefore, the ear does not perceive sounds with the same intensity at different frequencies across the spectrum as having equal loudness and the 'A-weighted' decibel scale is an attempt to accommodate this.

Equal loudness contours (Figure 5.4) have been obtained by investigation. In an experiment, large numbers of young people were asked to adjust the loudness level of pure sound tones at a series of frequencies until they were judged to be of 'equal loudness' to a 1,000Hz reference tone (Robinson & Dadson 1956). This was repeated at different sound levels in 10dB steps. The contour loudness level (in phons) is numerically equal to the sound level (in decibels) at 1,000Hz. This subjective assessment revealed that a doubling of sound intensity (ie a 3dB increase) was not judged as a doubling of subjective loudness, for which a 10dB increase in sound level was necessary.

A sound-level meter measures the loudness of a sound using an electronic weighting system at different frequencies to mimic the ear's response to sound across the audible spectrum. Since the ear is not equally sensitive to all frequencies, a meter which measured overall sound pressure level would not be a very good indication of the loudness of a sound. 'A-weighting' represents the equal loudness contour at 40 phons (see Table 5.2). It is important to use the designation dB(linear) and dB(A), as appropriate, when recording a sound level. For measuring the maximum value reached by the sound pressure at any instant during a measurement period, a linear (dB(linear)) value or 'C-weighting' (dB(C)) may be used. (C-weighting uses the 100 phon curve.)

FIGURE 5.4: Normal equal loudness contours for pure tones

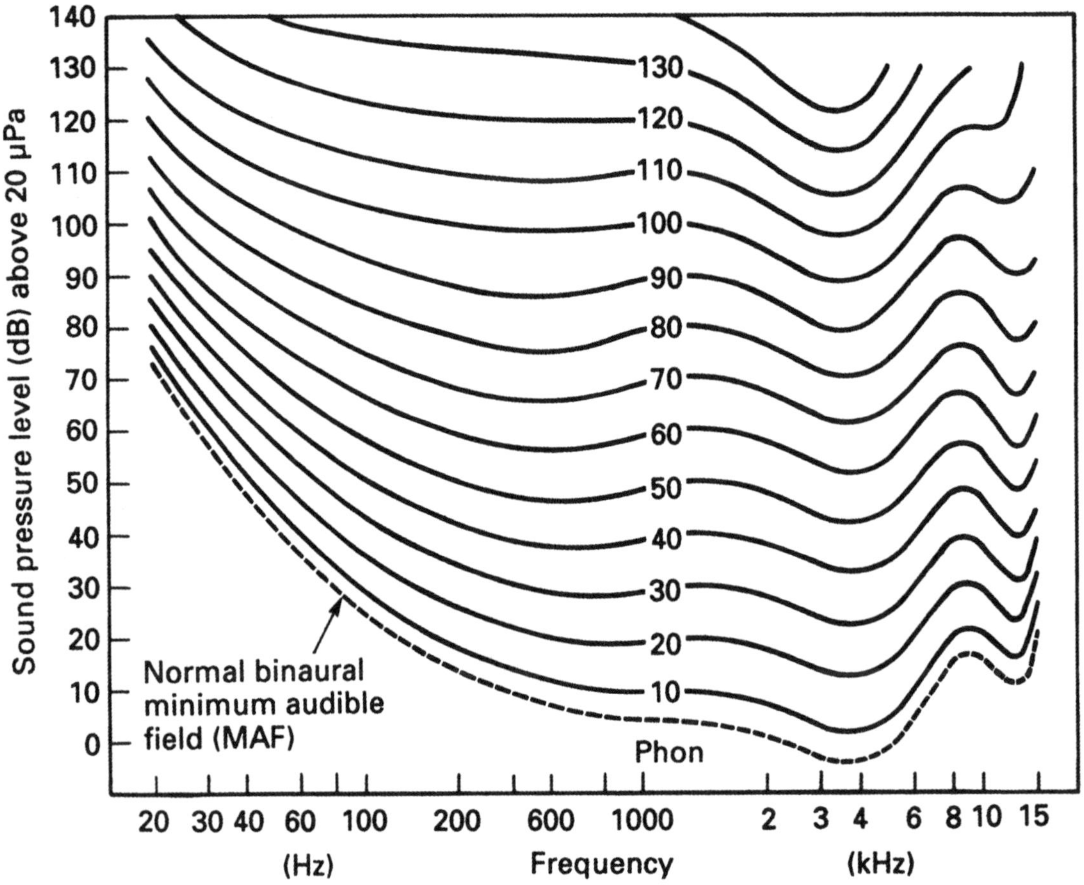

(Malerbi 1989. Reprinted by permission of Elsevier Limited.)

Frequency analysis

The perception of sound depends on loudness and frequency and a full investigation of a sound source examines both of these aspects. The ear is relatively insensitive to low and very high frequencies and the working range is normally taken from 45Hz to 11,200Hz. In frequency analysis, this range is divided into eight frequency groups, known as octave bands. An octave band is a frequency range in which the upper frequency is twice the lower. Each octave band is designated by its mid-frequency but this midpoint is not the arithmetic mean of the upper and lower frequencies, rather, it is the geometric mean, that is, (lower frequency x upper frequency)$^{1/2}$. For the eight octave bands of the normal hearing range, the mid-frequencies are: 63Hz, 125Hz, 250Hz, 500Hz, 1kHz, 2kHz, 4kHz and 8kHz. An octave band spectrum is illustrated in Figure 5.5.

Octave band data is useful in both the design of engineering noise control measures and the selection of appropriate personal hearing protection using a manufacturer's supplied sound attenuation data (see Chapter 13).

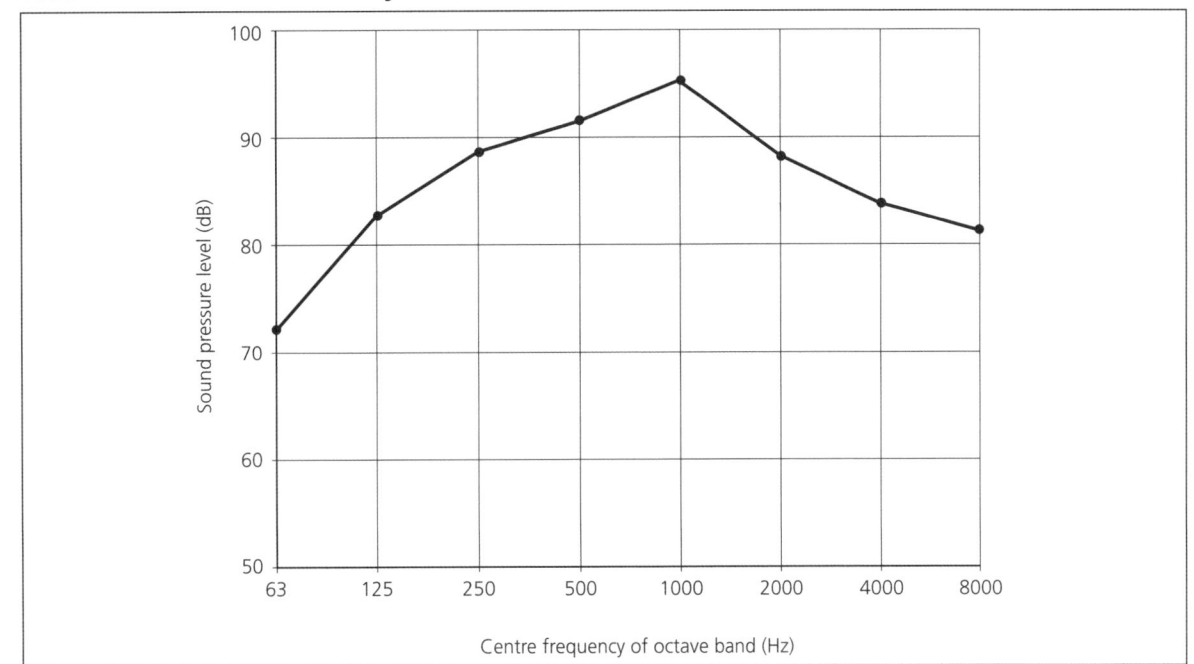

FIGURE 5.5: Octave band analysis of sound source

Estimating dB(A) level from octave band readings

The corrections shown in Table 5.2 are made to the decibel readings and the dB(A) level is found by combining the corrected octave band levels, using the rule of thumb method illustrated in Figure 5.6. A worked example is shown in Figure 5.7. When measuring across the whole audible spectrum with a sound-level meter, these corrections are automatically applied to the dB(linear) reading when the device is in the A-weighting setting.

TABLE 5.2: Octave band corrections for A-weighting

Octave band centre frequency (Hz)	63	125	250	500	1000	2000	4000	8000
Correction	-26	-16	-9	-3	0	+1	+1	-1

FIGURE 5.6: Rule of thumb for adding or subtracting decibels

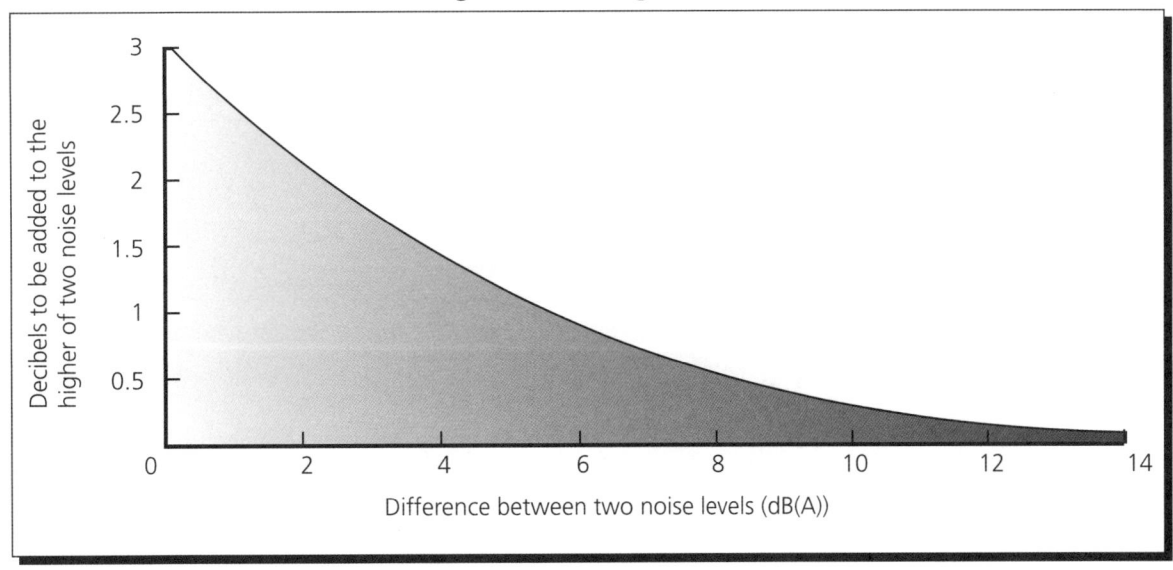

(Hassall & Zaveri 1979)

Using the correction factors in Table 5.2 and the rule in Figure 5.6, the corrected octave band decibel levels may be combined to give the overall dB(A) level. This is illustrated for the octave band spectrum (SPL) in Figure 5.7.

FIGURE 5.7: Estimating overall dB(A) from a frequency spectrum

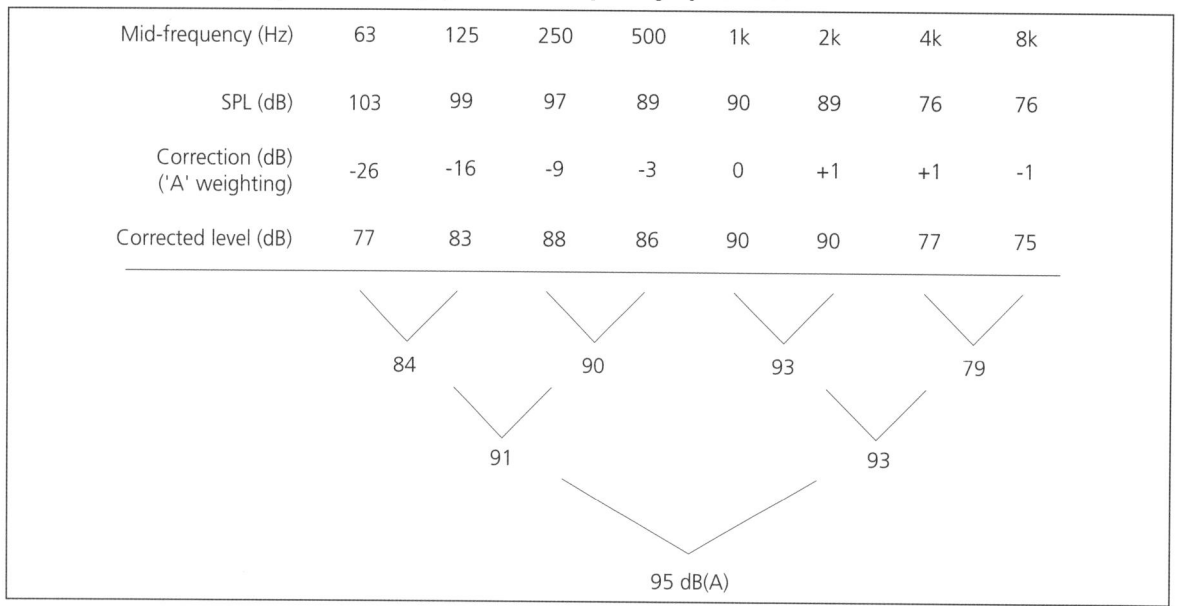

Mid-frequency (Hz)	63	125	250	500	1k	2k	4k	8k
SPL (dB)	103	99	97	89	90	89	76	76
Correction (dB) ('A' weighting)	-26	-16	-9	-3	0	+1	+1	-1
Corrected level (dB)	77	83	88	86	90	90	77	75

```
        84        90        93        79
           91              93
                   95 dB(A)
```

This method may also be used to calculate the protection given by hearing protectors in a noisy environment where octave band measurements have been taken. (This is discussed further in Chapter 13.)

Sound and materials

Materials may reflect, absorb and transmit sound and this is represented in Figure 5.8. The relative importance of each of these parameters depends on the nature of the material and the frequency spectrum of the noise. Absorption, reflection and transmission coefficients can be calculated for different materials and this information is used in the design of work environments and soundproofing structures such as enclosures.

FIGURE 5.8: Reflection, absorption and transmission of sound

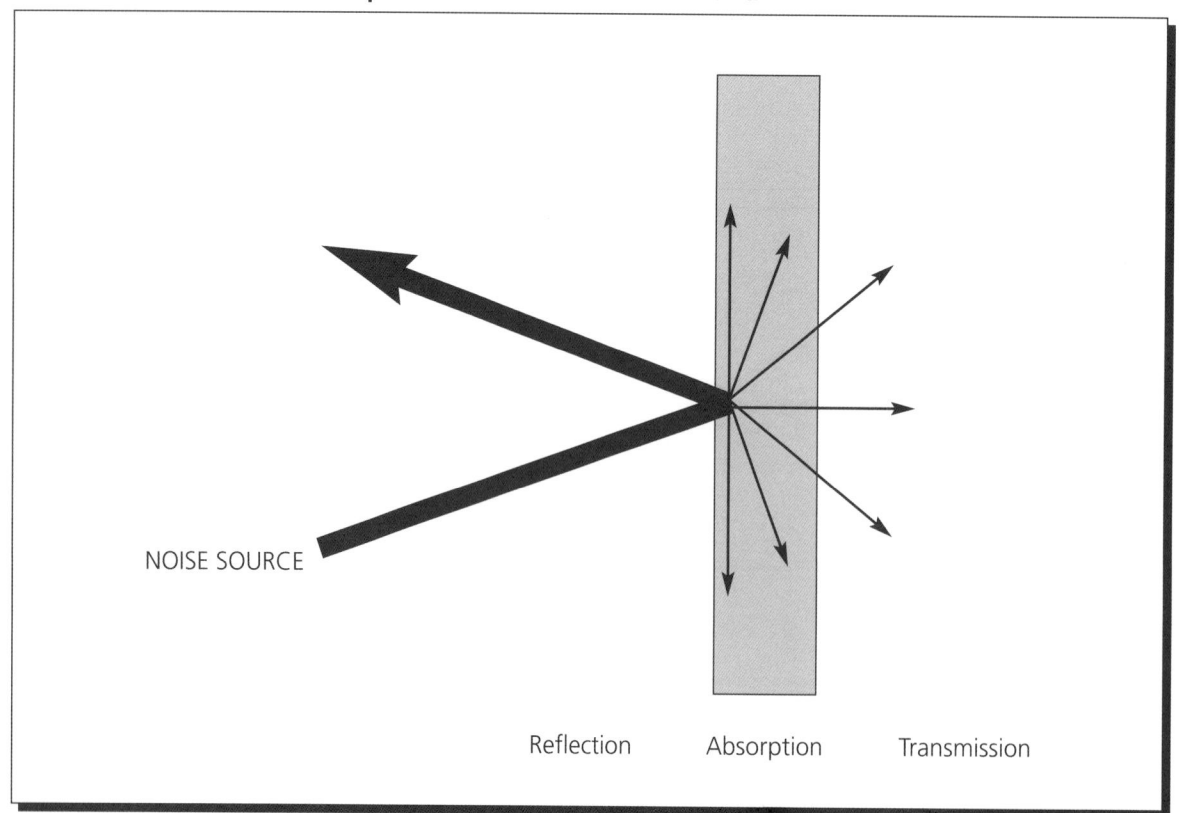

(Brüel & Kjaer 1982)

The absorption coefficient α (alpha) is defined as:

$$\frac{\text{Intensity of sound absorbed by material}}{\text{Intensity of sound incident on same area of material}}$$

The reflection coefficient ρ (ro) is defined as:

$$\frac{\text{Intensity of sound reflected by material}}{\text{Intensity of sound incident on same area of material}}$$

The transmission coefficient τ (taw) is defined as:

$$\frac{\text{Intensity of sound transmitted by material}}{\text{Intensity of sound incident on same area of material}}$$

(It follows that α + ρ + τ = 1.)

For many materials in practical use, τ is very much smaller than α and ρ. This enables the approximation α + ρ = 1 to be used in some situations. This is the position with the sound characteristics of an enclosure where there is transmission of very small amounts of noise through the walls.

Where sound is absorbed, it is converted to other forms of energy, principally heat. Materials which absorb sound can be divided into three categories:

1. **Porous materials** – sound energy enters the pores of the material and the viscous forces generated result in heat production (absorption coefficient greater at higher frequencies).
2. **Non-porous panels** – sound energy is converted into vibrational (mechanical) energy (absorption coefficient greater at lower frequencies).
3. **Perforated materials** – perforations act as cavity resonators, absorbing narrow bands of frequency.

The transmission coefficient (τ) for a material depends on its density and thickness and the frequency of the noise source. Since this is often very small, it is more convenient to express transmission as 'transmission loss' in decibels:

$$\text{Transmission loss (TL)} = 10\log_{10}\frac{1}{\tau}\,(\text{dB})$$

For example, the transmission coefficient for a brick wall is 0.0001 at 500Hz and when expressed as transmission loss this would be:

$$\text{TL} = 10\log_{10}\frac{1}{0.0001} = 40\text{dB}$$

Sound in an enclosed space

The total sound field produced in an enclosed space, as shown in Figure 5.9, consists of two components:

1. **Direct sound field** – this is the sound which travels directly from the source to the listener by the shortest route and does not encounter any room surface. This is the dominant component close to the source (in the 'near field').
2. **Reverberation sound field** – this is the sound which reaches the listener with at least one reflection from a room surface. This sound component dominates further away from the source (in the 'far field').

FIGURE 5.9: Direct and reverberation sound fields in an enclosed space

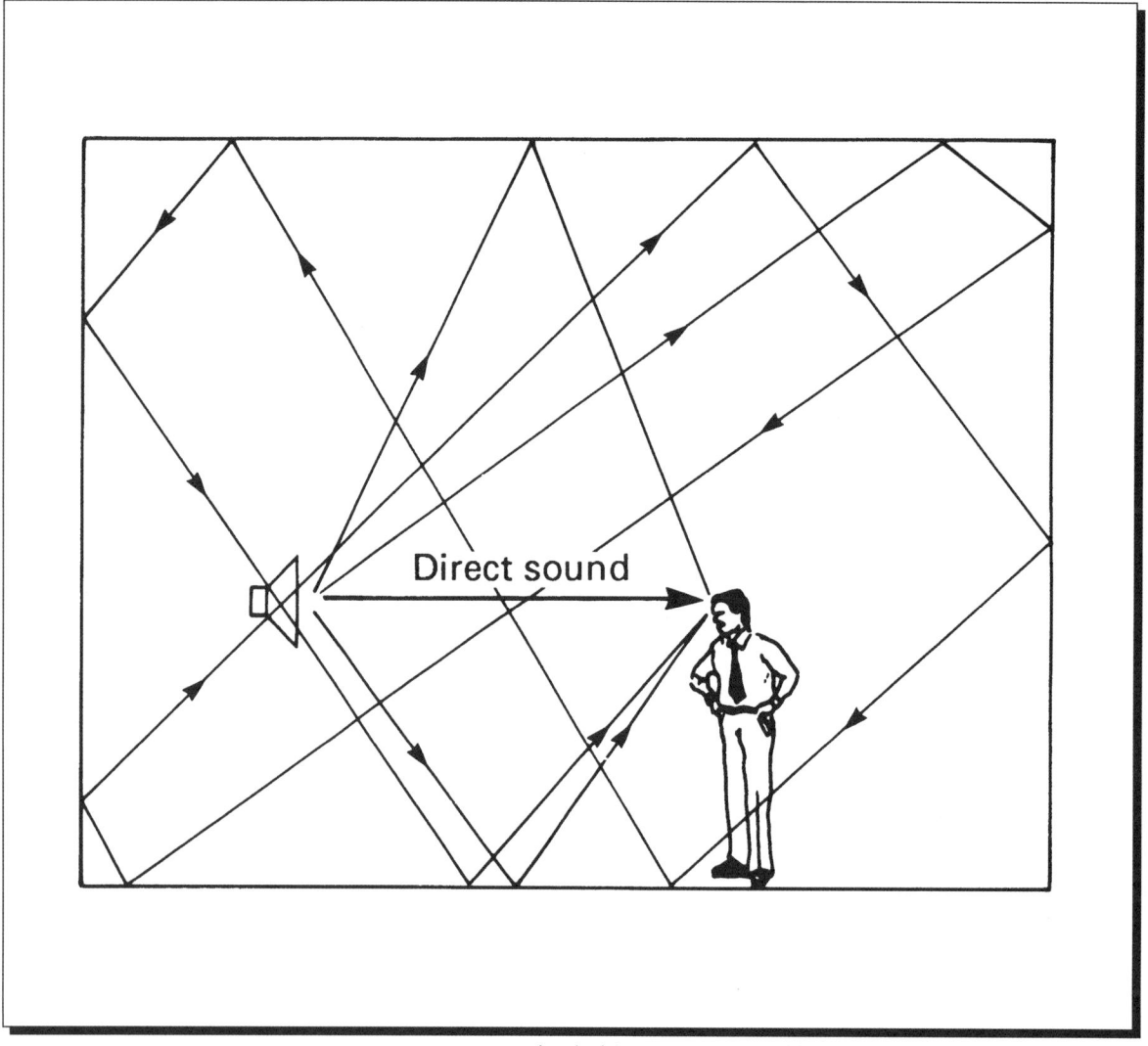

(Malerbi 1989. Reprinted by permission of Elsevier Limited.)

The size of the direct field depends on:
- the acoustic power of the source;
- the distance between the source and the listener; and
- the position of the source in the space.

The size of the reverberation component depends on:
- the amount of sound reflected at each reflecting surface; and
- the number of reflections of each sound wave before it reaches the listener.

The direct field and reverberation components are related to the average of the absorption coefficients and each of the surface areas of the room. Since absorption coefficients vary with frequency, reverberation time will vary across the frequency range. The reverberation component does not vary greatly for a given room, whereas the direct component for a point source varies inversely with the square of the distance from the source, that is, the sound level falls off rapidly. The different reverberation components of a noisy environment arrive at a given point at different times and, thus, the total sound field grows and decays. When a sound source is stopped, the sound heard does not stop immediately, but there is a finite time for it to be reflected off each surface where some is absorbed. The time for this decay depends on the sound absorption within the room. Reverberation time (RT) is defined as the time for a given sound to decay by 60dB and this is a useful guide to the acoustic quality of a room. It is possible to estimate reverberation times for planned rooms and incorporate necessary absorptive capacity into the design to achieve optimum RT values. Such values will depend on the size of the room and its intended use.

Exposure and health effects

The human hearing mechanism

The human ear converts pressure fluctuations in the air (generated by noise) which come into contact with the ear drum into audible noise by a complex mechanism. The basic structure of the ear is shown in Figure 5.10 and its function is outlined below. The hearing mechanism has four main components:

1. The external ear.
2. The middle ear.
3. The inner ear.
4. The auditory nerve pathway.

FIGURE 5.10: The human ear

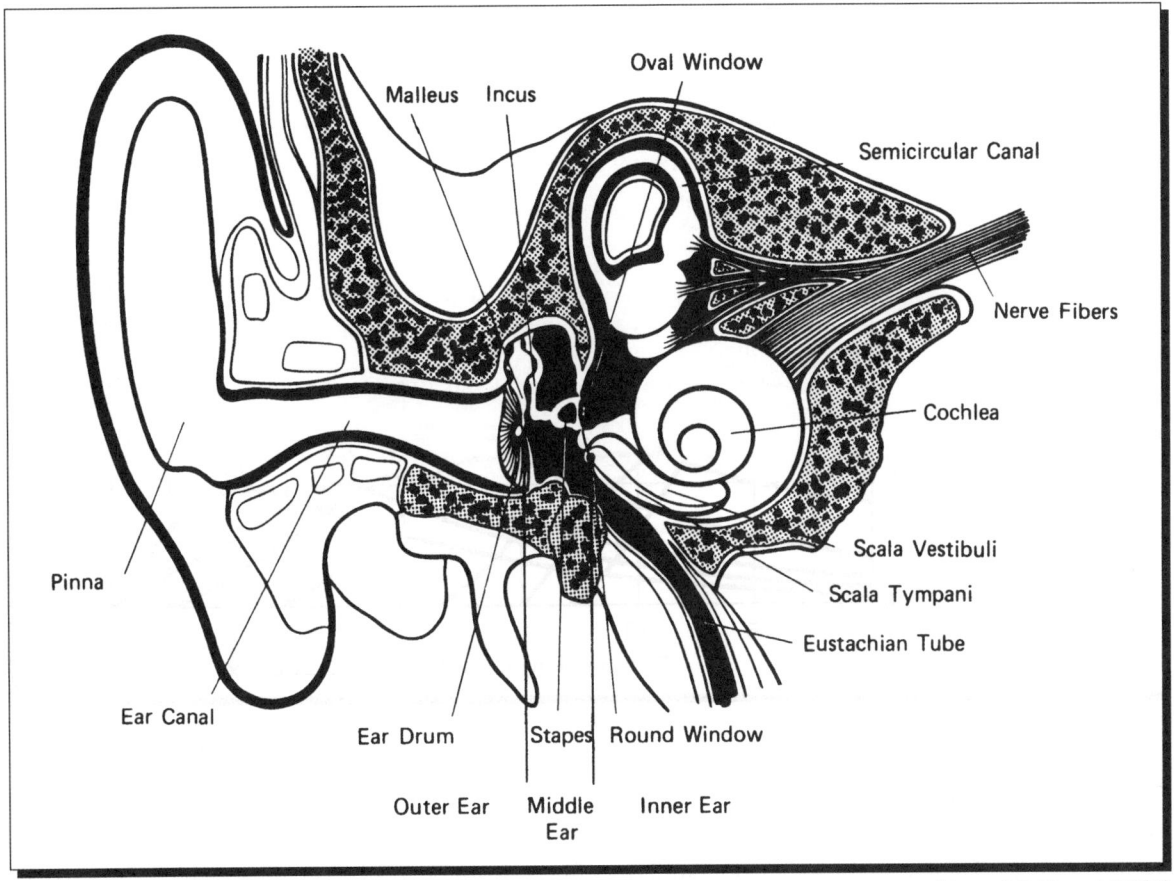

(Hassall & Zaveri 1979)

The external ear consists of the pinna and the external auditory canal. The external ear is separated from the middle ear by the ear drum (tympanic membrane). The middle ear contains three small bones – the hammer (malleus), the anvil (incus) and the stirrup (stapes) – which transmit noise to the inner ear. These bones have muscles attached to them and these perform a defensive function protecting the inner ear from loud noise. The inner ear has two structures: the cochlea (concerned with hearing) and the vestibulum (concerned with balance).

Sound pressure waves are generated by a noise source and these are transmitted through the air. They are received by the pinna which funnels them into the external auditory canal resulting in vibration of the ear drum. These vibrations are further transmitted by the middle ear bones to the entrance of the inner ear known as the 'oval window'. Vibrations are transmitted to the fluid inside the cochlea which, in turn, passes them to the sensitive hair cells inside the organ of Corti. These hair cells respond to different noise frequencies, as shown in Figure 5.11. The vibrations in the cochlear fluid are transformed by the hair cells into auditory nerve impulses which are sent to the brain, resulting in 'perception' of the noise. With excessive exposure to loud noise, the hair cells are damaged or destroyed, resulting in loss of hearing capacity.

FIGURE 5.11: Longitudinal section of the cochlea showing position of hair cell on membrane and relative noise frequency response

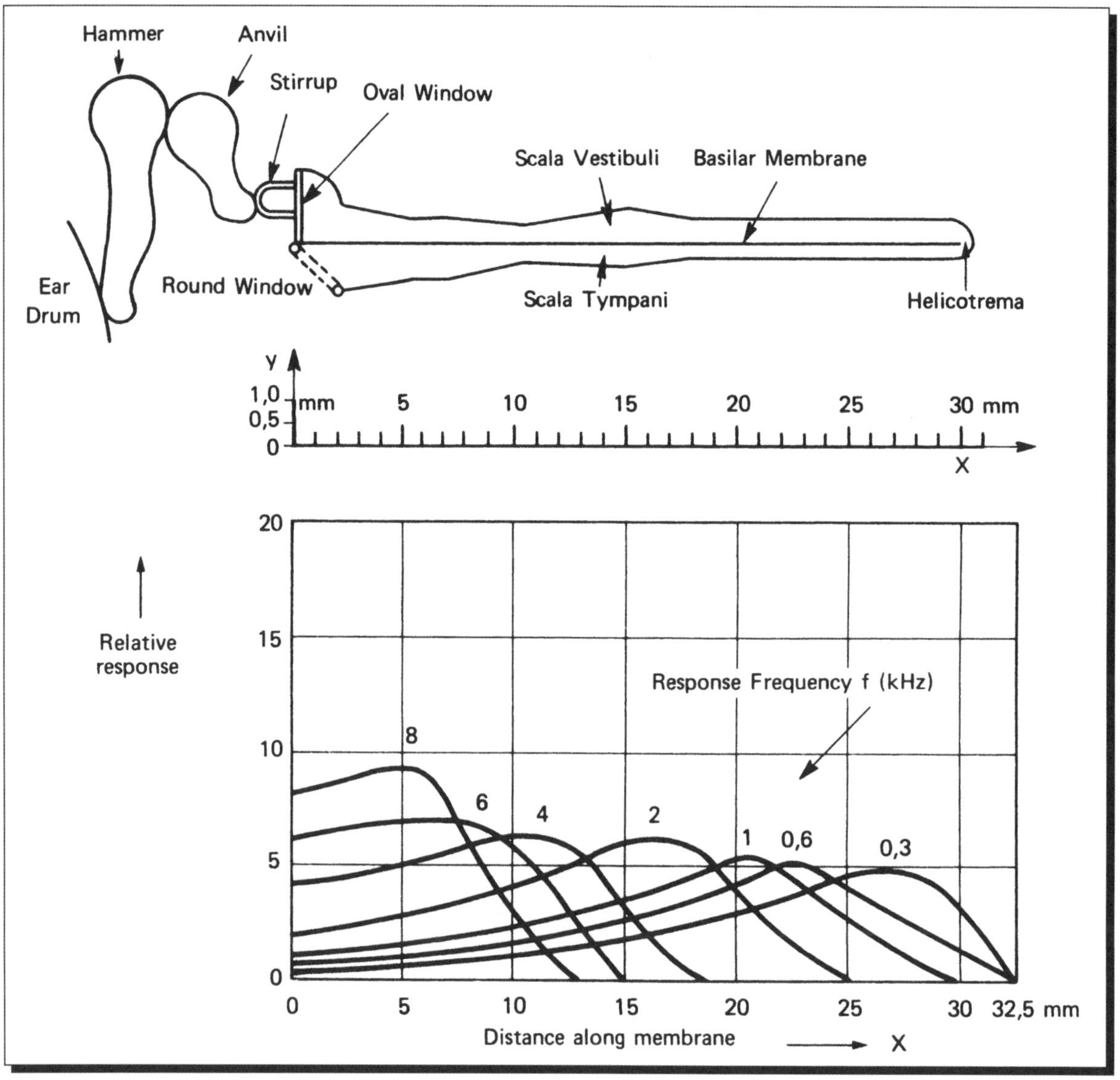

(Hassall & Zaveri 1979)

Health effects of noise

One of the consequences of exposure over many years to loud levels of noise is noise-induced hearing loss (NIHL). There are also other non-auditory effects. Noise levels below those which cause NIHL may cause irritation and annoyance, and impair concentration and communication.

It is important to understand that total elimination of noise is not the aim since this would result in silence, which itself is a source of stress. Also, some noise may be useful, for example, the nature of a noise change may give an early warning of a dangerous equipment failure.

Effects of noise other than hearing loss

Kjellberg (1997) identified the following effects of noise:
1. Non-auditory physiological and health effects – a range of effects have been studied but no clear pattern has emerged; cardiovascular and psychiatric effects have been given the most attention.
2. Annoyance and other subjective reactions to noise.
3. Interference with the perception of speech and other auditory signals.
4. Interference with the performance of non-auditory tasks – this is important since it may result in decreased productivity, increased errors and a perceived decrease in functional capacity.
5. Interference with sleep.

Hearing damage

Hearing damage may be divided into two major types: conductive and perceptive. NIHL is implicated only with perceptive hearing damage.

Conductive hearing loss

These disorders affect the outer and middle ear and some examples are given below:
1. Impacted wax – a foreign body in the ear canal reduces the amplitude of the noise entering the ear; it provides a sound barrier and may obstruct vibration of the ear drum.
2. Rupture of the ear drum – may be caused by an explosion or a bang on the head.
3. Measles – this may self-heal or surgery may be needed.
4. Eustachian tube blocked – when there is a discharge or swelling in the middle ear; the middle ear cannot make the pressure adjustment; the ear drum is under pressure and cannot respond effectively to sound.
5. The ossicles may be dislocated by the blast of an explosion.
6. Disease may cause fluid in the middle ear or articulated joint to become fixed (otosclerosis) – this can be treated by surgery.

Perceptive hearing loss

With these disorders, there is damage to the inner ear (the hair cells), the auditory nerve or the brain hearing centre. These conditions are inaccessible to medical intervention. Disorders include:
1. Congenital deafness which may be caused by rubella, influenza, or medication taken by the mother in early pregnancy.
2. An accident at birth; disease of the new-born or childhood; (drug-induced or viral conditions usually cause bilateral hearing loss, although mumps is normally unilateral).
3. Ototoxicity resulting from the side-effects of drugs and their action on the hair cells and/or auditory nerve (agents include anticancer drugs, alcohol, the contraceptive pill and streptomycin).
4. A fracture of the skull with damage to the delicate structures of the inner ear.
5. Acoustic neuroma – early detection needed and treatment by surgery; unilateral hearing loss.
6. 'Stone deafness' – the auditory nerve is disrupted and/or destroyed by disease and this results in complete hearing loss, while other conditions result in a patchy loss of hearing across the different frequencies of the audible range.

However, the most prevalent conditions which result in perceptive (sensorineural) hearing loss are presbyacusis and NIHL. NIHL is known as 'occupational deafness' when occurring as a result of exposure to noise at work. Other conditions associated with noise exposure are tinnitus, vertigo, loudness recruitment, masking, and effects associated with exposure to infrasound and ultrasound.

Presbyacusis

This is hearing loss due to ageing. The hearing loss begins at an early age with the loss of some higher frequency hearing capability (Figure 5.12). The hair cells near to the oval window are associated with higher frequencies and these are subjected to significant pressure changes in the fluid. Population studies have shown some high frequency impairment of hearing in the late teens. It is in later life, when the middle frequencies are affected and some speech becomes unintelligible, that a loss is perceived. Rosen & Plester (1962) (cited by Malerbi 1989) reported studies on a relatively 'noise-free' population. The Mabaan tribe who live in a remote part of Africa without Western-style stress and noise had an average hearing capability (level) in their 70 to 79-year-olds which was equivalent to that of 30 to 39-year-olds found in the US population. Presbyacusis is believed to be associated with the general stress of life.

The relationship between age and hearing loss is shown in the graph in Figure 5.12 where 12kHz can be seen to be the most age-sensitive hearing frequency.

NOISE

FIGURE 5.12: Graph showing hearing loss with age

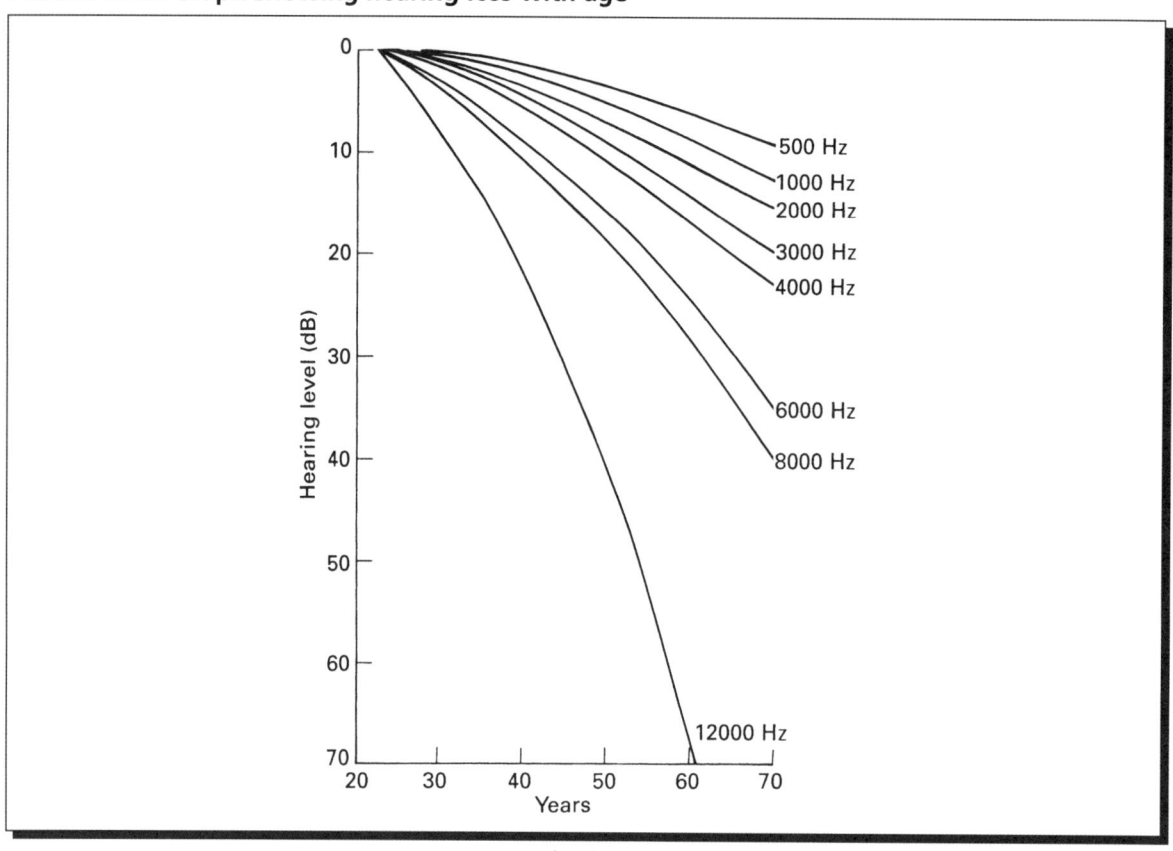

(Malerbi 1989. Reprinted by permission of Elsevier Limited.)

Noise-induced hearing loss (NIHL)

Noise-induced hearing loss (NIHL) is caused by degeneration of hair cells in the inner ear as a result of excessive exposure to loud noise. With exposure to typical industrial noise sources, loss of hearing level is characteristically first seen around the frequencies of 4kHz to 6kHz, as is illustrated in the pattern in Figure 5.13. In the cochlea, the site of damage caused by continuous pure tone or narrow band noise depends on the frequency of the noise. NIHL is not progressive (ie it is arrested on cessation of noise exposure) compared with presbyacusis, which continues through life. The effects of presbyacusis will be superimposed on any hearing decrement and will exacerbate the loss at 4kHz to 6kHz. (This often occurs in the mid-50s age range when the person discovers a loss of hearing.) The change in a person's hearing acuity, whether temporary or permanent, is known as a 'threshold shift'.

FIGURE 5.13: Audiograms showing the development of noise-induced hearing loss

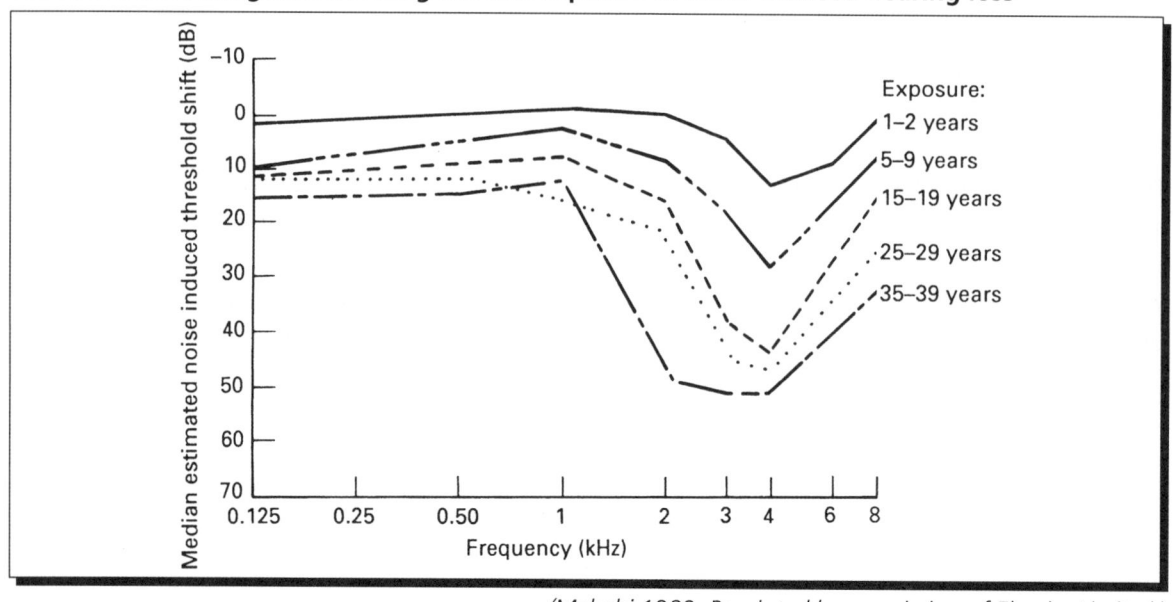

(Malerbi 1989. Reprinted by permission of Elsevier Limited.)

Temporary threshold shift (TTS)

This is a temporary sensation of deafness after high noise exposure, which will recover with time. The initial impact of loud noise is temporary; recovery time depends on the loudness of the noise and the duration of exposure and may be up to 48 hours. Overtime working may mean that recovery will not occur until the weekend and then only if this period is reasonably quiet. Temporary threshold shift is a body defence mechanism to protect against an injury and it is believed to be metabolically-induced. There is an aural reflex where if the ear is exposed to more than 90dB(A) in excess of 10 milliseconds (ms), then the muscles controlling the tension of the ear drum and the action of the bones of the middle ear will increase the tension of the ear drum. Action on the stapes will tighten and reduce movement of the mechanical parts of the ear, resulting in an attenuation of 12dB to 14dB. The 10ms delay means that this will not be a protective mechanism in an explosion. Another protective mechanism, above a noise level of 140dB, creates sideways movement of the middle ear bone ossicles, reducing the pressure transferred to the cochlea.

Permanent threshold shift (PTS)

This is permanent, irreversible deafness following prolonged exposure to loud noise. When there is incomplete recovery from TTS before further noise exposure, this may allow the residual threshold shift to become permanent. PTS will increase incrementally where this situation is repeated. The most rapid rate of increase is during the first 10 years of exposure. To estimate the extent of NIHL, the average expected hearing loss from presbyacusis is read from a standard graph (accounting for age and sex) and this is subtracted from the measurement of PTS.

Occupational deafness results from exposure to noise at work. It is impossible to quantify non-industrial noise exposure and unrelated causes of hearing loss (eg infection). Where the level and duration of occupational noise exposure is known, the data tables in BS 5330 (BSI 1976) can be used to estimate the likelihood that the mean hearing levels over 1, 2 and 3kHz will exceed 30dB of loss. This is a defined level of handicap in BS 5330 (BSI 1976). 'Hearing handicap' relates to a degree of impairment which will affect a person's normal social and/or domestic functioning, while the term 'disability' relates to employment. Estimating the percentage of an exposed population becoming handicapped in this way is based on a measure of their noise exposure, over a number of years, which is known as the 'noise immission level'.

Noise immission level (NIL)

$$\text{NIL} = L_{eq} + 10\log_{10} T/T_0$$

(Where: L_{eq} is equivalent continuous sound level in dB(A); T is duration of exposure in years; and T_0 is one year.)

Mechanism

Inner ear hair cells are damaged by high noise exposure but the exact mechanism is in doubt. A long-held theory has been that high noise exposure induces excessive movement of the hairs and causes cell damage. Others believe that this damage is a reaction to long-term stress (caused by excessive noise exposure) where hormone release disrupts and reduces blood flow to the inner ear. In PTS, these hormone levels do not return to normal and there is a permanent restriction of blood supply which leads to hair cell death. Blood hormones have been used as an early indicator of hearing impairment before audiometry was available. Attitude and perceived degree of control over noise are also believed to be linked to the level of hearing loss.

With PTS, there is a classic pattern of hearing loss focused on 4,000Hz to 6,000Hz. At first the speech frequencies (500Hz to 2,000Hz) are not affected, but as more cells are lost, discrimination and comprehension of speech suffers. These difficulties are exacerbated when there is significant background noise. Amplification may make the situation worse, since the remaining neurones become saturated with noise (known as recruitment), which results in an uncomfortable distortion. The separation between sufficient noise for comprehension and the onset of recruitment may be quite narrow and it can be very difficult to communicate with a person who has recruitment. (They cannot hear one minute and the next they accuse you of shouting!) There is a need to assess speech discrimination before a hearing aid is chosen. Individual susceptibility also plays a part in loss of hearing function.

Tinnitus

This is an unpleasant subjective sensation of noise in the head. It can be a high-pitched ringing, whistling or hissing, or a low-pitched rushing or buzzing. (Low-pitched tinnitus is not normally associated with NIHL.) Often a person may experience short periods of high-pitched tinnitus before the onset of PTS and this can be taken as a warning sign. In advanced cases of NIHL, tinnitus may be present continuously and this may obscure the amount of hearing damage.

When people with normal hearing enter an anechoic (sound-deadened) chamber, they experience tinnitus and this has led to the idea that tinnitus is always present but that the everyday noise of the world masks this, except where NIHL means that noise perception is insufficient to mask this.

Other health effects associated with noise

Loudness recruitment

Where someone has a high hearing threshold, with sound above this level, there is a rapid growth in perceived noise. This is thought to be due to damage to the organ of Corti in the inner ear.

Vertigo

Vertigo is often associated with deafness. Vertigo is not caused by NIHL but by a disturbance of the organ of balance and it is this which causes the deafness.

Infrasound and ultrasound

Infrasound, that is, sound below the audible range (less than 20Hz), is thought to have adverse effects. However, at high intensities even these low frequency sounds may be heard (Hinchcliffe 1987). The effects of low frequency noise are similar to those of higher frequency noise.

With ultrasound (ie sound above 20kHz), effects have included an unpleasant sensation of pressure in the ears, temporary tinnitus, nausea, headaches and possibly fatigue, and exposure criteria have been proposed based on these effects. According to Hinchcliffe (1987), hearing damage only occurs from exposure at much higher intensities.

Measurement of hearing loss

In 1886, Thomas Barr, a Scottish physician, measured hearing ability in three groups of workers, namely, boilermakers, foundrymen and letter carriers. He measured the number of inches at which the tick of a pocket watch could just still be heard in the case of each subject. The total number of 'inches of hearing' for each group was then calculated. The results were: letter carriers (5,694), foundrymen (3,291) and boilermakers (704). In a well-designed study, he also accounted for age as a factor between the different groups. He clearly showed that the noisier the job, the less hearing the occupational group possessed. It is worth pointing out that it still took another 103 years before the UK introduced comprehensive statutory noise regulations.

Audiometry

This is the standard technique for measuring the hearing level of an individual. Audiometry should be performed when the subject has not been exposed to loud noise for at least 16 hours or has worn high efficiency hearing protection before the test. This will minimise the impact of any TTS in lowering an individual's hearing threshold. The subject sits in a soundproof booth and listens to a series of signals across the audible frequency range. With each test frequency, the volume is progressively reduced and the subject indicates when a tone has just disappeared. The level is then increased again until the subject indicates that the tone has reappeared. A sweep is carried out in both directions through the audible frequency range and the average of the two is taken as the actual measured hearing level.

The audiometer generates a spectrum showing the individual's hearing level across the audible frequency range (Figure 5.14). This is plotted on a calibration chart which takes account of the 'normal' audiometric range, that is, the level of hearing in an otologically normal population represented by the zero level shown. An otologically normal person is defined as:

> ...a person in a normal state of health, who is free from all signs/symptoms of ear disease, and from obstructing wax in the ear canal and has no history of undue exposure to noise.
> (BS EN ISO 389-1: 2000)

The audiogram in Figure 5.14 is that of a 50-year-old man with a disability of 44dB. Disability is calculated from the average of hearing loss over the main speech frequencies, that is, 1, 2 and 3kHz.

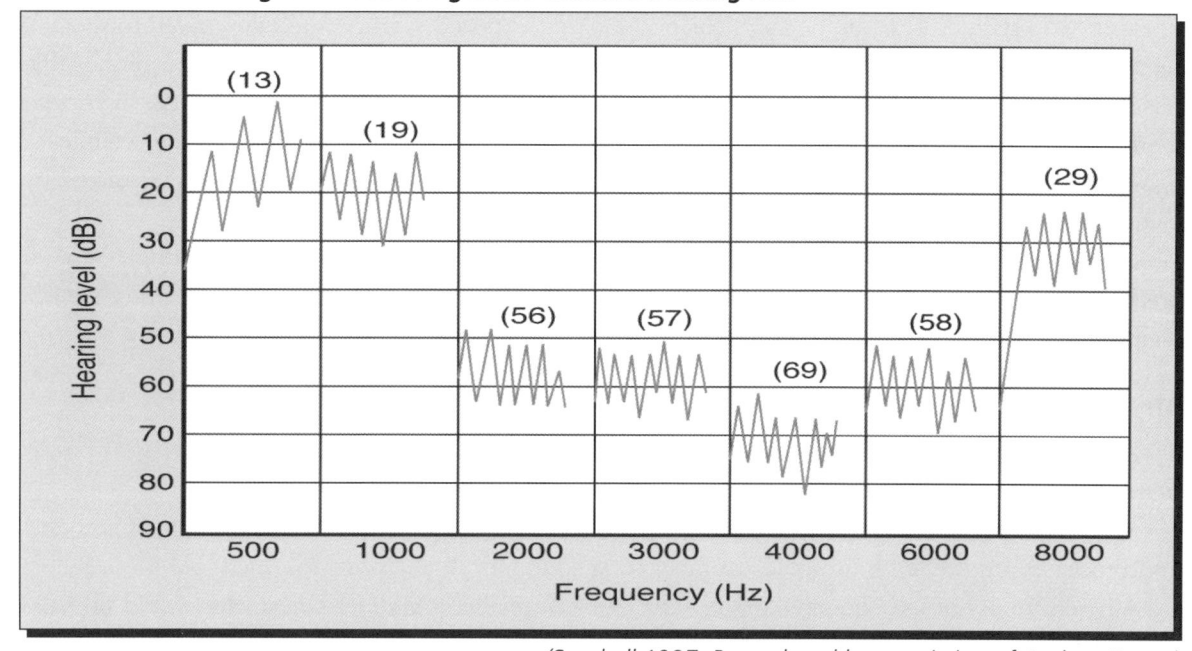

FIGURE 5.14: Audiogram illustrating noise-induced hearing loss

(Snashall 1997. Reproduced by permission of Anthea Carter.)

Interpretation of audiograms

The same effect is normally found in both ears and when there is a pattern in one ear only, other non-occupational causes may be implicated, for example, rifle shooting.

Often, as discussed above, with industrial noise exposure, there is a dip or notch at 4kHz or 6kHz with normal hearing levels around this region. A notch in the 1–3kHz region may indicate a familial cause of hearing loss (Snashall 1997). NIHL is distinguishable from presbyacusis by the upward slope of high frequencies. Although, as already noted above, presbyacusis will be superimposed on any NIHL later in life.

Assessment of audiograms

Three categories of audiogram can be identified:

1. **<20dB reduction in hearing level** – This is not regarded as outside the normal range and, therefore, does not represent NIHL or occupational deafness.
2. **>30dB reduction in hearing level across the 1, 2 and 3kHz frequencies** – This is the definition of hearing handicap defined in BS 5330 (BSI 1976) and is used in common law compensation cases.
3. **>50dB reduction in hearing level across the 1, 2 and 3kHz frequencies** – This represents a high level of hearing impairment. Hearing loss is averaged across both ears and this is the minimal level of hearing handicap to qualify a person for Industrial Injuries Disablement Benefit. In this context, this represents an overall defined disability of 20 per cent.

Measurement of exposure and analysis

Noise assessment survey

Exposure of people at work to loud noise can be measured in various ways depending on the objective of the survey. The NAW Regulations require an assessment of individual noise dose averaged over a nominal 8-hour day ($L_{EP,d}$), which can then be interpreted using the 'First' and 'Second' Action Levels specified in the Regulations. This may require a noise measurement survey to be carried out using technical equipment including a sound-level meter, an octave band frequency analyser and a personal dosimeter.

Fluctuating sound levels may be measured directly by an integrating sound-level meter and an 'equivalent continuous sound level' (known as the L_{eq} value) can be displayed. This is measured over a designated period of time and the L_{eq} is the theoretical sound level which would have emitted the same A-weighted sound energy over the same time as the actual noise. Measurements are taken at operator workstations near the person's ear position and exposed workers are interviewed to identify typical daily tasks, together with their frequency and duration. The noise surveyor also establishes that conditions on the day of the survey represent a typical daily personal exposure for the particular workplace. These measurements, together with knowledge of the worker's task routine, enables a computation to be made of a person's typical daily noise exposure ($L_{EP,d}$). This may be calculated by using the nomogram method described later in this chapter (see Figure 5.19).

Sound-level meters may also be fitted with an octave filter which allows the monitoring of sound levels over different frequency bands. This gives useful information for specifying engineering control measures and hearing protection equipment.

Noise measurement equipment

Sound-level meters (SLMs)

A wide range of sound-level meters are available which have different facilities and levels of accuracy and precision. In the UK, four grades of integrating sound-level meter are specified and these reflect the inherent errors of the equipment (see Table 5.3). Normally, a grade 1 or 2 meter would be used for a comprehensive noise assessment survey.

FIGURE 5.15: Sound-level meter

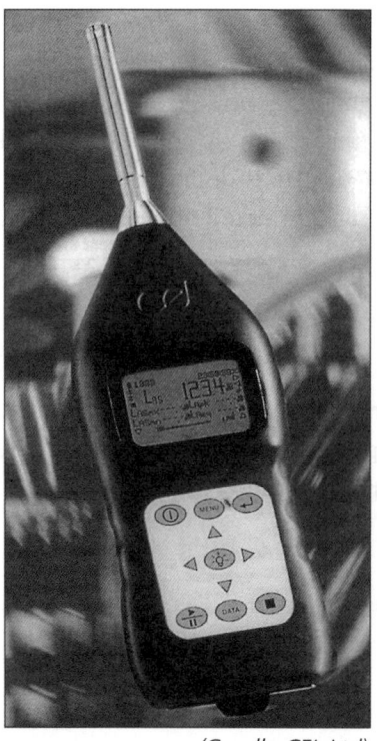

(Casella CEL Ltd)

TABLE 5.3: Sound-level meters and specification standards

Equipment type	Grades	Current standards	Old British standards
Sound-level meter	Type 0 (laboratory reference) Type 1 (laboratory and field) Type 2 (general field) Type 3 (field check)	BS EN 60651: 1994	BS 5969: 1981
Integrating sound-level meter	Type 0 (laboratory reference) Type 1 (laboratory and field) Type 2 (general field) Type 3 (field check)	BS EN 60804: 2001	BS 6698: 1986
Personal sound exposure meter (dosimeter)	Single grade only	BS EN 61252: 1997	BS 6402: 1994
Sound calibrator	Class 0 (most accurate) Class 1 Class 2 (least accurate)	BS EN 60942: 1998	BS 7189: 1989

(Modified from HSE 1998)

Personal noise dosimeters

Noise assessment can be carried out using personal noise dosimeters which exposed people are asked to wear for a period of time, possibly the whole working day. These devices will give an accumulated reading of total noise exposure (depending on the type of meter, the readout can be in percentage daily noise dose or $L_{EP,d}$). Some more sophisticated instruments will display a noise exposure history over the course of a day. These devices are particularly useful for itinerant workers who may work intermittently at different tasks and in different locations, for example, maintenance personnel and fork-lift truck drivers. They have the disadvantage that the final noise dose reading does not inform the surveyor as to where the worker received most of their noise exposure, although to some extent this information can be obtained from the workers themselves.

FIGURE 5.16: Personal noise dosimeter

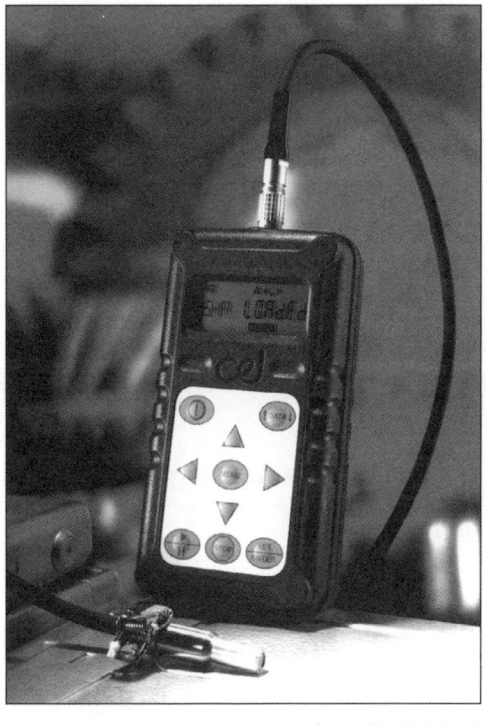

(Casella CEL Ltd)

NOISE

There is a range of devices available and when in use the microphone must be situated close to the operator's ear position, as shown in Figure 5.17. The microphone should be placed on the worker's side which is likely to receive the highest exposure.

FIGURE 5.17: Location of microphone for dosimeter

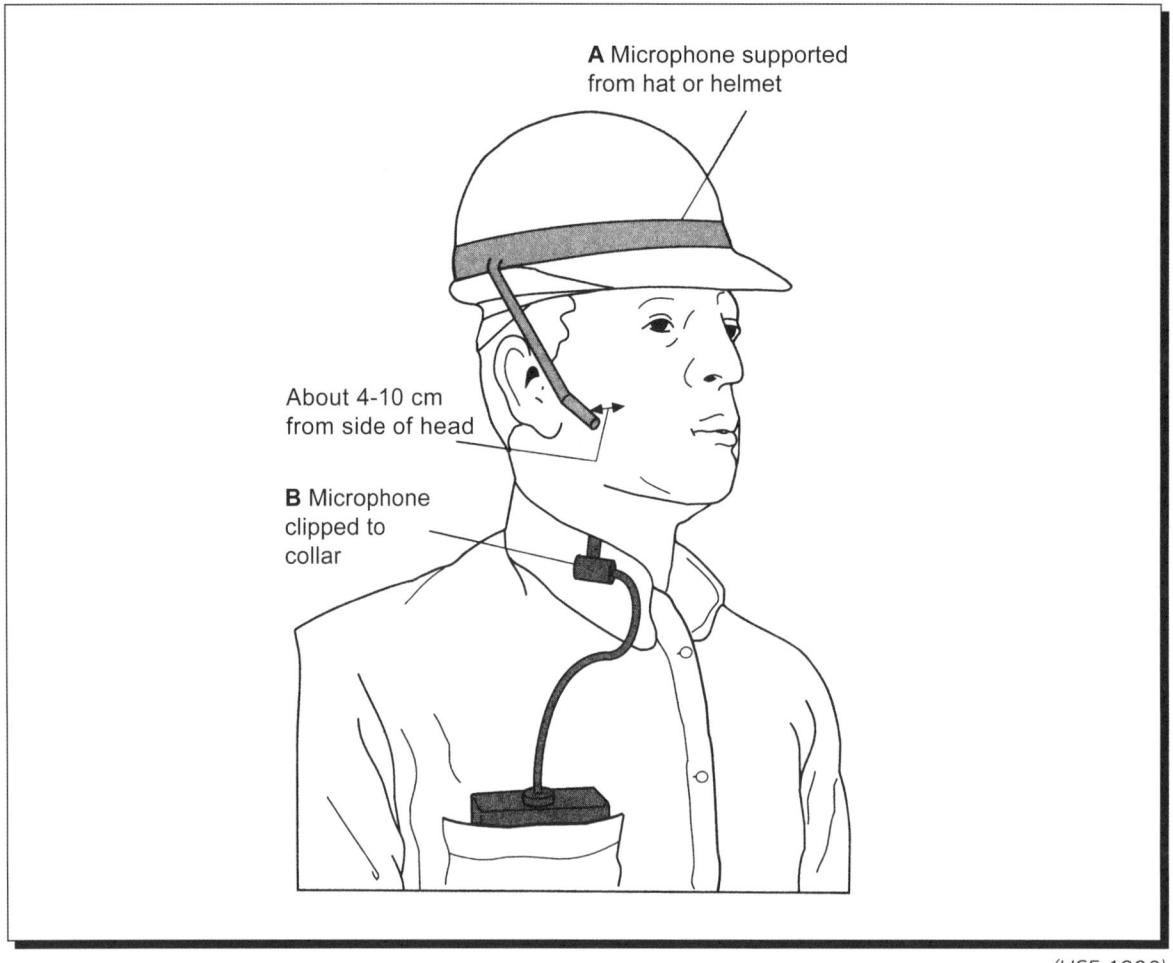

(HSE 1990)

Use of a sound-level meter is relatively flexible and it may allow noise dose estimates to be made for a group of workers over a relatively short period, while over the same period, less information may be obtained from using a dosimeter. However, overall, both types of equipment can be seen to complement each other. Sound-level meters and personal dosimeters need to be checked and calibrated regularly during a noise survey.

Calculation of $L_{EP,d}$

The nomogram in Figure 5.18 can be used for the calculation of $L_{EP,d}$ values. A straight line is drawn to connect the L-scale (noise level in dB(A)) with the t-scale (time) and the $L_{EP,d}$ value can be read off from the central scale. With more than one period of significant noise exposure, 'fractional exposures' using the f-scale can be calculated. Over the same day, values of 'f' can be added together and the result read as $L_{EP,d}$. A simple worked example is shown below:

TABLE 5.4: Calculation of $L_{EP,d}$ using the nomogram (Figure 5.18)

Task	Sound level (dB(A) Leq)	Duration	f-value
Hammering	100	15 minutes	0.3
Sanding	94	40 minutes	0.25
Sawing	87	3 hours	0.25
Maintenance work	75	4 hours	–

In the above calculation, the $L_{EP,d}$ (sum of f = 0.8) value is 89dB(A)

NOISE

FIGURE 5.18: Nomogram for calculation of $L_{EP,d}$

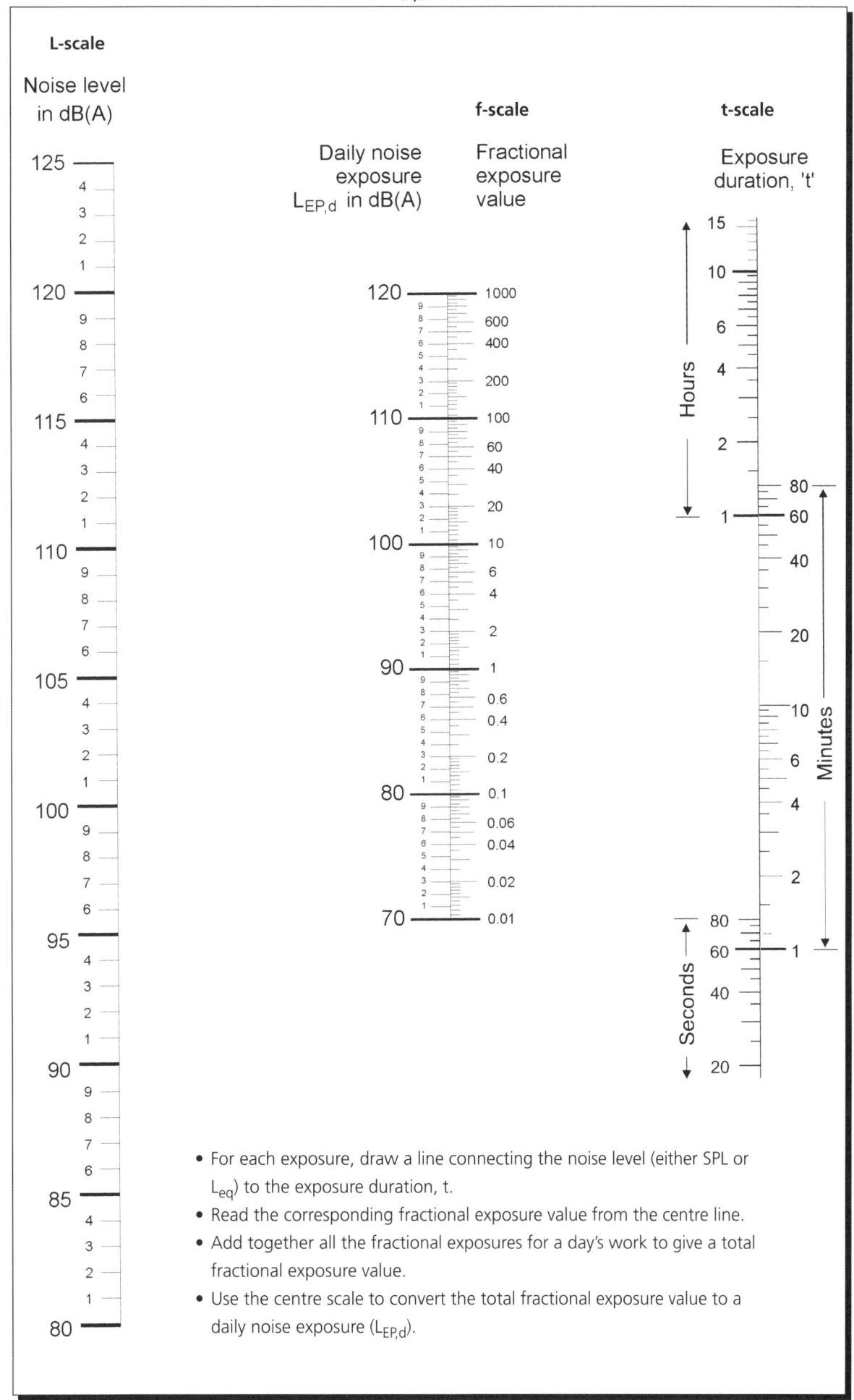

L-scale

Noise level in dB(A)

f-scale

Daily noise exposure $L_{EP,d}$ in dB(A)

Fractional exposure value

t-scale

Exposure duration, 't'

- For each exposure, draw a line connecting the noise level (either SPL or L_{eq}) to the exposure duration, t.
- Read the corresponding fractional exposure value from the centre line.
- Add together all the fractional exposures for a day's work to give a total fractional exposure value.
- Use the centre scale to convert the total fractional exposure value to a daily noise exposure ($L_{EP,d}$).

(HSE 1998)

NOISE

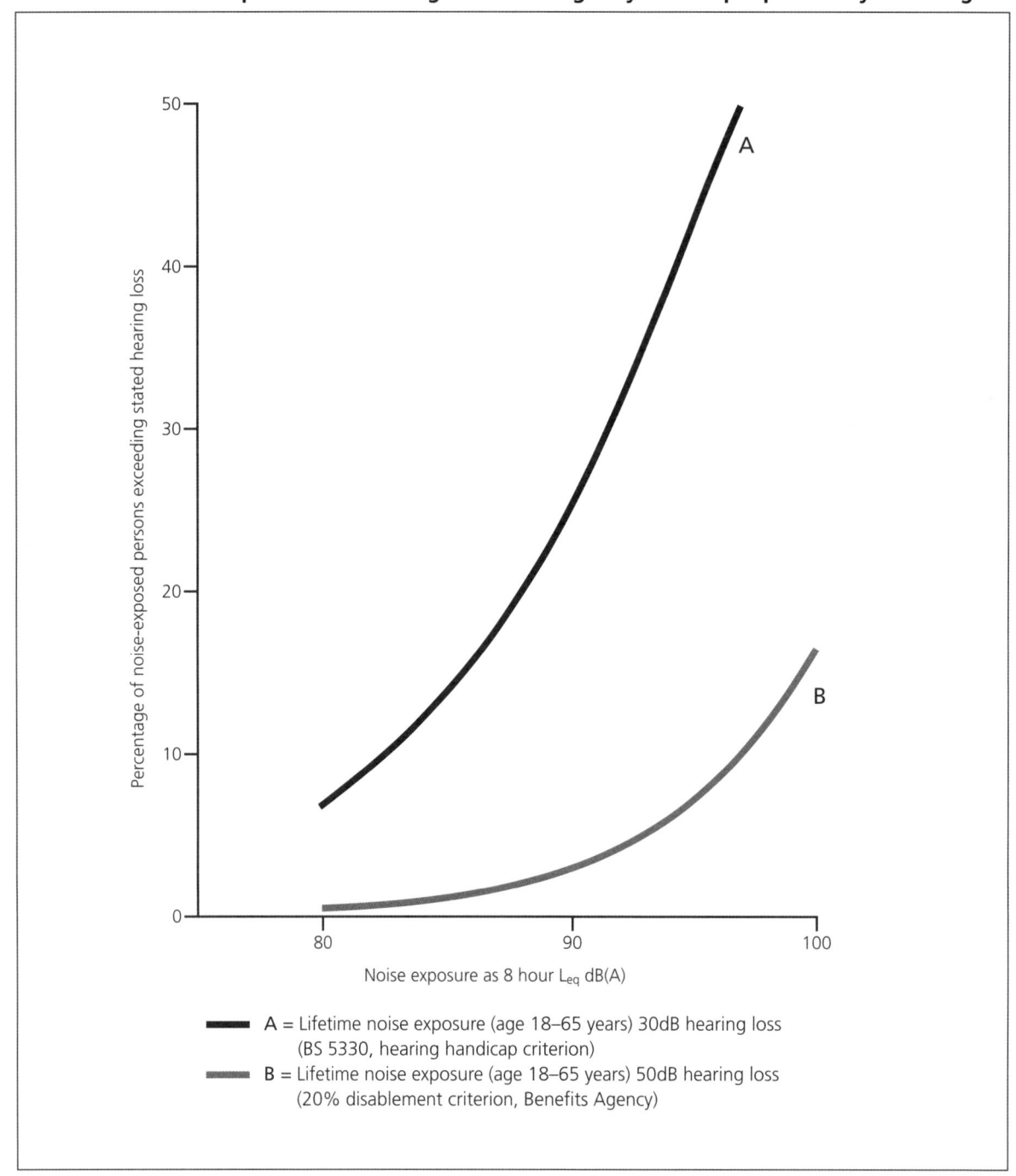

FIGURE 5.19: Noise exposure and hearing loss in otologically normal people at 65 years of age

[Graph: Percentage of noise-exposed persons exceeding stated hearing loss (y-axis, 0–50) vs Noise exposure as 8 hour L_{eq} dB(A) (x-axis, 80–100)]

- **A** = Lifetime noise exposure (age 18–65 years) 30dB hearing loss (BS 5330, hearing handicap criterion)
- **B** = Lifetime noise exposure (age 18–65 years) 50dB hearing loss (20% disablement criterion, Benefits Agency)

Based on data from NPL Acoustics Report Ac61; BS 5330 1976

Determination of risk tolerability

In NIHL, the risk of hearing impairment is assumed to be a direct function of total sound energy dose received (known as the 'equal energy principle'). This is believed to be the case with noise exposure levels up to 140dB. Above this value, acute hearing damage may occur. Below 140dB, hearing damage is independent of any temporal variation in exposure pattern and simply depends on overall dose of noise energy received. This implies that any permitted exposure time is halved when exposure level rises by 3dB, that is, a doubling of sound energy.

In 1971, the British Occupational Hygiene Society proposed an Equivalent Continuous Sound Level (L_{eq}) of 90dB(A), averaged over a nominal 8-hour working day, as a workplace noise standard (BOHS 1971). In 1972, this was adopted by the Department of Employment in its voluntary code of practice on exposure to noise (DoE 1972). In 1989, this level was included in the NAW Regulations as the Second Action Level.

There has been much criticism of the safety factor inherent in this limit and some of the HSC's previous publications have indicated the problem with this value (HSC 1981). Figures 5.19 and 5.20 illustrate

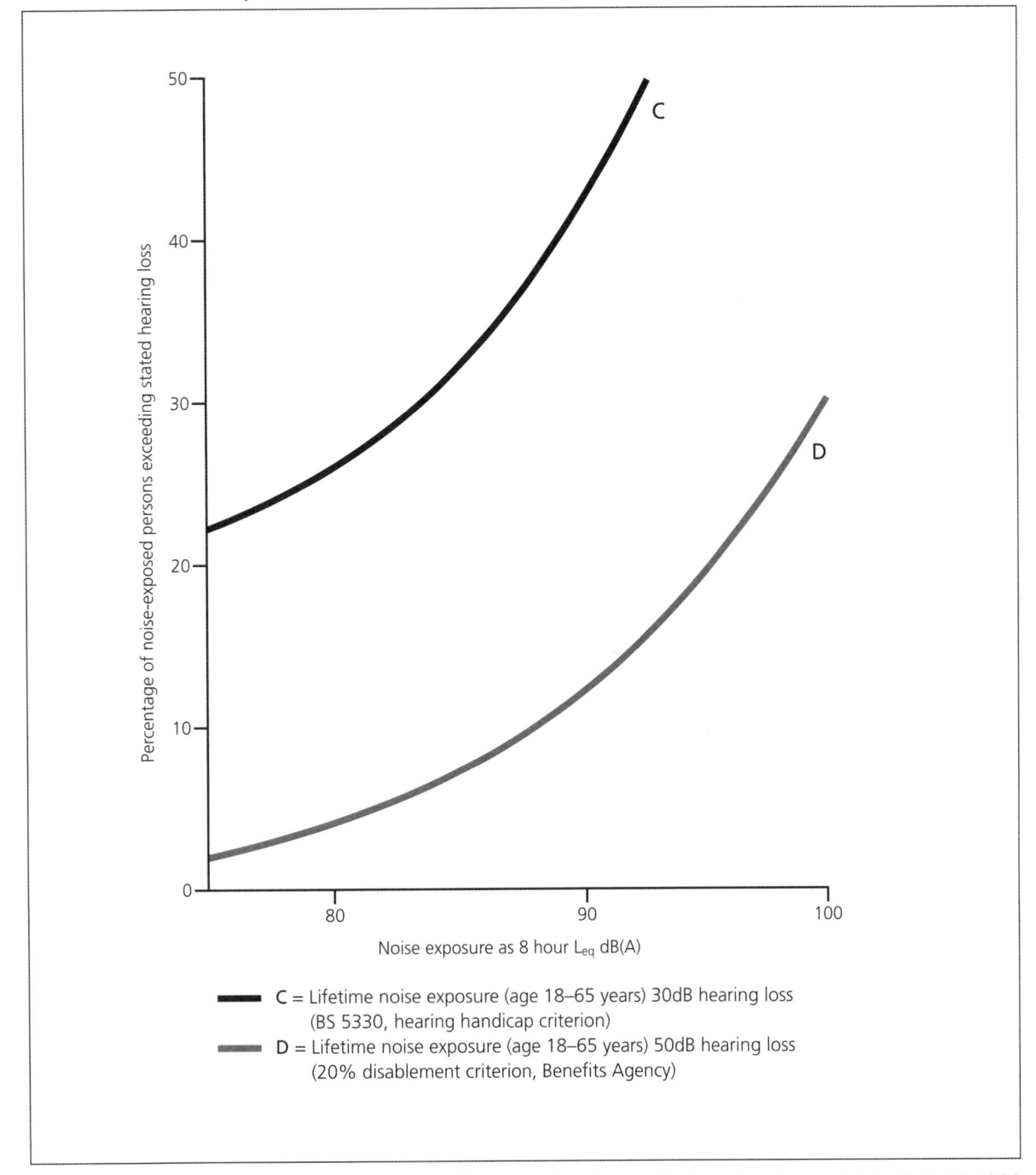

FIGURE 5.20: Noise exposure and hearing loss in a typical industrial population at 65 years of age

[Graph: Y-axis "Percentage of noise-exposed persons exceeding stated hearing loss" from 0 to 50; X-axis "Noise exposure as 8 hour L_{eq} dB(A)" from 80 to 100. Two curves labelled C and D.]

C = Lifetime noise exposure (age 18–65 years) 30dB hearing loss (BS 5330, hearing handicap criterion)

D = Lifetime noise exposure (age 18–65 years) 50dB hearing loss (20% disablement criterion, Benefits Agency)

Based on data from NPL Acoustics Report Ac61; BS 5330 1976

dose response information for noise, that is, at a given noise exposure level, the effect this would have on the exposed population. Figure 5.19 illustrates the dose/response relationship for noise with an otologically normal population, that is, all the hearing loss is due to noise exposure and average loss due to age. However, in the industrial population actually exposed to noise in the workplace, there is hearing loss caused by other factors, such as disease. Figure 5.20 illustrates the dose response information on a typical industrial population. Taking an example from Figure 5.20 (graph D), if an industrial population was exposed to noise at 90dB(A) for their entire working life, approximately 12 per cent would have hearing loss severe enough (ie 50dB) for them to qualify for industrial disablement benefit under social security legislation; from graph C, around 40 per cent would be above the threshold of loss for onset of disability as defined in BS 5330: 1976. (Note: much hearing loss by inherent disease.)

In 1987, a review of the contemporary data by Robinson clearly demonstrated the desirability of reducing noise exposure to 85dB(A) (HSE 1987). However, this did not prevent the subsequent NAW Regulations incorporating 90dB(A) (as averaged level over an 8-hour period) as the Second Action Level. This is in effect the maximum level permitted for unprotected exposure and is discussed next.

NOISE

The Noise at Work Regulations 1989 (NAW) and Action Levels

Within these Regulations, Action Levels are specified together with a general duty to reduce noise levels as low as is reasonably practicable. An assessment must be carried out where anyone is likely to be exposed in excess of the First Action Level.

The two Action Levels refer to daily personal exposure to noise ($L_{EP,d}$). The First Action Level is 85dB(A) ($L_{EP,d}$) and the Second Action Level is 90dB(A) ($L_{EP,d}$). The peak pressure is the highest pressure reached by the sound wave. The Peak Action Level means a peak sound pressure of 200 pascals. (This is 140dB for a reference pressure of 20μPa.) For practical purposes, the Peak Action Level is equivalent to a C-weighted peak of 140dB(C)[26]. The Peak Action Level could be important in a situation where there is very high impulse noise, for example, with a cartridge-operated tool which when operated on an occasional basis may not exceed the First Action Level of 85dB(A) ($L_{EP,d}$). A summary of the duties of imposed by the Noise at Work Regulations 1989 (NAW) with respect to the various Action Levels is given in Table 5.5.

New noise directive

A European Community directive has recently come into force regarding the exposure of workers to noise (EC 2003). This contains stricter noise exposure limits than those currently embodied in the NAW Regulations, which will need to be modified or replaced as the requirements of the directive must be enacted as UK domestic legislation by February 2006. (The HSC has issued a consultative document on this: *Proposals for new Control of Noise at Work Regulations implementing the Physical Agents (Noise) Directive 2003/10/EC*, CD 196, HSE Books 2004.) The directive contains noise 'Exposure Limit Values' and 'Exposure Action Values'. The Exposure Action Values are based on ambient noise levels and trigger different degrees of protective measures. The Exposure Limit Values lay down exposure limits which take account of the wearing of individual hearing protectors.

In each case, a daily, or weekly, average noise exposure value in dB(A) is accompanied by a peak sound pressure value (p_{peak}) to take account of high instantaneous noise levels.

The European Council of Ministers has reached agreement on the following noise exposure values:

- Exposure Limit Values of 87dB(A) and a peak sound pressure (p_{peak}) of 200Pa;
- upper Exposure Action Values of 85dB(A) and a peak sound pressure (p_{peak}) of 200Pa;
- lower Exposure Action Values of 80dB(A) and a peak sound pressure (p_{peak}) of 112Pa.

Where noise exposure exceeds the upper Exposure Action Values, workers are obliged to use the individual hearing protectors which the employer must make available to them when the lower exposure action value is exceeded.

Aural comfort

As well as limits to prevent NIHL, various yardsticks have been derived to provide guidance on maximum background noise levels for aural comfort. In general, the quieter the activity, the lower the acceptable background level. These noise levels are well below those which cause NIHL.

Noise criteria (NC) curves

Guidance has been provided on acceptable background noise levels. Work carried out by Beranek in the 1950s provided an indication of maximum sound levels allowable in the eight octave bands (63Hz to 2,000Hz) in order for there to be minimum interference with telephone conversations between females (Beranek 1956). A series of curves were derived (numbered from 15 to 70) which refer to the octave band dB level at a frequency of 1,000Hz. These are known as the noise criteria (NC) curves and they were produced to help achieve aural comfort.

They are most frequently used in office environments. The background noise levels are measured in dB(linear) and the sound intensity at each octave band plotted on a graph. The NC curve taken in a particular case is that above the highest decibel level across the spectrum. A number of different environments have been assigned appropriate specific NC levels and examples are given in Figure 5.22.

---

[26]C-weighted decibels are used to monitor peak noise exposure.

TABLE 5.5: Summary of the duties of the Noise at Work Regulations 1989 (NAW)

Action required where $L_{EP,d}$ is likely to be: (See note (1) below)	Below 85dB(A)	85db(A) First AL	90dB(A) Second AL
EMPLOYER'S DUTIES **General duty to reduce risk** Risk of hearing damage to be reduced to the lowest level reasonably practicable (regulation 6)	•	•	(2) •
Assessment of noise exposure Noise assessments to be made by a competent person (regulation 4). Record of assessments to be kept until a new one is made (regulation 5)		• •	• •
Noise reduction Reduce exposure to noise as far as is reasonably practicable by means other than ear protectors (regulation 7)			•
Provision of information to workers Provide adequate information, instruction and training about risks to hearing, what employees should do to minimise risk, how they can obtain ear protectors if they are exposed between 85 and 90db(A), and their obligations under the Regulations (regulation 11). Mark ear protection zones with notices so far as is reasonably practicable (regulation 9)		•	• •
Ear protectors Ensure so far as is reasonably practical that protectors are: • provided to employees who ask for them (regulation 8(1)) • provided to all exposed (regulation 8(2)) • maintained and repaired (regulation 10(1)(b)) • used by all exposed (regulation 10(1)(a)) Ensure so far as is reasonably practicable that all who go into a marked ear protection zone use ear protectors (regulation 9(1)(b))		• •	 • • • • (3)
Maintenance and use of equipment Ensure so far as is practicable that: • all equipment provided under the Regulations is used except for the ear protectors provided between 85 and 90dB(A) (regulation 10(1)(a)) • all equipment is maintained (regulation 10(1)(b))		• •	• •
EMPLOYEE'S DUTIES **Use of equipment** So far as practicable: • use ear protectors (regulation 10(2)) • use any other protective equipment (regulation 10(2)) • report any defects discovered to his/her employer (regulation 10(2))		 • •	• • •
MACHINE-MAKERS' AND SUPPLIERS' DUTIES **Provision of information** Provide information on the noise likely to be generated (regulation 12)		•	•

(HSE)

NOTES:
(1) The dB(A) Action Levels are values of daily personal exposure to noise ($L_{EP,d}$).
(2) All the actions indicated at 90dB(A) are also required where the peak sound pressure is at or above 200Pa (140db re 20μPa).
(3) This requirement applies to all who enter the zones even if they do not stay long enough to receive an exposure of 90dB(A) $L_{EP,d}$.

FIGURE 5.21: Noise criteria (NC) curves

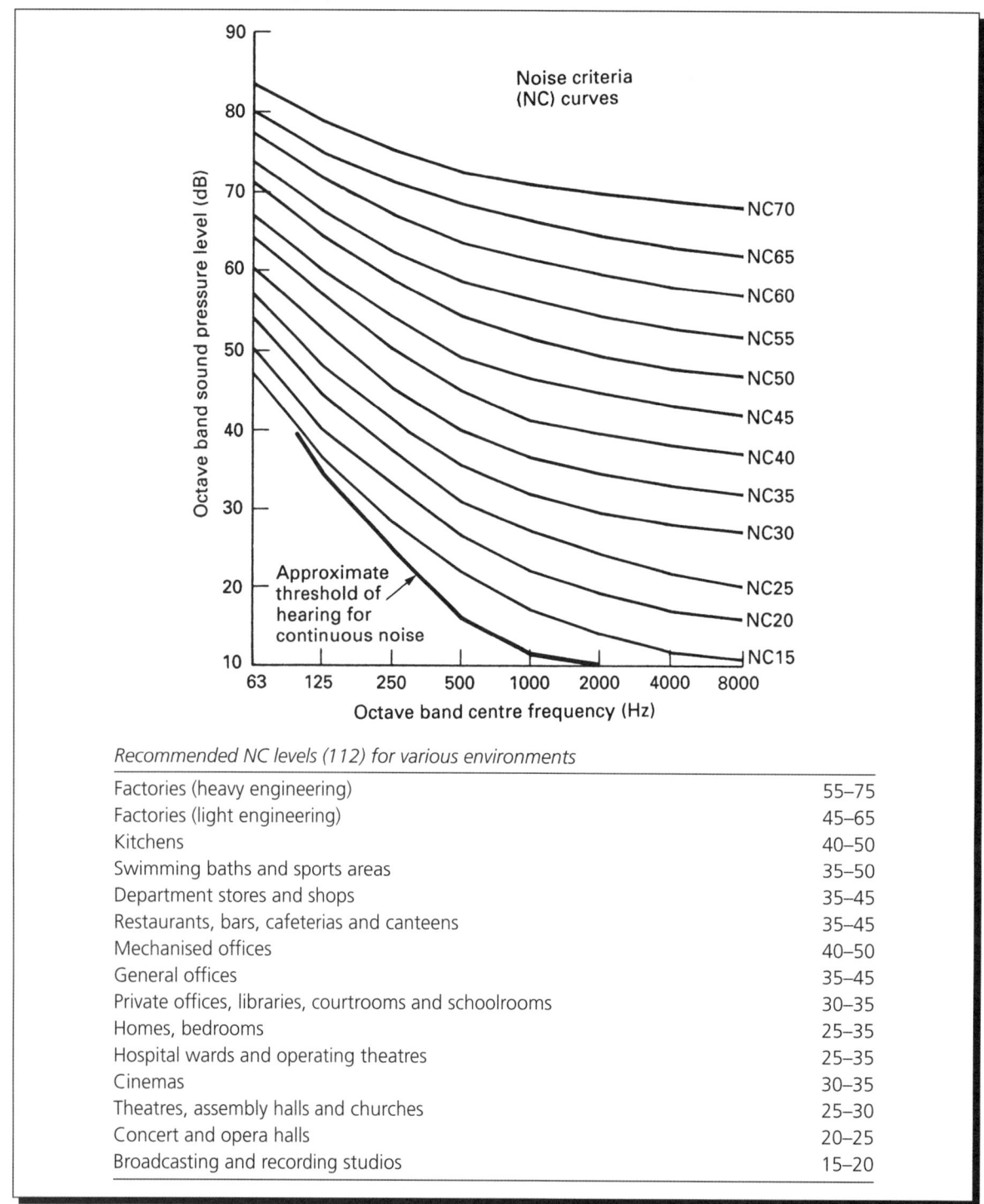

Recommended NC levels (112) for various environments

Environment	NC Level
Factories (heavy engineering)	55–75
Factories (light engineering)	45–65
Kitchens	40–50
Swimming baths and sports areas	35–50
Department stores and shops	35–45
Restaurants, bars, cafeterias and canteens	35–45
Mechanised offices	40–50
General offices	35–45
Private offices, libraries, courtrooms and schoolrooms	30–35
Homes, bedrooms	25–35
Hospital wards and operating theatres	25–35
Cinemas	30–35
Theatres, assembly halls and churches	25–30
Concert and opera halls	20–25
Broadcasting and recording studios	15–20

(Malerbi 1989. Reprinted by permission of Elsevier Limited.)

Noise rating (NR) curves

Noise rating (NR) curves are based on the same concept (Figure 5.22) as the NC system, but the curves are based on the results of a large-scale survey of the reaction of the community to noise (Kosten & van Os 1982). These give a similar rating to the NC curves, but they have a wider application to cover industrial use and community response. The main advantage of using octave band analysis data is that the frequencies of concern immediately become apparent.

Control strategy

Where it is not reasonably practicable to eliminate a noise risk (for example, by substituting an inherently noisy process with a quieter alternative), then it is necessary to adopt a strategy, preferentially applying engineering noise control measures followed by other measures applied from a control hierarchy.

FIGURE 5.22: Noise rating (NR) curves

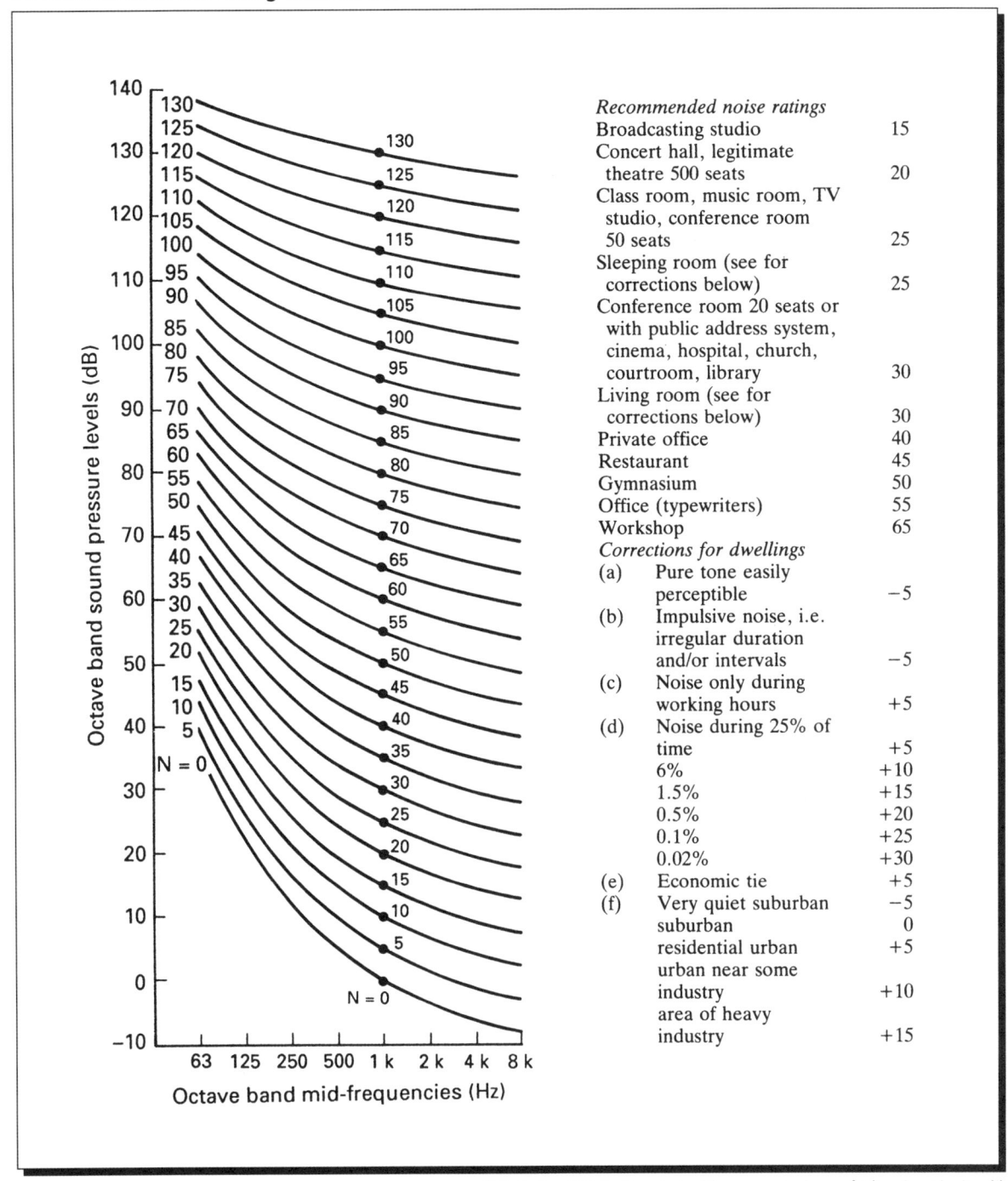

Recommended noise ratings	
Broadcasting studio	15
Concert hall, legitimate theatre 500 seats	20
Class room, music room, TV studio, conference room 50 seats	25
Sleeping room (see for corrections below)	25
Conference room 20 seats or with public address system, cinema, hospital, church, courtroom, library	30
Living room (see for corrections below)	30
Private office	40
Restaurant	45
Gymnasium	50
Office (typewriters)	55
Workshop	65

Corrections for dwellings

(a)	Pure tone easily perceptible	−5
(b)	Impulsive noise, i.e. irregular duration and/or intervals	−5
(c)	Noise only during working hours	+5
(d)	Noise during 25% of time	+5
	6%	+10
	1.5%	+15
	0.5%	+20
	0.1%	+25
	0.02%	+30
(e)	Economic tie	+5
(f)	Very quiet suburban	−5
	suburban	0
	residential urban	+5
	urban near some industry	+10
	area of heavy industry	+15

(Malerbi 1989. Reprinted by permission of Elsevier Limited.)

It is necessary to first identify each noise source and its pathway to the receiver. Sound transfer systems break down simply into three elements:

1. The noise source.
2. The transmission path (direct and reflected).
3. The receiver.

Industrial noise is produced from many different sources, for example, a power press generates impact noise when sheet metal is blanked off. (This is usually the principal noise source.) However, such machines may also generate gear, motor, materials handling and pneumatic exhaust noise.

Noise from individual sources may reach the receiver by different pathways (see Figure 5.23). Some of the impact noise will reach the operator directly and some will travel through the machine frame and floor (as mechanical vibrations), which will eventually reach the person as noise radiated from the floor and walls. When each source of noise has been identified, together with its transfer pathway, priorities are determined for the application of control measures.

FIGURE 5.23: Sound transfer pathways

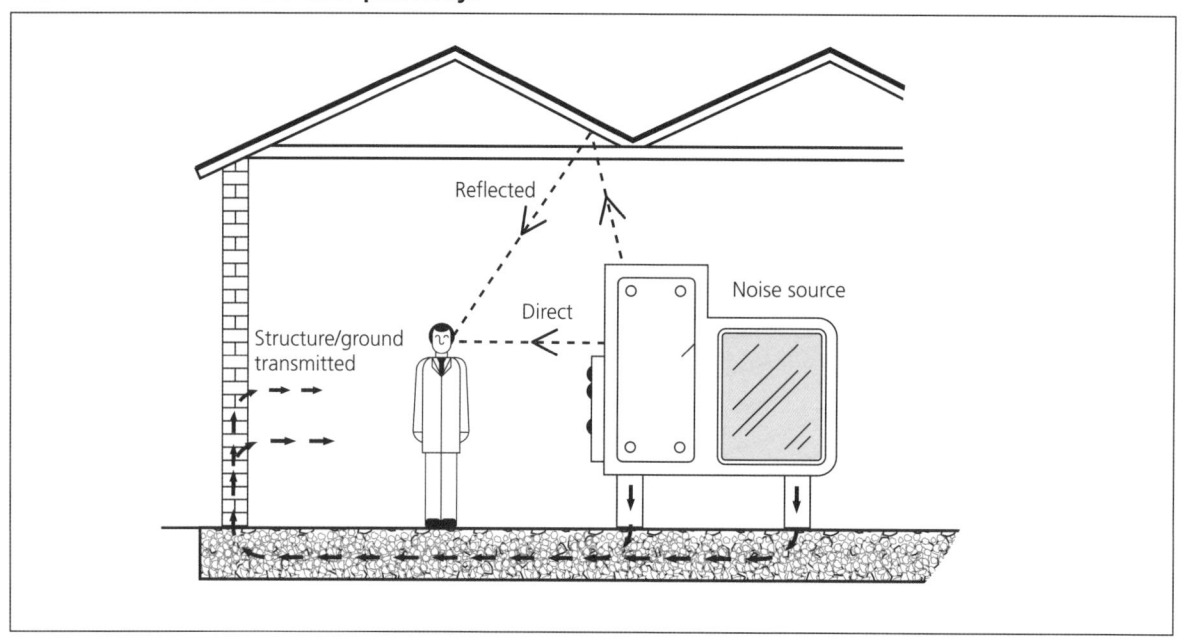

Noise control methods

Approaches to noise control can be conveniently grouped as follows:
1. Control the noise at source.
2. Prevent noise transmission through the machine and building.
3. Prevent the radiation of noise into the air.
4. Prevent the transmission of noise through the air to the receiver.

Initial measures

Before considering these four principles, it may be possible to reduce the number of people exposed to noisy machines by the simple expedient of moving all the noisy machines to one area. Unnecessary exposure of people other than operators is, thus, prevented and efforts and resources can be concentrated in one area. Similarly, it may be possible to reduce unnecessary exposure by removing people with inherently quiet jobs from noisy areas, for example, people performing inspection tasks close to noisy activities and processes.

Reducing the time of exposure to a particular noise source can be used as a dose-limiting control strategy. The dose is related to the intensity of the noise and the length of time a person is exposed. As indicated above, 90dB(A) $L_{EP,d}$ represents the energy level embodied in the Second Action Level of the NAW Regulations and this is the maximum level permitted for unprotected exposure by the Regulations. (Equal doses of noise energy are: 93dB(A) for four hours; 96dB(A) for two hours; 99dB(A) for one hour and so on.)

Design stage – Control of noise at source

Once the main sources of noise from a machine have been identified, then ways of modifying the design of noise-generating components can be considered. Potential noise sources are obviously best considered at the design stage (ie before construction of the machine or process), where a small change may eliminate or much reduce a problem, often with little consequent cost.

Most problems are concerned with machinery which is already in operation but there are still opportunities to reduce noise generation, for example, replacing steel gears with plastic alternatives, reducing operating air pressures and exhausts, cushioning impacts, and improved preventive maintenance procedures with timely replacement of noisy, worn parts. In the long term, it may be possible to fundamentally change a process, for example, replacing a riveting operation by a welding process. Two very useful collections of simplified noise control case studies have been published covering a wide range of examples (HSE 1986, 1995).

Prevent transmission through the machine

If control at source is not possible, then it may be practicable to prevent the spread of noise through the rest of the machine and into the floor by isolating the noisy part(s). Mechanical vibration tends to pass easily through rigid structures and isolators prevent structural vibration reaching efficient noise-radiating surfaces such as machine panels and guards. Isolators can be steel springs or inherently flexible materials such as rubber or neoprene. Whole machines may be mounted on rubber bushes to isolate their mechanical vibration and prevent transmission into the floor and/or walls and subsequent noise radiation into the air. Machine guards may be isolated by using rubber grommets between washers at panel fixing points.

Prevent radiation of noise

When the above approaches have been considered, the next step is to examine areas of the machine from which noise is radiated into the air. Two complementary approaches are possible:

1. Reduce the noise-radiating surface area.
2. Apply damping to residual radiating areas.

FIGURE 5.24: Saw blade sharpening – Application of damping

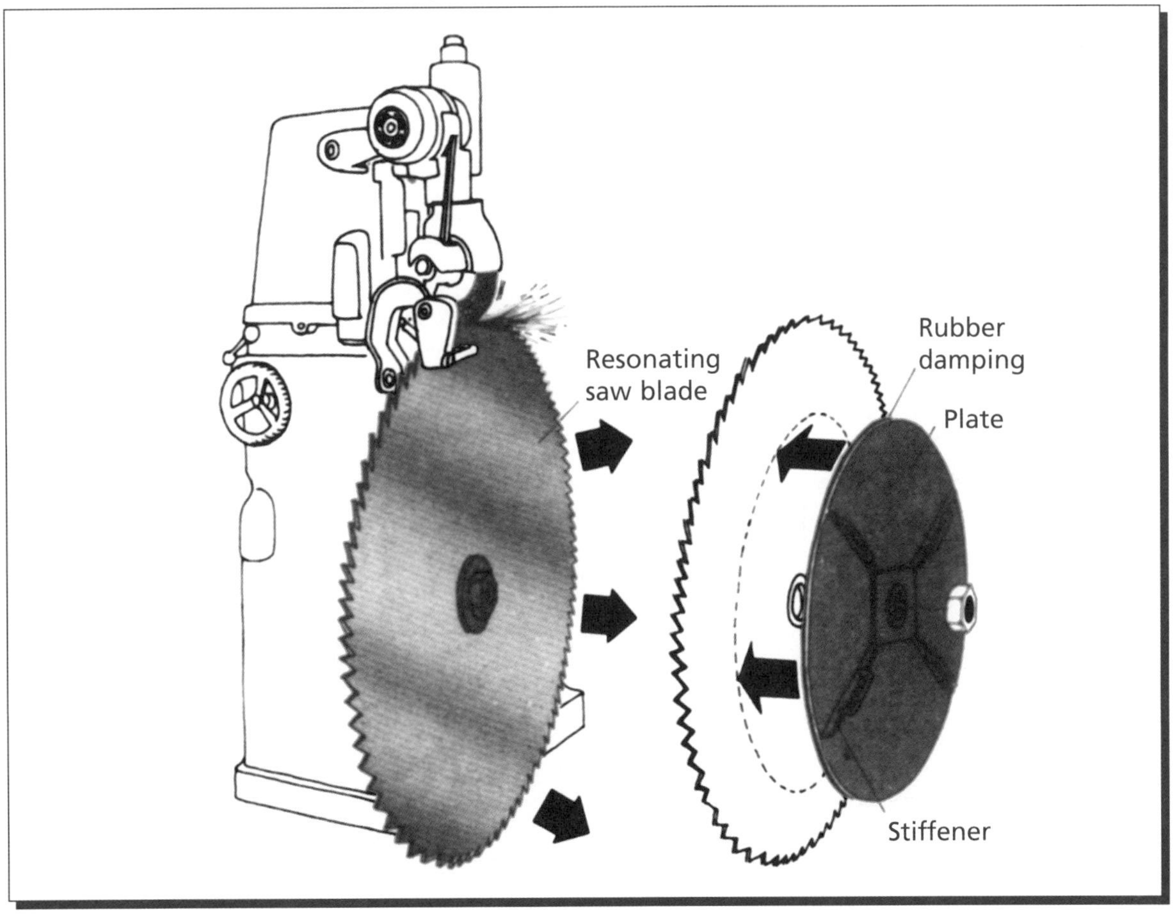

(UAW 1980)

Damping reduces the initial noise impact loading and the capability of surfaces to radiate noise into the air (Figure 5.24). For example, the steel panels that cover machinery often radiate large amounts of sound. Possible remedies are:

1. **Substitution** – using materials with a higher inherent damping capacity (eg cast iron has more damping capacity than steel).
2. **Applied damping treatment** – some plastics can be sprayed or glued on to the steel to increase the overall mass and increase stiffness. This causes the material to vibrate at a frequency greater than its natural frequency, which absorbs vibrational energy.
3. **Sandwich-type construction** – appropriate for structures with a thickness greater than three millimetres where the above damping treatment may not be effective; a composite

sandwich (two outer layers of steel separated by a viscose-elastic inner layer such as rubber or polyurethane).

4. **Stiffening ribs** – spot-welding steel ribs on to the panels will reduce noise radiation into the air.

Prevent transmission through the air to the receiver

Once the above possibilities have been considered and the sound is travelling through the air, the last option is to insulate operators and others from the sound and this can be accomplished by:

- enclosing the machine or its noisy parts;
- enclosing the operator in a noise haven;
- interrupting transfer pathways by use of acoustic screens and absorptive panels; and/or
- providing the operator with effective hearing protection.

Noise enclosures

A noise source can be attenuated by placing it inside an enclosure. This will control both the direct and reflected (reverberation) field noise. Features of enclosures are illustrated in Figures 5.25, 5.26 and 5.27.

FIGURE 5.25: Noise enclosure

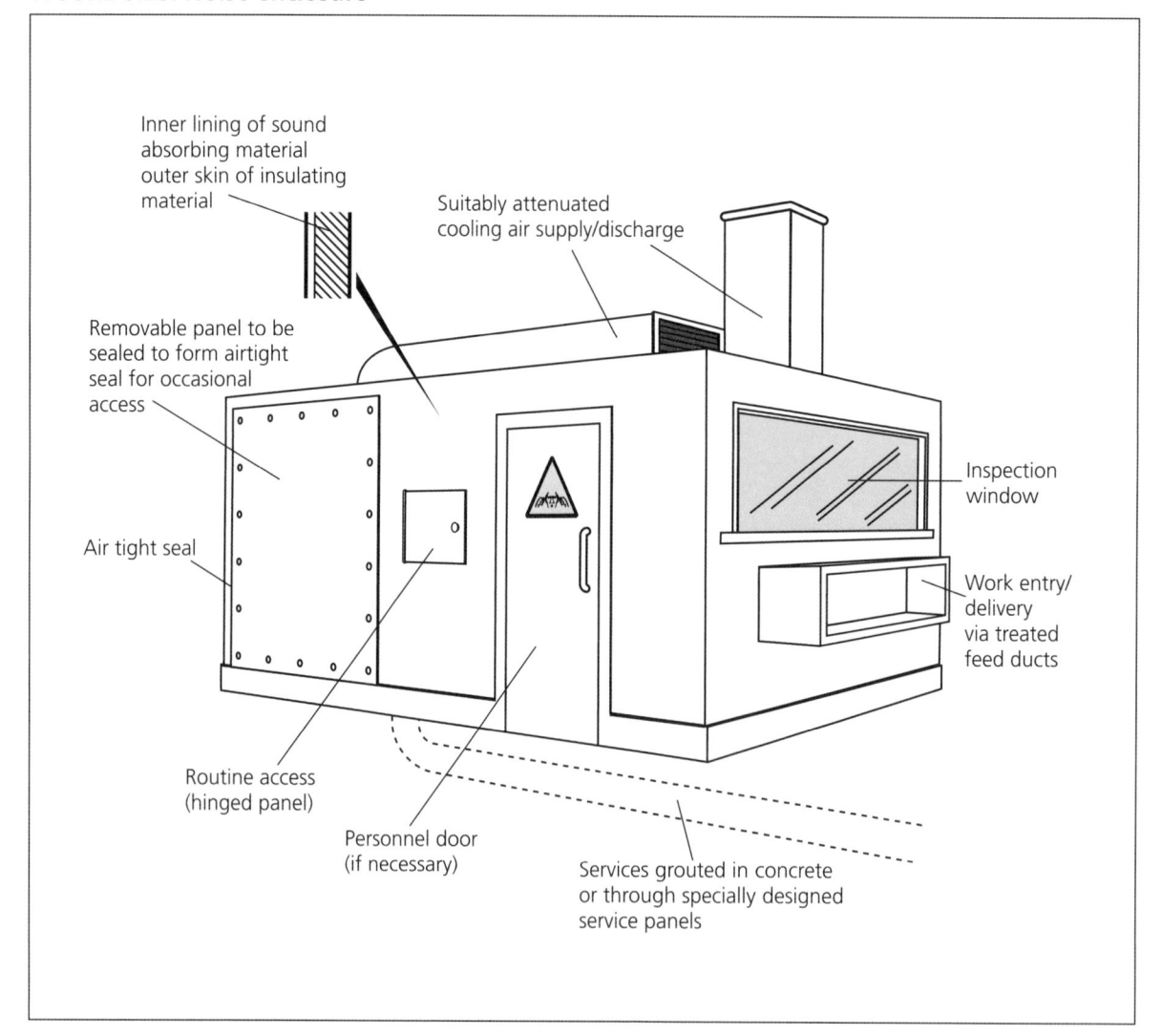

The typical features of an enclosure are:

- a heavy outer wall (steel, plasterboard or brickwork);
- an inner lining of an acoustically-absorbent material (eg mineral wool or rock wool); and
- an inner mesh or perforated panel to protect against mechanical damage.

FIGURE 5.26: Techniques to reduce the generation of airborne and structure-borne noise in machines

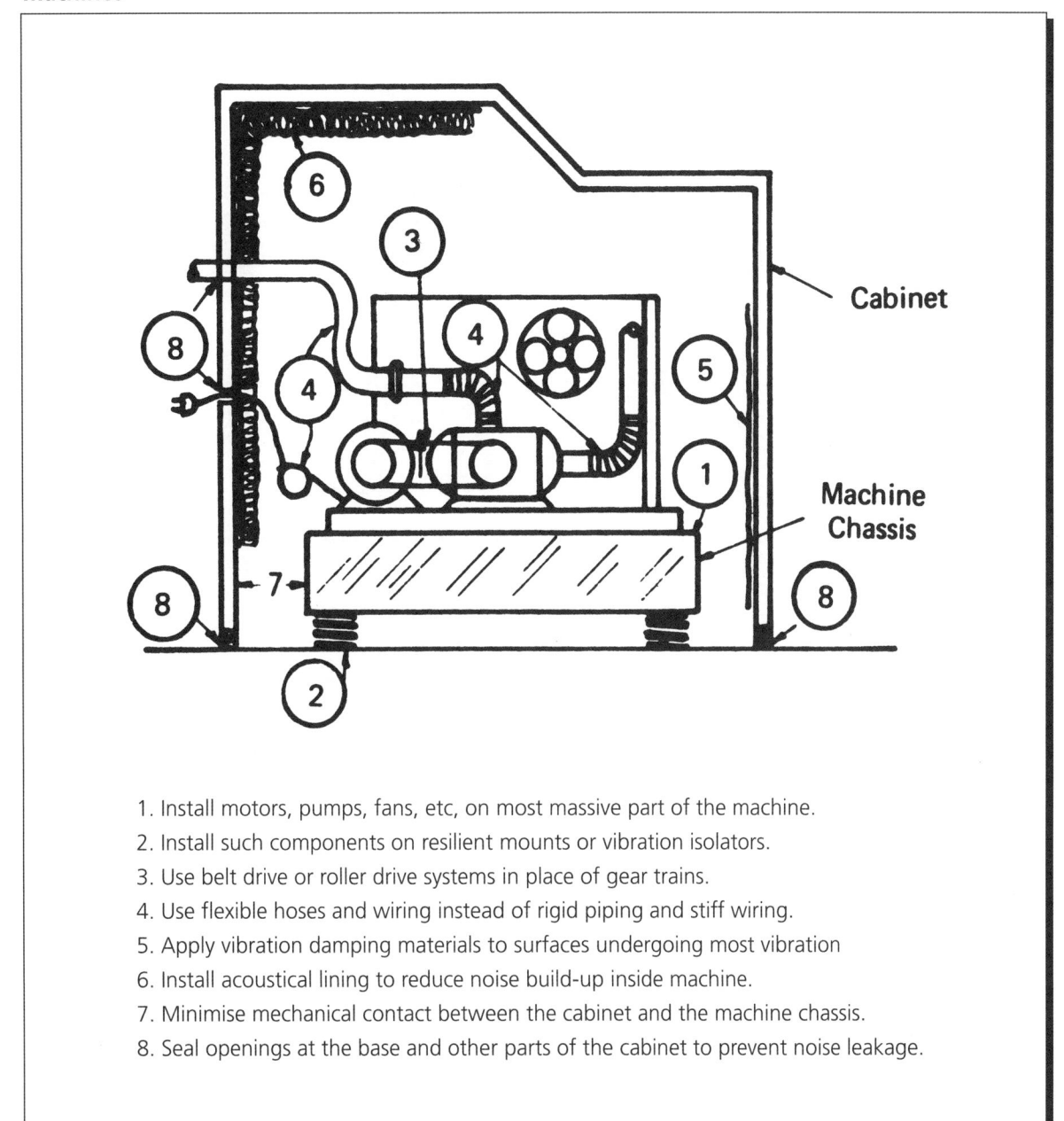

1. Install motors, pumps, fans, etc, on most massive part of the machine.
2. Install such components on resilient mounts or vibration isolators.
3. Use belt drive or roller drive systems in place of gear trains.
4. Use flexible hoses and wiring instead of rigid piping and stiff wiring.
5. Apply vibration damping materials to surfaces undergoing most vibration
6. Install acoustical lining to reduce noise build-up inside machine.
7. Minimise mechanical contact between the cabinet and the machine chassis.
8. Seal openings at the base and other parts of the cabinet to prevent noise leakage.

(UAW 1980)

Sound attenuation is the reduction in overall noise, which can be achieved by installation of an enclosure. The performance of an enclosure depends on the Sound Reduction Index (SRI), which is an alternative term for transmission loss described above. SRI values, at octave band frequencies, have been measured for a wide range of insulation materials (Sharland 1989). The inner surface of the enclosure is lined with sound-absorbent material in order to prevent reverberation build-up inside the enclosure. Sound absorption coefficients have been calculated for different materials. SRI and absorption coefficients are listed by Sharland (1989). Octave band measurements are used in the selection of both the outer wall material and the inner absorbent lining.

For an effective structure, careful design of an enclosure is required with adequate provision for:
- the ingress of raw materials and egress of product;
- adequate ventilation to prevent overheating of equipment;
- access for services;
- adequate silencing of any access conduits and vents;
- access for maintenance and repair work; and
- vision panels.

NOISE

FIGURE 5.27: Enclosure requiring air circulation for cooling

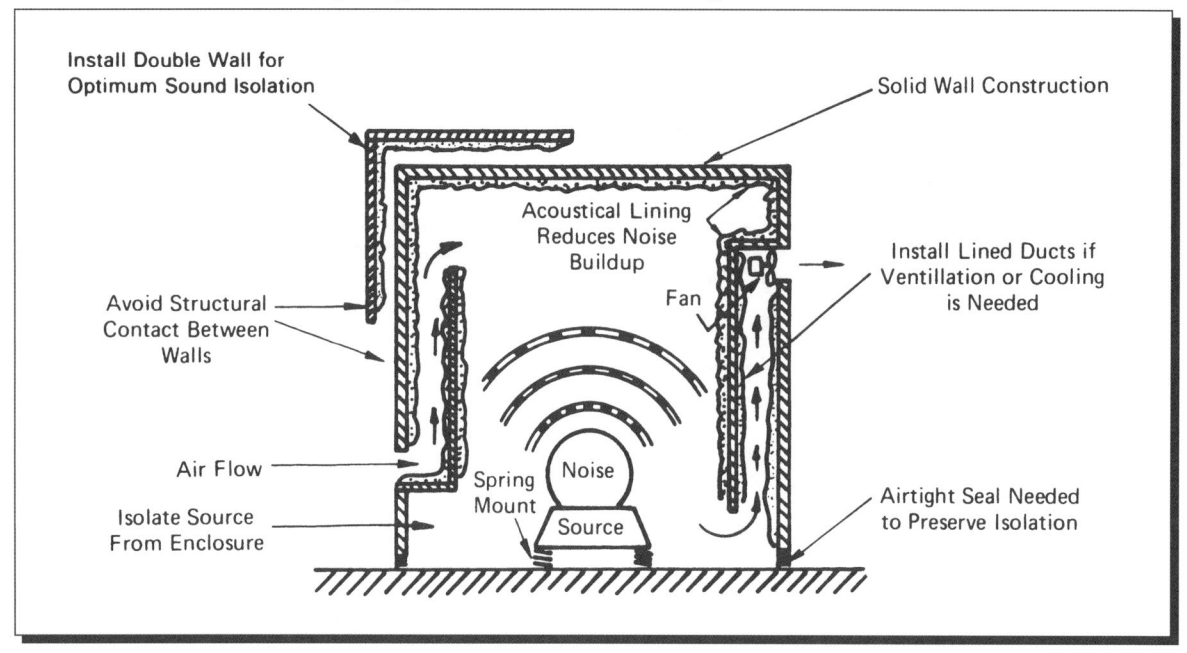

(UAW 1980)

It is important that a noise enclosure is as complete as possible since gaps (from damage or poor design and/or construction) will significantly reduce its effectiveness. As an illustrative example, an enclosure which theoretically could reduce noise by 50dB(A) may only achieve 20dB(A) due to the presence of gaps representing one per cent of total surface area.

Noise havens

A noise haven is an enclosure (Figure 5.28) where the sound-reduction process is carried out in reverse, that is, the purpose is to keep noise outside and achieve a suitable sound attenuation inside. Suitable conditions would be required for personnel with good door seals, adequate visibility and a reasonable thermal environment including ventilation provision.

FIGURE 5.28: Noise haven

(HSE 1998)

Lagging

Pipes carrying steam or heated fluids may be lagged, as an alternative to enclosure, with a sound reduction of 10 to 20dB(A). The lagging consists of a sound-absorbing material with an outer layer of aluminium, vinyl or lead. This is only effective with sound in excess of 500Hz and it is important that the lagged pipework does not come into direct contact with the outer layer of the lagging, since this itself could become a resonator and radiate noise.

Acoustic screens and absorptive panels

The principles of these are illustrated in Figure 5.29. Acoustic screens can be used to reduce direct field noise (up to 15dB(A)). They have most benefit against high frequencies and are least effective with low frequency noise. Their effectiveness decreases with distance from the noise source.

Absorptive panels consist of panels of sound-absorbent material fixed to walls or hung at ceiling height. They are useful where there is a significant reverberation build-up in a building with predominantly hard reflective surfaces and reductions of up to 15dB(A) have been reported. The absorptive lining dissipates the airborne sound energy, principally as heat. Examples of good sound-absorbent materials are unbonded glass fibre, mineral wool and rock wool.

FIGURE 5.29: Acoustic screen and roof absorption

(HSE 1998)

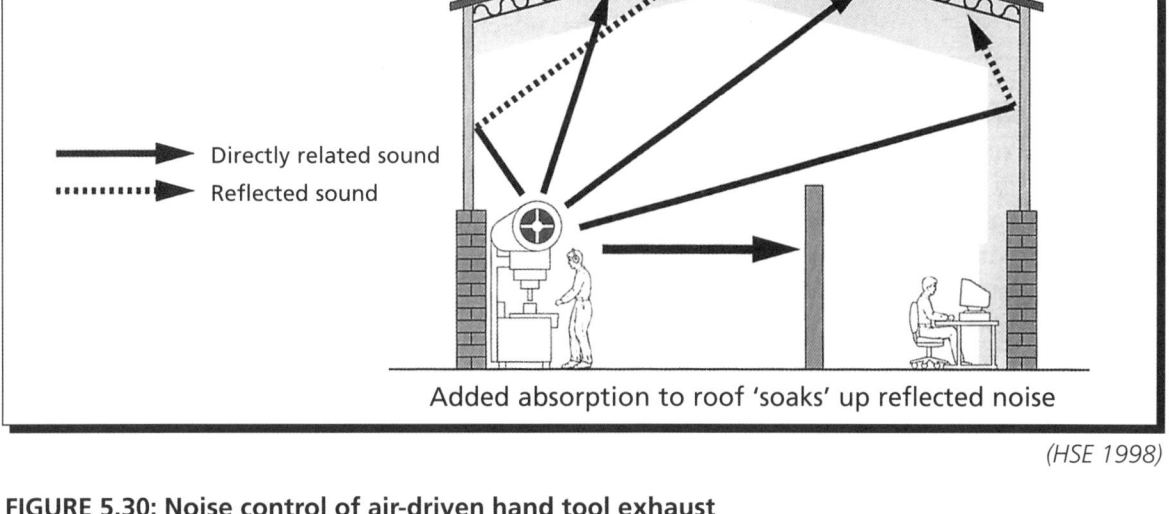

FIGURE 5.30: Noise control of air-driven hand tool exhaust

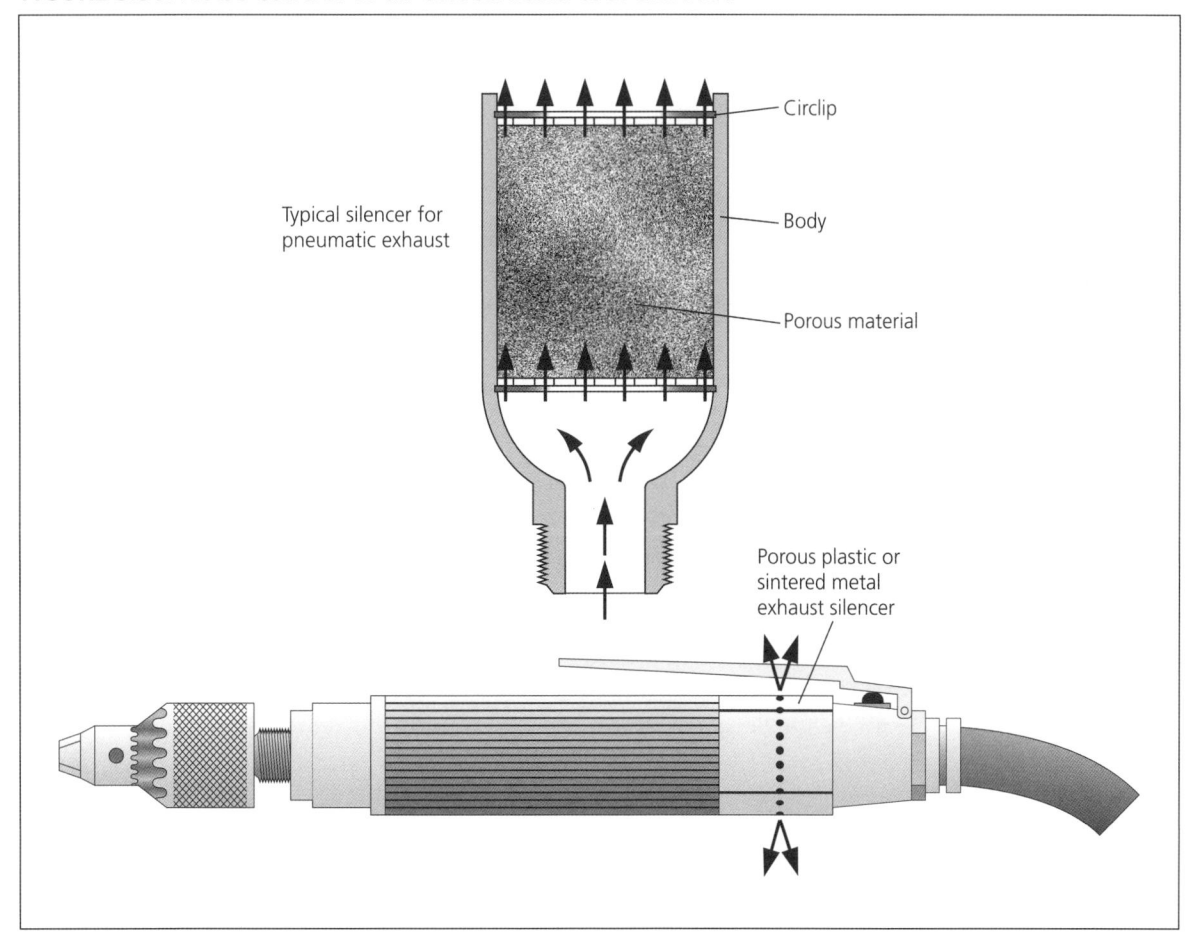

Silencers

The control of noise generated by air turbulence, for example, compressed air exhaust, relies on controlling the noise at source and preventing the transmission of noise through the air to the receiver. Methods of reducing compressed air turbulence at source can be considered such as reducing operating pressures and improving the aerodynamic design of equipment. Preventing the transmission of noise through the air to the receiver may be achieved by fitting a silencer.

Silencers can be used to suppress noise when air, gas and steam in pipes and ducts are vented to atmosphere. They can be divided into two basic types by their principle of operation, that is, absorptive and reactive:

1. **Absorptive** – These contain sound-absorbent material and are more effective for use with middle to high frequency noise. (An absorptive pneumatic exhaust silencer is shown in Figure 5.30.)
2. **Reactive** – These work on the principle of reflecting incident noise by their geometrical construction. They function best against lower frequency noise.

Silencers are available which combine both modes of operation.

Personal hearing protection

The different types of hearing protection and its selection and application is discussed in Chapter 13.

New machinery

Finally, it is important when embarking on a programme of controlling noise in the workplace to remember the noise output of newly-purchased machinery. There is little point in exercising a great deal of thought and time quietening existing noisy machinery and then going through the whole procedure again with new machinery.

To ensure that noise problems do not recur when new machines are installed, it is important to specify in the purchase contract the sound level of new machinery which is acceptable. When deciding what is an acceptable sound output rating, allowance should be made for where the machines are to be positioned, and how near to other machines they will be placed. Whatever the exact details, it is important that they are specified exactly in the contract and that the manufacturers understand that they will be held to the specification. Many progressive companies have incorporated noise checks into their buying policy and specify acceptable levels for the purchase of new machinery.

Associated control measures

Although the four principles of noise control have been presented as separate entities, the art, in fact, is selecting and using the correct blend of measures. Planning and execution of successful noise control requires training and skill and can be seen as part of a wider strategy including measures from the general hierarchy of control.

Information, instruction and training

The NAW Regulations require that adequate information, instruction and training is provided for employees. This includes the provision of information on risks to hearing and the basis for control measures. Employees should be informed on how to obtain and effectively use hearing protection equipment all the time they are at risk. They should also be informed as to their duties under the Regulations, that is, to wear hearing protection equipment when exposed above the Second Action Level, to use any other protective equipment and to report any defects in equipment.

Where noise levels are above the Second Action Level, the employer is required to mark ear protection zones.

Health surveillance and audiometry

Health surveillance is not specifically dealt with by the NAW Regulations. However, under the Management of Health and Safety at Work Regulations 1999 (MHSW) (regulation 6), employees exposed to certain types of risk, for example, high noise levels, should be provided with appropriate health surveillance. For people in noisy jobs, health surveillance usually means regular audiometric hearing tests, keeping records and receiving information about their test results. HSE (1995a) comments that it is good practice for employers to carry out regular hearing tests on workers exposed in excess of 90dB(A) $L_{EP,d}$, that is, in excess of the Second Action Level in the NAW Regulations.

REFERENCES

Beranek L L, 1956, Criteria for Office Quietening Based on Questionnaire Rating Status, *J Acoustical Soc Am*, **28**, 833.

British Occupational Hygiene Society, 1971, *Hygiene Standard for Wideband Noise*, Pergamon Press.

British Standards Institution, 1976, *Method of Test for Estimating the Risk of Hearing Handicap Due to Noise Exposure*, BS 5330: 1976, BSI, London.

British Standards Institution, 1993, *Sound Attenuation of Hearing Protectors – Methods of Measurement*, BS EN 24869-1, BSI, London.

British Standards Institution, 1994, *Specification for Sound-Level Meters*, BS EN 60651: 1994, BSI, London.

British Standards Institution, 1994a, *Hearing Protectors: Recommendations for the Selection, Use, Care and Maintenance*, BS EN 458: 1994, BSI, London.

British Standards Institution, 1997, *Specifications for Personal Sound Exposure Meters*, BS EN 61252: 1997, BSI, London.

British Standards Institution, 1998, *Sound Calibrators*, BS EN 60942: 1998, BSI, London.

British Standards Institution, 2000, *Acoustics. Reference Zero for the Calibration of Audiometric Equipment. Reference Equivalent Threshold Sound Pressure Levels for Pure Tones and Supra-Aural Earphones*, BS EN ISO 389-1: 2000, BSI, London.

British Standards Institution, 2001, *Integrating-Averaging Sound-Level Meters*, BS EN 60804: 2001, BSI, London.

Brüel & Kjaer, 1982, *Noise control: principles and practice*, Brüel & Kjaer, Naerum, Denmark.

Burns W, 1973, *Noise and Man*, Murray.

Department of Employment, 1972, *Code of Practice for Reducing the Exposure of Employed Persons to Noise*, HMSO, London.

European Community, 1980, *Framework Directive on the Harmonisation of Measures for the Protection of Workers with Respect to Chemical, Physical and Biological Agents at Work*, 80/1107/EEC, OJ L327/8.

European Community, 1986, *Directive on the Protection of Workers From the Risks Related to Exposure to Noise at Work*, 86/188, OJ L137/28.

European Community, 2003, *Directive on the Minimum Health and Safety Requirements Regarding the Exposure of Workers to the Risks Arising From Physical Agents (Noise)*, 2003/10/EC.

Hassall J R and Zaveri K, 1979, *Acoustic Noise Measurements* (4th edition), Brüel & Kjaer, Naerum, Denmark.

Health and Safety Commission, 1981, *Protection of Hearing at Work: Content of Proposed Regulations and Draft Approved Code of Practice and Guidance Note*, HMSO, London.

Health and Safety Executive, 1986, *101 Methods of Noise Control*, HMSO, London.

Health and Safety Executive, 1987, *Noise Exposure and Hearing – A New Look at the Experimental Data*, Robinson D W (Ed.), Contract Research Report 1, HSE Books, Sudbury.

Health and Safety Executive, 1990, *Noise at Work, Noise Assessment, Information and Control*, Noise Guides 3 to 8, HS(G)56, HSE Books, Sudbury.

Health and Safety Executive, 1995, *Sound Solutions*, HSG138, HSE Books, Sudbury.

Health and Safety Executive, 1995a, *Health Surveillance in Noisy Industries*, IND(G)193L, HSE Books, Sudbury.

Health and Safety Executive, 1996, *Noise at Work, Guidance on Regulations*, Noise Guides 1 and 2, L3, HSE Books, Sudbury.

Health and Safety Executive, 1998, *Reducing Noise at Work*, Guidance on the Noise at Work Regulations 1989, L108, HSE Books, Sudbury.

Hillage J, 1998, Noise at Work: The Effect of the Regulations on Employers (Institute of Employment Studies), *Occupational Health Review*, March 1998, IRS Publications.

Hinchcliffe R, 1959, The Threshold of Hearing as a Function of Age, *Acustica*, **9**, 303–308.

Hinchcliffe R, 1987, Sound, Infrasound and Ultrasound, Chapter 9 in *Hunter's Diseases of Occupations*, Raffle P A B, Lee W R, McCallum R I and Murray R I (Eds), Hodder and Stoughton, London.

Jones C M, 1997, Occupational Hearing Loss and Vibration-Induced Disorders, Chapter 2 in *ABC of Work-Related Disorders*, Snashall D (Ed.), BMJ Publishing Group, London.

Jones J R, Hodgson J T, Clegg T A and Elliot R C, 1998, *Self-Reported Work-Related Illness in 1995: Results from a Household Survey*, HSE Books, Sudbury.

Kjellberg A, 1997, Noise, Chapter 18 in *Occupational Health Practice* (4th edition), Waldron H A and Edling C (Eds), Butterworth-Heinemann, Oxford.

Kosten and van Os, 1982, Community Action Criteria for External Noises, in *Control of Noise* (conference proceedings), HMSO, London.

Malerbi B, 1989, Noise, Chapter 7 in *Occupational Health Practice* (3rd edition), Waldron H A (Ed.), Butterworths, London.

Robinson D W and Dadson R S, 1956, A Redetermination of the Equal Loudness Contours for Pure Tones, *British Journal of Applied Physics*, **7**, 166.

Rosen S and Plester D, 1962, Presbyacusis Study of a Relatively Noise-Free Population, *Annals of Otology, Rhinology and Laryngology*, September 1962.

Sharland I, 1989, *Practical Guide to Noise Control*, Woods, Colchester.

Snashall D, 1997, Occupational Hearing Loss and Vibration-Induced Disorders, Chapter 2 in *ABC of Work-Related Disorders*, Snashall D (Ed.), BMJ Publishing Group, London.

Taylor R, 1975, *Noise*, Penguin Books.

Union of Autoworkers, 1980, *Noise Control*, UAW, Detroit, MI, USA.

Webb J D, 1976, *Noise Control in Industry*, Sound Research Laboratories Ltd, Sudbury.

Wright F B, 1997, *Law of Health and Safety at Work*, Sweet and Maxwell, London.

LEGISLATION

Noise at Work Regulations 1989 (SI 1989/1790)

Provision and Use of Work Equipment Regulations 1998 (SI 1998/2306) (as amended by SI 1999/860 and SI 1999/2001)

Reporting of Injuries, Diseases and Dangerous Occurrences Regulations 1995 (SI 1995/3163)

Supply of Machinery (Safety) Regulations 1992 (SI 1992/3073) (as amended by the Supply of Machinery (Safety) Regulations 1994 (SI 1994/2063))

6: Vibration

(HSE 1996)

INTRODUCTION

Vibration is an oscillating motion of a particle or solid surface about a central point. Physical contact with a source of vibration can cause damage and vibration hazards occur in many occupations. High exposure to vibration has adverse effects on the hands and arms and it can cause harmful whole-body effects. Health effects include impaired blood circulation and damage to nerves and muscles; in the hands, this may result in tingling and numbness, finger blanching and the inability to grip properly. It is convenient to divide vibration risks into two categories:

1. Hand-transmitted vibration.
2. Whole-body vibration.

Hand-transmitted vibration exposure occurs where vibration is transmitted to the body through the hands when a vibrating tool or workpiece is grasped or pushed by the hands or fingers. Several ill health disorders occur as a result of exposure to hand-transmitted vibration, associated either with the use of hand-held power tools, for example, road-breakers, chain saws and lawn mowers, or when holding materials being processed by machinery, as in grinding operations. Whole-body vibration exposure occurs where the body is supported on a surface which is vibrating, for example, when sitting on a seat which vibrates or standing on a vibrating floor. To an extent, such exposure occurs in most forms of transport, inside buildings and when working close to machinery.

In a review (HSE 1994), it was concluded that vibration exposure was currently one of the 10 most important risks to health at work. According to recent HSE-supported research, more than one million workers are exposed to potentially harmful levels of hand-arm vibration, with around 300,000 showing symptoms of vibration white finger (VWF) and 380,000 exposed over the proposed EU Action Level for whole-body vibration (HSE 1999, 1999a).

The Physical Agents (Vibration) Directive (EC 2002) aims to protect workers from health risks arising from exposure to mechanical vibration. This includes both hand–arm and whole-body vibration. To comply with this Directive, the UK, following consultation (HSC 2003, 2003a), has recently enacted the Control of Vibration at Work Regulations 2005 (CVAW) (SI 2005/1093). At present in the UK, the principal published guidance on vibration exposure relates to hand–arm vibration (HSE 1994), with relatively little on whole-body vibration. Authoritative HSE guidance to accompany the new Regulations is expected to be published around the time of their implementation in July 2005. There is a useful source of information on current developments in the regulation of vibration risks on the HSE's website at www.hse.gov.uk/vibration/index.htm.

Vibration characteristics

In order to characterise a vibration source, it is necessary to evaluate the magnitude, frequency, direction and duration of the vibration.

Vibration magnitude

A vibrating object is constantly accelerating, first in one direction, and then in the opposite direction, with a nominal point in between where the object is at rest. Three waveforms can be visualised: displacement, velocity and acceleration. Quantification of a vibration source may be by measurement of displacement, velocity or acceleration. Usually, it is acceleration that is measured using an accelerometer and this parameter is expressed in metres per second squared (ms^{-2}) units. A decibel scale is sometimes used for expressing vibration magnitude.

Vibration acceleration

The magnitude of vibration acceleration is taken as the average measure, that is, the root mean square (rms) value[27] of the acceleration of the motion. As with the quantification of noise levels, it is possible to express vibration acceleration in decibels using a reference value and a logarithmic scale:

$$\text{Vibration acceleration } L_a = 20\log_{10}(a/a_0) \text{ dB}$$

(Where: a is measured acceleration (ms^{-2}); and a_0 is reference vibration (10^{-6}ms^{-2}). With this reference value, an acceleration of 1ms^{-2} corresponds to 120dB and 10ms^{-2} corresponds to 140dB.)

Vibration frequency

Vibration frequency, which is expressed in cycles per second, that is, hertz (Hz), influences the extent to which vibration is transmitted to the surface of the body, transmitted through the body, and the body's response. Oscillations below 0.5Hz cause motion sickness. With whole-body vibration, the most significant frequencies are between 0.5Hz and 100Hz. For hand-transmitted vibration, levels between 2Hz and 1,500Hz may have a detrimental effect. According to the HSE (1994), low frequency vibrating motions from 5Hz to 20Hz are more damaging than higher frequencies. To take account of this frequency effect, a frequency weighting is applied to measurements of vibration magnitude (see Figure 6.6).

Vibration direction

The response of the body depends on the direction of the motion. Vibration is usually measured at the point of contact of the body and the vibrating source in each of three orthogonal (right-angular) directions: front to back, side to side, and up and down. Figure 6.1 illustrates the axes of vibration used to measure hand-transmitted vibration.

The measurement devices (accelerometers) are sensitive to acceleration along a single axis. To assess total vibration entering the hand, measurements are taken along each of the three axes (x, y and z) and the results are combined to give the overall level of acceleration. A diagram is often necessary to define the axes of measurement for different vibration sources.

For whole-body vibration, principal measurement axes for seated and standing persons are fore and aft (x-axis), lateral (y-axis) and vertical (z-axis). These are shown in Figure 6.2. Again, vibration is measured at the point where the body is in contact with the vibrating source, in this case, on the seat or at the usual standing point.

---

[27] The rms is the square root of the mean value of the squares of the instantaneous values of a periodic quantity, in this case vibration acceleration. The rms value of a sine wave is the peak value divided by √2.

VIBRATION

FIGURE 6.1: Co-ordinate system for hand-transmitted vibration

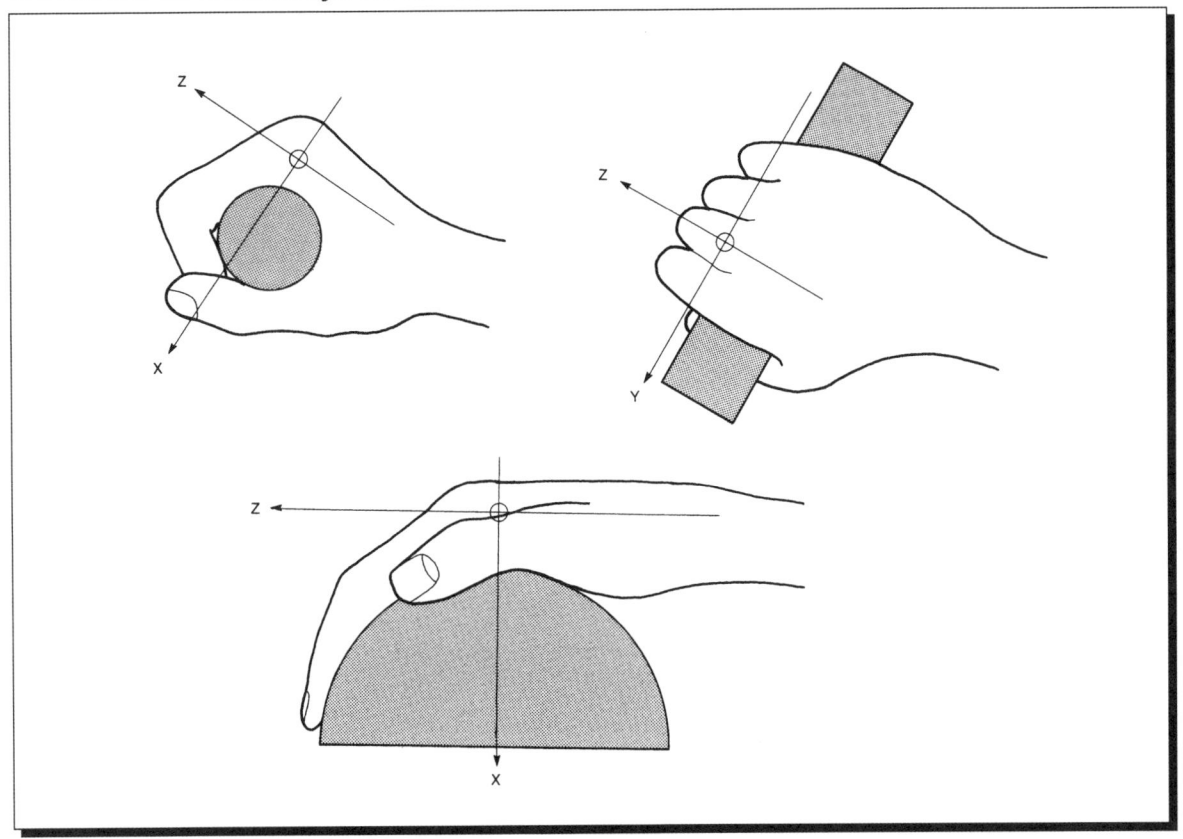

(HSE 1994 – rev. 2001)

FIGURE 6.2: Whole-body vibration – Measurement axes

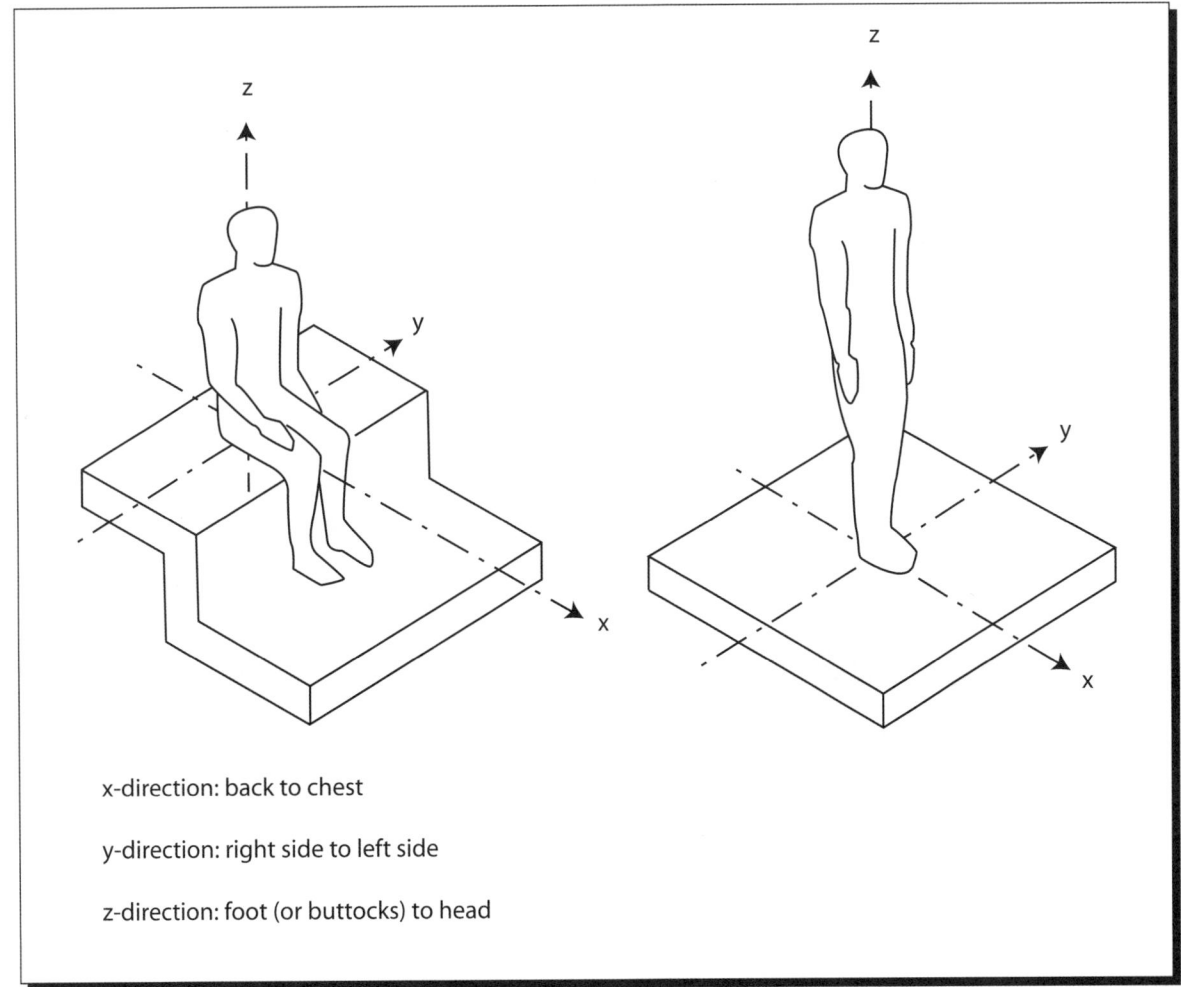

x-direction: back to chest

y-direction: right side to left side

z-direction: foot (or buttocks) to head

(BSI 2003)

Vibration duration

The total duration of vibration exposure is important. Also, the duration of measurements may affect the measured magnitude of the vibration – the rms (acceleration) may not provide a good indication of severity if the vibration is intermittent, contains shocks or varies in magnitude at different times.

Hand-transmitted vibration

There is a duty under the Control of Vibration at Work Regulations 2005 (regulation 5) to carry out a 'suitable and sufficient' assessment of risk from exposure to vibration and to identify required preventive/control measures with respect to vibration hazards.

Hazard identification

Tools and processes associated with hand-arm vibration

A large number of people in many industries are at risk of ill health resulting from exposure to hand-arm vibration. A selection of tools and processes associated with hand-arm vibration hazards are given in Table 6.1. With individual tools or processes, the important factors are the design of the tool, together with its method and frequency of use. Any tool which causes tingling or numbness after five to 10 minutes of continuous use is suspect.

TABLE 6.1: Tools and processes associated with hand-arm vibration hazards

Type of tool	Examples
Percussive metalworking tools	Riveting tools, chipping tools, fettling tools, swaging, jigsaws
Grinders and other rotary tools	Pedestal grinders, hand-held portable grinders
Percussive hammers and drills	Hammers, road drills
Forest and garden machinery	Chain saws, mowers
Other processes	Concrete saws, motorcycle handlebars, floor polishers

(Adapted from Griffin 1995)

FIGURE 6.3: Hand-transmitted vibration with power tools

(HSE 1996)

Exposure and health effects

Prolonged exposure to hand-transmitted vibration results in various signs and symptoms of hand-arm vibration syndrome (HAVS), an umbrella term for a group of clinical disorders. HAVS is widespread and it is believed to affect many thousands of workers. Jones *et al.* (1998) estimated that 36,000 people have an advanced stage of vibration white finger (VWF), which is the most well-known form of hand-arm vibration syndrome. Furthermore, Griffin (1990) estimated that up to 50 per cent of all foundry workers exposed to hand-arm vibration show symptoms of VWF.

Various factors are linked to HAVS including the characteristics of the vibration, the dynamic response of the fingers, the person's individual susceptibility to damage and other aspects of the environment, for example, ambient temperature. Griffin (1990) groups disorders associated with hand-transmitted vibration exposure as follows:

1. Circulatory (Type A).
2. Neurological (Type B).
3. Muscular (Type C).
4. Bones and joints (Type D).
5. Other general disorders (eg central nervous system) (Type E).

HAVS normally involves a combination of these disorders.

Circulatory disorders – Vibration white finger (VWF)

Vibration white finger (VWF) results in painful attacks and a loss of ability to grip. The person initially notices tingling or 'pins and needles' towards the end of the day, sometimes with numbness. With continued exposure, there is a loss of dexterity in the affected fingertips, clumsiness and a reduced ability to grip in the cold. 'Blanching', a white discolouration of the fingers, which starts at the tip but may extend to all of one or more digits with continued exposure, is precipitated by cold conditions or handling a cold object. It will last until the return of warmer temperatures when the blood vessels vasodilate, which allows more blood flow to tissues near the skin surface. There may have been years of exposure before blanching is noticed. It is associated with numbness, tingling, cyanosis (blueness) and, very rarely, gangrene. The severity of the effect of VWF may be assessed by the stage of the disorder. Several classification systems have been developed and Table 6.2 illustrates the Stockholm Workshop scale (Gemne *et al.* 1987).

TABLE 6.2: Stockholm Workshop System

Stage	Grade	Description of condition
0		No attacks
1	Mild	Occasional attacks affecting only the tips of one or more fingers
2	Moderate	Occasional attacks affecting distal and middle (rarely proximal) phalanges of one or more fingers
3	Severe	Frequent attacks affecting all phalanges of most fingers
4	Very severe	As 3, with trophic skin changes in finger tips

(Gemne et al. 1987)

Griffin (1990) proposes a 'simple scoring system', which is illustrated in Figure 6.4. The magnitude of blanching for a digit is given and a total score for each hand can be computed.

VWF is a 'reportable' disease under the Reporting of Injuries, Diseases and Dangerous Occurrences Regulations 1995 (RIDDOR). This condition is also a 'prescribed' disease for compensation purposes under the Industrial Injuries Disablement Benefit scheme and thousands of cases are assessed each year by the Department for Work and Pensions. (Although, as discussed in Chapter 1, very few of these 'assessed' cases are successful in actually obtaining disablement benefit.)

FIGURE 6.4: Numerical scoring of vascular symptoms (blanching) in VWF

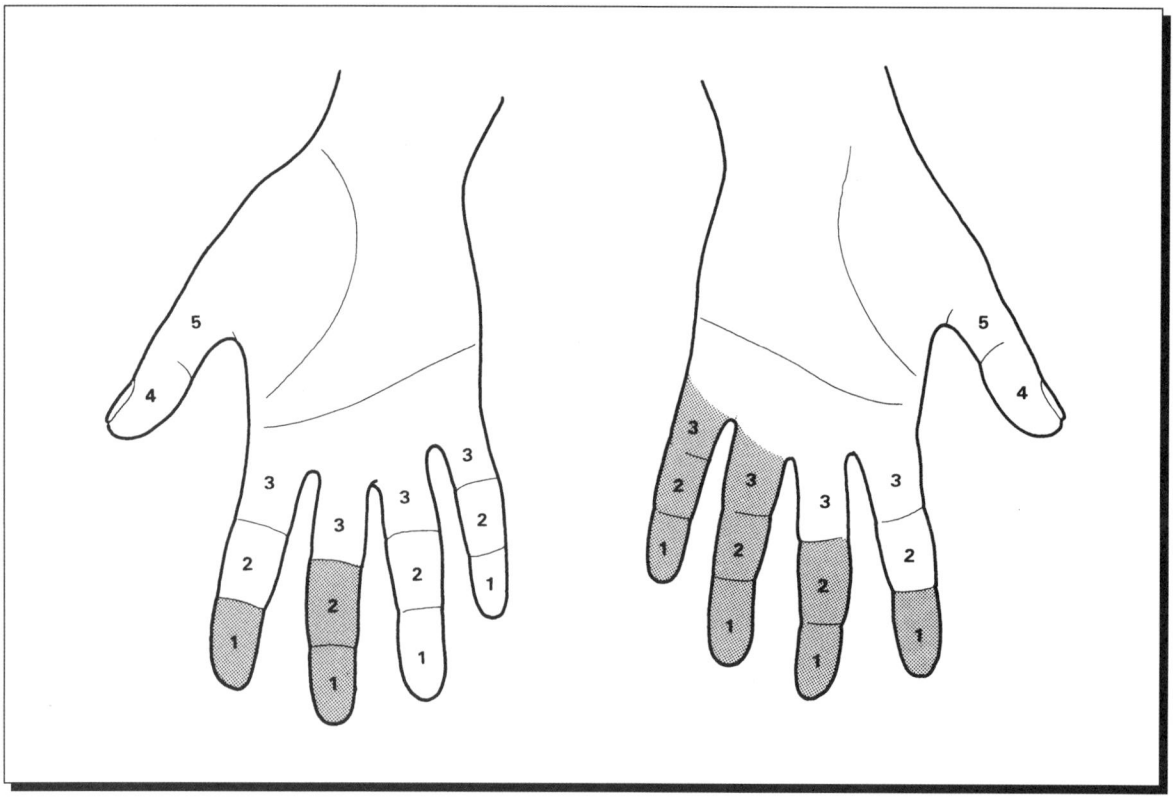

(HSE 1994 – rev. 2001)

Neurological disorders

According to Griffin (1990), neurological disorders are a separate effect of vibration exposure and not simply a symptom of VWF. Numbness, tingling and a heightened sensation for touch, vibration, temperature and pain, in the fingers and hands, are the prevalent symptoms. With these disorders, as well as heightened sensation, there is a reduction in grip strength and dexterity. Table 6.3 illustrates a subjective scale (from Brammer *et al.* 1987) which may be used to assess the 'stage' of neurological disorders.

TABLE 6.3: Subjective evaluation sensorineural disorder

Stage	Symptoms
0_{SN}	Exposed to vibration but no symptoms
1_{SN}	Intermittent numbness with or without tingling
2_{SN}	Intermittent or persistent numbness – reduced sensory perception
3_{SN}	Intermittent or persistent numbness, reduced tactile discrimination and/or manipulative dexterity

(Brammer et al. 1987)

Muscular effects

Muscular degeneration and problems with grip are associated with exposure to hand-transmitted vibration. The latter may be a protective effect resulting in the transmission of less vibration, but it can also interfere with work and leisure activity.

Bone and joint effects

There is some evidence of bone and joint problems in people using percussive tools, that is, damage leading to pain and stiffness in the hands and joints of the wrists, elbows and shoulders.

Other effects

A high incidence of headaches and sleeplessness has been reported for people exposed to hand-transmitted vibration. However, according to Griffin (1995), there is currently no universal agreement on this.

Measurement of vibration exposure and analysis

Where there is a suspected hazard, there is a need to evaluate exposure and this may involve the direct measurement of vibration at the hand-tool interface. Normally, the acceleration of the surface in contact with the hand is measured. The duration and pattern of exposure of the individual should also be quantified to obtain representative measurements with typical operating conditions.

If machine manufacturers can provide sufficient data on vibration levels under standard conditions, then it is often possible to estimate vibration exposure from this information and how long workers are likely to use particular tools. This avoids the practical difficulties of measuring vibration, but it needs to be ensured that representative data is collected. A vibration monitoring device for hand-transmitted vibration is shown in Figure 6.5 and a schematic diagram is shown in Figure 6.7.

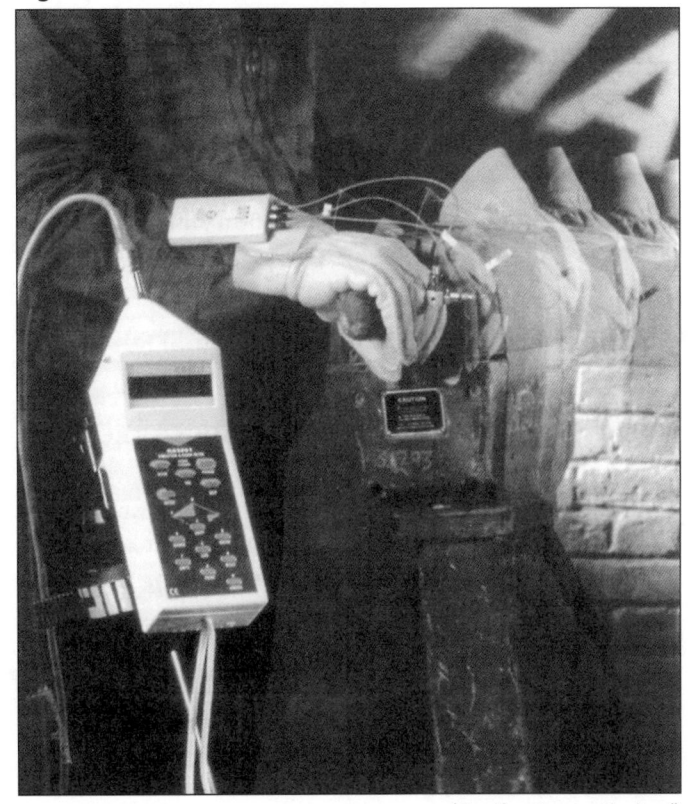

FIGURE 6.5: Monitoring hand-transmitted vibration

(Castle Group Limited)

The extent of damage caused to the hand and arm depends on the frequency of the energy being transmitted from the vibrating surface; 5–20Hz is thought to be more damaging than higher frequencies; below 2Hz and above 1,500Hz are not thought to cause damage (HSE 1994). A frequency-weighting is used during vibration measurement to account for this variation and this is shown in Figure 6.6. (This is analogous to the use of A-weighted decibels in the measurement of noise.)

The average acceleration level (rms) is measured, along each orthogonal axis, with a frequency-weighted accelerometer. Measurements from each axis – the x axis $(a_{x,h,w})$[28], the y axis $(a_{y,h,w})$ and the z axis $(a_{z,h,w})$ – are combined to give an overall frequency-weighted acceleration $(a_{h,v})$ in ms^{-2} as shown below:

$$a_{h,v} = \sqrt{(a^2_{x,h,w} + a^2_{y,h,w} + a^2_{z,h,w})}$$

This three-axis value (a_{hv}) is referred to as the 'vibration total value' or 'vector sum'. This is used to calculate the worker's vibration exposure, as a time-weighted average or A(8) value, at the hand position with the highest vibration. Measurements should be representative of the average vibration of the equip-

---

[28]Subscript 'h' is to indicate hand-transmitted vibration and 'w' to show that this value is frequency-weighted; 'v' indicates the vector sum.

VIBRATION

FIGURE: 6.6: Frequency weighting of vibration measurements

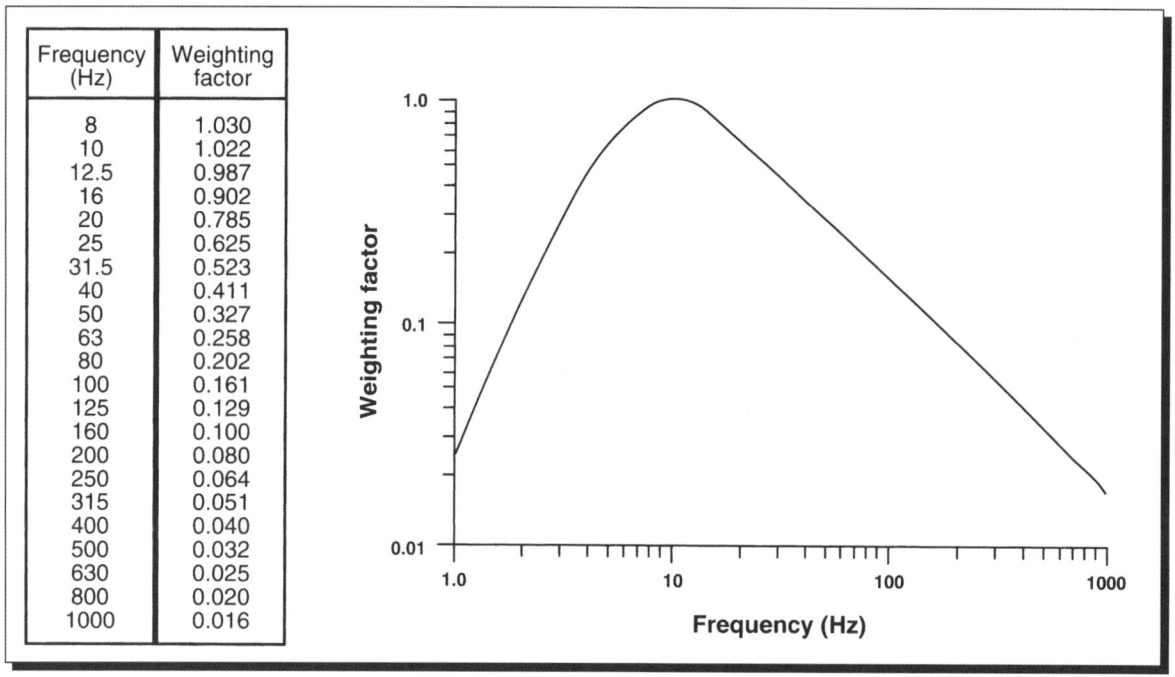

Frequency (Hz)	Weighting factor
8	1.030
10	1.022
12.5	0.987
16	0.902
20	0.785
25	0.625
31.5	0.523
40	0.411
50	0.327
63	0.258
80	0.202
100	0.161
125	0.129
160	0.100
200	0.080
250	0.064
315	0.051
400	0.040
500	0.032
630	0.025
800	0.020
1000	0.016

(HSE 1994 – rev. 2001)

FIGURE 6.7: Schematic diagram of vibration monitoring instrument

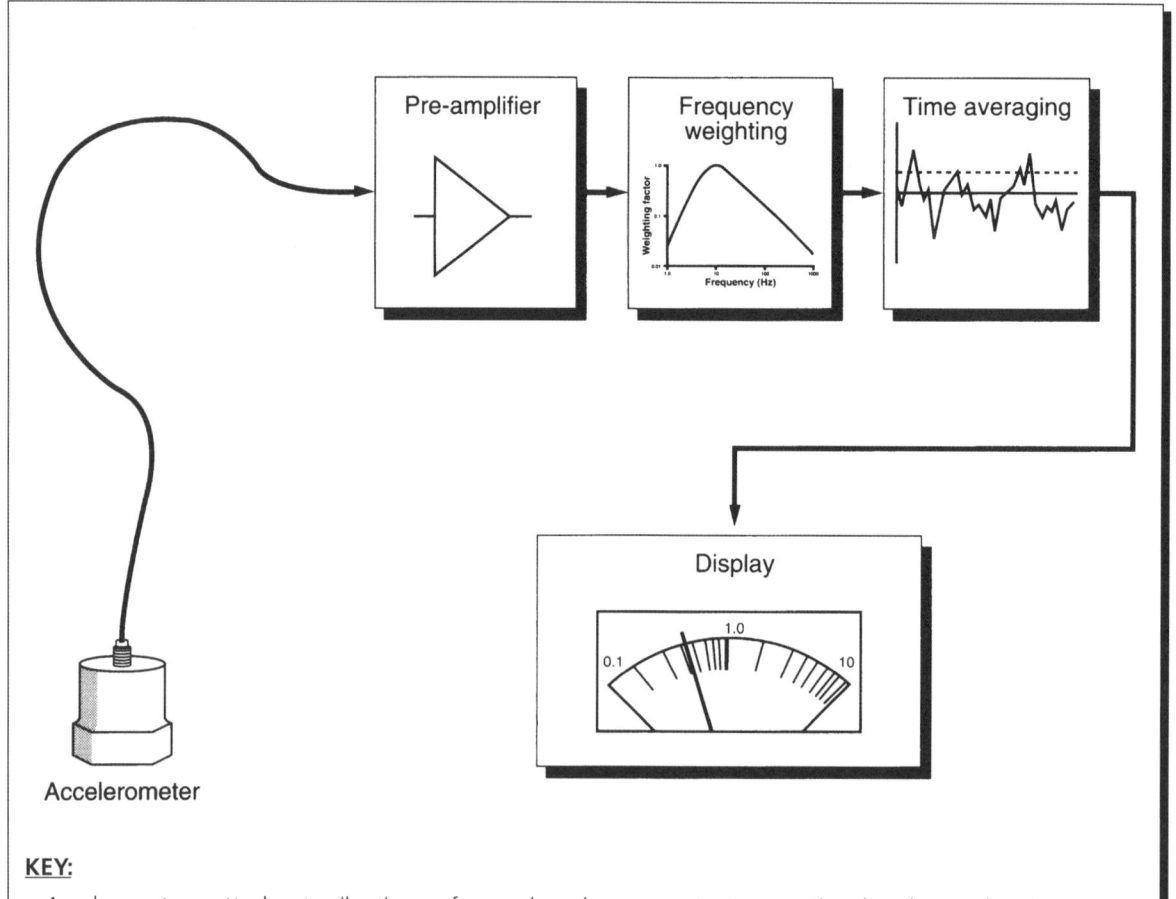

KEY:

- Accelerometer – attaches to vibrating surface and produces an output proportional to the acceleration
- Pre-amplifier – amplifies signal from accelerometer and converts this into a voltage proportional to acceleration
- Frequency-weighting (hand-transmitted vibration) – frequency-weighting of acceleration signal
- Time averaging – averages acceleration signals
- Display – shows measured vibration level in ms^{-2} or $L_{h,w}$ in decibels

(Specification for vibration measurement instrumentation given is BS 7482: 1991)

(HSE 1994 – rev. 2001)

ment used during the operator's work period. The Standard, BS EN ISO 5349 Part 1, defines the procedure for making these measurements (BSI 2001) and further detailed practical guidance on using the method is given in BS EN ISO 5349-2:2002 (BSI 2002). Vibration instrumentation should meet the appropriate specification for the measurement of hand–arm vibration, namely ISO 8041:2005 *Human response to vibration – measuring instrumentation* (expected to be incorporated as BS EN ISO 8041 later in 2005). An alternative to making technical measurements of vibration is to calculate levels (displacement, velocity or acceleration) using test data supplied by machine manufacturers.

Vibration exposure 'dose' depends on the duration of the exposure as well as the magnitude of the vibration source. Vibration levels are adjusted to a standard reference period of eight hours to give the 'A8' value, analogous to $L_{EP,d}$ and noise dose, and this allows different exposure patterns to be compared. Under the Control of Vibration at Work Regulations 2005 (regulation 4), the tolerability standards for frequency-weighted acceleration, adjusted to daily exposure, are an Exposure Action Value (EAV) of $2.5 ms^{-2}$ A(8) and an Exposure Limit Value (ELV) of $5 ms^{-2}$ A(8).

The measurement process can be divided into several stages:

1. identifying tasks which represent a vibration hazard
2. measuring the vibration for each task[29] identified (measured at the point of entry of vibration to the hand in each of the three axes)
3. estimating daily exposure time for each task
4. calculating partial vibration exposure for each task contributing to the 8-hour exposure
5. calculating daily 8-hour vibration exposure level (A(8)) for each operator, based on individual task profiles. This can be carried out using the nomogram in Figure 6.8.

Daily 8-hour vibration exposure levels are then interpreted in terms of health risk using the above EAV and ELV criteria for hand–arm vibration.

Vibration assessment survey

Any worker who uses a hand-held power tool as a major part of his/her job may be at risk of vibration injury to their hands or arms. People who spend long periods holding workpieces in contact with vibrating machinery are similarly at risk. These jobs are likely to cause noticeable symptoms such as tingling, numbness or finger blanching. The CVAW Regulations 2005 (regulation 5) require an assessment of health risks arising from hand–arm vibration exposure. Daily exposure should be assessed by:

1. observation of working practice;
2. reference to information supplied on probable magnitude of exposures; and
3. where necessary, measurement of the individual's exposure with technical equipment.

The assessment should be systematic and examine the work activity (tool and task), the operators and their practice, together with any current control measures that have been applied. Consideration should be given to the magnitude, pattern and duration of vibration exposure, including intermittent work and shocks. During the survey symptoms of hand-transmitted vibration in operators should be noted. The effects on employees whose health is at particular risk should also be considered, eg pregnant women, people with neck or back problems and young people, whose bones and muscles are not fully developed.

Vibration exposure may be evaluated indirectly using manufacturers' data sheets as indicated above, or measured directly using accelerometers. Sometimes technical measurement of vibration sources may be necessary, for example where exposure levels are thought to be high and the information supplied by a mnufacturer is not thought to represent the actual conditions of usage of the equipment. However, the HSE (2003) envisages that much of the work of assessment will be able to make use of supplied emission data. The assessment should also consider any impact of vibration on the workplace and work equip-

---

[29] It is difficult to obtain valid measurements with appropriate operating conditions, particularly where there are high shock levels. It is prudent to obtain acceleration data from tool manufacturers. The use of frequency-weighted acceleration allows the vibration of different tools to be compared. Where two tools expose the hand to vibration for the same period of time, then the one having the lowest frequency-weighted acceleration is less likely to result in injury and disease.

VIBRATION

FIGURE 6.8: Nomogram for calculating daily vibration exposure

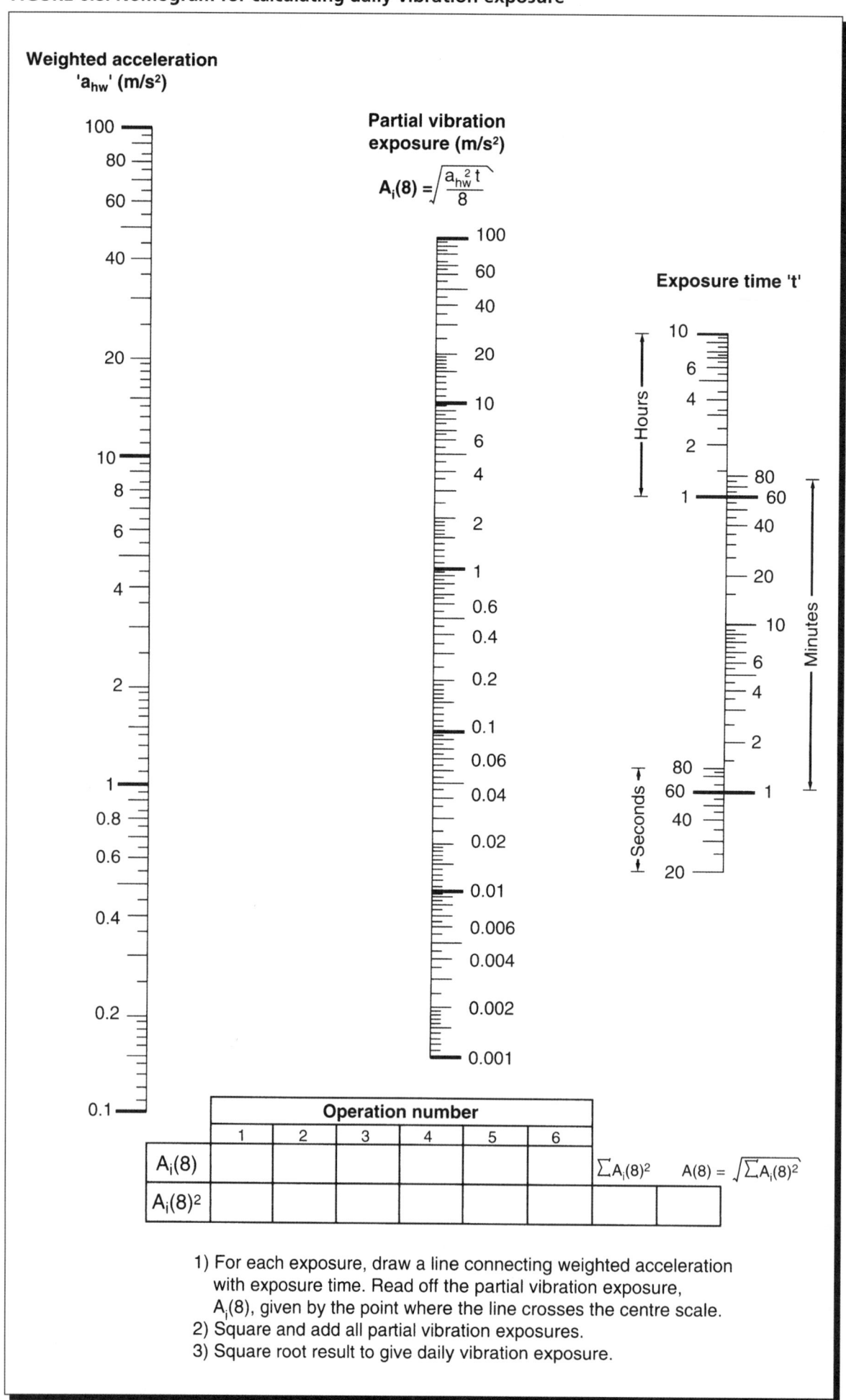

Weighted acceleration 'a_{hw}' (m/s²)

Partial vibration exposure (m/s²)

$$A_i(8) = \sqrt{\frac{a_{hw}^2 t}{8}}$$

Exposure time 't'

— Hours —
— Minutes —
— Seconds —

	Operation number							
	1	2	3	4	5	6	$\sum A_i(8)^2$	$A(8) = \sqrt{\sum A_i(8)^2}$
$A_i(8)$								
$A_i(8)^2$								

1) For each exposure, draw a line connecting weighted acceleration with exposure time. Read off the partial vibration exposure, $A_i(8)$, given by the point where the line crosses the centre scale.
2) Square and add all partial vibration exposures.
3) Square root result to give daily vibration exposure.

(HSE 1994 – rev. 2001)

ment. For example, is there any interference with the proper handling of controls and could vibration exposure cause damage to safety-critical equipment? The assessment should further consider the availability of low-vibration alternatives with regard to future machinery replacement. Following consideration of the risk factors, vibration exposure should be interpreted using the EAV and this should be recorded. Where exposure is thought to be above the EAV, possible control measures and an action plan need to be considered. The assessment should be recorded and regularly reviewed.

Determination of risk tolerability

In the workplace the use of vibrating tools varies widely from a few seconds in one case to a whole day in another, with many workers having intermittent exposures. Tolerability standards attempt to quantify the severity of hand-transmitted vibration over the frequency range 8Hz–1,000Hz. A common frequency weighting is applied to acceleration measurements in each of the three axes of vibration at the point of entry into the hand. Tolerability standards refer to 8-hour exposures.

The CVAW Regulations 2005 define the following compliance standards: an Exposure Action Value (EAV) of 2.5ms^{-2} A(8) and an Exposure Limit Value (ELV) of 5ms^{-2} A(8). Both of these limits are based on 'vibration total value', an averaged vibration magnitude obtained from measurements in all three orthogonal axes. This follows the method specified in the standard BS EN ISO 5349-1:2001 (BSI 2001). (The previous HSE A(8) action level of 2.8ms^{-2} (HSE 1994) referred to daily exposure obtained using the method of the (now withdrawn) British Standard BS 6842:1987. Under this Standard, vibration was measured in three directions, but exposure was calculated from the magnitude of vibration only in the dominant axis.) Figure 6.9 gives the vibration magnitudes and duration equivalents for the EAV of 2.5m^{s-2} A(8) and ELV of 5ms^{-2} A(8).

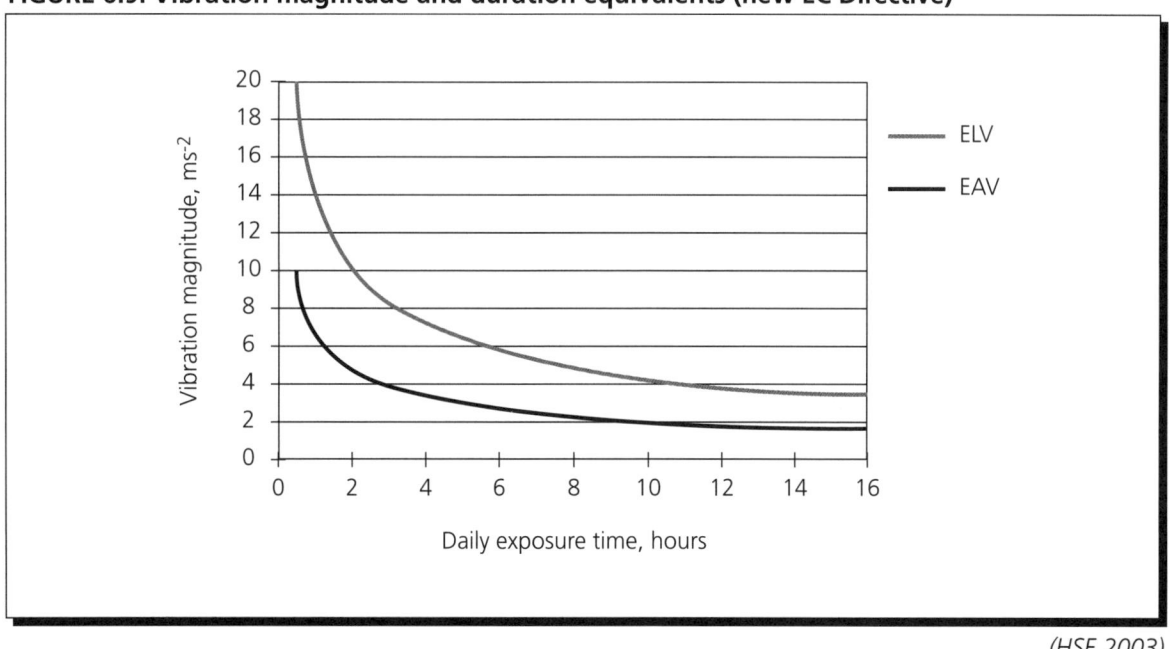

FIGURE 6.9: Vibration magnitude and duration equivalents (new EC Directive)

(HSE 2003)

Application of vibration standards

The risk from vibration exposure should be eliminated at source, but if this is not reasonably practicable, then reduction to a level as low as is reasonably practicable is required (regulation 6). If the EAV is reached or exceeded then the employer must reduce exposure as low as reasonably practicable by organisational and technical measures. The ELV should not be exceeded and if this occurs, immediate reduction below the limit is required, with identification of the cause and appropriate measures being taken. Where there is intermittent high exposure, under specified circumstances exposure may be averaged over one week. Compliance measures must be adapted for those particularly susceptible to risk. Health surveillance (regulation 7) and information, instruction and training (regulation 8) are required where the risk assessment indicates a health risk or the exposure is likely to be in excess of the EAV.

Control and preventive measures for hand-transmitted vibration

In controlling hand–arm vibration risks, effective measures need to be implemented and these are summarised in Table 6.6.

TABLE 6.6: Summary of hand-transmitted vibration control measures

Control measure	Comment
Management	Implement a vibration risk management strategy; reduce vibration exposure times; formulate machinery purchase policy with selection criteria[30]; ask for vibration data before purchase
Elimination	Process change to eliminate vibrating equipment; automation and robots
Substitution	Replace tools and equipment with alternatives which create less vibration
Tool manufacture and design	Measure tool vibration; design tools to minimise vibration and its transmission; reduce grip, push and other forces the worker must apply; design to keep hands warm; provide guidance on tool maintenance; provide warning of dangerous vibration
Engineering control	Remote handling and isolation; planned maintenance procedures; process automation; effective tool design
Health surveillance	Pre-employment screening; regular medical monitoring; recommended if people regularly exceed the EAV of $2.5 ms^{-2}$; identify workers with a predisposition for harm; policy on removal from work
Information, instruction and training	Required where the risk assessment indicates exposure in excess of EAV (regulation 8): Information on the nature of the hazard and the consequences of exposure; precautions to be taken and their basis, ie minimise grip and push forces; check condition of tools; keep hands warm and wear gloves (maintain good circulation in fingers); avoid pneumatic exhausts which discharge near the hands
Personal protective equipment	Wear gloves and warm clothing

(Adapted from Griffin 1995)

Whole-body vibration

Hazard identification

Whole-body vibration (WBV) is produced by various types of industrial machinery and different forms of transport. Several groups of workers are at risk from whole-body vibration hazards, particularly those involved in transport such as drivers of lorries, fork-lift trucks and off-road vehicles such as agricultural tractors and earthmovers. When vehicles are driven across rough terrain, often at speed, operators are exposed to significant seat-transmitted whole-body vibration. Similarly, exposure to WBV hazards occurs where a person is sitting or standing on a vibrating surface such as a machine or platform. Over 1.3 million workers are thought to be exposed in excess of the action level set in the CVAW Regulations 2005, with 20,000 male drivers exposed in excess of the ELV (HSE 2003a). Those principally exposed include

---

[30]The Machinery Safety Directive (89/392/EEC) states that the design and construction of machinery must ensure that vibration hazards are reduced as low as practicable taking into account technical progress and the availability of the means of reducing vibration. This directive has been implemented in the UK by the Supply of Machinery (Safety) Regulations 1992 (as amended by the Supply of Machinery (Safety) Regulations 1994). Transposed harmonised standards specify test conditions, for example, BS EN ISO 8662-4 applies to vibration testing of hand-held portable grinders. Furthermore, hand-held or guided machinery must display information on the vibration levels to which the hands and arms are subject and whether or not this exceeds some stated value (currently $2.5 ms^{-2}$ rms), as determined by the specified test method.

HGV, bus and other commercial drivers, together with fork-lift truck operators and off-road drivers (HSE 1999a).

Exposure and health effects

Exposure to whole-body vibration may affect the health, comfort and performance of workers. Subjective comments generally refer to the sensation caused by the vibration, rather than knowledge that it is causing harm.

Health effects

Disorders of the back – including back pain, displacement of intervertebral discs, degeneration of spinal vertebrae and osteoarthritis – can be associated with whole-body vibration exposure. Alternative explanations include heavy lifting tasks and poor sitting postures. In the above study (HSE 1999a), the association between lower back pain and sciatica with exposure to whole-body vibration was weaker than in previous work. Stronger associations were found between these conditions and manual handling lifting operations and work above shoulder height.

Other disorders associated with whole-body vibration exposure include abdominal pain, digestive tract disorders, urinary system dysfunction, prostatitis, haemorrhoids, balance and visual problems, headaches and sleeplessness.

TABLE 6.7: Vibration magnitude and its observed effect

WHOLE-BODY VIBRATION EXPOSURE (Frequency range 0–100Hz) (ms^{-2} rms)	OBSERVATION
0.01	Absolute threshold for perception of vibration
0.1	Easily noticeable level of vibration
1	Uncomfortable
10	Dangerous

Comfort

A doubling of vibration magnitude represents a doubling of subjective discomfort, which also depends on vibration frequency and direction. Vibration-induced discomfort increases with exposure time. With very low vibration magnitudes, it is possible to estimate the percentage of people able to feel vibrations and those who do not, while with higher magnitudes, estimates of discomfort can be assessed using a subjective scale (BSI 1992). Exposure limits applied to control vibration-induced discomfort vary between different environments, for example, those used for buildings and in a transport context.

Performance

Vibration interferes with visual perception, hand and/or foot movements, and complex cognitive processes such as learning, memory retention and decision-making. The major effects of whole-body vibration are on vision and continuous hand control.

Measurement of vibration exposure and analysis

The Standard ISO 2631 (ISO 1997) defines several different methods for evaluating whole-body vibration with respect to health effects and comfort requirements, amongst other things.[31] The Standard specifies methods for exposure assessment and gives guidelines on expected exposure effects. The assessment methods are applied to vibration transmitted to the whole body in standing, seated and recumbent positions (see Figure 6.2). It considers the acceleration, frequency, direction and duration of exposure together with the location and duration of measurements. Different frequency weightings are used for different axes of the body. This is to account for the differing sensitivity of the body to vibration transmitted via the different axes.

---

[31] According to Griffin (1998), ISO 2631 (1997) is complicated and 'difficult to summarise'. It is concerned with standardisation of the measurement, evaluation and assessment of whole-body vibration. It proposes 'Health Guidance Caution Zones' for use in interpreting whole-body vibration measurements.

VIBRATION

Several methods are described for measuring WBV including the rms or A(8) method and the vibration dose method which measures 'Vibration Dose Values' (VDVs). The Physical Agents (Vibration) Directive includes the option for member states to apply either approach, and the UK has opted for the A(8) rms method.

Vibration assessment survey

Any worker who drives a vehicle, particularly off-road and over rough terrain, as a major part of his/her work may be at risk of back injury resulting from exposure to whole-body vibration. This is especially the case where there is a significant shock or jolt component to the vibration exposure. The CVAW Regulations 2005 (regulation 5) require an assessment of risks to health arising from exposure to WBV.

Daily exposure should be assessed by similar principles as discussed for hand–arm vibration, ie by observing work practice, referring to manufacturers' vibration data and, where necessary, by actual measurement. With WBV particular attention should be paid to identifying shocks and jolts, as these are very important risk factors associated with vibration-induced back injury. The compliance limits in the CVAW Regulations 2005 are expressed in terms which require the A(8) method to be adopted for vibration exposure measurement. However, this is not the preferred method for measuring shocks and jolts, which are more important in the context of WBV. The shocks and jolts component of WBV exposure should be identified by carefully observing work under representative conditions and interviewing workers. Where there are particularly high levels of shocks and jolts, WBV could be measured using the VDV method (ISO 1997) and results interpreted using the VDV compliance rules (discussed below) in the Physical Agents (Vibration) Directive (EC 2002), but this would not be required for compliance with the CVAW Regulations 2005. The HSE has recommended that manufacturers and designers should measure vibration using both VDV and A(8) approaches to provide useful data to identify the risks from shocks and jolts. Where exposure is likely to be above the EAV, possible control measures and an action plan should be considered. The assessment must be recorded and reviewed at regular intervals.

Determination of risk tolerability

The Vibration Directive (EC 2002) has compliance standards for exposure to whole-body vibration which are expressed in terms of an A(8) rms value and as a VDV:

- **Exposure Action Value** – daily exposure action value, standardised to an 8-hour reference period, expressed as an A(8) rms value of $0.5 ms^{-2}$ or a VDV of $9.1 ms^{-1.75}$
- **Exposure Limit Value** – daily exposure limit standardised to an 8-hour reference period, expressed as an A(8) rms value of $1.15 ms^{-2}$ or a VDV of $21 ms^{-1.75}$.

There has been consultation as to how this choice of compliance limits should be incorporated into UK legislation, given that this will determine the required measurement approach in each case. The two approaches are:

- **A(8) rms method** – produces a cumulative exposure using an average acceleration adjusted to represent the 8-hour working day; results are expressed as ms^{-2};
- **VDV method** – measures 'total' exposure rather than 'average' exposure; results are expressed as $ms^{-1.75}$. VDV is defined as 'the magnitude of a one-second duration of vibration, which will be equally severe as the measured vibration' (BSI 1987).

The two methods are described in detail in ISO 2631-1 (ISO 1997) and the key features are compared in Table 6.8 opposite.

In the past, the HSE has commented that the VDV could be used for the EAV, in order to identify risks from shocks and jolts and to focus on their control, while on the other hand the ELV could be set using the A(8) rms method, which would be less restrictive in daily vehicle usage terms. Nevertheless, the balance of opinion on consultation supported both limits being set as A(8) rms values and this is what has been incorporated into the CVAW Regulations 2005 (regulation 4).

TABLE 6.8: Comparison of VDV and A(8) rms methods

VDV	A(8) rms
VDV is sensitive to individual high acceleration events and produces a cumulative dose over a working day	A(8) rms gives an average level of vibration over the working day
VDV gives a good representation of shocks and steady state levels; health risk – shocks and jolts transmitted to the vehicle operator are believed to pose a greater risk to health than lower magnitude steady state vibration; VDV is probably a better indicator of risk than A(8)	A(8) rms produces reasonable steady state information but poor representation of shocks and jolts
Correlates well with subjective comfort	A(8) rms can provide a guide to subjective comfort
VDV is an unfamiliar method	A(8) rms is a familiar approach from use in hand-arm vibration
Using VDV for EAV would be less restrictive on low vibration vehicles, eg lorries may not exceed EAV even when driven for 13 to 14 hours in a 24-hour period	Using A(8) for EAV would probably be less restrictive for older vehicles without suspended cabs or unloaded lighter trucks with higher vibration levels
Off-road vehicles have higher vibration levels and they are likely to exceed the EAV using the VDV method	Off-road vehicles are likely to exceed the EAV with A(8) rms method
Small choice of measurement instrumentation	Some choice of measurement instrumentation

(Adapted from HSE 2003)

Prevention and control of whole-body vibration

The CVAW Regulations 2005 require elimination of vibration hazards where this is reasonably practicable. Where this is not possible, then exposures should be reduced as low as is reasonably practicable and below the ELV (regulation 6). Furthermore, where exposure is in excess of the EAV, health surveillance (regulation 7) and information, instruction and training (regulation 8) are required. There are many appropriate measures which can be adapted from those listed above in Table 6.6 relating to the control of hand-transmitted vibration. Reducing whole-body vibration exposure requires analysis of the environment and identification of sources and routes for transmission to the body.

First, consideration should be given to eliminating or reducing vibration at source. With transport applications, it may be possible to level a road or track and/or reduce the speed of vehicles. Using additional mass to change the vibration emission characteristics of machinery may also be possible. The next step is to consider methods of reducing the transmission of vibration, for example by improving vehicle suspension, by isolating the driver's cab from the vehicle's chassis, or by designing the seat to attenuate vibration. It is important that vehicle, machinery and seating manufacturers should seek to minimise whole-body vibration in their products at the design stage and give clear instructions on maintenance. Ergonomic designs should be employed, taking into account the need for good posture while sitting. Procedures for purchasing new machinery and seating should employ appropriate selection criteria to minimise whole-body vibration hazards.

REFERENCES

Brammer A J, Taylor W and Lundborg G, 1987, Sensorineural Stages of the Hand-Arm Vibration Syndrome, *Scand J Wk Env Hlth*, **13**, 279–283.

British Standards Institution, 1987, *Guide to the Measurement and Evaluation of Human Exposure to Whole-Body Mechanical Vibration and Repeated Shock*, BS 6841, BSI, London.

(References continued on p. 229)

TABLE 6.9: Control of Vibration at Work Regulations 2005

Regulation	Requirement
1. Citation and commencement	Control of Vibration at Work Regulations 2005; in force from 06 July 2005
2. Interpretation	Definition of terms used in the Regulations
3. Application and transitional provisions	Specifies lead-in times for particular work equipment. Employers' duties to employees apply to any other person, whether at work or not, except as to provision of health surveillance (reg. 7) or provision of information, instruction and training (reg. 8)
4. Exposure limit and action values	**Hand–arm vibration** • Daily Exposure Limit Value 5ms^{-2} A(8) • Daily Exposure Action Value 2.5ms^{-2} A(8) **Whole-body vibration** • Daily Exposure Limit Value 1.15ms^{-2} A(8) • Daily Exposure Action Value 0.5ms^{-2} A(8)
5. Assessment of risk to health created by vibration at the workplace	'Suitable and sufficient' assessment of risk and identify measures required by these Regulations **Assess daily exposure** • observation of working practice • reference to information on probable magnitude of exposure • if necessary, technical measurement Further risk assessment information specified; regular review and recording of findings
6. Elimination or control of exposure to vibration at the workplace	Elimination of vibration risk at source or where this is not reasonably practicable, reduction to as low a level as is reasonably practicable **EAV**: if this is reached or exceeded – must reduce exposure ALARP through organisational and technical measures **ELV**: exposure must not exceed this; if exceeded, immediate reduction of exposure to below the limit is required; identify reason and take appropriate measures **Intermittent high exposure**: under specified circumstances, exposure may be averaged over one week Compliance measures must be adapted for those particularly at risk
7. Health surveillance	Required where risk assessment indicates a risk to health or exposure is likely to be in excess of EAV To prevent or diagnose a health effect Where a health effect is found, employee must be informed of results; employer must take appropriate action
8. Information, instruction and training	Required where risk assessment identifies a risk to health or exposure is likely to be in excess of EAV Specifies the required measures
9–11. Exemption certificates	Emergency services; air transport; Ministry of Defence
12. Extension outside Great Britain	
13. Amendments	
Schedule 1	Daily and weekly exposure to hand–arm vibration
Schedule 2	Daily and weekly exposure to whole-body vibration

British Standards Institution, 1987a, *Guide to the Measurement and Evaluation of Human Exposure to Vibration Transmitted to the Hand*, BS 6842, BSI, London.

British Standards Institution, 1991, *Instrumentation for the Measurement of Vibration Exposure to Human Beings*, BS 7482, BSI, London.

British Standards Institution, 1992, *Evaluation of Human Exposure to Vibration in Buildings*, BS 6472, BSI, London.

British Standards Institution, 2001, *Mechanical Vibration: Measurement and Evaluation of Human Exposure to Hand-Transmitted Vibration – General Requirements*, BS EN ISO 5349-1, BSI, London.

British Standards Institution, 2003, *Mechanical Vibration: Testing of Mobile Machinery in order to Determine the Vibration Emission Value*, BS EN 1032, BSI, London.

European Community, 2002, *Directive on the Minimum Health and Safety Requirements Regarding the Exposure of Workers to the Risks Arising from Physical Agents (Vibration)*, 2002/44/EC.

Gemne G, Pyykko L, Taylor W and Pelmear P, 1987, The Stockholm Workshop Scale, *Scand J Wk Env Hlth*, **13**, 275–278.

Griffin M J, 1990, *Handbook of Human Vibration*, Academic Press, London.

Griffin M J, 1995, Vibration, Chapter 10 in *Occupational Hygiene* (2nd edition), Harrington J M and Gardiner K (Eds), Blackwell Science, Oxford.

Griffin M J, 1998, Predicting the Hazards of Whole-Body Vibration, *Industrial Health*, **36**, 83–91.

Health and Safety Commission, 2003, *Proposals for new Control of Vibration at Work Regulations implementing the Physical Agents (Vibration) Directive (2002/44/EC) Hand–arm vibration*, CD190, HSE Books, Sudbury.

Health and Safety Commission, 2003a, *Proposals for new Control of Vibration at Work Regulations implementing the Physical Agents (Vibration) Directive (2002/44/EC) Hand–arm vibration*, CD191, HSE Books, Sudbury.

Health and Safety Executive, 1994, *Hand-Arm Vibration*, HS(G)88, HSE Books, Sudbury.

Health and Safety Executive, 1996, *Hazards Associated with Foundry Processes: Hand-Arm Vibration – Symptoms and Solutions*, Foundries Sheet No 9, HSE Books, Sudbury.

Health and Safety Executive, 1997, *Vibration Solutions*, HSG170, HSE Books, Sudbury.

Health and Safety Executive, 1999, *Hand-Transmitted Vibration: Occupational Exposures and Their Health Effects in Great Britain*, Contract Research Report 232/1999, HSE Books, Sudbury.

Health and Safety Executive, 1999a, *Whole-Body Vibration: Occupational Exposures and Their Health Effects in Great Britain*, Contract Research Report 233/1999, HSE Books, Sudbury.

Health and Safety Executive, 2003, Vibration (webpages), www.hse.gov.uk/vibration/index.htm.

International Standards Organisation, 1989, *Evaluation of Human Exposure to Whole-Body Vibration*, Part 2, ISO 2631.

International Standards Organisation, 1989a, *Mechanical Vibration – Guidelines for the Measurement and Assessment of Human Exposure to Hand-Transmitted Vibration*, ISO 5349.

International Standards Organisation, 1997, *Mechanical Vibration and Shock – Evaluation of Human Exposure to Whole-Body Vibration*, Part 1 General Requirements, ISO 2631-1.

Jones J R, Hodgson J T, Clegg T A and Elliot R C, 1998, *Self-Reported Work-Related Illness in 1995: Results from a Household Survey*, HSE Books, Sudbury.

LEGISLATION

Control of Vibration at Work Regulations 2005 (SI 2005/1093)

Management of Health and Safety at Work Regulations 1999 (SI 1999/3242)

Provision and Use of Work Equipment Regulations 1998 (SI 1998/2306) (as amended by SI 1999/860 and SI 1999/2001)

Reporting of Injuries, Diseases and Dangerous Occurrences Regulations 1995 (SI 1995/3163)

Supply of Machinery (Safety) Regulations 1992 (SI 1992/3073) (as amended by the Supply of Machinery (Safety) Regulations 1994 (SI 1994/2063))

7: Thermal environment

(Hunter 1978. Reproduced by permission of Hodder Arnold.)

INTRODUCTION

Problems generated by the thermal environment are common in workplaces as diverse as foundries, steelworks, brick factories, hospital laundries, light industrial units, offices, cold stores and outdoor working areas. The photograph above illustrates the work of a stoker on an old coal-fired ship where thermal conditions commonly gave rise to a debilitating condition known as 'stoker's cramp'.

It is useful to distinguish between thermal environments at work which:

- cause extreme physiological strain and may lead to severe heat or cold stress illness;
- lead to feelings of mild to moderate discomfort;
- represent a 'comfort zone' where people generally express satisfaction or neutrality with respect to their thermal environment.

This is represented in the diagram below.

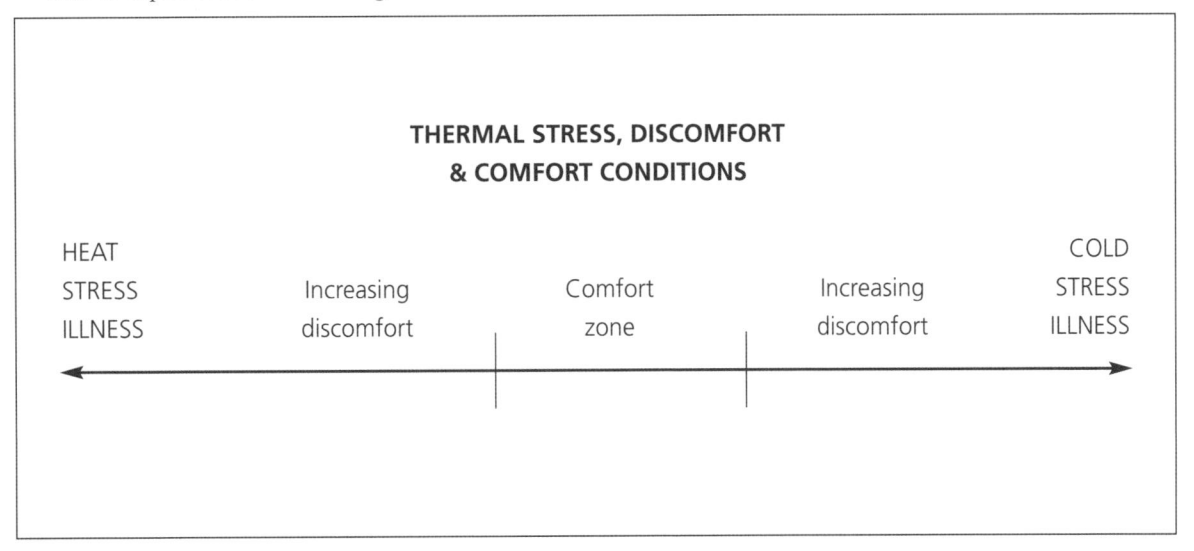

THERMAL STRESS, DISCOMFORT & COMFORT CONDITIONS

| HEAT STRESS ILLNESS | Increasing discomfort | Comfort zone | Increasing discomfort | COLD STRESS ILLNESS |

THERMAL ENVIRONMENT

Physiological thermal balance

Man is a homeothermal animal, that is, he maintains a near constant body temperature which is independent of the ambient environmental temperature. Core temperature is maintained by physiological control of body heat gain and loss. Humans are warm-blooded animals and core body temperature has to remain within a narrow range (37±0.5°C). This temperature represents optimum thermal conditions for human metabolic (biochemical) reactions.

The maximum permitted deviation from this temperature in fit people is ±2°C. A fall to a core temperature of 31°C leads to loss of consciousness and death of the person, while levels above 43°C lead to a total failure of the thermoregulatory mechanism. The body continuously generates heat by the conversion of food into usable energy and applying this to do work, that is, carry out normal activities.

There needs to be control of the balance between overall heat gain and heat loss, otherwise core temperature cannot be maintained within this narrow range. There are three major mechanisms by which the body maintains thermal balance:

1. The regulation of peripheral blood flow in the skin – vasoconstriction and vasodilation.
2. The production of sweat – this cools the surface of the skin by evaporation.
3. Involuntary skeletal muscle contraction (shivering).

Sources of heat gain and loss are summarised in Table 7.1.

Heat gain

The body generates heat by metabolism and there may be a heat gain from the ambient environment, by conduction, convection and radiation, where this is at a higher temperature than the body surface. There is also a small heat gain from hot food or liquid which is ingested. If the heat production is insufficient to maintain the body temperature, further metabolism is brought about by the involuntary contraction of the skeletal muscles.

Heat loss

Heat loss from the skin occurs by the processes of conduction, convection, radiation, and the evaporation of surface sweat. The rate of heat loss depends on the temperature difference between the skin and the environment. The skin temperature is lower than the core body temperature and it is regulated by the amount of warm (core) blood flow to the skin surface. With low blood flow (vasoconstriction), skin temperature is lowered and heat loss to the environment is minimised. With high blood flow (vasodilation), skin temperature is high and approaches the core temperature with heat loss maximised.

TABLE 7.1: Summary of source of body heat gain and heat loss

Heat gain	Heat loss
Body metabolic reactions	Production and evaporation of sweat from the skin surface
Heat gain from ambient environment by: conduction; convection; radiation	Heat loss to ambient environment by: conduction; convection; radiation
Ingestion of hot food or liquid	Exhalation of air
Involuntary skeletal muscle contraction (shivering)	Removal of waste products

Heat balance equation

The body's core temperature remains constant when there is an equilibrium between internal heat production and heat loss (mainly from the body's surfaces). Metabolism generates heat, some of which is lost to the environment in a controlled manner in order to maintain a stable core temperature. This allows humans to live in a range of temperature extremes. The heat balance equation below describes this relationship:

$$M = \pm K \pm C \pm R \pm S - E$$

(Where: M is the rate of metabolic heat production; K is conduction; C is convection; R is radiation; S is the rate of change in the store of body heat (= zero at thermal equilibrium); and E is evaporative heat loss from the skin and respiratory tract.)

Where there is a temperature difference between a body and the environment, heat transfer processes (ie conduction, convection, radiation and evaporation) try to reduce this difference. In the heat exchange relationship between the human body and the environment, the body normally shows a net heat loss.

Metabolic rate and heat production

Metabolic heat production is largely determined by muscle contraction during physical work but can be increased under cold conditions by shivering. The basal metabolic rate of the 'physically and mentally resting' body is 41Wm^{-2} for a young adult female and 45Wm^{-2} for a young adult male. For this purpose, the total surface area of the 'typical' body is estimated at 1.8m^2, which is known as the standard Du Bois area. Maximum values of 900Wm^{-2} for metabolic activity can be attained, but only for short periods; 400–500Wm^{-2} represents very heavy exercise which may be maintained for about an hour (BOHS 1996).

TABLE 7.2: Metabolic rates for different activities

Activity	Typical rate per person (W)	Rate per square metre of body surface area (Wm^{-2})
Resting	75	43
Light work	160	90
Heavy work	450	250
Running	1000	600
Very hard exercise (five to 10 minutes)	1600	900
Shivering	1000	600

(Adapted from Youle 1995)

Conduction

Conductive heat exchange occurs when there is physical contact between the skin, or clothing, and a surface in the environment. For example, heat is conducted from the hand when in contact with a cold surface, or from the body when sitting on a chair.

The rate of heat transfer depends on the temperature difference between the two surfaces in contact and the conductance of the contact area. Some materials such as metals are good heat conductors while others such as air are very poor. Clothing, because it contains a layer of trapped air, is a poor conductor of heat.

When considering conductance at the body surface, it is usually convenient to refer to insulation (I) as a measure of heat flow (expressed in m^2 °C W^{-1}).

There are three components of insulation for the human body surface:
1. The insulation of tissues affecting the flow of heat from the body core to the skin.
2. The insulation provided by the layer of air trapped by clothing.
3. The insulation value of the clothing material itself.

These are shown schematically in Figure 7.1.

THERMAL ENVIRONMENT

FIGURE 7.1: Insulation of the human body surface

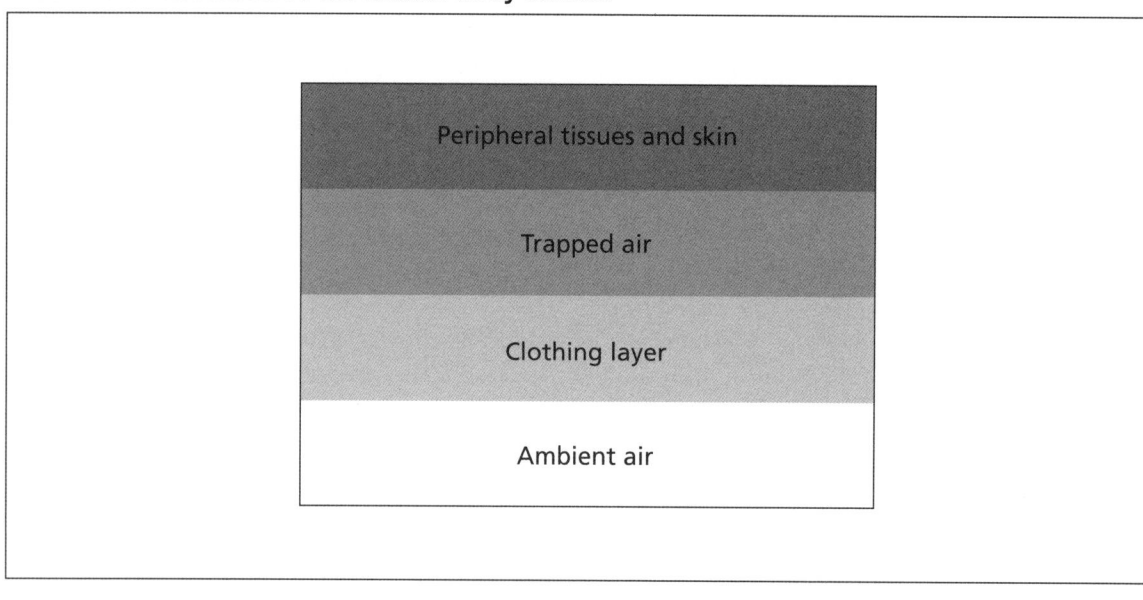

[Diagram showing horizontal layers from top to bottom: Peripheral tissues and skin; Trapped air; Clothing layer; Ambient air]

As concerns the conduction of heat at the body surface through clothing, it is more appropriate to refer to resistivity, which is expressed as resistance (or insulation) to heat flow across a given thickness of material. An arbitrary unit, the 'clo', is used to express the insulation value of clothing. One clo will provide insulation sufficient to allow a person to be comfortable when sitting in still air at a uniform temperature of 21°C. (One clo has an insulation value of $0.155 m^2$ °C W^{-1}.) This in effect means that heat will flow across the clothing (per square metre) at a rate of 0.155 joules/sec for each degree Celsius difference in temperature between the two sides.

TABLE 7.3: Clothing insulation values

Clothing ensemble	Clo
Naked	0
Light summer clothing	0.5
Indoor clothing	1
Heavy suit	1.5
Polar clothing	3–4

(Adapted from Youle 1995)

(In the peripheral region of the skin, full vasoconstriction will provide the equivalent of 0.6clo of insulation, while with vasodilation this will reduce to 0.15clo and, with heavy exercise, further still to 0.075clo.)

In most situations, the level of conductive heat exchange is reduced by personal discomfort, meaning that people will withdraw from contact. However, where there is immersion in cold water, heat losses can be severe because there is whole-body surface contact.

Convection

Convection occurs when there is heat transfer (either gain or loss) between a body and the surrounding liquid or gas. When there is heat transfer from a solid to cooler air, then the air warms up, its density decreases and it rises and is replaced by cooler air from below. In other words, convection heat transfer initiates an air circulation. Because convective heat transfer initiates an air flow over the cooling body, it follows that if this air flow (or more accurately, the relative air flow) is increased, then more cooling will take place. It is generally accepted that if the relative air speed is less than $0.1 ms^{-1}$, then natural or free ventilation is taking place. If the relative air speed is greater than this, then forced ventilation is taking place. The relative air speed over the arms or legs can be increased by walking or running faster.

Radiation

Thermal radiation (ie infrared radiation) refers to the transfer of heat energy in the infrared region – wavelength range from 10^{-6}m to 10^{-3}m of the electromagnetic spectrum (see Chapter 8). It differs crucially from conduction and convection in that no physical contact is required between the bodies concerned. In addition, radiant energy can be transmitted through a vacuum. The most well-known source of radiant energy is the sun. The amount of radiant energy emitted by a body is proportional to the fourth power of the absolute temperature of the body and a factor, its emissivity, which is a function of the surface characteristics of the emitting body. For practical purposes, emissivity is measured by reference to a black body, which is given a relative emissivity value of one. Dark, rough surfaces have emissivities approaching one and light-coloured, smooth surfaces have much lower values. As well as emitting thermal radiation, bodies also absorb thermal radiation. The amount absorbed by a body is proportional to the fourth power of the absolute temperature of the body and a factor, its absorptivity, which is a function of the surface characteristics of the body. Emissivity is numerically equal to the absorptivity of a body and again dark, rough surfaces have higher absorptivity than light-coloured, smooth surfaces.

Radiation exchange is particularly relevant when dealing with objects of high surface temperature, for example, red-hot molten steel. However, in many indoor environments, the surrounding surfaces are at a fairly uniform temperature and an emissivity factor is not normally used for determining wall temperature. Due to the way this is measured, wall temperature can more correctly be referred to as the Mean Radiant Temperature (MRT). MRT is the integrated temperature of uniform surrounding surfaces which will result in the same heat exchange by radiation from an object in the actual environment.

The relative heat loss by convection and that by radiation are directly related and radiative loss is normally twice convective loss.

Evaporation

The body loses heat by two processes known as insensible heat loss and sensible heat loss. Sensible heat loss is associated with temperature changes which are detectable by the senses, for example, heat loss by conduction, convection and radiation. Insensible heat loss is associated with cooling by the evaporation of water from the surface of the skin. At rest, in a comfortable ambient temperature, an individual loses moisture by the evaporation of water diffusing through the surface of the skin (cutaneous loss) and from the surfaces of the respiratory system (in exhaled breath). Total water loss is approximately $30gh^{-1}$. Water diffusion through the skin is equivalent to a heat loss of about $10Wm^{-2}$ (BOHS 1996).

When water evaporates from the surface of the skin, heat energy is absorbed from the body during the transition from liquid to the gaseous (vapour) state. This energy is called the latent heat of vaporisation; for water, this is 2,453kJkg (at 20ºC). Sweat is principally a weak solution of sodium chloride (approximately 3g per litre) generated by the sweat glands in the skin. A high sweat rate of one litre per hour will dissipate 680W of heat over the whole body. This corresponds to the metabolic rate for high work activity. In order to achieve maximal heat loss, the sweat needs to evaporate and not simply drip off the body's surface.

Sweat will only evaporate if there is a water vapour pressure gradient between the partial pressure of water vapour at the skin surface and the partial pressure of water vapour in the ambient air. The larger the gradient, the more efficiently sweat will evaporate from the skin. Air velocity also influences the rate of evaporation since this will determine the rate at which the skin boundary layer of air, which quickly saturates with water vapour and impedes further evaporation, is removed. Water vapour pressure is determined by the relative humidity of the air. This is the quantity of water vapour in air expressed as a percentage of what it would contain if the air were saturated at the same temperature.

The above discussion demonstrates that the environmental factors determining heat exchange between the body and the environment are air temperature, air speed, radiant temperature and water vapour pressure.

THERMAL ENVIRONMENT

Heat storage

The body has a definable capacity for storing heat since it can tolerate moderate deviations around normal body temperature (37°C). This has practical importance since it allows people to enter extreme environments for a short period of time, during which they are protected from the true thermal impact by this protective heat 'sink'.

Human heat balance

Under normal sedentary conditions approximating to a metabolic rate of 100 to 120W, the following contributions to heat exchange are typical: conduction (0 per cent); convection (25 per cent); radiation (45 per cent); and evaporation (30 per cent). With an increase in ambient temperature, radiation and convection decrease while there is an increase in evaporative heat loss. As ambient temperature rises, eventually heat loss by radiation and convection will reach zero and only evaporative heat loss will still occur.

Hot environments

Hazard identification

Whenever heat stress is imposed on the human body, there is a resulting physiological strain which results in reactions such as sweat production, increased heart rate, etc. The greater the heat stress load, the greater the heat strain, and in certain environments people may suffer severe heat stress illness or even death. To avoid heat stress illness, the 'heat balance' equation (see page 233) must balance. Thermal stress hazards may exist in many industries and occupations as illustrated in Table 7.4.

TABLE 7.4: Typical occupational examples of heat stress hazards

Heat stress	Radiant temp.	Air temp.	Wet bulb temp.	Air velocity	Metabolic rate	PPE
Glass-making	H	h	m	l	h	+
Handling molten metal	H	h	m	m	h	+
Welding, brazing	h	m	m	m	m	+
Boiler/furnace maintenance	h	h	m	l	h	+
Face-work – deep mines	m	h	m	l/m	h	+
Laundries	m	m	h	l	m	
Kitchens	h	h	h	l	m	
Firefighting	h	h	h	l/m	h	+
Asbestos removal	m	h	h	l	h	+
Outside hot work – agriculture, quarrying, fishing, oil rigs, construction	H	h	m	m	h	+

(H = very high; h = high; m = medium; l = low; + = situations where PPE may contribute significantly to heat strain)

(Adapted from Youle 1995)

Heat exposure and health effects

Heat stress disorders

These are summarised in Table 7.5.

TABLE 7.5: Heat disorders

Clinical name	Mechanism
Acute exposure to hot work Heat stroke Heat syncope Heat exhaustion Heat fatigue Prickly heat	Thermoregulatory failure Circulatory instability Salt and water imbalance Behavioural disorder Skin disorders and sweat gland injury
Chronic after-effects of acute heat illnesses Reduced heat tolerance	Associated with various symptoms linked to specific acute heat stress illnesses
Chronic exposure to hot work Thermal cataract Cardiovascular disorders Other disorders	Enhanced lenticular opacity caused by infrared radiation Myocardial damage Hypertension and digestive system problems

(Dukes-Dubos 1981)

Acute disorders

Heat stroke

Heat stroke is a rare but very serious heat disorder. Central nervous system (CNS) control of thermoregulation is overcome by excessive heat stress conditions. This may result in irreversible CNS damage and/or death. It is very important that signs and symptoms are recognised and the patient treated very rapidly. Symptoms such as collapse, delirium, convulsions and hallucinations may occur. External signs are hot, flushed and dry skin and a core temperature above 40.5°C. With convulsions and coma, core temperature may reach 45°C. The condition often leaves residual damage to the brain and kidney.

Heat stroke may occur with very hard physical work under very hot conditions when heat acclimatisation is lacking. When the heat source is the sun, this condition is normally referred to as sunstroke. Treatment requires a rapid reduction in core temperature with active cooling by immersion of the whole body in an ice water bath with active massage of the skin.

Heat syncope

This is caused by excessive strain on the circulatory system with symptoms such as pallor, sweaty skin, dizziness and headache. Heat stress conditions result in peripheral vasodilation and this may significantly reduce blood flow to the vital organs, which may lead to oxygen deficiency to which the brain and heart are particularly sensitive. This situation can be exacerbated by the demands of the muscles for oxygen during hard physical work. The affected individual should rest in the supine position (lying on their back with their face upwards) in a cool area but cooling should not be too rapid. The core temperature is usually normal in these cases.

Heat exhaustion

This is caused by a salt and water imbalance and there are two subtypes:
1. **Water depletion heat exhaustion** – Where water lost from the body is not replaced, the total content of body water will decrease reaching dangerous levels when fluid loss exceeds 10 per cent of total body weight. Moderate water loss (ie around five per cent of total body weight) is usually accompanied by a strong sensation of thirst, irritability, fatigue, and eventually exhaustion and clinical dehydration. This results in decreased heat tolerance with a raised heart rate and body temperature. The individual should rehydrate in a cooler area.
2. **Salt depletion heat exhaustion** – In this case, water is replaced but salt is not and this

results in typical symptoms of fatigue, giddiness, nausea and cramps. Cramps are caused by a salt and water imbalance which results in sharp pains in active muscles, particularly in the thighs and abdomen where there are high physical demands. The condition results from heavy sweating and the taking of unsalted fluids.

Non-acclimatised individuals usually lose high levels of salt in sweat and a high intake of salted fluids is required. These are preferable to salt tablets since these may induce nausea and vomiting, thereby exacerbating the negative salt balance. However, salt supplementation is usually unnecessary in acclimatised individuals (assuming a normal intake of around 10g per day).

Prickly heat

This condition results in a skin rash and prickly sensation during sweating. It is caused by prolonged heat exposure in high humidity conditions with continuous wetting of the skin or where sweat cannot evaporate freely. This results in the blocking of sweat gland ducts and, sometimes, the total cessation of sweating over some areas of skin.

Chronic health effects

Chronic heat illnesses have been subdivided into those which are the after-effects of acute heat stress illnesses and those which result from long-term exposure to work in hot conditions (Dukes-Dubos 1981).

Chronic after-effects of acute heat stress illnesses

These are the chronic after-effects of prickly heat, heat rash, heat exhaustion and heat stroke. It is well established that a person who has suffered an acute heat stress illness (except heat cramps) has a reduced heat tolerance for some time. After heat rash, this may be due to a reduced sweating capacity, although after heat stroke, this may be the consequences of irreversible cell damage in the brain, liver, kidney and other organs.

Chronic disorders and long-term exposure to hot work

Cataract
This is a degenerative disease of the lens of the eye which occurs in workers exposed to high radiant heat sources with significant infrared radiation, for example, glassblowers. Individuals should not look at high infrared sources and where this is unavoidable, then suitable eye protection is required.

Susceptibility to other diseases
Various studies have shown that groups of workers with long-term heat exposure have increased levels of cardiovascular disease when compared with other groups. Other reported chronic effects in 'hot' workers include hypertension and digestive system problems.

Decreased performance capacity
Research studies have shown that workers in hot environments tend to make more errors and generally work less efficiently. However, the relationship between human performance and exposure to heat is complex, involving (among other things) many psychological and physiological factors (BOHS 1996).

Thermal environment risk assessment

The Management of Health and Safety at Work Regulations 1999 (MHSW) (regulation 3) require a risk assessment of workplace hazards including those related to the thermal environment. The basic steps in the risk assessment and control process are represented below:
1. Collect information.
2. Define work process.

3. Identification of thermal environment hazards.
4. Analysis of risks and monitoring of environmental/personal parameters relating to the thermal environment. Interpretation of risks using thermal indices.
5. Review current practice and controls.
6. Draw intermediate conclusion about risk to health.
7. Apply prevention and control measures.
8. Review and audit.

Thermal environment survey – Measurement of heat exposure and analysis

To carry out a thermal environment survey, it is necessary to have information on the following environmental parameters[32]:

- air temperature;
- radiant temperature;
- air velocity; and
- humidity.

Information is also required on the person's work rate (metabolism) and the level of insulation afforded by their clothing. With the above data, it is possible to determine the degree of thermal stress exerted by an environment. (Information on the same factors is also combined in assessment of cold stress and thermal comfort conditions.) Thermal environment conditions change with time and the tasks and/or processes being carried out. Climatic conditions also vary spatially in a workplace given the distribution and location of heat and/or cold sources.

According to the BOHS (1996), environmental measurements should be taken at three heights for each sampling position:

- ankle height (0.1m);
- abdomen height (0.6m for sitting and 1.1m for standing); and
- head height (1.1m for sitting and 1.7m for standing).

Measurement times and positions should be selected depending on spatial distribution of heat sources and tasks and/or processes, and taking account of variations in climatic conditions. The objective is to assess the thermal exposure of individuals – although this does not normally involve personal monitoring where the worker actually wears the measurement device. However, the aim is to determine thermal environment exposure conditions on as near as an individual basis as practical constraints will allow. It is the thermal load (or dose) on the individual that is of interest when results are compared with derived tolerability standards. The practical determination of the various environmental and personal factors is discussed below.

Air temperature

The temperature of the air affects convective exchange between the human body and the ambient environment. This can be measured by various devices including a mercury in glass thermometer (most common), a thermistor or a thermocouple. It is important to prevent heat from radiant sources affecting the accuracy of air temperature measurements and this is achieved principally by shielding the sensor. Thermometers need a short period of time to reach equilibrium before a reading is taken.

Radiant temperature

For many indoor environments, the surrounding surfaces are at a fairly uniform temperature and radiant heat load can be described by the Mean Radiant Temperature (MRT). As mentioned earlier in this chapter, MRT is the integrated temperature of uniform surrounding surfaces which will result in the same heat exchange by radiation from a person as in the actual environment (BOHS 1996). The MRT is estimated from the temperature of the surrounding surfaces, according to their relative influence on

---

[32]The method for measuring the physical parameters is documented in BSI (1994).

THERMAL ENVIRONMENT

the person with respect to the orientation of the person to the radiating surfaces, for example, their posture and location in the room.

Monitoring instruments are available which allow the radiant heat load to be integrated into a single displayed value.

The globe thermometer (see Figure 7.2) can provide a good indication of radiant heat exchange likely to be found at a point. The device consists of a hollow black copper globe of 150mm in diameter with a temperature sensor (normally a thermometer) mounted in the middle. The temperature reading can be influenced by air velocity but tables are available to adjust for this. The diameter of the globe is arbitrary but nomograms have been derived for interpreting 150mm globe temperatures in terms of MRT. Smaller globes are available but these are more affected by air velocity. The advantage of a smaller globe is that it will reach equilibrium temperature sooner. The globe temperature will come to equilibrium with the radiant heat load from the various sources and convective heat exchange. Radiant heat is often a critical factor in stressful thermal environments and it is important that conditions are accurately determined. Where radiant heat originates from various sources, measurements are normally taken at the three standard heights.

FIGURE 7.2 Globe thermometer

(Casella Ltd)

In normal conditions, the mean of the three measurements is taken; in 'stress' conditions, the abdomen-height readings have twice the weighting of the ankle- and head-height measurements (BOHS 1996). The response time for the 150mm black globe is 20 to 30 minutes and this is not a useful instrument where radiant temperatures are changing rapidly.

Air velocity

Air velocity or windspeed is an important factor in determining convective and evaporative heat transfer. Air velocity may fluctuate widely and it is the mean value which is of interest. Windspeed monitoring devices may be classified into those with directional sensors and those which are omnidirectional.

Directional

A hot-wire anemometer (Figure 7.3) works on the principle of a wire (sensor) heated by an electric current to above ambient temperature and this is cooled by the movement of the air. The amount of cooling depends not only on air velocity but also on ambient air temperature and the physical characteristics of the heated element. These effects are compensated for by having two identical sensors, one of which measures the ambient air temperature. At high air temperatures, convection will affect the measurement of low air velocities.

FIGURE 7.3: Hot-wire anemometer

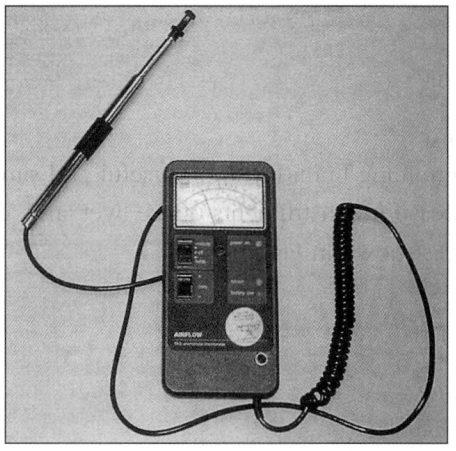

(Airflow Developments Ltd)

Omnidirectional

The Kata ('down' or 'falling') thermometer (Figure 7.4) is used for measuring air velocity. It consists of a reservoir of liquid and thin glass stem with upper and lower calibration points which correspond to a drop of 3°C. The thermometer is warmed up by immersion in hot water. It is then dried and allowed to cool and the time period is measured for the liquid to fall between the two calibration points.

FIGURE 7.4: Kata thermometer

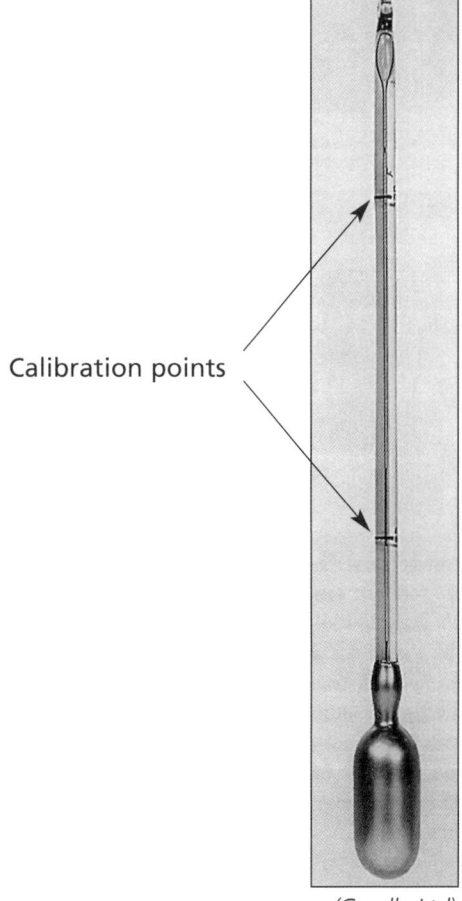

Calibration points

(Casella Ltd)

The air velocity is derived from a nomogram or formula which takes into account cooling time, the dry bulb temperature and the calibration factor for the particular Kata thermometer, representing heat loss per unit surface area. This device has a long response time and averages air movement values. It is not suitable for use where there is large or rapid variation in air velocity levels.

Air distribution patterns and local movement may be followed visually by means of smoke-generating devices such as tubes, bombs or pellets.

THERMAL ENVIRONMENT

Humidity

Humidity, or absolute humidity, is the concentration of water vapour in a given volume of air. Relative humidity is the ratio (expressed as a percentage) of the concentration of water vapour in a given volume of air at a given temperature compared with the concentration of water vapour when the air is saturated at the same temperature.

There are many ways of determining humidity and a useful and simple method involves using psychrometry and thermometers. Measuring instruments utilise 'wet' and 'dry' bulb thermometers and one of these, a whirling hygrometer, is shown in Figure 7.5.

FIGURE 7.5: Whirling hygrometer

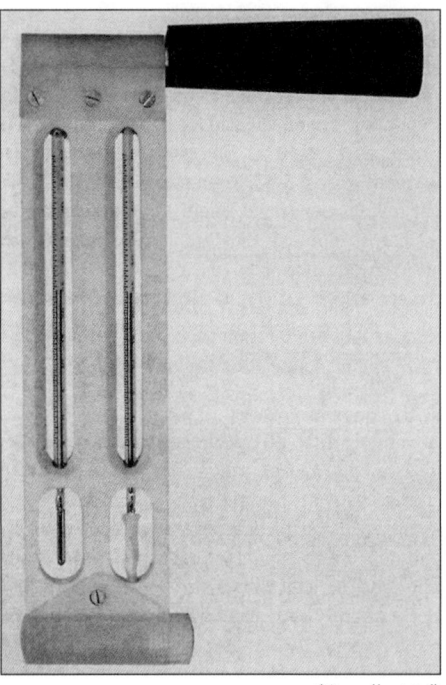

(Casella Ltd)

FIGURE 7.6: Psychrometric chart

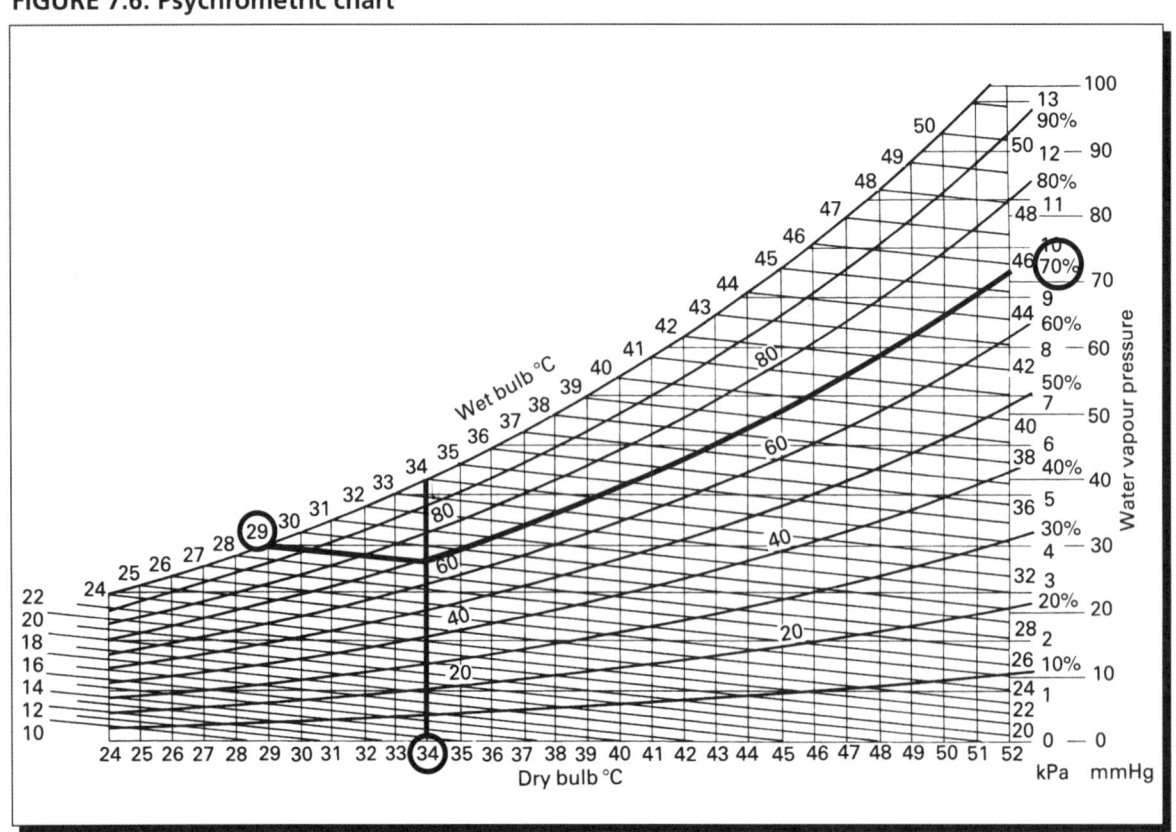

(Allan 1989. Reprinted by permission of Elsevier Limited.)

A whirling hygrometer consists of two standard, identical mercury in glass thermometers mounted in a frame, which can be rotated like a rattle. One of the thermometers, the wet bulb thermometer, has a cotton wick over the bulb, which is kept wet by capillary action with distilled water contained in a small reservoir. Water evaporates from the wet bulb thereby cooling it to below the temperature recorded on the dry bulb. The amount of cooling depends on the evaporation rate which itself is a function of the relative humidity of the air. To get reliable results, the hygrometer must be rotated vigorously either on a horizontal or vertical axis. A psychrometric chart is used to read off the relative humidity, as illustrated in Figure 7.6.

A psychrometric chart allows the determination of both absolute and relative humidity in an environment. The force which makes water evaporate is the difference in vapour pressure between the water in the air and at the surface of the water. The maximum water vapour pressure which can occur at any temperature is known as the saturation vapour pressure. This varies with temperature as shown by the 100 per cent saturation curve in Figure 7.6. The vapour pressure (in kPa or mmHg) and relative humidity (percentage saturation) contours are both shown on the right vertical axis of this diagram. The chart allows the relative humidity value for a given environment to be found by combining measured dry bulb and wet bulb temperatures. The worked example in Figure 7.6 shows an environment with a dry bulb temperature of 34°C and a wet bulb temperature of 29°C. Using the chart, this corresponds to a relative humidity of 70 per cent.

There are two types of wet bulb measurements: 'natural' (non-aspirated) and 'forced' (aspirated). Natural wet bulb temperature is the measurement taken with the wet bulb in a static position while forced wet bulb temperature is the reading taken immediately following the rotating of the hygrometer. Both thermometers should be shielded from radiant heat sources and the wick kept clean. Natural wet bulb temperature is more influenced by local air movements and is less predictable than forced wet bulb temperature. It is used in the Wet Bulb Globe Temperature (WBGT) index (discussed below) since it is believed to reflect localised conditions more accurately.

Integrating climate measurement devices

Indoor climate analyser

There are devices available which will give measurements of thermal environment parameters and also display integrated indices for both thermal stress and thermal comfort applications. These are generally used by technical specialists and vary in their complexity. An example of an indoor climate system device is shown in Figure 7.7.

FIGURE 7.7: Indoor climate system

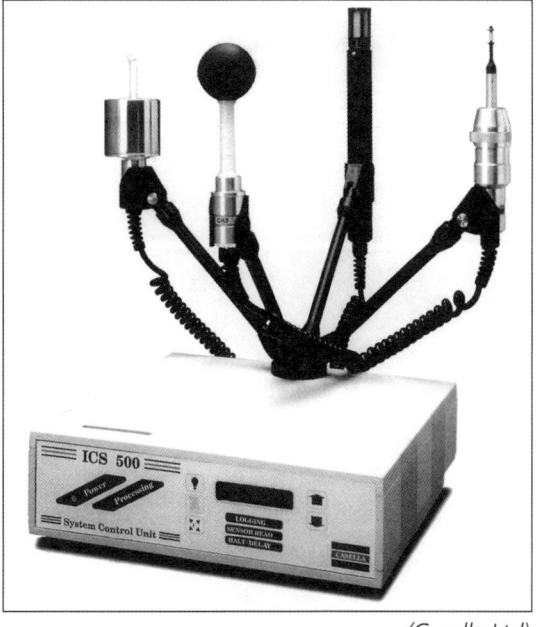

(Casella Ltd)

THERMAL ENVIRONMENT

Wet bulb globe temperature meter

This instrument measures the natural (non-ventilated) wet bulb temperature, air temperature and globe temperature using a 40mm diameter globe and incorporating correction factors. The display is in units of degrees Celsius WBGT. The sensors can be positioned remotely with continuous monitoring and the monitoring systems can be fitted with an alarm. The instrument can be used to evaluate the work environment and changes in the effectiveness of control measures.

FIGURE 7.8: Direct reading WBGT meter

(Casella Ltd)

Determination of risk tolerability

As previously mentioned in this chapter, whenever heat stress is imposed on the human body, there is a resulting physiological strain which results in reactions such as sweat production and increased heart rate. The greater the heat load, the greater the heat strain, and to avoid heat stress illness the 'heat balance' equation must balance. Thermal stress indices attempt to predict the effect of hot environments, particularly with respect to the impact on a person's core temperature. Environmental parameters (air temperature, radiant temperature, air velocity, relative humidity) and personal factors (clothing, metabolic rate) are taken into account in these predictions. Various attempts have been made to combine these determinants of heat exchange into a single number or index, which summarises the relative severity of an environment in order to predict its effect on exposed people. (Thermal stress indices aim to protect people from harmful thermal environments while thermal comfort indices (see page 256) attempt to define conditions necessary for a 'comfortable' thermal environment and these are discussed below.)

A number of thermal stress indices have been derived to evaluate heat exposure, principally to prevent heat stroke (where there is a significant rise in core temperature), but not to protect against the less well-documented chronic effects of exposure. The principal aim is to prevent core body temperature from exceeding 38°C. Thermal stress indices can be classified into direct, empirical, and analytical subgroups (Youle 1995).

Direct

These are measurements taken on a simple instrument which responds to similar environmental parameters to which humans respond, that is, air temperature, radiant temperature, air velocity and relative humidity. For example, wet bulb temperature may be used to assess heat stress and predict heat strain when radiant heat load and air velocity are low and humidity is high. For normally clothed individuals at low air velocities, a wet bulb temperature (aspirated) of around 30°C is the upper limit for unimpaired performance in sedentary tasks while 27°C is the upper limit for moderate levels of physical work (NIOSH 1986). Wet bulb temperature has been used as a predictive index to assess thermal conditions in mines and during tunnelling operations.

The integrated value of the temperature of a wet bulb thermometer and the temperature of a thermometer placed at the centre of a black copper globe comprise the Wet Bulb Globe Temperature (WBGT) index, which is the most widely-used thermal stress index (discussed on page 247).

Empirical

Empirical indices have been derived from assessing human physiological effects following exposure to varying test thermal environments. Examples include the Effective Temperature (ET) and Corrective Effective Temperature (CET) indices. Here, environments providing the same thermal sensation were given equal ET or CET values. Empirical indices do not show detailed physical components of the thermal environment but they have been widely used as the basis of standards since they are derived from practical experience.

Analytical

This group of thermal indices takes into account detailed theoretical considerations of the heat balance equation. This allows consideration of the factors controlling body heat balance, which is useful when assessing environmental or process changes. These indices are generally based on less practical data and only one has been used for standard-setting, namely, ISO 7933: 1989 (ISO 1989).

Empirical indices

Effective Temperature (ET) and Corrected Effective Temperature (CET)

These indices are based on human exposure to a range of environmental conditions and they have been used in both thermal stress and thermal comfort contexts.

Effective Temperature (ET) is an index which has been used to evaluate the warmth of an environment. ET takes account of the air temperature, humidity and the rate of movement of the air. Standard conditions of still and water-saturated air are used as reference points. The ET of an environment refers to the temperature of still air, saturated with water vapour, in which an equivalent sensation of warmth was experienced by test subjects. Although ET is based on subjective sensation, further work has shown that physiological parameters closely correlate with the index. A limitation of ET is that it does not take into account radiant heat load. Using a globe thermometer rather than a dry bulb thermometer led to the development of the index known as Corrected Effective Temperature (CET).

The nomogram for CET (and ET) is shown in Figure 7.9. This index takes limited account of clothing and a scale has been added for work rate. The CET scale tends to overestimate the effect of high humidity, underestimate the effects of air velocity and generally overestimate heat stress conditions.

In general, if the CET exceeds 30°C, then performance and productivity decreases. According to NIOSH (1986), the World Health Organisation has recommended that CET values for heat-unacclimatised personnel are unacceptable if they are greater than 30°C for sedentary activities, 28°C

THERMAL ENVIRONMENT

for moderate work and 26.5°C for hard work. For fully heat-acclimatised individuals, these tolerable limits can be increased by 2°C. Although the CET index has been widely used in coal mines to predict heat stress conditions, at present it is principally used as a guideline for comfort conditions. There are recommended levels for different occupations and Youle (1995) gives a CET range of 16–18°C for comfort conditions in typical office environments, but it is cautioned that values given for the UK are 2–4°C lower than those given for the USA.

FIGURE 7.9: Normal scale of Corrected Effective Temperature (lightly clothed) with additional nomogram including work rate

Air velocity			
ft min^{-1}	m s^{-1}	m s^{-1} plotted	m s^{-1} error
20	0.1016	0.100	0.0016
100	0.508	0.500	0.008
200	1.016	1.000	0.016
300	1.524	1.500	0.024
400	2.032	2.000	0.032
500	2.540	2.500	0.040
600	3.048	3.000	0.048
700	3.556	3.500	0.056
800	4.064	4.000	0.064
1000	5.080	5.000	0.080
1200	6.096	6.000	0.096
1500	7.620	7.500	0.120

Conversion factor
 ft min^{-1} × 0.00508 = m s^{-1}
Factor used
 ft min^{-1} × 0.005 (error 1.6%)

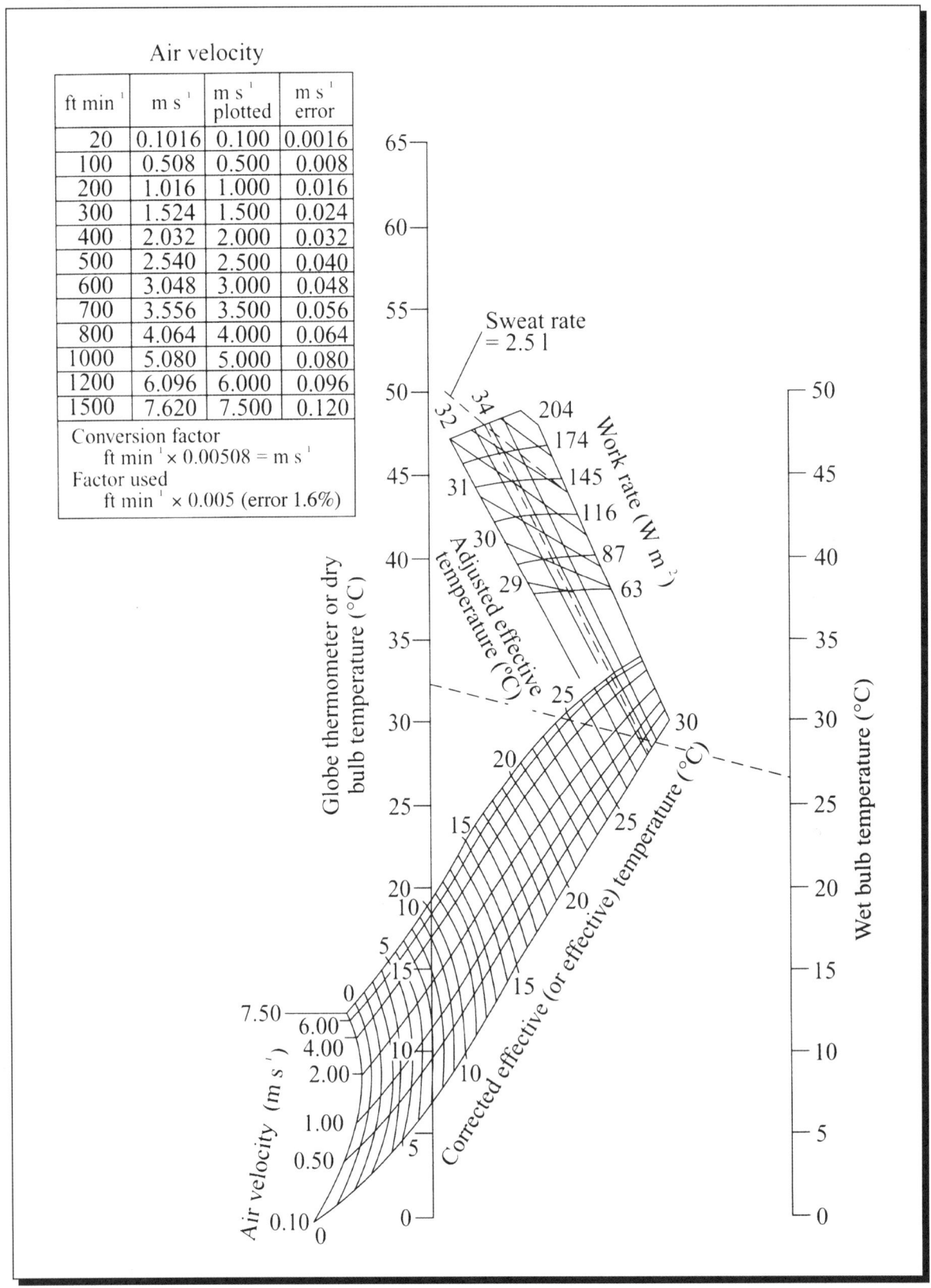

(Ellis et al. 1972)

THERMAL ENVIRONMENT

Example using the normal scale of Corrected Effective Temperature (after Ashton & Gill 2000)

Measure the wet bulb and globe temperature and air velocity. In this example, the following results were obtained: wet bulb temperature 27°C, globe temperature 32°C, and air velocity 0.5ms^{-1}.

Procedure

1. On the chart draw a line joining the wet bulb temperature with the globe temperature (or dry bulb if the globe is not used).
2. Where this line crosses the air velocity line, the normal Corrected Effective Temperature can be read off as 28°C from the central grid of the chart.
3. Where a correction for work rate is made (in this example, 204Wm^{-2}), a line is extended from the intersection with the air velocity up to the work rate extension to the chart until it intersects with the 204 line. The normal Corrected Effective Temperature adjusted for work rate is read as 33°C.

Wet Bulb Globe Temperature

Wet Bulb Globe Temperature (WBGT) is the most widely-used thermal stress index. It is the basis of an international standard, that is, ISO 7243 (BSI 1994a), and this index is also used by the American Conference of Governmental Industrial Hygienists (ACGIH) as the basis for its Threshold Limit Value (TLV) for heat stress conditions (ACGIH 2002).

Two categories of index are available as shown below:

$$WBGT\ (indoors) = 0.7WB + 0.3GT$$

$$WBGT\ (outdoors) = 0.7WB + 0.2GT + 0.1DB$$

(Where: WB is natural wet bulb temperature; GT is globe temperature; and DB is dry bulb temperature.)

Other indices are used to permit work at higher temperatures without harm and these are discussed by BOHS (1996). The WBGT indices (indoors and outdoors) are both very useful, practical thermal stress indices. However, care needs to be taken when impervious personal protective equipment is used where there is a high radiant heat load or a high air temperature and wind speed.

The WBGT index was originally derived to prevent heat stress casualties during US military training. It takes account of radiant temperature, air temperature, humidity and low air velocity (1ms^{-1}). The figures are reasonably conservative and believed to be safe for most people.

TABLE 7.6: TLV for heat exposure – Screening criteria for heat stress exposure (WBGT values in °C)

Work demands	ACCLIMATISED				UNACCLIMATISED			
	Light	Moderate	Heavy	Very heavy	Light	Moderate	Heavy	Very heavy
100% work	29.5	27.5	26		27.5	25	22.5	
75% work 25% rest	30.5	28.5	27.5		29	26.5	24.5	
50% work 50% rest	31.5	29.5	28.5	27.5	30	28	26.5	25
25% work 75% rest	32.5	31	30	29.5	31	29	28	26.5

(ACGIH 2002)

In its TLV standard (Table 7.6), the ACGIH (2002) has introduced guidance for different clothing ensembles when using the WBGT index (Table 7.7). The index is applied directly for 'light' clothing with an insulation value of 0.6clo and appropriate corrections must be made with alternative clothing.

For continuous work lasting more than eight hours, the figures represent the upper limit for combinations of environmental heat load and work activity which will not cause an increase in core temperature (above 38°C) in 95 per cent of acclimatised individuals.

TABLE 7.7: Additions to measured WBGT values (°C) for some clothing ensembles

Clothing type	WBGT addition
Summer work uniform	0
Cloth (woven material) overalls	+3.5
Double-cloth overalls	+5

(ACGIH 2002)

Analytical indices

Required sweat rate

The index embodied in BSI (1997) balances heat from the environment with sweat required from the exposed person. It applies the heat balance equation by balancing the heat load on a person, from the environment and metabolic rate, with the heat loss required by the evaporation of sweat. The method requires information on all the environmental factors, work rate and clothing. Recommendations are based on limiting the rise in core temperature and evaluating the strain induced by the sweating process. It is a complex index which is difficult to apply and it is generally used by technical specialists.

Heat Stress Index (HSI)

This represents a similar but simpler approach than BSI (1997). The index is based on the heat balance equation and relates the evaporative capacity required by a person (in a given work situation) to the maximum evaporative capacity of their environment (Belding 1972). It enables consideration of the contributing components of the thermal environment. The calculation is as follows:

$$\text{Heat Stress Index (HSI)} = (E_{req}/E_{max}) \times 100$$

The HSI (see Figure 7.10) represents thermal environments on a scale of 0–100 and a value of less than 40 is thought to represent an insignificant health risk. Above 40, the resulting heat strain and health risk increases proportionally until a value of 100 is reached, which is believed to be the maximum that can be tolerated by fit, acclimatised, young men[33]. Above 100, the body is unable to lose sufficient heat unless exposure time is limited. Allowable Exposure Time (AET) in this situation can be calculated using the following equation:

$$\text{Allowable Exposure Time (AET)} = 2440/(E_{req} - E_{max})$$

(Where: E_{req} is required evaporative (sweat) loss (= M - R - C, ie the net sum of metabolic heat gain (M) and radiant (R) and convective (C) heat loss); and E_{max} is maximum evaporative (sweat) loss (390Wm^{-2} as an upper limit). This upper limit is equivalent to a sweat loss of one litre per hour. It assumes a maximum allowable body temperature rise of 1.8°C, due to heat storage over a one-hour period. This is combined with an appropriate rest period to allow this stored heat to be lost.)

The method for calculating the HSI is summarised in Figure 7.10.

---

[33]This is the basis of the standard's original derivation.

FIGURE 7.10: Heat Stress Index

$$\text{Heat Stress Index} = (E_{req}/E_{max}) \times 100$$

Where:

E_{req} = Required evaporative (ie sweat) loss (W.m^{-2})
= M - R - C (see below)

E_{max} = Maximum evaporative (ie sweat) loss (W.m^{-2})
= $7.0 \, v^{0.6} (56 - P_a)$ ...clothed
= $11.7 \, v^{0.6} (56 - P_a)$ ...unclothed

with upper limit of 390W.m^{-2}

M = Metabolic rate (W.m^{-2})

R = Radiation rate (W.m^{-2}) = $4.4 (35 - t_r)$ ...clothed
= $7.3 (35 - t_r)$ ...unclothed

C = Convection rate (W.m^{-2}) = $4.6 \, v^{0.6} (35 - t_a)$ ...clothed
= $7.6 \, v^{0.6} (35 - t_a)$ ...unclothed

and

P_a = Water vapour pressure (mb)

t_r = Mean Radiant Temperature (°C)

t_a = Dry bulb (ie air) temperature (°C)

(BOHS 1996)

Predicted 4-Hour Sweat Rate (P4SR)

This index is based on physiological response to heat stress and enables a nominal sweat rate, as an index of heat strain, to be predicted from environmental and individual factors (MacPherson 1960). Environmental factors are measured and clothing and activity are taken into account by making adjustments to wet bulb temperature. A chart is used to compute the predicted sweat rate. A P4SR value of 4.5 litres is often given as a maximum for acclimatised young men, while a maximum of 2.7 litres is applied to clothed industrial workers. This index is inaccurate below a relative humidity of 40 per cent and it is not applicable to work with variable intermittent heat exposure.

Regulation and the thermal environment

Table 7.8 summarises the main legislative requirements with regard to the thermal environment.

TABLE 7.8: Legislation and the thermal environment

Statute	Comment
Health and Safety at Work etc Act 1974	Duty to provide a safe and healthy workplace
Management of Health and Safety at Work Regulations 1999	Require 'suitable and sufficient assessment' of risks with the identification of measures for controlling thermal environment hazards; provide health surveillance as appropriate

Table continued overleaf

THERMAL ENVIRONMENT

Workplace (Health, Safety and Welfare) Regulations 1992	Temperatures must be 'reasonable'; sufficient numbers of thermometers must be provided; no specification of maximum and minimum temperatures in the Regulations. (NB: The accompanying ACoP specifies a minimum ambient temperature value of 16°C and this reduces to 13°C where there is severe physical work.)
Control of Substances Hazardous to Health Regulations 2002, Control of Asbestos at Work Regulations 2002	Thermal conditions may be important factors in risk assessment and application of controls as required by these sets of Regulations
Personal Protective Equipment Regulations 1992	Requirements as regards the selection and implementation of a personal protection scheme
Building Regulations 1991 (Parts L & F)	Thermal aspects of building design

Prevention and control measures

Environmental measures

Process design and planning

Designing or changing processes to reduce operating temperatures enables the reduction of heat stress at source. Adequate insulation of exposed heat sources will reduce surface temperatures and radiant heat emission. For radiant heat control, bright, shiny surfaces have lower emissivities than dark or dull ones. For example, consider the emissivities of the following: aluminium (0.10); rusted iron (0.85); and rough bricks (0.93).

Process mechanisation with remote handling operations and the use of CCTV lessens the need for operator exposure to hot work processes. Similarly, the maintenance and repair of hot equipment and other short duration tasks should be planned to reduce operator exposures to a minimum.

Circulation of air

Faster air movement will increase convective and evaporative heat loss. However, if the air temperature is in excess of 35°C, convective heat gain will occur. Nevertheless, unless relative humidity is high, evaporative loss will outweigh this convective heat gain. Where the wet bulb temperature is below 36°C, increasing the air velocity is beneficial, while above this temperature, an increased air velocity will be detrimental to thermal balance (this is because the skin temperature will now be below air temperature and the skin will gain heat by convection).

Ventilation

The purpose is to remove hot and/or humid air and replace this with cooler and/or drier air and, thus, increase operator heat loss by convective and/or evaporative modes.

Shielding

Barriers can be erected to shield operators from radiant heat sources. They should have a low emissivity (high reflectivity) and be constructed out of materials which have good insulating properties. This is important so that the barriers themselves do not become secondary radiant heat sources or a contact hazard. Cold water radiators can act as 'heat sinks' to remove heat.

Air conditioning

This can be applied in extreme thermal environments, for example, in the provision of air-conditioned control rooms for process operatives.

Rest areas and welfare facilities
All eating, drinking, washing and rest facilities should be, if possible, at a cooler temperature than work areas.

Work organisation
In highly stressful hot environments, there should be a high level of worker supervision with no lone workers. Procedures should be in place to ensure that heat casualties are detected quickly and a permit-to-work system should be enforced in extreme environments. Where this is feasible, work should be planned for cooler times of the day or year.

Work-rest regimes
Work-rest regimes are usually structured to prevent core body temperature rising above 38°C with rest breaks taken in a cooler place. However, the 'rest area' in BSI (1994a) is assumed to be at the same WBGT as the work area and the figures calculated accordingly. Where the work environment is more extreme, an alternative tolerability index may be needed, coupled with a greater emphasis on medical screening and supervision. A physiological approach can be taken with 'return to work', for example, no return until a person's pulse or temperature has returned to a safe level.

Personal measures

Training
Workers and supervisors should be trained to recognise the symptoms of heat stress illness and the precautions that need to be taken. They should understand the precautions and how to minimise their exposure.

Health surveillance
Medical preselection and monitoring of workers is important for working in very hot environments. Cardiovascular, kidney and respiratory function testing are important, and age and general fitness are also relevant where operators are carrying out work in extreme thermal environments.

Acclimatisation
Procedures should be in force to ensure that workers acclimatise to hot work as appropriate and also that they re-acclimatise following significant absences. With continued exposure to hot environments, the body develops some tolerance to high ambient temperatures. Acclimatisation is characterised by an increased ability to sweat, a reduced core temperature, a reduced pulse rate, the process of sweating beginning at lower body temperatures, and a lower salt content in sweat. (Salt supplementation is usually unnecessary in acclimatised individuals, assuming a normal intake of 10g per day.) Acclimatisation can be achieved by gradually increasing controlled exposure to hot work, and tolerance is fully developed after about 10 days. Heat tolerance will begin to decline with absence from the work of more than a week and it will completely disappear after about one month.

Salt and water uptake
Serious heat disorders can arise from an imbalance of water and salt intake. Supplies of palatable, salted drinks should be available to exposed workers and they should be encouraged to consume these. (Salted fluids are preferable to salt tablets since the latter may induce nausea and vomiting, thereby exacerbating negative salt balance.)

Personal protective equipment and clothing
Personal protective clothing may have an adverse effect on body heat balance since it creates an insulation layer and will reduce evaporative heat loss. Where clothing which is impervious to moisture is used, then this may create a significant hazard at air temperatures as low as 21°C, particularly in unacclimatised or less fit individuals (BOHS 1996).

Respirators may cause significant discomfort and skin rashes. They will restrict airflow during breathing, further increasing cardiovascular strain. A positive pressure respirator is very desirable when working in stressful hot environments.

Clothing (natural fibre) may provide some protection against contact burns and radiation. Where very hot surfaces or sources (such as molten metal) are present, special clothing assemblies are required, as specified in BSI (1993). Aluminised surfaces and visors will protect against radiation hazards.

Heat-resistant clothing will only protect for limited periods and where there is prolonged exposure to heat, artificially cooled or air-conditioned clothing is required. Ice-cooled jackets (cotton with ice-packs) and air-cooled suits are the most commonly used in this context. Air-cooled suits may be coated with a reflective material to protect against radiant heat sources. Cooled air is supplied with a connecting hose and they may be worn for long periods at high temperatures. The hose, however, may restrict the operator's mobility.

In Chapter 13, a range of personal protective equipment for hazardous thermal environments is listed in Table 13.8.

Cold environments

Hazard identification

In a cold environment, the skin temperature falls and there is increased insulation in the body shell which maintains core temperature. With prolonged exposure to cold stress conditions, body heat production will increase (oxygen consumption may increase five-fold with intense shivering).

Heat is lost from the body by conduction, convection, radiation and evaporation. Body heat is also lost from the respiratory tract depending on the humidity of the air and respiratory ventilation rate. A mean skin temperature of less than 33°C is associated with increasing cold discomfort. Physiological responses, clothing and physical activity enable most people to maintain deep body temperature in cold environments. (Mean skin temperature may fall to 12°C in obese people and 25–30°C in thin individuals.) Most adults can tolerate an ambient temperature of 5°C (with 1clo of clothing insulation) in still air for several hours and maintain deep body temperature. However, they cannot tolerate much colder or wet and windy environments.

FIGURE 7.11: Pipeline worker dressed for cold/dry conditions

(Raffle et al. 1987. Reproduced by permission of Hodder Arnold.)

TABLE 7.9: Typical occupational examples of cold stress hazards

Cold stress	Radiant temp.	Air temp.	Wet bulb temp.	Air velocity	Metabolic rate	Water
Outdoor cold work – agriculture, quarrying, fishing, oil rigs, construction	l	l	l	m	h	h
Diving	l	l	l	l	l	h
Cold stores	l	l	l	m	l	l

(H = very high; h = high; m = medium; l = low; heat loss due to water conduction or evaporation from wet clothing is indicated in the 'water' column) *(Adapted from Youle 1995)*

Cold exposure and health effects

Hypothermia
This is a general lowering of core body temperature to below 35°C and this can occur in conditions well above freezing and can occur where people are immersed in water, exposed to very cold winds, or in an exhausted physiological state. It may develop insidiously without the person being aware of the risk. As the core temperature falls further, mental confusion and disorientation develop and below 30°C there is a progressive loss of consciousness and muscular rigidity.

Local cold injury
Frostbite involves the freezing of the extremities of the body, such as fingers, toes, nose or cheeks. It can be superficial or may constitute a deep injury and this normally depends on the duration of exposure. Frozen body extremities should be protected from further cold injury but no attempt should be made to thaw them except under controlled conditions.

Other effects of cold
There does not seem to be a process of 'cold acclimatisation' comparable to that induced by heat exposure. However, there appears to be some adaptation to cold conditions by local changes in the extremities, that is, an increased ability to maintain blood flow to maintain dexterity.

Measurement of exposure and analysis – Cold environments

Cold stress survey
A survey to evaluate cold stress involves the collection of information on environmental and personal factors (as with heat stress assessments described above). The exact nature of the information needed will depend on the risk tolerability index to be used. Determination of the Wind Chill Index involves the measurement of air speed and ambient temperature, and radiant temperature is needed for the use of Still Shade Temperature.

Determination of risk tolerability
In this context, there are less well-validated standards than there are for hot environments. There is greater scope for behavioural thermoregulation in maintaining core temperature. The objective of standards is to prevent core temperature falling below 35°C and to prevent cold injury to the extremities. Cold stress is evaluated for:
- general cooling (Still Shade Temperature; Required Clothing Insulation); and
- local cooling of body extremities (Wind Chill Index).

Still Shade Temperature
This index takes account of actual outdoor conditions and expresses them as an 'equivalent temperature'

THERMAL ENVIRONMENT

with no solar heat exchange and no wind effect (Burton & Edholm 1955). Corrections are applied for solar heat gain and measurements are standardised to zero air movement. A correction is applied for solar heat absorbed by the body, that is, the Thermal Radiation Increment (TRI). The factors that are taken into account include the solar heat absorbed by clothing, the posture of the subject and the reflecting power of the surface. The TRI (°C) is added to the measured temperature and in correcting for air movement, the thermal wind decrement (°C) is subtracted to give the equivalent shade temperature. Thus, environmental conditions can be converted to a single index figure and exposure can be regulated as with other indices.

Required Clothing Insulation (IREQ)

This is the resultant clothing insulation required to maintain the body in thermal equilibrium under steady-state conditions when sweating is absent and peripheral vasoconstriction is present. Clothing insulation is used to express cold stress as general body cooling and the insulation required to maintain thermal balance (Holmer 1984). Thus, the higher the value of IREQ at any given activity level, the greater the cooling power of the environment. An increase in metabolic rate will reduce the IREQ value for a given situation.

Wind Chill Index

Wind Chill Index (WCI) is an index of heat loss from the body and is the same as the wind chill correction factor applied to environmental conditions (Siple & Passel 1945). The WCI was derived to identify potential risk from the combined cooling effect of wind speed and air temperature using an artificial human model. The WCI correlates well to human response to temperature and wind combinations and, importantly, it identifies dangerous situations for exposed skin, since it is good for estimating local cooling of the hands, feet and head.

The relationship between cooling power and air speed is not linear with the greatest increase over the 0–2ms^{-1} range. The equivalent 'chilling temperature' produces the same cooling power as the actual environmental conditions.

The chart in Figure 7.12 shows cooling rate contours, in kcal m^{-2} h^{-1} units, for different combinations of wind speed and ambient temperature. With this index, the amount of clothing is not taken into account. However, it has proved to be useful, since given adequate dietary nutrients, cold tolerance is determined by the exposed parts of the body. This index becomes redundant where full-face protection and gloves are worn.

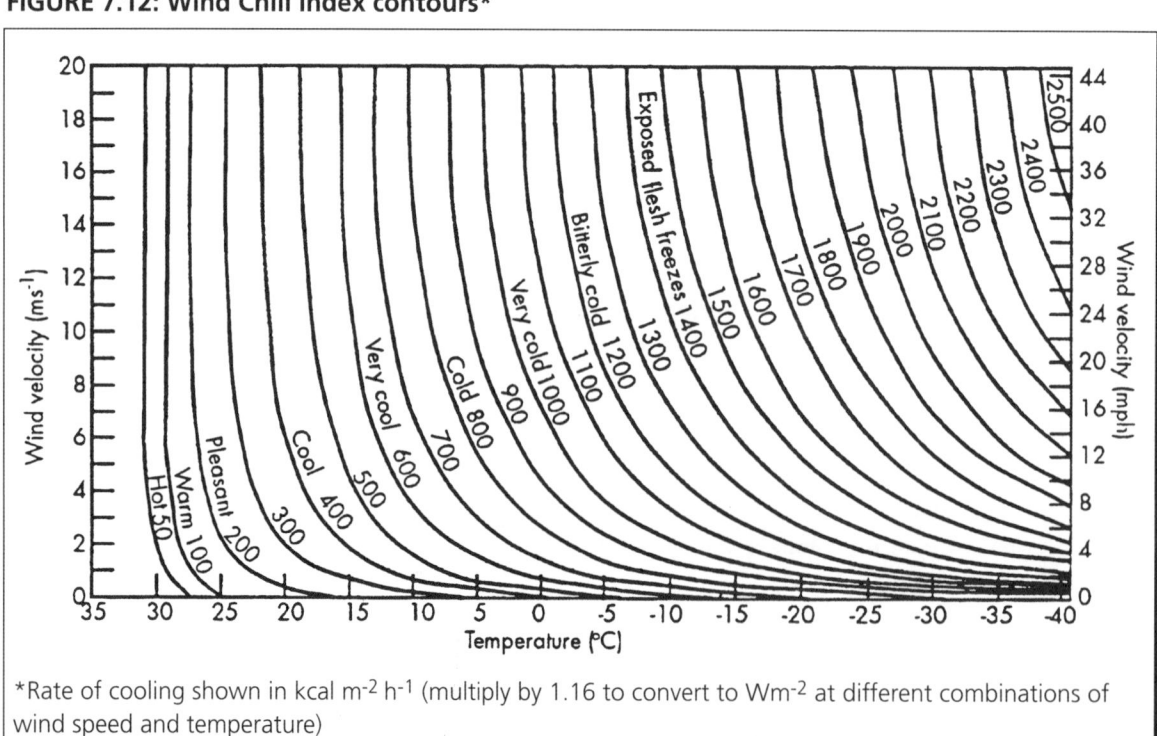

FIGURE 7.12: Wind Chill Index contours*

*Rate of cooling shown in kcal m^{-2} h^{-1} (multiply by 1.16 to convert to Wm^{-2} at different combinations of wind speed and temperature)

(BOHS 1996)

Threshold Limit Values (TLVs) are intended to protect workers from severe hypothermia and cold injury. In the case of repeated exposure, the objective is to prevent core temperature falling below 36°C and to prevent cold injury to body extremities, that is, the hands, feet and face/head. With a single or occasional exposure to extreme cold, the ACGIH (2002) recommends that core body temperature should be not be allowed to fall below 35°C, the point at which maximum severe shivering develops. Table 7.10 applies to any four-hour work period with moderate to heavy work activity and only to workers in dry clothing. The TLV specifies warm-up periods (10 minutes in a warm location) and an extended rest period at the end of the four-hour work period.

TABLE 7.10: Threshold Limit Values – Work/warm-up values for four-hour shifts

Air temperature – Sunny sky	No noticeable wind		5mph wind		10mph wind		15mph wind		20mph wind	
°C (approx.)	Max. work period	No. of breaks	Max. work period	No. of breaks	Max. work period	No. of breaks	Max. work period	No. of breaks	Max. work period	No. of breaks
-26° to -28°	(Norm. breaks)	1	(Norm. breaks)	1	75min	2	55min	3	40min	4
-29° to -31°	(Norm. breaks)	1	75min	2	55min	3	40min	4	30min	5
-32° to -34°	75min	2	55min	3	40min	4	30min	5	Non-emergency work should cease	
-35° to -37°	55min	3	40min	4	30min	5	Non-emergency work should cease			
-38° to -39°	40min	4	30min	5	Non-emergency work should cease					
-40° to -42°	30min	5	Non-emergency work should cease							
-43° and below	Non-emergency work should cease									

(ACGIH 2002)

Prevention and control measures

Environmental

The cooling effect of the environment is increased by air movement since this disturbs the insulating boundary layer outside of clothing and may penetrate clothing itself. This may require additional shielding or extra layers of wind-resistant personal protective equipment.

Radiant heat exchange for people working out of doors may also be an important factor – up to 95 per cent of incident radiation can be absorbed by a person wearing black, as compared with 30 per cent for white reflecting clothing.

Work activity

A worker dressed for thermal comfort during periods of inactivity in cold environments will be overdressed for hard physical work. Therefore, intermittent work schedules present difficulties in cold environments.

Clothing

Clothing is a very important control measure in cold environments. Whole-body protection is needed to prevent hypothermia. The aim is to maintain a core temperature above 36°C and outdoors, waterproof and windproof clothing may be required. A disadvantage of impermeable clothing is that this is also impermeable to water vapour escaping from the skin surface. Eventually, this will condense and eliminate the insulation provided by the layer of trapped air. Gore-Tex® and similar fabrics allow the passage of water vapour while remaining waterproof and windproof. Protection of the extremities, especially the hands, feet and head, is also very important in cold environments. Electrically-heated suits and gloves have also been developed for work activities in the cold (see Table 13.8).

Local cold injury

There is a high risk of cold injury to the hands and face since these are the areas most exposed in cold environments. Metal handles on tools should be covered with insulating material where work is at temperatures below -1°C. Gloves should be worn where some loss of manual dexterity is not a problem.

Work-rest regimes

For continuous work carried out in cold environments with an equivalent chill temperature below -7°C, warm refuges should be available. In working environments below -12°C, for example, cold stores, workers need to be under constant supervision. Work rates should not be high enough to induce heavy sweating, but if this is unavoidable, then frequent rest pauses and dry changes of clothes are necessary. Sitting and standing still should be avoided and air movement in general should not exceed $1ms^{-1}$ in the work area.

Thermal comfort

With large groups of modern indoor workers, the aim is to achieve optimum 'thermal comfort' conditions – where this is a reasonable expectation. Thermal comfort conditions are defined as those where people express satisfaction with their thermal environment or are neutral about it. The American Society of Heating, Refrigerating and Air-Conditioning Engineers (ASHRAE) (1993) defines thermal comfort as:

> ...that condition of mind which expresses satisfaction with the thermal environment.

The subjective approach to determining comfort conditions is to ask people what they think about their thermal environment (Figures 7.14 and 7.15). Various rating scales have been developed for this purpose and two examples are given in Table 7.11.

FIGURE 7.13: Work environment where thermal comfort is expected

(HSE 1997 – rev. 2003)

TABLE 7.11: Subjective thermal comfort scales

SUBJECTIVE SCALES FOR THERMAL COMFORT			
Bedford (Chrenko 1974)		ASHRAE (1993)	
Much too warm	7	Hot	3
Too warm	6	Warm	2
Comfortably warm	5	Slightly warm	1
Comfortable	4	Neutral	0
Comfortably cool	3	Slightly cool	-1
Too cool	2	Cool	-2
Much too cool	1	Cold	-3

(From BOHS 1996)

It is convenient to divide thermal discomfort into whole-body discomfort and local (body-site) discomfort. Field studies have found a range of 'neutral' temperatures in different climates. It is useful to complement objective physical measurements of thermal environments with subjective data. Comfort indices link measures of the physical environment to subjective feelings of comfort and discomfort. Physiological preconditions for thermal comfort are:

- thermal heat balance;
- sweat rate within limits; and
- mean skin temperature within limits.

A range of thermal indices have been used to evaluate comfort conditions. This is a complicated subject area and only one comfort index will be introduced and discussed below, namely that forming the basis of BS EN ISO 7730 (BSI 1995).

Thermal comfort survey

As in the case of thermal stress environments, similar questions arise with comfort surveys: When to measure? Where to measure? What to measure? The two protocols in Figures 7.14 and 7.15 have been used for subjective assessment of workplaces with respect to the perceived thermal comfort of their occupants (BOHS 1996).

Fanger (1970) defined physiological 'comfort' conditions in terms of mean skin temperature (during comfort) and sweat secretion (during comfort). These values were incorporated into a complex heat balance equation for the human body. The comfort equation establishes those combinations of activity, clothing and the four environmental variables – air temperature, radiant temperature, air velocity and relative humidity – which will provide thermal comfort. This information has been plotted in a series of 28 comfort diagrams for practical use (Fanger 1970). The activity level and clothing are first defined and then the comfort diagrams are used to find the combination of the four environmental variables which will provide thermal comfort.

When evaluating a workplace for thermal comfort, the work activity level and clothing insulation are first determined, together with values of the above four environmental variables at suitable positions. The thermal comfort equation is then used to determine the degree of thermal comfort offered by this combination of parameters in this particular workplace. This may be done in practice by using data tables or with a thermal comfort meter. Deviation from optimal comfort conditions can be evaluated and the Predicted Mean Vote (PMV) index has been developed for this purpose. This index gives the PMV of a large group of people on the following psychophysical scale:

Hot	+3
Warm	+2
Slightly warm	+1
Neutral	0
Slightly cool	-1
Cool	-2
Cold	-3

THERMAL ENVIRONMENT

FIGURE 7.14: Subjective evaluation of thermal comfort (I)

Form 1

Please answer the following questions concerned with your THERMAL COMFORT.

1. Indicate on the scale below how you feel NOW:

    Hot   ❑
    Warm   ❑
    Slightly warm   ❑
    Neutral   ❑
    Slightly cool   ❑
    Cool   ❑
    Cold   ❑

2. Please indicate how you would like to be NOW:

    Warmer   No change   Cooler

3. Please indicate how you GENERALLY feel at work:

    Hot   ❑
    Warm   ❑
    Slightly warm   ❑
    Neutral   ❑
    Slightly cool   ❑
    Cool   ❑
    Cold   ❑

4. Please indicate how you would GENERALLY like to be at work:

    Warmer   No change   Cooler

5. Are you GENERALLY satisfied with your thermal environment at work?

    Yes   No

6. Please give any additional information or comments which you think are relevant to the assessment of your thermal environment at work (eg draughts, dryness, clothing, suggested improvements, etc).

(BOHS 1996)

FIGURE 7.15: Subjective evaluation of thermal comfort (II)

Form 2

Please answer the following questions concerned with your THERMAL COMFORT.

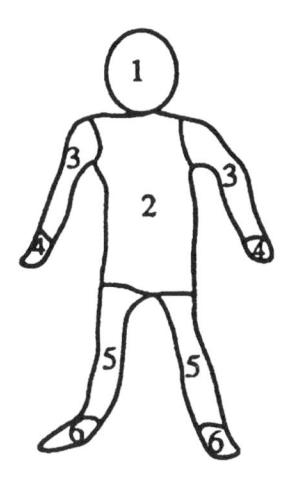

1. With reference to the above diagram, please indicate on the scales below how you feel NOW:

	Overall	Head 1	Trunk 2	Arms 3	Hands 4	Legs 5	Feet 6
Very hot	❏	❏	❏	❏	❏	❏	❏
Hot	❏	❏	❏	❏	❏	❏	❏
Warm	❏	❏	❏	❏	❏	❏	❏
Slightly warm	❏	❏	❏	❏	❏	❏	❏
Neutral	❏	❏	❏	❏	❏	❏	❏
Slightly cool	❏	❏	❏	❏	❏	❏	❏
Cool	❏	❏	❏	❏	❏	❏	❏
Cold	❏	❏	❏	❏	❏	❏	❏
Very cold	❏	❏	❏	❏	❏	❏	❏

2. Please indicate how you would like to be NOW:

   Warmer   No change   Cooler

3. Are you GENERALLY satisfied with your thermal environment?

   Yes   No

4. Please give any additional information or comments which you think are relevant to the assessment of your thermal environment at work (eg draughts, dryness, clothing, suggested improvements, etc).

(BOHS 1996)

THERMAL ENVIRONMENT

The PMV is determined from tables and it is then possible to determine the Predicted Percentage Dissatisfied (PPD) from Figure 7.16. According to Fanger (1970), the lowest value of PPD that can be expected with a working group is five per cent, that is, it is not possible to satisfy everyone's requirements for thermal comfort in the same environment.

This method is the basis of BS EN ISO 7730: 1995 which incorporates PMV into a comfort index (BSI 1995). The PMV is calculated from measurements of air temperature, MRT, humidity and air velocity of the environment, taken together with estimates of work activity and clothing insulation. Direct reading instruments are available which simulate the thermal characteristics of the human body and give values of PMV and PPD for a given environment.

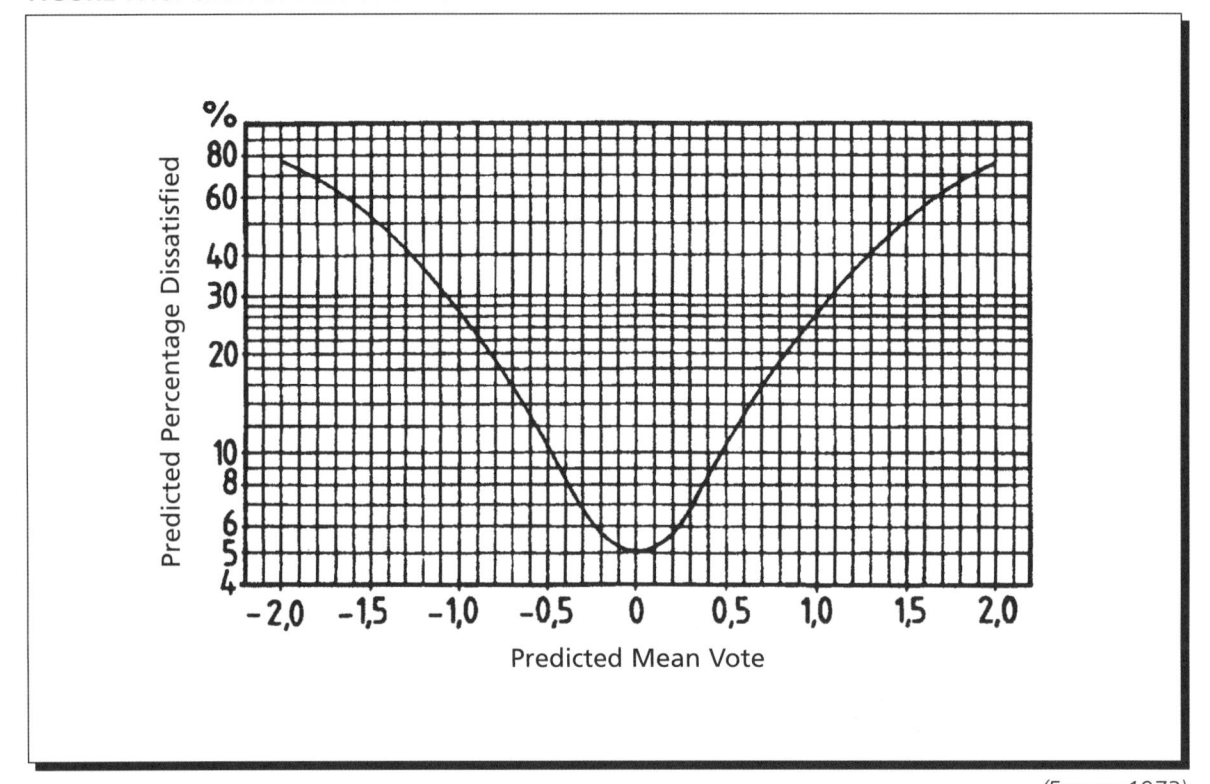

FIGURE 7.16: Chart of PMV and PPD

(Fanger 1973)

For each measurement point, air temperature, MRT, humidity, air velocity, clothing and work activity values are determined. The next stage is to predict the degree of whole-body discomfort (as PMV) using this information. Subjective information from returns of the forms similar to those illustrated in Figures 7.14 and 7.15 provides independent and complementary data on thermal comfort. As well as whole-body thermal sensation, environments with draughts and asymmetric temperature conditions may cause local discomfort. ISO 7730 considers factors relating to local thermal discomfort such as vertical temperature gradients and asymmetric radiant heat loads, together with discomfort caused by draughts. Recommended limits for air movement and temperature gradients are also given in this standard.

Comfort conditions lie between a PMV of -0.5 and +0.5 where the PPD is less than 10 per cent. This index allows the identification of the relative contribution of the different components of the thermal environment, enabling it to be used for design purposes.

Control measures

With the large increase in modern times in the numbers of indoor and office workers, much attention has been devoted to determining what constitutes a thermally comfortable internal environment. Many factors can be potentially involved in causing thermal discomfort conditions which are in need of rectification. These include the fabric of the building, the heating system, the ventilation system (the air-conditioning system where appropriate), control systems and plant maintenance. Particular control measures will be determined by the specific situation.

REFERENCES

Allan J R, 1989, Thermal Stresses in Occupations, Chapter 9 in *Occupational Health Practice* (3rd edition), Waldron H A (Ed.), Butterworths, London.

American Conference of Governmental Industrial Hygienists, 2002, *Threshold Limit Values for Chemical and Physical Agents and Biological Exposure Indices*, ACGIH, Cincinnati, OH, USA.

American Society of Heating, Refrigerating and Air-Conditioning Engineers, 1993, Thermal Comfort Conditions, *ASHRAE Standard*, **55**, New York.

Ashton I and Gill F S, 2000, *Monitoring for Health Hazards at Work* (3rd edition), Blackwell Science, Oxford.

Belding H S, 1972, Engineering Approach to Analysis and Control of Heat Exposure, *Industrial and Environmental Health*, Academic Press, New York.

British Occupational Hygiene Society, 1996, *The Thermal Environment* (2nd edition), Youle A, Collins K J, Crockford G W, Fishman D S, Mulhall A and Parsons K C (Eds), British Occupational Hygiene Society Technical Guide No 12, H & H Scientific Consultants Ltd, Leeds.

British Standards Institution, 1993, *Protective Clothing: Protection Against Heat and Fire*, BS EN 366: 1993, BSI, London.

British Standards Institution, 1994, *Thermal Environments – Instruments and Methods of Measuring Physical Quantities*, BS EN 27726, BSI, London.

British Standards Institution, 1994a, *Hot Environments – Estimation of the Heat Stress on the Working Man Based on the WBGT Index*, BS EN 27243: 1994 (ISO 7243 1989), BSI, London.

British Standards Institution, 1995, *Moderate Thermal Environments – Determination of the PMV and PPD Indices and Specification of the Conditions for Thermal Comfort*, BS EN ISO 7730, BSI, London.

British Standards Institution, 1997, *Hot Environments – Analytical Determination and Interpretation of Thermal Stress Using Calculation of Required Sweat*, BS EN 12515 (endorsement of ISO 7933: 1989), BSI, London.

Burton A C and Edholm O G, 1955, *Man in a Cold Environment*, Arnold, London.

Chrenko F A, 1974, *Bedford's Basic Principles of Ventilation and Heating* (3rd edition), H K Lewis, London.

Crockford G W, 1981, The Thermal Environment, Chapter 19 in *Occupational Health Practice* (2nd edition), Schilling R S F (Ed.), Butterworths, London.

Dukes-Dubos F N, 1981, Hazards of Heat Exposure: A Review, *Scand J Wk Env Hlth*, **7**, 73–83.

Ellis F P, Smith F E and Walters J D, 1972, Measurement of Environmental Warmth in SI Units, *Brit J Industr Med*, **29**, 361–377.

Fanger P O, 1970, *Thermal Comfort*, Danish Technical Press.

Fanger P O, 1973, Assessment of Man's Thermal Comfort in Practice, *BJIM*, **30**, 313–324.

Gill F S, 1980, Heat, Chapter 9 in *Occupational Hygiene* (1st edition), Waldron H A and Harrington J M (Eds), Blackwell Scientific Publications, Oxford.

Goelzer B, 1984, *Evaluation of Heat Stress in the Work Environment*, Office of Occupational Health, World Health Organisation, Geneva.

Health and Safety Executive, 1997, *Lighting at Work* (2nd edition), HSG38, HSE Books, Sudbury.

Holmer I, 1984, Required Clothing Insulation (IREQ) as an Analytical Index of Cold Stress, *ASHRAE Trans 90*, **Part 1**, 116–128.

Hunter D, 1978, *The Diseases of Occupations*, The English Universities Press Ltd, London.

International Standards Organisation, 1989, *Hot Environments – Analytical Determination and Interpretation of Thermal Stress Using Calculation of Required Sweat Rate*, ISO 7933: 1989, ISO, Geneva.

MacPherson R K, 1960, *Physiological Responses to Hot Environments*, MRC Special Report 298, HMSO, London.

National Institute for Occupational Safety and Health, 1986, *Criteria for a Recommended Standard, Occupational Exposure to Hot Environments*, DHHS, 86–113, Cincinnati, OH, USA.

Raffle P A B, Lee W R, McCallum R I and Murray R, 1987, *Hunter's Diseases of Occupations*, Hodder and Stoughton, London.

Siple P A and Passel C F, 1945, Measurement of Dry Atmospheric Cooling in Sub-Freezing Temperatures, *Proc Amer Phil Soc*, **89**, 177–199.

Youle A, 1995, The Thermal Environment, Chapter 12 in *Occupational Hygiene* (2nd edition), Harrington J M and Gardiner K (Eds), Blackwell Science, Oxford.

LEGISLATION

Management of Health and Safety at Work Regulations 1999 (SI 1999/3242)

Reporting of Injuries, Diseases and Dangerous Occurrences Regulations 1995 (SI 1995/3163)

Workplace (Health, Safety and Welfare) Regulations 1992 (SI 1992/3004)

8: Non-ionising radiation

INTRODUCTION

Over the last 75 years, there has been a vast increase in the number of man-made sources and applications of non-ionising radiation. This includes the many uses of laser and radio frequency radiation in industrial, scientific, medical and military applications. Considerable attention has been focused on the possible health effects of exposure to natural and man-made sources of non-ionising radiation. With current projections of a very large increase in the personal use of devices which create non-ionising radiation, especially the mobile phone, this is likely to be an increasingly important subject of interest.

The electromagnetic spectrum

From Figure 8.1, it can be seen that the electromagnetic (EM) spectrum can be divided into different regions and that any specific location can be characterised by:

1. **Wavelength** – the distance between the ends of one complete cycle of a wave.
2. **Frequency** – the number of complete wave cycles that pass a point in space in one unit of time. The time is normally one second with units in hertz (Hz).
3. **Photon energy** – the energy possessed by a discrete quantum or packet of radiation. This is measured in electronvolts (eV). (Photon energy is generally only of significance for non-ionising radiation in the ultraviolet region.)

The non-ionising radiation spectrum is very large, spanning about 15 orders of magnitude in frequency and wavelength. It includes the low frequency, radio frequency (RF), infrared (IR), visible and ultraviolet (UV) regions. It is common practice to describe the IR, visible and UV regions in terms of 'wavelength' and the low frequency/RF region in terms of 'frequency' (see Table 8.1).

NON-IONISING RADIATION

FIGURE 8.1: The electromagnetic spectrum

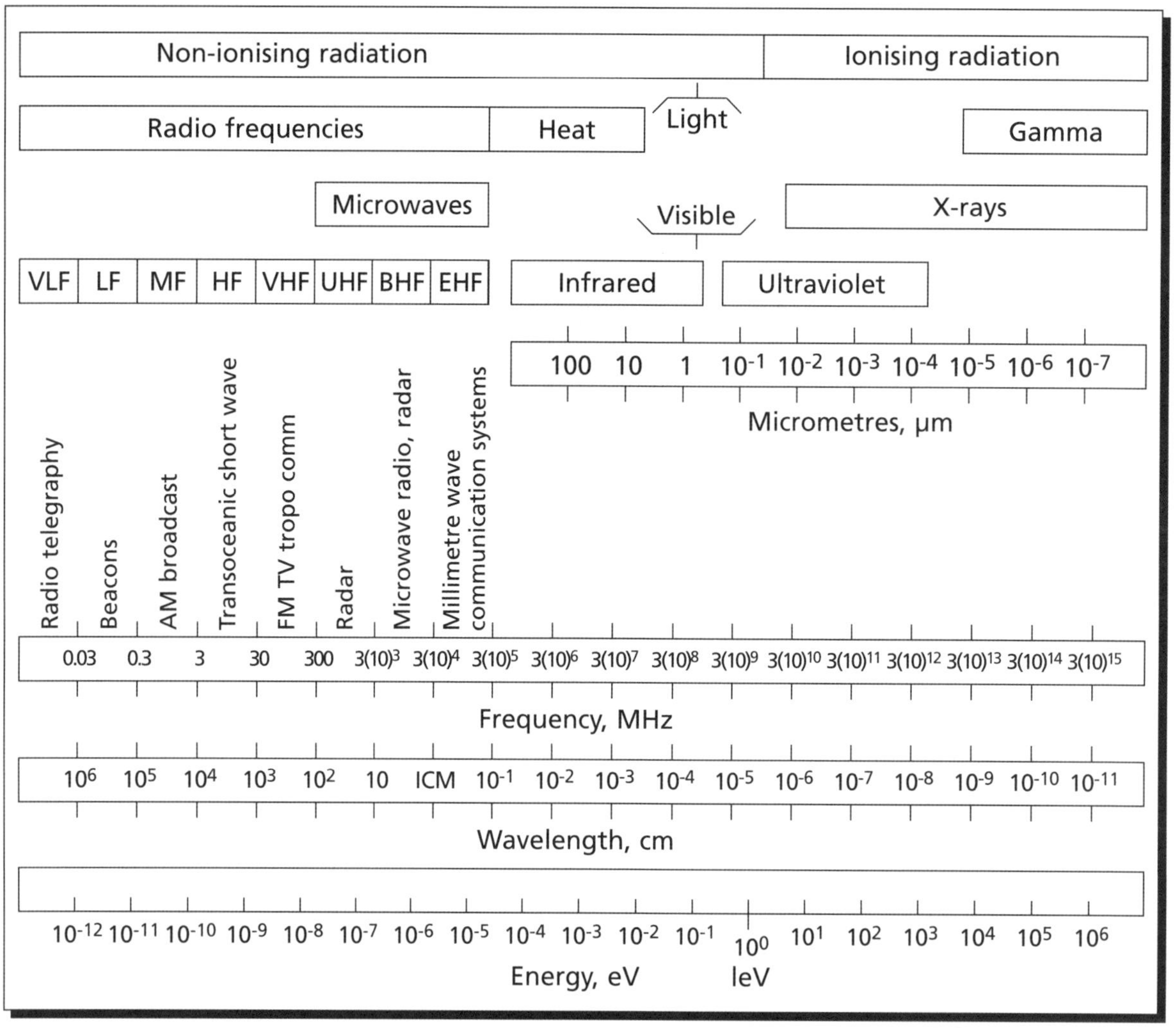

(After Mumford 1969)

Non-ionising radiation basics

Electromagnetic fields

Electric and magnetic fields, radiowaves, light, X-rays and gamma rays are all manifestations of electromagnetism.

Electromagnetic radiation is the transfer of energy through space (ie across a vacuum) and matter at a speed of $3 \times 10^8 ms^{-1}$, that is, the speed of light through space. This energy is generated by the acceleration of charged particles. There are two ways of visualising the transfer: as sinusoidal waves and as packets of energy called photons. When considered as waves, two wave fields (in phase) are identified: an electrical one and a magnetic one – at right angles to each other and at right angles to the direction of propagation (see Figure 8.2). A field line can be visualised by a theoretical cylindrical envelope surrounding the axis of propagation. A 'field' is a difficult concept; it may be defined as a region under the influence of either an electric charge or a magnetic dipole. An electromagnetic field has both magnitude and direction.

The frequency of the oscillations of a field best characterises its nature. The order of magnitude of these frequencies varies widely across the EM spectrum. These range from static fields through extremely low frequency (ELF) fields of 30–300Hz, to high energy gamma (γ) fields with frequencies of up to 10^{22}Hz. Electromagnetic radiation does not require any medium for its existence and it may be transmitted across a vacuum (unlike the transmission of sound waves). However, absorption, reflection, refraction and diffraction of the radiation can occur depending on the objects that it may encounter.

Electromagnetic waves obey the standard relationship between speed, wavelength and frequency, that is, speed = frequency x wavelength ($c = v\lambda$). This speed (c) is related to the frequency (v) in hertz and the wavelength (λ) in metres. They have the same speed in free space, that is, $3 \times 10^8 ms^{-1}$.

FIGURE 8.2: Electromagnetic radiation is composed of electric and magnetic fields

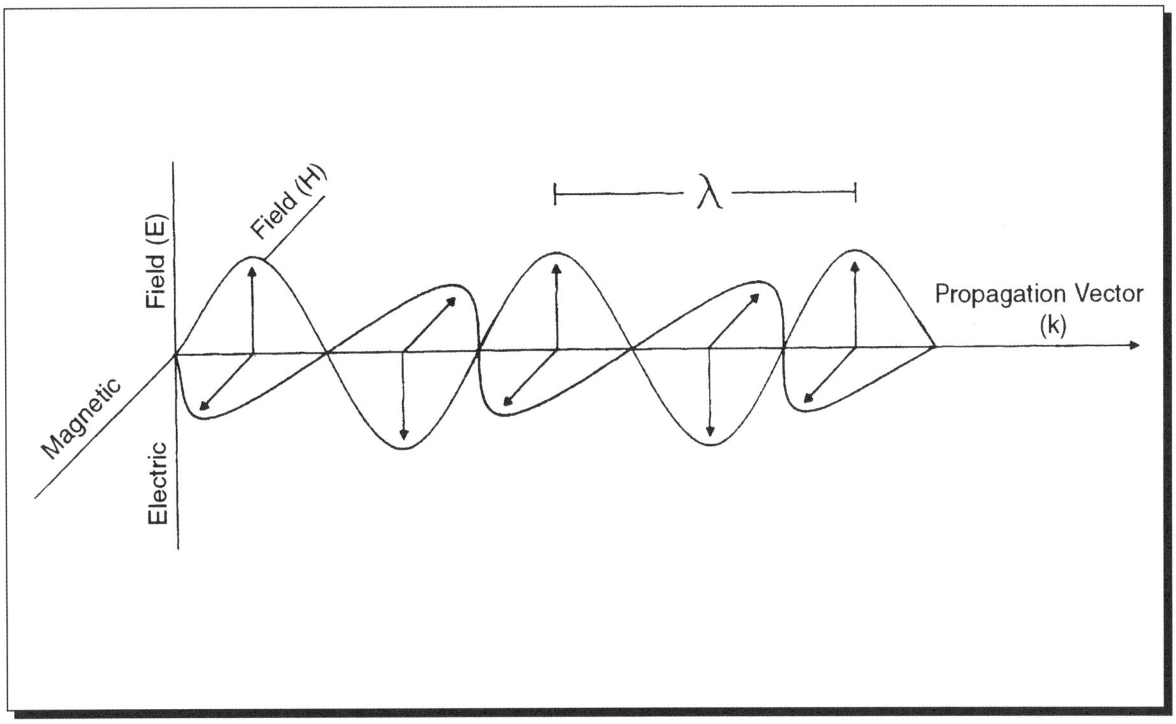

(After Sienkiewicz 1998)

If the radiation is travelling in a medium (rather than a vacuum), the speed is reduced by an amount which may depend on the frequency and the particular medium. With propagation through air, this change can normally be neglected.

At frequencies above 100kHz, fields are predominantly radiating, that is, dispersing energy from their source. At still higher frequencies, around those of the visible region, energy is emitted in quanta. The smallest quantum of energy is called a photon. The energy of a photon depends on the frequency of the electromagnetic radiation, as shown by the following expression:

$$\text{Energy} = \text{Planck's constant} \times \text{Frequency} \ (E = h\nu)$$

(Where: E is the energy in joules; h is Planck's constant (6.63×10^{-34} Js); and ν is the frequency.)

Electric and magnetic fields will exert a force on electric charges, and this is the basis for interactions with biological matter. Because the energies involved are so small, when considering the interaction of electromagnetic radiation with matter, a special energy unit is used for convenience, that is, the electronvolt (eV). An electronvolt is equivalent to 1.6×10^{-19} joules. This is the energy acquired by a single electron when accelerated through a potential difference of 1V. The EM spectrum (Figure 8.1) can be broadly divided into regions of ionising and non-ionising radiation, with the dividing line conventionally set at a photon energy of 12.4eV. This energy level is equivalent to the energy required to remove an electron from a hydrogen atom. Since hydrogen occurs in all biological material, photons of 12.4eV are thought to represent the lower energy limit for causing ionisation in biological systems.

For photons of 12.4eV, the frequency is 3×10^{15}Hz and the wavelength is 100nm (0.1µm).

This wavelength is near the middle of the ultraviolet region of the spectrum. At higher frequencies (ie above 3×10^{15}Hz), photons increasingly have sufficient energy to eject electrons from atoms, that is, to ionise them. This mechanism causes ionisation effects in biological tissues which are qualitatively different from those effects caused by the absorption of non-ionising radiation (see Chapter 9).

Risk assessment and management

Although an EC directive on physical agents is planned for the future, at present there is no specific

NON-IONISING RADIATION

UK legislation dealing with non-ionising radiation. However, the Health and Safety at Work etc Act 1974 and the Management of Health and Safety at Work Regulations 1999 (MHSW) apply in the case of exposure to non-ionising radiation. First, with the Health and Safety at Work etc Act 1974, section 2, there is the general duty of employers to protect the health of employees. Second, with the MHSW Regulations 1999, regulation 3, there is the duty to carry out a risk assessment for exposure to non-ionising radiation hazards and to make suitable arrangements for prevention and/or control, with reviews at appropriate intervals.

The risk assessment and management aspects for the non-ionising regions of the EM spectrum are discussed separately below. For this purpose, the non-ionising spectrum is divided into:
1. Low frequency radiation.
2. Radio frequency radiation.
3. Optical radiation including infrared radiation, visible radiation and ultraviolet radiation.

The characteristics of these regions are shown in Table 8.1. In the discussion below, low and radio frequency radiation will be identified by frequency, and optical radiation by wavelength. Later in this chapter, lasers are discussed as an important specialist application of optical radiation.

TABLE 8.1: The non-ionising electromagnetic spectrum

Spectral region		Frequency	Wavelength	Energy
Static fields				
Low frequencies		0–100kHz		
Radio frequencies		100kHz–300GHz		
Optical			Overall 1mm to 100nm	
Infrared	IR-C		1mm to 3μm	
	IR-B		3μm to 1.4μm	
	IR-A		1400nm to 780–760nm	
Light			780–760nm to 400–380nm	
Ultraviolet	UV-A		400–380nm to 315nm	
	UV-B		315nm to 280nm	
	UV-C		280nm to 100nm	
Nominal boundary				
Non-ionising and ionising radiations			100nm	12.4eV
Ionising radiation			Below 100nm	Above 12.4eV

Low frequency radiation

Low frequencies extend from zero (static fields) up to about 100kHz. Above 100kHz up to 300GHz is the zone of radio frequency radiation. Table 8.2 illustrates the range and uses of low frequency and radio frequency radiation.

In the low frequency region of the spectrum, electric and magnetic components are considered separately. Fields which oscillate at 'power' frequencies are called extremely low frequency (ELF) and these are found wherever electricity is supplied and used. The magnetic field arises from the alternating current (AC) and the electrical field arises from the alternating voltage. The electricity generation frequency is 50Hz in the UK, Europe and many other parts of the world, and 60Hz in North America. Below 100kHz, there is essentially no radiation (ie dispersion of energy) and, strictly speaking, 'non-ionising radiation' is an inappropriate label here.

The earth has a permanent static magnetic field and other examples are permanent magnets including magnetic resonance imaging (MRI) equipment and electrolytic processes using direct current. Static electrical fields arise where there is an accumulation of electric charge, for example, thunder clouds, in synthetic fibres, in visual display units, TV screens and near high-voltage direct current (DC) power systems.

TABLE 8.2: Low frequency and radio frequency radiation

Range	Frequency	Uses – Near field	Uses – Far field radiation
Extremely Low Frequency (ELF)	30Hz to 300Hz	Electric power systems, railways, industrial processes, melting	
Voice Frequency (VF)	300Hz to 3kHz	Electric furnaces, induction heating, hardening, melting	
Very Low Frequency (VLF)	3kHz to 30kHz	Induction heating, hardening, melting	Long-range radio navigation
Low Frequency (LF)	30kHz to 300kHz	Induction heating, melting, power inverters	Radio navigation
Medium Frequency (MF)	0.3MHz to 3MHz	Industrial RF equipment	AM broadcasting
High Frequency (HF)	3MHz to 30MHz	Medical diathermy, magnetic resonance imaging, wood drying and gluing, dielectric heating	Short wave radio
Very High Frequency (VHF)	30MHz to 300MHz	Magnetic resonance imaging, plastic welding, food processing, plasma heating	FM broadcasting, police, fire, air traffic control
Ultra High Frequency (UHF)	0.3GHz to 3GHz	Medical diathermy, cooking	TV broadcasting, microwave communications, mobile radio, mobile phones, radar
Super High Frequency (SHF)	3GHz to 30GHz		Radar, satellite communications, microwave relays, anti-intruder alarms
Extremely High Frequency (EHF)	30GHz to 300GHz		Radar, radio navigation, satellite communications, microwave relays

(Adapted from Maddock 1995)

Fields are often thought of as lines of force; electric field strength is expressed in volts per metre (Vm^{-1}) and magnetic field strength in amps per metre (Am^{-1}). For magnetic fields, the flux density in Teslas (T) is frequently used, since this most characterises the interaction of the field with conducting objects ($1\mu T = 10^{-2}$ Gauss (G), which approximates to $796 Am^{-1}$). Field strengths in the normal environment cover a very wide range, for example, at 50Hz, from $1-100 Vm^{-1}$ and $0.01-5mT$ up to at least $10kVm^{-1}$ and $1mT$ near heavy electrical plant. Both electric and magnetic field strength depend critically on the distance from the source and fall off rapidly, according to the inverse square law.

As a general rule, fields less than 1–2 wavelengths from a source, that is, in the near field, are non-radiating, while radiation occurs further away in the far field. In the near field, the electric and magnetic fields are treated separately, while in the far field these are coupled and are proportional to each other.

Health effects

At power frequencies, strong electric fields are perceived by a tingling of exposed skin or by the vibration of fine hairs on the back of the hand or neck. Occasionally, small electrical discharges occur between the edges of clothing and the skin, which are mainly perceived as an irritation. Induced currents may be felt if they are strong enough to stimulate nerve or muscle cells, with a threshold (10Hz to 1kHz) of $1Am^{-2}$ current density.

No adverse health effects have been established in such fields (Maddock 1995). In the past, some epidemiological studies have shown an association between childhood cancer and the proximity of homes to overhead power lines, and some did not. However, a five-year study in the UK (UKCCS 1999) did not find such an association between exposure to power frequency magnetic fields and childhood cancer (leukaemia). Other studies have also shown an increase in some cancers for 'electrical workers', but at present it is not clear whether this relates to electric or magnetic fields, or some other feature of working conditions. Electric and magnetic fields and radiations do not have sufficient energy to damage DNA directly (in the causation of cancer), but they may have other effects on the body and it has been suggested that they may 'promote' cancer which has been initiated by other factors.

According to the National Radiological Protection Board (NRPB) (1998), the international consensus is that there is insufficient available data for setting electric and magnetic field exposure standards relating to cancer promotion. Exposure guidelines for electric and magnetic fields, issued by the NRPB and others, are based on limiting or preventing acute health effects. For extremely low frequency (ELF) fields, as generated by power lines, these are effects on the central nervous system caused by the induction of electric currents in the body, or perception effects due to the build-up of electric charge on the surface of the body. In addition, there is a need to prevent shock effects arising from contact with metal objects in the field.

Measurement

Most low frequency electric field meters consist of two metal plates and a device to measure the induced current between them. Care needs to be taken with measurements of low frequency and static electric fields, as the presence of nearby objects and the person carrying out the measurements may influence results.

Tolerability of risk

Guideline values and limits from various different bodies have been proposed. The NRPB's Investigation Levels and the American Conference of Governmental Industrial Hygienists (ACGIH) Threshold Limit Values (TLVs) for static and low frequency electric and magnetic fields are given below (NRPB 1993; ACGIH 2002).

Investigation Levels

In 1993, the NRPB recommended the following Investigation Levels (Tables 8.3 and 8.4) for electric and magnetic fields over a frequency range of 0–12MHz. Investigation Levels are values provided for comparison with quantities measured in the field to investigate whether compliance with basic restrictions has been achieved. These guidelines are the same for exposure of workers as for members of the public.

TABLE 8.3: Investigation Levels – Electric fields (0–12MHz)[34]

Frequency range	Electric field strength E (Vm⁻¹)
<24Hz	25,000
24–600Hz	600/f (kHz)
600Hz–600kHz	1000
600kHz–12MHz	600/f (kHz)

(NRPB 1993)

---

[34] In Tables 8.3 and 8.4, the 'f' represents frequency.

TABLE 8.4: Investigation Levels – Magnetic fields (0–12MHz)

Frequency range	Magnetic field strength H (Am^{-1})	Magnetic flux (µT)
<0.4Hz	160,000	200,000
0.4–1kHz	64,000/f (Hz)	80,000/f (Hz)
1–535kHz	64	80
0.535–12MHz	18/f^2 (MHz)	23/f^2 (MHz)

(NRPB 1993)

Threshold Limit Values

Threshold Limit Value (TLV) standards have been proposed for static and low frequency radiation electric and magnetic fields.

TABLE 8.5: TLVs for sub-RF radiation exposure

Region of EM spectrum	Nature of exposure	TLV
Magnetic fields		
Static magnetic fields	Whole-body (routine)	60mT
	Whole-body (ceiling)	2T
Static magnetic fields	Limbs (routine)	600mT
	Limbs (ceiling)	5T
Static magnetic fields	Medical electronic device wearers (ceiling)	0.5mT
Magnetic fields (ELF) (1Hz to 300Hz)	Whole-body (ceiling) (The exposure of the extremities can be increased by a factor of 10 (hands and feet) and a factor of 5 (arms and legs))	60/f mT (f = frequency in Hz)
Magnetic fields (300Hz to 30kHz)	Partial and whole-body (ceiling)	0.2mT
Electric fields		
Static/electric fields (0Hz to 100Hz)	Partial and whole-body (ceiling)	25kV/m
Electric fields (100Hz to 4kHz)	Partial and whole-body (ceiling)	2.5 x 10^6/f
Electric fields (4kHz to 30kHz)	Partial and whole-body (ceiling)	625kV/m

(Adapted from ACGIH 2002)

Strong electric fields may interfere with the operation of some implanted pacemakers and suitable precautions need to be taken in the use of these. According to the ACGIH (2002), pacemaker wearers should not be exposed to magnetic field levels exceeding 0.5mT (5G).

Control

Electric fields can be reduced or screened either beside the source or around the person. With work on live high-voltage electric power lines, it is necessary to use personal conducting suits. This is a complete body ensemble fabricated with conducting fibre, which charges up during line working. It operates as a Faraday cage and there is no electric field within the suit. This will protect the operator during line working and when engaging and disengaging with a live line. Magnetic fields in the low frequency radiation region are more difficult to control and a thick sheet of aluminium may be needed to protect potentially exposed personnel.

Radio frequency radiation

This is defined as any frequency where electromagnetic radiation is used for telecommunication, that

is, 100kHz to 300GHz, which includes microwaves. Based on its uses, RF radiation may be conveniently divided into two categories:
1. Uses which rely on the radiated nature of the waves (far field), eg radio and TV broadcasting.
2. Uses where the electromagnetic fields are used close to the source or confined in some way (near field), eg heating applications.

The strengths of the electric and magnetic fields vary widely. At the lower frequencies of this region, the electric and magnetic fields must still be considered separately, but as the frequency increases, they become increasingly coupled together until true radiation is dominant. Which aspect dominates depends on several factors including the wavelength, distance from the source and the size of the source. The region close to the source is known as the 'near field' and consists of non-propagating and radiating components, depending on the specific situation. At the more distant 'far field', only the radiating component still persists.

The field intensities vary inversely with the square of the distance from the source, hence, the power density varies with the square of the distance from the source. Power density is the quantity of radiation arriving at a surface (with time) divided by the cross-sectional area of that surface. This is illustrated in Figure 8.3. Power density is normally expressed in Wm^{-2} or $mWcm^{-2}$. Absorption of energy in biological tissue is characterised by the Specific Absorption Rate (SAR) expressed in Wkg^{-1}. With the absorption of higher frequency radiation in thin layers, an absorbed power density is used, expressed in Wm^{-2}.

FIGURE 8.3: Application of the inverse square law for a point source of radiation

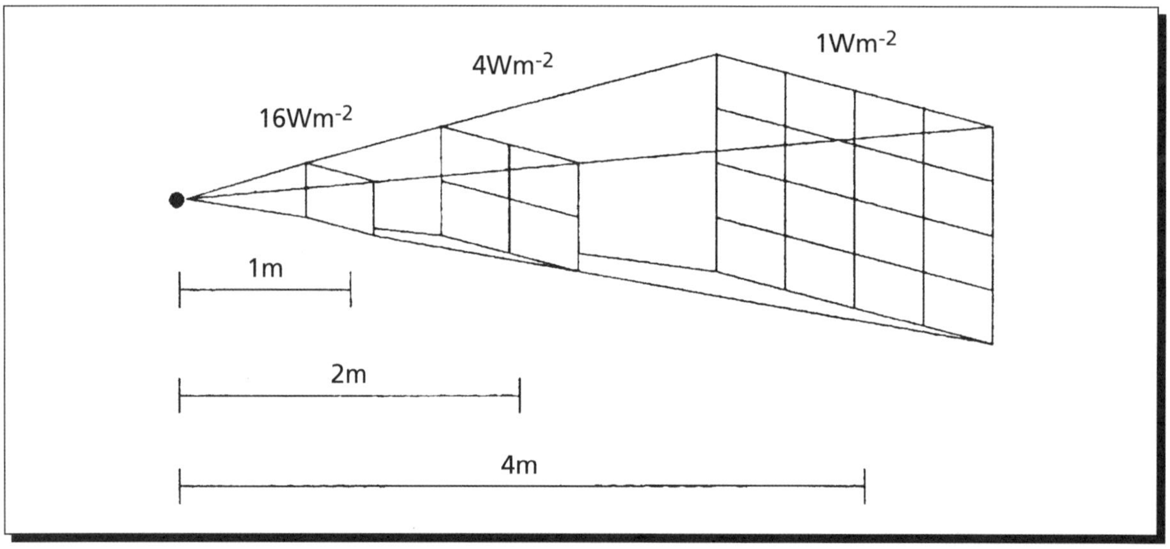

(Hitchcock 1998)

Health effects

The principal health effect from RF radiation exposure is an increased body temperature. As with low frequency radiation, RF fields can induce voltages on objects, which if touched cause burns resulting from discharge current. Currents may be induced in conducting objects including people, which result in heating effects. The thermoregulatory system adjusts, up to a point, by increasing blood flow to the skin surface and by the evaporation of sweat, both enhancing body heat loss. Above a SAR of $4Wkg^{-1}$, this becomes more difficult and hyperthermia may result in the exposed person. In an international context, there are more exposure standards for RF fields than for low frequency fields. According to Maddock (1995), a consensus has developed on this. A whole-body SAR of $0.4Wkg^{-1}$ is widely accepted to be about one-tenth the absorption level where significant changes in body temperature occur. If the absorption is restricted to a region of the body, for example, a limb, then considerably higher values can be tolerated. However, in some parts of the body, for example, the eye, heat removal is markedly poor and here lower SARs need to be applied. This is primarily a problem at higher frequencies where absorption is at the surface of the body with burns and other tissue damage occurring.

It is generally accepted that overheating effects pose a health hazard to exposed people. Maddock (1995) acknowledges suggestions of potentially harmful, non-thermal health effects at levels of field or power densities well below those associated with overheating. However, he asserts the current expert consensus that harmful non-thermal effects have not been scientifically established.

Measurement

It is convenient to divide RF radiation monitoring equipment into the two following categories:
1. Equipment where the field is sensed and displayed as power density.
2. The quantity of power is absorbed and a thermistor or thermocouple measures the resulting proportional temperature rise.

Most measurement devices respond to broad frequency bands of non-ionising radiation.

Tolerability of risk

A whole-body Specific Absorption Rate (SAR) of $0.4Wkg^{-1}$ is generally accepted to be about one-tenth the absorption level where significant changes in body temperature occur. Exposure guidelines have been proposed by various authoritative bodies, which seek to define a tolerable SAR in terms of measurable quantities such as field strength and power density.

There are around 47 million mobile phones and 35,000 base relay stations currently in use in the UK. Following public concern, an independent expert group has recently reviewed the evidence and concluded that thermal effects remain the best basis for setting exposure limits for RF radiation (NRPB 2000). The International Commission on Non-ionising Radiation Protection (ICNIRP) has proposed limits for exposure to RF radiation (100kHz to 10GHz), as a whole-body SAR, of $0.4Wkg^{-1}$ for people at work and $0.08Wkg^{-1}$ for the general public averaged over any six-minute period (ICNIRP 1998). Other specific localised SAR values are proposed for 'head and trunk' and 'limbs'. Following the report of an independent expert group (NRPB 2000), the NRPB supports these limits.

Threshold Limit Values

The Threshold Limit Values (TLVs) for RF/microwave radiation (ACGIH 2002) are expressed in terms of root-mean-square (rms) electric (E) and magnetic (H) field strengths, equivalent power densities (S) and induced currents (I) in the body associated with exposure to such fields. The TLVs are given in Tables 8.6 and 8.7 and Figure 8.4 as a function of frequency (f) in MHz. The TLVs in Table 8.6 refer to exposures obtained by spatially averaging over an area equivalent to the vertical cross-section of the human body. In the case of partial body exposure, these TLVs can be relaxed. Access should be restricted to limit induced and contact RF body currents and potential for electrostimulation (Table 8.7).

TABLE 8.6: Threshold Limit Values for whole-body RF/microwave radiation (I)

Region of EM spectrum	Power density (S) ($mWcm^{-2}$)	Electric field** strength (Vm^{-1})	Magnetic field** strength (Am^{-1})	Averaging time (minutes)
30kHz to 100kHz		614	163	6
100kHz to 3MHz		614	16.3/f*	6
3MHz to 30MHz		1842/f*	16.3/f*	6
30MHz to 100MHz		61.4	16.3/f*	6
100MHz to 300MHz	1	61.4	0.163	6
300MHz to 3GHz	f/300*			6
3GHz to 15GHz	10			6
15GHz to 300GHz	10			$616,000/f^{1.2}$*

*f is frequency in MHz
**Whole-body exposure values measured as electric and magnetic field strengths are obtained by spatially averaging values over an area equivalent to the vertical cross-section of the human body

NON-IONISING RADIATION

TABLE 8.7: Induced and contact RF currents – Maximum current (mA)

Frequency	Through both feet	Through either foot	Contact	Averaging time
30kHz to 100kHz	2000f	1000f	1000f	1 second
100kHz to 100MHz	200	100	100	6 minutes

The ACGIH (2002) asserts that these represent conditions under which nearly all workers may be repeatedly exposed without adverse health effects. These values are to be averaged over six-minute periods, apart for radiation above 15GHz, which is computed as shown. Higher exposure values may be permitted where absorption is confined to a restricted region of the body and specific peak SARs are cited for body tissues in general, the hands, wrists, feet and ankles.

FIGURE 8.4: Threshold Limit Values for RF/microwave radiation (II)*

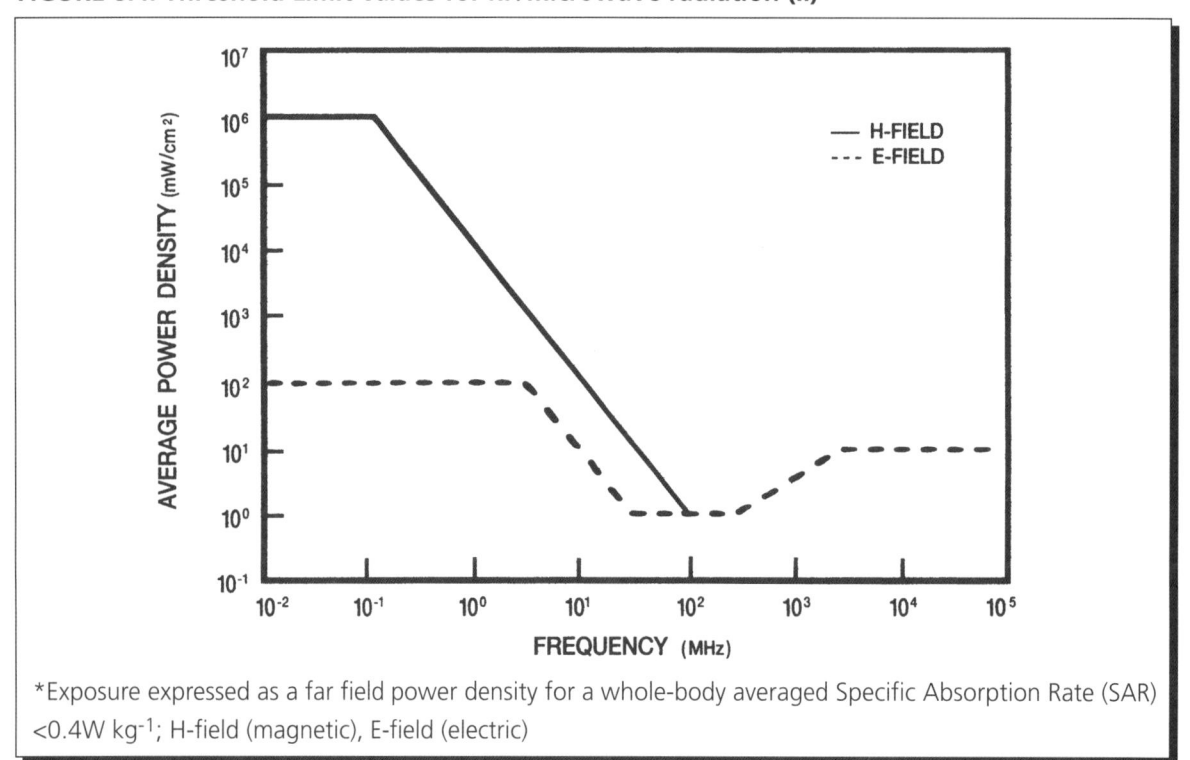

*Exposure expressed as a far field power density for a whole-body averaged Specific Absorption Rate (SAR) <0.4W kg^{-1}; H-field (magnetic), E-field (electric)

(From ACGIH®, 2002 TLVs® and BEIs® book. Copyright 2002. Reprinted with permission.)

These guidelines for power levels are for application in moderate thermal environments; under moderate to severe heat stress conditions, the guide numbers need to be appropriately reduced.

Prevention and control measures

Prevention and control measures for limiting occupational exposures to radio frequencies are shown in Table 8.8. Careful design and siting of RF radiation sources are very important for limiting exposure.

TABLE 8.8: Controlling exposure to RF emissions

Type of control
Engineering controls
• Directional aerials for communication systems
• Reduction of stray RF fields from industrial heating equipment
• Effective earthing of equipment and metal objects
• Screening out radio frequencies using metallic meshes (the mesh is smaller than the wavelength of the radiation), eg the perforated screens on the doors of microwave ovens
• Using absorptive material to avoid undesired reflective effects

Table continued opposite

NON-IONISING RADIATION

Administrative controls
• Exclusion of personnel from high-field areas
• Provision of warning signs
• Safe systems of work

Personal controls
• Provision of information, instruction and training, particularly about potential biological effects
• PPE including RF protective clothing (polyester fabric around stainless steel fibres), eye protection, insulating gloves and rubber-soled shoes

Optical radiation

Optical radiation is usually characterised by its wavelength rather than its frequency. The optical radiation range extends from a wavelength of 1mm, at the end of the RF range, through the infrared, visible and ultraviolet regions, down to a wavelength of around 100nm, which overlaps with the bottom of the soft X-ray region. As noted above, radiation with wavelengths of less than 100nm make up the ionising part of the spectrum. The principal wavelength regions of the optical region are given in Table 8.1. Although the regions of optical radiation are considered separately here, many sources radiate over a broad range of wavelengths and hazards should be considered separately and collectively for possible synergistic effects.

FIGURE 8.5: Health effects of optical radiation

	UV-C 100 to 280NM	UV-B 280 to 315NM	UV-A 315 to 380–400NM	Visible light 380–400 to 760–780NM	IR-A 760–780 to 1400NM	IR-B 1400 to 3000NM	IR-C 3000 to 10^6NM
Skin	Erythema Increased pigmentation Faster skin ageing Cancer	Erythema Increased pigmentation Faster skin ageing Cancer	Erythema Increased pigmentation Darkening of pigment Photosensitivity Faster skin ageing Cancer	Burn Darkening of pigment Photosensitivity	Burn	Burn	Burn
Eye	Photokeratitis	Photokeratitis Cataract (Photochemical)		Retinal damage Photochemical retinal damage	Burn (cornea) Cataracts (thermal) Retinal damage	Burn (cornea) Cataracts (thermal)	Burn (cornea)

Infrared radiation

Thermal effects are associated with radiation exposure throughout the infrared (IR) region and into the red end of the visible spectrum. The skin and the eye are principal targets and consequent health effects are summarised in Figure 8.5. The main hazard to both target sites is from heating effects. Normal reflexes, for example, blinking, eye movement and turning the head away, provide reasonable protection except in the case of strong laser sources.

The three components of the IR radiation region are: IR-C (1mm to 3μm); IR-B (3μm to 1.4μm); and IR-A (1,400nm to 760–780nm). With exposure to IR-C radiation, a corneal burn may result, since the cornea is opaque to radiation in this region and shields the rest of the eye. In addition, the natural film of tears provides an important cooling mechanism for the eye. In the IR-A and IR-B regions, corneal absorption is lower and there is significant absorption in the lens and adjacent tissues. Prolonged exposure to IR-A/IR-B radiation causes chronic lenticular opacity (thermal cataracts) and in the past 'glassblower's cataract' was a common condition in this group of workers. According to Maddock (1995), there is little evidence that IR-A and IR-B arising from modern sources, for example, welding activities, are a significant cause of cataracts. In the IR-A and visible region, radiation will reach the retina and it is usually focused on it. This results in a greatly increased level of irradiation and an intense source may lead to retinal damage due to local burning.

Visible radiation

This visible region is characterised by light radiation with a wavelength range of 780–760nm to 400–380nm. It can be seen from Figure 8.5 that the main target sites for overheating effects are the eye and the skin. Radiation at the blue end of the spectrum is a hazard to the retina and can result in photochemical damage. As noted above, the eye is protected by normal aversion responses from the extreme effects of intense light and IR sources. When the eye is subject to high levels of illumination, particularly in an unchanging field, then retinal degeneration occurs and it is probable that repeated exposure to ambient light plays a role in the ageing process. Although humans are well adapted to living in sunlight, this radiation source still causes damage to the eye. Furthermore, some artificial light sources, such as lasers, may cause harm within the time of the aversion reflex.

Ultraviolet radiation

The properties of ultraviolet (UV) radiation are used in a range of applications including arc welding (carbon, xenon and other arcs), polymerising systems in printing and dentistry, and sterilisation in the food industry (bacterial lamps).

The UV radiation region extends over the wavelength range from 400nm to 100nm. For direct harmful effects, 200nm can be regarded as a practical limit, since optical radiation at shorter wavelengths is only transmitted through a vacuum and it is attenuated by passage through the air. Short wavelength UV radiation creates another hazard when propagated through air, since it partially converts oxygen into ozone, a toxic gas.

Health effects

UV radiation is non-penetrating and it causes damage at the surface of the skin and eyes. Most body surface epithelial cells are replaced every one to two days and, therefore, superficial damage is repaired quickly. However, harmful changes at a deeper level take longer to repair. Acute effects include skin pigment darkening (associated with UV-A radiation) and 'tanning' with the production of extra melanin and the migration of melanin from deeper to surface layers in the skin (associated with UV-B radiation). Sunburn or erythema is the most obvious acute result from excessive UV radiation exposure.

Much of the ageing, that is, the coarsening, drying and wrinkling of skin, is attributed to long-term exposure to sunlight and specifically its constituent UV radiation. This interaction involves complex photochemical and biochemical reactions which produce the initial reddening and some tanning.

The most serious chronic effect of exposure to UV radiation is the development of several types of skin cancer. UV, particularly UV-B, is associated with the relatively common non-melanoma type of skin cancer. For most people this will be due to solar UV radiation. The more serious malignant melanoma is believed to be associated with exposure to high levels of solar UV-A, particularly at an early age. In this context, non-tanning white populations living in tropical climates are an identified high-risk group. Where a person works intermittently with UV sources, it is likely that their background solar exposure to UV is relatively much more important. The individual risk of malignant melanoma is higher in people with a large number of moles on the skin, who sunburn easily and tan poorly or where there is a family history.

The eye is also a target site and photo-keratitis (inflammation and damage to the cornea and conjunctivitis) occurs with exposure throughout the UV region, especially to UV-B and UV-C radiation with a threshold level of 30Jm^{-2}. Snow blindness (from strong, scattered blue and UV radiation) and welder's arc eye can occur with exposures at just above this threshold. Symptoms occur after several hours and persist for a few days. For direct sunlight, but not necessarily for occupational exposure to UV, the cornea is reasonably well protected by the position of the eye. Only a small proportion of UV radiation reaches the retina because of absorption in the anterior part of the eye. For people who have had a lens removed (aphakes) and for children, the risk to the retina from UV-A radiation exposure is higher.

Chronic effects of excessive UV exposure include photochemical cataract of the lens of the eye and, in animal studies, exposure to UV-B radiation has been demonstrated to induce lenticular opacities at 5,000Jm^{-2}. According to Wilkening (1991), an important conclusion about the effects of exposure to UV on biological systems is that tissue damage appears to depend on the total energy absorbed (dose) rather than the rate of energy absorption. Hence, the essential aim is to suitably control dose to give adequate protection.

Measurement

The biological effects of optical radiation clearly depend heavily on the particular wavelength or waveband under consideration. Complete assessment of a source or location may require sophisticated spectoradiometers to obtain the irradiance spectrum of interest. Spectral filters are available for simpler measurement devices, which may be used in many situations. Dose may be assessed by a variety of methods, for example, a film badge is available for assessing UV exposure dose.

For the longer IR wavelengths, thermal measurement devices are normally employed. The principle is that the incident energy increases the temperature of the absorbing medium in the measurement device, which is calibrated and displayed. These devices tend to be broadband, slower in response and not particularly sensitive. Photonic detectors respond to the photons of incident radiation and can be fast, sensitive but with narrower bandwidths.

Tolerability of risk

For IR and visible sources of radiation, there are no internationally agreed standards for exposure from non-laser sources. The TLV system (ACGIH 2002) has adopted standards for occupational exposure to optical radiation including IR, visible and UV regions. The avoidance of thermal injury to the eye and photochemical injury to the retina are the basis of these standards.

Threshold Limit Values

For the near-UV spectral region (UV-A, wavelength 400nm to 315nm), an exposure of the unprotected eye should not exceed 1.0mWcm^{-2} for periods greater than 10^3 seconds and 1.0Jcm^{-2} for exposure times of less than 10^3 seconds (ACGIH 2002). The TLV standard for exposure to UV radiation over the wider wavelength range of 400nm to 180nm is also specified for unprotected skin or eyes. This standard takes into account the relative biological effectiveness of UV radiation at different wavelengths. The standard also gives a formula for determining exposure standards for broadband sources.

These values apply to the exposure of the eye or skin from various UV sources, including arc and gas welding, fluorescent and incandescent sources and solar radiation, but excluding lasers. These limits should not be applied to the exposure of identified photosensitive individuals nor where there is simultaneous exposure to other photosensitising agents. In addition, these values should not be applied to aphakes (people who have had a lens removed, for example, following cataract surgery).

ICNIRP guideline

Maddock (1995) cites the occupational standard for UV exposure proposed by the ICNIRP which contains the following restrictions:
   1. Unprotected exposure of skin at all UV wavelengths and of unprotected eyes to UV-B and UV-C should not exceed 30Jm^{-2} over an eight-hour period.

2. Total exposure of the eye to UV-A radiation should not exceed $10 Jm^{-2}$ over an eight-hour period.

Prevention and control measures

The major concern with exposure to optical radiation is the protection of the skin and the eyes from excessive exposures. Where elimination of the source is not possible, control measures include the provision of effective enclosures and reflective screens, control by distance from source and personal protective equipment. These should be complemented by administrative measures including provision of appropriate systems of work and information, instruction and training for exposed personnel.

Enclosures and reflective screens

Exposure to optical radiation can be controlled by the use of enclosures and reflective screens. Where UV radiation is present, then suitable glass or plastic absorbers are required to attenuate the source.

Distance

The radiating power of a source is inversely proportional to the square of the distance from the source, so that safety may be attained by removal of exposed personnel to a suitable distance. Maddock (1995) cautions that special care must be taken with retinal hazards because of the focusing mechanism of the eye, which means harmful levels may occur over a small area of the retina.

Personal protective equipment (PPE)

It may be necessary for personnel to wear personal protective equipment (PPE), for example, sun hats, glasses and protective clothing, if prolonged exposure to outdoor sources of sunlight is likely. Not all fabrics provide adequate shielding for UV and this is particularly the case when they are wet. Reflective clothing may be necessary where there are strong radiant sources.

Similarly, goggles may be necessary where there is exposure to strong light sources. Care must be taken to ensure that the temperature rise in any goggles does not facilitate re-radiation of energy to the cornea. Goggles with an outer reflective coating can be used to protect against this possibility.

Helmets and face shields with filter windows are also available for this purpose and these are used in welding and plasma spraying. Some are now fitted with auto-darkening filters. Here, the welder can see the work immediately before lighting the arc. Their use means that welders do not have to raise and lower their visors repeatedly. These auto-darkening applications are still being developed and it is necessary to ensure that the darkening speed is fast enough for the work in hand. Switching times of 100μs are now available.

Lasers

The laser is a device which emits radiation as an intense beam of light of a very narrow wavelength spread. (The acronym 'LASER' stands for Light Amplification by Stimulated Emission Radiation.) Electromagnetic radiation is emitted over the wavelength range of 400nm to 700nm, as visible light, and where above 0.7μm, as invisible optical radiation. The intense beam of light can vaporise the hardest and most resistant of materials. These devices are used in many different sectors including manufacturing, retail, research, medicine, dentistry, the security industry, discotheques and other entertainment venues. Lasers have many applications including, deep penetration welding, drilling holes in diamonds, microsurgery, holography, and optical fibre communications and display equipment.

There are different types of laser and the degree of hazard varies with the characteristics of the particular equipment. The hazard will depend on:
- the wavelength of the transmitted radiation;
- the energy content of the radiation; and
- the pulse length of the laser beam.

FIGURE 8.6: Laser displays

(HSE 1996)

Lasers generate almost parallel beams of radiation (low divergence) with a narrow wavelength spread (monochromatic) and the light is all in phase in space and time. Light radiation may be reflected, diffracted and refracted. Lasers are particularly hazardous to the eye and the skin because they generate high brightness and high energies which they can deliver to the body from a long range.

Laser radiation may cause the same biological effects as optical radiation except that damage may be more severe because of the high energy densities and extreme localisation. Dangerous reflections of laser radiation also need to be prevented because they can be more hazardous than those from conventional light sources.

Health effects

The health hazards of lasers are principally surface (skin) burning and damage to the eye. The damage caused by surface burning depends on the level of incident energy falling per unit area of surface and this is illustrated in Figure 8.7. Retinal images of only a few microns are typical and this means that the power density of the radiation entering the eye may have been multiplied by 100,000 because of the focusing effect of the lens. Damage to the central field of view of the retina may cause severe and permanent damage to vision.

NON-IONISING RADIATION

FIGURE 8.7: Direct laser viewing

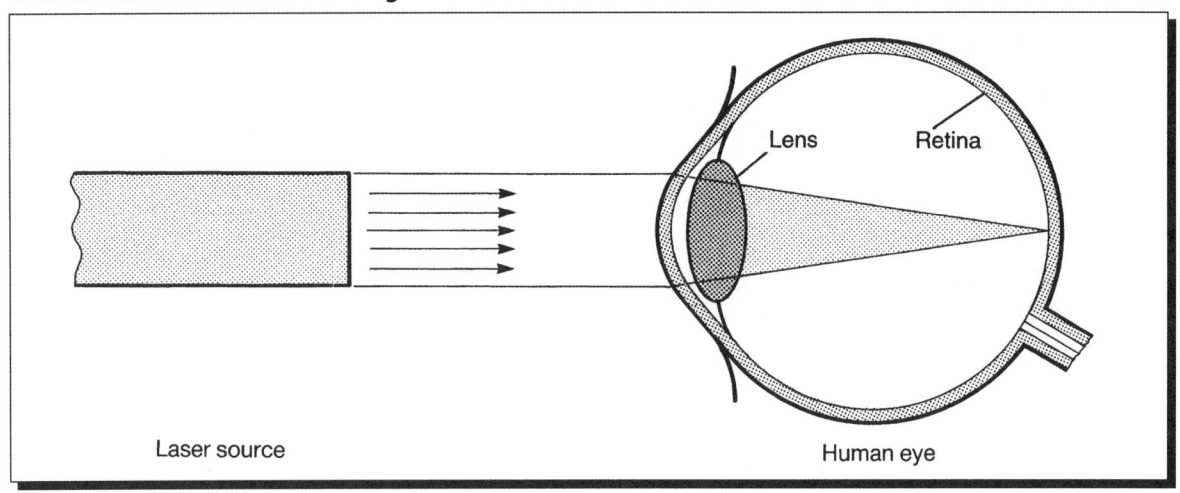

(HSE 1996)

Viewing a non-coherent source such as a light bulb forms an extended image on the retina, rather than a narrowly focused point image, with a much lower power density than that generated by the laser.

FIGURE 8.8: Extended source viewing

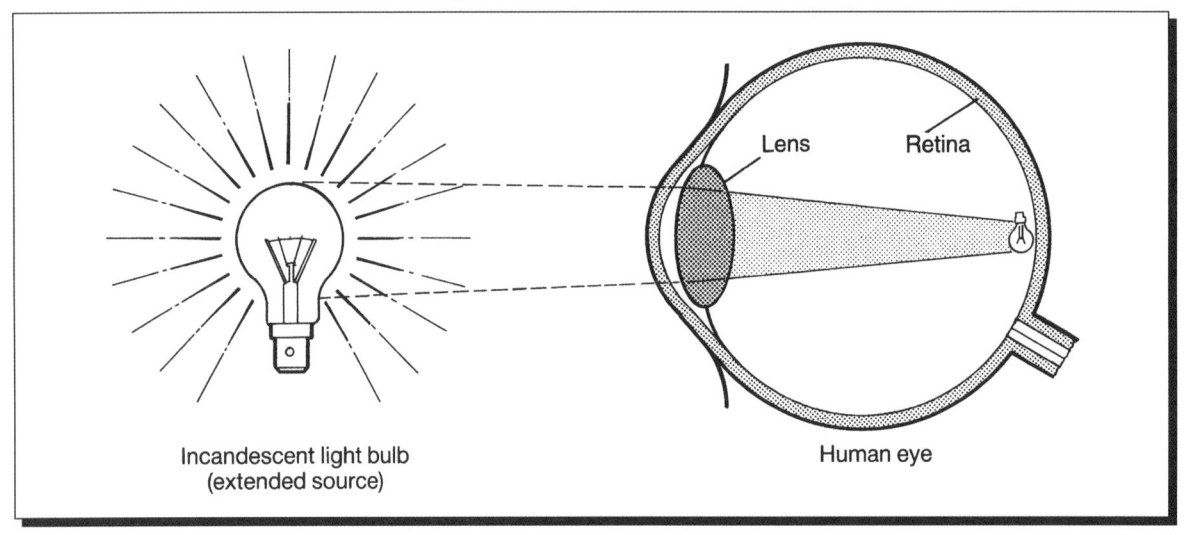

(HSE 1996)

Laser powers of a few milliwatts can damage the retina before the protective natural aversion reflex can occur. Effects on the eye vary from mild retinal burns to permanent blindness. Laser emissions may cause cataracts, and the likelihood of this depends on the quantity and duration of radiation exposure.

Laser devices

With general optical radiation, a large number of photons are emitted spontaneously, distributed randomly in time. In contrast, with laser stimulation of atoms or molecules, the consequent photons are coherent in phase with time and space. This results in radiation with a very specific wavelength.

A laser has three basic components:

1. **Initial source of energy** – this may be electrical, optical or chemical.
2. **Lasing medium** – this consists of atoms where electrons are raised to a higher energy level and stimulated to emit energy and return to a lower level.
3. **Resonance produced at the designated wavelength** – this is generated by placing a mirror at each end of the lasing medium and the radiation is reflected many times. One mirror only partially reflects and this allows some of the energy to emerge in a beam of light radiation.

Classes of laser

A classification system for lasers has been developed which aims to ensure that these devices are used safely with minimum effort (see Table 8.9). Most laser users will not have to make exposure measurements and can concentrate on developing safe working practices appropriate to the class of the laser. This classification system takes into account the capacity of the laser as well as the protective features provided. The manufacturer must determine the class of the laser, label it and provide the necessary user information (BSI 1994).

TABLE 8.9: Classes of lasers and their hazards

Class	Specification	Hazard
1	Lasers that are inherently safe, either due to low output power or protective features, eg totally enclosed system	No hazard to eye or skin
2	Low power devices which emit visible radiation; not inherently safe but eye protection normally by the aversion response, including the blink; not capable of causing damage to the skin	Eye hazard if viewed for more than 0.25 seconds (blink response); no skin hazard
3A	Emit higher levels of radiation; higher power in beam of larger cross-section; output viewed directly; the power of the beam entering the eye does not exceed Class 2; low/medium power lasers	Eye hazard with optical aids; no skin hazard
3B	Output invisible (ie no aversion response) or beam power causes damage in a shorter period than the blink reaction (<0.25 seconds)	Capable of causing eye injury; high power lasers in this class may also cause skin burns; for those lasers which do not emit UV, there would be sufficient discomfort to expect skin withdrawal
4	Most hazardous class of laser with high power devices	May cause immediate injury to the eyes and skin; exposure to diffuse reflections may be hazardous

(After Maddock 1995)

FIGURE 8.9: Laser classification system

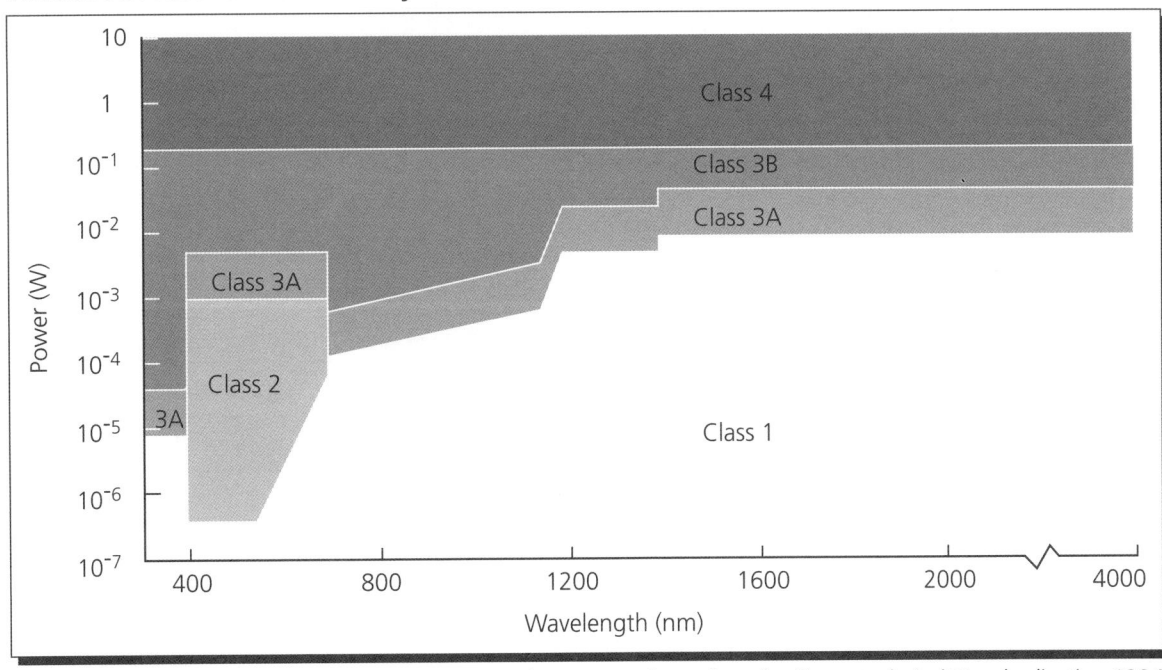

(International Electrotechnical Commission 1993 and European Committee for Electrotechnical Standardization 1994)

Measurements

The measurement of laser emissions is a complicated process requiring sophisticated equipment because of the wide range of conditions met and there are many sources of error in such evaluations. As noted above, the manufacturer's classification of a device should, in most instances, allow safe systems to be applied without the actual measurement of emissions.

Tolerability standards

These standards are complicated and difficult to interpret. There is a wide range of possible biological effects associated with exposure to lasers. These effects are dependent on many factors including, wavelength, power, pulse duration and beam geometry. The ACGIH (2002) has published TLV standards for laser emissions for both ocular (ie of the eye) and skin exposures. These encompass IR, light and UV exposures arising specifically from viewing a laser beam.

Prevention and control measures

Prevention and control measures applied to laser operations are listed in Table 8.10 and these are generally applied to the different classes of laser device as shown in Table 8.11. The principal aim is to prevent exposure of the eye and the skin to laser emissions.

TABLE 8.10: Prevention and control measures

Type of measure	Measure
Administrative	Organisation; appointment of laser safety officers; designated users; controlled areas; warning signs; information, instruction and training
Engineering	Control at source; interlocked safety enclosures; remote interlocks; key control; physical barriers; emergency stop buttons
Personal	Eye protection; other protective clothing and equipment; medical surveillance

TABLE 8.11: Control measures when using lasers

Protective measure	Laser class				
	1	2	3A	3B	4
Remote interlock	Not required		Connect to door		
Key control	Not required		Remove key when laser not in use		
Beam attenuator	Not required		Prevents inadvertent exposure		
Emission indicator	Not required		Indication required		
Warning signs	Not required	Provide signs plus precautions			
Beam termination	Not required	Terminate beam			
Specular reflection	No hazard	Care required	Prevent unwanted reflections		
Eye protection	No special precautions			Special precautions required	
Protective clothing	No special precautions			Sometimes req'd	Recomm'ed
Training	Not necessary		Required for all users		

(Adapted from Ashton & Gill 2000)

REFERENCES

American Conference of Governmental Industrial Hygienists, 1990, *A Guide for Control of Laser Hazards*, ACGIH, Cincinatti, OH, USA.

American Conference of Governmental Industrial Hygienists, 2002, *Threshold Limit Values for Chemical and Physical Agents and Biological Exposure Indices*, ACGIH, Cincinnati, OH, USA.

Ashton I and Gill F S, 2000, *Monitoring for Health Hazards at Work* (3rd edition), Blackwell Science, Oxford.

British Standards Institution, 1994, *Safety of Laser Products: Equipment Classification, Requirements and User's Guide*, BS EN 60825-1, BSI, London.

European Committee for Electrotechnical Standardization, 1994, *Safety of Laser Products, Equipment Classification, Requirements and User's Guide*, EN 60825-1, CENELEC, Brussels.

Health and Safety Executive, 1996, *The Radiation Safety of Lasers Used for Display Purposes*, HS(G)95, HSE Books, Sudbury.

Hitchcock R T, 1998, *General Concepts for Non-Ionising Radiation Protection*, American Industrial Hygiene Association, AIHA Press.

International Commission on Non-Ionising Radiation Protection, 1998, Guidelines for Limiting Exposure to Time-Varying Electric, Magnetic and Electromagnetic Fields (up to 300GHz), ICNIRP, *Health Physics*, **74**, 494–522.

International Electrotechnical Commission, 1993, *Safety of Laser Products, Equipment Classification, Requirements and User's Guide*, IEC 825-1, IEC, Geneva.

Maddock B J, 1995, Non-Ionising Radiation, Chapter 13 in *Occupational Hygiene* (2nd edition), Harrington J M and Gardiner K (Eds), Blackwell Science, Oxford.

Mumford S S, 1969, Heat Stress Due to RF Radiation, *Proceedings IEEE 57*, 171–178.

National Radiological Protection Board, 1993, Restrictions on Human Exposure to Static and Time-Varying Electromagnetic Fields and Radiation, *Documents of the NRPB*, **4**(5).

National Radiological Protection Board, 1998, *National and International Exposure Standards for Electric and Magnetic Fields*, Response Statement 7/7/98, NRPB.

National Radiological Protection Board, 2000, *The Stewart Report – Mobile Phones and Health*, Report of the Independent Expert Group, NRPB.

Sienkiewicz Z, 1998, Biological Effects of Electromagnetic Fields, *Power Engineering Journal*, June 1998.

United Kingdom Childhood Cancer Study, 1999, Exposure to Power Frequency Magnetic Fields and the Risk of Childhood Cancer, *The Lancet*, **354**, 1925–1931.

Wilkening G W, 1991, Non-Ionising Radiation, Chapter 39 in *Patty's Industrial Hygiene and Toxicology*, Clayton G W and Clayton F E (Eds), Wiley-Interscience.

LEGISLATION

Management of Health and Safety at Work Regulations 1999 (SI 1999/3242)

Reporting of Injuries, Diseases and Dangerous Occurrences Regulations 1995 (SI 1995/3163)

9: Ionising radiation

(Hunter 1978. Reproduced by permission of Hodder Arnold.)

INTRODUCTION

Ionising radiation refers to radiant energy which either directly or indirectly produces ionisation of the matter in which it is absorbed or through which it passes. It can be particulate or high frequency electromagnetic radiation.

The term 'radioactive' refers to those substances which contain atoms the nuclei of which are unstable and undergo spontaneous disintegration with the emission of radiation to form more stable atoms. Radioactive decay is accompanied by the emission of charged particles and/or gamma rays.

Radioactivity may have both natural and artificial origins. Natural radiation arises from several sources including radiations from materials in the earth's crust, radioactive gases in the atmosphere and cosmic radiations from outer space. Humans have always lived with this natural background radiation and by far the greater proportion of the general public's exposure is from this source. The photograph above shows an early hospital X-ray machine with minimal protection for staff and patients.

Between 1992 and 1997, the average annual dose to a member of the UK general population was estimated at 2.6mSv and Table 9.1 shows the percentage breakdown of this figure (NRPB 1999).

TABLE 9.1: Exposure of the public to radiation sources

Natural	%	Artificial	%
Radon	50	Medical	14
Gamma background	13.5	Occupational	0.2
Internal (food and drink)	10	Fallout	0.2
Cosmic	12	Disposals	<0.1
		Consumer products	<0.1

(NRPB 1999)

IONISING RADIATION

Hazard identification

Basic atomic theory

A simple explanation of the structure of the atom and nuclear disintegration is useful for an understanding of radioactivity and the production of ionising radiation. The atom consists of a central positively-charged nucleus surrounded by negatively-charged orbital electrons (*cf.* planets orbiting around the sun in the solar system). Each electron is held in a discrete orbital shell each with its own energy level. The nucleus is densely packed with two types of particles: protons (positively charged) and neutrons (neutral, with no charge). The nucleus is very small, that is, 10^{-12}mm, with the radius of the orbital shells relatively much larger at 10^{-8}mm. On the other hand, the nucleus is very dense and contains most of the mass of the atom. With an atom in its normal state, the number of orbiting electrons equals the number of nuclear protons and the atom is uncharged. A neutron can decay into a proton and a very high energy electron.

TABLE 9.2: Atomic particles

Particle	Relative mass	Electrical charge
Proton (p)	1	Positive (+1)
Neutron (n)	1	Neutral (0)
Electron (e)	1/1840	Negative (-1)

Two numbers are used to describe the nucleus: the atomic number (Z) and the mass number (A). The atomic number is the number of protons in the nucleus and is numerically equal to the charge on the nucleus and, hence, the number of orbital electrons. The atomic number is the same for every atom of the same element. For example, for carbon atoms, Z = 6; for oxygen atoms, Z = 8. Furthermore, when Z = 1, the element is hydrogen; when Z = 2, this is helium; and when Z = 24, this is chromium. The mass number is the total number of protons and neutrons in the nucleus, that is:

$$\text{Mass number (A)} = \text{Atomic number (Z)} + N$$

(Where: N is the number of neutrons.)

Nuclear symbols identify the mass number and the atomic number, as shown below:

$$^{12}_{6}\text{C}$$

(Where: C is the chemical symbol (in this case, carbon); 12 is the mass number; and 6 is the atomic number.)

Although all atoms of a particular element contain the same number of protons, they may occur with different numbers of neutrons. This means that the same element can have several different *types* of atom. For example, the element phosphorus has an atomic number of 15, that is, each atom has 15 protons, but it can occur with a differing number of neutrons (ranging from 13 to 19). Each of these forms is called an 'isotope' of the element. For example, the isotope phosphorus-32 has 15 protons and 17 neutrons and, therefore, has a mass number of 32. Isotopes are labelled by their mass number and the isotope carbon-12 is shown in the example above.

Most elements exist naturally as a mixture of isotopes, usually with the one isotope the more prevalent. Isotopes may be produced artificially, for example, by bombarding isotopes with neutrons. Some isotopes of some elements are unstable with their nuclei breaking down spontaneously and these are described as radioactive. Nuclides[35] are not always radioactive, for example, the isotopes oxygen-16, oxygen-17 and oxygen-18 are not radioactive, but oxygen-19 is radioactive. The isotopes of an element are chemically identical, since chemical properties are determined by the atomic number.

---

[35] A nuclide is an atom of an element with a specified mass number.

Radioactivity

Some isotopes disintegrate spontaneously with the loss of energy through the emission of a charged particle and electromagnetic radiation (gamma rays). Virtually all nuclides with an atomic number greater than 83 are radioactive. Radioactive decay is a random process and is a function of the nucleus and nothing else, such as temperature and pressure. The decay follows an exponential curve and the time for half of all nuclei to decay is known as the isotope's 'half-life'. This is fixed for each radioactive isotope and Table 9.3 gives the half-lives for some isotopes.

Similarly, the disintegration rate or activity of the sample is proportional to the number of unstable nuclei; this will also vary exponentially with time and mathematically this can be expressed as:

$$A = A_o e^{-\lambda t}$$

(Where: A is the activity at time t; A_o is the activity of the sample initially; and λ is the radioactive decay constant.)

The variation of activity with time showing exponential decay is illustrated in Figure 9.1 below.

FIGURE 9.1: Variation of activity with time

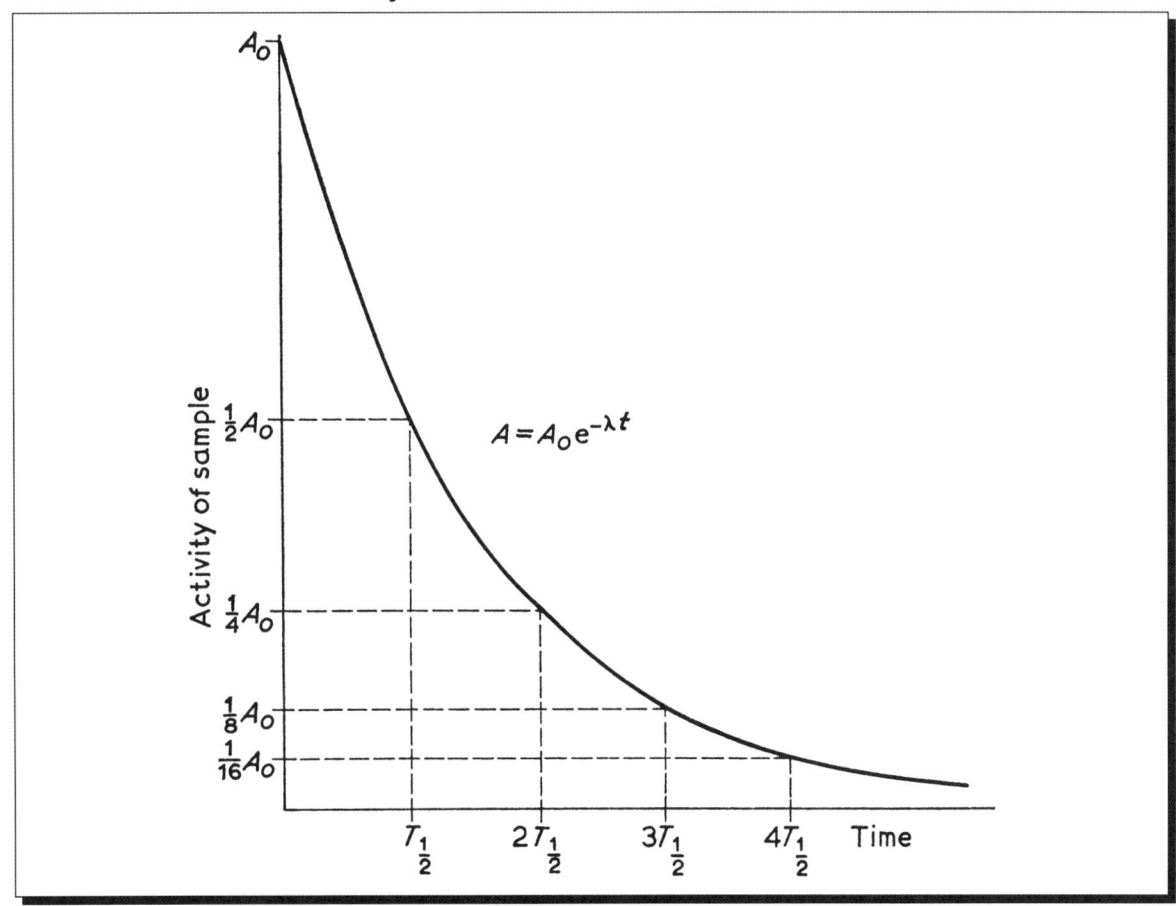

(After Martin & Harbison 1986)

TABLE 9.3: Isotope half-lives

Isotope	Half-life
Uranium-238	4.5×10^9 years
Carbon-14	5.7×10^3 years
Strontium-90	28 years
Iodine-131	8.1 days
Bismuth-214	19.7 minutes
Polonium-214	1.5×10^{-4} seconds

IONISING RADIATION

People may be irradiated by external sources, that is, located outside the body, and internal sources, that is, radioactive substances which gain entry to the body. Ionising radiation causes changes in cells and tissues which may later lead to demonstrable dysfunction and health effects.

The penetrative power of external radiation depends on whether it can reach the basal layer of the skin epidermis. Internal radiation may gain access to the body by inhalation, ingestion and skin absorption and, via the body's systemic circulation, may reach sensitive internal organs, tissues and cells.

The principal agents of ionising radiation are listed and discussed below:
1. Alpha (α) particles.
2. Beta (β) particles.
3. Gamma (γ) radiation.
4. X-ray radiation.
5. Neutron radiation.

Alpha (α) particles

Alpha (α) particles are helium nuclei, with two protons and two neutrons bound together very tightly. These are large particles which travel slowly through matter. An α-particle behaves as if it is a fundamental particle (mass number is four, with two positive charges). The release of an α-particle results in a decrease of two in the atomic number and a new element has been created. The nuclei of the heavier elements found in nature are inherently unstable and some will release an α-particle in order to achieve greater stability. For example, plutonium-239 ($Z = 94$; $A = 239$) emits an α-particle and is transformed into uranium-235 ($Z = 92$; $A = 235$).

There is a high chance of an interaction with atoms in matter and α-particles will give up some of their energy in these collisions. Their action on orbital electrons causes excitation or ionisation in the matter it is passing through (see Table 9.4). In a dense medium, such as human tissue, energy is lost very rapidly and α-particles only travel a short distance. They are stopped easily by dead skin, paper or even as little as 4cm of air. If α-particles are present as an 'internal' hazard, they will lose energy very rapidly, causing intense and damaging local ionisation in body tissues.

Beta (β) particles

Beta (β) particles are high-speed electrons which have their origin in the disintegration of a neutron into a proton and an electron. Being much smaller than α-particles, they travel much faster with fewer interactions per unit path length. Fewer interactions mean that energy is lost more slowly and they penetrate more deeply into matter than α-particles. Their range depends on their energy level; over the range 0.07–2.5MeV, they will penetrate up to 1.25cm in soft body tissue.

In the case of β-emission, the original element is transformed into an element with an atomic number one unit higher, but with the same mass number. For example, lead-210 is transformed into bismuth-210 with the emission of a β-particle. β-particles lose energy by interacting with orbital electrons in the absorbing medium causing excitation or ionisation.

Gamma (γ) radiation

Gamma (γ) rays are electromagnetic radiation which originate in a radioactive nucleus. They occur because either the nucleus undergoes a spontaneous rearrangement to a lower energy state or as a result of the release of α- or β-particles. The emission of γ-radiation does not result in any change in atomic number. For example, when cobalt-60 decays, two γ-rays having energies of 1.33MeV and 1.17MeV are emitted by the daughter nickel-60 settling into its ground state.

For the present circumstances, γ-rays can be considered as electromagnetic radiation with a very short wavelength and, hence, very high frequency. Like all electromagnetic radiation, its velocity through free space is $3 \times 10^8 ms^{-1}$ and its energy is inversely proportional to the wavelength. When γ-rays interact with matter, energy is transferred to the orbital electron and they are either moved to a higher energy level (excitation) or are removed from the atom which then becomes an ion (ionisation). γ-rays travel large distances in dense matter and are difficult to absorb completely.

TABLE 9.4: Interaction of radiation with matter

Radiation	Mechanism	Comments
Alpha (α) (particle – two protons and two neutrons)	Interactions with orbital electrons	Energy transferred to electrons leads them to be transferred to a higher energy level (excitation) or separated from the atom altogether (ionisation)
		Alpha particles are large particles which travel slowly through matter and have a high chance of interacting with atoms on their pathway. They give up their energy during these interactions, thus energy is lost rapidly and alpha particles travel only short distances in dense media (see Table 9.5)
Beta (β) (particle – high-speed electron)	(i) Interaction with orbital electrons	Leads to excitation and ionisation
	(ii) Charged particles slowing down very rapidly in the field of the nucleus emit energy as X-rays	Leads to emission of braking radiation (bremsstrahlung)
		Beta particles are much smaller than alpha particles and travel much faster; they undergo far fewer collisions with atoms (per unit path length) and thus give up their energy much more slowly and travel further than alpha particles (see Table 9.5)
X-ray or gamma (γ)	(i) Photoelectric effect	All the energy of an X- or γ-photon is completely absorbed by an orbital electron, which is ejected from its parent atom
	(ii) Compton effect	Only part of the photon energy is absorbed; the X- or γ-photon is scattered with a reduced energy
	(iii) Pair production	An energetic γ-photon is converted into a positron-electron pair; the two particles share the available energy; only part of the photon energy is absorbed
		All three mechanisms lead to energy being transferred to atomic electrons, which undergo excitation or ionisation. γ-radiation loses energy mainly by interacting with orbital electrons; it travels very large distances in dense media and is very difficult to absorb completely (see Table 9.5)
Neutron	Variety of mechanisms	Neutrons are uncharged particles and cannot cause ionisation directly; as with γ-radiation, neutrons ultimately transfer their energy to charged particles; they may also be captured by the nucleus resulting in γ-emission. Neutrons are very penetrating and will travel large distances in dense media

(Adapted from Martin & Harbison 1986)

IONISING RADIATION

Radiation energy

An electronvolt (eV) is the energy gained by an electron in passing through a potential difference of one volt. However, as the electronvolt is a very small unit, radiation energies are normally expressed in kiloelectronvolts (keV) or megaelectronvolts (MeV). One advantage in the use of electronvolts is that the same unit can be applied to the energy of different particles, that is, alpha, beta and electromagnetic radiation.

X-ray radiation

X-rays, another class of electromagnetic radiation, are in many respects similar to γ-rays but are less penetrating and have a longer wavelength. However, X-rays can still travel long distances in dense media and they are very difficult to absorb completely. X-rays are produced from an atom when orbiting electrons move from a higher energy level into a lower one, in contrast to γ-rays which originate from the nucleus itself. When X-rays interact with matter, energy is transferred to orbital electrons resulting in excitation or ionisation.

Neutron radiation

Neutron radiation is produced naturally from spontaneous fission and it is also produced in nuclear reactors and accelerators. It is not directly ionising but does induce ionisation by its interaction with matter (when neutrons are absorbed by a nucleus, this becomes radioactive). Because of this effect, all containers used for the transport and storage of neutron sources become radioactive. Neutrons are very penetrating and, thus, will travel long distances in dense media. The practice is to describe neutron energy as one of three broad bands: fast, intermediate or thermal.

TABLE 9.5: Properties of nuclear radiation

Radiation	Relative mass	Charge	Range (air)	Range (tissue)
α	4	+2	3cm	0.04mm
β	1/1840	-1	3m	5mm
γ, X	0	0	Very large	Through body
Fast neutron	1	0	Very large	Through body
Thermal neutron	1	0	Very large	15cm

Occupational exposure

In an occupational context, people are exposed to ionising radiation from a wide variety of sources in industry, medicine and research.

TABLE 9.6: Uses of ionising radiation

Use	Example
Medicine	Diagnosis (X-rays), treatment (radiotherapy), sterilisation of medical products (γ-radiation), medical research purposes
Power generation	Nuclear power stations
Industrial photography	Non-destructive testing of welds and structural integrity
Research	Various applications
Surveillance systems	Smoke detectors, baggage examination systems

In 1895, Röntgen discovered X-rays and in the following year natural radiation was observed by Becquerel who reported the blackening of photographic emulsion in the presence of a uranium compound. Radiation was thought to be emitted by the uranium compound. Over the next 10 years, the research of Rutherford and Soddy, together with the Curies, established the presence of certain unstable nuclei which emitted different types of radiation: alpha, beta and gamma.

The health risks of exposure to ionising radiation have long been recognised and include both acute harm (from very high levels of exposure over a short period of time) and chronic effects such as cancer (discussed further on page 291). Concern about the health risks arising from exposure to ionising radiation led to the establishment of the International Commission on Radiological Protection (ICRP) in 1928. Since this time, the ICRP has published many recommendations on the broad principles of radiation protection along with detailed guidance on methodological issues, for example, the estimation of exposure dose. In 1977, it published recommendations (known as ICRP26) outlining three axioms of radiation protection:

1. **Justification** – the process of showing that the work involving exposure to radiation produces sufficient benefit both to the exposed individuals and to society to offset the radiation detriment it causes.
2. **Optimisation** – keeping all exposures 'as low as reasonably achievable' (ALARA) with economic and social factors being taken into account.
3. **Dose limitation** – keeping exposures received by workers and the general public within relevant specified dose limits.

The ICRP's recommendations were very influential and ICRP26 led to the adoption in 1980 of European Directive 80/836/Euratom (later amended by 84/467/Euratom) which laid down safety standards for the protection of the health of workers and the general public against the risk of exposure to ionising radiation. In the UK, the Ionising Radiations Regulations 1985 (IRR) (HSC 1985) were introduced mainly to implement the provisions of the 1980 directive. During the 1980s, the ICRP recognised that exposure risks from ionising radiation were greater than was previously thought and it published new general recommendations in 1991 (known as ICRP60). This resulted in a further directive (EC 1996) – which revised the 1980 directive and was based on the recommendations in ICRP60 – and this, in turn, resulted in the current Ionising Radiations Regulations 1999 (IRR) (HSC 2000).

Sealed and unsealed radioactive sources

Radioactive sources are not pure elements but substances with chemical and physical properties and they may exist in any one of the three basic states of matter: solid, liquid or gas. Sealed or closed sources are those which remain intact in all situations. They may be encapsulated or a non-friable (ie non-dust generating) solid. Before a source can be classified as a 'sealed source', it has to conform to strict criteria, that is, remain intact when dropped, immersed in water, or exposed to high temperature or pressure. Unsealed sources are those which give rise to radioactive contamination such as powders, dust, solutions, gases, vapours, friable solids and those solids with an easily removable oxide layer.

Radioactive contamination

This arises from (unwanted) unsealed radioactive sources. X-rays, γ-radiation or a sealed source in contact with a surface will not give rise to contamination. Exposure to high energy X-rays or neutrons may induce radioactivity in an exposed material, but this is a different situation to what is normally regarded as contamination.

Radiation units

Quantity of radioactivity

The quantity of radiation is measured in terms of the number of disintegrations per unit time. One bequerel (bq) represents one disintegration per second (dps). Because the bq is a very small unit, radioactivity is more often expressed in gigabequerels (1Gbq = 10^9dps), megabequerels (1Mbq = 10^6dps) and kilobequerels (1Kbq = 10^3dps).

Radiation absorbed dose

Radiation absorbed dose is the measure of energy deposition in any irradiated material by all types of ionising radiation. This is measured in grays (Gy) and one Gy represents the equivalent of 1 joule kg^{-1} of energy deposition.

Dose equivalent

In biological systems, the degree of damage depends on the absorbed dose and the type of radiation. To compensate for this, a 'quality factor' (QF) is used in the determination of 'dose equivalent'. Dose equivalent is measured in sieverts (Sv) and this is the absorbed dose in grays multiplied by the QF, which is determined by the type of radiation:

$$\text{Dose equivalent} = \text{Absorbed dose (grays)} \times \text{QF}$$

(The QF adjusts for the different types of harm likely to result when the same dose of radiation is received by the same amount of human tissue due to the action of the different types of radiation.)

TABLE 9.7: Type of radiation and the quality factor

Type of radiation	Quality factor (QF)
γ-rays, X-rays and electrons	1
Thermal neutrons	5
Fast neutrons	20
α-particles	20

(Martin & Harbison 1986)

Radiation dose rate

The absorbed dose measures the total amount of radiation absorbed in a given period of time. The dose rate is the amount of radiation absorbed in unit time and is expressed as microsieverts per hour (μSv h^{-1}). Statutory dose limits for UK workers are given in Tables 9.10 and 9.11 (see page 299), which are expressed in millisieverts per year (mSv Y^{-1}).

Biological effects

Biological effects are caused by the interaction of ionising radiation – from internal and external sources – with body tissues and cells. The severity of health effects is related to radiation exposure dose and dose rate; health effects include radiation sickness, cataracts and cancer (discussed below).

External and internal sources

External radiation is that arising from sources located outside the body while internal radiation is that arising from sources which have gained entry into the body systems via inhalation, ingestion or skin absorption. Absorbed radioactive substances may be retained in the body or excreted rapidly with other metabolic waste products depending on their chemical properties. Those retained become internal radioactive sources until their activity becomes very low (this depends on the half-life of the particular isotope).

External sources

This generally refers to ionising radiation coming from outside the body, particularly X-rays, γ-rays, beta particles and neutrons. Some external sources of radiation, such as X-rays, γ-rays and neutrons, are very penetrating and can pass right through the body, irradiating internal organs in their path. Alpha particles do not penetrate very far into the body and are not normally significant external sources.

Internal sources

Potential internal sources of radiation can gain entry to the body by inhalation, ingestion or skin absorption. The degree of absorption and metabolic handling of a radioactive substance will depend on the physical and chemical properties of the substance, as discussed in Chapter 2. Once a harmful substance has gained entry to the body by one of the above routes, it can reach the bloodstream (the body's systemic circulation) and be transported around the body to vulnerable and sensitive soft tissues. Some contaminants concentrate in specific tissues or organs and this increases their potential to cause radioactive and toxicological damage.

Radiation and cells

There are detectable biological effects caused by the interaction of the ions created by radiation and the body's biochemical processes. The clinical symptoms and signs depend on the amount of absorbed radiation and the dose rate. Radiation interacts with biological tissue by ionising atoms within cells, which results in the deposition of energy.

Radiation effects may be divided into two broad categories:
1. **Somatic effects** – where the exposed individual suffers tissue damage.
2. **Hereditary effects** – where future descendants of the individual may be affected.

In both cases, the basic mechanism is believed to be the disruption of DNA molecules which control the growth and development of cells. (The basic structure and function of a generalised cell is discussed in Chapter 2.) This may affect the way a cell divides or it may result in the death of the cell. If enough cells are damaged, this loss of capacity will have an effect on tissue or overall organ function.

In the short initiation stage of the radiation damage process, energy is deposited in target cells causing ionisation and the resulting ions interact with water molecules and produce free radicals. These chemical species are very reactive and attach themselves to the large protein and/or nucleic acid molecules which make up the chromosomes in the nucleus of the cell. These structures are intimately involved in the processes of cell division in somatic body cells (mitosis) and reproductive germ cells (meiosis). Such interaction with chromosomal material (DNA and protein) may cause early cell death, prevention or delay of cell division, and mutations (some of which may result in cancer). This may occur in both body (somatic) cells and germ (reproductive) cells. This second, biological, stage of the radiation damage process can last from a short period to many years.

Based on their mechanism of causation, health effects can be divided into non-stochastic and stochastic:
1. **Non-stochastic (deterministic) effects** do not occur until a certain *threshold* of radiation dose is exceeded.
2. **Stochastic effects** are those where there is a probability of them occurring at *any* dose, ie there is no threshold dose below which exposure has no effect. This probability increases with increasing dose. Cancer caused by radiation exposure is regarded as a stochastic effect.

Somatic effects – Chronic

Effects arise from the depletion of mitotic cells or from interference with the process of mitotic cell division. Damage is most likely in cells which undergo mitotic division more frequently, for example, the epithelial lining cells of the gut or respiratory system. Here, at any time a large number of cells are undergoing mitotic division.

Early last century, it became apparent that radiologists and their patients suffered a higher level of certain cancers in comparison to other groups not exposed to radiation. There have been other studies of groups exposed to high levels of ionising radiation and these include atomic bomb victims, patients treated by radiotherapy and, in an occupational context, uranium miners. These studies have confirmed that ionising radiation causes cancer, principally in the white blood cells and/or bone marrow and soft tissues, and have reported dose estimates. (Leukaemia is cancer of the white blood cells and bone marrow.) It is believed that most types of cancer can be induced by radiation and that an increased dose will increase the prevalence of a cancer above spontaneous levels.

Another health effect of exposure to ionising radiation is cataract formation, which is believed to be non-stochastic, with a dose threshold of 15Sv over a person's working lifetime. This means that this radiation dose threshold must be exceeded before this condition will develop.

Somatic effects – Acute

Where a large dose of radiation is received over a short time period, the first symptoms are due to depletion of cells which normally have a short life span. The most important of these are the white blood cells (whose precursors are in the bone marrow) and the epithelial cells lining the gastrointestinal tract. This depletion in cells results from damage to both the bone marrow and the gastrointestinal tract. Acute absorbed doses of about 1Gy of radiation give rise to nausea and vomiting (radiation sickness) which occur several hours after exposure. Acute doses over 2Gy may lead to death 10 to 15 days after exposure. For doses up to 10Gy, death is normally caused by secondary infections due to the depletion of defensive white blood cells. (Gray units are used in the above discussion since the sievert incorporates a quality factor and this is only intended to be applied to radiation doses within normally applied limits.)

Normal radiation exposures in both radiation workers and the public are far below these dose levels. Such levels could only conceivably occur following a serious nuclear accident. However, low doses arising from normal operations may cause serious health effects in exposed workers in the long term.

Hereditary effects

Hereditary effects are caused by genetic mutations in reproductive cells (ie male sperm and female ova). In this case, harmful changes can be passed on to the next generation and so on. There is a general working assumption that all mutations are harmful (not strictly true with respect to the theory of evolution) and since ionising radiation causes an increase in mutation rate, there needs to be strict control of exposure of the general population as well as people at work. Protection against such effects is incorporated into the prescribed dose limits for exposed workers (see page 299).

Measurement of exposure and analysis

Radiation assessment survey

Before any work with radioactive substances is commenced, the identification of hazards and evaluation of prospective risks must be carried out. A "suitable and sufficient" risk assessment is required under IRR 1999 (regulation 7) to identify control measures to restrict exposure. This complements the requirements of the Management of Health and Safety at Work Regulations 1999 (MHSW), the Control of Substances Hazardous to Health Regulations 2002 (COSHH) and other risk assessment legislation. Under IRR 1999, regulation 7(1), a new activity involving work with ionising radiation may not commence until a risk assessment has been carried out. Following this assessment of radiation risks, control measures for the proposed process can be determined. This usually involves the demarcation of specific areas and the classification of personnel by their expected degree of exposure. Where significant quantities of radioactive substances are involved, the impact on the environment and the public need to be considered.

Exposure of people at work to ionising radiation can be measured in various ways depending on the objective of the survey. IRR 1999 require an assessment of individual radiation dose averaged over a specified time period, which can then be interpreted using the dose limits specified in regulation 11. Since the human body cannot sense ionising radiation, this usually (unless insignificant quantities are involved) requires a radiation monitoring survey to be carried out using technical equipment, including ionising radiation contamination monitors and personal dosimeters.

There are many types of monitoring instruments available and these devices utilise the chemical and physical effects of ionising radiation. Instruments are based on several types of detector (with associated electronic circuitry) and can quantify incident radiation as a count rate, dose rate and accumulated dose (see Table 9.8).

It is necessary to calibrate monitoring instruments against a standard source. All monitors depend on the response of the detector to ionisation produced due to the interaction between the ionising radiation and matter. Alpha and beta radiation are detected by their direct ionising properties in that the media in which they move becomes ionised and, thus, electrically conducting. X-rays and γ-rays produce electrons as they move through matter and these are detected. From neutron radiation, a variety of charged particles are produced and these can be detected. The detectors are linked via electronic circuitry which amplify the signal and this is then displayed. The principal types of detector in use are listed in Table 9.8.

TABLE 9.8: Principles of radiation detection

Principle of detection	Type of instrument	Comment
Gas ionisation	Ionisation chamber (IC)	Radiation ionises the air and the ions are attracted to electrodes causing a current to flow in the chamber. The magnitude of current is a mean value measure of radiation intensity
	Proportional counter (PC)	This is similar to an ionisation chamber but operates at a higher potential difference and secondary ionisation (gas amplification) occurs; a single particle of IR can produce a pulse of detectable current, therefore the PC counter is more sensitive than the IC
	Geiger-Müller (GM) tube	Operates at an even higher potential difference and ions produced are accelerated to high velocities; the result – a single ionising particle produces secondary ionisation and a very large pulse of current
Solid state detectors	Scintillation detector	Some substances when exposed to ionising radiation emit light. This light is energy absorbed from ionising radiation; emitted light is amplified and displayed as a visual or audible signal
	Thermoluminescent detector	In some substances, ionising radiation causes the trapping of electrons (a stable state at room temperature); the device is heated and the trapped electrons return to their original state with the emission of a light photon, the energy of which is proportional to the radiation dose received
Change in chemical systems	Photographic effect	Ionising radiation causes a similar effect on photographic film as does visible light. Following processing the optical density of the film is measured, which can be converted to radiation dose by comparison with calibration films
Neutron activation	Neutron meter	Bombardment of elements by neutrons produces radionuclides; the degree of activation allows estimation of neutron flux

Approaches to monitoring ionising radiation

It is convenient to divide approaches to monitoring ionising radiation into those appropriate for external and internal sources, as explained below. Approaches to monitoring are summarised in Figure 9.2.

External sources

Approaches can be subdivided into area monitoring and personnel monitoring.

Area monitoring

The purpose of area monitoring is to measure radiation levels at various points in the workplace to check controls are functioning as intended in order to regulate ionising radiation exposure dose. Monitoring is carried out during the commissioning of a new process facility and routinely during normal operations. Tasks can be selected for specific evaluation. Various instruments are available to carry out this monitoring and selection depends on the type of radiation, its energy level and the required

IONISING RADIATION

FIGURE 9.2: Approaches to monitoring ionising radiation

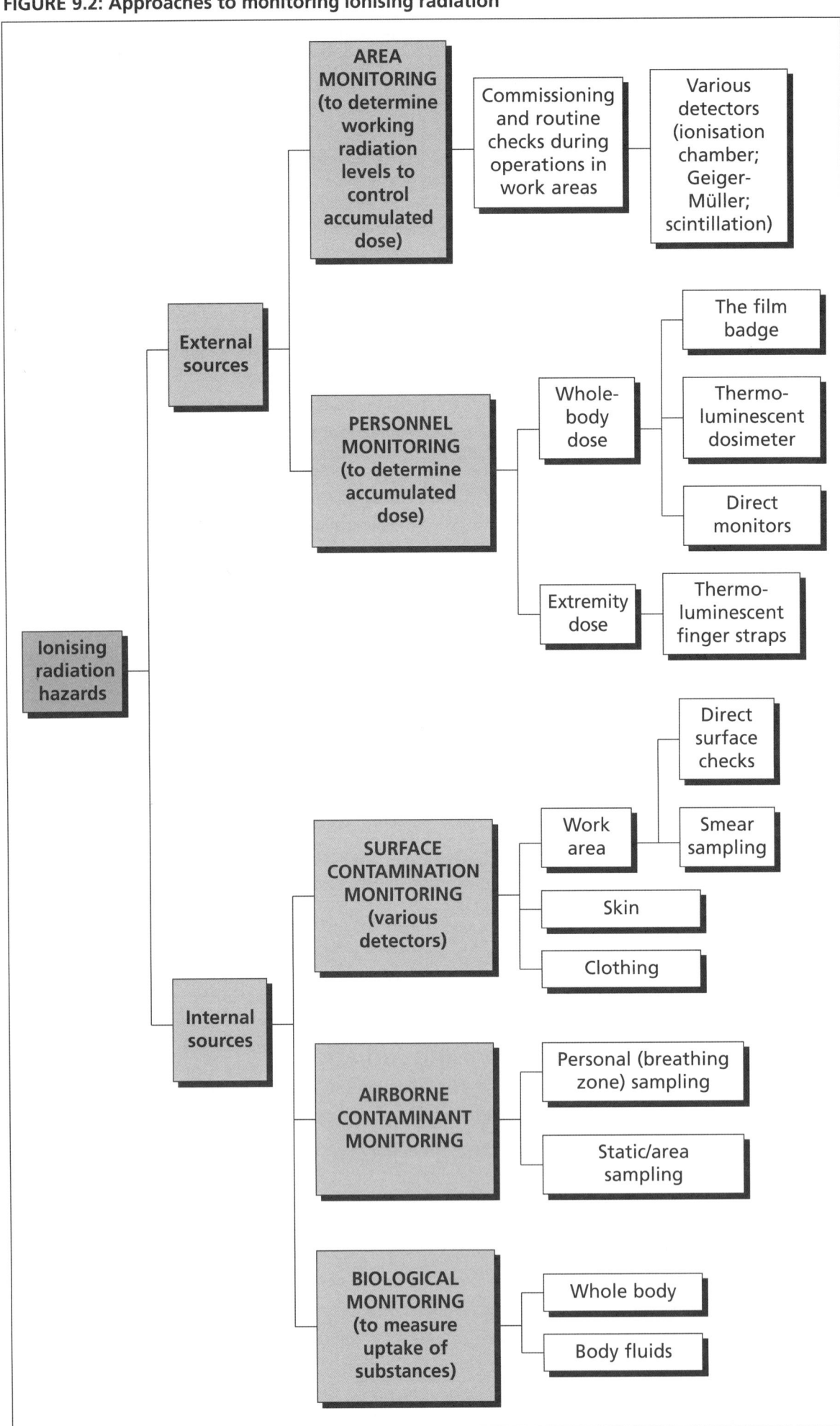

```
Ionising radiation hazards
├── External sources
│   ├── AREA MONITORING (to determine working radiation levels to control accumulated dose)
│   │   ├── Commissioning and routine checks during operations in work areas
│   │   └── Various detectors (ionisation chamber; Geiger-Müller; scintillation)
│   └── PERSONNEL MONITORING (to determine accumulated dose)
│       ├── Whole-body dose
│       │   ├── The film badge
│       │   ├── Thermo-luminescent dosimeter
│       │   └── Direct monitors
│       └── Extremity dose
│           └── Thermo-luminescent finger straps
└── Internal sources
    ├── SURFACE CONTAMINATION MONITORING (various detectors)
    │   ├── Work area
    │   │   ├── Direct surface checks
    │   │   └── Smear sampling
    │   ├── Skin
    │   └── Clothing
    ├── AIRBORNE CONTAMINANT MONITORING
    │   ├── Personal (breathing zone) sampling
    │   └── Static/area sampling
    └── BIOLOGICAL MONITORING (to measure uptake of substances)
        ├── Whole body
        └── Body fluids
```

sensitivity of detection. Examples include monitors based on the ionisation chamber, the Geiger-Müller tube and scintillation detectors.

FIGURE 9.3: Portable Geiger-Müller counter

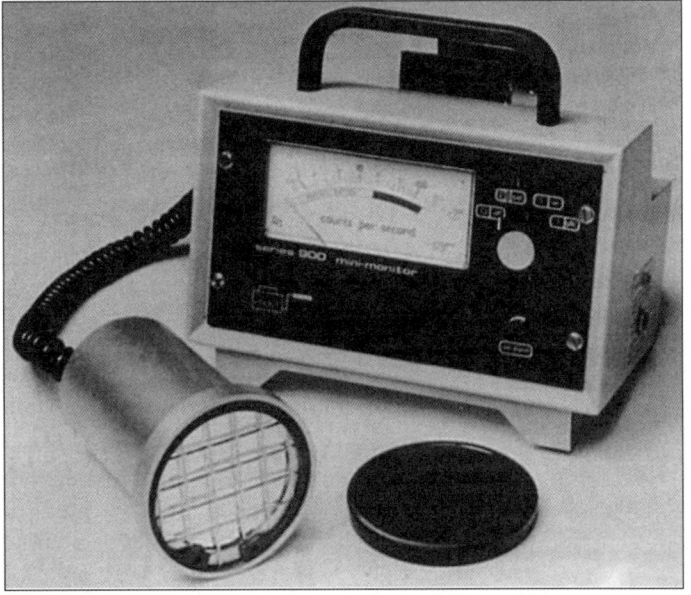

(Mini Instruments Ltd)

Personnel monitoring

This is carried out to determine the exposure of employees to external radiation sources. Employees move around during their work and spend varying times on different tasks and these devices give an integrated measure of exposure dose. It is useful to divide this monitoring into whole-body dose and extremity dose monitoring. Results are expressed as accumulated dose and dose rate. A range of personal dosimeters is illustrated in Figure 9.4.

Whole-body dose monitors

There are three types of whole-body dose monitors:
1. The film badge.
2. Thermoluminescent dosimeter.
3. Direct monitoring dosimeters.

The film badge

Commonly, a film badge is used to monitor exposure to X-rays, γ-rays and high energy β-emitters. The dosimeter must be worn all the time the person is working, as it is evaluating the integrated dose for the whole body.

Radiation-sensitive film is housed in a plastic casing with windows of various materials which filter out different types of radiation. The device is worn during normal work where radiation exposure arises and a badge normally lasts for one week. The film is analysed in a laboratory to quantify the accumulated dose of the different types of radiation. Following processing, the film is evaluated by passing a beam of light through it and measuring the resulting optical density. The observed density is converted to radiation dose using calibration films (ie films exposed to known quantities of radiation). The detection sensitivity of this method depends on the grain size of the film and ranges from radiation levels of 50μSv to 50mSv. From the exposed film, information about the type and energy of radiation can be deduced. This can be stored and scrutinised later. A disadvantage of this method is that the films are not amenable to rapid or direct reading.

Thermoluminescent dosimeter

These devices can be used to measure dose over the short and long term, and are used both in whole-body and extremity (fingers) monitoring.

These dosimeters use materials such as lithium fluoride crystals and are based on an electron trapping process as described in Table 9.8. The degree of irradiation can be related to the amount of light produced on heating.

One disadvantage of these devices is that the analytical process destroys the collected information, unlike the film badge which forms a permanent record. However, this is currently the most popular approach to personal monitoring, partly because analysis can be quickly and automatically performed. Thus, this is a convenient method of short-term dose control.

FIGURE 9.4: Personal dosimeters (a) Radon sampler; (b) Film badge holder; (c) Thermoluminescent dosimeter; (d) Neutron film badge holder; (e) Thermonluminescent dosimeter finger strap in holder; (f) Thermoluminescent finger strap

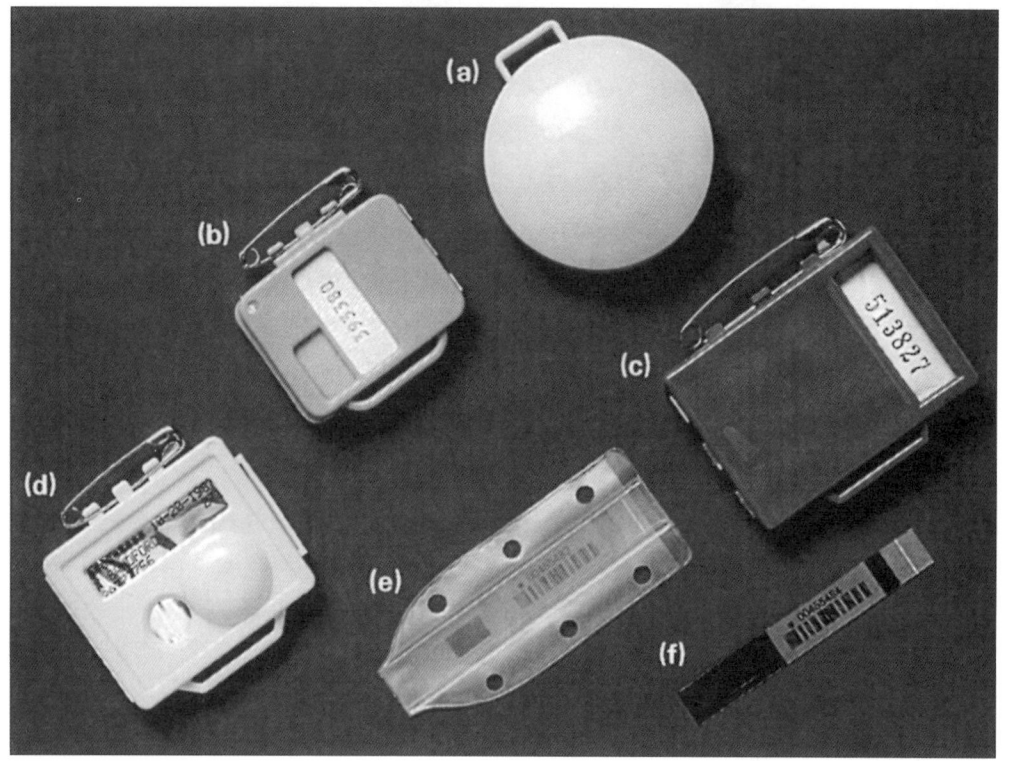

(NRPB Dosimetry Service)

Direct monitoring dosimeters

In situations where an immediate indication of X- or γ-dose rate is required, then direct reading dosimeters are used. They are particularly useful in situations where the dose rate is high, since a continuous watch can be kept on the accumulation of dose. Personal alarm monitors are available which give an audible warning of a preset threshold being reached (Figure 9.5).

FIGURE 9.5: Personal dose rate meter with alarm

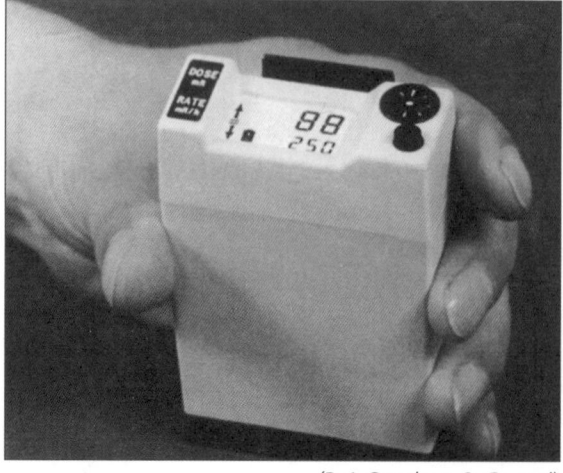

(R A Stephen & Co Ltd)

FIGURE 9.6: Pocket radiation monitor

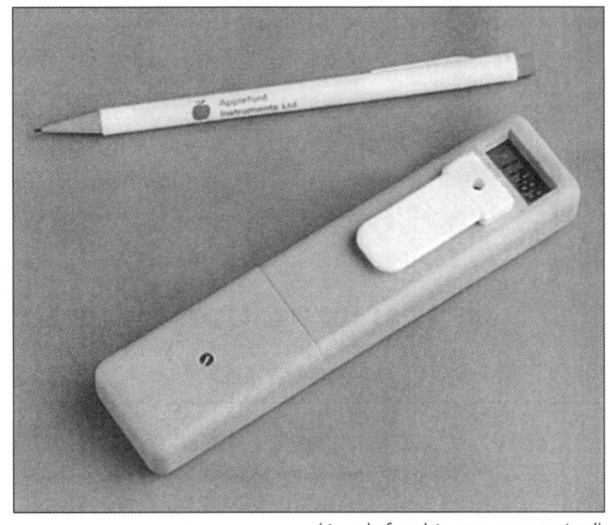

(Appleford Instruments Ltd)

Extremity dose

Thermoluminescent monitors are available for extremity dose monitoring. A finger-strap monitor is shown in Figure 9.4(e) and (f).

Internal sources

With internal sources, the objective of monitoring is to identify and quantify radioactive substances which can gain entry to the body via inhalation, ingestion and contact with damaged skin. The potential for this to occur will depend on the employee's exposure to contaminated air and surfaces in the work area. Annual limits of intake (ALIs) for inhalation and ingestion have been established by the ICRP for a wide range of radionuclides. Limits for tolerable air concentration and surface contamination have been derived from these ALIs. These are used in the interpretation of internal source monitoring results.

Surface contaminant monitoring

Activity is monitored on the surfaces in the work area, and on the employee's skin and clothing. In the latter case, this is routinely carried out by fixed monitors when an employee leaves a 'controlled' area. There are sophisticated contamination checks where the employee enters a booth and, if there is an unacceptable level of contamination, he or she is not able to leave the area until satisfactory decontamination measures have been applied. Surface contamination checks are carried out with portable monitors and in 'smear sampling', the activity level per unit surface area is determined.

FIGURE 9.7: Fixed contamination monitor

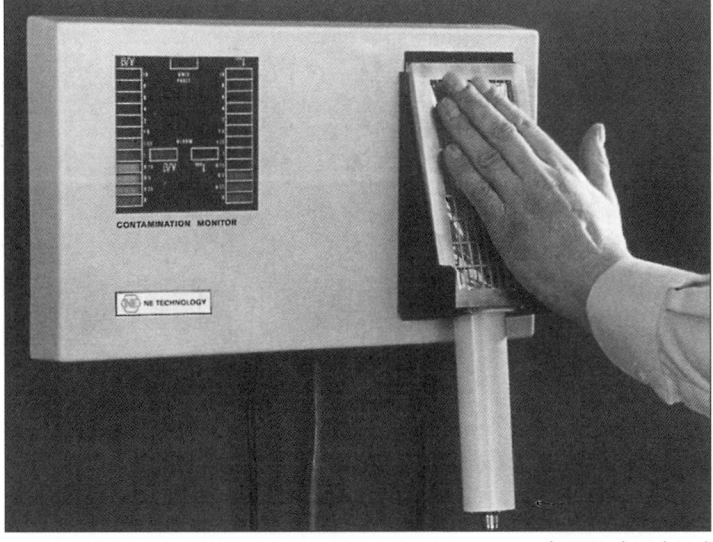

(NE Technology)

Airborne contaminant monitoring

This is carried out to quantify unsealed sources which may become airborne, for example, dusts and gases. For dusts, a pump is used to draw air through a filter to collect a sample of the airborne contaminant (Figure 9.8). The activity on the filter is quantified and knowledge of the collected air volume (from pump flow rate and sampling time) allows the concentration of the activity in the air to be determined. The sampling device can be positioned in the person's breathing zone (personal sampling) or in the general work area (area or static sampling). For gases and vapours, monitoring can also be carried out with a collection device and an air sampling pump. However, a passive monitor may also be used for sampling collection where no pump is involved. For example, passive samplers can be used for radon gas monitoring.

FIGURE 9.8: Static air samplers

(Negretti Automation Ltd)

Biological monitoring

This quantifies radiation sources which have gained entry to the body by the modes of entry discussed above. Whole-body monitoring can be carried out to evaluate some sources (eg γ-radiation). Also, urine and other body fluids can be monitored as an index of total absorbed dose using appropriately derived standards to interpret such measurements.

Determination of risk tolerability

Dose limits

International Commission on Radiation Protection (ICRP)

The ICRP aims, by dose limitation, to prevent non-stochastic (deterministic) effects and limit stochastic effects to exposed individuals and second generation offspring to tolerable levels using the guideline 'as low as is reasonably achievable' (ALARA) (Table 9.9). In ICRP60, there are no special dose limits for women who are not pregnant. In pregnant women, the dose to the abdomen is limited to 2mSv for the rest of the pregnancy (once the pregnancy has been declared). There were no changes in the dose limits for individual organs or the lens of the eye. (The dose limits for whole-body exposure are lower than for a single organ because all organs and tissues are exposed in a whole-body exposure, while only a single organ is involved in the single organ exposure limits.)

TABLE 9.9: Dose limits – ICRP60 (1991)

Category of person	Dose limit
Radiation workers	50mSv in any one-year period but not more than 100mSv in any five-year period (implied annual dose 20mSv/year)
General public	1mSv/year; in special circumstances a higher effective dose is allowed; average dose must not exceed 1mSv/year in the person's lifetime

Current UK dose limits

The dose limits used in the Ionising Radiations Regulations 1999 are listed in Tables 9.10 and 9.11.

TABLE 9.10: Dose limits (IRR 1999, regulation 11(1); Schedule 4, Part I)

Category	Whole body (mSv/year)	Lens of the eye (mSv/year)	Skin (mSv/year)	Hands, forearms, feet and ankles (mSv/year)
Employees (over 18)	20	150	500	500
Trainees (under 18)	6	50	150	150
Others	1	15	50	50

(The dose limit to the abdomen of a woman of reproductive capacity is 13mSv in any consecutive 13-week period. The dose limit to the abdomen of a pregnant woman must not exceed 10mSv during the period of the pregnancy. After the employer is informed of the pregnancy (regulation 8(5)), the equivalent dose to the foetus should not exceed 1mSv for the remainder of the pregnancy.)

Regulation 11(2) is concerned with dose limitation in special cases where the above dose limits are deemed impracticable. If the employer can demonstrate this because of the nature of the work, then the following limits may be applied (Table 9.11).

TABLE 9.11: Dose limits – Special cases (IRR 1999, regulation 11(2); Schedule 4, Part II)

Category	Whole body (mSv/year)	Lens of the eye (mSv/year)	Skin (mSv/year)	Hands, forearms, feet and ankles (mSv/year)
Employees (over 18)	100 in any period of 5 consecutive calendar years (maximum effective dose of 50 in a calendar year)	150	500 (1cm^2)	500

These limits do not take into account exposure in medical and dental practice and exposure to high natural background radiation. Some further control may be necessary for persons exposed to:
- materials containing elevated levels of natural radionuclides;
- cosmic rays to aircrew and frequent fliers in jet aircraft;
- radon gas and daughters.

It is required that doses must always be 'as low as is reasonably practicable' (ALARP) which is equivalent to the ICRP's ALARA principle.

National Radiological Protection Board (NRPB)

In the UK, the National Radiological Protection Board (NRPB) advises the Government on matters concerned with radiological protection. The NRPB's principal objectives are:
- to advance knowledge on human protection from radiation hazards;
- to provide information and advice for those with responsibilities in radiological protection;
- to provide technical services for those dealing with radiation hazards (including external and internal dose assessments, analyses of dose in employees, and assessment of

sources of general public exposure); and
- to provide training in radiological protection.

The NRPB is supported by an Advisory Committee which provides advice on the practical aspects of applying current knowledge to the control of radiation hazards.

The Ionising Radiations Regulations 1999 (IRR)

Until the enactment of the initial Radioactive Substances Act in 1960, there was no statutory regulation on how work with ionising radiation should be carried out. In the 1960s, regulations were applied only to factories while other places including hospitals and dental and veterinary surgeries had advisory codes of practice. The Health and Safety at Work etc Act 1974 brought statutory regulation to virtually all work activities – including work with ionising radiations. However, it was not until the enactment of the initial Ionising Radiations Regulations in 1985 (together with the associated Approved Codes of Practice (ACoPs)) that detailed legal coverage was brought over all users of ionising radiation. These have now been replaced by the Ionising Radiations Regulations 1999 and the requirements of these Regulations are summarised in Table 9.12. Other selected legislation dealing with ionising radiation is listed in Table 9.13.

TABLE 9.12: Summary of the Ionising Radiations Regulations 1999 (IRR)

Regulation	Requirement
Part I 1–4	Interpretation and general Citation and commencement; Interpretation; Application; Duties
Part II 5–12	General principles and procedures Specified practices; Notification of special procedures; Prior risk assessment; Restriction of exposure; Personal protective equipment; Maintenance and examination of controls; Dose limitation; Contingency plans
Part III 13–15	Arrangements for the management of radiation protection Radiation protection adviser; Information, instruction and training; Co-operation between employers
Part IV 16–19	Designated areas Controlled or supervised areas; Local rules and radiation protection supervisors; Additional requirements for designated areas; Monitoring of designated areas
Part V 20–26	Classification and monitoring of persons Designation of classified persons; Dose assessment and recording; Estimated doses; Dosimetry for accidents; Medical surveillance; Investigation and notification of overexposure; Dose limitation for overexposed workers
Part VI 27–33	Arrangements for the control of radioactive substances, articles and equipment Sealed sources; Accounting for radioactive substances; Keeping and moving radioactive substances; Notification of certain occurrences; Duties of manufacturers of articles for use with ionising radiation; Equipment used for medical exposure; Misuse or interference with sources of ionising radiation
Part VII 34–41	Duties of employees and miscellaneous Duties of employees; Approval of dosimetry services; Defences; Exemption certificates; Extension outside Great Britain; Transitional provisions; Modification for MoD; Modification, revocation and saving
Schedules 1–9	Miscellaneous Work not required to be notified under regulation 6; Particulars for notification; Additional particulars; Dose limits; Matters for radiation protection advisers; Radiation passbook; Health records; Quantities and concentrations of radionuclides; Modifications
Appendix 1 Appendix 2	Estimating effective and equivalent dose from external radiation Explanation of terms

IRR 1999 implement most of the Basic Safety Standards Directive 96/29/Euratom, which reflects the recommendations of the ICRP in 1990 (ICRP60). This directive specifies basic safety standards for the protection of the health of workers and the general public from the hazards of ionising radiation. Overall, the new Regulations reflect previous British legislation as well as incorporating European developments.

TABLE 9.13: Other legislation dealing with ionising radiation

Statute	Notes
The Radioactive Substances Act 1993	Before a person uses radioactive material they must register with the Environment Agency and obtain authorisation for its use, storage, accumulation and disposal of waste. One essential requirement is that of meticulous record-keeping
Ionising Radiation (Medical Exposure) Regulations 2000	These apply to medical and dental personnel and require that people conducting medical exposures must have acquired prescribed core knowledge and have adequate training records
Radiation (Emergency Preparedness and Public Information) Regulations 2001	Employers and local authorities have duties; deals with the distribution of information to the public
The Radioactive Material (Road Transport) Act 1991	This incorporates previous Atomic Energy Authority advice into UK law

Control of exposure

Following assessment of the risk arising from exposure to radioactive sources, it is then necessary to consider prevention and control measures. The general hierarchy of control can be applied to radiation with elimination of the hazard considered first, followed by substitution of materials by less radioactive alternatives. Application of the control hierarchy to radiation hazards, in particular, is discussed below. Broadly, precautions can be divided into administrative and practical.

Administrative arrangements

The precise arrangements necessary will depend on a particular situation but many of the following measures are likely to be needed including:

1. Demarcating specific areas and the classification of personnel based on their radiation exposure. It is necessary to decide which employees are to be designated 'classified' radiation workers and for whom health surveillance and personal dosimetry is required by IRR 1999.
2. Appointing radiation protection advisers (RPAs) and radiation protection supervisors (RPSs), as defined in the Regulations.
3. Designing and arranging appropriate radiation monitoring programmes including possible measurements of air contaminants.
4. Formulating waste disposal arrangements.
5. Preparing written systems of work for each location and making these available to the workforce.
6. Arranging for the training of personnel working with radiation on safe working procedures, the nature of the hazard and the necessity for precautions.

Practical measures

It is convenient to consider practical control measures as they are applied to external and internal radiation hazards.

External radiation hazard

This is where the hazard arises from sources outside the body from exposure to beta, gamma, X-ray or neutron radiation (alpha radiation is not normally an external radiation hazard as it cannot penetrate the outer layers of the skin). Principal control measures for sealed sources are by time of exposure, distance of person from radioactive source and degree of shielding.

Time

Cumulative radiation dose is a function of exposure time and dose rate. If an employee reduces the time they spend in an active area, then their total dose will be proportionately reduced.

Distance

The greater the distance that the exposed employee is from the source, the lower will be their exposure. This reduction follows the inverse square law, that is, if the distance between a point source of radiation and the object irradiated (in this case, the employee) is doubled, then the dose rate at the target will be one quarter of the original. (Conversely, if the distance is halved, then exposure will increase four-fold.) This emphasises the importance of ensuring that there is no direct hand contact with radioactive sources, which should always be handled remotely with tongs or tweezers with the worker wearing gloves.

Shielding

This is used to attenuate radiation and involves placing a shield between the source and the exposed employee. Due to the different penetrating powers of the different radiations, different amounts and types of shielding are required. The thickness of the shielding will depend on the energy of the radiation, the quantity present and the tolerable dose rate at the point of interest. (For occupied zones, this is normally taken as less than 2.5mSv h^{-1} and as far as reasonably practicable less than 1.0mSv h^{-1}.) The thickness required in a given situation will also depend on the shield material, for example, under standard conditions, half the thickness of lead is required when compared with steel. Concrete shields are used in the case of large sources.

TABLE 9.14: Radiation and shielding

Radiation	Shielding
α-radiation	Particles are very easily absorbed – thin piece of paper or foil, layer of skin or 3cm of air are normally sufficient
β-radiation (in the energy range of β-radiation normally encountered, ie 1–10MeV)	β-radiation requires up to 10mm of perspex for complete absorption; ease of shielding implies it is less dangerous than γ or neutron sources and an important problem is the generation of secondary X-rays (from bremsstrahlung); a β-shield should be constructed of materials of low mass number, ie aluminium or perspex to reduce the bremsstrahlung radiation emitted
γ-rays and X-rays	These are attenuated exponentially when they pass through any material; they may lose energy in a few interactions but they can travel a long distance before interacting; penetration depends on their radiation energy; stopped effectively by 'heavy' materials such as lead, steel and concrete
Neutrons	Often used with a neutron moderator (to reduce energy); material for neutron capture (to capture low energy electrons) and γ-shields; a combination of heavy and light materials is used and concrete is often chosen and boron in some cases

Personal dose control

Routine dose control is based on a system of area classification. The objective is to segregate areas based on their degree of radiological hazard.

The IRR 1999 specify a:
1. **Controlled area** – The purpose of a controlled area is to restrict exposure and potential spread outside the work area. These should be designated where exposures are likely to exceed an effective dose above 6mSv/year or an equivalent dose greater than three-tenths of any relevant dose limit (Schedule 4) for an employee aged over 18 years. For employees over 18 years, the current whole-body dose limit is 20mSv/year and, therefore, a controlled area would be required where exposures are likely to be in excess of around 6mSv/year. The ACoP recommends a controlled area be designated where the external radiation dose rate exceeds 7.5μSv/h and workers should have routine medical surveillance and personal dosimetry. Under regulation 17, every employer should make local rules with respect to both controlled and supervised areas.
2. **Supervised area** – This is where exposures for employees over 18 years are likely to be an effective dose above 1mSv/year or an equivalent dose greater than one-tenth of any relevant dose limit (Schedule 4), ie 2mSv/year. This designation depends on the assessment of likely doses and the possibility that conditions might change.
3. **Classified person** – This is an employee (over 18) who is likely to receive an effective dose in excess of 6mSv/year or an equivalent dose which exceeds three-tenths of any relevant dose limit (Schedule 4). Such employees must be informed that they have been designated a classified person (regulation 20).

A regular survey of areas should be undertaken to confirm designated classifications and that precautions are adequate. In controlled and supervised areas, film badges and TLD devices are used, often in conjunction with direct reading radiation dosimeters.

Internal radiation hazard

This arises from a radioactive source which has gained entry to the body. Once this has occurred, the source will continue to irradiate the body until the isotope either decays sufficiently or is excreted from the body. Material can enter the body by several routes including:
- inhalation by breathing in airborne contaminants;
- ingestion via the mouth and gastrointestinal tract;
- through skin wounds or other lesions;
- penetrating intact skin.

Assessment is required and risks are controlled by limiting airborne concentration and surface contamination. Risk assessments under IRR 1999 should be integrated, taking into account risk assessments required under the COSHH Regulations 2002. As with external radiation, the objective is to limit the dose to various organs of the body to permitted levels. For this purpose, derived limits for surface contamination (expressed in Bqm^{-2}) and airborne concentration (using the ICRP's annual limit of intake (ALI) for the nuclide and expressed in Bqm^{-3}) are used as tolerable levels.

An internal radiation source will only arise if the radioactive material escapes into the air or contaminates surfaces and containment efforts need to be applied to the processing of the material to prevent this occurring. For example, possibly the task in question could be carried out in a glove box or a suitable fume cupboard. Supporting measures such as air and surface contamination monitoring are also applied; results are compared with derived limits to determine if current control measures are adequate. Where unsealed sources are involved, there should be strict controls on food consumption and smoking. Employees should be encouraged to have high standards of personal hygiene and there should be strict control of items leaving contaminated areas.

There should be careful design of areas intended for radioactive work. Where possible, surfaces should be easy to clean and non-porous; glove boxes, fume cupboards and other local exhaust systems should be used where practicable. Appropriate personal protective equipment should be selected and applied in a well-managed scheme (Chapter 13). Specific requirements will depend on the nature and the amount of the contamination. Where there are significant amounts of airborne contamination, it is usually necessary to have a whole-body suit fitted with a respirator or air supply unit. With this equipment, changing, decontamination and maintenance facilities are required. Emergency plans and procedures are necessary for dealing with contaminated personnel.

REFERENCES

Building Research Establishment, 1995, *Radon in the Workplace*, BR 293, HMSO, London.

Clayton R F, 1995, Ionising Radiation, Chapter 14 in *Occupational Hygiene* (2nd edition), Harrington J M and Gardiner K (Eds), Blackwell Science, Oxford.

European Community, 1980, *Basic Safety Standards*, Council Directive 80/836/Euratom (later amended by 84/467/Euratom).

European Community, 1996, *Laying Down Basic Safety Standards for the Protection of the Health of Workers and the General Public Against the Dangers of Ionising Radiation*, Council Directive 96/29/Euratom.

European Community, 1997, *Health Protection of Individuals Against the Dangers of Ionising Radiation in Relation to Medical Exposure*, Council Directive 97/43/Euratom.

Health and Safety Commission, 1985, *The Protection of Persons Against Ionising Radiation Arising From Any Work Activity*, The Ionising Radiations Regulations 1985, Approved Code of Practice, L58, HSE Books, Sudbury.

Health and Safety Commission, 2000, *Work With Ionising Radiation*, The Ionising Radiations Regulations 1999, Approved Code of Practice and Guidance, L121, HSE Books, Sudbury.

Hunter D, 1978, *The Diseases of Occupations*, The English Universities Press Ltd, London.

International Commission on Radiological Protection, 1991, *Recommendations of the International Commission on Radiological Protection*, ICRP Publication 60, Annals of the ICRP, **21**, 1–3.

Martin A and Harbison S A, 1986, *An Introduction to Radiation Protection* (3rd edition), Chapman and Hall, London.

National Radiological Protection Board, 1999, *Ionising Radiation Exposure of the UK Population: 1999 Review*, NRPB-R311, NRPB.

LEGISLATION

Ionising Radiation (Medical Exposure) Regulations 2000 (SI 2000/1059)
Ionising Radiations Regulations 1999 (SI 1999/3232)
Radiation (Emergency Preparedness and Public Information) Regulations 2001 (SI 2001/2975)
Reporting of Injuries, Diseases and Dangerous Occurrences Regulations 1995 (SI 1995/3163)
The Radioactive Material (Road Transport) Act 1991
The Radioactive Substances Act 1993

10: Lighting

(HSE 1997 – rev. 2003)

INTRODUCTION

This chapter is concerned with what constitutes 'good lighting' and 'bad lighting', the improvement of unsatisfactory lighting from a health and safety point of view and, in a positive sense, creating pleasant, efficient and comfortable lighting conditions. Light is essential for sight and too much in the wrong place or wrong direction or with an unsuitable spectral composition may impair visual performance as well as health and safety.

Poor lighting may cause problems such as eyestrain, migraine and headaches, decreased efficiency and productivity, and it may result in an increased level of accidents. In new and refurbished buildings, unsatisfactory lighting has been linked with sick building syndrome and associated with symptoms of lethargy, irritability and poor concentration (HSE 1997). People need to move around in the workplace and good lighting is essential if they are to see and avoid obstacles. Work needs to be adequately illuminated so that people can see at an appropriate level of detail in order to carry out tasks correctly and efficiently. Lighting conditions which lead to stroboscopic effects and glare need to be minimised. (Process-generated visible light hazards arising from the use of lasers and from welding activities are considered in Chapter 8.)

According to the Workplace (Health, Safety and Welfare) Regulations 1992 (regulation 8(1)):

Every workplace shall have suitable and sufficient lighting.

Other requirements of regulation 8 are that, as far as is reasonably practicable, lighting provision should be by natural light and that suitable and sufficient emergency lighting must be provided, where people may be exposed to special danger, following the failure of artificial light sources. There are also requirements for lighting under other legislation. "Suitable and sufficient" is concerned with the amount of light reaching the task, its direction, the size of the source, its spectral composition and colour-rendering properties.

The Management of Health and Safety at Work Regulations 1999 (MHSW) require employers to

LIGHTING

assess risks in the workplace including whether lighting arrangements are adequate and do not create significant risks for employees.

Light

Light is a form of energy which manifests itself as electromagnetic radiation and has a speed of transmission of $3 \times 10^8 \text{ms}^{-1}$. The visible segment of the electromagnetic spectrum is highlighted below (Figure 10.1) and this makes up a wavelength range from 380nm (ultraviolet region) to 760nm (deep red region). Within this range, a change in wavelength will produce a change in colour. It is helpful to define some important lighting terms and the definitions below are from Kroemer & Grandjean (1995).

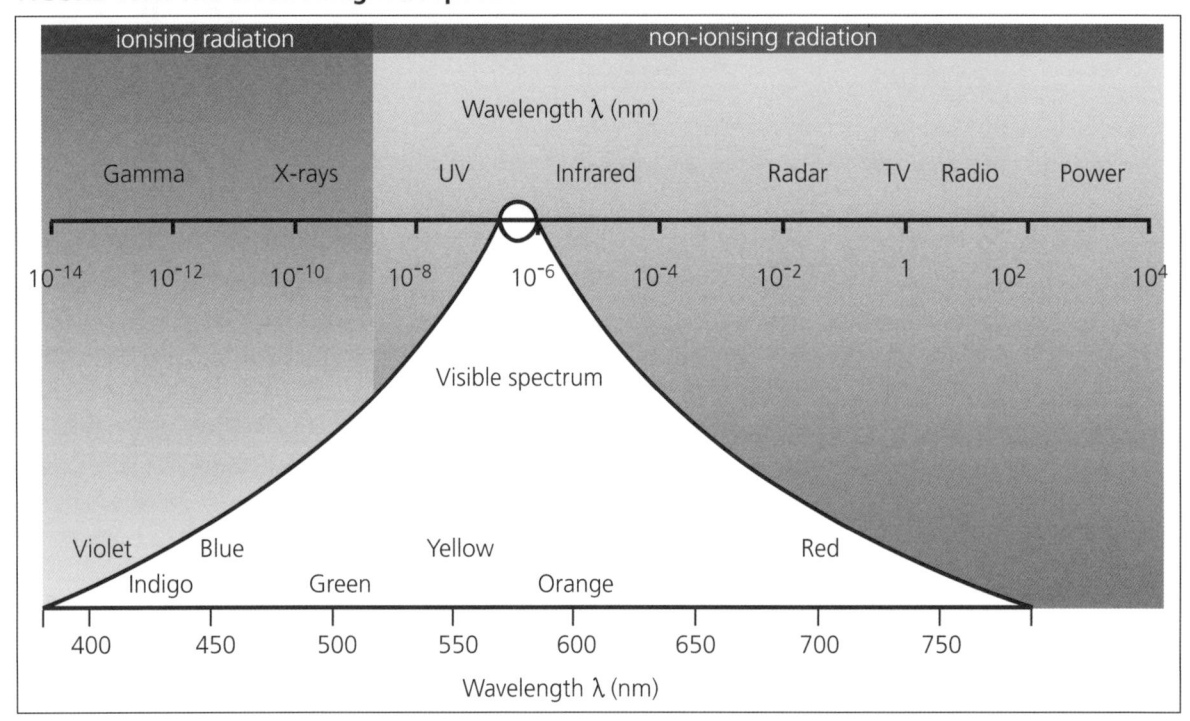

FIGURE 10.1: The electromagnetic spectrum

Illumination or illuminance

Illumination or illuminance is the amount of light falling on a surface. The unit of measurement is the lux:

1 lux (lx) = 1 lumen (lm) per square metre; the lumen is the unit of luminous flux

The eye responds to a very wide range of illumination levels, from a few lux in a darkened room to hundreds of thousands of lux outside in bright sunlight. Illumination levels in the open vary between 2,000–100,000lx during the day; at night, artificial lighting levels of 50–500lx are normal.

Luminance

Luminance is the amount of light reflected or emitted from a surface. The unit of measurement is the candela per m² (cdm^{-2}). This is the light which is seen on the surfaces of walls, furniture and other objects and depends on the absorptive or, conversely, reflective properties of the surface. The luminance of a lamp is an exact measure of the light emitted.

For example, in an office with an illumination of 300lx, the luminance of some common surfaces is given below:

- window surface – 1,000–4,000cdm^{-2};
- white paper – 78–80cdm^{-2};
- table surface – 40–60cdm^{-2}.

A typical fluorescent lamp would have a luminance of 10,000cdm^{-2}.

Smith (2000) distinguishes between illuminance and luminance in the diagram below (Figure 10.2).

FIGURE 10.2: Illuminance and luminance at a petrol forecourt

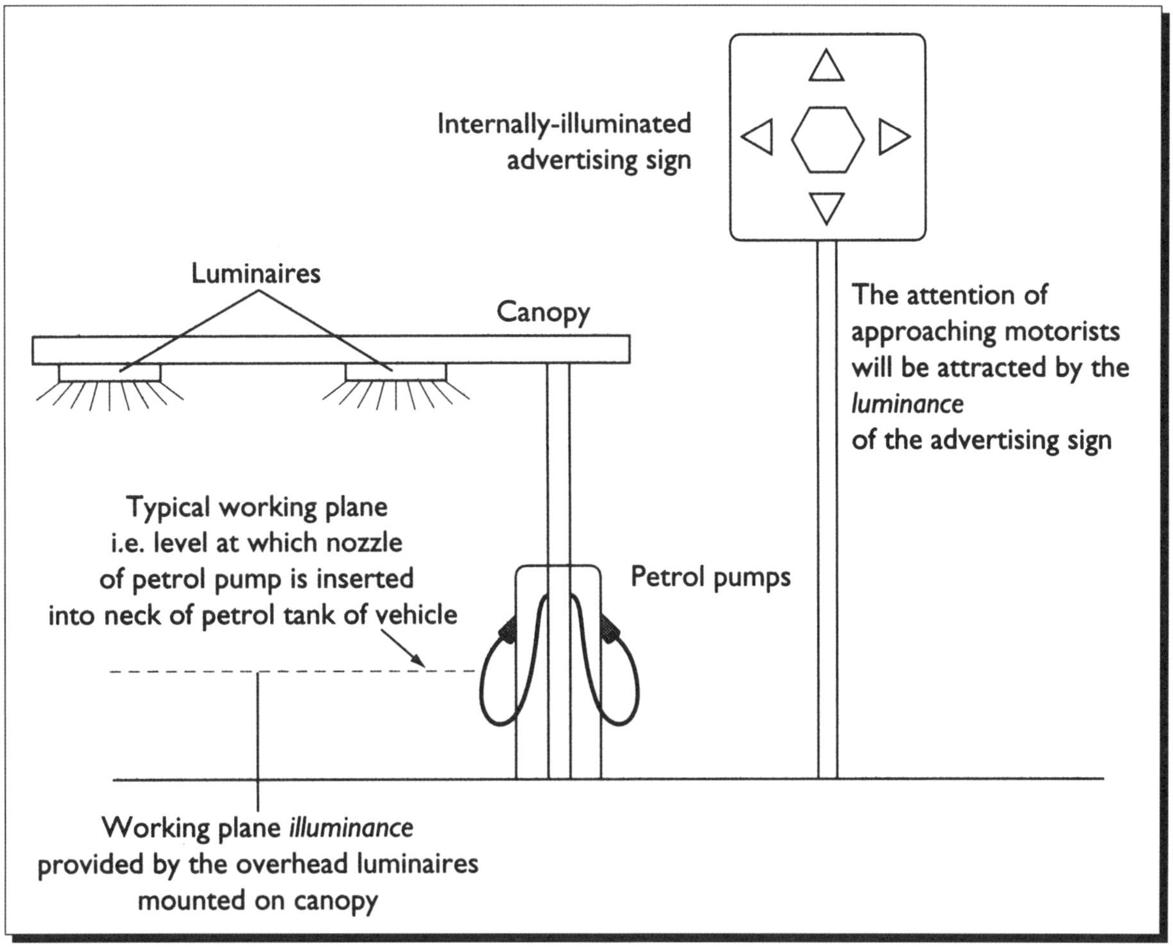

(Smith 2000. Reprinted by permission of Elsevier Limited.)

Reflectance

Different surfaces absorb varying amounts of the incident light. For example, a dark surface absorbs relatively more and, therefore, reflects less than a light-coloured surface. Reflectance is the ratio of incident light to reflected light. The reflectance of different surfaces can be measured and compared.

The visual process

A person can only see an object (see Figure 10.3) when light from the object enters the special sense organ, the eye, which collects light rays and focuses them into an image on the retina. The eye functions in a similar way to a camera.

Light enters the eye through the cornea and lens and falls on the retina which is the light-sensitive region of the eye. Light passes through the iris which functions like the diaphragm on a camera in controlling the amount of light passing through. The size of the pupil is controlled by the iris. The curvature of the lens can be varied so that an image can be focused on the retina. The retinal image is converted into nerve impulses which are transmitted to the brain by the optic nerve. These signals are interpreted by the brain and presented as the image we actually 'see'.

The retina consists of light-sensitive cells known as rods and cones. Cone cells work optimally at high levels of light and allow humans to see in colour (photopic vision), while at intermediate lighting levels, it is mainly the rod cells operating (mesopic vision). At low levels of illumination, only the rods function (grey or scotopic vision). Specialised cone cells are sensitive to red, green and blue light respectively. Cones are concentrated in the fovea region of the retina and this represents the centre of colour and the area of sharpest vision. (The eye is very sensitive to yellow-green colours at the centre of the visible spectrum and much less sensitive to reds and blues at the periphery.) Under certain conditions, the nerves of the retina will become fatigued and this results in distorted visual perception.

LIGHTING

FIGURE 10.3: Structure of the eye

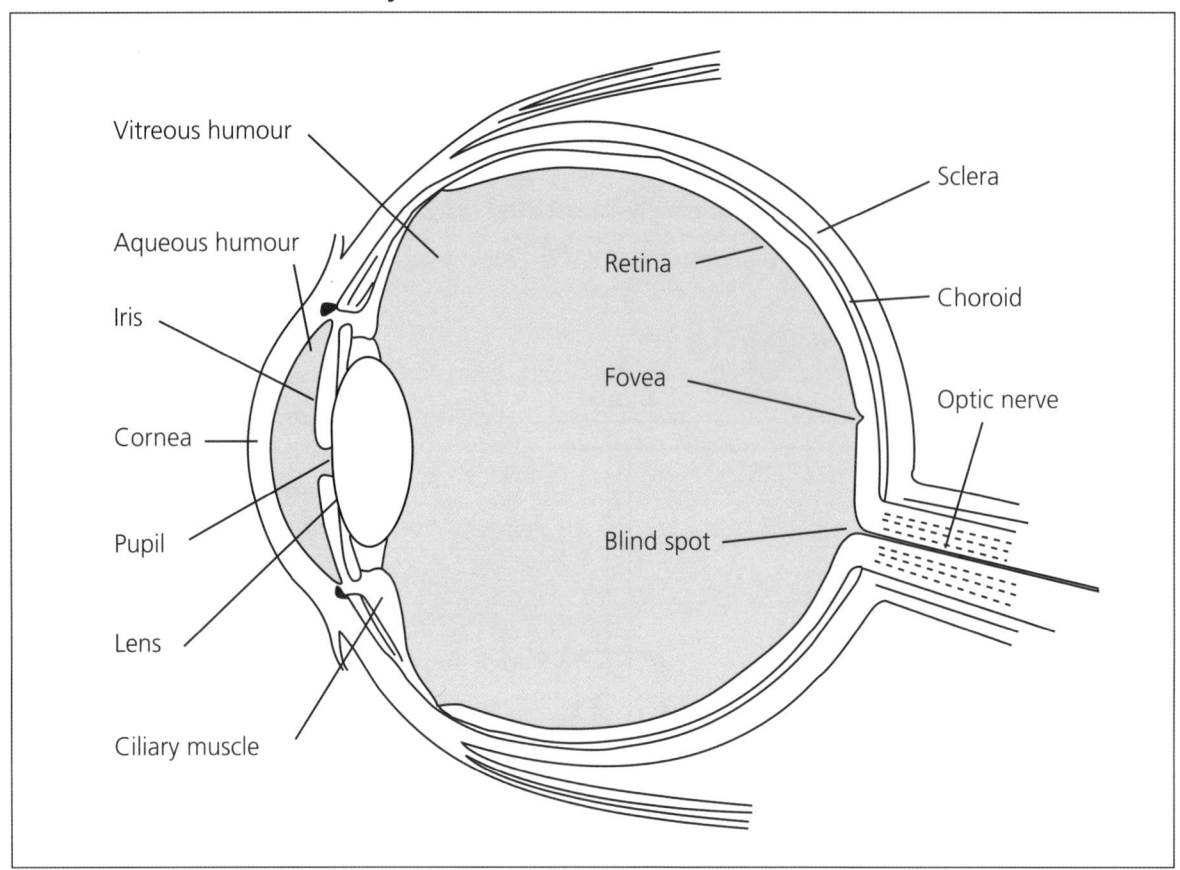

The stages of visual process are listed below:
1. Emission of light from a source or the reflection of light from an object.
2. Light reaches the eye and is absorbed by the retina.
3. Nerve impulses initiated by the retina are transmitted to the brain by the optic nerve.
4. The signals are interpreted by the brain as the 'seen' image.

Other important features of visual function are accommodation, adaptation and acuity, and these are discussed below.

Accommodation
This is the ability to focus on an object and involves two separate, automatic operations:
1. The adjustment of the lens to ensure that the image formed is sharp.
2. The convergence of the signals from both eyes to ensure that there is only one actual image seen.

Adaptation
By this process, the eye can focus over a wide range of brightness sources simultaneously. It responds to variations in brightness by changing its sensitivity to the brightness of the object being viewed. A low to high adaptation generally occurs in seconds, while a high to low adaptation may take several minutes.

The iris of the eye is a muscular diaphragm with a central opening (the pupil). The iris controls the amount of light entering the eye. The iris aperture opens and closes quickly in response to perceived brightness while the retina changes its sensitivity to light by a slower process. The iris compensates for small changes in brightness while the retina responds to large changes. Extensive adaptation uses significant amounts of energy and may result in visual fatigue. Under normal daylight conditions, the sensitivity of the eye peaks for light at a wavelength of 555nm, while under dark conditions this peak shifts to 505nm (Purkinje shift).

Visual acuity
This is the ability to discern detail and it is influenced by the luminance of the object being viewed. Visual acuity initially increases rapidly with task illumination and levels off at higher illumination.

Visual fatigue
This can be due to several factors including overall state of health and wellbeing, general deterioration in vision, for example, with ageing, and the levels of illuminance in a task environment. This fatigue can be subdivided into fatigue due to the visual task itself and that due to the task environment.

Visual task
In low levels of light, the brain amplifies signals by feedback to the eye and when this feedback becomes continuous, it causes eyestrain often resulting in headaches. Features of the visual task which lead to this are:
- minute detail being handled;
- very low contrast between task and background;
- movement of the task; and
- the nature of the surface of the task.

Task environment
Similarly, the features of the visual environment which lead to eyestrain are:
- inadequate illuminance;
- very high contrast between the task and the background;
- glare;
- flicker from fluorescence sources;
- stroboscopic effects; and
- a poor quality environment in general.

Light and lighting applications
Lighting conditions are composed of natural and artificial light sources[36]. The sky determines the level of natural light and the quantity entering a workplace depends on external reflections caused by obstructions and the number, size and cleanliness of doors, windows and skylights.

The daylight factor
Daylight illuminance levels vary greatly. In the UK (Southeast), for example, it ranges from a monthly average of 8,000lx in winter to 35,000lx in summer with a peak value of 50,000lx. Where external natural illuminance levels are below 5,000lx, then artificial lighting will be needed within a building. Indoor, natural lighting has three components, as illustrated in Figure 10.4.

FIGURE 10.4: Daylight factor components

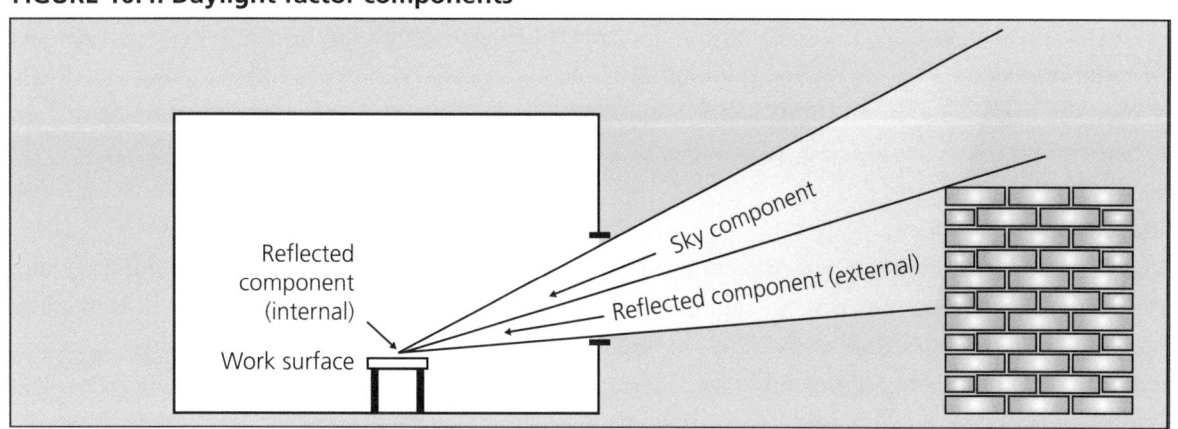

---

[36]Only electrically-powered light sources will be dealt with here.

LIGHTING

The amount of external natural light admitted to a building is rarely more than 10 per cent of the external value with much lower levels at points further from the windows. Because of variation in sky illuminances, interior natural light is expressed as a percentage of the outdoor value and this is known as the 'daylight factor'. Normally, for assessing interior environments, an average daylight factor is used. Where it is in excess of 5 per cent of the external value, then this is generally regarded as satisfactory whereas less than 2 per cent is regarded as unsatisfactory and further interior lighting would be needed.

Lighting installations

Exterior and interior lighting installations consist of a lamp, a luminaire and a control system. The aim of a lighting installation is to achieve a reasonably uniform illuminance in all relevant working areas.

Lamps

The lamp is the primary generator of the light source. Lamps can be broadly divided into two types: filament and discharge lamps. In the filament lamp, a metallic filament is heated by an electric current until it becomes candescent. This type is inefficient in energy terms since only about half of the electrical energy input is converted into heat.

With discharge lamps, electricity is passed through a gas (argon or neon) or a metal vapour (mercury or sodium) enclosed in a glass tube. The atoms of the gas or vapour absorb energy and electrons move to higher energy levels. When these electrons fall back to their normal energy level, electromagnetic radiation is released in the form of light. The wavelength of the light emitted (and thus colour) is determined by the particular gas or vapour used in the lamp. In discharge lamps, there is no direct electrical contact within the lamp, as is the case with filament lamps.

Discharge lamps can be subdivided into low pressure and high pressure lamps. Examples of low pressure lamps are sodium (SOX) lamps and the common fluorescent tube (low pressure mercury). Low pressure sodium lamps are monochromatic, emitting light at one wavelength only, that is, 589nm. At this frequency, the eye has maximum sensitivity and, therefore, these devices are very effective. However, their colour-rendering properties are very poor and with everything except yellow appearing as brown or black.

The inside of the discharge tube may be coated with a fluorescent substance, which converts the ultraviolet rays of the discharge into visible light. The colour of the visible light is determined by the chemical composition of the fluorescent material.

Fluorescent tubes have some advantages:
- high output and a long life;
- low luminance when adequately shielded;
- their light can be matched to daylight or similar conditions; and
- they have good colour-rendering properties.

The disadvantages of flicker and stroboscopic effects associated with fluorescent tubes are discussed later in this chapter.

Mercury vapour and metal halide lamps are examples of high pressure discharge lamps.

The typical characteristics and applications of a range of lamp types are listed in Table 10.1.

Luminaire

This is the actual light fitting, which provides support, fixing and an electrical connection for the lamp. Lighting is used in different activities and in different environments and the luminaire controls the flow of light, its direction on to the work and the brightness output. The luminaire facilitates the appropriate distribution of the light, sometimes by screening the lamp from direct view, minimising particulate deposition in dusty environments, and providing protection against flammable and corrosive atmospheres. Flameproofing, pressure protection and dustproofing measures are all specified in appropriate manufacturing standards for this equipment (BSI 1997).

TABLE 10.1: Typical lamps and their application

Lamp type and symbol	Typical lamp efficacy (lumens per watt)	Typical lamp life (hours)	Typical applications
Tungsten filament (GLS)	8–18	1,000–2,000	Domestic, display
Tungsten halogen (TH)	18–24	2,000–4,000	Display, traffic signals, overhead projectors (OHPs)
Mercury vapour (MB)	40–60	5,000–10,000	Industrial, road lighting
Metal halide (MBI)	65–85	5,000–10,000	Floodlighting and amenity lighting
Fluorescent (MCF)	50–100	5,000–10,000	Domestic, commercial
Low pressure (SOX)	100–175	6,000–12,000	Road lighting
High pressure sodium (SON)	65–120	6,000–12,000	Industrial, road lighting, civic and amenity lighting

(Smith 1995)

Lighting design

The amount of light on a surface affects the ability of people to see. If greater detail is needed, then a higher illuminance is required. The aim is to achieve a reasonably uniform illuminance recognising and minimising the effects of any shadows. Many factors will affect the choice of a specific lighting installation for a particular site. These include:

- physical constraints;
- the purpose of the installation; and
- suitability of the installation.

There are three basic types of lighting installation in commercial and industrial premises, namely, general, localised and local, and these are illustrated in Figure 10.5.

General

This seeks to provide an even level of lighting over the whole work area. It allows a relatively flexible plant layout but may provide more light than is needed in some areas. Therefore, this type of lighting is generally more costly than the other two approaches.

Localised

This is where there is preferential lighting of work task areas with lower levels in gangways and adjacent areas.

Local

This is lighting close to the work task to supplement general or localised lighting. Local lighting should not be used alone, since the high contrasts may cause eyestrain when looking up from work.

Lighting applications

Office lighting

In the past, lighting was principally concerned with visual tasks (mainly reading and writing) carried out on a horizontal surface (plane). The modern office has a much wider variety of tasks and a larger

LIGHTING

FIGURE 10.5: Types of lighting installation

General lighting

Localised lighting

Local lighting

(HSE 1987 – rev. 2003)

range of office machines (photocopiers, computers, etc) and work is carried out in different planes. Continuous use of artificial lighting has allowed flexibility in the use of office space. However, energy conservation constraints encourage the use of more localised lighting installations.

In an office environment, many tasks involve reading typed information and the visual task is influenced by the size of the type, the clarity of the type, and the reflectance of the type and paper. When analysing a task, an assessment needs to be made of the adaptation and accommodation required as well as the frequency of the particular activity.

Factory lighting

In factories, there is a very wide variation in the visual difficulty and character of work tasks. This requires a wide range of illuminance levels and specialised lighting installations. Factories commonly receive daylight from roof glazing and they tend to have large areas of space without many windows.

Light is required mainly where people are working and in traffic routes such as corridors or gangways. Different illuminances are appropriate in amenity and functional areas of the factory. Appropriate illuminance is the aim, since excessive levels of lighting are not cost-effective. In areas of automated production plant, higher lighting levels may only be necessary during inspection, maintenance and repair activities. As indicated above, lighting may have to operate in a variety of hostile environments, for example, dusty, wet, corrosive and/or explosive work areas. The lighting installations for such areas are highly specified.

Emergency lighting

This is a very important application especially in windowless work areas. Emergency lighting comes into action following the failure of mains electricity. The aim is to achieve a general level of one to two per cent of mains lighting, particularly for circulatory and escape routes. Emergency lighting in occupied work areas is a legal requirement under certain circumstances (Workplace (Health, Safety and Welfare) Regulations 1992, regulation 8(3)) and it needs to:

- clearly indicate escape routes;
- provide illumination for safe passage to exits; and
- enable fire alarm call points and firefighting equipment to be readily located.

Minimally, the centre-line limit for an escape route should be at a lower limit of 0.2lx and come into action within five seconds of mains failure (BSI 1999).

Standby lighting (five to 20 per cent of the lighting level generated by the mains electricity supply) enables essential work to continue and equipment and machinery to be rendered safe.

Lighting for areas with display screen equipment (DSE)

Where display screen equipment (DSE) is used, task or room lighting must achieve satisfactory lighting conditions and an appropriate level of contrast between the display screen and its background environment (HSE 1992). This takes into account the type of work and the visual requirements of the task operator. Glare and veiling reflections on the display screen should be prevented by appropriate arrangement of the workstation, work area, artificial lighting equipment and other light sources. Windows should be fitted with a suitable adjustable covering so that the amount of light falling on a DSE workstation can be controlled. Illuminance in the vicinity of display screen equipment should be between 300–500lx. DSE screens should be located as far from windows as is possible and the operator's viewing position should be parallel to the window wall. Furthermore, screens should be capable of being tilted, have an adjustable contrast control and be fitted with an anti-glare device.

The HSE in its guidance refers to the "specific and detailed guidance" given in the Chartered Institution of Building Services Engineers lighting guide for workstations with DSE equipment (CIBSE 1996, 2001).

In the provision of direct lighting in DSE areas, knowledge of the particular display screens and software in use (or to be used) is very important. This enables the selection of appropriate luminance values in the work area. Luminance limit angles are applied to avoid the high luminance parts of luminaires being reflected on the display screens. The limit angle is the angle above which luminance will not rise above a specified luminance limit. This is illustrated in Figure 10.6, which also shows the approach where the lighting engineer does not know the type of screens to be used in an area.

However, this concern with the light distribution of luminaires as regards DSE tasks should not compromise the overall risk assessment, which should take into account lighting provision for other non-DSE tasks carried out in the work area.

LIGHTING

FIGURE 10.6: Specifying downlighter luminaires in DSE areas

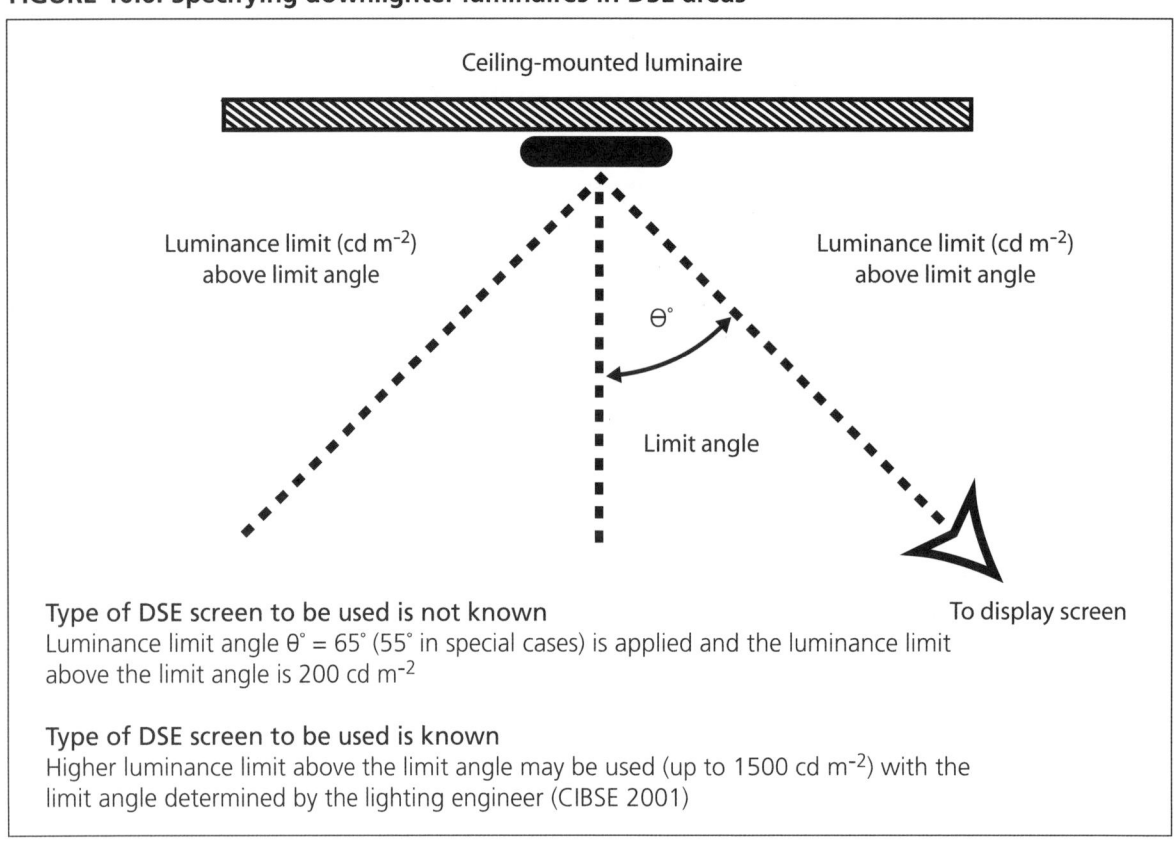

```
                    Ceiling-mounted luminaire
        ▨▨▨▨▨▨▨▨▨▨▨▨▨▨▨▨▨▨▨▨▨▨▨▨▨▨▨

  Luminance limit (cd m⁻²)              Luminance limit (cd m⁻²)
     above limit angle                      above limit angle
                              θ°
                           Limit angle
                                                  ▶
                                          To display screen
```

Type of DSE screen to be used is not known
Luminance limit angle θ° = 65° (55° in special cases) is applied and the luminance limit above the limit angle is 200 cd m⁻²

Type of DSE screen to be used is known
Higher luminance limit above the limit angle may be used (up to 1500 cd m⁻²) with the limit angle determined by the lighting engineer (CIBSE 2001)

Uplighters are often installed in areas where display screen equipment is used. Here, light is projected on to the ceiling and some is reflected back down into the room. This overcomes the problem of direct light falling on a screen causing glare and problematic reflections.

Exterior lighting

With outside workplaces, there is an absence of reflecting surfaces and much larger areas need to be illuminated with the luminaires often on high supports. Exterior lighting is used in goods yards, storage depots, construction sites, and car and lorry parks. Commonly, lighting is provided for the relatively few employees who are carrying out tasks which normally present little visual difficulty. Exterior installations often employ direct lighting, which causes sharp shadows and glare. The shadows may be a hazard and the glare causes visual discomfort. Increasing the mounting height will reduce shadows but higher-rated lamps may then be required for the same level of illumination. The likely positions of stored goods and parked vehicles should be taken into account when planning the position of luminaires.

Mobility is an important issue in construction site lighting, since it is common for luminaires to be relocated regularly as work progresses.

Hazardous area lighting

In the Dangerous Substances and Explosive Atmospheres Regulations 2002, Schedule 2, hazardous areas are classified as follows:

Classification of hazardous places
Hazardous places are classified in terms of zones on the basis of the frequency and duration of the occurrence of an explosive atmosphere.

Zone 0
A place in which an explosive atmosphere consisting of a mixture with air of dangerous substances in the form of gas, vapour or mist is present continuously or for long periods or frequently.

Zone 1

A place in which an explosive atmosphere consisting of a mixture with air of dangerous substances in the form of gas, vapour or mist is likely to occur in normal operation occasionally.

Zone 2

A place in which an explosive atmosphere consisting of a mixture with air of dangerous substances in the form of gas, vapour or mist is not likely to occur in normal operation but, if it does occur, will persist for a short period only.

Zone 20

A place in which an explosive atmosphere in the form of a cloud of combustible dust in air is present continuously, or for long periods or frequently.

Zone 21

A place in which an explosive atmosphere in the form of a cloud of combustible dust in air is likely to occur in normal operation occasionally.

Zone 22

A place in which an explosive atmosphere in the form of a cloud of combustible dust in air is not likely to occur in normal operation but, if it does occur, will persist for a short period only.

As well as using the above zoning, BS EN 60079-14 classifies the luminaires which may be used in specific hazardous atmospheres (BSI 1997a).

Effects of lighting

Visual fatigue

Glare

Glare is most commonly experienced when lamps are directly visible close to the line of sight. It occurs when one part of the visual field is brighter than the level to which the eye has become adapted. There are two important sources of this excessive luminance, first, direct glare (eg the sun or a car headlight), and second, indirect or reflected glare from polished or glossy surfaces.

There are two types of glare:

1. **Discomfort glare** – this is where glare only causes discomfort, ie irritability and annoyance.
2. **Disability glare** – this is where glare causes direct interference with visual performance.

Overall, discomfort glare has been studied more extensively than disability glare. The distinction is often blurred and some light sources cause both types of glare. Under conditions of glare, there is often distraction from the work task, since the eye tends to move to the brightest part of the visual field, in a response known as the 'phototropic effect'. This can result in visual fatigue and with prolonged exposure, this commonly results in eyestrain and headache. It is possible to assign a numerical value to discomfort glare, which may then be compared with published standard values (CIBSE 1994).

Flicker

Fluorescent lighting operates from an alternating current and tubes produce a flickering light at a frequency of 100Hz (in Europe). Where this frequency is reduced to 50Hz or less, the flicker becomes visible to most people. This may happen with old or defective fluorescent tubes. Also, with some apparently normal tubes, small 50Hz fluctuations may be superimposed on the normal 100Hz cycle. Flicker causes harmful effects resulting from repetitive overexposure of the retina. This is a source of visual discomfort causing annoyance, fatigue and occasionally epileptic seizures (typically at frequencies between 5Hz and 25Hz). Stroboscopic effects are discussed below and are included in Table 10.4.

Veiling reflections

These are high luminance reflections which obscure task details, affecting task performance and causing visual discomfort. A common example is a reflected window on a dark DSE screen. The bright reflection may be a source of disabling glare and may also put a veil of light over the display.

Tissue damage

Infrared radiation and ultraviolet radiation

Some lamps produce significant emissions at infrared (IR) and ultraviolet (UV) wavelengths, both of which are invisible and, therefore, people could be unknowingly exposed. For example, tungsten-halogen lamps operate at high temperatures and emit high levels of UV radiation, consequently a filter should be incorporated into the luminaire. Similarly, high-powered lamps, as used in theatres and studios, have a very high output of IR and UV radiation and these are a hazard to the skin and the cornea of the eye when used at close proximity for extended periods. The hazards of these and other types of non-ionising radiation are discussed in Chapter 8.

Visible radiation

With visible radiation, people will look away from a very bright light source and will, therefore, be protected. With high-powered lamps, eyesight can sometimes be damaged before people can look away. The risks arising from the use of lasers are discussed in Chapter 8.

Health and safety hazards

Colour effects

A surface lit by different artificial light sources or by daylight, under changing lighting conditions, may appear to vary in colour. Variation in the perception of colour may have implications for health and safety, for example, in some electrical work. However, for most light sources, the change in the appearance of colour is not significant enough to cause problems. With monochromatic light sources (eg sodium discharge lamps), colours are not identifiable. Also, with very low levels of illuminance, colour vision doesn't function. When a significant risk arises from colour effects, then lighting conditions which will prevent this need to be determined and introduced.

Stroboscopic effects

This occurs where lights are powered by an alternating electricity supply which produces oscillations in light output. Where the rate of flicker exactly matches the speed of a moving object, the object will appear stationary (stroboscopic effect). For example, this causes machines to appear stationary or moving slowly either forwards or backwards where there is a small mismatch. These effects need to be prevented where they create a significant health and safety risk.

Tolerability standards for lighting conditions

As first discussed at the start of this chapter, the Workplace (Health, Safety and Welfare) Regulations 1992 specify that workplaces shall have "suitable and sufficient lighting"[37]. The HSE gives guidance on minimum acceptable illumination conditions for interior and exterior lighting installations (HSE 1997). These recommendations cover both illuminance on the task and illuminance ratios (see Tables 10.2 and 10.3). Average illuminance levels and minimum levels of illuminance are specified, both for the workplace as a whole and for any position in the workplace.

---

[37]The phrase "suitable and sufficient lighting" has been interpreted under the Factories Act 1961 to apply not just to the lighting installation, but also to mean that all practicable steps must be taken to ensure that lights are switched on whenever appropriate or reasonably accessible light switches are provided.

TABLE 10.2: Recommended task illuminance levels

Activity	Typical locations/ type of work	Average illuminance (lux) lx	Minimum measured illuminance (lux) lx	Comments
Movement of people, machines and vehicles	Lorry park, corridors, circulation routes	20	5	No perception of detail needed here so only safety hazard is considered; higher level needed where perception of detail is required
Movement of people, machines and vehicles in hazardous areas; rough work – no perception of detail required	Construction site clearance, excavation and soil work, loading bays, bottling and canning plants	50	20	Aim is prevention of visual fatigue; adequate levels for safety purposes
Work requiring limited perception of detail	Kitchens, factories assembling large components, potteries	100	50	Aim is prevention of visual fatigue; adequate levels for safety purposes
Work requiring perception of detail	Office work, sheet metal work, bookbinding	200	100	Aim is prevention of visual fatigue; adequate levels for safety purposes
Work requiring perception of fine detail	Drawing offices, factories assembling electronic components, textile production	500	200	Aim is prevention of visual fatigue; adequate levels for safety purposes

(From HSE 1997 – rev. 2003)

TABLE 10.3: Maximum illuminance ratios for adjacent areas

Applicable situations	Location	Maximum ratio of illuminance working area:adjacent area
Where each task is individually lit and the area around the task has a lower illuminance	Local lighting in an office	5:1
Two working areas are adjacent, but one has a lower luminance than the other	Localised lighting in a works store	5:1
Two working areas are lit to different illuminances and separated by a barrier, but there is frequent movement between them	Storage area inside a factory and a loading area outside	10:1

(From HSE 1997 – rev. 2003)

LIGHTING

The illuminance level needed depends on how much detail needs to be seen in a given task situation. It also depends on the speed and efficiency at which the work is required to be performed. Detailed performance-related requirements and lighting levels are specified by the Chartered Institution of Building Services Engineers (CIBSE) (1994).

The CIBSE Guides specify the lighting conditions for a wide variety of premises and give guidance on achieving the desired levels (CIBSE 1989, 1993).

Glare index

The glare index is a numerical value assigned to the level of discomfort glare following a method specified by CIBSE. Such values are then compared with those listed in the CIBSE Code (CIBSE 1994). To avoid discomfort glare, the values listed in the CIBSE index list should not be exceeded.

Management of risks from lighting

An assessment of the visual environment is needed in two situations: first, in a design context where the purpose is to create an environment to ensure visual comfort and efficiency; and second, where an environment already exists and the aim is to assess and control risks arising from lighting hazards. The latter situation is that most likely to be encountered by health and safety specialists.

Hazard identification

It is important to examine lighting in the work environment closely in order to identify what may cause harm or injury.

Typical risks from lighting originate from:

- lighting effects (glare, colour effects, flicker and stroboscopic effects, veiling reflections, radiation effects);
- poor lighting design;
- improper lighting installation, maintenance, replacement and disposal; and
- improper selection of emergency lighting.

Measurement and analysis of risk factors

Assessment of lighting levels

The aim of a lighting survey is to understand the lighting distribution levels in a workplace, to determine whether these are suitable for the intended work, and to ensure that they do not pose significant health and safety risks by suggesting control measures. A survey could involve a single workstation or the whole work area. An assessment form and a checklist is useful for the evaluation of lighting conditions.

The principal objectives of the assessment are to decide whether:

- illuminances are sufficient and identify deficiencies;
- lighting is suitable for the workroom's function;
- there are excessive and undesirable shadows or reflections on work surfaces; and
- colour rendering is satisfactory.

Where interiors are lit by discharge lamps, there should be a check for flicker or stroboscopic effects near moving machinery.

Measurements of daylight factor values in a workplace may be required for several reasons. For example, the erection of a new building or other structure nearby may affect the amount of natural light entering a workplace, and where planned control measures for one workstation may affect the amount of natural daylight reaching other parts of the workplace.

It is helpful to have an initial walk-through survey of the work area to gain a subjective impression of lighting conditions, noting areas where detailed assessment is necessary. The second stage involves systematic measurement and evaluation of lighting conditions.

Information collection and walk-through survey

This initially involves collection of information on the following (where appropriate):

- type of workspace and its use;
- principal visual tasks and the plane(s) on which they are carried out;
- recommended illuminance levels or daylight factors;
- nature of lighting (natural, artificial or both);
- type of luminaires;
- type of lamps and wattage;
- condition of lighting (whether all lamps are working, whether lamps, luminaires and windows are clean);
- reflectances of principal room surfaces (assessed subjectively);
- the use of the work space, and the range, timing and severity of environmental problems (obtained by interviewing task operators);
- dimensions of the workroom and its furniture and layout;
- the layout of the workroom;
- principal working surfaces and their relationship with the windows, luminaires and other features; and
- overlay plans of workroom and ceiling.

Lighting measurement

Measurements should be carried out on an overcast day. Illuminance and luminance measurements are made at workstations and surfaces under normal lighting conditions. General and local lighting is measured separately to assess the contribution of each. A grid measurement method is commonly employed for taking and recording measurements.

Instrumentation

Photometers contain a photocell which converts light into an electric current and this is measured on a display in lx. For workplace assessments, a suitable range device will measure up to 2,500lx. Some very sensitive photometers are available which can measure down to very low levels (0.2lx or less) and these are used in the assessment of emergency lighting. Some devices will measure up to 100,000lx.

In devices where the photocell and the meter are connected by a cable, the display can be read without the observer overshadowing the cell. A basic photometer does not have the same response to light spectra as the eye. (The eye is very sensitive to yellow-green colours at the centre of the visible spectrum and much less sensitive to reds and blues at the periphery.) However, photometers can be corrected by the use of appropriate filters (colour correction). Instruments are also 'cosine-corrected' to compensate for the arrival of light at the sensor from different directions. As illustrative examples, two photometers are shown in Figure 10.7.

FIGURE 10.7: Examples of photometers

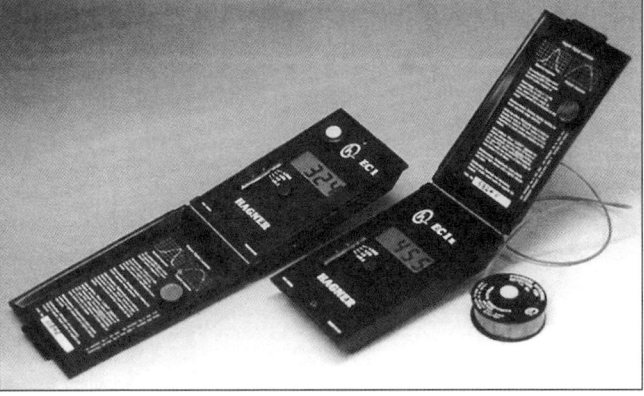

(Hagner Photometric Instruments Ltd)

TABLE 10.4: Integrated lighting control measures

Hazard from which a health and safety risk may arise	Risk control measures
Insufficient light on task – illuminance too low	• Clean lamp and luminaire • Replace failed lamps • Increase reflectance of the room surfaces (dark to light) • Remove obstructions • Decrease spacing of luminaires • Provide more local lighting • Move work area
Uneven lighting	• Replace failed lamps and clean luminaires • Provide additional luminaires • Decrease spacing of luminaires • Change luminaires to give wider light distribution and more upward light without causing glare • Increase reflectance of room surfaces • Remove obstructions
Luminaire too bright, resulting in glare	• If bare lamp, fit light controller • Move luminaire outside exclusion zone • Change orientation of luminaire for an end-on view • Raise height of luminaire • Increase reflectance of room surfaces against which luminaires are seen
Reduced contrast by task veiling reflections	• Change to matt finish • Move workstation • Move any bright sources • Increase local lighting • Increase luminance by increasing reflectance of room surfaces
Flicker	• Planned maintenance to change lamps near to the end of their service life • Check for electrical faults • Use high frequency control gear • Supply adjacent rows of luminaires from different phases of the electricity supply
Stroboscopic effects	• Supply adjacent rows of luminaires from different phases of the electricity supply • Use high frequency control gear • Provide a high frequency supply • Replace or remove local lighting
Tasks difficult to see	• Ensure task background is clear • Provide sufficient lighting • Increase contrast between task and background • Provide magnification

(Adapted from HSE 1997 – rev. 2003)

A daylight factor survey is normally carried out with a standard light meter. A specific daylight factor meter may be used, although these are relatively rare. The results are normally expressed as contours, that is, lines of equal daylight plotted on a plan of the work area. It is important to emphasise that daylight factors should only be measured under an overcast sky.

Prevention and control measures

A range of prevention and control measures can be applied to lighting hazards.

Workplace design

By careful design of workplaces and workstations, it is often possible to reduce the need for artificial lighting, but complete elimination is not usually a realistic option. Lighting conditions prevailing must be appropriate for the tasks taking place in a given area.

Integrated application of lighting controls

Table 10.4 summarises the application of a range of integrated process and environmental controls to lighting hazards.

Legal requirements

The legal requirements relating to lighting conditions are summarised in Table 10.5.

TABLE 10.5: Legal requirements for lighting conditions

Regulations	Requirement
Health and Safety at Work etc Act 1974	Duty to ensure health, safety and welfare of employees and others
The Management of Health and Safety at Work Regulations 1999	Duty to assess risks to health and safety arising from lighting conditions
The Workplace (Health, Safety and Welfare Regulations) 1992	Every workplace shall have 'suitable and sufficient lighting'; also emergency lighting where people are specially exposed to danger
The Docks Regulations 1988	Premises for dock operations shall be 'suitably and adequately lighted'
The Construction (Health, Safety and Welfare) Regulations 1996	Every working place and approach shall have 'suitable and sufficient lighting'
The Health and Safety (Display Screen Equipment) Regulations 1992	Detailed requirements for lighting conditions in rooms where DSE is to be used

REFERENCES

Ashton I and Gill F S, 2000, *Monitoring for Health Hazards at Work* (3rd edition), Blackwell Science, Oxford.

British Standards Institution, 1997, *Luminaires: General Requirements and Tests*, BS EN 60598-1, BSI, London.

British Standards Institution, 1997a, *Electrical Apparatus for Explosive Gas Atmospheres. Electrical Installations in Hazardous Areas (Other Than Mines)*, BS EN 60079-14, BSI, London.

British Standards Institution, 1999, *Emergency Lighting: Code of Practice for the Emergency Lighting of Premises Other Than Cinemas and Other Specified Premises Used for Entertainment*, BS 5266-1, BSI, London.

Chartered Institution of Building Services Engineers, 1989, *The Industrial Environment*, CIBSE Lighting Guide 1.

Chartered Institution of Building Services Engineers, 1993, *Lighting for Offices*, CIBSE Lighting Guide 7.

Chartered Institution of Building Services Engineers, 1994, *Code for Interior Lighting*.

Chartered Institution of Building Services Engineers, 1996, *The Visual Environment for Display Screen Use*, 3rd edition, CIBSE Lighting Guide 3.

Chartered Institution of Building Services Engineers, 2001, *The Visual Environment for Display Screen Use – A New Standard of Performance*, Addendum to CIBSE Lighting Guide 3.

Health and Safety Commission, 1992, *Workplace Health, Safety and Welfare*, Approved Code of Practice, L24, HSE Books, Sudbury.

Health and Safety Executive, 1987, *Lighting at Work* (1st edition), HS(G)38, HMSO, London (out of print).

Health and Safety Executive, 1992, *Display Screen Equipment Work*, The Health and Safety (Display Screen Equipment) Regulations 1992, Guidance on Regulations, L26, HSE Books, Sudbury.

Health and Safety Executive, 1997, *Lighting at Work* (2nd edition), HSG38, HSE Books, Sudbury.

Kroemer K H E and Grandjean E, 1995, *Fitting the Task to the Human* (5th edition), Taylor and Francis, London.

Oborne D J, 1995, *Human Factors in Design and Development* (3rd edition), Wiley, Chichester.

Smith N A, 1995, Light and Lighting, Chapter 11 in *Occupational Hygiene* (2nd edition), Harrington J M and Gardiner K (Eds), Blackwell Science, Oxford.

Smith N A, 2000, *Lighting for Health and Safety*, Butterworth-Heinemann, Oxford.

LEGISLATION

Dangerous Substances and Explosive Atmospheres Regulations 2002 (SI 2002/2776)

Management of Health and Safety at Work Regulations 1999 (SI 1999/3242)

Workplace (Health, Safety and Welfare) Regulations 1992 (SI 1992/3004)

Provision and Use of Work Equipment Regulations 1998 (as amended) (SI 1998/2306)

11: Agents of physical misfit

(Else)

INTRODUCTION

Poor work design may lead to a physical misfit between workers and the tasks they are required to carry out and this may result in the development of work-related musculoskeletal disorders (WMSDs). The back, neck, shoulders and upper limbs are particularly at risk, together with injuries to the hips and knees. The picture above illustrates an uncomfortable posture taken up during welding work, which puts considerable strain on the person's lower back. Some musculoskeletal disorders develop as chronic conditions following a long period of exposure to mechanical stresses from hazardous work, or they may occur as acute injuries resulting from an accident, for example, a fall.

The 1990 Labour Force Survey estimated that 5.4 million working days were lost due to musculoskeletal disorders "caused or made worse by work". This included 2.8 million days lost due to back problems (Hodgson *et. al* 1993). In the 1995 survey of self-reported, work-related ill health (SWI95), there was an estimated overall prevalence of 1,155,000 for musculoskeletal conditions including back injuries (508,000), upper limb and neck disorders (375,000) and lower limb conditions (100,000). Other categories of mixed musculoskeletal disorders (where an individual has more than one condition) make up the residue of total cases (Jones *et al.* 1998).

Paoli (1997), in a large representative survey of the EU workforce, reported that 17 per cent of workers experienced muscular pain in the arms and legs and 30 per cent suffered from backache. There is evidence that exposure to risk factors leading to WMSDs is increasing. Paoli (1997) showed that the prevalence of WMSD risk factors – such as painful posture, high musculoskeletal demands and high-speed work with tight deadlines – increased between 1992 and 1996.

In response to European directives, specific UK regulations concerned with the prevention and control of WMSDs have been enacted, namely, the Health and Safety (Display Screen Equipment) Regulations 1992 and the Manual Handling Operations Regulations 1992. These supplement the general requirements of the Management of Health and Safety at Work Regulations 1999 and the Health and Safety at Work etc Act 1974.

The employer's common law duty of care is also relevant to the prevention of WMSDs and requires the application of reasonably practicable control measures. In a recent civil law case, it was held that five bank encoders suffered WMSDs caused by repetitive work under intensive pressure with insufficient work breaks and sustained bad posture (*Alexander et al. -v- Midland Bank*).

AGENTS OF PHYSICAL MISFIT

FIGURE 11.1: Work-related musculoskeletal disorders

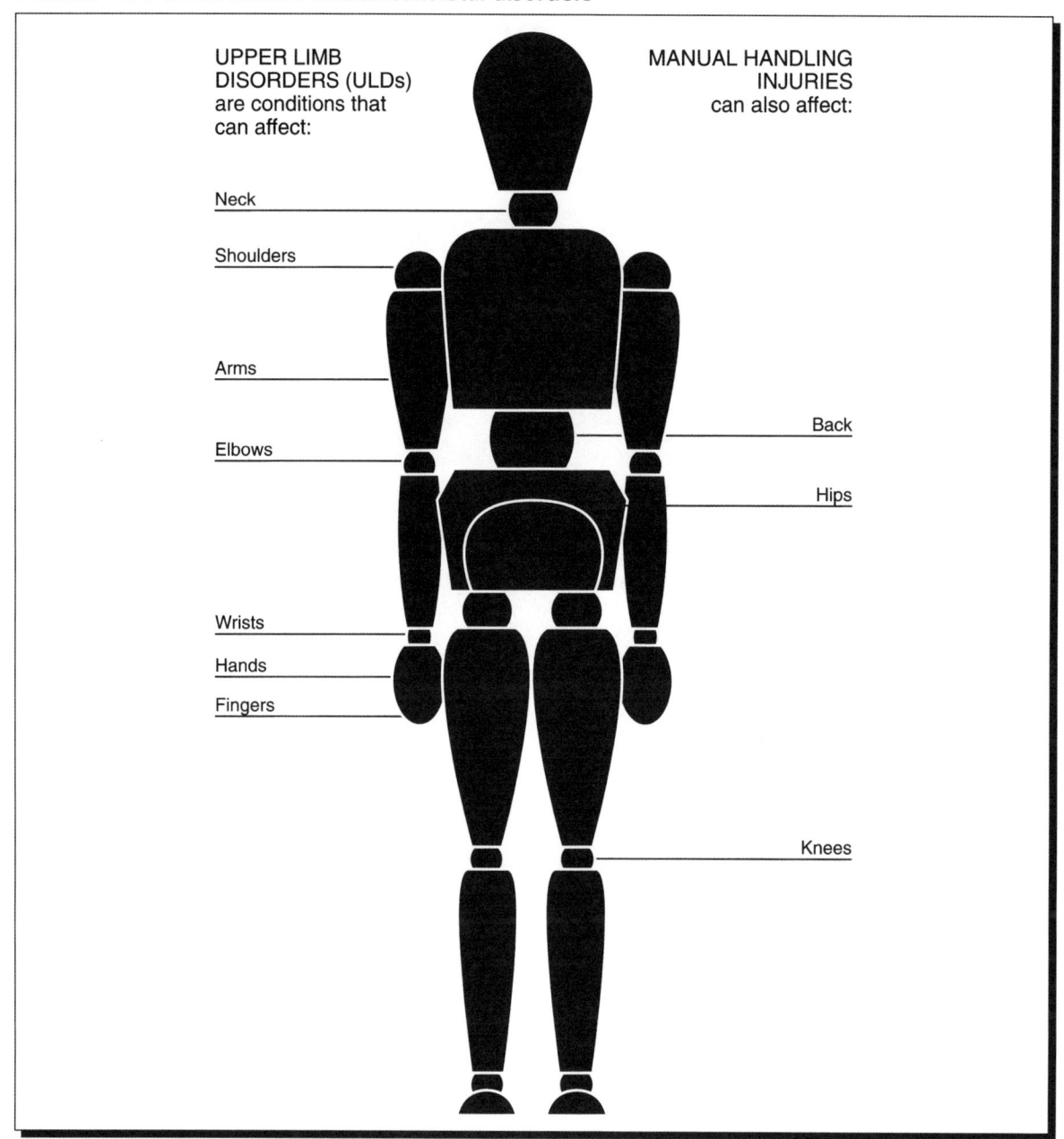

UPPER LIMB DISORDERS (ULDs) are conditions that can affect:
- Neck
- Shoulders
- Arms
- Elbows
- Wrists
- Hands
- Fingers

MANUAL HANDLING INJURIES can also affect:
- Back
- Hips
- Knees

(HSC 1996)

In this chapter, the ergonomics approach to risk assessment is applied in the prevention and control of risk of WMSDs. As well as considering the risks from work environments in general, particular attention will be given to work with display screen equipment (DSE) and to manual handling operations.

In the prevention of WMSDs, it is necessary to identify misfit hazards, both physical and psychosocial, in order to assess risks, determine tolerability and decide on the appropriateness of further preventive measures. The assessment of physical agents of misfit is discussed in this chapter while psychosocial aspects are dealt with in Chapter 12.

The HSE has recently revised its guidance on upper limb disorders in the workplace (HSE 2002) and this presents a risk management-based cycle which acknowledges the importance of psychosocial as well as physical risk factors. This approach is based on a seven-stage management cycle:

1. Understand the issues and commit to action.
2. Create the right organisational environment.
3. Assess the risk of upper limb disorders in your workplace.
4. Reduce the risks of upper limb disorders.
5. Educate and inform your workforce.
6. Manage any episodes of upper limb disorders.
7. Carry out regular checks on programme effectiveness.

The ergonomics approach

Fitting the task to the worker is the concern of ergonomics. Ergonomics identifies the workload, activities and objectives of work to identify where these do not fit human characteristics. According to Clark & Corlett (1984), ergonomics is:

> ...the study of human abilities and characteristics which affect the design of equipment, systems and jobs... and its aims are to improve efficiency, safety and wellbeing.

Ergonomics focuses on human characteristics, capabilities and limitations when considering the design and assessment of work. It is an interdisciplinary subject including aspects of human psychology, anatomy, physiology, mathematics, physics and related disciplines. Ergonomics data comprises information on human characteristics and capabilities including data on body size, body forces, sensing capacity (ie the detection and relay of signals by the central nervous system), information processing and mental capacity.

Parsons (1995) identifies four general categories of approach to collecting information in ergonomics and these are outlined below:

1. **Objective methods** – direct measurement of human characteristics.
2. **Subjective methods** – this is where people report their impressions, verbally or in questionnaires.
3. **Behavioural methods** – behaviour of humans is observed by a trained observer and inferences are drawn.
4. **Predictive modelling** – a model of a human system is used to predict a human response.

It is also important to note that task analysis is a fundamental tool in ergonomics and this is used to break down, systematically, the different steps that are involved in tasks at work (Kirwan & Ainsworth 1993). In the context of health and safety, task analysis can be used as a basis for risk assessment, since it can highlight the problems that can arise when performing a particular task.

Ergonomics data and methods have contributed very widely to enlightened design of work and working systems and Parsons (1995) identifies some of the important contributions. First, in the design of office and computerised workstations, second, the use of ergonomics data in the development of safe handling techniques, and third, in the design and application of effective personal protective equipment.

In summary, ergonomics is concerned with the use of scientific data on human physical and mental capacities and performance for the design of work and working systems. Ergonomics relates closely with agents of physical misfit.

Risk management and WMSDs

In order to understand the types of WMSDs, and their causation and prevention, it is helpful to understand the basic features of the musculoskeletal system and a typical joint. The muscular and skeletal systems are common targets in many occupational ill health disorders. The skeleton provides a framework for muscles to achieve the maintenance of posture, movement and manipulation of the environment. The musculoskeletal system includes:

- bones;
- joints;
- cartilage (rubbery smooth tissue on the end of bones in joints);
- ligaments (fibrous cords which bind the bones together at joints); and
- muscles and tendons.

Joints occur where two or more bones touch. There are several types: fixed, slightly moveable and freely moveable or synovial. With fixed joints, such as those which form the roof of the skull, no movement is possible. With a slightly moveable joint, a degree of movement is possible, as, for example, in the vertebrae of the spinal column which can move slightly against the cartilaginous disks located between them. There are around 70 freely movable or synovial joints in the body. The shoulder, knee and elbow are examples and a generalised example is shown in Figure 11.2. Where the ends of the bones rub together, they are covered with a slippery cartilage and the joint is lubricated by synovial fluid. This fluid is sealed in the joint by the surrounding synovial membrane. The bones of the joint are held in place by the fibrous ligaments while at the same time, depending on the type of joint, they are allowed extensive freedom of movement.

FIGURE 11.2: Structure of a freely movable (or synovial) joint

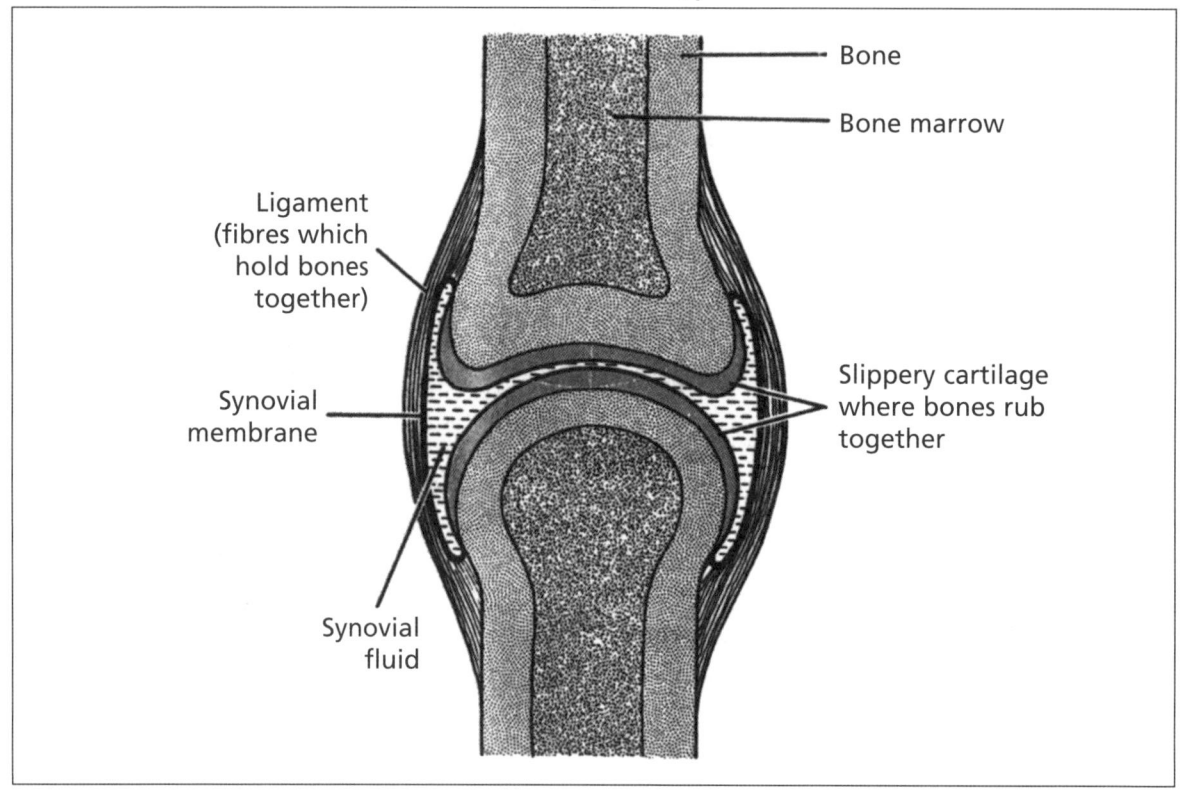

The ligaments are fibrous cords which bind the bones together at joints, and the elbow joint is presented as an illustrative example in Figure 11.3. Sprains occur when ligaments of a joint are overstretched and torn, causing swelling and pain.

FIGURE 11.3: Ligaments holding the elbow joint together

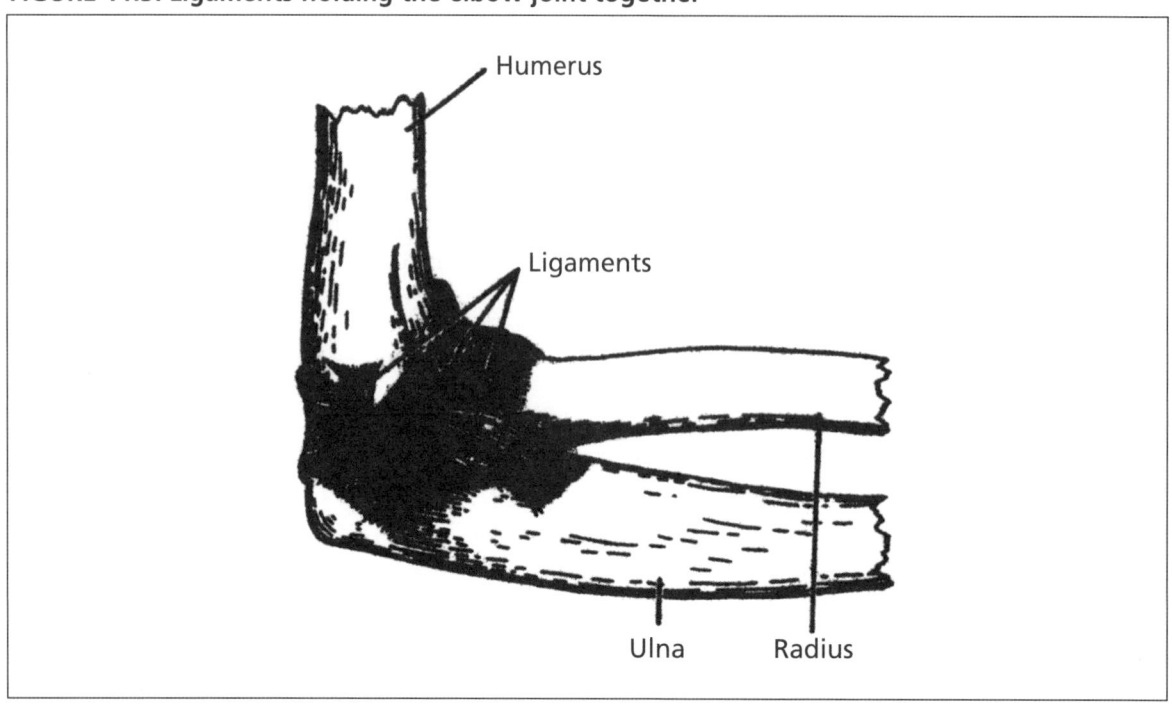

The arrangement of the muscles and bones in the arm is shown in Figure 11.4.

FIGURE 11.4: Muscles in the arm

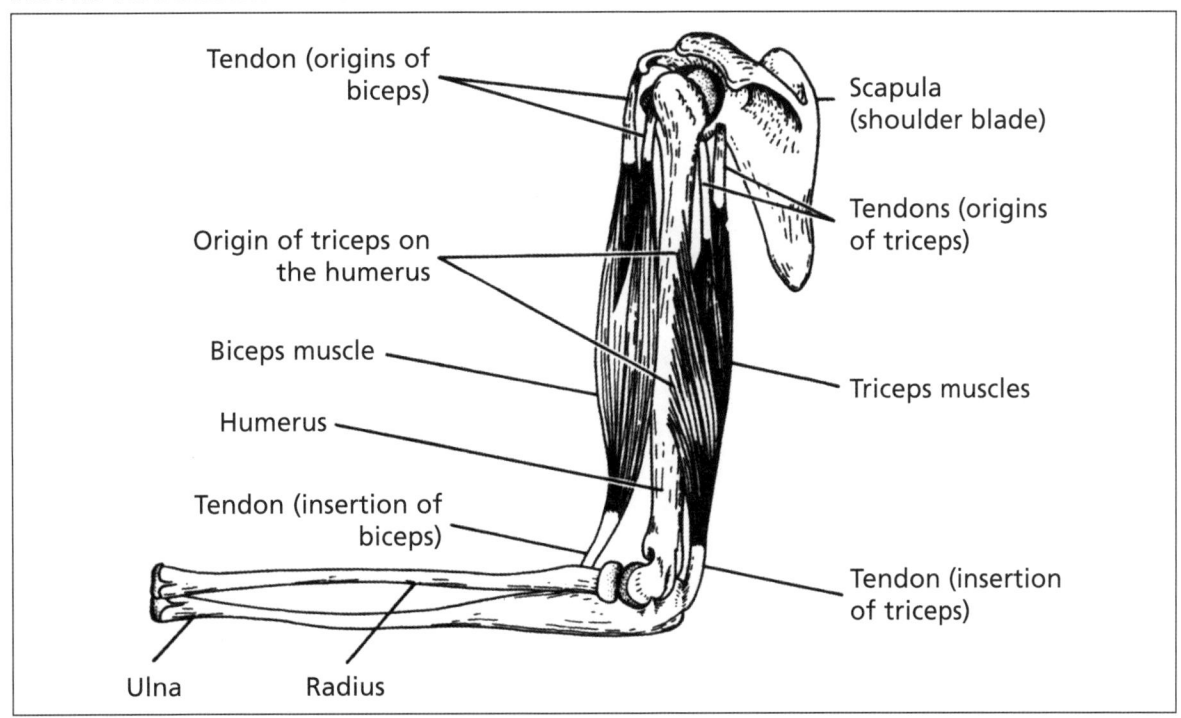

There are three types of human muscle: skeletal, smooth and cardiac. Only skeletal muscle is relevant to this discussion as this is the only type under voluntary control. Skeletal muscles are attached to bones, which act as levers and this allows human beings movement. Skeletal muscle cells are very long and are known as muscle fibres or myofibrils. Muscle fibres taper into a tendon which is attached to a bone. There are around 400 skeletal muscles in the body acting in pairs or more, either together (synergists) or against each other (antagonists). They constitute about 40 to 50 per cent of total body weight and are responsible for the production of considerable amounts of body heat.

Muscles cause movement in the body by contracting, so shortening their length. They can only pull a bone (not push); in bending and straightening a joint, they work in antagonistic pairs, that is, when one muscle is contracting, the other is relaxing. In the case of the arm, the biceps is the flexor muscle (ie it contracts and bends the joint) and the triceps is the extensor muscle (ie it contracts and straightens the joint). The tendons make the connection between the muscles and the bones. The tendon at the end of the muscle closest to the joint it moves is called the 'insertion' of that muscle and the tendon at the opposite end is the 'origin' of the muscle. During muscular contraction, the insertion moves and the origin remains fixed as the anchoring point of the muscle.

Dynamic and static muscular effort

In order to understand the mechanism of damage involved in WMSDs, it also useful to have information on static and dynamic muscular effort. There are two kinds of muscular effort: dynamic (motion) effort and static (posture) effort. These are outlined below:

1. **Dynamic muscular effort** – the muscle length changes with an alternation of contraction and extension, which is often rhythmical.
2. **Static muscular effort** – a prolonged state of contraction, which usually maintains a postural stance.

There are important differences between dynamic and static muscular efforts. With strong static effort, the internal pressure of the muscle tissue compresses blood vessels and blood does not flow. There is also a build-up of metabolic waste products and the muscle will soon feel painful and fatigued. In dynamic muscular effort, the muscle acts as a pump; blood is squeezed out of the muscle on contraction and fresh blood enters on relaxation (this may reach up to 20 times the resting level). A muscle carrying out dynamic work, therefore, has a plentiful supply of freshly-oxygenated blood and efficient removal of metabolic waste products. The converse is true for muscles carrying out static work, that is, poor supply of fresh blood and build-up of waste products. For this reason, static muscular effort cannot continue for a long period, since pain and fatigue will set in. On the other hand, dynamic muscular work can be carried on for long periods, providing an appropriate rhythm is chosen for the work.

Static efforts are common in everyday life, most notably in the maintenance of body posture.

Kroemer & Grandjean (1997) identify the following examples of considerable static effort:
- high effort maintained for more than 10 seconds;
- moderate effort for more than one minute; and
- slight effort for more than five minutes.

There is a static component in many forms of work and the following are some common examples:
- jobs where the back bends forwards or sideways;
- holding things in the hands;
- manipulations with the arms stretched out, or above shoulder height;
- standing in one place for long periods;
- pushing or pulling heavy objects;
- tilting the head strongly forwards or backwards; and
- raising the shoulders for long periods.

Constrained postures are frequently found in static work where the head, trunk or limbs are carried in unnatural positions. Most work tasks have both dynamic and static components. For example, keyboard operators use both dynamic and static muscular efforts:
- the back, shoulders and arms use static effort to hold the hands in position over the keyboard;
- the digits operate mainly by dynamic muscular effort as they operate the keys.

The static component is important in postural fatigue while the muscles and tendons operating the digits and thumbs may suffer from repetitive motion strain.

Work-related musculoskeletal disorders (WMSDs)

Work-related musculoskeletal disorders (WMSDs) are "diseases of the musculoskeletal system that have a causal determinant that is work-related, that is, concerned with the performance of the work or the work environment" (International Commission on Occupational Health (ICOH) 1996).

WMSDs involve the nerves, tendons, muscles, circulatory system and supporting structures such as the inter-vertebral disks of the spinal column. The musculoskeletal system may be overloaded by a series of small traumas, which by their cumulative effects may become significant. The risk of damage to muscles and joints is not confined to any particular occupational sector or jobs. In an occupational environment, mildly adverse physical mismatches may lead to musculoskeletal problems due to the repetitive nature of the work. Repetitive actions are widely distributed in modern work, for example, in food and meat processing, supermarket checkout operations, factory assembly lines, typing and computer keyboard operations. WMSDs resulting from these cumulative traumas are now presenting a large occupational health problem. In the early 1980s, there was some optimism about the imminent elimination of many repetitive tasks, however, this has not occurred in practice.

Some WMSDs have a well-defined clinical pattern (eg carpal tunnel syndrome), while others are much less well defined and are known as non-specific WMSDs. In 1997, the US National Institute for Occupational Safety and Health (NIOSH) carried out a review of the evidence of disorders of the neck, upper extremities and lower back (Bernard & Putz-Anderson 1997). The authors found a strong link between these medical conditions and high exposure to work risk factors. These included psychosocial work organisation aspects, for example, high workload, low job control and low job satisfaction, as well as physical factors such as load, work equipment and work environment. The risk of WMSDs is believed to be highest where there is exposure to a high level of agents of both physical and psychosocial misfit. Where there is exposure to both types of agent, the risk is believed to be more than additive.

AGENTS OF PHYSICAL MISFIT

FIGURE 11.5: General classification of WMSDs

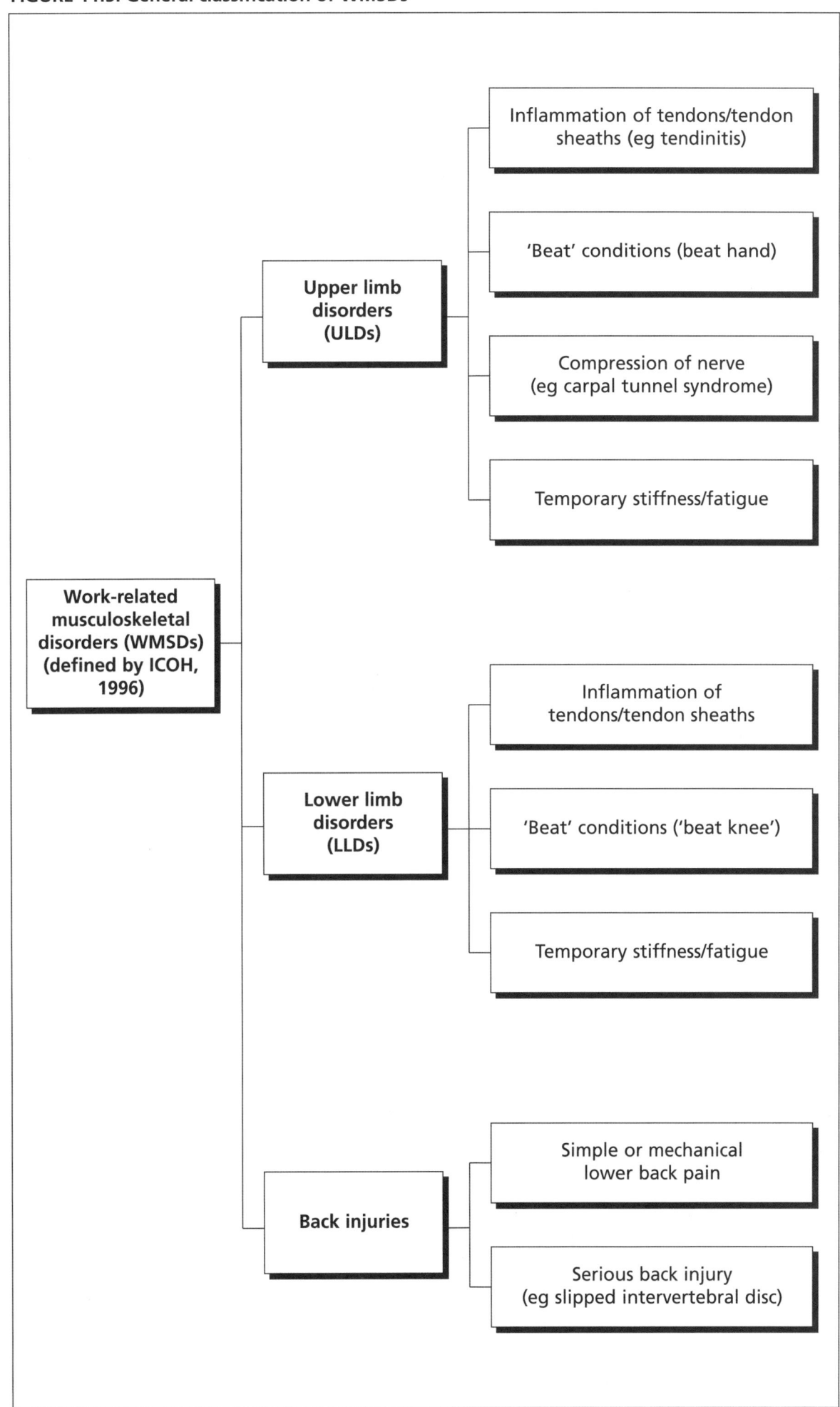

- **Work-related musculoskeletal disorders (WMSDs) (defined by ICOH, 1996)**
  - **Upper limb disorders (ULDs)**
    - Inflammation of tendons/tendon sheaths (eg tendinitis)
    - 'Beat' conditions (beat hand)
    - Compression of nerve (eg carpal tunnel syndrome)
    - Temporary stiffness/fatigue
  - **Lower limb disorders (LLDs)**
    - Inflammation of tendons/tendon sheaths
    - 'Beat' conditions ('beat knee')
    - Temporary stiffness/fatigue
  - **Back injuries**
    - Simple or mechanical lower back pain
    - Serious back injury (eg slipped intervertebral disc)

AGENTS OF PHYSICAL MISFIT

The severity of these disorders varies from mild periodic symptoms to chronic disabling and painful ill health. Examples are carpal tunnel syndrome, tenosynovitis and lower back pain. The link between some types of work and certain musculoskeletal disorders has long been recognised (eg cotton twister's wrist, telegraphist's cramp and writer's cramp); although automation has reduced the prevalence of these examples, similar conditions still exist. A general classification of WMSDs is given in Figure 11.5 with a detailed list of disorders given in Table 11.2 (on page 336).

WMSDs of the upper and lower limbs (excluding the back) are illustrated in Figures 11.6 and 11.7. Here, these disorders are grouped by tissue type, that is, tendon, ligament, vascular, nervous, muscular and bursae.

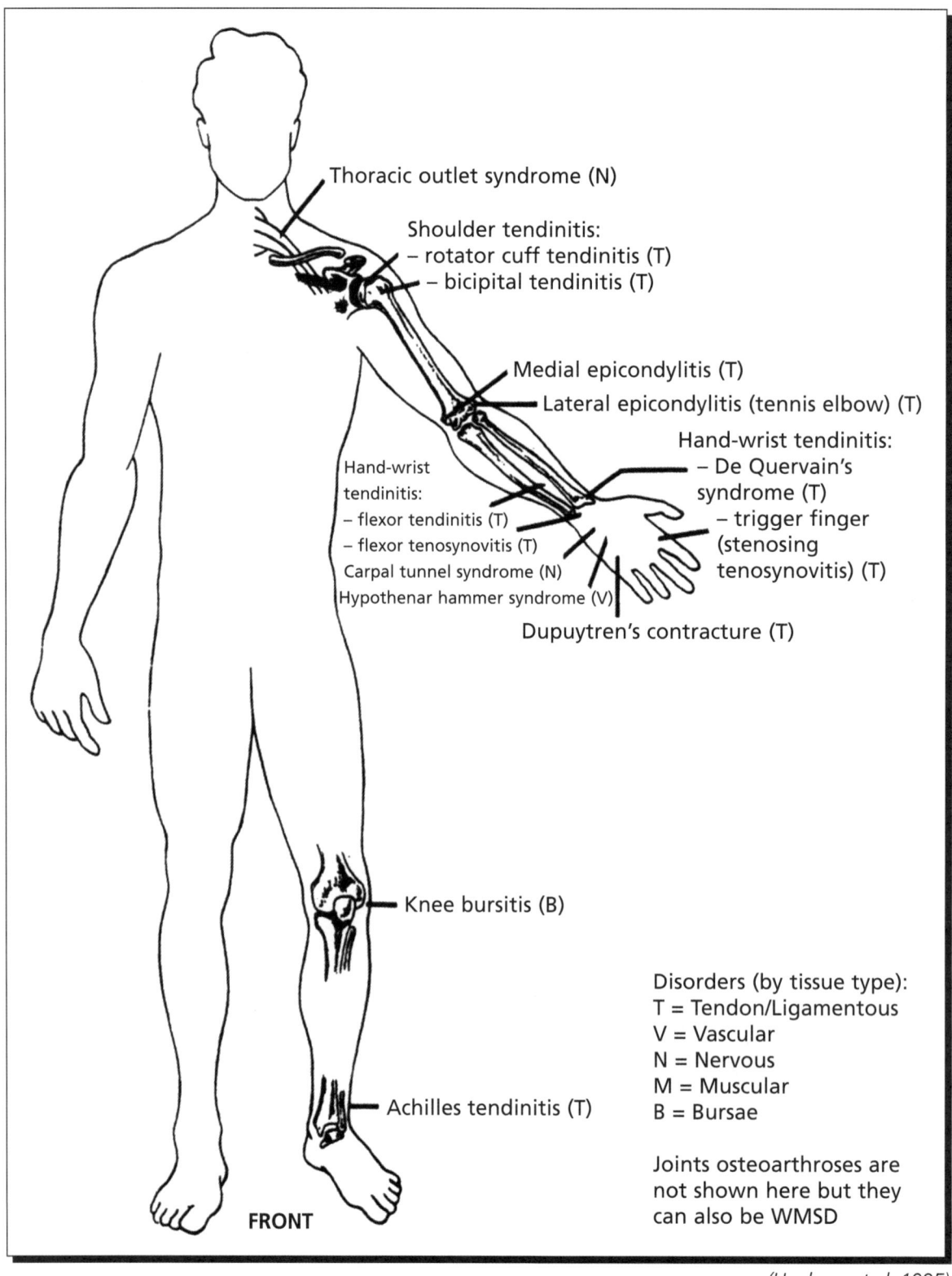

FIGURE 11.6: Examples of WMSDs (Front)

Thoracic outlet syndrome (N)

Shoulder tendinitis:
– rotator cuff tendinitis (T)
– bicipital tendinitis (T)

Medial epicondylitis (T)
Lateral epicondylitis (tennis elbow) (T)

Hand-wrist tendinitis:
– De Quervain's syndrome (T)
– trigger finger (stenosing tenosynovitis) (T)

Hand-wrist tendinitis:
– flexor tendinitis (T)
– flexor tenosynovitis (T)
Carpal tunnel syndrome (N)
Hypothenar hammer syndrome (V)

Dupuytren's contracture (T)

Knee bursitis (B)

Achilles tendinitis (T)

Disorders (by tissue type):
T = Tendon/Ligamentous
V = Vascular
N = Nervous
M = Muscular
B = Bursae

Joints osteoarthroses are not shown here but they can also be WMSD

FRONT

(Hagberg et al. 1995)

FIGURE 11.7: Examples of WMSDs (Back)

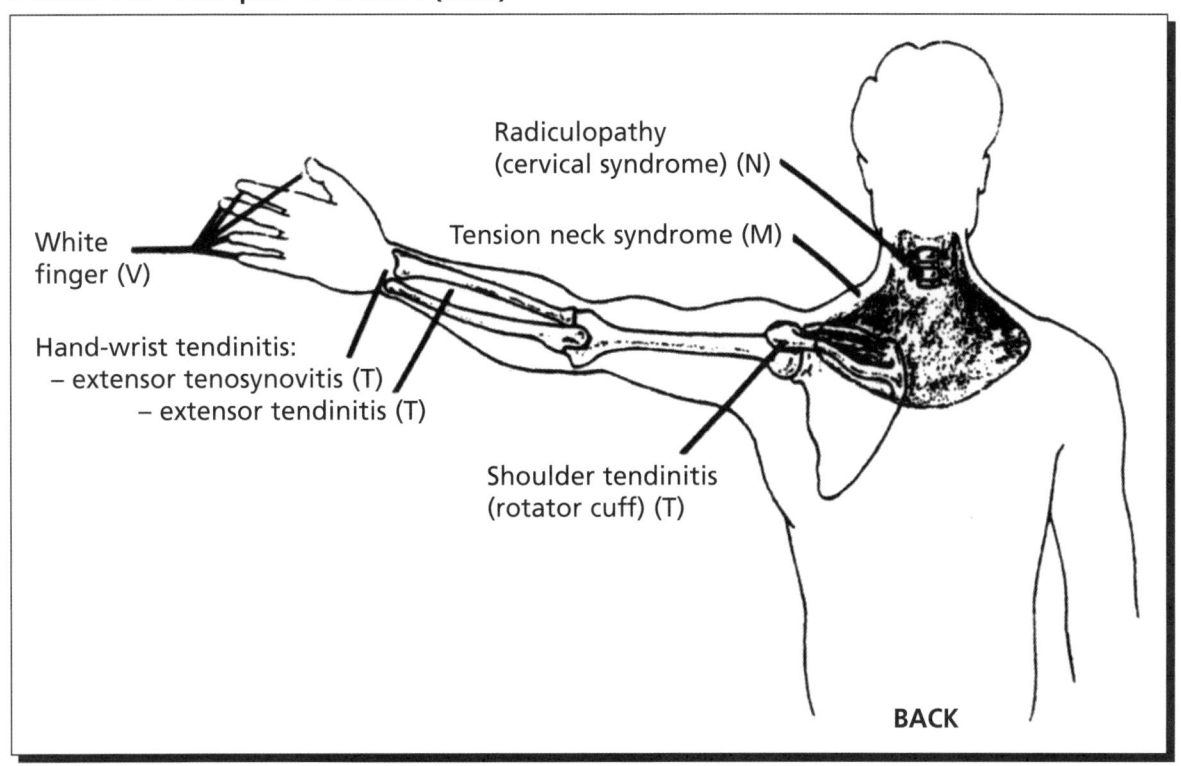

(Hagberg et al. 1995)

The following factors are important in the causation of musculoskeletal disorders:

Poor job design:
- awkward or static postures;
- the requirement for high levels of force;
- the requirement for a high level of repetition;
- high exposure to above risk factors.

Poor work environment:
- inadequate lighting;
- uncomfortable thermal environment.

Poor work organisation:
- high workload and low job control;
- low job satisfaction.

Repetitive Strain Injury (RSI)

Repetitive Strain Injury (RSI) is a term that has been used widely during the 1980s and 1990s. It refers to a group of painful disorders of muscles, tendons and nerves which are caused by frequent and repetitive work activities. However, the term is limited in that it only focuses on injuries that are caused by frequent and repetitive work activities when these are only a proportion of all WMSDs. Another problem with the term is that there is no general agreement as to its definition. Other terms have been used to cover these types of disorder, for example, cumulative trauma disorder (mostly used in the USA), occupational overuse syndrome (mostly used in Australia), and occupational cervicobrachial disorder (mostly used in Japan).

Work-related upper limb disorders (WRULDs)

In the UK, the term 'work-related upper limb disorders' (WRULDs) has been used to describe musculoskeletal disorders of the upper limbs (Figure 11.1). Almost all work involves the use of the hands and arms and, therefore, most disorders involving the musculoskeletal system occur in the hands, elbows, neck and shoulders. Where work involves the lower body, similar disorders can occur in the knees, hips, ankles and back. Generally, there has been much less research information generated about WMSDs affecting the lower limbs.

Primarily affected are the soft tissues, particularly tendons which connect muscle to bone. The muscles themselves and connecting nerves are also often affected. With continuing exposure, the disorder may progress from minor aches and pains to chronic disease and severe disabling injury.

Symptoms of upper limb disorders

These are principally pain, restriction of joint movement and soft tissue swelling. At an early stage, there is no visible sign of joint swelling and bruising. With some conditions, the sense of touch and manual dexterity is reduced. With the slow onset of the condition, adaptation to the way in which work is performed may lead to complex symptom patterns. With repeated sprains and strains (overexertion injuries), tissue inflammation and chronic injury occurs. The HSE (1990) comments that there is no consensus on classifying upper limb disorders, but suggests they can be conveniently grouped as follows:

1. **Inflammation/trauma of the tendons, muscle tendon junction or surrounding tissues, particularly the tendon sheath** – this is usually temporary but may become chronic (permanent).
2. **Inflammation of the hand tissue** – constant bruising and/or friction of the hand, elbow and knee; these are known as 'beat conditions'.
3. **Compression of peripheral nerves serving the upper limbs** – carpal tunnel syndrome may arise spontaneously in normal populations and be exacerbated by work.
4. **Temporary fatigue/stiffness** – this may occur following extended absence from work; no permanent pathological condition will result and there will be full recovery after resting.

WMSDs and RIDDOR 1995

Some WMSDs are reportable under RIDDOR 1995 and these are shown in Table 11.1.

TABLE 11.1: WMSDs and RIDDOR 1995

Condition	Type of work
8. Cramp of the hand or forearm due to repetitive movements	Work involving prolonged periods of handwriting, typing or other repetitive movements of the fingers, hand or arm
9. Subcutaneous cellulitis of the hand (Beat hand)	Physically demanding work causing severe or prolonged friction or pressure on the hand
10. Bursitis or subcutaneous cellulitis arising at or about the knee due to severe or prolonged external friction or pressure (Beat knee)	Physically demanding work causing severe or prolonged friction or pressure at or about the knee
11. Bursitis or subcutaneous cellulitis arising at or about the elbow due to severe or prolonged friction or pressure at or about the elbow (Beat elbow)	Physically demanding work causing severe or prolonged external friction or pressure at the elbow
12. Traumatic inflammation of the tendons of the hand or forearm or of the associated tendon	Physically demanding work, frequent or repeated movements, constrained postures or extremes of extension or flexion of the hand or wrist
13. Carpal tunnel syndrome	Work involving the use of hand-held vibrating tools

Hazards associated with WMSDs

Predisposing work factors include ordinary movements such as forceful and repetitive gripping, twisting, reaching and moving. Commonly, an important hazard factor is the prolonged repetition, often in

AGENTS OF PHYSICAL MISFIT

a forceful and awkward manner with insufficient rest or recovery time. Occupational factors can be conveniently grouped into three principal categories:

1. **Force** – the application of undesirable force.
2. **Frequency and duration of movement** – this includes an unsuitable rate of working or the repetition of a single task or subtask.
3. **Awkward posture** – of the hand, wrist, forearm or shoulder during the task.

In some tasks, only one of these elements may be significant, but in others, there may be two or more. For example, a task where there is a need to maintain a stressful or tiring grip can be seen as a combination of force requirements, awkward posture and long duration. The physical work demands inherent in each of these factors is outlined below.

Force

Body forces are transmitted to the workpiece via tools or the hands. Often, because of poor design of the tool, workplace or job itself, excessive force may be needed to overcome resistance posed by a task. Particular problems may arise where high force is required combined with a static posture. The characteristics of the material being handled are relevant to the required application of force. Figure 11.8 illustrates a sewing task where a high level of force must be applied to a material to hold it in position for sewing.

FIGURE 11.8: Forceful grip

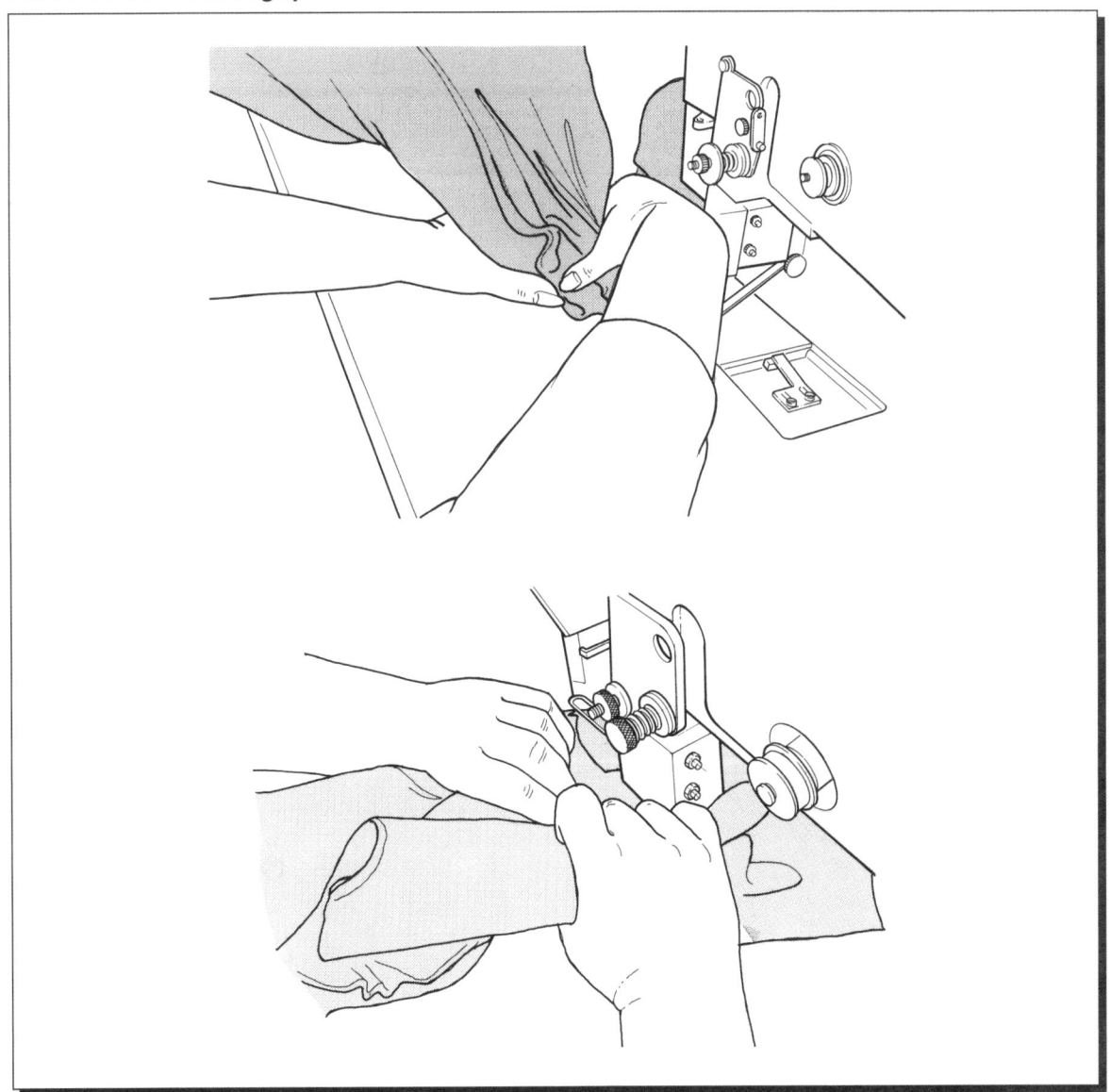

(HSE 1990 – rev. 2000)

Frequency and duration

Tasks that require repetitive motions combined with short cycle times need to be carefully examined. The muscles required to contract at high speed develop less tension if they contract at a lower speed for the same force. More effort per unit time is required and, therefore, a greater recovery period is needed.

With machine pacing, there is a higher level of risk than with self-pacing because in the latter the individual can distribute his or her effort over a given time. Other important factors are the payment system and productivity targets, the number and distribution of rest breaks, and the degree of job rotation.

FIGURE 11.9: Frequent and awkward postures and movement

(HSE 1990 – rev. 2000)

Awkward posture

Certain tasks require the person to take up an awkward posture that may cause significant stress to the joints of the upper limb and its soft tissues. An awkward posture is any fixed or constrained body position that:

- overloads the muscles and tendons;
- loads the joint in an uneven or asymmetrical manner; or
- involves a static load on the body where the limb is held in a fixed position over a sustained period.

FIGURE 11.10: Awkward static posture and possible solution

(HSE 1990 – rev. 2000)

AGENTS OF PHYSICAL MISFIT

Highly paced repetitive work, particularly where it occurs in combination with awkward movements of the upper limbs, can lead to upper limb disorders (Figure 11.9). In Figure 11.10 (left illustration), an awkward static posture is shown. Figure 11.10 (right illustration) shows that changing the position of the control panel greatly reduces the need for prolonged work in a static posture. A combination of harmful factors in a task involving a power-operated hand tool is illustrated in Figure 11.11.

Other factors

Exposure to vibration that imposes higher handgrip force requirements and cold environments may be relevant factors and increase risks. Work organisational factors and psychosocial aspects such as stress can also be important contributory factors to WMSDs.

FIGURE 11.11: Combination of factors – Shoulder and elbow extension, forceful grip and static posture

(HSE 1990 – rev. 2000)

A summary is given in Table 11.2 of risk factors and symptoms associated with important musculoskeletal disorders.

Evaluation of exposure and analysis

An assessment needs to be carried out on tasks from which the risk of WMSDs may arise. This focuses on identifying the presence of specific risk factors and the degree to which they affect the likelihood of injury. The process or task is defined and an ergonomics checklist may be used for collecting information. If the assessment is thought to be too complex, then help should be sought from an ergonomics specialist. A generic version of an ergonomics checklist is given in Table 11.3. The objective of the assessment is to draw a conclusion on the tolerability of the risk of developing WMSDs and to identify preventive measures.

Checklist questions address task and equipment, organisational, environmental, and personal and/or anthropometric factors, and are grouped in these categories in Table 11.3.

TABLE 11.2: Musculoskeletal disorders, risk factors and symptoms

Upper limb disorder	Risk factors and symptoms
Tendinitis	Inflammation of a tendon **Symptoms** – Pain, weakness, swelling, lack of sensation or dull ache over affected area **Tasks** – Repetitive wrist motions; repetitive shoulder motions; sustained hyperextension of the arms; prolonged load on the shoulders
Tenosynovitis	Inflammation of the synovial sheath **Symptoms** – Pain, weakness, swelling, lack of sensation or dull ache over affected area **Tasks** – Repetitive wrist motions; repetitive shoulder motions; sustained hyperextension of the arms; prolonged load on the shoulders
Epicondylitis	Inflammation of the tendons which attach muscles to the elbow (eg tennis elbow) **Symptoms** – Pain, weakness, swelling, lack of sensation or dull ache over affected area **Tasks** – Repeated or forceful motions of the forearm and bending of the wrist at the same time
De Quervain's disease	Affects the tendon sheath in the thumb and nerve endings **Symptoms** – Pain at the base of the thumb **Tasks** – Repetitive hand twisting and forceful gripping
Carpal tunnel syndrome	The carpal tunnel (space in the wrist surrounded by the wrist bones) links the bones together and through this passes the flexing tendons of the fingers and the median nerve. The tendons of the fingers surround the median nerve and swelling of the tendons compresses the median nerve and can injure it **Symptoms** – Numbness, tingling, pain and lack of co-ordination of the hand. This combination of symptoms is known as carpal tunnel syndrome. Tasks such as unscrewing bottle tops, fastening buttons and turning keys become difficult **Tasks** – Repetitive hand positions; awkward hand position; strong gripping; mechanical stress on palm; vibration; also many non-occupational factors
Thoracic outlet syndrome	**Symptoms** – Pain, numbness, swelling of the hands **Tasks** – Prolonged shoulder flexion; extending arms above shoulder height; carrying loads on the shoulder
Bursitis elbow[38]	Swelling at the elbow **Symptoms** – Subcutaneous cellulitis **Tasks** – Severe or prolonged friction or pressure at the elbow
'Beat hand'	Swelling of the hand **Symptoms** – Subcutaneous cellulitis **Tasks** – Severe or prolonged friction or pressure on the hand
Tension neck syndrome	**Symptoms** – Neck pain **Tasks** – Prolonged restrictive posture

[38] Also a similar condition, 'beat knee' – bursitis at the knee.

TABLE 11.3: Ergonomics assessment checklist

General category	Question
Task and equipment	**Applied forces** Is there a need for the operator to use a lot of force? Do tasks involve static muscle loads? Are forces applied by the arms or joints at the extremes of their range of movements? **Movements** Is there regular repetition of the same movements? Are the movements rapid? Are the following movements present: • forceful twisting of the wrist as in wringing out clothes? • rotation of the wrist particularly when it is bent? • movement of the wrist from side to side? • highly flexed fingers and wrist? • hand or arm motions beyond a comfortable range? **Posture** Are the arms raised high or stretched out at the shoulder? Is the upper arm held away from the vertical? Is poor posture caused by other factors such as seating and/or inappropriate equipment? **Duration of effort** Are tasks performed for long periods without breaks? Are there short intensive periods during the longer period of activity? **Tools and equipment factors** Are women using tools designed for men? Do tools vibrate significantly? Do the tools impose shock loading on the user? Do the tools have to be held very firmly? Do the tools have a jerky action? Is considerable pressure needed to hold and operate the tools? Are the handles of appropriate dimensions? Do operators twist or turn frequently in carrying out their tasks? Do operators wear gloves? Are the tools well designed?
Organisational	Is there adequate training? Are there adequate breaks? Are changes made after consulting the workforce? Do payment systems encourage safe working practice? Does management activity create unnecessary stress for workers?
Environmental	Are noise levels sufficient to cause stress or irritation? Are lighting levels causing operators to adopt unsafe postures? Is the air temperature adequate for the work? Are there other problems with the work environment?
Personal and/or anthropometric	Do operators suffer from anxiety because of difficulties at home or work? Could out-of-work activities exacerbate potential work-related problems? Are operators at the extremes of the normal range for height in the working population? Are operators at the extremes of the normal range for strength in the working population?

The HSE (2002) has published revised guidance on managing the risks of WRULDs. This document incorporates a 'risk filter' and risk assessment worksheets. The stated aim of the risk filter is to set out an approximate threshold below which the risk of upper limb disorders is likely to be low. This is provided as an aid to risk assessment. The risk filter and the risk assessment worksheets provide a two-stage assessment process:

- **Stage 1** – The risk assessment filter helps in the identification of situations where a more detailed risk assessment is required.
- **Stage 2** – The risk assessment worksheets are used to conduct a more detailed risk assessment.

Tolerability of risk

Following analysis of the responses to the risk assessment checklist, a conclusion is made on the tolerability of risk for the defined task-worker combination and whether further preventive measures are needed. The degree of risk is broadly indicated by the extent to which risk factors are identified by the checklist. The principal target is to eliminate as many of these risk factors as possible. This will give an indication of the residual risks. Where factors cannot be eliminated, their effects should be mitigated as far as possible, for example, with adequate rest breaks, job rotation and effective training.

Preventive measures

These can be conveniently divided into two categories: those concerned with ergonomic work design; and those concerned with organisational change. The HSE has published a useful collection of case studies to illustrate the practical application of preventive measures to ergonomics problems (HSE 1994).

Work design

Improving the design of work involves:

- reducing the levels of force needed in tasks;
- reducing highly repetitive movements; and
- introducing improved postural requirements.

Reduction of force levels

General approaches to reducing force levels include:

- reducing the force required;
- spreading the force;
- better mechanical advantage (using stronger muscle groups and more effective tools);
- maintenance of tools; and
- training.

Reduction of highly repetitive movements

Methods of reducing highly repetitive movements include:

- minimising repetitive motions;
- job enlargement with restructuring, so that each employee has a larger and more varied series of tasks to perform;
- mechanisation and the use of special tools to reduce repetition;
- automation;
- use of pre-assembled subcomponents if possible; and
- reducing machine pace and using self-paced systems where possible.

Postural changes

Methods of introducing postural changes include:

- redesigning the operation or product; and
- altering tools or controls.

Organisational changes

Today much evidence points to the fact that in order to be effective, prevention strategies must involve work organisational and psychosocial improvements as well as ergonomic improvements.

Hagberg et al. (1993) suggest job rotation, job enlargement, incorporating flexibility in production planning and giving increased responsibility to employees.

Consultation with task operators
Workers should be consulted about any redesign of equipment and changes to work. This has been shown to have several benefits which includes encompassing the creative suggestions of operators for carrying out their tasks.

Training
It is very important to teach employees to perform tasks in a safe and healthy way. Training by 'sitting with Nellie' is not satisfactory since bad habits may be learned by this method. Training should aim to reduce, to as few as possible, the number of hazardous body movements and postures, and programmes should emphasise the risk factors which contribute to WMSDs.

Following the analysis of existing jobs during the assessment of risks, undesirable postures are identified using appropriate ergonomics and/or biomechanical guidelines. With this information, work methods can be modified and specific training objectives developed. It is very important that operators can set up and carry out their work satisfactorily, as judged by ergonomics criteria. This is the essential outcome of a training programme. Therefore, clear guidelines on the ergonomics aspects of tasks should be given to operators, together with the signs and symptoms of WMSDs to look out for and the importance of early reporting. Training should also emphasise the need for taking adequate rest breaks and job rotation.

New employees
New employees may have a higher risk of developing WMSDs than more experienced workers. It may be that it is the 'survivors' who remain in the job, that is, those who are most able to cope. Special provision needs to be made for new employees; they should be introduced to a slower rate of production with gradually increasing demands. The staged introduction of new employees allows them to develop better work practices and techniques. Similarly, special provision is needed for people returning to work following injury, particularly if WMSDs are involved.

Job rotation
Increasing the variability of work and job rotation should be applied wherever this is practicable. In the case of work with display screen equipment, this is an explicit requirement of the Health and Safety (Display Screen Equipment) Regulations 1992 (DSE).

Health surveillance
This aims to link the occurrence of WMSDs with work-related risk factors. Effective health surveillance depends on the keeping of reliable and accurate health records. These are very important in monitoring ill health trends and the effectiveness of applied prevention and control measures.

Risks from work with DSE – Assessment and management
There are concerns about the health of people working at computer workstations. Although the risks are thought to be very low, the actual numbers affected could still be quite high due to the overall number of DSE workers. Many millions of people in Europe and around the world use display screen equipment on a daily basis, primarily in office environments with desks and tables. Computers are used in a wide range of settings for a variety of jobs and this poses challenges in devising principles for good workstation design.

The definition of 'display screen equipment' (under the DSE Regulations, regulation 1) includes conventional cathode-ray tube (CRT), liquid crystal display (LCD) and other display screen technology. The screens included are those used to display text, line drawings, graphs, charts, but not screens where the main use is to display television or films. However, the definition also covers non-electronic display equipment, for example, microfiche readers.

AGENTS OF PHYSICAL MISFIT

In the traditional office, employees would have carried out a wide range of tasks during which they would have adopted many different postures. Here, the suboptimal ergonomic design of furniture and equipment is not likely to have created a high degree of annoyance and discomfort in employees. However, in offices which have computer workstations, the operator is much more 'tied' to the equipment, with fewer tasks and less scope for physical movement. The operator's attention must be directed towards the monitor and viewing may be required continuously for several hours. In these circumstances, the task environment and ergonomic characteristics of the furniture and equipment make operators much more susceptible to musculoskeletal disorders and other health problems.

This concern about the health of such a large section of the workforce using computer workstations has led to statutory control. The DSE Regulations were enacted to implement the requirements of European Directive 90/270/EEC. The Regulations (as amended by the Health and Safety (Miscellaneous Amendments) Regulations 2002) are summarised in Table 11.6 (page 344) and they are accompanied by authoritative guidance. Regulation 1 defines the important terms used:

DISPLAY SCREEN EQUIPMENT
Any alphanumeric or graphic display screen regardless of the display process involved.

USER
An employee who habitually uses display screen equipment as a significant part of his/her normal work.

OPERATOR
A self-employed person who habitually uses display screen equipment as a significant part of his/her normal work.

WORKSTATION
Means an assembly comprising:
(i) display screen equipment (whether provided with software determining the interface between the equipment and its operator or user or any other input device);
(ii) any optional accessories to the display screen equipment;
(iii) any disk drive, telephone, modem, printer, document holder, work chair, work desk, work surface or other item peripheral to the display screen equipment; and
(iv) the immediate work environment around the display screen equipment.

An assessment of DSE workstations is required by the DSE Regulations to determine whether people are exposed to significant health risks and, where appropriate, risk reduction measures should be applied (regulation 3). The risks arising from DSE work are associated principally with musculoskeletal disorders, visual fatigue and mental stress. These disorders can be prevented by applying ergonomics principles to the design, selection and installation of display screen equipment, job design and the work organisation.

The requirements of the DSE Regulations should be read in conjunction with the Management of Health and Safety at Work Regulations 1999 (MHSW), the Workplace (Health, Safety and Welfare) Regulations 1992 (WHSW), and the Provision and Use of Work Equipment Regulations 1998 (PUWER).

Health effects associated with DSE work

WMSDs

The symptoms of upper limb WMSDs have been discussed in detail earlier in this chapter. Disorders among DSE users range from aches, temporary soreness and fatigue in limbs to chronic conditions, such as peritendinitis and carpal tunnel syndrome; some also suffer from cramp of the hands.

The contribution of individual risk factors is not clear and it is likely that a combination of causes is involved such as:

- keying-in speed;

- prolonged static posture of the back, neck and head;
- awkward positioning of the hands and wrist (from poor working technique or inappropriate work height);
- high workload and tight deadlines, lack of control over work, lack of rest breaks and job rotation.

Visual effects

DSE work is not associated with damage to the eyes or eyesight, nor is it thought to worsen existing eye conditions. It may make workers with pre-existing eye conditions more aware of them (HSE 1992). Some workers may suffer temporary visual fatigue leading to a range of symptoms such as:

- impaired visual performance;
- red or sore eyes;
- headaches.

The risk factors linked with visual fatigue are:

- keeping the same eye position or focus for a long period of time;
- poor positioning of the display screen equipment;
- poor legibility of the information on the screen;
- poor lighting conditions with glare or reflective surfaces;
- drifting or flickering on-screen images.

General fatigue and stress

Many symptoms described by DSE workers reflect the demands of their tasks. Symptoms may be linked with musculoskeletal or visual problems, but more often they are connected with poor job design or work organisation. There is often a lack of control of work by the user and other factors include:

- under-utilisation of skills;
- high-speed repetitive work;
- social isolation.

These factors have been linked with stress in DSE work, but linking individual symptoms with specific aspects of the work is often difficult.

Other health effects

Other health concerns with DSE work are summarised in Table 11.4.

TABLE 11.4: Other health concerns with DSE work

Health effect	Comments
Epilepsy	Not known to induce seizures; people with photosensitive epilepsy can work safely with DSE
Skin disease	No evidence that electromagnetic radiation causes skin disease, but it may exacerbate existing skin conditions; occasional itching on the face or neck may be due to low relative humidity or static electricity near the screen
Electromagnetic radiation	Concerns about effects on pregnant women have been widespread, but levels of ionising and non-ionising EM radiation are not thought to pose a significant risk to health; no special measures needed to protect people from this radiation; no increased disposition to cataract formation has been detected
Health effects in pregnancy	No observed increased risk of spontaneous abortions or birth defects in women using DSE during pregnancy (Doll 1994)

AGENTS OF PHYSICAL MISFIT

Exposure assessment and analysis

Competent ergonomic design is required in all aspects of the DSE work activity. To evaluate this in practice, an assessment can be carried out using an ergonomics checklist (broadly similar to that illustrated in Table 11.3) but specifically designed for use with DSE workstations. An example is given in Table 11.5. Using appropriate criteria, it is necessary to identify DSE 'users' under the DSE Regulations. An assessment is carried out for each DSE workstation and information is collected on the following subjects as indicated. The assessment should identify the presence of risk factors at a workstation together with the presence of desirable ergonomic features. Assessments should be reviewed at appropriate intervals or when a major alteration in work occurs, for example, a change in software, hardware, furniture, time on display screen equipment, task requirements or environmental conditions.

TABLE 11.5: Sample DSE workstation questionnaire

Subject	Sample questions
Time spent using DSE and type of work (% of time on the computer)	Audio typing? Data entry? Copy typing? Graphics editing? Direct input and text editing (ie text not copied)? Mouse use? Comments?
Posture	Are shoulders relaxed? Are the elbows at about right angles? Are the wrists straight/flat? Are the wrists in a neutral posture (ie no deviation)? Is the lumbar spine supported? Are the thighs supported equally? Are the knees at about 90°? Are the feet flat on the floor or a stable footrest? Comments?
Desk	Is there enough desktop space for the flow of work? Is their adequate leg room under the desk? Is the layout of the desktop equipment satisfactory? Does the desk have a matt surface finish? Is the desk height adjustable? Comments?
Chair	Is the chair comfortable for the user? Is the chair stable? Does the chair swivel? Does the chair have a five-star base with castors? Can the seat be adjusted in seat height? Can the seat be adjusted in backrest height? Can the seat be adjusted in backrest angle? Can all the adjustments be made easily when seated? Is the chair undamaged? Comments?
Footrest	With the seat adjusted correctly, are the feet firmly on the floor or a footrest? Where a footrest is required, is an appropriate one present? Comments?
Display screen equipment	Is the monitor at the correct viewing angle? Is the monitor height adjustable? Can the monitor be tilted sufficiently? Can the monitor be adjusted sufficiently side to side? Is the information on the screen well defined and easy to read? Is the brightness and contrast easy to adjust? Is the image stable and flicker-free? Is the screen free from glare and reflections? Comments?
Keyboard	Is the keyboard separate from the screen? Is it easy to adjust the angle of tilt of the keyboard? Are the key symbols adequately contrasted? Does the keyboard have a matt surface? Comments?
Document holder	Can documents be viewed with the head in a balanced upright posture? Where

Table continued opposite

	necessary, has a stable document holder been provided? Does the document holder suit user requirements (adjustable, large enough)? **Comments?**
Other equipment	Are the mouse, CPU, modem, and telephone appropriate for use? Is extra equipment located in a position that is stable and suitable for use? **Comments?**
Space and room layout	Is there adequate access to the workstation? Is there enough space to manoeuvre the chair? Does the work area layout allow the task to be done efficiently? Is there sufficient storage space? Is the work area free from obstructions? Is the work area free from tripping hazards? Is the position of the cabling safe? Is the work area free from any electrical hazards? **Comments?**
Lighting	Is there adequate lighting for all the tasks? Is additional task lighting supplied where necessary? Is the lighting positioned to avoid glare and reflections? Are blinds/curtains provided at the windows to reduce glare? Do all the wall surfaces minimise reflections falling on the workstation? **Comments?**
Noise	Is the workstation free from noise interference? Are sources of noise located away from the workstation? Have noise sources been reduced where possible? **Comments?**
Temperature and humidity	Is the work area temperature and humidity comfortable most of the time? Can the temperature be adjusted locally? Can the humidity be adjusted locally? Is the work area free from draughts? **Comments?**
Software	Is the software suitable for tasks? Is the software easy to understand and use? Does the software reduce/eliminate delays in tasks? **Comments?**
Work organisation	Are there adequate breaks from the screen? Are off-screen activities incorporated into daily routines? Have peaks and troughs in workload been eliminated where possible? **Comments?**
Training and information	What does the user know about the possible risks of DSE work? Has the user had an eyesight test in the last two years? Has the user had instruction in how to adjust their workstation? Is the user aware of the importance of a comfortable posture? Is the user aware of the importance of off-screen breaks? Has the user any persistent pains or discomfort at work? Does the user know where to report a workstation hazard? **Comments?**

(Gannon)

Tolerability of risk

The assessment should conclude on the tolerability of risks arising from the DSE work and determine whether further preventive measures are needed. As with other risk assessment-driven legislation, such as the Control of Substances Hazardous to Health Regulations 2002 (COSHH) or the Noise at Work Regulations 1989, the DSE Regulations require that risk is reduced "to the lowest extent reasonably practicable". Minimum requirements for workstations are specified in the Schedule to the DSE Regulations. In the context of DSE use, the elimination of some risk factors will be possible in many cases with small, inexpensive changes to the work situation. A summary of the DSE Regulations is given in Table 11.6.

TABLE 11.6: Summary of the Health and Safety (Display Screen Equipment) Regulations 1992 (as amended) (DSE)

Regulation	Requirement
Regulation 1: Citation, interpretation, commencement and application	Defines what display screen equipment is covered and who is a DSE 'user' or 'operator' under the Regulations; defines where the Regulations are not to be applied
Regulation 2: Analysis of workstations	Suitable and sufficient analysis and systematic risk assessment; reduce risks identified to the lowest extent reasonably practicable; review assessment
Regulation 3: Requirements	Workstations must meet requirements laid out in the Schedule for workstations
Regulation 4: Daily work routine of users	DSE work should be periodically interrupted by breaks or changes in activity
Regulation 5: Eyes and eyesight	Provide users who request it with an eye and eyesight test; provide corrective appliance where appropriate
Regulation 6: Provision of training	Adequate health and safety training for those starting DSE work and when a particular workstation is to be substantially modified
Regulation 7: Provision of information	Provide information to operators and users on: risks arising from DSE work; the protective measures taken; the provision of breaks or changes in activity; and the entitlement to eye and eyesight tests
Regulation 8: Exemption certificates	
Regulation 9: Extension outside Great Britain	
Schedule:	Employer must ensure that workstation meets the minimum requirements for workstations laid down in the Schedule. These apply to the following: • Equipment – display screen; keyboard; work desk or work surface; work chair • Environment – space requirements; lighting; reflections and glare; noise; heat; radiation; humidity • Interface between computer and operator/user
Annex A: Guidance on workstation minimum requirements	Gives background information regarding the content of the Schedule to the Regulations
Annex B: Display screen equipment – possible effects on health	
Annex C: Further sources of information	

Ergonomics specifications for the use of display screen equipment are contained in European and British standards including BS EN 29241, BS 7179 and BS EN ISO 9241-1: 1997 (BSI 1990a, 1990b, 1993, 1993a, 1997). These standards contain specifications for screen and keyboard design (including other data input devices), software design and its usability, workstation arrangements and environmental conditions. Other standards, such as BS 3044: 1990, give guidance on ergonomics principles for the design and selection of suitable office furniture (BSI 1990). There are also standards for more specialised applications of display screen equipment, such as in process control where there are machinery safety implications and the use of programmable electronic systems.

Minimum standard requirements for DSE workstations

Figures 11.12 and 11.13 summarise the principal features of workstations as required by the DSE Regulations.

FIGURE 11.12: Subjects dealt with by the Schedule to the DSE Regulations

- There should be adequate lighting
- There should be adequate contrast with no glare or distracting reflections
- Distracting noise should be minimised
- Legroom clearances should allow postural changes
- Window covering should be provided if needed to minimise glare
- Software should be appropriate to the task, adapted to the user and provide feedback on system status. There should be no undisclosed monitoring

- Display screen – should have a stable image with no flickering, it should be adjustable, readable, glare-free and reflection-free
- Keyboard should be usable, adjustable, detachable and legible
- Work surface – should allow flexible arrangements and be glare-free
- Work chair – should be stable and adjustable
- Footrest should be provided if required

(Adapted from HSE 2003)

AGENTS OF PHYSICAL MISFIT

FIGURE 11.13: Seating and posture for typical office tasks

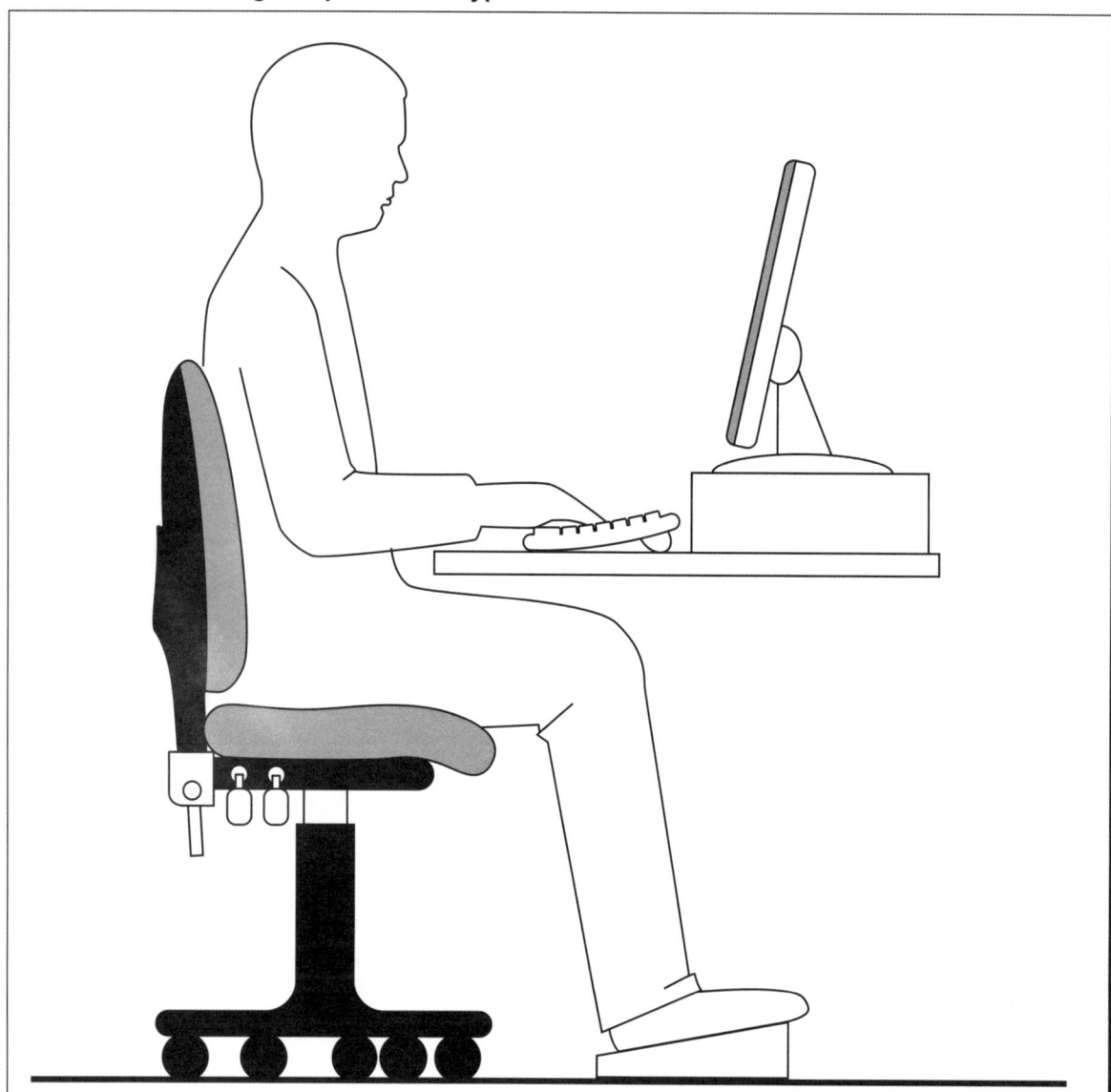

- The seat back should be adjustable
- Good lumbar support should be provided
- The seat height should be adjustable
- There should be no excess pressure on the underside of the thighs and the backs of the knees
- Foot support should be provided if needed
- There should be space for postural changes with no obstacles under the desk
- Forearms should be approximately horizontal
- There should be minimal extension, flexion or deviation of the wrists
- Screen height and angle should allow a comfortable head position
- There should be space in front of the keyboard to support hands and wrists during pauses in keying

(Adapted from HSE 2003)

Prevention and control of risk

Health risks arising from DSE work can be prevented by applying ergonomics principles to the design, selection and installation of display screen equipment, the design of the work, and the design and organisation of the task.

The prevention strategy requires application of an appropriate blend of the following types of measure:
- ergonomic design of tasks;
- improving the equipment and layout of the workstation (minimum standards laid down in the Schedule to the Regulations);
- improving the work environment;
- improving work organisation.

Postural problems

As indicated above, the minimal requirements for a workstation are specified in the Schedule (and are required by regulation 3). New workstations with more appropriate equipment may be constructed using ergonomics guidelines and suitable equipment and layout. Sometimes, problems with posture may be overcome with simple adjustments to the workstation. This could involve simply repositioning equipment or adjusting the chair. New equipment such as a document holder or footrest may by needed in some cases. Training is very important and is formally required under regulation 6. It is vital that operators and users are trained in taking up the correct hand position and posture as well as understand how to adjust the workstation.

Visual problems

Visual problems can be eliminated or reduced by simple modifications such as repositioning the screen to avoid reflections or installing window blinds to prevent glare. In some situations, lighting that is more appropriate may be required. Users who request an eye and eyesight test must be provided with this as specified under regulation 5.

Fatigue and stress problems

These can be tackled by eliminating obvious workstation defects as indicated above. Good design of tasks is important in preventing stress and fatigue. This should include, as far as possible, giving workers control over their work with adequate organisational arrangements for job rotation and rest breaks (regulation 4), information (regulation 7) and training (regulation 6).

Risks from manual handling operations – Assessment and management

Manual handling is the transporting or supporting of loads by human effort as opposed to mechanical handling by cranes or hoists. The manual handling of loads often involves a good deal of static and dynamic effort – enough to be classified as heavy work, that is, an activity characterised by high energy consumption and severe stresses on the heart and lungs.

More than one-quarter of reportable accidents reported each year are associated with manual handling (HSE 1998). Manual handling accidents resulting in a major injury are common, accounting for more than 10 per cent of all major injuries recorded in 1996–97. The vast majority of reported manual handling accidents result in 'over-three-day' injuries, most commonly a sprain or strain, often of the back.

In the SWI95 survey, musculoskeletal injuries represented the largest group in the survey with an estimated national prevalence of 1,155,000 individuals (Jones *et al.* 1998). Of survey respondents in this category, 52 per cent attributed their injury to manual handling, illustrating the extent of injury caused by this activity.

The incorrect application and/or prolonged use of bodily force will cause strains and sprains. Poor posture and excessive repetition of movement can also be factors in their onset. Manual handling injuries are often cumulative rather than caused by one single event and there is not always a full recovery of function.

Concerns about the magnitude of manual handling accidents and injuries have resulted in specific legislation to control this problem, namely, the Manual Handling Operations Regulations 1992 which implemented European Directive 90/269/EEC. These Regulations require that manual handling risks be reduced to the lowest level reasonably practicable. These Regulations (as amended) need to be read in conjunction with the general duties of the Health and Safety at Work etc Act 1974 and the requirements of the MHSW Regulations 1999.

The Manual Handling Regulations (regulation 4) require a suitable and sufficient risk assessment to be carried out for all manual handling operations. Where a manual handling task cannot be eliminated, the application of reasonably practicable control measures must be applied. An ergonomics approach to risk assessment can be applied to manual handling, that is, examining the overall fit between the individual and the handling operation. This includes analysing the nature of the task, the load involved, the working environment and individual's personal capability.

AGENTS OF PHYSICAL MISFIT

The following definition is given in regulation 2 of the Manual Handling Operations Regulations 1992:

"Manual handling operations" means any transporting or supporting of a load (including the lifting, putting down, pushing, pulling, carrying or moving thereof) by hand or bodily force.

Manual handling and the spine

In order to understand the nature of manual handling risks, particularly as they relate to the back, there now follows a brief introduction to the structure and function of the spinal column.

The spine is made up of the following groups of vertebrae: cervical vertebrae (7), thoracic vertebrae (12), lumber vertebrae (5) and the sacrum. Its structure is shown in Figure 11.14.

FIGURE 11.14: Structure of the spinal column

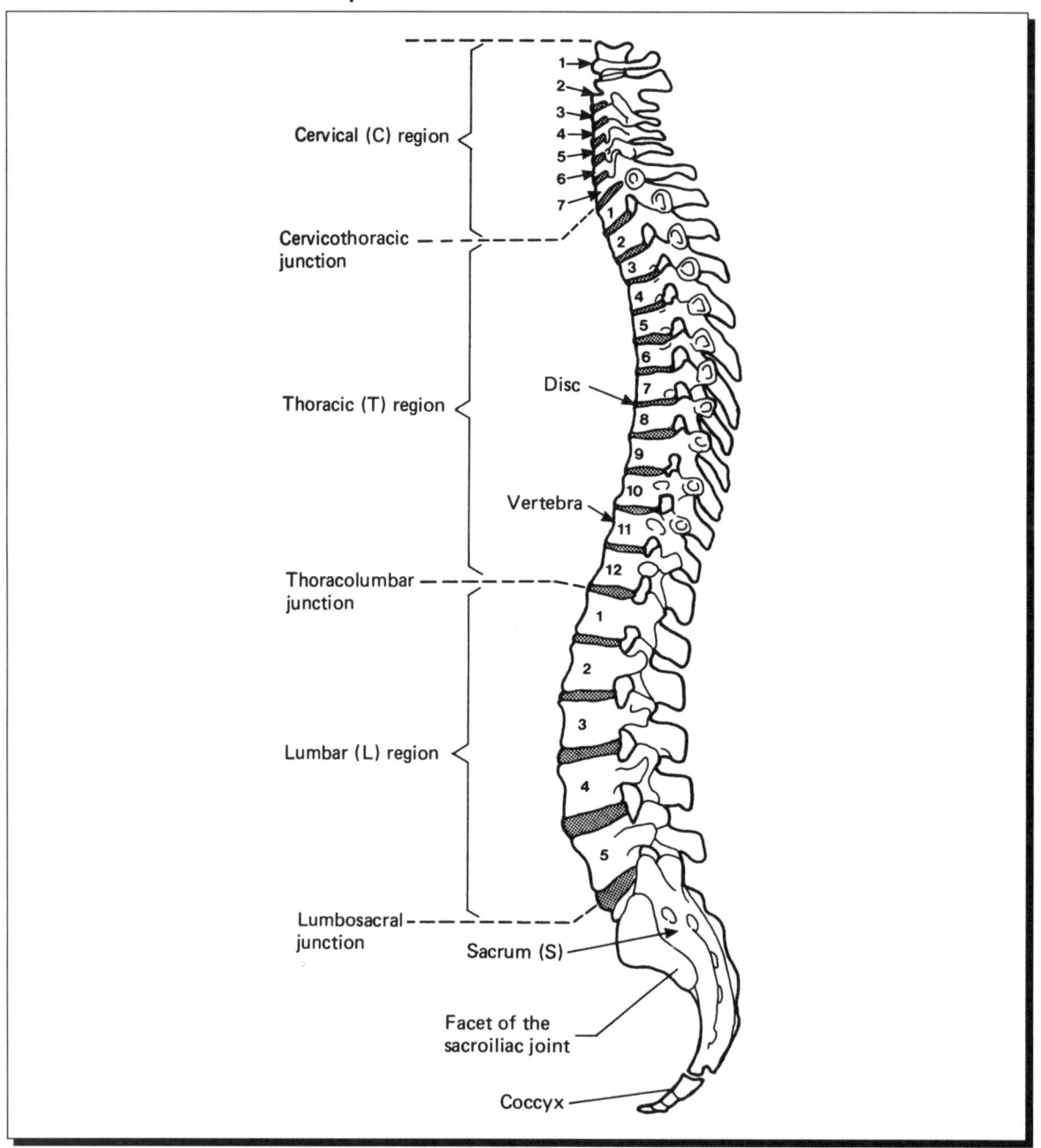

(Troup & Edwards 1985)

The spinal nerve cord passes down the vertebral column and at each intervertebral joint there is a disc between the two vertebrae. In Figures 11.14 and 11.15, the discs are shown as shaded zones. With an erect posture, due to the weight of the body, the load on the spine increases progressively downwards to a maximum in the lumbosacral region. Forces arising in the upper limbs are transmitted to the lower limbs via the sacroiliac joint and the pelvis.

AGENTS OF PHYSICAL MISFIT

FIGURE 11.15: Section of the spine and intervertebral disc

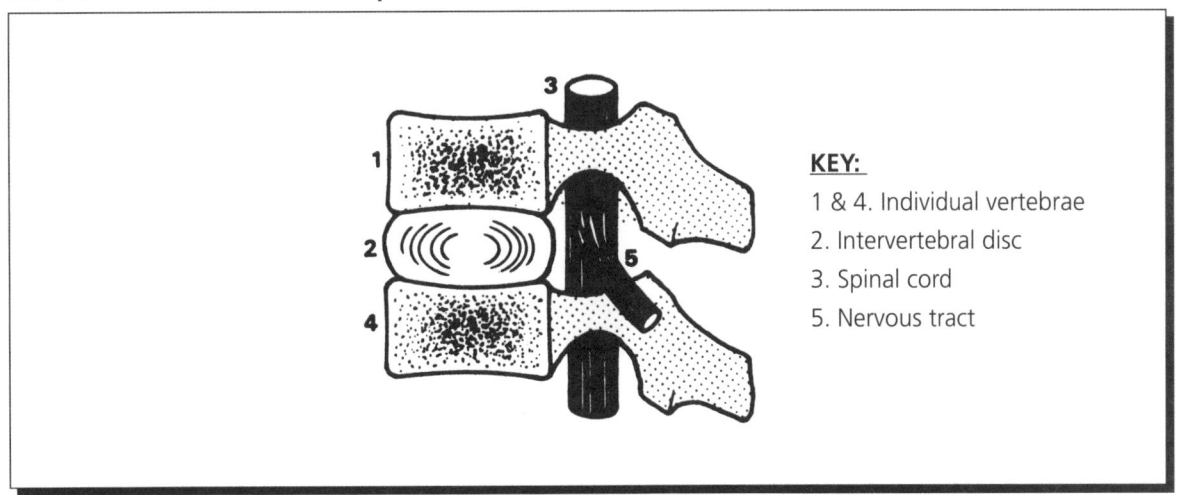

KEY:
1 & 4. Individual vertebrae
2. Intervertebral disc
3. Spinal cord
5. Nervous tract

(Kroemer & Grandjean 1997)

The discs make up about one-quarter of the total length of the spine. Each disc consists of a gel-like matrix with a fibrous outer coat. The discs cushion and transmit compressive load between the vertebrae. Disc degeneration is common with age and this alters the dynamic response of the disc under loading, that is, the response becomes more rapid. Unnatural postures, heavy lifting and bad seating can speed up deterioration of discs. The study of different pairs of vertebrae is difficult due to their complex movements in many different physical planes. Figure 11.16 illustrates that disc pressure can be greater when sitting (without a back rest) than when standing. Compared with standing, the increase in intervertebral disc pressure is 40 per cent when sitting and 90 per cent when leaning forward. An angle greater than 90 degrees between the back and the thighs helps to decrease pressure on the lumbar vertebrae.

FIGURE 11.16: Increased intervertebral lumbar disc pressure and activity

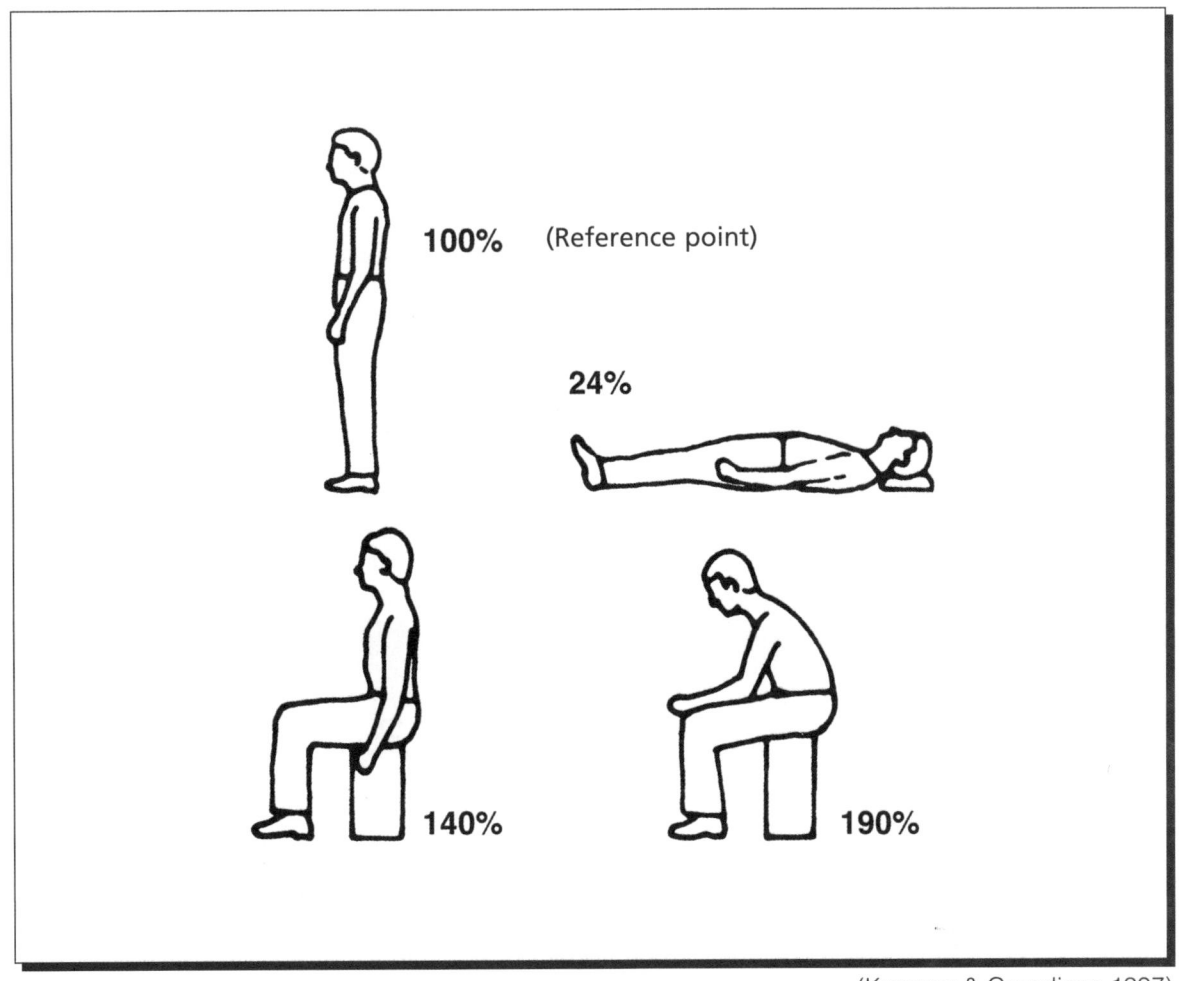

100% (Reference point)

24%

140%

190%

(Kroemer & Grandjean 1997)

AGENTS OF PHYSICAL MISFIT

Figure 11.17 illustrates that bending the back while keeping the legs straight during a manual lifting operation puts a much higher stress on the lumbar discs than keeping the back as straight as possible and bending the legs.

FIGURE 11.17: Intervertebral disc stress and body posture

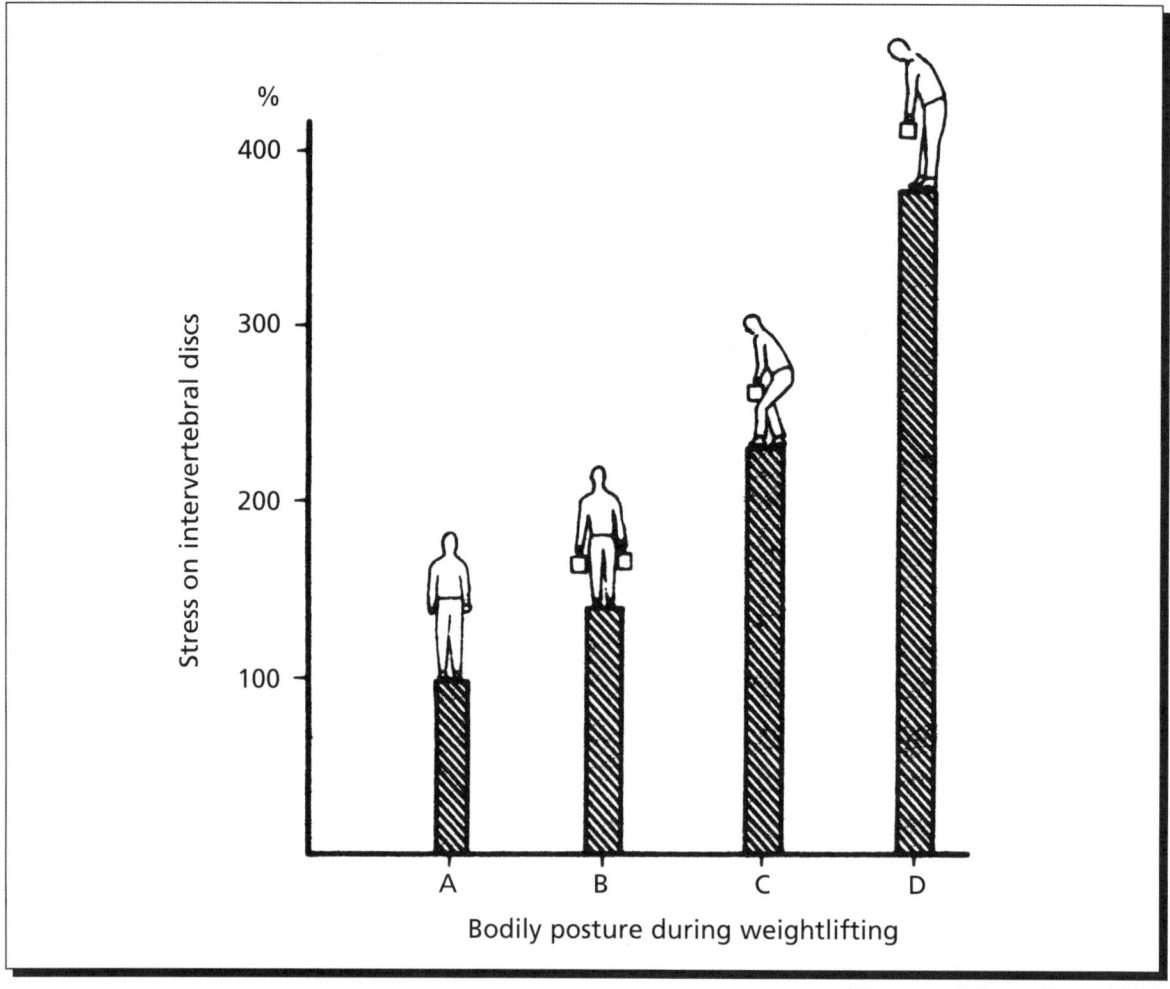

(Kroemer & Grandjean 1997)

FIGURE 11.18: Intervertebral disc pressure and two approaches to a work task

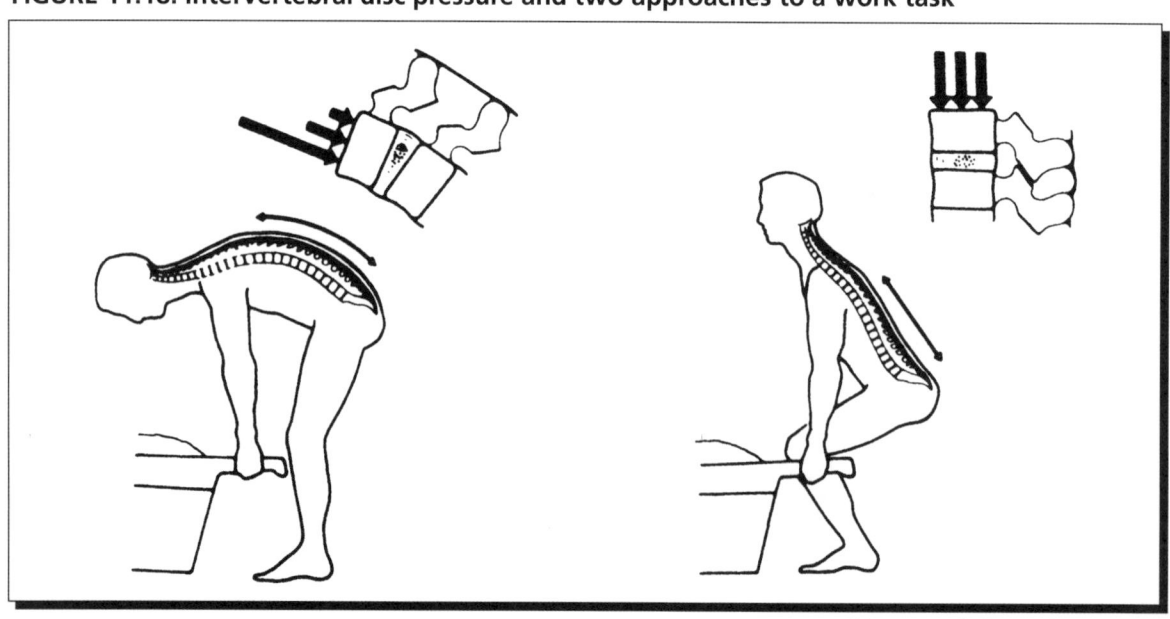

(Kroemer & Grandjean 1997)

In Figure 11.18, the rounded back on the left can be seen to lead to higher pressures on the front edge of the disc. The straight back ensures that the loads on the disc are distributed more evenly.

Gradually, there is fibrosis of the annulus (the ring of the disc). The outer ring becomes worn and tattered and fails to contain the gel-matrix inside and this may press on the cord or a nerve ganglion. (The annulus may heal with the fluid plug out of position, a condition known as a prolapsed or slipped disc.) There is also wear and tear on the joints between the vertebrae (facet joints), which are lubricated by synovial fluid and held in place by a cartilaginous sheath. Ligaments become stretched permanently by poor posture, putting extra pressure on the joints and discs and this produces a permanently distorted posture. There is cumulative damage until a final trauma (incident) brings on a chronic back condition.

Health effects

Of all musculoskeletal injuries, back pain makes up the largest single category and this is experienced by 80 per cent of the working population during their working lives (Wynn & Pilling 1999). Some lower back pain has serious underlying causes such as cancer, abscess or ankylosing spondylitis (less than one per cent) or prolapsed intervertebral disc (15 per cent). However, most back pain is classed as simple or 'mechanical' lower back pain, although only a small proportion of cases has an identifiable mechanical abnormality. Work involving manual handling operations increases the risk of back injury. The frequent bending and twisting movements in many occupations have been shown to increase the risk of lower back injury and disability.

The causal mechanism is not clear in many disorders resulting in back pain, and which is experienced in a wide range of activities from heavy industrial work to light office duties. Some estimates for the general population attribute only 20 per cent of back pain to manual handling causes (Wynn & Pilling 1999). The highest risk factors for developing back pain are:

- previous history of the condition;
- smoking;
- suffering excessive psychological stress at work (including job dissatisfaction, high work load and monotony);
- operating vibrating machinery; and
- undertaking lengthy commuting journeys.

In people who develop lower back pain, those who exercise and keep active experience a more rapid recovery and earlier return to work.

Evaluation of exposure and analysis

The Manual Handling Operations Regulations 1992 require that, where reasonably practicable, a hazardous manual handling operation should be avoided. Where an operation cannot be avoided, then a suitable and sufficient assessment is required and the risk of injury should be reduced "to the lowest extent reasonably practicable".

Risk assessment filter

To avoid carrying out a detailed risk assessment for every manual handling operation, the HSE has published guidance on filtering out operations where this is not appropriate (HSE 1998). This screening filter uses numerical guidelines as an approximate boundary and it is thought to be suitable for the protection of 95 per cent of men and women in the workforce. They caution that the values do not constitute a 'safe weight' for lifting. It is important to note that the risk assessment filters the lifting and lowering operations, which cover only one aspect of manual handling activities. (These activities also include, among other things, pushing, pulling, carrying and moving.)

The guidelines make certain assumptions, that is, the load is easy to grasp with both hands, the operation is taking place in reasonable working conditions, and the handler has a stable body position. The guidelines take account of the vertical and horizontal position of the hands as they move during the operation as well as the height and reach of the handler. When the load is at arm's length or above shoulder height, there is a reduced capacity to lift. The effect of horizontal distance on individual capacity is shown in Figure 11.19.

AGENTS OF PHYSICAL MISFIT

FIGURE 11.19: Reduction of individual handling capacity with distance

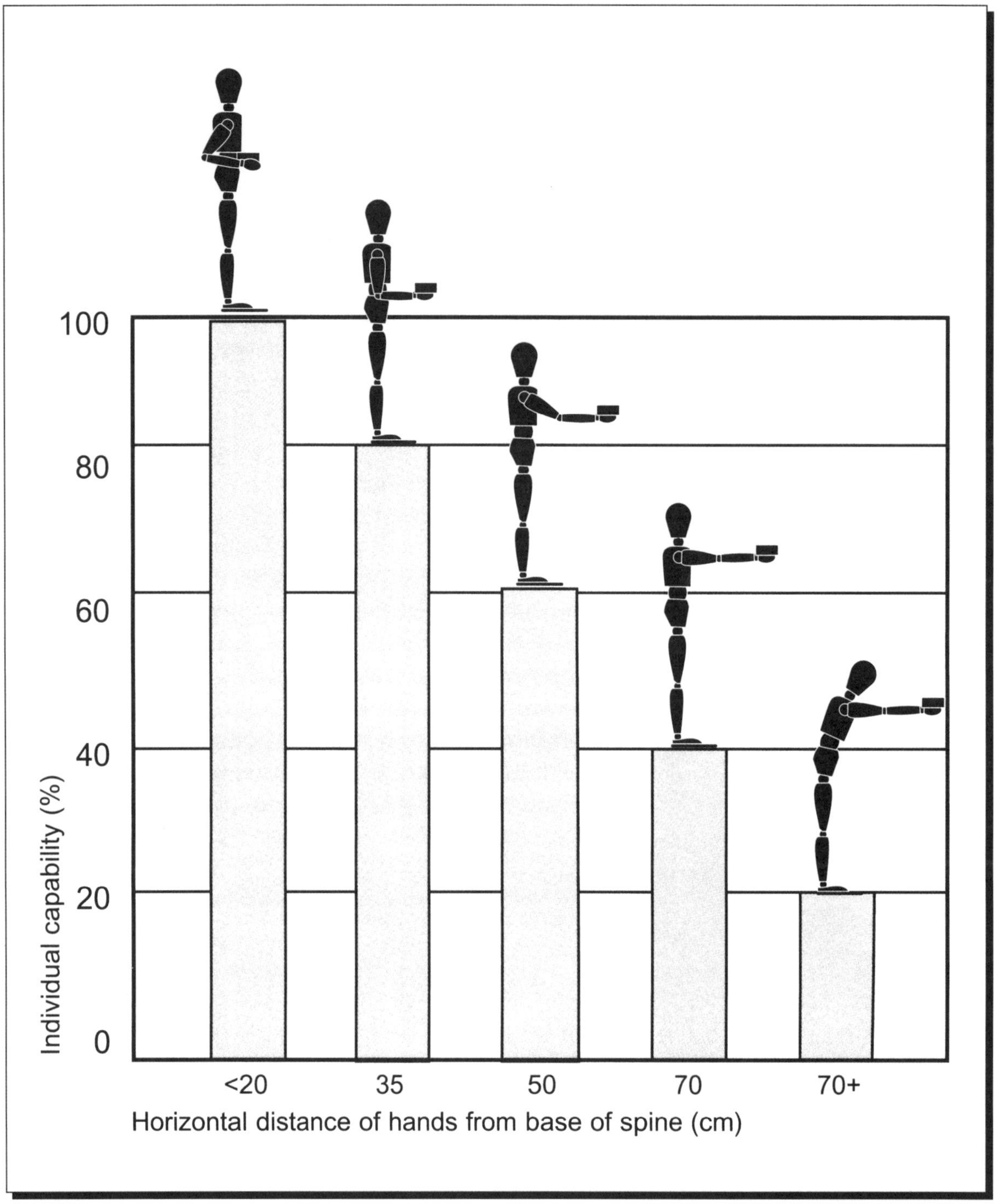

(HSE 1998 – rev. 2003)

The filter guidelines for lifting and lowering are shown in Figure 11.20. If the operator's hands enter more than one of the boxed zones in the diagram, then the smallest figures apply. When lifting or lowering beyond the boxed zones, then a risk assessment should always be made. These guidelines assume a frequency of less than 30 repeat operations per hour and where a higher rate is envisaged, then the figures should be reduced accordingly. With one or two operations per minute, the reduction should be 30 per cent; with five to eight operations per minute, the reduction should be 50 per cent; and with 12 operations per minute, the reduction should be 80 per cent. Even if the above guidelines are satisfied, a detailed risk assessment should always be made where:

- the operator does not control the work pace;
- there are inadequate rest pauses;
- there is no change of work activity (which would provide the opportunity to use different muscles);
- the operator supports the load for a significant period of time.

AGENTS OF PHYSICAL MISFIT

FIGURE 11.20: Guidelines for lifting and lowering

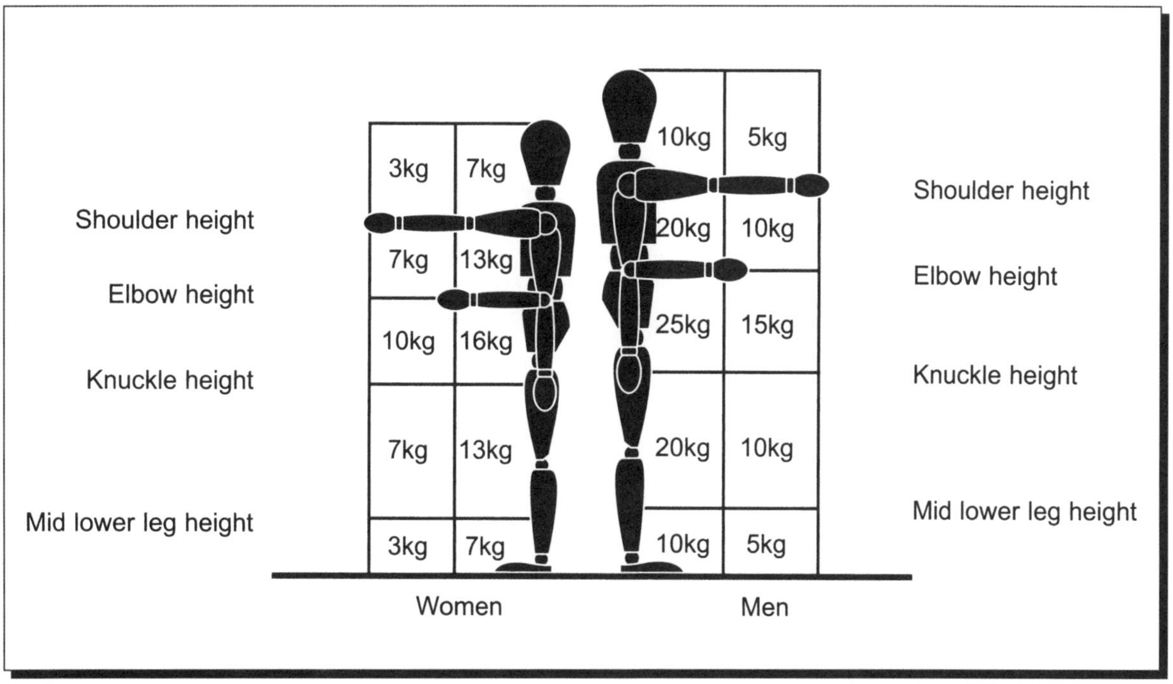

	Women			Men	
Shoulder height	3kg	7kg	10kg	5kg	Shoulder height
Elbow height	7kg	13kg	20kg	10kg	Elbow height
Knuckle height	10kg	16kg	25kg	15kg	Knuckle height
Mid lower leg height	7kg	13kg	20kg	10kg	Mid lower leg height
	3kg	7kg	10kg	5kg	

(HSE 1998 – rev. 2003)

The HSE (1998) gives additional guidelines for carrying where the load is held against the body and carried no further than about 10 metres. There are further guidelines given for pushing and pulling operations and for handling while in a seated position. Many manual handling operations involve twisting or turning and this increases the risk of injury. It is recommended, as a general rule, that these figures should be reduced by 10 per cent where the operator twists through 45 degrees, and 20 per cent where the operator twists through 90 degrees. Where a task involves frequent twisting and turning, a detailed risk assessment would normally be carried out.

Manual handling injuries are usually associated more with the nature of the operations rather than with the individual capability of the operators. However, general lifting ability will vary between males and females. There are age differences in that people aged less than 20 years and above 50 years are likely to have a lower lifting ability than those between these ages. With people involved in a high level of manual handling and physical exertion, there is often some element of self-selection, that is, those who are not happy with the activity will leave this type of work. Special consideration must also be given to those individuals with relevant health problems and to pregnant women.

Risk assessment

The risk assessment needs to evaluate the following aspects:
- the task;
- the load;
- the working environment; and
- the capability of the individual.

Basically, the risk assessment involves asking questions about each of the above aspects of the work in order to determine how well is the fit between the individual and the work situation overall. The greater the degree of misfit, then the higher the risk of manual handling injuries. Schedule 1 of the Manual Handling Operations Regulations 1992 (Figure 11.21) lists the factors and questions which the employer must have regard for when carrying out a manual handling risk assessment. A checklist (Table 11.7) can be used for risk assessment based on the above Schedule.

The essential stages in a detailed risk assessment are:
1. Describe the manual handling task.
2. Evaluate the level of risk (low/medium/high) associated with each item on the checklist.
3. Decide whether the overall level of risk is high, medium or low.

FIGURE 11.21: Manual Handling Operations Regulations 1992 (MHOR), Schedule 1

Schedule 1	Factors to which the employer must have regard and questions he must consider when making an assessment of manual handling operations

Regulation 4(1)(b)(i)

Column 1	Column 1
Factors	Questions
1 The tasks	Do they involve:
	- holding or manipulating loads at distance from trunk?
	- unsatisfactory bodily movement or posture, especially:
	- twisting the trunk?
	- stooping?
	- reaching upwards?
	- excessive movement of loads, especially:
	- excessive lifting or lowering distances?
	- excessive carrying distances?
	- excessive pushing or pulling of loads?
	- risk of sudden movement of loads?
	- frequent or prolonged physical effort?
	- insufficient rest or recovery periods?
	- a rate of work imposed by a process?
2 The loads	Are they:
	- heavy?
	- bulky or unwieldy?
	- difficult to grasp?
	- unstable, or with contents likely to shift?
	- sharp, hot or otherwise potentially damaging?
3 The working environment	Are there:
	- space constraints preventing good posture?
	- uneven, slippery or unstable floors?
	- variations in level of floors or work surfaces?
	- extremes of temperature or humidity?
	- conditions causing ventilation problems or gusts of wind?
	- poor lighting conditions?
4 Individual capability	Does the job:
	- require unusual strength, height, etc?
	- create a hazard to those who might reasonably be considered to be pregnant or to have a health problem?
	- require special information or training for its safe performance?
5 Other factors	Is movement or posture hindered by personal protective equipment or by clothing?

(HSE 1998 – rev. 2003)

AGENTS OF PHYSICAL MISFIT

TABLE 11.7: Risk assessment checklist for manual handling

Key aspects	Question checklist	Risk (Low, Medium, High)
Tasks	Do they involve: • Holding loads away from the trunk? • Twisting? • Stooping? • Reaching upwards? • Large vertical movements? • Long carrying distances? • Strenuous pushing and pulling? • Unpredictable movement of loads? • Repetitive handling? • Insufficient rest or recovery? • A work rate imposed by a process?	
The loads	Are they: • Heavy? • Bulky/unwieldy? • Difficult to grasp? • Unstable/unpredictable? • Intrinsically harmful (eg sharp/hot)?	
The working environment	Are there: • Constraints on posture? • Poor floors? • Variations in levels? • Hot/cold/humid conditions? • Strong air movements? • Poor lighting conditions?	
Individual capability	Does the job: • Require unusual capability? • Hazard those with a health problem? • Hazard those who are pregnant? • Call for special information/training?	
Other factors	Is movement or posture hindered by clothing or PPE	

(Adapted from HSE 1998 – rev. 2003)

The next step is to decide on the overall level of risk for the task taking into account the answers to the checklist questions. This will determine whether preventive measures are required.

Tolerability of risk

Manual handling tasks, as pointed out by Pheasant (1986), are often 'undesigned' one-off operations. For such occasional tasks, it is difficult to set up standards, although with frequent repetitive work, various limits have been produced. The limits in the HSE's filter guidelines were cited above (HSE 1998).

In 1981, the US National Institute for Occupational Safety and Health (NIOSH) reviewed the scientific literature and produced standards in terms of a lifting equation to rate lifting tasks in terms of whether the loads were excessive. The equation, revised on several occasions, takes into account six key factors in defining a Recommended Weight Limit (RWL) for the lifting and lowering of loads. The formula is designed to assess only certain lifting and lowering tasks (eg standing, two-handed, smooth lifting of stable objects in unrestricted spaces). The six factors, each of which requires actual measurements or numerical ratings on a scale, are as follows:

1. Horizontal position of the load relative to the body.
2. Vertical position of the load relative to the floor.
3. Vertical distance the load is moved.
4. Frequency and duration of lifting task.
5. Asymmetry (lifts requiring twisting or rotation of the trunk or body).
6. Quality of the operator's grip on the load.

The RWL is thought to represent a load that nearly all (ie 90 per cent of the adult population) can lift for up to eight hours without significantly increasing the risk of lower back disorders. When the actual load weight for a given task is compared with the computed RWL, this represents an estimate of the risk presented by the task. Where loads exceed the RWL for a task, factors contributing to the excess risk can be identified and this helps target the application of control measures (NIOSH 1999). The equation permits the lifting of a load which will give a maximum compression force in the lumbar vertebrae of 3,400 newtons (3.4kN).

The limits apply to both lifting and lowering and the maximum recommended weight is 23kg under the most favourable conditions. It is worth pointing out that there is no such thing as a 'safe' load; for example, someone could reach out awkwardly and injure their back even with the most trivial of loads.

Following the assessment analysis, a decision needs to be taken on the degree of misfit between the task operator and the work. This, in turn, will determine whether the risk of manual handling injury arising from the work is deemed tolerable or further precautions are needed.

Prevention and control measures

The specific measures taken in a given situation will obviously depend on the results of the risk analysis. The analysis will address the adequacy and evaluate each of the task and/or operator elements identified above.

According to Bridger (2001), the practice of training workers in lifting techniques, for example, 'kinetic lifting', is still widespread despite the lack of scientific evidence that these techniques really do protect people from injury. He asserts that successful strategies in reducing injuries are holistic, involving the redesign of tasks, the redesign of work areas where manual handling takes place, the provision of lifting aids, and training in the use of lifting aids. He further states that training in lifting techniques alone appears ineffective.

Application of ergonomic job design principles

This aims to match employees better with their work situation with the aim of minimising manual handling risks. The principal aim is to eliminate the manual handling task, where this is possible, and where not, minimise the inherent risks in a task by, for example, using mechanical assistance to help with the task. This is the most effective approach for minimising levels of lower back pain in employees.

Information and training

Although manual handling training is important, to be successful it needs to be applied as part of a whole work system strategy. Information and training should be given to task operators and include the following topics:

- caring for the back – normal function and how problems arise, personal fitness;
- ergonomics and the identification of hazardous handling operations;
- good manual handling techniques and the proper use of handling devices;
- factors affecting individual capability;
- the proper use of personal protective equipment;
- good housekeeping.

As regards training in lifting and handling techniques, Kroemer & Grandjean (1997) cite the following handling rules which are based on both scientific knowledge and general experience:

1. Seize the load and lift it with a straight back and bent knees.
2. Get the load to as close to the body as possible and whenever possible between the knees.
3. The hold on the load should not be lower than knee height.
4. If the load does not have handles, use mechanical assistance if practicable.
5. Avoid rotating or twisting movement of the trunk when lifting or lowering a load.
6. Wherever possible, use mechanical aids such as a hoist.
7. Try to replace lifting and lowering by pushing and pulling.

TABLE 11.8: Generic questions – Application of ergonomics to job design

Aspect	Control item
Task	Can mechanical assistance be used with this task?
	How can task lay-out be improved?
	How can the body be used more efficiently?
	How can the need for stooping, twisting, and stretching be reduced?
	How can the load be held closer to the body?
	Where can lifting operations be replaced with controlled pushing and/or pulling operations?
	How can work posture be improved?
	How can fixed postures be minimised?
	How can the frequency of handling be reduced?
	How can breaks and job rotation be implemented?
	How can variation of work ensuring use of the different muscle groups be implemented?
	How can handling where seated be achieved?
	Is team handling practicable?
	How can interference by PPE and other clothing be prevented?
Load	How can the load be made lighter?
	How can the load be made smaller and easier to manage?
	How can the load be made easier to grasp?
	How can the load be made more stable?
	How can the load be made less damaging to hold?
Work environment	How can any space constraints be removed?
	How can the nature and condition of the floor be improved?
	How can working at different levels be eliminated?
	How can the thermal environment be made adequate?
	How can ventilation conditions be improved?
	How can wind speed be reduced?
	How can the lighting conditions be made adequate?
Individual capability	How can the operator improve his/her general state of health and fitness?
	How can the confidence and motivation of the operator be improved with respect to handling heavy loads?
	How can the individual be trained to carry out competent manual handling?

(Adapted from HSE 1998 – rev. 2003)

Health surveillance

Whether the task operator is pregnant, or has a history of back problems, hernias or other health effects, is highly relevant in the management of manual handling operations. A medical history is important since the strongest predictor for lower back pain is the individual's previous history of this condition. A question about this is often included in pre-employment questionnaires, however, it may not always be answered with complete honesty.

Wynn & Pilling (1999) point out that a clinical examination and review of specialist reports on potential employees with severe back problems (by occupational physicians) will allow recommendations to be made regarding suitability or job adaptation. These authors caution that this could be seen as discriminatory against older workers who are more likely to have had an episode of lower back pain. The Disability Discrimination Act 1995 requires that those with a disability should not be excluded from work that they may be able to perform, with or without reasonable adaptation.

Fitness and general state of health are also important factors with respect to handling of loads and these are monitored by routine health surveillance.

Manual Handling Operations Regulations 1992 (MHOR)

A summary of the requirements of the Manual Handling Operations Regulations 1992 is given in Table 11.9.

TABLE 11.9: Summary of the Manual Handling Operations Regulations 1992 (MHOR) (as amended)

Regulation	Requirement
Regulation 1: Citation and commencement	
Regulation 2: Interpretation	Defines manual handling operation
Regulation 3: Disapplication of the Regulations	Do not apply to a seagoing ship
Regulation 4: Duties of employers	• Avoidance of manual handling • Assessment of risk • Reducing the risk of injury • The load – additional information • Additional factors related to employees • Reviewing the assessment
Regulation 5: Duty of employees	Proper use of any system of work provided
Regulation 6: Exemption certificates	
Regulation 7: Extension outside Great Britain	
Regulation 8: Repeal and revocations	
Schedule 1: Factors to which an employer must have regard and questions when making an assessment	See Figure 11.21
Schedule 2: Repeals and revocations	
Appendix 1: Numerical guidelines for assessment	See Figure 11.20
Appendix 2: Example of an assessment checklist	
Appendix 3: References and further information	

REFERENCES

Alexander et al. -v- Midland Bank plc, Court of Appeal, 22 July 1999, CCRTF98/1014–1018.

Bernard B P and Putz-Anderson V, 1997, *Musculoskeletal Disorders and Workplace Factors: A Critical Review of the Epidemiological Evidence for Work-Related Musculoskeletal Disorders of the Neck, Upper Extremities and Lower Back*, National Institute for Occupational Safety and Health, Cincinnati, OH, USA.

Bridger R S, 2001, Lifting the Load, *Health and Safety at Work*, June 2001.

British Standards Institution, 1990, *Guide to Ergonomics Principles in the Design and Selection of Office Furniture*, BS 3044 1990, BSI, London.

British Standards Institution, 1990a, Ergonomics of Design and Use of Visual Display Terminals (VDTs), in *Offices, Part 5: Specification for VDT Workstations*, BS 7179, BSI, London.

British Standards Institution, 1990b, Ergonomics of Design and Use of Visual Display Terminals (VDTs), in *Offices, Part 6: Code of Practice for the Design of VDT Work Environments*, BS 7179, BSI, London.

British Standards Institution, 1993, *Ergonomic Requirements for Office Work With Visual Display Terminals (VDTs), Part 2: Guidance on Task Requirements*, BS EN 29241-2: 1993, BSI, London.

British Standards Institution, 1993a, *Ergonomic Requirements for Office Work With Visual Display Terminals (VDTs), Part 3: Visual Display Requirements*, BS EN 29241-3: 1993, BSI, London.

British Standards Institution, 1997, *Ergonomic Requirements for Office Work With Visual Display Terminals (VDTs), Part 1: General Introduction*, BS/EN/ISO 9241-1: 1997, BSI, London.

Clark T S and Corlett E N, 1984, *The Ergonomics of Workspaces and Machines: A Design Manual*, Taylor and Francis, London.

Doll R, 1994, *Health Effects Related to the Use of Visual Display Units*, National Radiological Protection Board, HMSO, London.

European Community, 1990, *Council Directive on the Minimum Safety and Health Requirements for Work With Display Screen Equipment*, 90/270/EEC.

European Community, 1990a, *Council Directive on the Minimum Requirements for the Manual Handling of Loads Where There is a Risk Particularly of Back Injury to Workers*, 90/269/EEC.

Hagberg M, Kilbom A and Buckle P, 1993, Strategies for the Prevention of Work-Related Musculoskeletal Disorders – A Consensus Paper, *Int J Ind Erg*, **11**, 77–81.

Hagberg M, Silverstein Wells R, Smith M J, Dendrick H W, Carayon P and Perusse M, 1995, *Work-Related Musculoskeletal Disorders (WMSDs): A Reference Book for Prevention*, Taylor and Francis, London.

Health and Safety Commission, 1996, *Picking up the Pieces – Prevention of Musculoskeletal Disorders in the Ceramics Industry*, HSE Books, Sudbury.

Health and Safety Commission, 1998, *Manual Handling in the Health Services*, HSE Books, Sudbury.

Health and Safety Executive, 1990, *Work-Related Upper Limb Disorders – A Guide to Prevention*, HS(G)60, HMSO, London.

Health and Safety Executive, 1992, *Display Screen Equipment at Work*, The Health and Safety (Display Screen Equipment) Regulations 1992, Guidance on Regulations, L26, HMSO, London.

Health and Safety Executive, 1994, *A Pain in Your Workplace – Ergonomic Problems and Their Solution*, HSG121, HSE Books, Sudbury.

Health and Safety Executive, 1997, *Seating at Work*, HSG57, HSE Books, Sudbury.

Health and Safety Executive, 1997a, *Lighting at Work*, HSG38, HSE Books, Sudbury.

Health and Safety Executive, 1997b, *Well Handled – Offshore Manual Handling Solutions*, HSG171, HSE Books, Sudbury.

Health and Safety Executive, 1998, *Manual Handling* (2nd edition), The Manual Handling Operations Regulations 1992, Guidance on Regulations, L23, HSE Books, Sudbury.

Health and Safety Executive, 2002, *Upper Limb Disorders in the Workplace* (2nd edition), HSG60(rev), HSE Books, Sudbury.

Health and Safety Executive, 2003, *Work with Display Screen Equipment: Health and Safety (Display Screen Equipment) Regulations 1992 as Amended by the Health and Safety (Miscellaneous Amendments) Regulations 2002 – Guidance on Regulations*, L26, HSE Books, Sudbury.

Hodgson J T, Jones J R, Elliot R C and Osman J, 1993, *Self-Reported Work-Related Illness*, Research Paper 33, HSE Books, Sudbury.

International Commission on Occupational Health, 1996, Musculoskeletal Disorders, *Int J Occ & Env Hlth*, **2**, 239–246.

Jones J R, Hodgson J T, Clegg T A and Elliot R C, 1998, *Self-Reported Work-Related Illness in 1995: Results from a Household Survey*, HSE Books, Sudbury.

Kirwan B and Ainsworth L K, 1993, *A Guide to Task Analysis*, Taylor and Francis, London.

Kroemer K H E and Grandjean E, 1997, *Fitting the Task to the Human* (5th edition), Taylor and Francis, London.

Mital A and Nicholson A S, 1997, *A Guide to Manual Materials Handling*, Taylor and Francis, London.

National Institute for Occupational Safety and Health, 1991, *Work Practices Guide for Manual Lifting*, Cincinatti, OH, USA.

National Institute for Occupational Safety and Health, 1999, *Applications Manual for the Revised NIOSH Lifting Equation*, National Technical Information Service, Springfield, VA, USA.

Paoli P, 1997, *Second European Survey on Working Conditions 1996*, European Foundation for the Improvement of Living and Working Conditions, Dublin.

Parsons K C, 1995, Ergonomics, Chapter 15 in *Occupational Hygiene* (2nd edition), Harrington J M and Gardiner K (Eds), Blackwell Science, Oxford.

Pheasant S, 1986, *Bodyspace: Anthropometry, Ergonomics and Design*, Taylor and Francis, London.

Pheasant S and Stubbs D, 1991, *Lifting and Handling – An Ergonomic Approach*, National Back Pain Association.

Troup J D G and Edwards F C, 1985, *Manual Handling – A Review Paper*, HSE Books, Sudbury.

Wynn P and Pilling K, 1999, Risk Management and Manual Handling, Chapter 22 in *Occupational Health – Risk Assessment and Management*, Sadhra S S and Rampal K G (Eds), Blackwell Science, Oxford.

LEGISLATION

Disability Discrimination Act 1995

Health and Safety (Display Screen Equipment) Regulations 1992 (SI 1992/2792) (as amended by the Health and Safety (Miscellaneous Amendments) Regulations 2002 (SI 2002/2174))

Management of Health and Safety at Work Regulations 1999 (SI 1999/3242)

Manual Handling Operations Regulations 1992 (SI 1992/2793) (as amended by the Health and Safety (Miscellaneous Amendments) Regulations 2002 (SI 2002/2174))

Provision and Use of Work Equipment Regulations 1998 (SI 1998/2306) (as amended by SI 1999/860 and SI 1999/2001)

Reporting of Injuries, Diseases and Dangerous Occurrences Regulations 1995 (SI 1995/3163)

Workplace (Health, Safety and Welfare) Regulations 1992 (SI 1992/3004)

12: Agents of psychosocial misfit

(Hulton Getty Picture Collection)

INTRODUCTION

The aim of this chapter is to consider the assessment and management of risks arising from exposure to harmful psychosocial environments which result in work-induced stress and workplace violence. Such environments are believed to represent a significant and growing problem. Although stress and violence are treated separately here, sometimes there is a close link between work-induced stress levels and violent incidents.

Stress at work

The UK survey of self-reported work-related ill health carried out in 1995 (SWI95) estimated a national prevalence of 515,000 cases in the category labelled 'stress, depression, anxiety or physical condition ascribed to stress' (Jones *et al*. 1998). The subcategory 'stress, depression and anxiety' was the second most commonly reported condition, with 14 per cent of all respondents who reported a work-related illness mentioning this condition. Based on this evidence, a corresponding national prevalence of 279,000 was estimated for this subcategory. Furthermore, in this survey the occupational groups with the highest prevalence of work-related stress included doctors, teachers, nurses and road transport workers. A recent study carried out for the HSE (Smith *et al*. 2000) evaluated the severity and scale of occupational stress in the UK. It was found that 20 per cent of UK workers (equated to be around five million) were very or extremely stressed by their work.

Kompier & Cooper (1999) cite a study of 15,000 European workers where 28 per cent reported stress as a work-related problem for them (Paoli 1997). These authors estimated the total cost of 'workplace pressure' at 10 per cent of GDP in developed countries. These costs involved sickness absence, loss of turnover, increased insurance premiums and treatment.

In a report commissioned by the HSE, Cox (1993) cites official figures showing that, in 1989–90, approximately 80 million working days were lost due to 'mental disorder', thought mainly to be due to stress and stress-related conditions.

There are many factors linked to this very high level of work-related stress. Over the last 20 years, there have been many changes in employment practice with contracting out of labour, downsizing, delayering and multiskilling, all of which can lead to job insecurity. For those who remain in work, the demands are becoming ever larger. According to Demos (1995), 70 per cent of workers in the UK would like to work a 40-hour week but only 30 per cent achieve this, and 20 per cent of all manual workers work in excess of 50 hours per week and 12.5 per cent of managers work in excess of 60 hours per week.

In the SWI95 survey mentioned above, reported by Jones *et al.* (1998), causal factors mentioned by the 'stress, depression and anxiety' group are shown in Table 12.1.

TABLE 12.1: SWI95 survey – 'Stress, depression and anxiety' group and causative factors

Causative factor	Percentage of group mentioning this factor
'Workload and pace'; 'Pressure of work'; 'Too much work'	50
'Lack of support'	25
'Change' (eg reorganisation of work, career change or instability)	20
'Work schedule' (eg long hours, shiftwork, limited rest breaks)	14
'Contact with members of the public' (eg conflict, poor relationships, attacked or threatened)	11
'Relationships at work' (eg attacked or threatened by colleagues, bullying, harassment)	10

(Data from Jones et al. 1998)

The problems arising from contact with the public and relationships at work are also relevant in consideration of violence at work, which is discussed in the second part of this chapter.

Stress research

Occupational stress has been a very popular research area in recent years. However, Kompier & Cooper (1999) comment that, although there has been much research aimed at identifying sources of workplace stress and its links with adverse personal and organisational factors, relatively little work has focused on prevention and control strategies. They draw three related conclusions:

1. There has been considerable activity in 'stress management', mainly aimed at reducing the *effects* of stress rather than reducing the presence of causes, ie stressors (psychosocial work hazards).
2. Most interventions have been aimed at the individual rather than the workplace or organisation (eg improving the employee's *coping* skills rather than changing the management style or approach).
3. There has been a noticeable lack of application of systematic risk assessment and a lack of research on the effectiveness of stress prevention and control strategies (often termed 'interventions' in the stress literature). This is despite the clearly established link between psychosocial work hazards, stress and ill health. This also contrasts with the current widespread international emphasis on applying risk assessment and control to other types of hazard, eg physical and chemical agents.

Overall, Kompier & Cooper (1999) conclude that systematic risk assessment, with a combination of work-directed and worker-directed control measures and the commitment and involvement of management and employees, is vital for success in preventing occupational stress. In recent HSE-sponsored research, Cox *et al.* (2000) applied a general risk management model to the challenge of reducing work stress in a group of large UK private sector organisations.

Stress interventions
Approaches to preventing and controlling occupational stress have been classified into primary, secondary and tertiary interventions (Murphy 1988).

Primary
Interventions aimed at eliminating, reducing or altering stressors in the workplace.

Secondary
These are strategies to help prevent employees who are showing early signs of stress from becoming ill by, for example, increasing their coping capacity.

Tertiary
These activities involve the treatment of people with stress-related health problems and include stress counselling, employee assistance programmes, and rehabilitation after long-term absenteeism.

European context
In a European context, Kompier & Cooper (1999) identify three clusters of countries by their activity on occupational stress:
- **Group 1** (includes the Netherlands and Scandinavian countries) – These countries pay a lot of attention to preventing work stress and consider stress a relevant health and safety issue.
- **Group 2** (includes the UK and Germany) – These countries take an intermediate position; stress is considered a policy issue but there are no specific legal regulations on stress at work. With regard to stress monitoring, good preventive practice and interventions, and cost benefit analyses, these countries are not as advanced as Group 1.
- **Group 3** (includes Southern European countries including Spain, Greece and Italy) – Work stress is not recognised as an important policy or real issue. There is little information on risk groups and risk factors and more emphasis is put on typical blue-collar hazards.

UK developments
The HSE has recently developed 'management standards' for work-related stress, originally proposed in guidance (HSE 2001). The standards are based on identified possible sources of stress: demands (of the job); control (employee control over how work is carried out); support (from management and work colleagues); relationships (at work); role (clarity of definition); and change (organisational).

At present, there is no legislation which specifically cover the risks from work-related stress. However, in the general duties of employers to their employees under the Health and Safety at Work etc Act 1974, the term 'health at work' can be considered to include mental health. Consequently, the risk assessment required under the Management of Health and Safety at Work Regulations 1999 (MHSW) (regulation 3) should also consider risks to mental health.

UK employers are becoming increasingly aware that their common law duty of care and statutory obligations extend to psychosocial factors. There have been high profile and influential civil law cases concerned with the effects of stress. The case of *Johnstone -v- Bloomsbury Health Authority* (1992) was brought by a junior hospital doctor who claimed that his schedule had damaged his health. The case of *Walker -v- Northumberland County Council* (1995) was brought by a social worker who had suffered a nervous breakdown and on returning to work had suffered another one, it was argued, due to the demands of work and the inadequate work system provided by his employer. In a recent combined case, the Court of Appeal has issued comprehensive new guidelines on damages claims for work-related stress *(Hatton -v- Sutherland* (2002)). Cases heard since *Hatton* have emphasised the burden on the claimant to prove that it was foreseeable to the employer that the claimant would suffer from a stress-related illness.

Stress intervention programmes tend to be confined to large organisations, usually with more than 500 employees and these are typically the secondary and tertiary intervention type as classified above. The most popular forms of intervention in the UK include stress management and health enhancement programmes which aim to improve coping skills. Generally, 'stress management' tackles symptoms and not causes. However, factors related to an individual can play an important role in the development of stress and this needs to be taken into account in a prevention strategy.

Definitions of stress

There are many definitions of stress. However, for current purposes the definition used by the HSE is clear and useful:

> *Stress is the adverse reaction people have to excessive pressure or other types of demand placed upon them.* (HSE)

For our purposes, occupational stress exists where the demands of the workplace are outside the capacity of the individual to adjust. Stress is a person's response to psychosocial hazards in a workplace which may lead to ill health.

FIGURE 12.1: Stress model

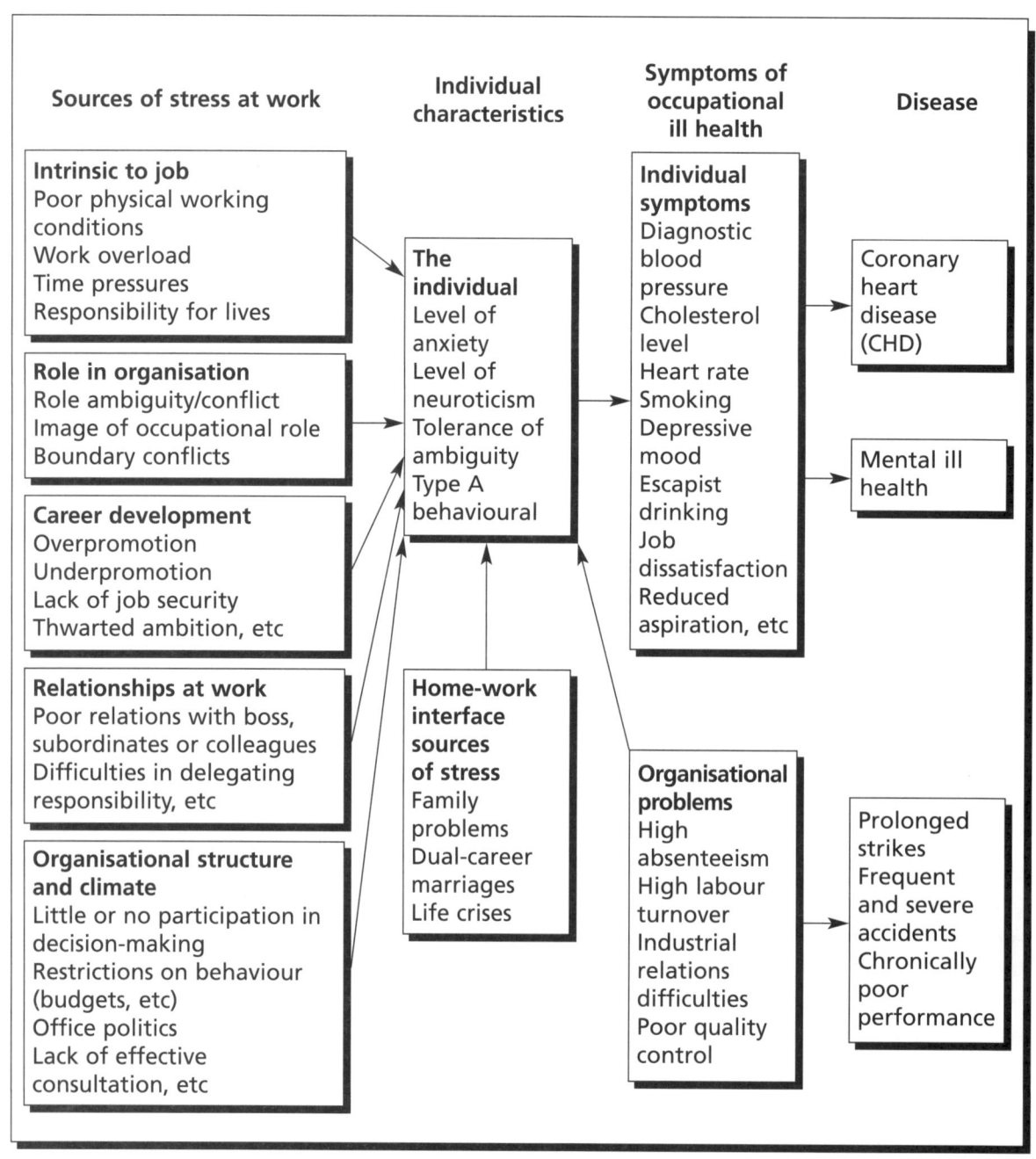

Sources of stress at work	Individual characteristics	Symptoms of occupational ill health	Disease
Intrinsic to job Poor physical working conditions Work overload Time pressures Responsibility for lives	**The individual** Level of anxiety Level of neuroticism Tolerance of ambiguity Type A behavioural	**Individual symptoms** Diagnostic blood pressure Cholesterol level Heart rate Smoking Depressive mood Escapist drinking Job dissatisfaction Reduced aspiration, etc	Coronary heart disease (CHD) Mental ill health
Role in organisation Role ambiguity/conflict Image of occupational role Boundary conflicts			
Career development Overpromotion Underpromotion Lack of job security Thwarted ambition, etc			
Relationships at work Poor relations with boss, subordinates or colleagues Difficulties in delegating responsibility, etc	**Home-work interface sources of stress** Family problems Dual-career marriages Life crises	**Organisational problems** High absenteeism High labour turnover Industrial relations difficulties Poor quality control	Prolonged strikes Frequent and severe accidents Chronically poor performance
Organisational structure and climate Little or no participation in decision-making Restrictions on behaviour (budgets, etc) Office politics Lack of effective consultation, etc			

(Cooper 1986)

Stressors and stress differ in important ways from physical and chemical agents which are normally the subject of the risk assessment and control process. Stressors for an individual are often complicated by some arising outside the workplace, that is, from home and social life, where they are less accessible to preventive action. Also, different individuals have different thresholds for coping with stress.

It is not easy to apply risk assessment and management to occupational stress. Howe (1999) cautions that in examining occupational hazards likely to cause stress, for example, inappropriate culture or poor management policies, it is difficult to state, with any certainty, that the stress experienced by an individual or a group is caused by workplace factors or to assign a numerical value to them. Furthermore, management is likely to be less willing to accept that the company's policies or management style may be significant in causing occupational stress. On the other hand, they may be much more receptive to non-work aspects of stress causation. According to Howe (1999), this influences the type of action that is ultimately initiated, that is, the more preferable support for the individual (with personal troubles) rather than the identification and elimination of basic organisational causes.

Hazard identification

The stress model in Figure 12.1 (Cooper 1986) attempts to highlight the major sources of stress (from work and home), the relevant individual characteristics, the symptoms of ill health and the serious diseases which may result.

The general characteristics of occupational stressors are illustrated below by Cox (1993) (Table 12.2). In an occupational context, there is particular interest in the sources of stress listed.

TABLE 12.2: Stressful characteristics of work

Work characteristics	Conditions defining hazard (demands, control and support)
Context	
Organisational function and culture	• Poor task environment and lack of definition of objectives
	• Poor problem-solving environment
	• Poor development environment
	• Poor communication
	• Non-supportive culture
Role in organisation	• Role ambiguity
	• Role conflict
	• High responsibility for people
Career development	• Career uncertainty
	• Career stagnation
	• Poor status or pay incongruity
	• Pay
	• Job insecurity and redundancy
	• Low social value to work
Decision latitude control	• Low participation in decision-making
	• Lack of control over work
	• Little decision-making in work
Interpersonal relationships at work	• Social or physical isolation
	• Poor relationships with superiors
	• Interpersonal conflict or violence
	• Lack of social support
Home/work interface	• Conflicting demands of work and home
	• Low social or practical support at home
	• Dual career problems

Table continued overleaf

AGENTS OF PSYCHOSOCIAL MISFIT

Content	
Task design	• Ill-defined work
	• High uncertainty in work
	• Lack of variety or short work cycles
	• Fragmented or meaningless work
	• Underutilisation of skills
	• Continual exposure to customer/client groups
Workload/work pace – quantitative and qualitative	• Lack of control over pacing
	• Work overload or underload
	• High levels of pacing or time pressure
Work schedule	• Shift working
	• Inflexible work schedule
	• Unpredictable long hours
	• Long or unsocial hours

(Cox 1993)

In a workplace situation, the aim is to pinpoint the stressors and apply risk assessment and control. The more of these stressors that are present in a given situation (and the greater their magnitude), then the more likely it will be that people are suffering from occupational stress and are at risk of the associated health effects.

Health effects of stress

The 'fight or flight' stress reaction is a traditional response to danger. However, this reaction is not a socially acceptable display in the modern work environment and it may be translated into an 'accept or avoid' response to a challenge.

Physiological responses

A range of physiological responses are associated with the stress response. In the production of the aroused state, there is a release of the catecholamines, adrenalin and noradrenalin, and cortisol is also generated. Noradrenalin is concerned with the physical aspects of the stress response and adrenalin with perceived feelings of effort.

Other changes in physiological parameters include increased heart rate and increased blood pressure with sweaty palms and dry mouth, warm and clammy feelings, tense muscles, and senses on full alert. These may ultimately result in adverse cardiovascular changes and serious heart disease.

Endorphins and acetylcholine are generated by the parasympathetic nervous system and function to moderate this aroused, stress-induced state. Normally, throughout the day and night, the stress response is switched on and off depending on demands. If this aroused state persists, then a chronic stress state occurs and mental faculties will begin to deteriorate rapidly. The individual worries that they cannot cope.

Psychological changes

1. Anxiety.
2. Depression.

Mental health problems

1. Mental health breakdown.
2. Somatic symptoms (physical manifestations where there is no organic basis – headaches, rashes, even paralysis).
3. The consequences of alcoholism and smoking.

Other ill health conditions

1. Heart disease.

2. Cancer and infectious diseases – the immune system's capability is lowered in people found to have been highly stressed; thus, they have been found to have a greater likelihood of contracting these conditions.

Overall, stress is thought to be a contributory factor in the development of many ill health conditions.

Stress risk assessment

Risk assessment is carried out to identify the presence of hazards and evaluate the risk of stress occurring. In the approach to the assessment survey, it is necessary to look at the organisation as a whole and also break this down into smaller, manageable units. The objectives are to identify the prevalence of the range of stress hazards (listed in Table 12.2) and assess the mental health state and performance of the workforce. The more stress hazards that are identified in a given situation, then the greater the risk of the symptoms of stress occurring. With this in mind, the following general types of information are collected:

- mental health and performance indicators for the workforce;
- the presence of workplace stress hazards (objective);
- the perceptions of the workforce (subjective); and
- the levels of errors and accidents, work efficiency and risk-taking.

This information is collected systematically using checklists and questionnaires. Addley (1997) includes a useful a range of relevant, targeted questionnaires. Checklists are a simple means of collecting information for subsequent analysis of the following aspects:

- job content (monotony, time pressure, poor work organisation, inadequate support, emotionally demanding);
- working conditions (recognised hazards and ergonomic problems);
- terms of employment (career opportunities, pay and conditions, training); and
- social relations at work (communication and support issues).

Further information on the following aspects is then obtained using detailed, targeted questionnaires:

1. **Stress in the workplace** – this covers job demands, levels of decision-making, skill requirements, terms of employment and support issues.
2. **Health complaints** – to help determine individual stress-related health problems.
3. **Employee job stress evaluation** – to help employees determine how stressful their work is. This provides the means of diagnosing role ambiguity, overload, time pressure, conflict and responsibility stressors.
4. **Personality type assessment** – this is thought to be an important factor in determining an individual's susceptibility or vulnerability to stress.

Cooper *et al.* (1988) have produced the Occupational Stress Indicator – a battery of questionnaires which are used to identify stress hazards and evaluate their impact. This integrated method (or tool) is used to gather information on groups of individuals and consists of six questionnaires and the collection of general biographical data. The questionnaires are entitled:

1. How you feel about your job.
2. How you assess your current state of health.
3. The way you behave generally.
4. How you interpret events around you.
5. Sources of pressure in your job.
6. How you cope with stress you experience.

This battery of questionnaires has been found to be too time-consuming for practical risk assessment purposes and it may be necessary for the assessor to develop their own survey questionnaires from published material. A useful and practical approach to stress risk assessment and management was applied by Toll (2001) and is illustrated in Figure 12.2.

The HSE Stress Management Standards (see www.hse.gov.uk/stress/index.htm) are presented as goals to be achieved by risk assessment and continuous improvement. Six key areas of work are identified: demands, control, relationships, change, role and support. Each standard contains simple statements about good management practice in the six areas and the stated aim is to prioritise stress risk issues. Collection of data is recommended by both qualitative methods – for example workplace talks and focus groups – and quantitative methods – for example sickness data and questionnaires. The HSE has developed an 'Indicator Tool' (questionnaire) specifically for use with the standards. It is emphasised that senior management commitment and employee consultation are crucial to the success of this approach.

One factor which could be important in the evaluation of stress is the view of the prevailing workplace culture towards stress. It may be that anyone reporting stress would be regarded as weak or inadequate at coping with their job and this may lead to underreporting of true levels.

FIGURE 12.2: Stress risk assessment and management framework

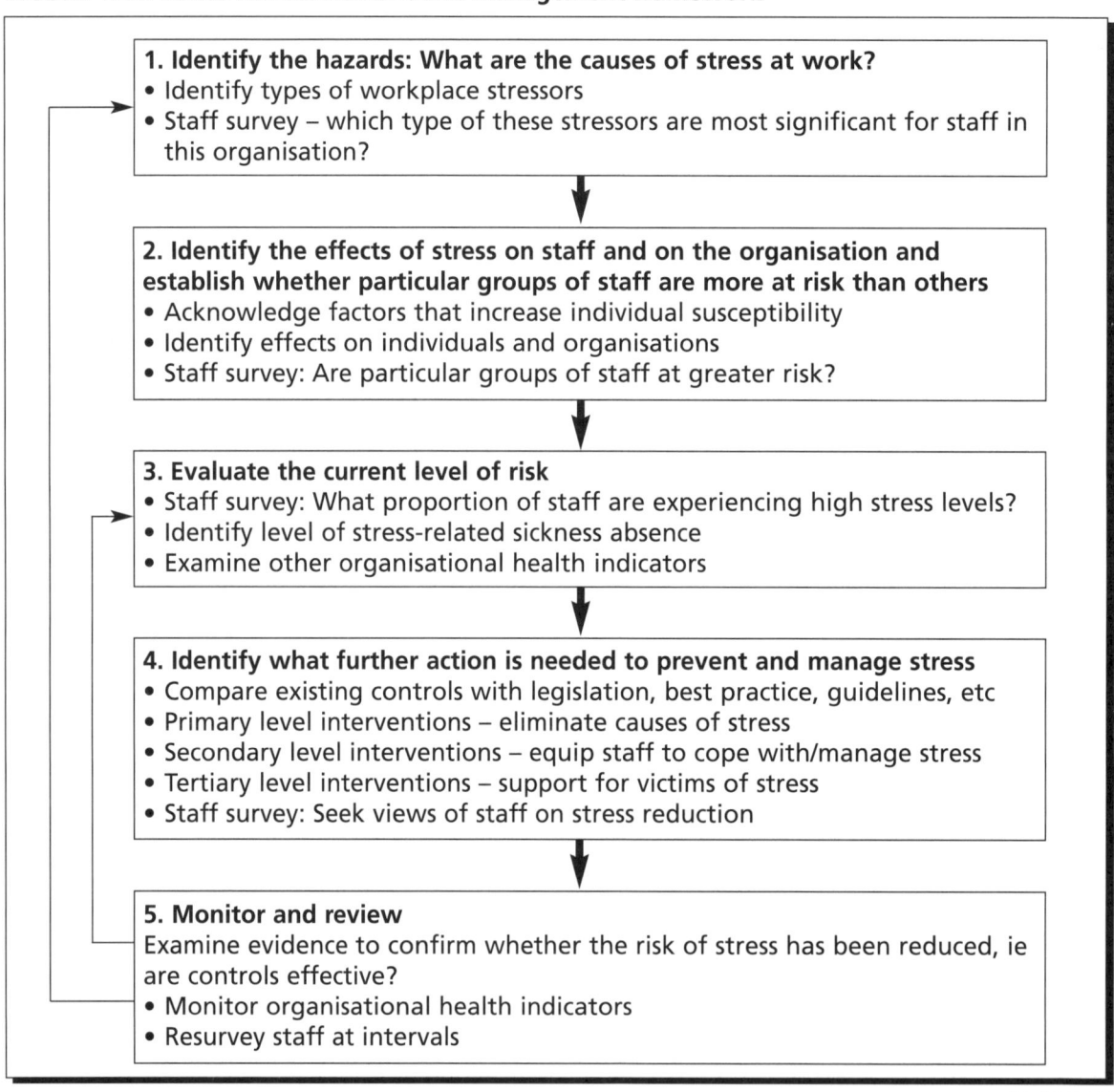

1. **Identify the hazards: What are the causes of stress at work?**
   - Identify types of workplace stressors
   - Staff survey – which type of these stressors are most significant for staff in this organisation?

2. **Identify the effects of stress on staff and on the organisation and establish whether particular groups of staff are more at risk than others**
   - Acknowledge factors that increase individual susceptibility
   - Identify effects on individuals and organisations
   - Staff survey: Are particular groups of staff at greater risk?

3. **Evaluate the current level of risk**
   - Staff survey: What proportion of staff are experiencing high stress levels?
   - Identify level of stress-related sickness absence
   - Examine other organisational health indicators

4. **Identify what further action is needed to prevent and manage stress**
   - Compare existing controls with legislation, best practice, guidelines, etc
   - Primary level interventions – eliminate causes of stress
   - Secondary level interventions – equip staff to cope with/manage stress
   - Tertiary level interventions – support for victims of stress
   - Staff survey: Seek views of staff on stress reduction

5. **Monitor and review**
   Examine evidence to confirm whether the risk of stress has been reduced, ie are controls effective?
   - Monitor organisational health indicators
   - Resurvey staff at intervals

(Toll 2001)

Tolerability of risk

There is some difficulty in defining tolerable levels of stress due to the interplay between non-work stress hazards and work stress hazards. This is further complicated by the differing inherent capacity of individuals to cope. In terms of work-generated stress, the aim should be to reduce adequately the risk of stress and related health effects, with all reasonably practicable prevention and control measures in place.

The HSE's management standards will provide a yardstick for organisations to measure performance in tackling work-related stress (HSE 2001). Following consultation with key stakeholders, the current HSE Stress Management Standards omit the numerical guidelines that appeared in the earlier draft version. The Standards – relating to demands, control, support, relationships, role and change – would be achieved in an organisation where employees indicate that:

- they are able to cope with the demands of the job (demands);
- they are able to have a say about the way they do their work (control);
- they receive adequate information and support from their colleagues and superiors (support);
- they are not subjected to unacceptable behaviour at work (relationships);
- they understand their role and responsibilities (role); and
- the organisation engages them frequently when undergoing an organisational change (change).

In addition, each Standard requires local systems to be in place to respond to any individual concerns.

Stress prevention and control

Effective preventive action must deal with underlying organisational causes and not wholly focus on stress management. Admittedly, this is not a simple objective to achieve, since often management is inherently more receptive to the option of stress management, as discussed above. Organisations need to develop their own strategic approach to dealing with stress.

Stress policy

Increasing numbers of organisations are developing a stress policy and Addley (1997) lists some of the benefits of such a policy. For example, there is an opportunity to examine the organisation's view of stress and this may identify relevant training and allow areas of responsibility among management to be demarcated. Importantly, as far as employees are concerned, it promotes communication and understanding within the workplace and it shows that management is taking the problem of stress seriously.

The key stages in drafting a policy have been identified as:

1. Consult widely with all interested parties.
2. Seek help from external experts, if appropriate.
3. Initial estimation of stress problem – questionnaire assessment (attitude survey) or more formal stress audit.
4. Consult and agree final draft of policy (ensure objectives and actions are achievable, effective and relevant).
5. Evaluate implementation of policy.
6. Regular review.

Elimination

In dealing with work stress hazards, the first priority should always be their elimination so far as is reasonably practicable.

Organisational change

The stress risk assessment should give an indication of the source and extent of stress generation. This is taken into account when looking at ways of introducing a change in management approach and systems.

Most organisations generate stress in their employees and it should be explicitly acknowledged, by the organisation, that stress is a health and safety problem and a policy objective. Managers need to understand the practical implications of stress and that no single management style is guaranteed to eliminate stress.

Overall, a participative management style and supportive culture are more likely to develop a sense of control in individual employees and, thus, reduce the risk of stress. That is not to say, of course, that sometimes there will still be a need for clear direction of staff. Effective two-way channels of communication between management and workforce are essential in helping to reduce stress risks and organisational culture should facilitate better inter-employee relationships at all levels.

Management training
Training should enable managers to identify stress in individuals and groups and to identify jobs where stress could be a problem. This would enable them to take action to reduce the risks of stress and to understand staff training needs as job specifications and demands change.

Work design
The prevention of occupational stress can be facilitated by the design of work, for example, the incorporation of ergonomic features in machinery and in the structure of tasks. The involvement of operators in task design has also been found to be beneficial in the prevention of stress, since it is important to allow operators as much control over their tasks as is practicable.

Systems of work
This involves developing good employment practices to help reduce the prevalence of stress, for example, in recruitment and selection, induction, training, performance management, absence management, shift systems, and regular review of assessments for stress. This includes monitoring systems for detecting significant levels of stress in the workforce.

Systems should be in place to deal with the emotional problems following traumatic incidents, for example, a serious occupational accident. Also, there should be systems for ensuring the rehabilitation of workers following absence from work due to stress-induced ill health.

Employee training
Training aims to develop stress fitness and threshold levels in individual employees for inherent job stress hazards (which cannot by definition be eliminated). This is to enable employees to develop more effective coping strategies.

Legal requirements
As noted above, under the Health and Safety at Work etc Act 1974, section 2, there is the general duty of employers to protect the (mental) health of workers. In addition, under the MHSW Regulations 1999 (regulation 3), there is a duty to carry out a risk assessment of employees' health and safety (which includes stress) and to put suitable arrangements for prevention in place, with reviews at appropriate intervals.

Non-work stress
For stress generated in individuals, arising from outside of work, the following measures may be suggested or offered to employees:
1. **Counselling** – this involves the discussion of personal emotional issues in a free, non-judgmental and supportive atmosphere. The aim is to achieve personal resolution of conflict in a confidential setting.
2. **Personal stress management training** – this involves health promotion initiatives and has an important role in developing general health and creating a 'health culture' in employees.

Violence at work
There is increasing concern about the levels of work-related violence both in the UK and internationally. According to Upson (2004), the 2002/2003 British Crime Survey (BCS) estimated that there were just over 849,000 incidents of violence at work in England and Wales in 2002/2003, which consisted of 431,000 physical assaults and 418,000 threats. The BCS estimates that approximately 376,000 workers in England and Wales experienced at least one violent incident in 2002/2003 while they were working. The risk seems to have spread from sectors with a traditional high risk of violence, such as prisons and law enforcement, into other areas such as healthcare, education and retail. Standing & Nicolini (1997) comment that there is currently more awareness of violence with more casual work and looser network types of organisation. It is also thought that the greater number of self-employed workers may add to those at risk in vulnerable occupations. In some sectors, there is a growing fear of violence at work and indications that there is underreporting of incidents. Overall, a dramatic increase in the number of incidents has been observed across a wide

range of occupational groups. There have been a few well-publicised incidents, though in the majority of cases, victims do not need hospital in-patient care.

The only direct reference to violence in occupational safety and health law occurs in the Reporting of Injuries, Diseases and Dangerous Occurrences Regulations 1995 (RIDDOR), where, in regulation 2, the word accident is defined to include 'an act of non-consensual physical violence done to a person at work'.

As with stress, violence is considered to be a part of the overall requirements dealing with health and safety at work, therefore, the Health and Safety at Work etc Act 1974 applies to such situations, as does the MHSW Regulations 1999. The common law duty of care is also relevant.

There is a general lack of legislation at the European level and only the Netherlands and Sweden have a specific regulatory body concerned with violence at work. However, it is believed that in the near future European Union guidance will be issued on this subject.

Poyner & Warne (1988) point out that the problem of controlling violence is not new and that violence and aggression has received a good deal of attention from various professions in the past including law enforcement, criminology, education, and psychiatry. Many theories of violence causation with possible solutions have been advanced over the years. Poyner & Warne (1988) observe that much of the research literature proposes that there is a need to understand the causes of violence before we can do anything about it. However, they themselves take a more pragmatic view, in that it is preferable to find solutions to work-related violence whether or not the true causes of the violence are known.

As with other hazards, a systematic risk-based approach is needed for the management of work-related violence. This involves identifying hazards, evaluating risks, and designing and implementing prevention and/or control measures, together with monitoring the effectiveness of the strategy.

Definitions of violence

It is useful to explore what the term 'violence' constitutes. There have been many definitions of violence and the HSE has published several versions in different sector-targeted publications:

Any incident in which a person is abused, threatened or assaulted in circumstances relating to their work. (HSE 1997)

Whitaker (1999) cites the following definition:

Violence is behaviour which produces damaging or hurtful effects physically or emotionally on other people. The definition is not limited simply to physical assault, but permits the inclusion of equally distressing and intimidating verbal aggression. (Association of Directors of Social Services)

The BCS, from 1998 onwards, defines a 'violent incident' as:

All assaults or threats which occurred while the victim was working that were perpetrated by members of the public.

It can be seen in all these definitions that there is concern, not only with physical acts, but also with verbal abuse and threatening behaviour.

Violence leads to a range of effects including personal trauma suffered by the victim, sickness absence, decreased work performance, high staff turnover, increased insurance premiums, compensation costs, and litigation. There are concerns about both the physical and psychological harm suffered by the victim. Predictably, the response to harm of individual employees varies and some are less sensitive than others. However, some victims may suffer severe mental trauma some time after the incident. This may impair both their work and their personal life. Employees may not report violent incidents or traumatic consequences because they believe they should be able to cope. Where the potential for violence is continuous, there is the problem of repeat exposure and the consequent health effects. The long-term impact of violent incidents is not known.

Violence statistics

National data collection by the annual BCS has shown that the number of victims of at least one violent incident at work rose by 30 per cent between 1991 and 1997 (from 423,000 to 551,000). However, since this peak there has been a fall of 32 per cent to 376,000 victims, as recorded by the 2002/2003 survey (Upson 2004). This indicates that 1.7 per cent of working adults were the victim of at least one violent incident at work. Of these victims, 196,000 were physically assaulted and 203,000 were subjected to threats. Some individuals suffered more than one violent incident over the preceding year.

TABLE 12.2A: Occupations most at risk of violent incidents at work

Occupational sector	Employees suffering at least one violent incident (%)	
	Assaults	Threats
Protective services (eg police, fire, prison officers)	12.6	3.0
Health and social welfare (eg nurses, paramedics)	3.3	2.3
Transport drivers	1.9	1.3
Managers in agriculture and services	1.8	2.2
Health professionals (eg doctors, dentists)	1.4	2.3
Caring personal services (care/nursing assistants)	1.3	0.9
Teachers and research professionals	1.0	1.3
Sales	0.5	1.3
All groups	0.9	1.0

(Upson 2004)

This general picture has been confirmed by a range of surveys on the extent of workplace violence in different sectors including healthcare, education, retail, transport and the emergency services.

The Criminal Injuries Compensation Authority (CICA) provides some additional data on occupational violence due to injuries inflicted by the public. According to Standing & Nicolini (1997), around 10 per cent of total claims submitted to the CICA are for incidents of occupational violence and this represents about 8,000 cases per year.

Proportionally, the breakdown of the figures has remained constant over recent years: around eight per cent are police claims with the remaining two per cent from firefighters, psychiatric nurses, and bank and building society employees.

Models for workplace violence

Poyner & Warne (1988) proposed an analytical model for a violent incident which has been very influential in determining the direction of research into this problem. Their model highlights the key factors involved in some violent incidents. It is directed towards a violent incident occurring in an interaction between the public and the employee. The framework aims to bring together as many of the relevant factors as possible. What is proposed is a method of analysis which is able to take into account the different aspects of this interaction. Poyner & Warne's hope was that this relationship could be made 'satisfactory' and less likely to result in violence. The basic problem in the violent situation is the assailant, although the employee may contribute to the final outcome. Their generic model is shown in Figures 12.3 and 12.4 and illustrates its application in highlighting factors in violent incidents in the health services (HSE 1997). According to this model, to help understand how violent incidents can happen, it is necessary to focus on the five basic elements shown: the assailant, the employee, the type of interaction, the situation and the outcome. Standing & Nicolini (1997), while accepting the usefulness of this model, suggest some additional perspectives be added, including shifting the emphasis from the assailant-victim relationship towards the organisational context, classifying different types of violent incident, and distinguishing between organisational parameters which are unchangeable and those which may be altered.

AGENTS OF PSYCHOSOCIAL MISFIT

FIGURE 12.3: Model for a violent incident

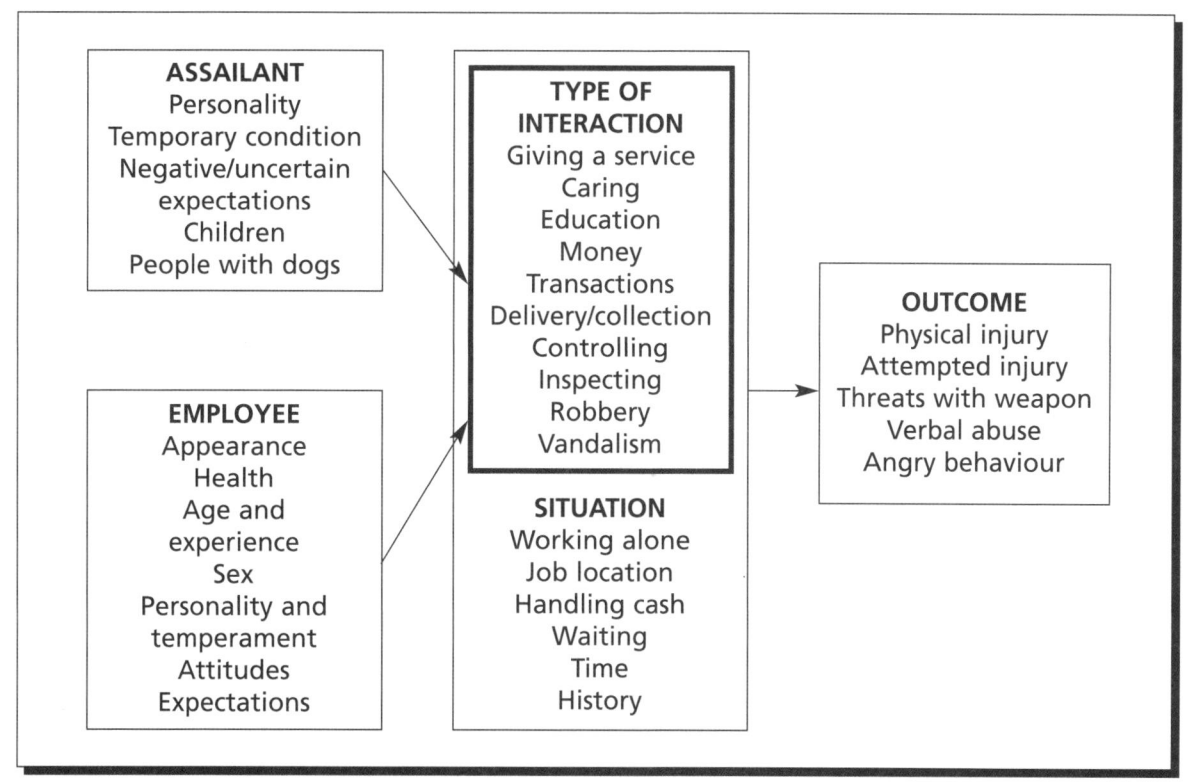

ASSAILANT
Personality
Temporary condition
Negative/uncertain expectations
Children
People with dogs

EMPLOYEE
Appearance
Health
Age and experience
Sex
Personality and temperament
Attitudes
Expectations

TYPE OF INTERACTION
Giving a service
Caring
Education
Money
Transactions
Delivery/collection
Controlling
Inspecting
Robbery
Vandalism

SITUATION
Working alone
Job location
Handling cash
Waiting
Time
History

OUTCOME
Physical injury
Attempted injury
Threats with weapon
Verbal abuse
Angry behaviour

(Poyner & Warne 1988)

FIGURE 12.4: Application of model to violent incidents in the health services

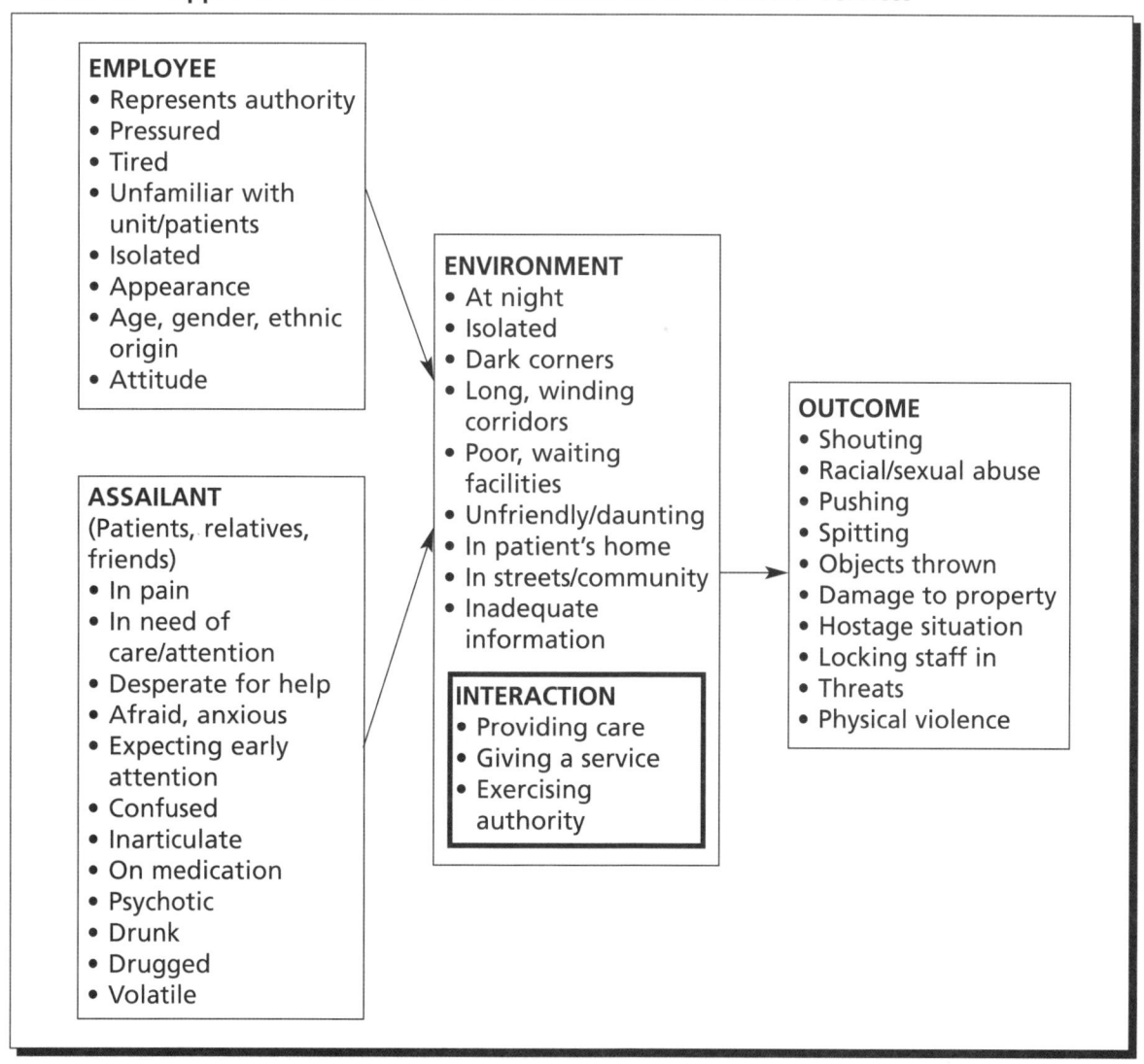

EMPLOYEE
- Represents authority
- Pressured
- Tired
- Unfamiliar with unit/patients
- Isolated
- Appearance
- Age, gender, ethnic origin
- Attitude

ASSAILANT
(Patients, relatives, friends)
- In pain
- In need of care/attention
- Desperate for help
- Afraid, anxious
- Expecting early attention
- Confused
- Inarticulate
- On medication
- Psychotic
- Drunk
- Drugged
- Volatile

ENVIRONMENT
- At night
- Isolated
- Dark corners
- Long, winding corridors
- Poor, waiting facilities
- Unfriendly/daunting
- In patient's home
- In streets/community
- Inadequate information

INTERACTION
- Providing care
- Giving a service
- Exercising authority

OUTCOME
- Shouting
- Racial/sexual abuse
- Pushing
- Spitting
- Objects thrown
- Damage to property
- Hostage situation
- Locking staff in
- Threats
- Physical violence

(HSE 1997)

Poyner & Warne (1988) focused on assaults on staff by members of the public while Standing & Nicolini (1997) categorise three types of violent incident and discuss the different aspects of prevention and management for each type:

- **Type 1 violent incident** – The violent agent has no legitimate connection with the organisation and target-hardening is one response.
- **Type 2 violent incident** – The violent agent is a receiver of a service; violence from clients can be prevented by physical and personnel controls, security and training.
- **Type 3 violent incident** – This involves violent behaviour by someone with an employment relation with the affected workplace.

Features of prevention strategies

Standing & Nicolini (1997) found that prevention policies targeted at Type 1 and 2 incidents typically combine some of the following actions:

1. Explicit management commitment.
2. Violence-related reporting system.
3. Written programmes and policy.
4. Work site analysis and site improvement.
5. Decrease in the degree of organisational isolation and/or increase in community links.
6. Security awareness committees.
7. Training and educational actions.
8. Modification of working procedures and standard operating procedures.
9. Modification of staffing procedures.
10. Strengthening of security measures.
11. Pre-emptive employee screening strategies.
12. Zero tolerance measures policy.
13. Changes in the job climate and stress level.
14. Post-incident response plans.

Because the service industries, particularly the public services, have relatively high levels of violent incidents, Standing & Nicolini (1997) have listed the prominent features of prevention strategies in this sector:

1. Action for clarifying existing regulations constraining provision of services, in order to help the public to approach the service with realistic expectations.
2. Strategic deployment of staff.
3. Proper information to staff.
4. Training for improving interpersonal skills and aggression diffusion techniques.
5. Selection of personnel especially to withstand stressful and potentially aggressive situations.
6. Design of work to eliminate risk factors such as cash handling.
7. Modify layout and/or setting with physical and environmental measures (reduce noise, allow for privacy, improve waiting areas).
8. Introduction of emergency devices.
9. Appropriate choice of location and time.

The frequency of Type 3 violent incidents is believed to be closely related to the general state of employer-employee relations. To prevent these incidents may require broad changes in management style, work climate, and human resources policies including recruitment and methods of information communication.

According to Standing & Nicolini (1997), characteristics linked with Type 3 incidents are:

1. Organisational problems regarding personnel are largely ignored.
2. Chronic labour-management conflict.

3. Preferential treatment of a few because of title and responsibility.
4. Employees perceive themselves as tools in the workplace.
5. Ineffective employee grievance procedures.
6. Lack of mutual respect in the department among employees.
7. Ineffective horizontal and vertical communication.
8. Lack of consistency in management's action.
9. Increased workload with greater expectations; fewer resources and fewer rewards.
10. Working atmosphere that is repetitive and unfulfilling.
11. Overly aggressive authoritarian management style.
12. Insufficient attention to the physical environment and security measures.
13. Ineffective pre-employment screening.
14. Inconsistent application of organisational policies and procedures.

Applying risk management to workplace violence

There is a need to apply the risk management framework to identify hazards and apply prevention and/or control measures in high risk situations. The Poyner & Warne model can be used to identify the main features of risk situations.

Predictably, some jobs are very high risk and Whitaker (1999) cites the example of social workers removing children from their parents with a court order as one task with a high risk of violence and the consequent need for appropriate control measures. High risk jobs tend to involve dealing with the public or where there is a high risk of robbery.

If the hazard of violence cannot be eliminated, then the foreseeable risks should be controlled so far as is reasonably practicable. There is a need to collect systematic information on all violent incidents that occur to the employees of an organisation.

Violence can occur in many different contexts, including at virtually any point where staff serve the public, where large sums of money are involved, or in workplaces where interpersonal relationships are very strained. The motive or reason for violence varies and includes robbery, anger, mental illness, and alcohol or drug abuse.

Exposure assessment and analysis

Each organisation needs to look at its own activities and decide where there is a significant risk of violence occurring. The analysis should include any historical data on previous violent incidents to identify the tasks where there is a foreseeable risk. Consideration should also be given as to the definition to be used for a violent incident, and whether people are reporting or are containing and/or coping with incidents. In some cases, violence may be suspected and in others not. However, it is suggested that where there is just a suspicion, initial information is collected informally so as not to alarm people.

The aim is to identify situations where employees are exposed to violence hazards while at work. As well as considering previous incident data, discussions should be held with managers and employees with the aim of identifying tasks which involve exposure to a violence hazard and the factors affecting the likelihood of violence occurring in practice.

The general type of questions which would be relevant in this risk assessment are illustrated in Table 12.3, which is based on the Poyner & Warne model. The questions asked in a real situation would obviously be tailored to the particular sector, for example, the healthcare sector would collect data on factors arising from the aspects illustrated in Figure 12.4.

Furthermore, it is necessary to assess the adequacy of any current prevention and/or control measures. The next stage is to evaluate the tolerability of the residual risk of violence arising from these task-employee situations while taking into account any current controls. At this point, it is necessary to come to a conclusion on the acceptability or unacceptability of the risk of violence, and to recommend further controls, if appropriate.

As mentioned above, this model is principally concerned with analysis of violent incidents in the service industries.

TABLE 12.3: Identification of violence risk factors using the Poyner & Warne model

ASPECT OF MODEL		CHECKLIST QUESTION
Assailant	**Personality** – In some jobs employees deal with clients who react more violently or aggressively than on average, eg a local authority home care unit or mass transit systems where there will be a few people predisposed to violence	Are employees carrying out this job likely to encounter people predisposed to violence?
	Temporary state – Temporary state induced by drugs, alcohol, illness or stress. Behaviour is unpredictable and less well controlled	Are employees carrying out this job likely to encounter people in a temporary state?
	Negative/uncertain expectations – From their experience people may expect difficulties, eg where a claimant is repeatedly refused a benefit, where they believe they are entitled to the benefit	Are the expectations of the public likely to lead to violence with respect to the task under consideration?
	Immaturity – The behaviour of children and young people is not expected to be as good as adults	Are immature individuals likely to be encountered in this task?
	Possession of dogs – May use these animals as a threatening weapon	Is contact with people owning dogs likely in this task?
Employee	**Appearance** – First impressions can set the tone for an interaction; height (tallness), build and uniform may all have some influence in different situations	Is the employee's appearance likely to increase the risk of a violent incident?
	Health – Mild mental illness, stress, anxiety, overwork and work pattern may influence behaviour	Is there health surveillance for staff carrying out this task?
	Age and experience – More experienced staff are generally more wise, more confident with the public. There are certain expectations of behaviour of staff at different ages, eg there have been more assaults and verbal abuse aimed at student nurses than at their elders, similarly with staff of mass transit systems	Have staff been appropriately deployed for this task?
	Sex – This may also influence behaviour in a given situation	Have staff been appropriately deployed for the task?
	Attitude – Staff attitude and tolerance is important	Have staff been appropriately trained?
	Expectations – Job expectations will influence the situation	Is this likely to be a factor with this task?

Table continued opposite

Interaction	Most violent incidents involve direct contact. Violence or aggression when a member of the public believes employee or organisation is not being fair or reasonable	Is this likely with this task?
Work environment	Total environment of the task	
	Working alone – Many jobs at risk require people to work alone	Do people work alone on this task?
	Job location – Local knowledge may be important in reducing risks; the risk of different locations, eg bus routes vary depending on the area of the city they serve	Where is the job location?
	Cash handling – Target for robbery	Is cash handled?
	Waiting and queueing – Reducing the level of tolerance of the individual	Is the task associated with waiting and queuing?
	Time – Important risk factor for violent incidents, eg late at night after public houses close	When is the task carried out?
	Territory – Staff may feel more secure in their offices, however, some members of the public behave better in their own homes	On whose territory is the interaction? Is this significant?
	Protective measures – May not prevent violence, but may ameliorate the effects	What are the current protective measures?
	Privacy – If the interaction involves confidential and sensitive information, a large amount of stress/aggression may be caused if there is a lack of privacy	Is sensitive information likely to be discussed? Is there an appropriate level of privacy?
Outcome	Previous incidents	Have there been any previous incidents of violence? If so, what was the outcome?

(Based on the model of Poyner & Warne 1988)

Tolerability of risk

The only tolerable level for violent incidents is zero. However, in the protection of people at work, the aim is that all reasonably practicable measures should be implemented to reduce the foreseeable risk of employees being exposed to violence at work.

Prevention and control measures

General measures

A wide range of work situations may lead to a violent incident and approaches to prevention and control measures will obviously be specific to the given situation. The general types of measure that can be applied are listed in Table 12.4. Where alternative measures exist, these need to be compared and evaluated for cost-effectiveness and their acceptability to staff.

TABLE 12.4: General prevention and control measures for violent incidents

Point of application	Detailed measures
Organisation	• Develop and apply organisational policy on violence, thus recognising the problem; involves consultations between management and staff; positive commitment from senior staff is very important • Monitoring the effectiveness of implementation of policy and arrangements
Design of work	• Avoid face-to-face encounters • Free travel on public transport • Eliminate night services • Eliminate/introduce home visits (depends on specific situation) • Introduce cash-free work • Potential assailants (general public) should be given clear information
Workplace	• Physical protection with barriers and screens • Monitoring measures – security cameras and alarms • Environmental calming measures – pleasant, bright, quiet, designed to control movement and degree of crowding; environment; consider client privacy aspects • Consider home visits
Work systems	• Monitoring and information systems – clear reporting system for incidents; good records kept on previous violent incidents • Effective channels of communication between managers and employees – to ensure full reporting of incidents • Sensitive selection and deployment of staff – do not put junior staff in the most dangerous situations; select appropriate experienced staff • Good staff monitoring systems – to check on the location of vulnerable staff
Personal	• Personal protective equipment (does not prevent violence but may reduce severity) • Personal body alarms • Information, instruction and training – how to avoid incidents (the use of body language and posture); improvement of interpersonal skills; how to give information clearly to the public; looking for warning signs; how to deal with an incident; self-defence training • Post-incident counselling for employees

Legal requirements

Both the Health and Safety at Work etc Act 1974 and the MHSW Regulations 1999 apply in the case of violence at work.

Under the Health and Safety at Work etc Act 1974, section 2, there is the general duty of employers to protect the health of workers. Furthermore, with the MHSW Regulations 1999, there is a duty to carry out a risk assessment (for violence) and to put suitable and sufficient arrangements for prevention in place, with review at appropriate intervals.

REFERENCES

Addley K, 1997, *Occupational Stress – A Practical Approach*, Butterworths, London.
Budd T, 1999, *Violence at Work: Findings from the British Crime Survey*, HSE/Home Office.
Budd T, 2001, *Violence at Work: New Findings from the British Crime Survey 2000*, HSE/Home Office.
Cooper C L, 1986, Job Distress: Recent Research and the Emerging Role of the Clinical Occupational Psychologist, *Bulletin of the British Psychological Society*, **39**, 325–331.
Cooper C L, Sloan S J and Williams S, 1988, *Occupational Stress Indicator: Management Guide*, NFER-Nelson.

Cox T, 1993, *Stress Research and Stress Management: Putting Theory to Work*, Contract Report 61/1993, HSE Books, Sudbury.

Cox T, 1998, Work-Related Stress: From Environmental Exposure to Ill Health, Chapter 7 in *The Changing Nature of Occupational Health*, HSE Books, Sudbury.

Cox T, Griffiths A, Barlowe C, Randall R, Thomson L and Rial-Gonzalez E, 2000, *Organisational Interventions for Work Stress – A Risk Management Approach*, Contract Research Report 286/2000, HSE Books, Sudbury.

Demos, 1995, *Freedom's Children*, Wilkinson H and Mulgan G, Demos Policy Group, London.

Forbes R, 1979, *Corporate Stress*, Dolphin, New York.

Hatton -v- Sutherland, Barber -v- Somerset County Council, Jones -v- Sandwell Metropolitan Borough Council, Bishop -v- Baker Refractories Ltd, Court of Appeal (Civil Division), (2002) EWCA Civ 76, (2002) 2 All ER 1, (2002) ICR 613, (2002) IRLR 263.

Health and Safety Commission, 1997, *Violence in the Education Sector*, HSE Books, Sudbury.

Health and Safety Executive, 1995, *Stress at Work: A Guide for Employers*, HSG116, HSE Books, Sudbury.

Health and Safety Executive, 1997, *Violence and Aggression to Staff in Health Services*, HSE Books, Sudbury.

Health and Safety Executive, 1998, *Mental Health in the Workplace: Management Training and Development*, HSE Books, Sudbury.

Health and Safety Executive, 1999, *Managing Stress at Work* (discussion document), HSE Books, Sudbury.

Health and Safety Executive, 2000, Secondary Analysis of the 1995 Self-Reported Ill Health Survey (SWI95), *Information Sheet 4/00/EMSU*, October 2000, HSE, Bootle.

Health and Safety Executive, 2001, *Tackling Work-Related Stress*, HSG218, HSE Books, Sudbury.

Howe W, 1999, Stress, Chapter 27 in *Occupational Health – Risk Assessment and Management*, Sadhra S S and Rampal K G (Eds), Blackwell Science, Oxford.

Johnstone -v- Bloomsbury Health Authority, (1992) QB 333.

Jones J R, Hodgson J T, Clegg T A and Elliot R C, 1998, *Self-Reported Work-Related Illness in 1995: Results from a Household Survey*, HSE Books, Sudbury.

Kompier M and Levi, 1994, *Stress at Work: Causes, Effects and Prevention – A Guide for Small and Medium-Sized Enterprises*, European Foundation for the Improvement of Living and Working Conditions, Dublin.

Kompier M and Cooper C, 1999, *Preventing Stress – Improving Productivity*, Routledge, London and New York.

Murphy L R, 1988, Workplace Interventions for Stress Reduction and Prevention, in *Causes, Coping and Consequences of Stress at Work*, Cooper C L and Payne R (Eds), 301–331, Wiley, New York and Chichester.

Paoli P, 1997, *Second European Survey on Working Conditions 1996*, European Foundation for the Improvement of Living and Working Conditions, Dublin.

Poyner B and Warne C, 1988, *Preventing Violence to Staff*, HSE Report, HMSO, London.

Smith A P, Brice C, Collins A, Mathews V and McNamara R, 2000, *The Scale of Occupational Stress: A Further Analysis of the Impact of the Demographic Factors and Type of Job*, HSE Books, Sudbury.

Smith A P, Wadsworth E S, Johal S, Davey-Smith G and Peters T, 2000a, *The Scale of Occupational Stress: The Bristol Stress and Health at Work Study*, HSE Contract Report CRRR 266/2000, HSE Books, Sudbury.

Standing H and Nicolini D, 1997, *Review of Workplace-Related Violence*, Contract Report 143/1997, HSE Books, Sudbury.

Sutherland V J and Cooper C L, 1990, *Understanding Stress*, Chapman & Hall.

Toll M H, 2001, *Occupational Stress* (unpublished MSc thesis), Aston University.

Upson A, 2004, *Violence at work: findings from the 2002/2003 British Crime Survey*, Home Office online report 04/04.

Walker -v- Northumberland County Council, (1995) 1 All ER 737, (1995) ICR 702, (1995) IRLR 35, (1995) ELR 231, (1994) NLJR 1659.

Whittaker S C, 1999, Violence at Work, Chapter 28 in *Occupational Health – Risk Assessment and Management*, Sadhra S S and Ramphal K G (Eds), Blackwell Science, Oxford.

LEGISLATION
Management of Health and Safety at Work Regulations 1999 (SI 1999/3242)
Working Time Regulations 1998 (SI 1998/1833)

13: Personal protection

(Hunter 1978. Reproduced by permission of Hodder Arnold.)

INTRODUCTION

Where risk reduction by other means is impracticable, then personal protective equipment is used to protect people from workplace hazards. It includes both protective clothing (overalls, aprons, gloves, footwear and helmets as well as clothing for adverse thermal environments and weather conditions) and protective equipment (respiratory protection, hearing protection and eye protection). The term is used here to cover a wide range of equipment specifically with reference to occupational health hazards. Hearing protection, respiratory protection, eye and face protection, body and whole-body protection, skin protection, skin barrier preparations, and protective clothing (such as overalls and gloves) are all included and discussed in this chapter.

In the Personal Protective Equipment at Work Regulations 1992 (PPE), regulation 2, "personal protective equipment" means:

> ...all equipment (including clothing affording protection against the weather) which is intended to be worn or held by a person at work and which protects him against one or more risks to his health or safety, and any addition or accessory designed to meet that objective.

Personal protective equipment (PPE) is widely used in workplaces and it is perceived by many employers to be an easy and cheap control option. However, as will be shown below, effective and continuing risk protection by means of a PPE scheme is difficult to achieve. The principal aim of this chapter is to apply general principles to the selection of appropriate equipment and implementation of an effective personal protection scheme. Largely, these principles are not dependent on the particular hazard. Obviously, with different types of hazard, the detailed protective requirements will vary, driven by the overall risk assessment. This chapter reviews the different types of PPE, principally with reference to occupational health hazards.

PERSONAL PROTECTION

A safe workplace strategy, that is, making the workplace safe, should be the first consideration (see Figure 13.2), but if it is not possible to reduce risks sufficiently by controlling hazards at source, then the use of personal protective equipment is an important control measure in the achievement of tolerable levels of risk.

Personal protective equipment is best seen as one option in the overall portfolio of control measures. The aim is to apply an optimal blend of control measures in a given risk situation. The simplistic and well-worn cliché that personal protection is 'always the last resort' ignores the fact that PPE is sometimes the best and indeed the only resort, for example, when dealing with a chemical spillage or when carrying out some short-term maintenance task. Having said that, prevention or controlling risks at source, for example, by design or the application of engineering measures, should always have the highest priority – an approach required by the relevant legislation. Only where control at source is not thought to be reasonably practicable is the use of PPE permitted.

FIGURE 13.1: Some tasks require several types of PPE

(Else)

An effective PPE strategy is difficult to achieve and requires considerable management commitment with the allocation of adequate resources. The provision of adequate information, instruction and training for all relevant work groups is vital to success. The wearing of PPE at work is not an ideal situation and, generally, people need to be persuaded that it is necessary. It is important that the wearer's views are taken into account when deciding which protective device to provide, particularly where there is scope for choice. Protective equipment needs to be worn all the time that the person is at risk or the actual level of protection achieved will be unacceptable. The use of personal protective equipment has long been recognised as a difficult control measure to incorporate into an effective protection strategy. Else & Hale (1984) cite the following to support this:

> *The old difficulty of getting the workers to use the respirators provided for them is instanced by several of the inspectors.* (Annual Report of the Chief Inspector of Factories, 1908)

And also a comment of Sir Thomas Legge, the first Medical Inspector of Factories:

> *Respirators, therefore, except for work lasting a short time – half an hour to an hour – cannot be considered an effective or sufficient means of protecting the worker against dust.* (Legge & Goadby 1912)

TABLE 13.1: Summary of the Personal Protective Equipment at Work Regulations 1992 (as amended)

Regulation	Requirement
1. Citation and commencement	Personal Protective Equipment at Work Regulations 1992 came into force on January 1 1993
2. Interpretation	Defines the term 'personal protective equipment'
3. Disapplication of these Regulations	The Regulations do not apply in certain specified circumstances (eg seagoing ships) and where other regulations apply which may require the provision of PPE
4. Provision of PPE	Requires the provision of suitable PPE except where the risks have been adequately controlled by other means; clarifies 'suitable': • Appropriate to risk, workplace conditions, time period worn • Takes account of ergonomic aspects, health of person, workplace characteristics • Fits the wearer • Effective to prevent or adequately control risk • Where hygiene requires – PPE for personal use only
5. Compatibility of PPE	Items of PPE protecting against different risks must be compatible with each other
6. Assessment of PPE	Selecting PPE must include: • The identification of hazards and the assessment of risks • Consideration of the characteristics of the PPE to determine whether it will be effective for the risk, ie reduce exposure to a tolerable level • Must consider compatibility of other PPE where required simultaneously
7. Maintenance and replacement of PPE	PPE must be maintained (including replaced or cleaned as appropriate) in an efficient state, in efficient working order and in good repair
8. Accommodation for PPE	Appropriate accommodation must be provided for the PPE when it is not being used
9. Information, instruction and training	This should be adequate and include: • The risk(s) the PPE is protecting against • The way the PPE is to be used • Action the employee needs to take to ensure the PPE is maintained in an efficient state • Information and instruction must be comprehensible to employees and others to whom equipment may be provided; information must be kept available to employees • Demonstrations in wearing PPE at suitable intervals
10. Use of PPE	• Employer should ensure PPE is used • Employee should use any PPE provided • User should return PPE to accommodation provided
11. Reporting loss or defect	Employee must report obvious defect or loss of PPE
12. Exemption certificates	
13. Extension outside GB	
14. Modifications, repeal and revocations	Dispensed with much miscellaneous legislation, eg the Protection of Eyes Regulations 1974

PERSONAL PROTECTION

The Personal Protective Equipment at Work Regulations 1992 (PPE) were enacted to cover situations concerning PPE where other legislation did not apply, for example, the need for safety footwear and the use of whole-body protection in hot environments. The PPE Regulations are complemented by useful guidance on how to achieve an effective personal protection scheme (HSE 1992). These Regulations implement a European directive[39] on the use of personal protective equipment at work into UK legislation. The following legislation contains requirements relating to PPE:

1. The Control of Substances Hazardous to Health Regulations 2002 (as amended).
2. The Noise at Work Regulations 1989.
3. The Control of Lead at Work Regulations 2002.
4. The Control of Asbestos at Work Regulations 2002.
5. The Ionising Radiations Regulations 1999.
6. The Construction (Head Protection) Regulations 1989.
7. The Confined Spaces Regulations 1997.

In situations where the above legislation is relevant, then the PPE Regulations (as amended) do not apply. However, for exposure to hazards not covered by the above (and some other miscellaneous legal provisions), the PPE Regulations (as amended) apply in conjunction with the Management of Health and Safety at Work Regulations 1999 (MHSW), for example, the provision and use of suitable protective clothing for workers in an extreme thermal environment.

It is also worth noting that the Health and Safety at Work etc Act 1974 (section 9) forbids charging employees for the provision of personal protective equipment where the provision is necessary for the protection of their health and safety at work.

Safe person versus safe workplace strategy

As shown in Figure 13.2, a PPE strategy is a 'safe person' approach and this has several disadvantages when compared with the 'safe workplace' option. First, PPE may transfer responsibility for protection from the employer to the employee. Second, only the employee who uses the PPE is protected and there is no protection for others in the surrounding work area. Third, if the PPE fails, then the individual worker may be put at increased risk since they may believe (falsely) that they are still protected.

However, once a PPE strategy has been adopted, it is crucial to its success that adequate resources are provided and there is strong management commitment at all levels.

FIGURE 13.2: Safe person and safe workplace strategy

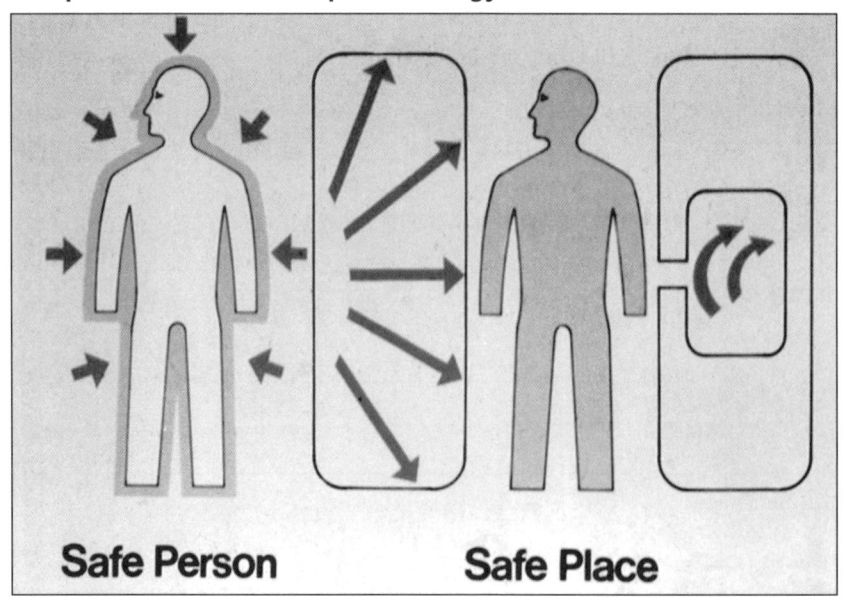

(Else)

---

[39]Personal Protective Equipment Directive (89/656 EEC).

Depending on the nature of the hazard and risk, suitable protective equipment needs to be chosen, provided to workers and then worn during the *whole* period that they are exposed to the hazard. A PPE programme needs to be carefully planned, managed and monitored for the strategy to be successful.

The key stages for achieving an effective PPE scheme are discussed below. This is followed by a description of the general technical features of selected types of PPE.

Key elements of effective PPE schemes

In order for a PPE scheme to be an effective control measure, a high level of management commitment is essential. Adequate resources and competent people are required to select equipment and administer the PPE scheme.

Control of risks by PPE is not an easy option and it is important that appropriate equipment is provided for a particular hazard, together with suitable support for the scheme overall, for example, the provision of the correct eye protection filter for a welding operation, adequate hearing protection prescribed after octave band measurements of a high noise source, or supplying suitable protective clothing following a thermal environment assessment survey. These must be accompanied by adequate equipment maintenance, storage, replacement and other relevant arrangements.

The design and implementation of an effective personal protection scheme can be broadly divided into two principal stages:

- **Stage One** – Selection of suitable protective device.
- **Stage Two** – Consideration of other relevant factors to achieve an effective protection scheme in practice.

Stage 1 – Selection of suitable PPE

Else (1981) outlines three essential elements of information required for a personal protection scheme and these are shown in Figure 13.3.

FIGURE 13.3: Stage 1 – Selection of theoretically adequate PPE

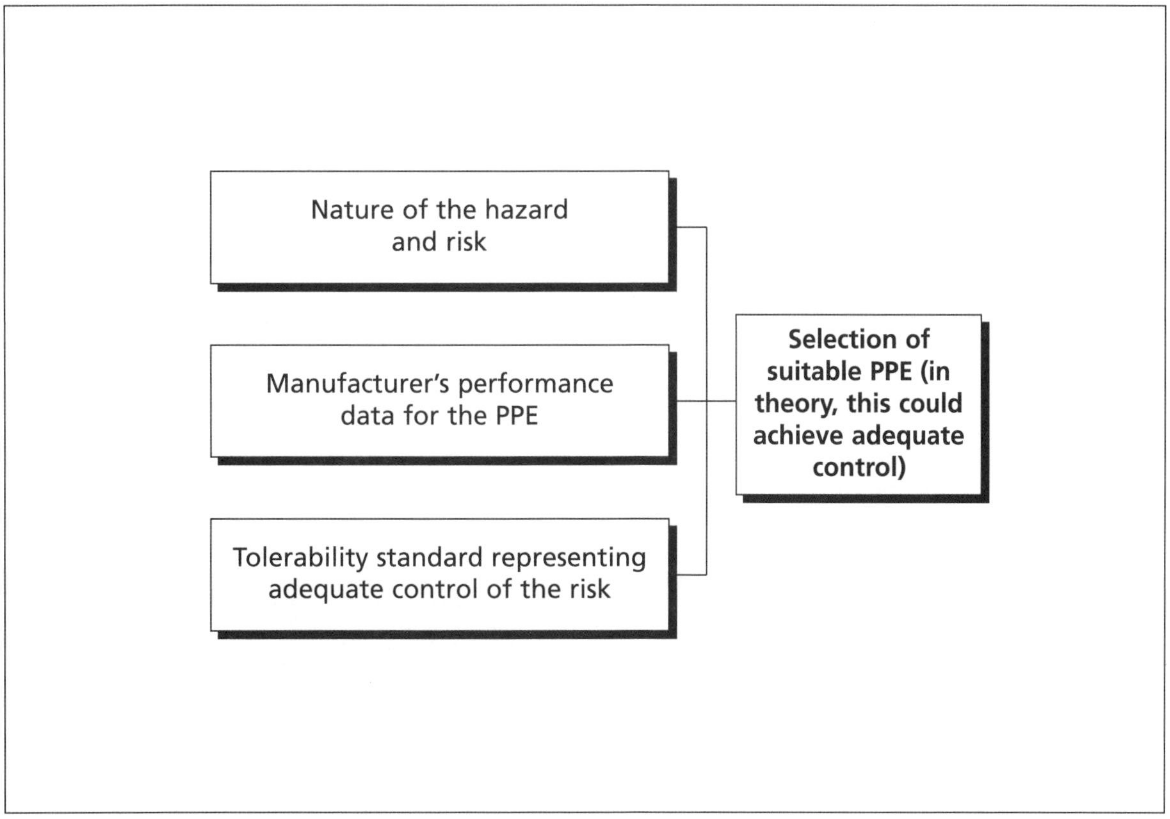

- Nature of the hazard and risk
- Manufacturer's performance data for the PPE
- Tolerability standard representing adequate control of the risk

→ Selection of suitable PPE (in theory, this could achieve adequate control)

Nature of the hazard and risk

First, hazards need to be identified and the risks assessed, for example, in the case of air contaminants, the nature of the substance(s) present and their estimated concentration and the extent of

PERSONAL PROTECTION

exposure. With a noise hazard, there is measurement of sound levels and its frequency characteristics generated by the noise source(s).

Manufacturer's performance data for PPE

Data are required about the ability of equipment to protect against a particular hazard and manufacturers carry out tests under controlled conditions which are often specified in national or international standards. In the UK, the British Standards Institution (BSI) is the predominant standard-setting body. For example, BS EN 149: 2001 specifies the performance requirements of filtering half-masks for protection against particles. Furthermore, the standard method used to determine the sound-attenuation capability of hearing protectors at different frequencies (octave bands) throughout the audible range is specified in BS EN 24869-1: 1993.

Tolerability standard representing adequate control of the risk

For some risks, such as exposure to potent human carcinogens or protection of eyes against flying metal splinters, the only tolerable level of risk is as near to zero risk as possible. The prudent application of the relevant limits thought to embody 'tolerable' exposure is relevant here, for example, the occupational exposure limits prescribed in the Control of Substances Hazardous to Health Regulations 2002 (COSHH), the noise Action Levels in the Noise at Work Regulations 1989 (NAW), or the dose limits prescribed by the Ionising Radiations Regulations 1999.

These three elements of information outlined above are needed to decide whether the PPE in question could *in theory* provide adequate control of a particular risk.

Stage 2 – Factors relevant to an effective PPE scheme

Once theoretically suitable PPE has been chosen, the factors shown in Figure 13.4 need to be considered if the personal protection scheme is to be effective in practice.

In the following section, specific examples of PPE are used to illustrate the general principles involved.

FIGURE 13.4: Stage 2 – Achieving an effective PPE scheme

Achieving an effective personal protection scheme in practice – factors to consider:
- Fit of the equipment
- Comfort of the equipment
- Maintenance
- Information, instruction and training
- Interference with the function of other PPE
- Interference with the perception of warning signals
- Percentage time the equipment is worn of total time the person is at risk
- Management commitment

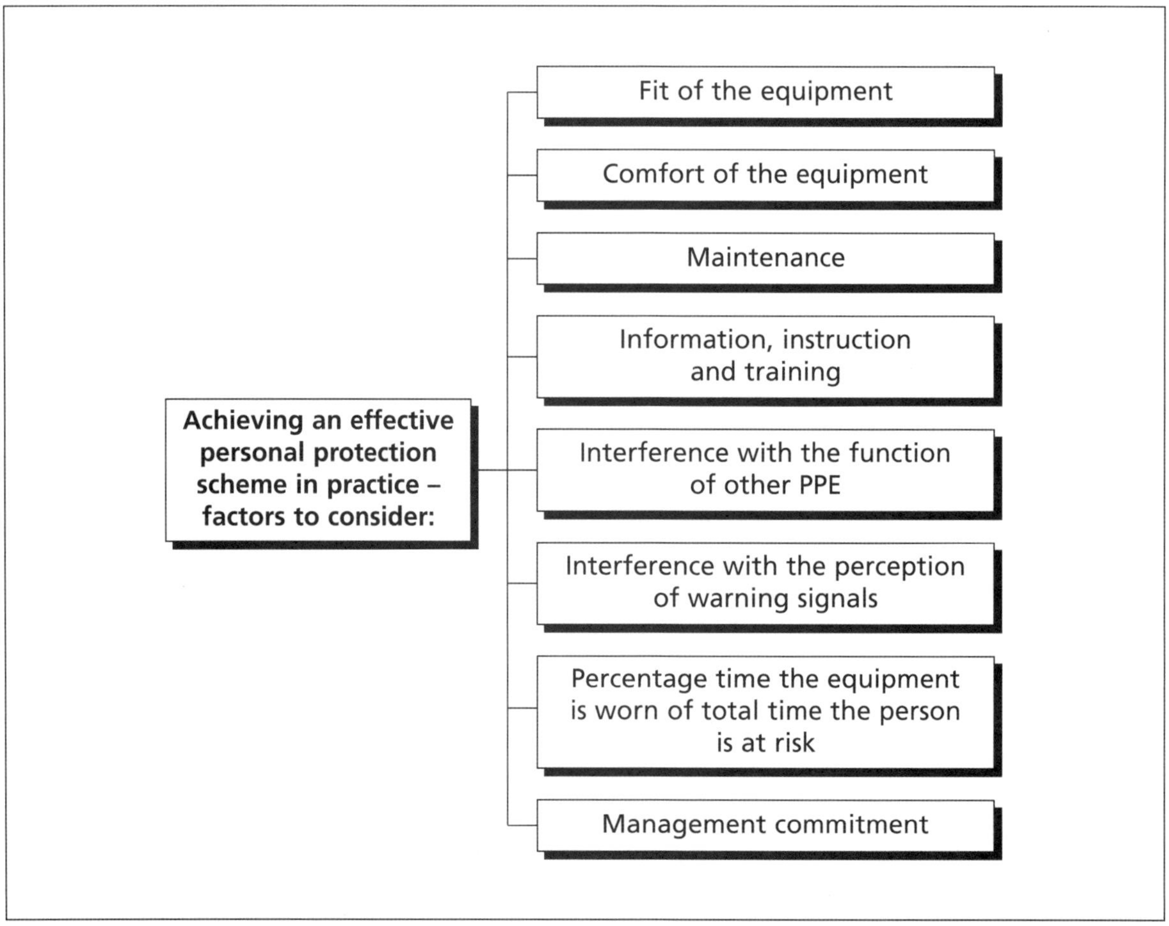

Fit of the equipment

A good fit between the protective equipment and the person is essential to ensure maximum protection is achieved. For example, this is particularly important with respiratory protection face-seals, as can be seen in Figures 13.5 and 13.6. As with other types of PPE, this needs to fit or it will not be effective and possibly not worn.

The fit of PPE is not as important in some other situations, for example, in the fit of protective footwear or overalls. Here, while a good fit is highly desirable, it may not be as crucially important to protection.

FIGURE 13.5: Poor fit (respirator too large)

(Else)

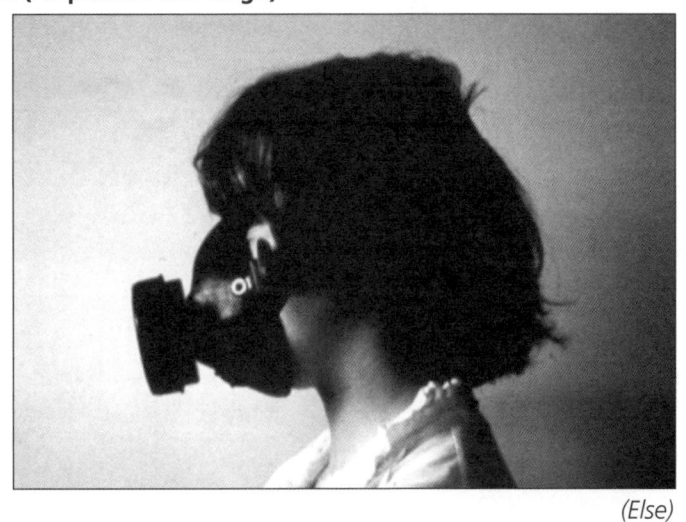

FIGURE 13.6: Poor fit (beard growth)

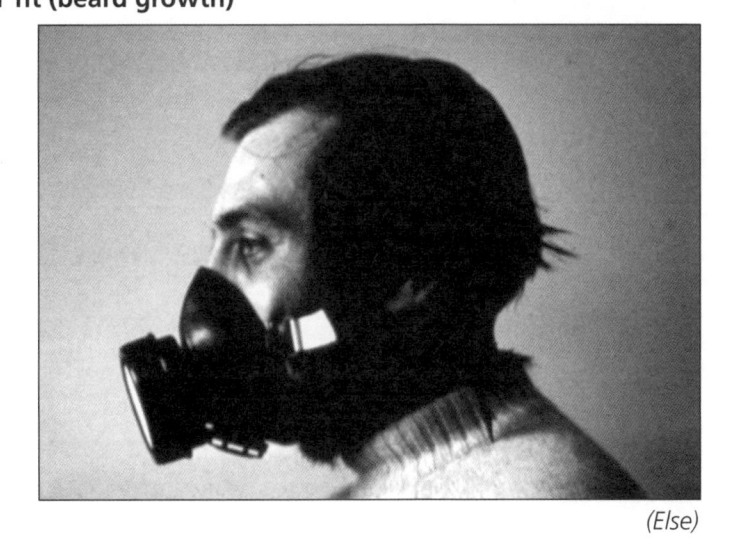

(Else)

Comfort of the equipment

Equipment that is comfortable is more likely to be worn. Where possible, the user should be given a choice of alternatives from a range which afford an equal level of protection. User trials have also been found to be beneficial in helping to ensure the acceptability of the equipment to the wearer. For example, in the case of hearing protection equipment, some people prefer earplugs and some prefer earmuffs.

Maintenance

Personal protective equipment needs to be adequately maintained and regulation 7(1) of the PPE Regulations 1992 requires that:

> *Every employer shall ensure that any personal protective equipment provided to his employees is maintained (including replaced or cleaned as appropriate) in an efficient state, in efficient working order and in good repair.*

PERSONAL PROTECTION

In the case of hearing protective equipment, Figures 13.7 and 13.8 illustrate the reasons for this maintenance requirement. In Figure 13.7, the left picture shows the earplugs when new, while the right picture shows the state of the same plugs after several days of use.

FIGURE 13.7: Disposable earplugs

(Else)

Figure 13.8 shows the impact of wear and tear on hearing protector seals, illustrating the need for regular replacement. The seal on the left was used for three months in a foundry.

FIGURE 13.8: Hearing protector seals

(Else)

Information, instruction and training

Training should be given to all those who use personal protective equipment and to their supervisors. This needs to cover the theory and practice of the PPE and will normally incorporate the recommendations of the PPE manufacturers. A typical training programme would normally include a selection of the subjects listed below (HSE 1998a):

1. Reasons why PPE is needed and when it should be used.
2. Principles of operation of the PPE and its limitations.
3. Practice in putting on and removing the equipment.
4. How to obtain a good fit with the equipment (where appropriate).
5. Factors which will affect the degree of protection afforded.
6. Procedures for safe working and any specific emergency procedures.
7. User maintenance, correct cleaning, inspection and storage.
8. Technical instruction for maintenance staff.
9. Selection of the best type of equipment for individuals (for managers).

The amount and level of training will depend on the type and complexity of the equipment, how often it is being used and the needs of the people being trained. For example, contrast the needs of people using complex self-contained breathing apparatus in a very high risk situation and those using disposable respirators. The frequency of training also has to be addressed, since some workers will need refresher courses. Apart from users, it is important that everyone else involved in the PPE scheme undergoes appropriate training, and this may include the people who select the PPE, buyers, stores personnel, maintenance staff, management and supervisors.

Interference with the function of other PPE

It is vital that the equipment selected is compatible with other protective equipment. For example, interference in the fit of hearing protectors by eye protection is illustrated below.

FIGURE 13.9: Eye protection resulting in a poor earmuff seal

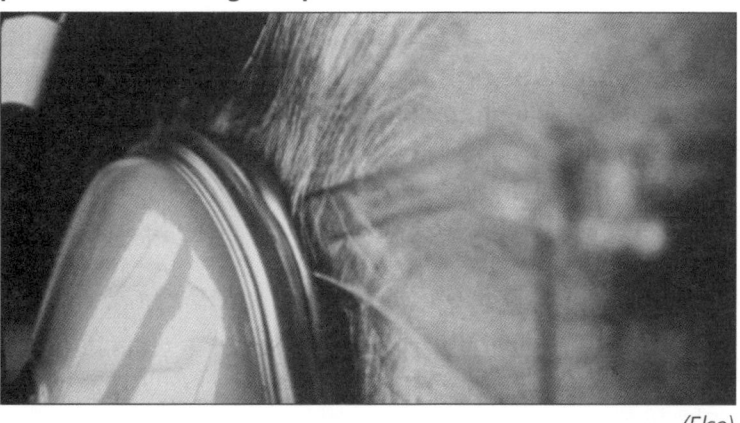

(Else)

Interference with the perception of warning signals

Some eye protectors and helmets may interfere with the peripheral visual field. Respirators and breathing apparatus interfere with olfactory senses and may reduce safety factors.

FIGURE 13.10: Impact of time worn on actual protection

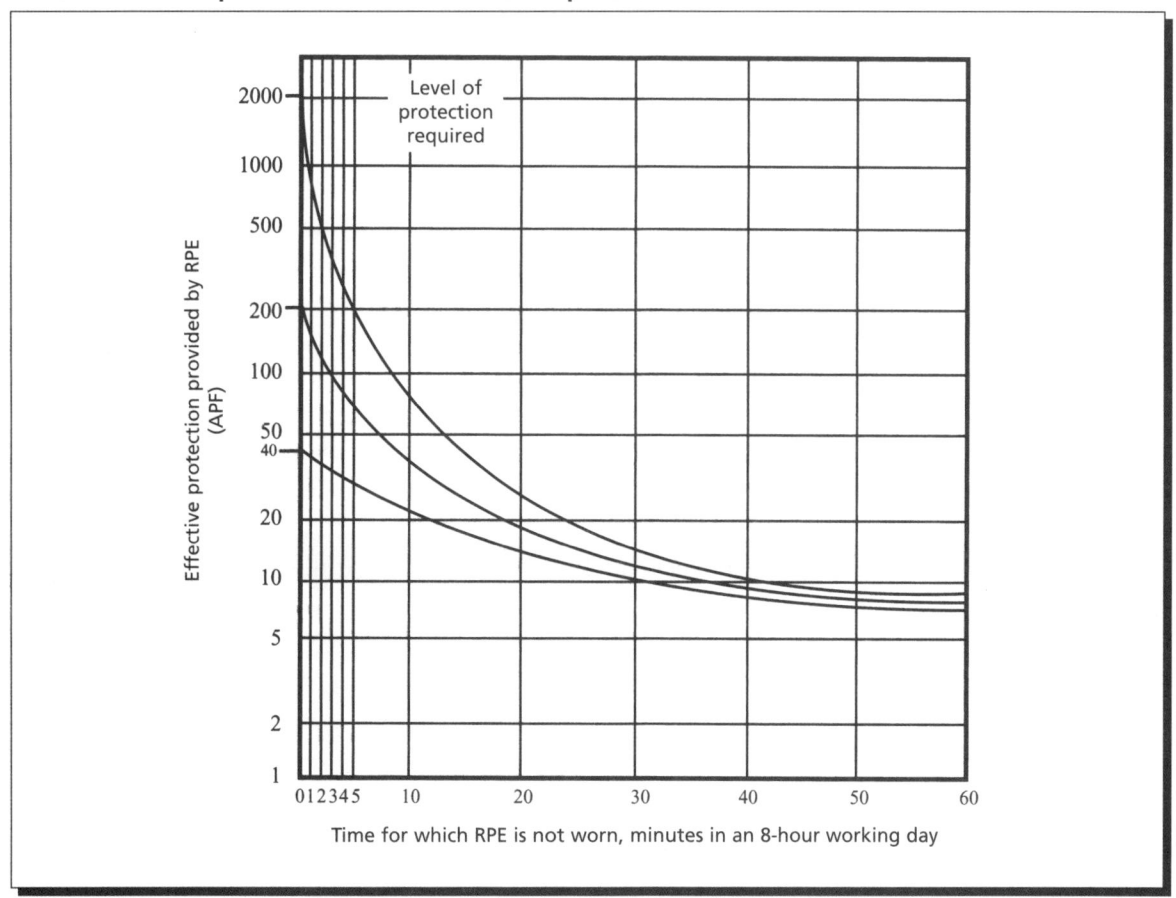

(HSE 1998a)

Percentage time worn

The maximum degree of protection will not be achieved unless the equipment is worn *all* the time the wearer is at risk. Where this is not the case, then the level of protection achieved will be much reduced. This can be observed diagrammatically in Figure 13.10. Here, the impact of reduced wearing time can be seen on the actual level of protection achieved with three respiratory protective devices. Respiratory protection is used here simply as an example and the principle is valid for other types of personal protection, such as hearing protection equipment.

Management commitment

Management commitment is crucial to the success and effectiveness of a personal protection scheme. Once the decision has been taken to rely on personal protection as a control choice, it is crucial that the strategy has sufficient management support and resources. The effectiveness of the scheme should be monitored and reviewed at suitable intervals as with any management policy. The difficulties in achieving an effective protection scheme should be recognised and managers should support the scheme at every opportunity, for example, by managers wearing suitable protective equipment when they enter hazardous areas, even for short periods. Such behaviour is known to increase the success of PPE schemes.

Types of personal protective equipment

It is convenient to divide PPE into the following groups:
1. Hearing protection.
2. Respiratory protection.
3. Eye (and face) protection.
4. Protective clothing (and whole-body protection).
5. Skin protection.

Hearing protection

The NAW Regulations 1989 require that hearing protection equipment (HPE) be made available for use where workers are exposed in excess of an $L_{EP,d}$ of 85dB(A) (First Action Level) and this must be worn where exposure is in excess of an $L_{EP,d}$ of 90dB(A) (Second Action Level) (see Chapter 5). Detailed guidance concerned with the selection, use, care and maintenance of hearing protection is given in BS EN 458 (BSI 1994). There are many types of ear protection devices and all protection provided should have a 'CE' mark. As with other protective equipment, this needs to fit, be in good condition and, above all, be worn all the time the person is at risk. There are three principal types of ear protectors with high, medium and low noise reduction devices available in each case:

1. **Earmuffs** – cover the external ear.
2. **Earplugs** – inserted directly into the ear canal.
3. **Semi-inserts** – premoulded ear caps attached to a headband and inserted into the ear canal.

Assessment of hearing protection

The different types and makes of ear protectors attenuate (reduce) noise with varying efficiency at different frequencies. Given the octave band analysis of a sound and the attenuation values of a hearing protector at these frequency ranges, the overall sound level in dB(A) within the hearing protection can be calculated. These calculations take into account the variability in protection a population of people using the hearing protection will experience. Sound attenuation data is provided by all manufacturers for all hearing protection equipment. This data is collected by a standard method specified in BSI (1993). The method involves a subjective 'threshold shift' procedure in which the faintest sound audible for 16 test subjects is found. The procedure is repeated with and without the protectors. The difference between the results is taken as the sound attenuation of the protectors. There are variations in the measurement of attenuation for different individuals and, therefore, for each octave band frequency, the attenuation measurement is given as a mean and standard deviation. The assumed protection at each frequency band is usually taken as the mean attenuation value minus one standard deviation, known as the Assumed Protection Value (APV) (see Table 13.3).

TABLE 13.2: Noise source octave band

Octave band centre frequency (Hz)	63	125	250	500	1,000	2,000	4,000	8,000
Sound pressure level of source (dB)	90	92	94	94	96	98	96	94

TABLE 13.3: Sample octave band data supplied with hearing protection

Octave band centre frequency (Hz)	63	125	250	500	1,000	2,000	4,000	8,000
Mean attenuation (dB)	7.4	10.0	14.4	19.6	22.8	29.6	38.8	34.1
STD deviation (dB)	3.3	3.6	3.6	4.6	4.0	6.2	7.4	5.2
Assumed Protection Value (APV) (dB)	4.1	6.4	10.8	15.0	18.8	23.4	31.4	28.9

TABLE 13.4: Noise level inside protector

Octave band centre frequency (Hz)	63	125	250	500	1,000	2,000	4,000	8,000
Sound pressure level inside protector (dB)	85.9	85.6	83.2	79	77.2	74.6	64.6	65.1

FIGURE 13.11: Graphical octave band method – Predicted sound attenuation of HPE using the data from Tables 13.3 and 13.4[40]

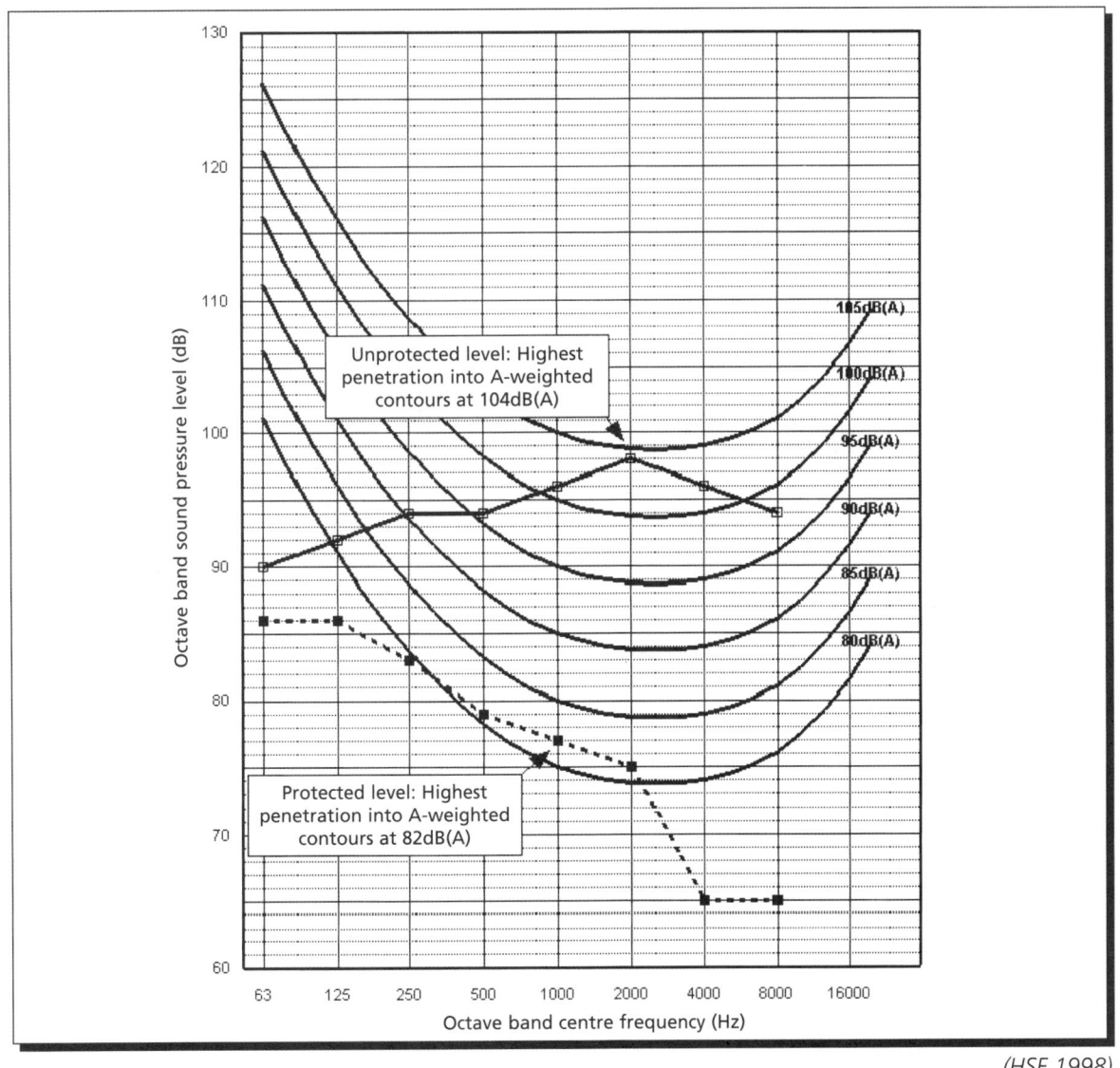

(HSE 1998)

[40]The octave band levels from the data above have been plotted with and without the hearing protector APVs applied. The graph shows the predicted spectra at the ear for protected and unprotected conditions. Noise levels within the ear protection device are also shown in Table 13.4. In addition to this graphical method, the approach outlined in Chapter 5 (Figure 5.6) can be used to estimate overall dB(A) levels from octave band data.

PERSONAL PROTECTION

Using this data, it is possible to predict, for a given noise source (Table 13.2) where octave band measurements for the work environment are available, whether a particular hearing protection device is adequate, inadequate or overprotects[41].

The HSE (1998) gives practical guidance on several methods for predicting the reduction in $L_{EP,d}$ given by wearing hearing protection. The graphical method is illustrated in Figure 13.11. The octave band values for the noise source (Table 13.3) are plotted on the chart (top line). The Assumed Protection Value is then subtracted from each octave band value (Table 13.4) and, in turn, plotted on the chart (lower line). The value of the lower line, which penetrates the contours to the greatest extent, is the estimated dB(A) value, as measured using the contour scale. This is 82dB(A) in the example and represents the attenuated value achieved by the hearing protector.

Earmuffs

These consist of rigid plastic cups which cover the ears and are held in position by a sprung headband. The cup forms an acoustic seal to the head with soft plastic foam or a viscous liquid enclosed in an annular sac. The inner surface of the cups is covered with a sound-absorbing material, usually a soft plastic foam. A range of earmuffs is shown in Figure 13.12. Where earmuffs are attached to a hard hat or helmet, then the performance of the device will be different from the stand-alone version and this needs to be taken into account in selection. Sound attenuation data from the various types of earmuffs needs to be considered in selection.

FIGURE 13.12: Range of earmuffs

(HSE 1998)

Earplugs

Earplugs fit directly into the ear canal and they are sometimes worn with a cord or neckband to prevent loss. Several types of plug are shown in Figure 13.13. Various earplugs are available including disposable, re-usable and permanent types. Disposable and re-usable earplugs are made from glass down, plastic-coated glass down or polyurethane foam. These are often a popular choice of plug. With re-usable earplugs, attention needs to be given to maintenance and their continued cleanliness. Permanent earplugs are usually available in a range of sizes and it is very important that the correct size is used; this is indicated by a slightly tight fit. Custom-made plugs may be made from silicone rubber and these are moulded to the individual's ears; these devices provide a good level of sound attenuation and they are relatively comfortable.

Before these devices are prescribed to workers, any medical problems with the ear need to be highlighted, for example, irritation of the ear canal, discharge from the ear or earache.

---

[41]Overprotection – this is where a protector reduces ambient sound to below 75dB(A) and workers may experience feelings of isolation which leads to them not wearing their hearing protection.

FIGURE 13.13: Earplugs

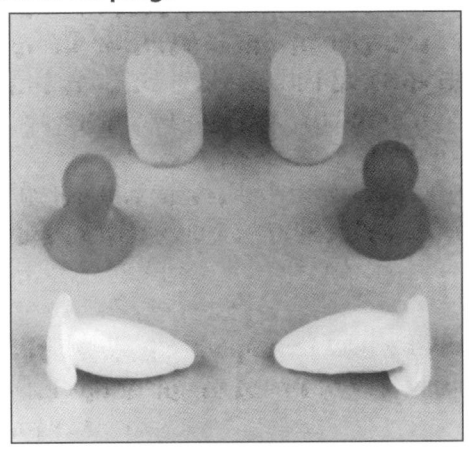

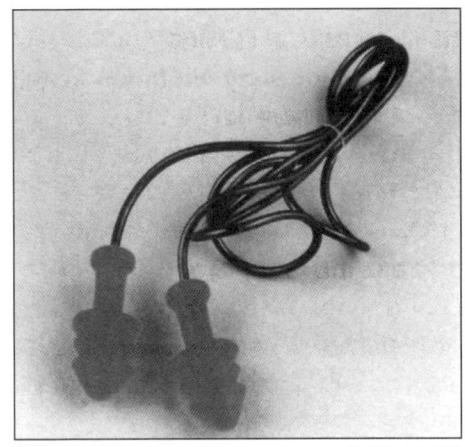

(HSE 1998)

Semi-inserts

Premoulded ear caps press against the entrance to the ear canal. These are useful for visitors to a work area who may only spend relatively short periods in ear protection zones. They are easy to put in and take out of the ear.

FIGURE 13.14: Semi-inserts

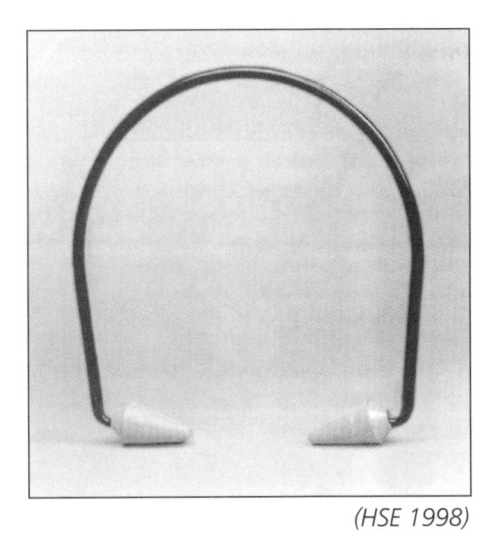

(HSE 1998)

Other types of protector

Several other types of hearing protector are available:

1. **Level-dependent protectors (amplitude-sensitive)** – These are designed to protect against high levels of noise and allow good communication during quieter conditions.
2. **Active noise reduction protectors** – These devices (usually earmuffs) incorporate electronic sound cancelling to achieve improved attenuation. They are particularly effective at lower frequencies (50–500Hz) where normal earmuffs are less effective. According to the HSE (1998), these devices improve sound attenuation by up to 15dB at frequencies below 160Hz.
3. **Flat-frequency response protectors** – Most protectors provide greater attenuation at high frequencies than they do at low frequencies. In some work situations, it may be important to hear the high frequency sound at the correct level relative to the low frequency sound. Where this is required, flat-frequency protectors can be used which give the same attenuation across the whole sound spectrum.

Dual protection

This is applicable to extreme noise hazard situations where earmuffs and earplugs are worn at the same time (above 115dB(A)) or at peak sound pressure levels of around 160dB. Usually, the best combination is a high-performance plug with a medium-performance muff, since this has often been found to be the most comfortable.

Factors likely to affect hearing protection equipment performance

Hearing protectors should be chosen to reduce the personal noise exposure level (as an $L_{EP,d}$) at the wearer's ear to at least below 85dB(A), but not below a noise level of 75dB(A). At this level, there is overprotection and the wearer may feel too isolated and remove the protection altogether.

With high ambient noise levels, the choice of HPE should not be based on simple A-weighted measurements of the noise because sound reduction will depend on the frequency spectrum. Octave band sound measurements provide information which can be matched against the overall sound attenuation characteristics of different hearing protectors claimed by the manufacturers in their test data. Manufacturers provide information on the noise reduction achieved by their devices under standard test conditions specified in BSI (1993).

The HSE (1998) gives guidance on the methods that can be used to estimate the noise reduction ($L_{EP,d}$) achieved by different hearing protectors in a noisy workplace (see the section on 'Assessment of hearing protection' earlier in this chapter). In practice, there are many reasons why devices may give less effective performance than that predicted by the manufacturer's data:

- earmuff incompatible with other equipment;
- some interference with muff seals;
- incorrect fitting of earplugs;
- failure to use protectors all the time in noisy areas (see Table 13.5).

TABLE 13.5: Predicted noise exposure and percentage time HPE is worn[42]

Percentage time HPE worn	Time worn during an 8hr day	Actual noise reduction (dB(A))
100	All day (8 hours)	30
99	7 hours 55 minutes	18.5
87	7 hours	9
50	4 hours	3

(Adapted from HSE 1998)

Overall, research has shown that there is 5dB less sound attenuation with hearing protection when used in the workplace than would be predicted from manufacturer's data. There was greater variability (up to 18dB) found with earplug use due to poor fitting of the devices (HSE 1998).

Information and training

Employees should understand why they are being issued with hearing protection equipment, where they should use it and when to replace it (Figures 13.7 and 13.8). Also, they should know how to wear hearing protection correctly and to maintain it in good condition. The importance of achieving a good fit and using the protection for the whole time that they are at risk needs to be emphasised to wearers.

Comfort and choice

As noted above, some workers prefer earplugs to earmuffs, and vice versa. Wearers should, wherever possible, be offered a choice between earplugs and earmuffs. Comfort is also an important factor, since where the hearing protection is perceived as comfortable, it is more likely to be worn. For example, earplugs are generally more comfortable than earmuffs in hot environments.

Maintenance

All re-usable equipment needs to be kept clean and stored in a suitable place. Earmuff seals should be inspected and replaced at regular intervals. There should be a visual inspection to detect any cracks and holes which could reduce effectiveness and the tension of the headband should be regularly checked. Re-usable earplugs should be carefully cleaned between periods of use.

---

[42]Example based on a protector capable of 30dB(A) attenuation at a continuous sound pressure level of 113dB(A).

Respiratory protection

Respiratory protective equipment (RPE) is designed to be worn in a contaminated atmosphere and permit the wearer to breathe safe air. Legislation in the UK requires that all personal protective equipment must be 'CE' marked. It is convenient to divide RPE into two broad classes:

1. **Respirators** – which purify the air by drawing it through a filter to remove the contamination.
2. **Breathing apparatus (BA)** – which supplies clean air from an uncontaminated source.

Within these classes there are many different subclasses of RPE and it is important to choose the correct type of equipment based on a risk assessment. (A full hierarchy of RPE is given in Figure 13.15.) From the risk assessment, it is necessary to decide whether to use a respirator or breathing apparatus. The Minimum Protection Required (MPR) for a given situation then needs to be considered and this is calculated as follows:

$$\text{Minimum Protection Required (MPR)} = \frac{\text{Concentration outside the facepiece of the RPE}}{\text{Concentration inside the facepiece of the RPE}}$$

The MPR values can then be compared with the Assigned Protection Factors[43] (APFs) for different types of respirator and breathing apparatus which are published in BS 4275 (BSI 1997). The APFs are intended to be used as a guide and these protection levels may not be achieved where the equipment is not suitable for the environment or the user. The appropriate respirator facepiece is combined with the filtering device (eg a cartridge or canister) to give the desired APF.

Respirators

There are many different types of respirator available.

FIGURE 13.15: Types and classes of RPE

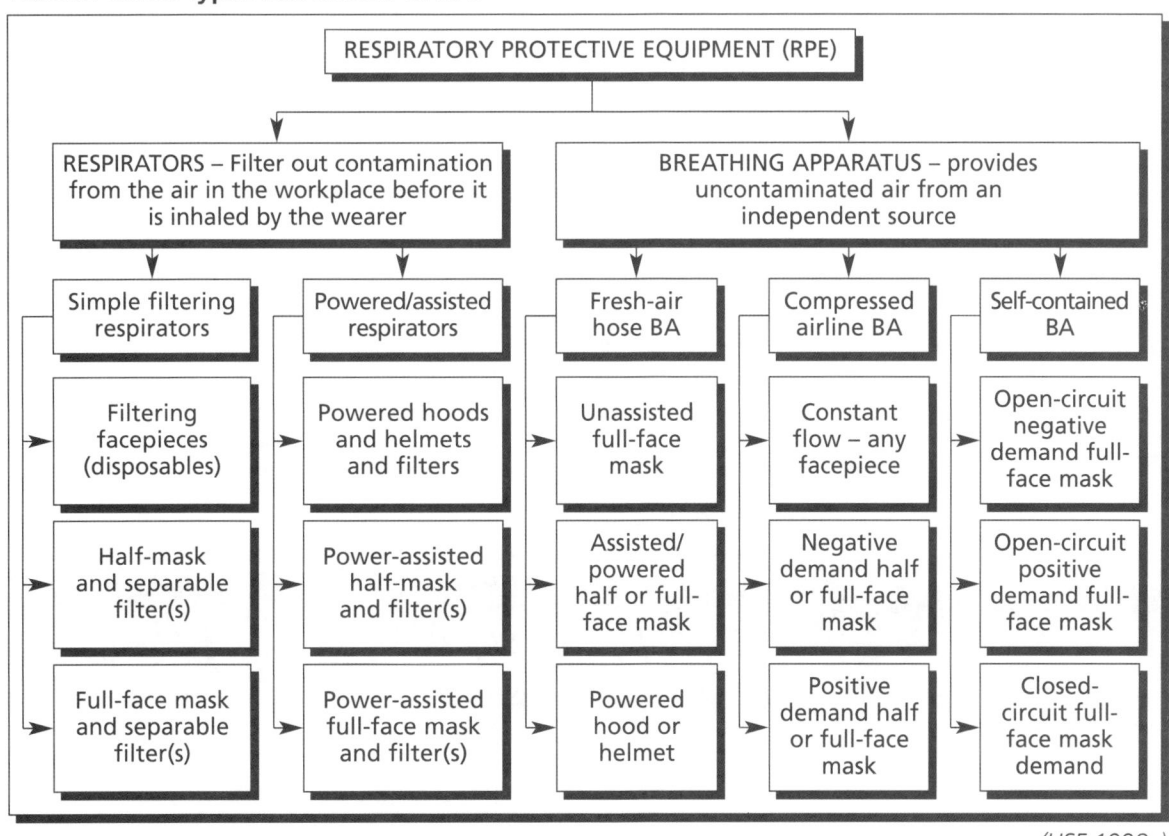

	RESPIRATORY PROTECTIVE EQUIPMENT (RPE)	
RESPIRATORS – Filter out contamination from the air in the workplace before it is inhaled by the wearer		**BREATHING APPARATUS** – provides uncontaminated air from an independent source

Simple filtering respirators	Powered/assisted respirators	Fresh-air hose BA	Compressed airline BA	Self-contained BA
Filtering facepieces (disposables)	Powered hoods and helmets and filters	Unassisted full-face mask	Constant flow – any facepiece	Open-circuit negative demand full-face mask
Half-mask and separable filter(s)	Power-assisted half-mask and filter(s)	Assisted/ powered half or full-face mask	Negative demand half or full-face mask	Open-circuit positive demand full-face mask
Full-face mask and separable filter(s)	Power-assisted full-face mask and filter(s)	Powered hood or helmet	Positive demand half or full-face mask	Closed-circuit full-face mask demand

(HSE 1998a)

[43]Nominal Protection Factors (NPFs) have been used in the past for identifying the capability of different types of RPE. However, this approach has changed because studies have shown that some wearers may not achieve the level of protection indicated by the NPF and so this could be misleading.

PERSONAL PROTECTION

Filtering half-masks

These are made from filtering material and are known as disposable respirators. The breathing action of the wearer draws air through the filter.

FIGURE 13.16: Filtering half-masks to protect against particles

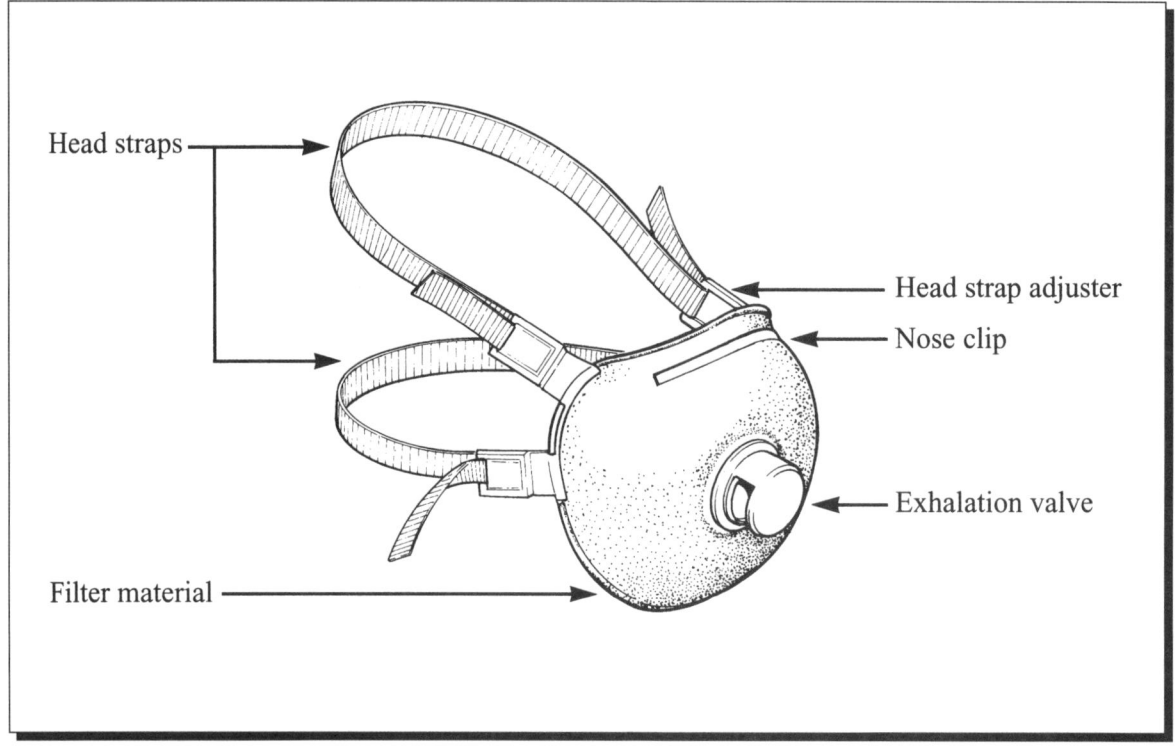

(HSE 1998a)

Half- or full-face masks

With separate filtering devices (filters or canisters), these rely on the breathing action of the wearer to draw air through the filtering device or there may be a powered filtering unit to assist breathing.

FIGURE 13.17: Half-mask reusable with filters

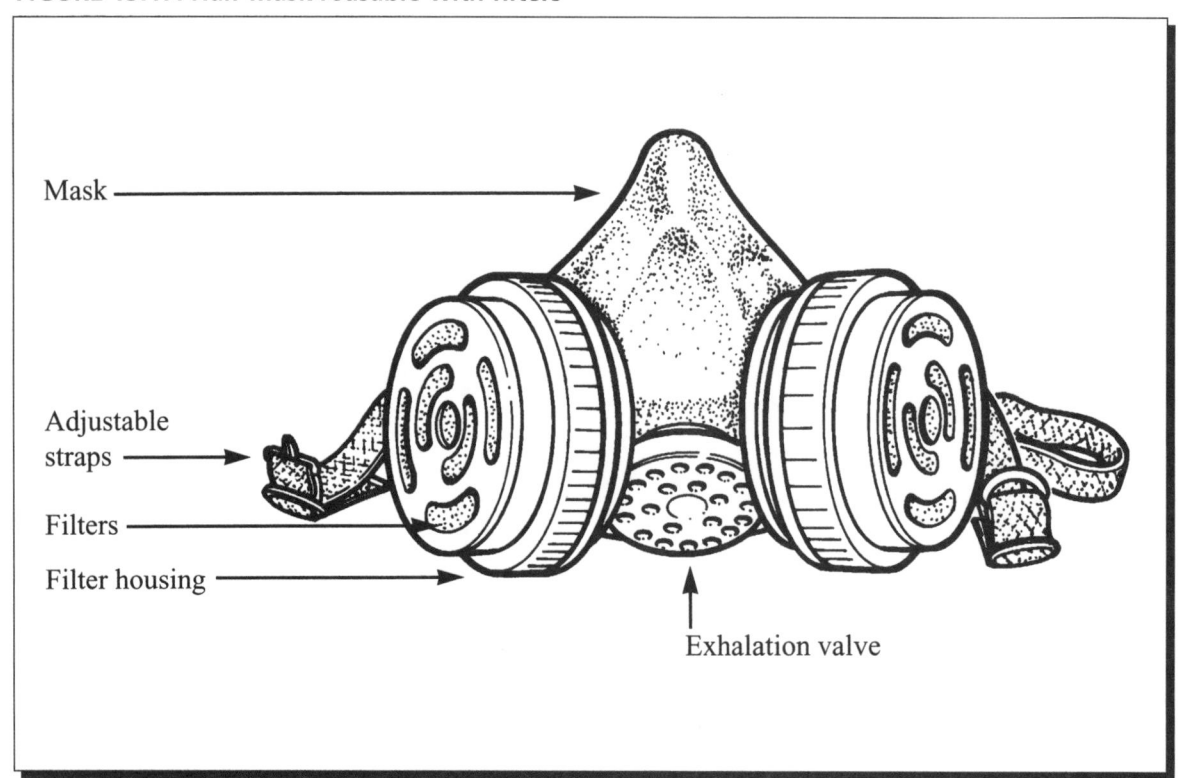

(HSE 1998a)

FIGURE 13.18: Full-face mask

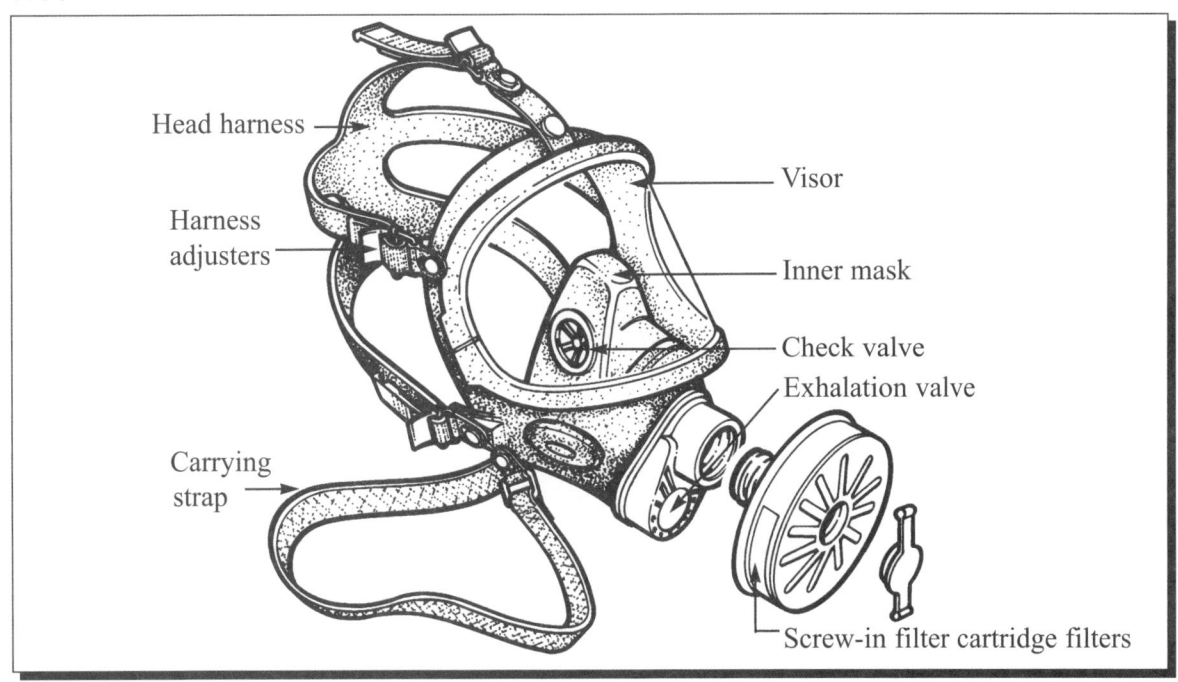

(HSE 1998a)

Hoods, helmets, visors and blouses

These are used with a battery-powered filtering unit. Respirators need to have the correct filtering capacity for the atmosphere in which they are to be used. Filters are available for particles, for gases and vapours, and for combinations of the two. Particle filters are classified on the basis of their filtration efficiency while gas and vapour filters are classified on the basis of their holding capacity (ie how much of the contaminant gas or vapour can they absorb or adsorb). Gas and vapour filters may only be effective within a narrow range of contaminants. The holding capacity of a given filter must not be exceeded or the gas or vapour will break through the filter and it may be breathed in. The wearer's sense of smell may not give sufficient warning in this situation since olfactory fatigue may set in very rapidly. In addition, many toxic substances are harmful at concentrations below their olfactory threshold.

Breathing apparatus

Breathing apparatus (BA) may be used to protect the wearer against particles, gases and vapours, and in environments where there is an 'immediate danger to life or health' (IDLH) or a lack of oxygen, or in situations where respirators cannot be used. There are several different forms of breathing apparatus:

- fresh-air hose equipment;
- continuous flow compressed airline equipment;
- compressed airline equipment with a demand valve;
- self-contained breathing apparatus; and
- self-contained breathing apparatus for escape purposes.

Breathing apparatus requires a source of clean air, either nearby or incorporated into the BA, for example, a compressed air cylinder. The system should ensure that the quality of the inspired air is suitable. The BSI (1997) specifies: air temperature comfortable and free of condensed water; oxygen level 20 to 23 per cent volume/volume; the carbon monoxide level at or below 5ppm volume/volume; carbon dioxide at or below 500ppm; oil mist level below $0.5 mgm^{-2}$; air without significant odour or taste; and with above exceptions, substances hazardous to health controlled to less than 10 per cent of OEL value. Test kits may be used to check the quality of the supplied air.

Some BA equipment is highly complex with consequent technical requirements for appropriate training and maintenance. In IDLH environments, a back-up emergency breathing facility is required, in case the breathing apparatus fails.

PERSONAL PROTECTION

FIGURE 13.19: Self-contained breathing apparatus (SCBA) – Open circuit

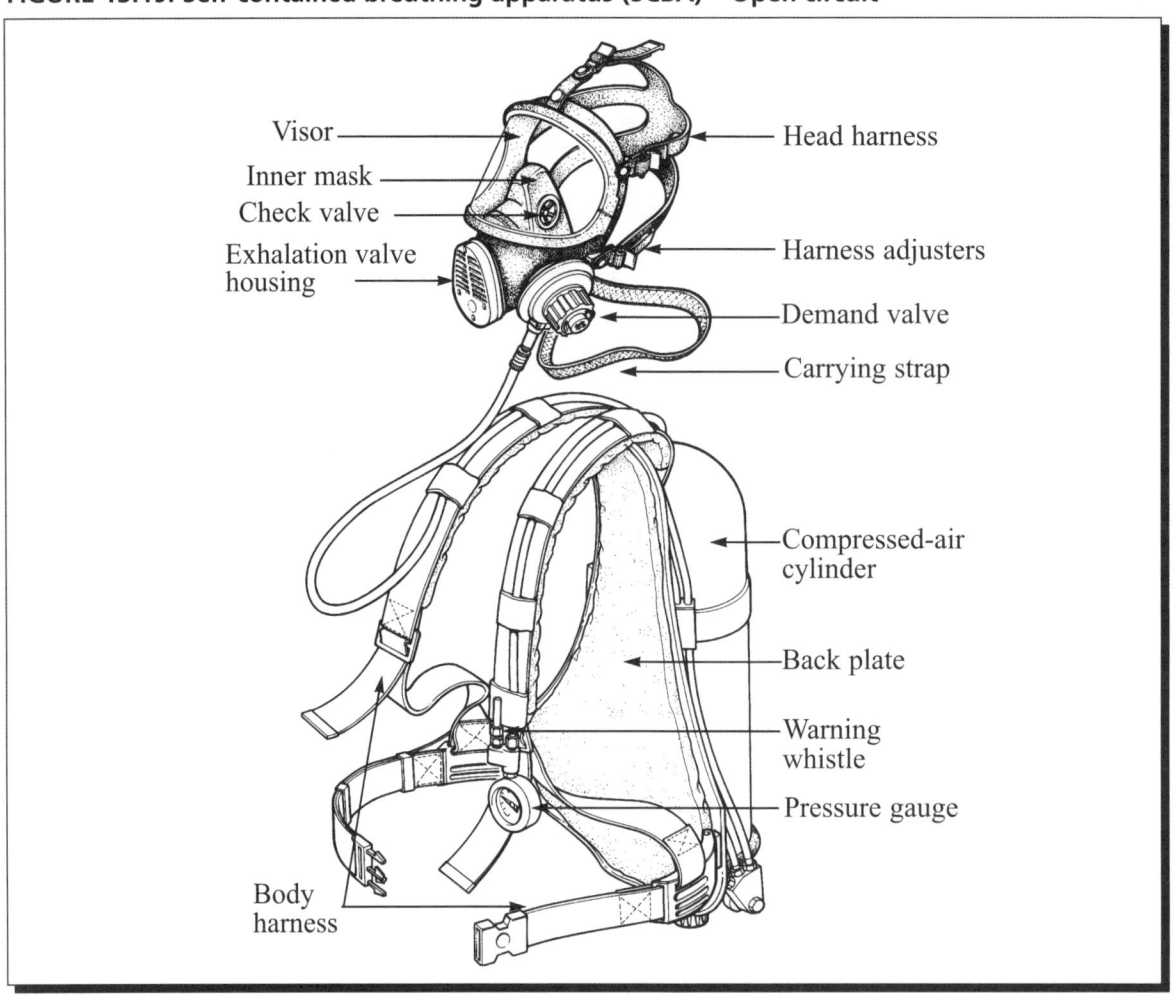

(HSE 1998a)

Personal and work-related factors in the selection of RPE

The wearer and the equipment need to be as well matched as possible for it is important that the equipment is worn whenever the wearer is at risk. The HSE (1998a) highlights the discomfort and various restrictions associated with the wearing of RPE including extra weight, higher breathing resistance, increased heat strain, poorer visibility, impaired communication and, with some devices, limited mobility. These factors should be considered during the risk assessment stage.

Health surveillance

The wearers of RPE should be assessed medically as suitable for this type of personal protection and able to cope with the physical and mental stresses. Because of the higher breathing resistance, RPE wearers should not have explicit heart or lung problems and, additionally, they should not be excessively overweight. Respiratory protection may make it difficult to see detail and lead to communication difficulties, feelings of isolation and discomfort.

Thermal strain

The risk assessment should consider the possibility that the proposed RPE may significantly affect the wearer's ability to lose heat effectively and the consequent increase in heat strain. This should be taken account of in the task and work system specification.

The removal of asbestos insulation materials in hot environments involves exposure both to asbestos and heat stress hazards. The wearing of RPE restricts breathing and in this type of environment either a powered respirator or an airline-fed BA is recommended. This equipment will reduce breathing effort and lessen potential heat strain. If the ambient temperature is above 31°C, then the supplied air should be artificially cooled. The selection of the operator for such a work situation should take into account their medical suitability for the task, as discussed above (HSE 1992a).

Respirator face seal

With this equipment, a good seal (fit) between the face and the respirator is essential or else there will be direct inward leakage of contaminant. The relevant factors to be considered include face size and shape, the amount of facial hair, and the wearing of spectacles.

Work factors

Personal protective equipment is first selected on the basis of the principal risk under consideration, for example, air contamination (Stage One, as discussed earlier in this chapter). Subsequently, Stage Two considers the factors relating to overall effectiveness of the equipment and the PPE strategy. With RPE, this includes possible considerations of physical work rate for the task, possible heat strain, mobility needs, impaired communication, impaired visibility and interference of other PPE. Explosive risks also have to be considered, since some RPE components may produce frictional or electrostatic sparks and could ignite highly flammable atmospheres.

Information, instruction and training

This must be given to all those who use the RPE or are involved in the administration of the protection strategy. It should include the subjects highlighted in Table 13.1 (on page 383), for example, adequate storage of respiratory protection is very important. Figure 13.20 shows a half-mask dust respirator used for protection against organophosphate pesticide being 'stored' on a drum of this very material. The surface of the drum was contaminated with pesticide granules.

FIGURE 13.20: Inappropriate storage of respirator

(Piney & Hartley)

Use of RPE

An RPE strategy requires inspection of the condition of vulnerable parts, ensuring air flow for powered devices, checking batteries, and the assessment of the age and condition of respirator filters. For face seals, a fit test should be carried out each time the equipment is used. Quantitative leak testing can also be carried out to check equipment performance in high risk situations.

Maintenance of RPE

This is required by legislation and the detailed maintenance programme will obviously vary with the type of RPE under consideration.

Specific applications of RPE

Radioactive substances

There are no specified values for allowable levels of radioactive aerosols and gases inside the respiratory protector facepiece. Exposure levels to radiation are required to be 'as low as reasonably practicable' (ALARP), so that the relevant personal radiation dose limits are not exceeded. In each case, an appropriate annual limit of intake needs to be established and the practical unit of control is the derived air concentration (see Chapter 9 for information on ICRP60 (reference 'ICRP 1991')). The environment is evaluated with airborne contaminant and surface monitoring. Respiratory protection may also be used when there is exposure to dust containing low levels of natural radioactivity, for example, some refractory products. It is important that RPE is selected to give protection against both radiation and other risks to health.

Biological agents

The level of protection required will depend on the assigned hazard group of the particular biological agent (see Chapter 4). When airborne, biological agents will always be in a particulate form. However, because there are no occupational exposure limits for biological agents, the normal procedure for RPE selection cannot be followed. Risk assessment considers the hazard group of the biological agent, the amount of the material to be handled, and the quantity of airborne particulate likely to be generated. Both respirators and breathing apparatus may be suitable in different risk situations.

Where there is exposure to biological agents, special training is necessary for RPE users. In this case, the cleaning, maintenance, storage and disposal of protective equipment are particularly important aspects of the programme. Training should include information on the health effects of the biological agent(s), the hygiene precautions necessary and emergency procedures. It should be emphasised that all used RPE must be regarded as potentially contaminated requiring thorough cleaning and disinfection, and that used respirator filters need to be disposed of with particular care.

Eye protection

Eye protection is needed to protect against a range of the different risks or risk combinations, each of which may require a different type of protective device. Hazards include:

- impact of particulate matter;
- splashing of hot or corrosive materials or molten metal;
- contact with irritant gases and vapours;
- contact with a source of non-ionising radiation;
- contact with harmful biological agents.

It is convenient to divide eye protection into three basic types:

1. **Spectacles** – These are used against large, relatively low energy projectiles, eg metal swarf. The lenses may be clear, clip-on, prescription or tinted. Specific lenses can be fitted to provide tougher impact resistance.
2. **Goggles** – These can be used against a wide range of hazards including chemicals, dusts, gases, welding, molten metal and general hazards.
3. **Face shields or visors** – With these the eye and the whole face is protected and they may be attached to a helmet or a headband.

As with other types of PPE, comfort and fit, together with inspection, cleaning, maintenance and replacement systems, are important for a successful eye protection strategy. A common problem found with eye protection is that devices may restrict the visual field, which is made worse when they become scratched and worn. Furthermore, eye protectors may interfere with other types of protection equipment, for example, respiratory protection and hearing protection (see Figure 13.9 on page 389). Where possible, the provision of spectacles or visors may be preferable in humid or hot conditions, as goggles tend to mist up. For people carrying out gas and/or arc welding or using lasers, special filtering lenses are required.

In turn, normal prescription spectacles may interfere with the use of eye protection. Here, the use of contact lenses could be considered, although these may create new hazards, for example, work with organic solvents where the eye may become contaminated.

TABLE 13.6: Eye hazards and personal protection

Hazard	Eye protection equipment	Examples
Impact	Spectacles with toughened lenses/side screens	Chiselling, flying swarf
	Goggles which give protection from side impact	Chiselling
	Face shields or visors	Grinding, cutting bricks
Dust	Goggles	Grinding
	Air-fed positive pressure hood with visor	Shot-blasting
Molten metal	Goggles	Casting and pouring
	Face shield or visor	Casting and pouring
Chemical/biological	Goggles	Exposure to: harmful gases, vapours, liquids and dusts; biological agents
	Face shield or visor	Exposure to toxic liquids
Radiation (ionising)	Face shield or visor	
Radiation (non-ionising)	Goggles – tinted	Welding and lasers (UV radiation)
	Spectacles – tinted	Welding and lasers (UV radiation)
	Goggles – tinted	Casting and pouring molten metal/glass (infrared radiation), furnace-viewing
	Face shield or visor with correct protective shade	Casting and pouring molten metal (infrared radiation), furnace-viewing

Protective clothing

Protective clothing systems are required for a wide range of hazards, as indicated by the list below:
- hostile environments (hot and cold, extremes of pressure);
- chemical agents (dermatitic or corrosive, systemic toxins);
- biological agents;
- other physical agents (ionising and non-ionising radiations); and
- physical safety risks.

For example, protective clothing is required for handling corrosive substances, butchery operations, using chain saws and stripping asbestos in hot environments. Well-designed and properly worn protective clothing provides a reasonably effective barrier. Regarding the selection of protective clothing, Howie (1995) recommends consideration of the overall level of protection and the likelihood of the clothing exacerbating heat stress (which may limit the length of time the clothing is worn).

Hostile environments

Two important factors – thermal insulation and clothing ventilation – will influence overall thermal strain and these can be adjusted by the selection of appropriate protective clothing ensembles. Furthermore, contact burns caused by contact with very hot surfaces (eg metals at 45°C or higher) or very cold surfaces (below minus 20°C) need to be prevented by the wearing of appropriate protective clothing, especially gloves. The characteristics of protective clothing used in hot and cold work environments are discussed below.

Hot

Thermal insulation from clothing may be reduced by increasing air penetration of the clothing, allowing the body to lose more heat. This can be enhanced by the inclusion of ventilation openings in the design of the clothing. With certain ambient temperature and relative humidity limits, increased clothing ventilation with workplace air will increase body heat loss by convection and sweat evaporation.

Personal protective equipment and clothing are worn for asbestos stripping in hostile thermal environments with consequent thermal stress and asbestos exposure hazards. (This situation was discussed with respect to RPE earlier in this chapter.) Protective clothing used for asbestos removal minimises bodily contamination and, typically, this is hooded with elastic cuffs and ankles. Air movement is restricted and there are limitations on cooling by the physiological sweating mechanism. For asbestos removal in hot environments, protective clothing is recommended which is loose fitting with good air and water permeability properties. At the same time, this material should be resistant to asbestos fibre penetration. Clothing that is impermeable to water vapour and air should not be worn unless it is adequately ventilated.

Temperature-controlled suits are required in extremely hot environments. Air-ventilated suits for personal cooling promote convective heat loss and/or sweat evaporation. Generally, air-ventilated suits are not used for heat gain purposes since high mass air flows would be needed to be effective. Liquid-conditioned suits with a network of small pipes, through which a liquid is circulated, are also used to achieve heat loss (or alternatively heat gain). Where there is a significant radiant heat load, the protective clothing should be made out of light-coloured or reflective material.

Cold

In cold environments, a cold weather assembly of PPE including protective clothing is vital for the prevention of cold injury. This provides a safe microclimate which limits the amount of heat loss to the cold environment. The still, trapped air between the skin and the material and within the layers of clothing provides an effective insulation barrier against heat loss. The thickness of this barrier will determine the relative thermal insulation. The presence of water (which ultimately evaporates), either from an external source or internally generated sweat, reduces this thermal insulation capacity. Furthermore, outer clothing layers which permit wind penetration also lead to a significant decrease in insulation capacity, since warm air will be removed from within the clothing. The level of thermal insulation required, from the clothing ensemble, will depend on the level of external cold stress and the metabolic demands of the work in question (ie the level of internal heat generation). The desired work-rest regime and requirements for manual dexterity are also considered in the choice of particular clothing ensembles.

Protective clothing where heat is actively generated is also available and these include electrically-heated whole-body suits as well as gloves, socks and other battery-powered apparel.

Chemical agents

A range of protective clothing will provide physical protection for the skin and body, but protection from chemical attack can be more difficult to achieve. The specification of the protective clothing ensemble will be determined by the risk assessment for the work activity. In the case of splash protection to prevent skin contact with toxic and corrosive substances, a wide range of gloves, sleeves, impervious aprons and overalls is available. The, feet, head and eyes also need to be considered. When selecting protective clothing for handling chemical agents, knowledge of the material is required since protective clothing may fail by:
- penetration of substances through small pinholes, imperfections and zips;
- degradation, ie change in the properties of the material with a reduction in resistance;
- permeation, where the substance passes through the protective material at the molecular level involving absorption, diffusion and desorption. (Where there is exposure to high temperatures, the permeation process speeds up.)

According to Allan (1989), PVC-based fabrics are useful for splash protection against acids, bases, oxidising agents and solvents. It is always necessary to check that a particular clothing fabric will protect against the chemical agent(s) in question. Where the chemical agent is present as an airborne contaminant, RPE may be required and, if sufficiently toxic, a whole-body protective suit may be required too.

Gloves

Virtually all jobs involve the hands and often these need to be protected from chemical agents with gloves. However, since common glove materials provide only limited protection against many chemicals, it is often necessary to select the most appropriate glove for a work task, giving guidance on how long the glove can be worn and if it may be re-used. Leinster *et al.* (1990) propose a guide for the selection of different glove materials, which in addition will give information on the useful life of the glove and whether it may be re-used. Selection is based on the toxicity of the chemical agent, the work activity and the degree of protection given by a particular glove material, based on standard test data.

Gloves are available in a variety of natural and synthetic materials. BS EN 420: 1994 defines the general requirements for all protective gloves (BSI 1994a). Other standards give guidance on the determination of the resistance of protective gloves to permeation by non-gaseous chemicals and micro-organisms (BSI 2003).

The HSE (2000) has recently published a brief guide to assist in the choice of the 'most suitable' glove materials to protect against particular groups of chemicals and this is given below as Table 13.7.

TABLE 13.7: Selection of appropriate gloves/chemical combinations

CHEMICAL GROUP	GLOVE MATERIAL					
	Natural rubber	Nitrile rubber	Neoprene™	PVC	Butyl	Viton™
Water-miscible substances, weak acids/alkalis	✔	✔	✔	✔		
Oils		✔				
Chlorinated hydrocarbons						✔
Aromatic solvents						✔
Aliphatic solvents		✔				✔
Strong acids					✔	
Strong alkalis			✔			
PCBs						✔

(HSE 2000)

Biological agents

Clothing for personal protection against biological agents includes gloves, coats, aprons, visors and boots. This is usually waterproof or water-resistant (in addition, of course, appropriate respiratory and eye and/or face protection may also be required). Detailed arrangements for the cleaning of protective clothing must be specified to prevent this, itself, becoming a site of infection. Specific protective clothing and its usage are prescribed by the defined containment levels in Schedule 3 of the COSHH Regulations 2002.

Ionising and non-ionising radiations

When handling radioactive sources, the use of protective clothing such as laboratory coats, gloves and overshoes should be confined to the active area to avoid the spread of contamination. Disposable handkerchiefs should be provided for use in the contaminated area only. Protective clothing should be designed for easy removal to lessen the potential for transfer of contamination.

Integrated whole-body protection

The integration and compatibility of the various components of a whole-body protection ensemble are very important in high risk situations, for example, in extreme thermal and hyperbaric environments, handling radioactive substances, toxic chemicals or hazardous biological agents.

FIGURE 13.21: Integrated whole-body protection

(AEA Technology)

Skin protection

Where protective clothing is impracticable due to the proximity of machinery or unacceptable restriction of the ability to manipulate, a barrier cream may be the preferred alternative. It is convenient to divide skin protection preparations into the following three groups:

1. **Water-miscible** – This group protects against organic solvents, mineral oils and greases, but not metal-working oils mixed with water.
2. **Water-repellent** – These protect against aqueous solutions, acids, alkalis, salts, oils and cooling agents that contain water.
3. **Special group** – These cannot be assigned to a group by their composition and they are formulated for specific applications.

Skin protection preparations should be applied before starting work and at suitable intervals during the day. However, these preparations are only of limited usefulness as they are rapidly removed by rubbing action. They should be carefully selected since with some solvents increased skin penetration can occur. The application of a moisturising cream, which replenishes skin oil, is beneficial after work.

Selected specification standards and personal protective equipment

In Table 13.8, there is a reference listing of selected specification standards for personal protective equipment. These are grouped into the following categories:

1. Eye protection.
2. Gloves.
3. Footwear.
4. Protective clothing.
5. Respiratory protection.
6. Head protection.
7. Hearing protection.

TABLE 13.8: Selected standards relating to PPE

Eye protection	
BS EN 166: 2002	Personal eye protection. Specifications
BS EN 167: 2002	Personal eye protection. Optical test methods
BS EN 168: 2002	Personal eye protection. Non-optical test methods
BS EN 169: 1992	Specification for filters for personal eye protection equipment used in welding and similar operations
BS EN 170: 1992	Specification for ultraviolet filters used in personal eye protection equipment
BS EN 171: 1992	Specification for infrared filters used in personal eye protection equipment
BS EN 172: 1995	Specification for sunglare filters used in personal eye protectors for industrial use
BS EN 175: 1997	Personal protection. Equipment for eye and face protection during welding and allied processes
BS EN 379: 1994	Specification for filters with switchable or dual luminous transmittance for personal eye protectors used in welding and similar operations
BS EN 1836: 1997	Personal eye protection. Sunglasses and sunglare filters for general use
BS 4110: 1999	Specification for visors for vehicle users
BS 7028: 1999	Eye protection for industrial and other uses. Guidance on selection, use and maintenance
Gloves	
BS EN 374-1: 2003	Protective gloves against chemicals and micro-organisms. Terminology and performance requirements
BS EN 374-2: 2003	Protective gloves against chemicals and micro-organisms. Determination of resistance to penetration
BS EN 374-3: 2003	Protective gloves against chemicals and micro-organisms. Determination of resistance to permeation by chemicals
BS EN 388: 1994	Protective gloves against mechanical risks
BS EN 407: 1994	Protective gloves against thermal risks (heat and/or fire)
BS EN 420: 1994	General requirements for gloves
BS EN 421: 1994	Protective gloves against ionising radiation and radioactive contamination
BS EN 455-1: 2000	Medical gloves for single use. Requirements and testing for freedom from holes
BS EN 455-2: 2000	Medical gloves for single use. Requirements and testing for physical properties
BS EN 455-3: 2000	Medical gloves for single use. Requirements and testing for biological evaluation
BS EN 511: 1994	Specification for protective gloves against cold
BS EN 60903: 1993	Specification for gloves and mitts of insulating material for live working
Footwear	
BS EN 344-1: 1993	Safety, protective and occupational footwear for professional use. Requirements and test methods
BS EN 344-2: 1997	Safety, protective and occupational footwear for professional use. Additional requirements and test methods
BS EN 346-1: 1993	Protective footwear for professional use. Specification
BS EN 346-2: 1997	Protective footwear for professional use. Additional specifications

Table continued overleaf

PERSONAL PROTECTION

Protective clothing	
BS EN 340: 1993	Protective clothing. General requirements
BS EN 341: 1993	Personal protective equipment against falls from a height. Descender devices
BS EN 361: 1993	Personal protective equipment against falls from a height. Full body harnesses
BS EN 366: 1993	Protective clothing. Protection against heat and fire. Method of test: evaluation of materials and material assemblies when exposed to a source of radiant heat
BS EN 367: 1992	Protective clothing. Protection against heat and fire. Method for determining heat transmission on exposure to flame
BS EN 368: 1993	Protective clothing. Protection against liquid chemicals. Test method: resistance of materials to penetration by liquids
BS EN 373: 1993	Protective clothing. Assessment of resistance of materials to molten metal splash
BS EN 381-5: 1995	Protective clothing for users of hand-held chain saws. Requirements for leg protectors
BS EN 381-7: 1999	Protective clothing for users of hand-held chain saws. Requirements for chainsaw protective gloves
BS EN 465: 1995	Protective clothing. Protection against liquid chemicals. Performance requirements for chemical protective clothing with spray-tight connections between different parts of the clothing (type 4 equipment)
BS EN 467: 1995	Protective clothing. Protection against liquid chemicals. Performance requirements for garments providing protection to parts of the body
BS EN 469: 1995	Protective clothing for firefighters. Requirements and test methods for protective clothing for firefighting
BS EN 470-1: 1995	Protective clothing for use in welding and allied processes. General requirements
BS EN 471: 1994	Specification for high-visibility warning clothing
BS EN 510: 1993	Specification for protective clothing for use where there is a risk of entanglement with moving parts
BS EN 531: 1995	Protective clothing for workers exposed to heat
BS EN 532: 1995	Protective clothing. Protection against heat and flame. Test method for limited flame spread
BS EN 533: 1997	Protective clothing. Protection against heat and flame. Limited flame spread materials and material assemblies
BS EN 702: 1995	Protective clothing. Protection against heat and flame. Test method. Determination of the contact heat transmission through protective clothing or its materials
BS 3314: 1982	Specification for protective aprons for wet work
BS 5426: 1993	Specification for workwear and career wear
BS 5438: 1976	Methods of test for flammability of vertically-oriented textile fabrics and fabric assemblies subjected to a small igniting flame
BS 5438: 1989	Methods of test for flammability of textile fabrics when subjected to a small igniting flame applied to the face or bottom edge of vertically-oriented specimens
BS EN ISO 6529: 2001	Protective clothing. Protection against chemicals. Determination of resistance of protective clothing materials to permeation by liquids and gases
BS 7184: 2001	Selection, use and maintenance of chemical protective clothing

Table continued opposite

Respiratory protection

BS EN 12941: 1999	Respiratory protective devices. Powered filtering devices incorporating a helmet or a hood. Requirements, testing, marking
BS EN 132: 1999	Respiratory protective devices. Definitions of terms and pictograms
BS EN 133: 1991	Respiratory protective devices. Classification
BS EN 134: 1998	Respiratory protective devices. Nomenclature of components
BS EN 135: 1999	Respiratory protective devices. List of equivalent terms
BS EN 136: 1998	Respiratory protective devices. Full-face masks. Requirements, testing, marking
BS EN 137: 1993	Specification for respiratory protective devices: self-contained open-circuit compressed air breathing apparatus
BS EN 138: 1994	Respiratory protective devices. Specification for fresh-air hose breathing apparatus for use with full-face mask, half-mask or mouthpiece assembly
BS EN 139: 1995	Respiratory protective devices. Compressed air line breathing apparatus for use with a full-face mask, half-mask or a mouthpiece assembly. Requirements, testing, marking
BS EN 140: 1999	Respiratory protective devices. Half-masks and quarter-masks. Requirements, testing, marking
BS EN 141: 2000	Respiratory protective devices. Gas filters and combined filters. Requirements, testing, marking
BS 7309: 1990, BS EN 142: 1989	Specification for mouthpiece assemblies for respiratory protective devices
BS EN 143: 2000	Respiratory protective devices. Particle filters. Requirements, testing, marking
BS EN 144-1: 2000	Respiratory protective devices. Gas cylinder valves. Thread connections for insert connector
BS EN 144-2: 1999	Respiratory protective devices. Gas cylinder valves. Outlet connections
BS EN 145: 1998	Respiratory protective devices. Self-contained closed-circuit breathing apparatus compressed oxygen or compressed oxygen-nitrogen type. Requirements, testing, marking
BS EN 146: 1992	Respiratory protective devices specification for powered particle filtering devices incorporating helmets or hoods
BS EN 147: 1992	Respiratory protective devices. Specification for power-assisted particle filtering devices incorporating full-face masks, half-masks or quarter-masks
BS EN 12942: 1999	Respiratory protective devices. Power-assisted filtering devices incorporating full-face masks, half-masks or quarter-masks. Requirements, testing, marking
BS EN 149: 2001	Respiratory protective devices. Filtering half-masks to protect against particles. Requirements, testing, marking
BS EN 269: 1995	Respiratory protective devices. Specification for powered fresh-air hose breathing apparatus incorporating a hood
BS EN 270: 1995	Respiratory protective devices. Compressed air line breathing apparatus incorporating a hood. Requirements, testing, marking
BS EN 271: 1995	Respiratory protective devices. Compressed air line or powered fresh-air hose breathing apparatus incorporating a hood for use in abrasive blasting operations. Requirements, testing, marking

Table continued overleaf

BS EN 371: 1992	Specification for AX gas filters and combined filters against low boiling organic compounds used in respiratory protective equipment
BS EN 372: 1992	Specification for SX gas filters and combined filters against specific named compounds used in respiratory protective equipment
BS EN 400: 1993	Respiratory protective devices for self-rescue. Self-contained closed-circuit breathing apparatus. Compressed oxygen escape apparatus. Requirements, testing, marking
BS EN 401: 1993	Respiratory protective devices for self-rescue. Self-contained closed-circuit breathing apparatus. Chemical oxygen (KO2) escape apparatus. Requirements, testing, marking
EN 404: 1993	Specification for respiratory protective devices for self-rescue: filter self-rescuer
BS EN 405: 1993	Respiratory protective devices. Valved filtering half-masks to protect against gases or gases and particles
BS 4275: 1997	Guide to implementing an effective respiratory protective device programme
BS 4400: 1969	Method for sodium chloride particulate test for respirator filters

Head protection

EN 397: 1995	Specification for industrial safety helmets
BS EN 12492: 2000	Mountaineering equipment. Helmets for mountaineers. Safety requirements and test methods

Hearing protection

BS EN 352-1: 1993	Hearing protectors. Safety requirements and testing. Earmuffs
BS EN 352-2: 1993	Hearing protectors. Safety requirements and testing. Earplugs
BS EN 352-3: 1997	Hearing protectors. Safety requirements and testing. Earmuffs attached to an industrial safety helmet
BS EN 352-4: 2001	Hearing protectors. Safety requirements and testing. Level-dependent earmuffs
BS EN 458: 1994	Hearing protectors. Recommendations for selection, use, care and maintenance. Guidance document
BS EN ISO 4869-2: 1995	Acoustics. Hearing protectors. Estimation of effective A-weighted sound pressure levels when hearing protectors are worn
BS EN ISO 4869-4: 2000	Acoustics. Hearing protectors. Measurement of effective sound pressure levels for level-dependent sound-restoration earmuffs
BS EN 24869-1: 1993	Acoustics. Hearing protectors. Sound attenuation of hearing protectors. Subjective method of measurement
BS EN 24869-3: 1994	Acoustics. Hearing protectors. Simplified method for the measurement of insertion loss of earmuff-type protectors for quality inspection purposes

REFERENCES

Allan J R, 1989, Protective Clothing, Chapter 21 in *Occupational Health Practice* (3rd edition), Waldron H A (Ed.), Butterworths, London.

Bednall A W, 1988, *Anti-Vibration Gloves*, Specialist Inspector Report 13, HSE Technology Division.

British Standards Institution, 1993, *Acoustics, Hearing Protectors, Sound Attenuation of Hearing Protectors, Subjective Method of Measurement*, BS EN 24869-1: 1993, ISO 4869-1: 1990, BSI, London.

British Standards Institution, 1994, *Hearing Protectors: Recommendations for Selection, Use, Care and Maintenance*, BS EN 458: 1994, BSI, London.

British Standards Institution, 1994a, *General Requirements for Gloves*, BS EN 420, 1994, BSI, London.

British Standards Institution, 1997, *Guide to Implementing an Effective Respiratory Protective Device Programme*, BS 4275, BSI, London.

British Standards Institution, 2001, *Respiratory Protective Devices: Filtering Half-Masks to Protect Against Particles – Requirements, Testing, Marking*, BS EN 149: 2001, BSI, London.

British Standards Institution, 2003, *Protective Gloves Against Chemicals and Micro-Organisms, Determination of Resistance to Permeation by Chemicals*, BS EN 374-3: 2003, BSI, London.

Else D, 1981, Personal Protection, Chapter 21 in *Occupational Health Practice* (2nd edition), Schilling R S F (Ed.), Butterworths, London.

Else D and Hale A R, 1984, *The Rôle of Training and Motivation in a Successful Personal Protective Equipment Program*, COPE, Toronto, Ontario, Canada.

Health and Safety Executive, 1992, *The Personal Protective Equipment at Work Regulations 1992*, Guidance on Regulations, L25, HSE Books, Sudbury.

Health and Safety Executive, 1992a, *The Problems of Asbestos Removal at High Temperatures*, Guidance Note EH57, HMSO, London.

Health and Safety Executive, 1998, *Reducing Noise at Work*, Guidance on the Noise at Work Regulations 1989, L108, HSE Books, Sudbury.

Health and Safety Executive, 1998a, *The Selection, Use and Maintenance of Respiratory Protective Equipment*, HSG53, HSE Books, Sudbury.

Health and Safety Executive, 2000, *Protective Gloves for Work with Chemicals*, INDG330, HSE Books, Sudbury.

Howie, 1995, Personal Protective Equipment, Chapter 23 in *Occupational Hygiene* (2nd edition), Harrington J M and Gardiner K (Eds), Blackwell Science, Oxford.

Hunter D, 1978, *The Diseases of Occupations*, The English Universities Press Ltd, London.

Legge T M and Goadby K W, 1912, *Lead Poisoning and Lead Absorption*, Edward Arnold, London.

Leinster P, Bonsall J L, Evans M J and Lewis S J, 1990, The Application of Test Data in the Selection and Use of Gloves Against Chemicals, *Ann Occ Hyg*, **34**, 85–90.

LEGISLATION

Confined Spaces Regulations 1997 (SI 1997/1713)

Construction (Head Protection) Regulations 1989 (SI 1989/2209)

Personal Protective Equipment at Work Regulations 1992 (SI 1992/2966) (as amended by the Health and Safety (Miscellaneous Amendments) Regulations 2002 (SI 2002/2174))

APPENDICES

1: NEBOSH syllabus

The National Examination Board in Occupational Safety and Health (NEBOSH) National Diploma syllabus is in a modular format that suits the requirements of the syllabus presentation. This format does not facilitate the preparation of a textbook to cover the material contained in the syllabus. For this reason, the tables that follow contain the 'Content' sections of the modules and units from the syllabus which are covered in this textbook, together with details of chapters and sections under which the relevant material appears. Where possible, syllabus items which form a natural group have been dealt with under a single section heading. Sometimes it has been more convenient to deal with one item of a group in a different section or chapter.

Part 1 – Module 1E: Agents

Unit 1E1: Occupational health risks

CONTENT	CHAPTER	SECTION HEADING
Nature and history of occupational health and hygiene		
Purposes and nature of occupational health and hygiene discipline	1	The whole chapter
Summary of the history of occupational health	1	Historical background and perspectives
Physiology		
Outline of human anatomical systems – respiratory, digestive, circulatory, nervous and the special sense organs, skin, eyes, ears, nose	2 10 5	Physiological systems The eye The ear
Routes of entry of harmful substances to the body	2	Modes of entry
General aspects of occupational health and hygiene		
Main types of occupational health hazards – chemical, physical, biological, ergonomic	1	Occupational health services
Stages of occupational hygiene practice – recognition/identification, measurement, evaluation, control	3	Workplace hazardous substance risk management
Chemical agents		
Forms: solids, liquids, dusts, fibres, mists, gases, fumes, vapours	3	Physical state

APPENDIX 1: NEBOSH SYLLABUS

Toxic – meaning of toxicity; examples of toxic effects of commonly occurring toxic substances – trichloroethylene, asbestos, carbon monoxide, isocyanates, siliceous dusts, lead	3	Common hazardous chemical agents
Corrosive – meaning of corrosive: effects of inhalation of and skin and eye contact with corrosive substances; examples of commonly occurring corrosive substances – acids, ammonia, sodium hydroxide	3	"
Dermatitic – primary/contact and secondary/allergic or sensitised forms of dermatitis; circumstances and substances likely to lead to dermatitis; typical workplace examples	3	"
Sensitisation – skin, respiratory system; typical workplace examples	3	"

Physical agents

Noise – basic concepts of sound, wavelength, amplitude, frequency, intensity, pitch; the decibel (dB) and A-weighting (dB(A)); acute/chronic effects of exposure to high noise levels; typical workplace examples	5	Basic acoustics Exposure and health effects
Vibration – sources and principal effects on the body	6	The whole chapter
Heat – factors affecting thermal comfort. Outline of main effects of working in high and low temperatures and humidities; typical workplace situations likely to lead to thermal discomfort	7	The whole chapter
Radiation – basic concepts of ionising and non-ionising radiation; general effects of exposure; typical workplace examples	8 and 9	The whole chapters
Light – glare and possible ill effects; possible ill effects of insufficient task illumination	10	The whole chapter

Biological agents

The more commonly occurring zoonoses and other occupational diseases resulting from exposure to micro-organisms – Weil's disease, anthrax, legionnellosis, hepatitis, HIV/AIDS, and occupational groups at risk	4	Biological agents and disease

Ergonomic considerations

Conditions likely to result from lack of attention to ergonomic principles: WRULDs, general musculoskeletal effects from poor posture; typical workplace examples	11	Work-related musculoskeletal disorders

Classification of hazardous substances

Health effects of substances classification	3	Classification of chemical agents

APPENDIX 1: NEBOSH SYLLABUS

CONTENT	CHAPTER	SECTION HEADING
Risk and safety phrases contained in the Approved Supply List; information approved for the classification and labelling of substances and preparations dangerous for supply	3	Classification of chemical agents
Requirements relating to safety data sheets	3	"

Main routes of attack on the human body

CONTENT	CHAPTER	SECTION HEADING
Main routes of entry of harmful substances to the body – inhalation, ingestion, skin pervasion, injection, implantation	2 3	Modes of entry Occupational toxicology
Site of absorption into blood of substances – lungs, gut, skin and mucous membrane of eyes	2	Physiological systems
Explanation of local and systemic effects with examples	3	Occupational toxicology

Defence mechanisms of the body

CONTENT	CHAPTER	SECTION HEADING
Natural defences – cough and sneeze reflex, mucous production, lachrymation, airways filter, phagocytosis, immune response, inflammatory response, fibrotic response	2	Physiological defence mechanisms

Unit 1E2: Measurement and evaluation of the working environment

CONTENT	CHAPTER	SECTION HEADING

Risk assessment

CONTENT	CHAPTER	SECTION HEADING
Factors to be considered in the assessment of risk to health from hazardous substances and agents: numbers exposed; personal factors, individual susceptibilities (eg atopic persons, women of child-bearing capacity); frequency and duration of exposure; continuing and contingent exposures; exposure levels and comparisons with standards	3	Workplace hazardous substance risk management

AIRBORNE CONTAMINANTS

Exposure limits for airborne contaminants

CONTENT	CHAPTER	SECTION HEADING
The meanings of Occupational Exposure Limit (OEL), Occupational Exposure Standard (OES), and Maximum Exposure Limit (MEL); the use of OELs to define 'adequate control' under the COSHH Regulations 2002; Guidance Note EH40	3	Determination of risk tolerability
Criteria by which OESs and MELs are established; the work of the Advisory Committee on Toxic Substances (ACTS) and the Working Group on the Assessment of Toxic Chemicals (WATCH)	3	"

APPENDIX 1: NEBOSH SYLLABUS

Short-term and long-term exposure limits (STEL, LTEL) and time-weighted average (TWA) values and their significance in occupational hygiene practice	3	Determination of risk tolerability

Measurement of airborne contaminants

Strategies for sampling: peak level and static measurements, personal sampling	3	Air monitoring techniques
Use of stain tube (colourimetric) detectors, applications and limitations. Use of passive devices. Personal sampling using activated charcoal tubes and pumps	3	"
Monitoring (Tyndall beam) and measurement (filtration methods) of airborne dusts	3	"
Direct reading instruments	3	"

NOISE

Exposure standards for noise at work

L_{eq} and $L_{EP,d}$	5	Exposure and health effects
Action Levels in the Noise at Work Regulations 1989 and the required action	5	The Noise at Work Regulations 1989 (NAW) and Action Levels

Noise measurement

Simple noise measurements at the workplace using a sound-level meter; application of measured values to legal standards	5	Measurement of exposure and analysis
Sound-level meter and dosimeter – advantages and limitations of use	5	"
Meaning and purpose of frequency band analysis	5	"

Thermal environment

Measurement and units of thermal environmental factors	7	Thermal environment risk assessment
Measurement of ambient temperature and radiant temperature, wind speed, and hygrometric values to determine relative humidity	7	"
Principal effects of air temperature, wind speed and humidity on thermal stress and comfort	7	Heat exposure and health effects Cold exposure and health effects

APPENDIX 1: NEBOSH SYLLABUS

| Exposure standard for the thermal environment; use of the Wet Bulb Globe Temperature (WBGT) thermal stress index | 7 | Thermal environment risk assessment |

Unit 1E3: Prevention and control measures

CONTENT	CHAPTER	SECTION HEADING
Hierarchy of control		
Elimination, control at source	1	Risk assessment and control
Substitution: one substance for a less harmful substance; one material for another (eg glass for plastic in a bottling plant)	3	Preventing and controlling exposure to chemical agents
Change of work method to minimise or suppress generation of harmful substance or agent (eg painting instead of spraying, pressing instead of beating)	3 5	Preventing and controlling exposure to chemical agents Noise control methods
Change of work patterns to reduce length of time of exposure	3 5	"
Isolation and segregation: remote handling systems; enclosure of process/plant producing harmful substances or agents; enclosure of persons (eg noise haven); reducing numbers exposed by segregation of process/persons	3 5	"
Engineering control methods; local exhaust ventilation (LEV) systems (captor, receptor, low-volume high-velocity) and dilution ventilation; noise and vibration damping and absorption	3 5	"
Personal protective equipment	13	The whole chapter
Monitoring and maintenance of control measures		
Visual inspection	3	Ventilation
Ventilation measurements: methods and equipment for measuring capture velocities, face velocities, transport velocities and static pressures	3	"
Periodic monitoring of exposures	3	"
Medical and health surveillance including audiometry	5	Audiometry
Statutory requirements for monitoring and maintenance	3	Preventing and controlling exposure to chemical agents

APPENDIX 1: NEBOSH SYLLABUS

The roles and functions of occupational health specialists

Content	Chapter	Section Heading
The roles and functions of: the occupational hygienist, the occupational health physician, the occupational health nurse, the Employment Medical Advisory Service (EMAS)	1	Occupational health services
The role, function and composition of an occupational health service in respect of, in particular, health promotion, pre-employment medical screening, medical/health surveillance and counselling	1	"

Unit 1E4: Personal protective equipment

CONTENT	CHAPTER	SECTION HEADING
General		
Role of personal protective equipment as a control measure	13	Introduction
Main legislative requirements relating to the provision and use of personal protective equipment	13	"
Relationship of the Personnel Protective Equipment at Work Regulations 1992 with other regulations requiring the provision of personal protective equipment	13	"
Eye protection		
Nature of hazards for which eye protection is available	13	Types of personal protective equipment – eye protection
Specification and standards for eye protection against impact, chemicals, dusts, molten metal, non-ionising radiations	13	"
Factors affecting choice of type of protection (eg spectacles, goggles)	13	"
Hearing protection		
Types of hearing protection; significance of attenuation data; factors affecting degree of protection in practice versus theoretical protection	13	Types of personal protective equipment – hearing protection
Skin protection		
Types of hand and lower arm protection; hazards protected against and limitations	13	Types of personal protective equipment – protective clothing

APPENDIX 1: NEBOSH SYLLABUS

Use of pre- and post-exposure skin creams	13	Types of personal protective equipment – skin protection

Respiratory protection

Respiratory protective equipment, applications and limitations	13	Types of personal protective equipment – respiratory protective equipment
Significance of applied protection factors	13	"
Factors affecting choice of respiratory protection and degree of protection afforded	13	"

Body and whole-body protection

Hazards protected against: impact, contact with sharp edges and dangerous parts of machinery, temperature extremes, inclement weather, chemicals, toxic particulates. Example applications such as construction work, asbestos-stripping, handling corrosive substances, butchery operations and chain saw use	13	Types of personal protective equipment – protective clothing
Types of equipment available, application and limitations	13	"

Management of personal protective equipment schemes

Introduction of PPE as a control measure; selection, choice and consultation; personal and workplace factors	13	Key elements of effective PPE schemes
Maintenance, instruction, information, supervision factors affecting management of PPE scheme and degree of protection afforded	13	"
Monitoring of use	13	"

Part 2: Module 2E

Unit 2E1: Chemical health hazards

CONTENT	CHAPTER	SECTION HEADING

Exposure to chemical agents

Main routes and mechanisms of attack by toxic, corrosive and dermatitic substances, dusts and fibres	3	Occupational toxicology

APPENDIX 1: NEBOSH SYLLABUS

Target organs and target systems, signs and symptoms, and the body's defence responses	3	Occupational disease and chemical agents
Carcinogenesis, mutagenesis	3	"
Occupations presenting exposure risks and typical substances	3	"
Factors which affect hazard/risk to individual: concentration, solubility in body fluids, synergy, age and susceptibility of individual, sensitisation, aerosol/particle size and morphology, exposure time	3	"
Use of risk phrases and safety phrases – Chemicals (Hazard Information and Packaging for Supply) Regulations 2002	3	Classification of chemical agents

Measurement and analysis

Purpose of sampling, Guidance Note HSG173, general strategies for surveys	3	Risk assessment survey
Solid particulate sampling, collection methods, gravimetric sampling, methods of determining dust mass/volume and fibre count/volume values	3	"
Principles of optical microscopy and infrared analytical techniques	3	"
Sampling for gases and vapours: bulk sampling, absorption, reactive methods, direct-reading instruments	3	"
Methods for the Determination of Hazardous Substances (MDHS) guidance on analysis	3	"
Gas liquid chromatography, atomic absorption spectroscopy, X-ray diffraction	3	"
Assessment of health risks presented by exposure to various agents	3	"

Hygiene standards

The general philosophy and application of the various types of hygiene standards relevant to chemical substances	3	Determination of risk tolerability

Controls

The range of engineering and procedural measures and strategies which can be applied to prevent or control the hazards/risks/effects associated with exposure to the various agents	3	Preventing and controlling exposure to chemical agents
Legal requirements: assessments, controls, information, hygiene standards, workplace monitoring and health surveillance	3	Risk assessment survey

APPENDIX 1: NEBOSH SYLLABUS

Unit 2E2: Noise and vibration

CONTENT	CHAPTER	SECTION HEADING
Noise		
Application of the basic concepts of sound physics to the evaluation of occupational noise; logarithmic scales; addition of combined sounds (equal and unequal); noise rating curves	5	Basic acoustics
Effects		
Acute and chronic physiological effects of exposure to high noise levels	5	Exposure and health effects
Assessment of degree of hearing loss in an individual; the role and principles of audiometry	5	Measurement of hearing loss
Measurement		
Instrumentation and measurement of noise; types, methodology, calibration, calculation of L_{eq} and $L_{EP,d}$, use of frequency analysis, background noise	5	Measurement of exposure and analysis
Noise surveys; planning/approach; interpretation/evaluation of results	5	Determination of risk tolerability
Controls		
Principles of noise reduction and their application to the control of occupational noise; transmission, reflection, absorption, damping, diffusion; use of sound reduction indices and sound absorption coefficients; design specifications	5	Noise control methods
Evaluation of noise control techniques to remedy specific problems: – control at source – eg relocation, redesign, maintenance; – along transmission path – eg isolation, barriers, enclosure; – at receiver – acoustic havens, ear protection (passive and active)	5	"
Vibration		
Vibration displacement, velocity and acceleration for oscillating particles	6	Vibration characteristics
Measurement of vibration, the accelerometer	6	Measurement of vibration exposure and analysis

APPENDIX 1: NEBOSH SYLLABUS

Effects

Significance of amplitude and frequency of vibrations on comfort levels	6	Exposure and health effects
Ill health effects and conditions produced by whole-body and segmental vibration; workers at risk	6	"

Controls

Control measures which may be applied in respect of whole-body vibration occupations such as farmers, construction workers and drivers, and segmental vibration occupations such as those handling vibrating tools	6	Determination of risk tolerability

Unit 2E3: Radiation and the thermal environment

CONTENT	CHAPTER	SECTION HEADING

Non-ionising radiation

Types of non-ionising radiation throughout the electromagnetic spectrum	8	The whole chapter
Workplace occurrences and applications	8	"
Possible biological effects	8	"
Assessment of risks and control strategies	8	"

Ionising radiation

Particulate and non-particulate types of ionising radiation, origins and sources	9	Basic atomic theory
Uses and applications	9	Occupational exposure
Units of radioactivity, radiation dose and dose equivalent	9	Radiation units
Biological effects of exposure, acute and chronic effects of irradiation, dose response and dose effect	9	Biological effects
Controls – radiological limits, practical control of external and internal radiation	9	Determination of risk tolerability
Role of the International Commission on Radiological Protection and the National Radiological Protection Board	9	"

Heat/Cold

Content	Chapter	Section Heading
Human body/thermal environment parameters – surrounding temperature, humidity, air velocity, metabolic rate, clothing, duration of exposure	7	Physiological thermal environment
Instruments and measurement	7	Thermal environment survey
Heat indices: Wet Bulb Globe Temperature (WBGT), Effective Temperature (ET), Corrected Effective Temperature (CET), Heat Stress Index (HSI), Predicted 4-Hour Sweat Rate (P4SR), Wind Chill Index (WCI)	7	Determination of risk tolerability
Assessment of exposures to thermal environment extremes	7	"
Control measures to improve unsatisfactory thermal environment parameters – for hot and cold environments	7	Prevention and control measures

Light

Content	Chapter	Section Heading
Necessity for lighting in workplaces, 'sufficient and suitable lighting', natural and artificial lighting	10	Introduction
Impact of lighting levels on safety issues – incorrect perception, failure to perceive, stroboscopic effects, colour assessment, effect on attitudes	10	Effects of lighting
Effects of brightness contrast – disabling and discomfort glare, tissue damage from light exposure, visual fatigue	10	"
Instrumentation, units and measurement of light, assessment of lighting levels and standards	10	Measurement and analysis of risk factors

Unit 2E4: Biological agents

CONTENT	CHAPTER	SECTION HEADING

Biological agents

Content	Chapter	Section Heading
Types of biological agent (yeasts, moulds, fungi, bacteria, viruses)	4	Basic microbiology
Principles of genetic manipulation	4	"
Endotoxins, exotoxins, enterotoxins, mycotoxins	4	"
Modes of transmission of disease; the body's defence mechanisms against attack on the body	4	Exposure and health effects
Signs and symptoms of disease; the body's defence mechanisms	4	"

APPENDIX 1: NEBOSH SYLLABUS

Zoonoses and other biological diseases (of occupation – brucellosis, farmers lung; of human contact – hepatitis, AIDS; of environmental exposure – legionnellosis, leptospirosis)	4	Biological agents and disease
Occupational groups at risk	4	Infectious occupational diseases
Sensitisation	4	Risk assessment

Assessment and control strategies

Risk assessment	4	Risk assessment Prevention and control of exposure Special control measures
Intentional work and opportunistic infection	4	"
Diagnostic laboratories	4	"
Laboratory work and containment	4	"
Scale-up	4	"
Animal houses	4	"
Baseline testing and health surveillance	4	"
Sharps control	4	"
Personal protection	4	"
Effluent and waste control	4	"
Decontamination and disinfection	4	"
Notification requirements to HSE	4	Specific legislative requirements

Unit 2E5: Toxicology and epidemiology

CONTENT	CHAPTER	SECTION HEADING
Toxicology		
Legal requirements for the testing of new substances	3	Occupational toxicology
Types of toxicity test performed	3	"

APPENDIX 1: NEBOSH SYLLABUS

Significance of LD_{50}, LD_{90}, LC_{50}, and LC_{90}	3	Occupational toxicology
Use of Ames assays for testing mutagenicity	3	"
Long-term toxicity tests	3	"
Limitations of animal testing	3	"
Significance of chemical analogy as a method of predicting hazards	3	"

Epidemiology

Methodology, uses and limitations of epidemiological studies	3	Occupational epidemiology
Reviews of occupational morbidity/mortality statistics, cross-sectional surveys, case control studies, retrospective/prospective cohort studies	3	"
Application of epidemiological techniques to health surveillance of a workforce	3	"

Application of toxicological and epidemiological data

Criteria for setting occupational exposure limits	3	Determination of risk tolerability
The work of the Advisory Committee on Toxic Substances (ACTS) and the Working Group on the Assessment of Toxic Chemicals (WATCH)	3	"

Unit 2E6: Violence at work

CONTENT	CHAPTER	SECTION HEADING

Occupations at risk from violence

Defining problems of violence: what constitutes violence, extent of problem, consequences for organisation and individuals	12	Definitions of violence
Risk factors: people working with public in caring/teaching professions, working with psychiatric clients or alcohol/drug impaired people, working alone, home visiting, handling money/valuables, inspection and enforcement duties	12	Models for workplace violence

Management actions to prevent and control violence

Legal duties to protect employees from violence	12	Prevention and control measures

APPENDIX 1: NEBOSH SYLLABUS

CONTENT	CHAPTER	SECTION HEADING
Defining risk factors: use of staff surveys, incident reporting and risk assessment	12	Applying risk management to workplace violence
Planning to cope with violence: guidance to staff post-incident including training for managers in counselling	12	"
Communication systems: passing on information on risks from individual clients, recording of staff whereabouts and recognition when staff are overdue, use of mobile communication equipment	12	"
Staff training: recognition of situations where violence could result, interpersonal skills to defuse aggression, use of language and body language	12	"

Physical measures to reduce risks of violence

CONTENT	CHAPTER	SECTION HEADING
Cash-free systems, layout of public areas and design of fixtures and fittings, use of cameras, protective screens and security-coded doors, use of panic buttons and personal alarms	12	Prevention and control measures

Unit 2E7: Stress at work

CONTENT	CHAPTER	SECTION HEADING

Definitions of stress

CONTENT	CHAPTER	SECTION HEADING
Ill health effects associated with stress	12	Health effects of stress
Causes of stress: organisational factors, personal relationships including bullying and harassment, physical factors in the workplace	12	Hazard identification
Legal obligations relating to stress	12	Stress prevention and control
Recognition of the problem: signs of stress at work	12	"
Control actions to reduce stress: organisation culture and management, management of change, clarity of roles, job design, staff selection, work schedules, relationships at work	12	"

2: Vocational standards knowledge requirements

INTRODUCTION

Structure of the units

The Scottish and National Vocational Qualifications (S/NVQs) in occupational health and safety practice are presented in a series of 16 Units of Competence. Each unit is divided into three parts: overview, elements, and knowledge requirements.

Overview

This contains three general headings, the first of which is a statement of the aim of the unit under the title 'This unit is appropriate for you if your role involves...'.

This is then followed by a list of typical activities under the title 'The activities you are likely to be involved in...'

The final general heading is 'What the unit covers', which lists the elements of the unit.

Elements

Each element contains a list of the required performance criteria which the person seeking to obtain the unit must be able to meet.

Knowledge requirements

The knowledge requirements for the whole unit are collected together under three headings: 'The nature and role of... [a summary of the title of the unit] ...within the organisation', 'Principles and concepts', and 'External factors influencing...'.

The knowledge requirements are headed by the following statement:

You need the following knowledge requirements to perform this Unit of Competence. You will show this through the outcome of your work activities and through evaluation of your systems and procedures. You need to be able to show that you have a general knowledge and understanding of the following...

The qualification structure

The Level 5 qualification contains nine mandatory units and three other units drawn from a list of 10 non-mandatory units. Units H1, H2 and H3 are listed as mandatory units and units H4 and H16 are contained in the non-mandatory list. The remaining units that are not referred to here are drawn from S/NVQs not directly concerned with occupational health and safety practice.

The Level 4 qualification has 13 mandatory units and four additional units that are not necessary for the achievement of the award. Included in the Level 4 mandatory list are units H2, H3, H4, H5, H6, H7, H8, H9, H10, H11, H12 and H13, and the additional list contains units H14, H15 and H16. In the list of additional units, there is one that is not directly concerned with occupational health and safety practice.

The Level 3 qualification is based on the eight 'stand-alone units' with the title 'Health and Safety for People at Work'. Units A, B, C, E, F, G and H are mandatory and unit D is an additional unit.

The role of the book

The contents of the book are of direct relevance to the knowledge requirements of the following three

APPENDIX 2: VOCATIONAL STANDARDS KNOWLEDGE REQUIREMENTS

Employment National Training Organisation (EMPNTO) standards:
- Unit H6: Identify and evaluate health and safety hazards;
- Unit H7: Assess health and safety risks; and
- Unit H8: Determine and implement health and safety risk control measures.

In health and safety, it is generally understood that the term 'health hazards' covers hazards to health from chemical, physical, biological, ergonomic and behavioural agents. In this book, 10 chapters are devoted to these agents, namely:

Chapter 3	Chemical agents
Chapter 4	Biological agents
Chapter 5	Noise [a physical agent]
Chapter 6	Vibration [a physical agent]
Chapter 7	Thermal environment [a physical agent]
Chapter 8	Non-ionising radiation [a physical agent]
Chapter 9	Ionising radiation [a physical agent]
Chapter 10	Lighting [a physical agent]
Chapter 11	Agents of physical misfit [ergonomics]
Chapter 12	Agents of psychosocial misfit [behavioural]

The remaining three chapters deal with the discipline of occupational health and hygiene (Chapter 1), human physiology (Chapter 2), and personal protection (Chapter 13).

Chapters 3 to 12 contain material concerned with identifying the specific hazards to health, the processes used to assess the risks, the control measures that are applicable and the relevant legal requirements. Therefore, for each hazardous agent, the knowledge requirements for each of the three units, H6, H7 and H8, are contained in the relevant chapter.

For the most part, occupational health is a science-based discipline concerned with the exposure of the person to the hazardous agents. Consequently, the risk assessment process, where relevant, is founded on the measurement, using appropriate instruments, of the exposure of the person or persons and the comparison of the measurement with numerical standards. This is a fundamentally different process to that for general safety in which the risk assessment process is based on the considered judgment of a specialist. Because of this fundamental difference, many of the risk assessment procedures described in the companion book to this, *Health and Safety: Risk Management*, are of little relevance, but all human and managerial aspects concerned with individuals and groups are of direct relevance.

For completeness, the knowledge requirements of the three units, H6, H7 and H8, are given below.

Unit H6: Identify and evaluate health and safety hazards

The nature and role of the identification of health and safety hazards within the organisation

1. How to inspect a workplace in order to identify and evaluate health and/or safety hazards
2. How to observe work activities in order to identify and evaluate health and/or safety hazards
3. How to carry out task analyses in order to identify and evaluate health and/or safety hazards
4. How to appraise designs and proposals in order to identify and evaluate health and/or safety hazards to employees and other people who may be affected by work activities
5. How to appraise designs and proposals in order to identify and evaluate the safety hazards to physical assets

Principles and concepts

6. How to carry out Hazard and Operability Studies and Failure Mode and Effect Analyses and similar hazard evaluation techniques

APPENDIX 2: VOCATIONAL STANDARDS KNOWLEDGE REQUIREMENTS

7 How to keep and utilise appropriate electronic and paper records of health and/or safety hazards and/or environmentally damaging hazards

External factors influencing the identification of health and safety hazards

8 How to identify and apply relevant health and safety statutory and common law requirements
9 How to apply quality management requirements to all health and safety documentation

Unit H7: Assess health and safety risks

The nature and role of assessing health and safety risks within the organisation

1 How to use risk assessment techniques
2 How to use instruments and survey techniques to determine the exposure of persons who may be affected

Principles and concepts

3 How to carry out qualitative and quantitative mode Fault Tree Analysis and Event Tree Analysis
4 How to carry out Hierarchical Task Analysis techniques
5 How to carry out human error predictions
6 How to involve managers, employee representatives and employees in the determination of health, and/or safety, and/or environmentally damaging risks
7 How to keep and utilise appropriate electronic and paper records of health, and/or safety, and/or environmentally damaging risks

External factors influencing the assessment of health and safety risks

8 How to identify and apply the relevant health and safety statutory and common law requirements
9 How to decide the tolerability/acceptability of risk
10 How to apply quality management requirements to all health and safety documentation

Unit H8: Determine and implement health and safety risk control measures

The nature and role of health and safety risk control measures within the organisation

1 How to evaluate the effectiveness of risk control measures, and/or safe systems of work
2 How to identify and evaluate appropriate risk control measures, and/or safe systems of work
3 How to prioritise risk
4 How to identify and obtain the necessary resources to implement risk control measures, and/or safe systems of work
5 How to determine any new and necessary competencies required for the implementation of risk control measures, and/or safe systems of work

Principles and concepts

6 How to carry out task analyses
7 How to determine the cost-effectiveness of risk control measures, and/or safe systems of work
8 How to involve managers, employee representatives and employees in the implementation of risk control measures, and/or safe systems of work

APPENDIX 2: VOCATIONAL STANDARDS KNOWLEDGE REQUIREMENTS

9   How to keep and utilise appropriate electronic and paper records of risk control measures, and/or safe systems of work

External factors influencing health and safety risk control measures

10   How to identify and evaluate the relevant risk control measures required by statutory and common law requirements and industry best practice

11   How to identify and evaluate the relevant safe systems of work required by statutory requirements and industry best practice

3: Selected list of websites

1. Health and Safety Executive (UK)
http://www.hse.gov.uk

2. Her Majesty's Stationery Office (UK legislation)
http://www.hmso.gov.uk/legis.htm

3. European Agency for Safety and Health at Work (Spain)
http://agency.osha.eu.int

4. National Library of Medicine USA (PUBMED)
http://www.ncbi.nlm.nih.gov/entrez/query.fcgi

5. National Institute for Occupational Safety and Health (US)
http://www.cdc.gov/niosh/homepage.html

6. Canadian Centre for Occupational Health and Safety (Canada)
http://www.ccohs.ca

7. National Radiological Protection Board (UK)
http://www.nrpb.org.uk

8. British Occupational Hygiene Society
http://www.bohs.org

9. COSHH Essentials (HSE UK)
http://www.coshh-essentials.org.uk

10. National Institute for Working Life (Sweden)
http://www.niwl.se

11. International Labour Organisation
http://www.ilo.org

12. World Health Organisation
http://www.who.int/en

13. European Trade Union Technical Bureau for Health and Safety
http://www.etuc.org/tutb/uk/index.html

14. European Chemical Bureau (Italy)
http://ecb.jrc.it

15. Health, environment and work (UK) (Gateway site)
http://www.agius.com/hew/index.htm

INDEX

A

A-weighted decibels, 181, 219
Absorption and metabolic handling of toxic substances, 65
Acoustic screen
– roof absorption, 209
– absorptive panels, 206, 209
Acquired immune deficiency syndrome (AIDS), 173
Adenocarcinoma of the nose, 88
Aerodynamic diameter, 49, 51
Aerosol(s), 48-51, 62-63, 97, 103, 132, 136, 147, 150, 153-154, 157, 162, 168, 170, 400, 420
Agricola, 8
Airborne contaminants
– classification, 63
Air cleaning devices, 124-125
Air monitoring, 14, 78-79, 94, 96-98, 106, 117, 157, 416
Air temperature
– loss of body heat, 235
– thermal comfort survey, 257
– thermal environment survey, 239, 423
– thermal indices, 239, 245, 257
– Wind Chill Index (WCI), 253-254, 423
Algae, 147-148, 150, 152, 168
Allergy, 56, 67, 89, 145
Alveoli, 37, 48, 50-51, 87, 153, 170
Ames test, 74-75
Animal studies, 70, 72-74, 107, 275
Anthrax, 10, 145, 149, 153-154, 165-167, 176, 414
– cutaneous, 153, 166
– pulmonary and gastrointestinal, 167
– wool-sorter's disease, 145, 166
Asbestos, 1, 7, 11-19, 21, 27-28, 51-52, 54, 56-57, 59-60, 65, 67-70, 86-88, 94-95, 97, 102-103, 109, 114, 117-118, 124-125, 143-144, 236, 250, 384, 398, 401-402, 409, 414
Asbestosis, 11-13, 67, 70, 84, 87, 109
Audiometry, 4, 191-192, 210, 417, 421
Avian chlamydiosis, 154, 165, 170

B

Bacteria, 7, 40, 63, 145-154, 160, 167-168, 171, 175, 423
Bacterial diseases, 154, 165-172
Basic atomic theory, 284, 422
Benign pneumoconiosis, 84, 87
Biological agents
– classification, 156
– COSHH Regulations, 154-164
– exposure and health effects, 153-154
– industrial processes, 161, 163-164
– infectious occupational diseases, 154, 424
– [and] pregnancy, 158
– special control measures, 161-163, 424
Biological monitoring, 4, 62, 64, 78-79, 94-95, 106-107, 144, 294, 298
– epidemiology, 78-79
– ionising radiation, 294-298
– toxicology, 62, 64
Bloodborne viral infections, 172
Bovine spongiform encephalopathy (BSE), 174
British Occupational Hygiene Society (BOHS), 5, 13, 27, 105, 114, 119-121, 139, 142, 198, 211, 233, 235, 238-240, 247, 249, 251, 254, 257-259, 261, 431
Bronchial carcinoma, 84, 87-88
Brucellosis, 149, 153-154, 165, 168, 424
Byssinosis, 18, 84, 86

C

Cancer, 8, 11-13, 17-19, 21, 28, 54, 65-70, 75, 77-78, 83, 85, 87, 89, 109, 111-112, 142, 172-173, 268, 274, 281, 289-291, 351, 367
Carcinogenicity, 68, 72, 74-75
Carcinogens, 14, 17, 65, 67-69, 72, 74, 111, 113, 386
– COSHH Regulations, 69
– exposure standards, 111
– genotoxic and epigenetic, 69
Cardiovascular system, 33, 45-46, 71
Cataract(s), 237-238, 274-275, 291, 341
– ionising radiation, 291
– thermal, 238, 273
– UV, 274-275
Chemical agents, 15, 17, 38, 52, 54, 56-57, 59-144, 154, 160, 174, 362, 365, 401-403, 413-415, 417, 419-420, 428
– characteristics of harmful effects, 66-69
– classification, 75, 414
– common hazardous, 69-70, 414
– common hazardous and work processes, 60
– exposure standards, 107-113
– immediate and delayed effects, 67
– main diseases and target sites, 84
– monitoring, 94
– personal protective equipment, 401-403
– physical factors, 110
CHIP, *see Legislation*
Chlamydiosis, 146, 150, 154, 165, 169-170
Clinical waste, 161, 173, 175
Clothing
– protective, 77, 116-117, 159-160, 166, 170-171,

173, 251, 261, 273, 276, 280, 381, 384-385, 390, 401-404, 406, 408, 418-419
– thermal environment, 233-234, 248-249, 251-255, 257-261
CNS effects, 84, 90
Cold exposure, 253, 416
– environments, 252-256
– injury, 253, 256
– protective clothing, 401, 405
– vibration white finger (VWF), 217
Comfort
– aural, 200, 202
– lighting, 318
– personal protective equipment, 386-387, 394, 400
– thermal, 256-260
– vibration, 225
Control measures
– biological agents, 154, 159-163
– chemical agents (workplace hazardous substances), 91-95, 113-117
– Display screen equipment (DSE), 346-347
– ionising radiation, 301-304
– lighting, 318-319, 321
– manual handling, 356-357
– noise, 204-211
– non-ionising radiation, 272, 275-276, 280
– stress at work, 369-370
– thermal environment, 250-252, 255-256
– vibration, 224, 227-228
– violence at work, 377-378
– work-related musculoskeletal disorders (WMSDs), 335-339
Conducting airways, 36-38, 48-50, 85
Control options, principal, 26
Corrected Effective Temperature (CET), 245-248
COSHH, *see Legislation*
COSHH Essentials, 113, 144, 431
Cyanobacteria, 148, 150

D

Daylight factor, 309-310, 318, 321
Dermatitis (contact), 22, 54, 56, 67, 71, 84, 88-89
Display screen equipment (DSE), 15-16, 313-314, 322-324, 339-342, 344-346, 359-360
– lighting, 313-314
– sample DSE workstation questionnaire, 342
Dust lamp, 97, 105, 134, 136-137, 144
Dust monitoring, 102-103
Dusts and fibres, 103, 105, 419
Dynamic and static muscular effort, 327

E

Earmuffs and earplugs, 390, 392-394, 408
Effective Temperature (ET), 245-248
EH40, 96, 107, 109-110, 112, 144, 415
Electromagnetic spectrum, 235, 263-264, 266, 306
Electromagnetic fields, 228, 264, 270, 281
Employment Medical Advisory Service (EMAS), 4
Enforcement of Occupational Exposure Limits, 112
Epidemiology, 6, 60-61, 72, 78, 80, 82, 107, 111, 424-425
– cohort study, 82-83
– cross-sectional studies, 83
– health outcome data, 79-80
– longitudinal studies, 83
– measures of frequency, 79-80
– measures of occurrence, 79-80
– measures of risk, 81
– validity, 82
Ergonomics, 6, 324-325, 335, 337-340, 342, 345-347, 356-360, 428
– assessment checklist, 337
– job design, 357
European Inventory of Existing Commercial Substances (EINECS), 7, 15, 59, 74
Eukaryotes, 148, 151
Exposure to mixtures of chemical agents
– additive effect, 69
– antagonism, 69
– calculation of exposure, 110
– duration and frequency, 66
– potentiation, 69
– synergistic effect, 69
Exposure limits, 64, 96, 100, 108-113, 118, 141, 143-144, 158-159, 200, 225-226, 271, 298, 386, 400, 415-416, 425
Extrinsic allergic alveolitis, 56, 84-85, 87, 152, 161, 170-172
Eye protection, 238, 273, 279-280, 381, 385, 389, 400-401, 404-405, 418

F

Farmer's lung, 84, 87, 165, 170-171
Fletcher nomogram, 138-139
Flicker, 309-310, 315-316, 318, 320
Full-face mask(s), 395, 397, 407
Fungi, 146, 148, 150-153, 160, 165, 171, 423

G

Gas and vapour monitoring, 100
Gas chromatography, 102

Gases and vapours, 51, 85, 97-99, 101, 103-104, 298, 397, 400, 420
Genetic engineering, 152
Glare, 305, 309, 313-316, 318, 320, 341-345, 347, 414, 423
Globe thermometer, 240, 245
Gloves, 77, 96, 160, 166-167, 169, 173, 224, 254, 256, 273, 302, 337, 381, 402-406, 408-409
Grab sampling, 97-99

H

Health and veterinary care facilities, 161-162
Health effects
– biological agents, 153-154
– chemical agents, 70-71, 109-112
– Display screen equipment (DSE), 340-341
– ionising radiation, 290-292
– lighting, 315-316
– manual handling, 351
– noise, 188-192
– non-ionising radiation, 268, 270-271, 273-275, 277-278
– stress at work, 361-370
– thermal environment, 236-238, 253
– vibration, 217-218, 225
– violence at work, 371
– work-related musculoskeletal disorders (WMSDs), 323-339
Health surveillance, 3-4, 79, 93, 117, 155, 158, 160, 171, 210-211, 221, 224, 227-228, 249, 251, 301, 339, 357-358, 376, 398, 417-418, 420, 424-425
Hearing protection, 116, 182, 192, 194, 206, 210, 381, 385, 387, 390-392, 394, 400, 404, 408, 418
– assessment of, 390-391
Heat balance equation, 232-233, 236, 244-245, 248, 257
Heat Stress Index (HSI), 248-249
Hepatitis, 145-146, 150, 154, 158, 165-166, 172-173, 175, 414, 424
Homeostasis, 31-32, 38, 47-48
Hot environments, 236, 238, 244, 251-253, 261, 384, 394, 398, 401-402
Hot-wire anemometer, 134, 136, 240-241
Human hearing mechanism, 178, 187
Humidifier fever, 152, 154, 171
Humidity, 110, 147, 235, 238-239, 242-245, 247, 249-250, 252, 257, 260, 341, 343-344, 402, 416, 423
Hypersensitivity, 56, 67, 71, 85, 88, 175

I

Illumination or illuminance, 306

Immune
– response, 48, 51, 54-56, 147
– system, 54-56, 67, 88, 173
Industrial Injuries Scheme, 18, 22
Infection, 48, 145, 147, 149-151, 153-158, 160-161, 165-170, 172, 174-176, 191, 403, 424
Inflammatory response, 48, 51, 53-54, 147, 415
Infrared radiation, 104, 235, 237-238, 266, 273, 316, 401
Infrasound and ultrasound, 178, 189, 192, 212
Integrated whole-body protection, 404
International Commission for Non-Ionising Radiation Protection (ICNIRP), 275
International Commission on Radiation Protection (ICRP), 298
Ionising radiation, 6-7, 34, 68, 79, 88, 264, 266, 283-304, 405, 422, 428
– alpha (α) particles, 286-287, 290
– beta (β) particles, 286-287, 290
– biological effects, 290-291
– dose limits, 289-290, 292, 298-300
– external radiation hazard, 302
– external sources, 290-291, 293-294
– gamma (γ) radiation, 286-287
– internal radiation hazard, 303
– internal sources, 290, 293-294, 297
– isotope half-lives, 285
– monitoring, 293-298
– neutron radiation, 286, 288, 292, 302
– personal dose control, 302
– radiation units, 289, 422
– surface contaminant monitoring, 297
– whole-body dose, 295, 303
– X-rays, 86-87, 264, 287-290, 292, 295, 302

J

Job rotation, 334, 338-339, 341, 347, 357

K

Kata thermometer, 241

L

Laboratories and animal rooms, 161-162
Labour Force Survey (LFS), 20-23
Lasers, 266, 274-277, 279-281, 305, 316, 400-401
– classification, 279-280
– devices, 278
– hazards, 279
Legionellosis (including legionnaire's disease), 146, 153-154, 165, 167-168
Legislation
– development of, 13-16

– Chemicals (Hazard Information and Packaging for Supply) Regulations 2002 (CHIP), 15, 59, 64, 67, 74-77, 111
Control of Asbestos at Work Regulations 2002 (CAW), 13, 15, 59, 94, 118, 143-144, 384
– Control of Lead at Work Regulations 2002 (CLAW), 15, 59, 94, 117, 143-144, 384
– Control of Substances Hazardous to Health Regulations 2002 (COSHH), 16, 23, 59, 69, 78, 93, 107-115, 117, 145-146, 154-156, 161-164, 292, 303, 343, 415
– Health and Safety (Display Screen Equipment) Regulations 1992 (DSE), 339-340, 342-345
Management of Health and Safety at Work Regulations 1999 (MHSW), 15, 24, 29, 210, 216, 229, 238, 262, 266, 281, 292, 305, 322-323, 340, 347, 360, 363, 370-371, 378, 380, 384
– Manual Handling Operations Regulations 1992 (MHOR), 15, 323, 347-348, 351, 353-354, 358-360
Ionising Radiations Regulations 1999 (IRR), 15, 289, 292, 299-301, 303-304, 384, 386
– Noise at Work Regulations 1989 (NAW), 15, 23, 27, 177, 194, 198-201, 204, 210-212, 343, 384, 386, 390, 409, 416
– Notification of New Substances Regulations 1993 (as amended) (NONS), 15, 59, 64, 74-75
– Personal Protective Equipment Regulations 1992 (as amended) (PPE), 381, 383-384, 387
– Reporting of Injuries, Diseases and Dangerous Occurrences Regulations 1995 (RIDDOR), 18-22, 28-29, 110, 144, 146, 164-170, 172-176, 212, 217, 229, 262, 281, 304, 332, 360, 371-372
Leptospirosis (Weil's disease and cattle leptospirosis), 146, 149, 153-154, 165-166, 414, 424
Light
– colour effects, 316, 318
– daylight factor, 309-310, 318, 321
Lighting, 105, 261, 276, 305-322, 331, 337, 341, 343-345, 347, 355, 357, 359, 423, 428
– assessment of lighting levels, 318
– design, 311, 318
– emergency, 313, 318, 320-321
– exterior, 310, 314, 316
– factory, 313
– hazardous area, 314
– measurement, 318, 320
– lamps, 274, 310-311, 314-316, 318-320
– luminaires, 310, 316, 320
– luminance, 306-307, 309-310, 313-317, 319-320
– office, 311
Liver, 35, 41, 56-57, 65, 67, 69-70, 74-75, 84, 89, 112, 166, 172, 238

Lyme disease, 154, 165, 170
Lymphatic system, 34, 40, 45-46

M

Malignant disease, 84-85, 87-90
Manual handling, 15-16, 225, 323-324, 347-348, 351, 353-360
– ergonomics approach, 324-325, 347
– guidelines for lifting and lowering, 352-353
– health effects, 351
– health surveillance, 357-358
– prevention and control measures, 356-357
– risk assessment, 353-356
– risk assessment filter, 338, 351
– structure of the spinal column, 348
Maximum Exposure Limit (MEL), 86, 107-113, 415
Mental health problems, 2, 366
Mesothelioma, 11, 13, 19, 70, 84, 87-88, 144
Micro-organisms
– family tree, 148
Metabolic transformation, 48, 56
– biotransformation, 56
– conjugation, 56-57
Modes of entry, 34, 116, 153, 298, 413, 415
Monitoring techniques, 6, 14, 64, 98, 108, 144, 160
– air, 94-106
– biological, 95, 106-107
– noise, 194-198
– vibration, 219-221
– thermal environment, 239-244
Muscular system, 43-44
Mutagenicity, 67, 74-75, 425

N

Narcosis, 66-67, 69-70, 84, 90, 109, 111-112
National occupational health statistics, 18
National Radiological Protection Board (NRPB), 268-269, 271, 281, 283, 299-300, 304, 359, 422, 431
Nervous system, 32-35, 40-42, 45, 65-67, 70, 84, 90, 149, 151, 217, 237, 268, 325, 366
Noise, 3, 6-7, 15, 23-24, 26-27, 79, 114, 130, 177-212, 214, 219, 221, 227, 337, 343-345, 374, 384-386, 390-394, 409, 414, 416-417, 421, 428
– A-weighted decibels, 181, 219
– Action Levels, 177, 194, 198-201
– basic acoustics, 178-186, 414, 421
– decibel scale, 179-181, 214
– frequency analysis, 182, 421
– sound transmission, 184-186
– octave band analysis, 183, 202, 390

Noise assessment survey, 194
- noise criteria (NC) curves, 200, 202
- dosimeters, 195-196
- nomogram for $L_{EP,d}$, 196-197
- noise rating (NR) curves, 202-203, 421
- sound-level meter(s), 180-181, 183, 194-196, 211, 416

Noise control methods, 204, 417, 421
- enclosures, 206
- havens, 208, 421
- hearing protection, 116, 182, 192, 194, 206, 210, 381, 385, 387, 390-392, 394, 400, 404, 408, 418

Noise exposure and health effects, 187-192
- audiometry, 4, 191-192, 210, 417, 421
- auditory effects, 189
- conductive hearing loss, 189
- human hearing mechanism, 178, 187
- loudness recruitment, 189, 192
- noise-induced hearing loss, 178, 188, 190, 193
- perceptive hearing loss, 189
- permanent threshold shift (PTS), 191
- presbyacusis, 189-191, 193, 212
- temporary threshold shift (TTS), 191
- tinnitus, 16, 21, 189, 192

Non-cellular infectious agents, 148, 150
Non-ionising radiation, 7, 263-281, 316, 400, 414, 422, 428
- electromagnetic fields, 228, 264, 270, 281
- electromagnetic spectrum, 235, 263-264, 266, 306
- infrared radiation, 104, 235, 237-238, 266, 273, 316, 401
- lasers, 266, 274-277, 279-281, 305, 316, 400-401
- low frequency radiation, 266-272
- radio frequency radiation, 269-272
- ultraviolet radiation, 38, 40, 266, 274, 316

O

Obstructive airways disease, 84-86
Occupational asthma, 71, 83, 85-86, 109, 143-144, 165, 175
Occupational exposure, 17, 26, 62, 86, 90, 98, 107-112, 143-145, 147, 158, 172, 261, 275, 288, 386, 400, 415, 422, 425
- by infection, 147
- by workplace, 147, 365

Occupational Exposure Limit (OEL), 61, 108, 110-112, 143-144, 158, 386, 400, 415, 425
Occupational Exposure Standard (OES), 107-113, 415

Occupational health
- disasters, 1, 10
- services, 3-7
- statistics, 16-23

Occupational hygiene, 5-6
Oil folliculitis and acne, 88
Optical radiation, 227, 266, 273-278
Orf, 149-150, 154, 174
Ovine chlamydiosis, 154, 165, 169-170
Oxygen analysers, 104

P

Paracelsus, 1, 8
Parkinsonism, 90
Passive badge monitor, 101
Period or shift sampling, 98-100
Personal hygiene, 26, 113, 116-117, 169-170, 172, 174-175, 303
Personal protective equipment (PPE), 26, 92, 94, 113, 116, 157, 159-160, 167, 169, 171, 173, 224, 247, 250-252, 255, 276, 300, 303, 325, 356, 378, 381-384, 387-388, 390, 395, 399, 402, 404, 406, 409, 417-419
- comfort of equipment, 387
- effective PPE schemes, 385, 419
- fit of equipment, 386-387
- information, instruction and training, 388-389
- impact of time worn on actual protection, 389
- interference with other PPE and warning signals, 389
- manufacturer's performance data, 385-386
- selected British Standards (BSI), 405-408

Personal protective equipment, types
- eye protection, 400-401
- hearing protection, 390-394
- protective clothing, 401-404
- respiratory, 395-400
- skin protection, 404

Phagocytosis, 51-52, 55-56, 415
Physiological defence mechanisms, 48
- ciliary escalator, 48-50, 70, 153
- deposition dynamics, 49

Physiological systems of the body, 34-35
- circulatory, 45-46
- digestive, 40-41
- endocrine, 45
- muscular, 43-44
- nervous, 41-42
- reproductive, 47-48
- respiratory, 36-38
- skeletal, 43

– skin, 38-40
– urinary, 47
Physiological thermal balance, 232
Pitot-static tube, 134-136
Pneumoconiosis, 16, 18, 21, 84-87
– asbestosis, 11-13, 67, 70, 84, 87, 109
– benign, 84, 87
– coal miner's, 86
– collagenous, 86
– non-collagenous, 87
– progressive massive fibrosis (PMF), 87
– silicosis, 8-9, 70, 84, 86, 153
– simple, 86-87
Polycyclic aromatic hydrocarbons, 72, 88-89
Posture, 9, 34, 43, 227, 240, 254, 323, 325, 327-328, 333-337, 341-343, 346-348, 350-351, 355, 357, 378, 414
Pott, Percival, 8
Pregnant women, 157-158, 170, 298, 341, 353
Prickly heat, 237-238
Primary irritant contact dermatitis, 84, 88
Prions, 151
Prokaryotes,, 148-149
Protective clothing, 77, 116-117, 159-160, 166, 170-171, 173, 251, 261, 273, 276, 280, 381, 384-385, 390, 401-404, 406, 408, 418-419
Protozoa, 146-148, 150, 152
Psychrometric chart, 242-243

Q
Q fever, 146, 150, 154, 165, 169

R
Rabies, 150, 154, 165, 174
Radiation, 3, 6-7, 34, 38, 40, 68, 79, 88, 102, 104, 204-206, 227, 232-233, 235-239, 249, 252, 254-255, 263-281, 283-304, 306, 310, 316, 318, 341, 344, 400-401, 405, 414, 422, 428
– ionising, 6-7, 15-16, 34, 68, 79, 88, 264-266, 273, 283-304, 341, 384, 386, 401, 403, 405, 414, 422, 428
– infrared, 97, 104, 235, 237-238, 263-264, 266, 273, 316, 401, 405, 420
– lasers, 266, 274-277, 279-281, 305, 316, 400-401
– low frequency, 266-272
– optical, 32, 227, 266, 273-279, 293, 295, 405, 420
– radio frequency, 269-272
– ultraviolet, 38, 40, 102, 110, 263-266, 273-274, 306, 310, 316, 405
– visible, 274

Radioactive substances, 286, 290, 292, 297, 300-301, 304, 400, 404
Radioactivity, 283-285, 289, 400, 422
Ramazzini, 8
Repetitive Strain Injury (RSI), 331
Reproductive system, 47-48, 84, 91
Respiratory protection, 106, 116, 160, 170-171, 173, 381, 387, 390, 395, 398-400, 404, 407, 419
– biological agents, 400-401
– breathing apparatus, 105, 389, 395, 397-398, 400, 407-408
– filtering half-masks, 386, 396, 407-409
– hoods, helmets, visors and blouses, 397
– maintenance of RPE, 399
– masks, half and full-face, 386, 396, 407-409
– selection of RPE, 398
Respiratory system, 31, 34-36, 49-51, 62, 65, 70-71, 84-85, 87-88, 153, 170, 235, 291, 414
– as a target, 85
Rickettsiae, 150, 154
Risk assessment, 2, 4-7, 10, 15, 24-25, 59-62, 68, 74, 78, 91-93, 95, 113-114, 142, 153-161, 164, 168, 175-176, 238, 265-266, 292, 300, 324-325, 337-338, 344, 347, 351-353, 355, 360, 362-363, 365-370, 372, 375, 378-381, 395, 398, 400, 402, 415-417, 420, 424, 426, 428-429
– biological agents, 157-165
– chemical agents, 61, 91-117
– Display screen equipment (DSE), 343-347
– ionising radiation, 292-302
– lighting, 318-321
– manual handling, 353-356
– noise, 194-203
– non-ionising radiation, 265-266, 271-272, 275-276, 280
– Personal protective equipment (PPE), 385-390
– stress at work, 365-370
– thermal environment, 238-250, 253-255
– vibration, 219-227
– violence, 375-378
– Work-related musculoskeletal disorders (WMSDs), 335-339
Rotating vane anemometer, 134-136

S
Safe person and safe workplace strategy, 384
Safety data sheet, 76
Sampling strategies (chemical agents), 96-106
Secondary allergic contact dermatitis, 84, 88
Self-reported work-related ill health survey 1995 (SWI95), 16, 21, 177, 323, 347, 361-362, 379

Sensitisation, 67, 71, 73, 75, 77, 86, 89, 110, 414, 420, 424
Sensory and motor neurones, 42
Silicosis, 8-9, 70, 84, 86, 153
Skeletal system, 43
Skin
– absorption, 34, 57, 65, 110
– as a target organ, 88
– irritation, 73, 75, 77
– protection, 116, 390, 404
– sensitisation, 73, 75, 77
Smoke tube, 134, 137
Somatic effects
– acute, 291
– chronic, 291
Sound level, 179, 181-182, 186, 191, 194, 196, 198, 210, 390
Sound-level meters, 180-181, 183, 194-196, 211, 416
Sound transfer pathways, 204
Specificity, 55, 73, 82
Stain detector tubes, 98
Standardised Mortality Ratio (SMR), 80-81
Streptococcosis, 169
Stress at work, 351, 361, 363-364, 368, 379, 426
– definitions, 364
– model, 364-365
– prevention and control, 362, 369
– risk assessment, 367-369
Stroboscopic effects, 305, 309-310, 316, 318, 320, 423
Systemic circulation, 35, 38-39, 41, 46, 65, 67, 153, 169, 286, 290

T
Target organ or site, 64-65
– blood, 90
– digestive system, 89
– nervous system, 90
– skin, 88-89
– reproductive system, 91
– urinary system, 90
Task environment, 309, 340, 365
Tetanus, 154, 165, 169
Thermal environment, 208, 231-262, 331, 357, 384-385, 416-417, 422-423, 428
– acclimatisation, 237, 251, 253
– acute disorders, 237
– air conditioning, 250
– analytical indices, 248
– chronic health effects, 238
– comfort, 115, 239, 243-245, 255-261

– empirical indices, 245
– physiological thermal balance, 232
– risk assessment, 238
– wet bulb globe temperature (WBGT) meter, 244
Thermoluminescent dosimeter, 294-296
Threshold Limit Values (TLVs), 107, 142, 255, 261, 268-269, 271-272, 275, 281
Threshold of harm, 111
Time-weighted average (TWA) concentration, 109
Tinnitus, 16, 21, 189, 192
Tissue damage, 54, 56, 271, 275, 291, 316, 423
Tolerability standards, 5-6, 61, 94, 221, 239, 280, 316
Toxicology, 6, 60-62, 64, 69, 78, 142, 281, 415, 419, 424-425
– animal studies, 72-74
– chemical analogy, 72
– dose response curve, 64
– subacute and subchronic toxicity testing, 73
– testing and hazard data, 72
Tuberculosis, 8, 146, 149, 153-154, 165, 167

U
Upper airways, 36, 49-51, 71, 85
Upper limb disorders, 324, 329, 331-332, 335, 337, 359
Urinary system, 47, 84, 90, 225

V
Veiling reflections, 313, 316, 318, 320
Ventilation, 3, 5-6, 8, 12, 14, 26, 61, 92, 94, 103, 113, 115-116, 119, 124-125, 129, 132-137, 140-144, 147, 157, 167, 170, 177, 207-208, 234, 250, 252, 260-261, 357, 401-402, 417
– dilution, 26, 115-116, 140-142
– local exhaust ventilation (LEV), 115, 119
– air cleaning devices, 124-125
– captor systems, 119-120, 122
– design of LEV systems, 132
– fans, 116, 129-130, 207
– evaluating performance, 132-140
– receptor systems, 119-120
Vertigo, 189, 192
Vibration, 7, 16, 19, 21, 40, 178, 180, 187, 189, 205, 207, 212-229, 268, 335-336, 414, 417, 421-422, 428
– bone and joint effects, 218
– characteristics, 214-216
– EC Vibration Directive, 227-228
– hand-arm vibration syndrome (HAVS), 217

– hand-transmitted, 213, 216-224
– measurement of exposure, 219-221
– muscular effects, 218
– neurological disorders, 218
– whole-body, 213, 224-228
– vibration white finger (VWF), 16, 19, 21, 213, 217
Violence at work, 362, 370-371, 377-378, 380, 425
– definitions, 371
– models for, 372-374
– risk management, 375-378
Viroids, 148, 151
Viruses, 7, 34, 63, 68, 146-150, 153, 157, 164, 172-174, 423
Visible radiation, 266, 274, 279, 316
Visual
– accommodation, 308
– acuity, 309
– adaptation, 308
– effects, 341
– fatigue, 309, 315-316, 341
– task, 309

W

Wet Bulb Globe Temperature (WBGT), 243-245, 247, 423
Whirling hygrometer, 242-243
Wind Chill Index (WCI), 253-254, 423
Wool-sorter's disease (anthrax), 166
Work-related musculoskeletal disorders (WMSDs), 323-325, 327-332, 335, 339-340, 359
Work-related upper limb disorders (WRULDs), 329, 331-332
Work-rest regimes, 251, 256